Contexts for Criticism

Contexts for Criticism

Donald Keesey
San Jose State University

Mayfield Publishing Company
Palo Alto, California

Library of Congress Catalog Card Number: 86-062997
International Standard Book Number: 0-87484-767-2

Manufactured in the United States of America
10 9 8 7 6 5 4 3 2 1

Mayfield Publishing Company
285 Hamilton Avenue
Palo Alto, California 94301

Sponsoring editor: C. Lansing Hays
Manuscript editor: Linda Purrington
Managing editor: Pat Herbst
Art director: Cynthia Bassett
Designer: Jeff Kelly
Cover designer: John Osborne
Production manager: Cathy Willkie
Compositor: Auto-Graphics, Inc.
Printer and binder: George Banta Company

Contents

Preface

As a teacher of courses in literary criticism, I have long felt the need for a book that would help readers focus on the fundamental issues of literary interpretation, first, by arranging the many competing theories in some clear and useable way, and second, by applying the different theories to the same literary texts. Ideally, such a book would also provide a sampling of current thinking on these issues. This last need has grown more pressing in the past decade, because new developments in reader-response, intertextual, and deconstructive criticism have been much debated in scholarly books and professional journals, but few books have appeared to bring these debates to a wider audience. I have fashioned *Contexts for Criticism* to meet these needs.

Arranging the various critical theories within five basic contexts, the book offers categories sufficiently large to contain the different voices, sufficiently few to give a useable order, and sufficiently parallel to make comparison easy. After a prologue setting forth the organizing principles, each chapter opens with an introductory essay that explains the assumptions and interests of the critics represented in that chapter, traces briefly the role the context has played in the history of criticism, and offers an assessment of its place in the contemporary scene. The emphasis in these introductory essays is on the general orientation that the critics in each context share rather than on matters that divide them, for the first task is to get a clear view of the basic approach. Suggestions for further reading follow every introduction. Each chapter next presents three "theoretical" essays chosen to represent strong contemporary arguments for a particular way of looking at literature. The es-

says are written by well-known critics who are themselves committed to the approach, and they often exhibit a somewhat polemical stance, for my goal has been to include essays that state the issues forcefully enough to provoke thought and clearly enough to give that thought some direction.

To further clarify the issues, each chapter concludes with three essays applying some version of the critical approach to the same three literary texts: *Hamlet*, *Lycidas*, and *Heart of Darkness*. These widely read works represent different periods and genres; equally to the point, they are rich enough to have inspired a variety of critical comment and short enough to be read and reread in conjunction with the critical essays. So, as readers see each theory applied to works they know well, they will better understand what it can do and how it might be used. Further, as they see the same three works from the perspective of the other contexts, they can more easily estimate each approach's relative strengths and possible uses. And they will be better equipped to make their own applications of the theories. Criticism, as this book seeks to show, is an activity, something one does; and when I have tried out versions of the book in classes, I have found it works best to have each student choose yet another target text and develop one more set of applications as we work through the various contexts.

The application essays, then, provide a way to clarify and test the theories. And because the same target texts appear in all chapters, they also open a dialogue between the contexts. This dialogue is carried out in the theoretical essays as well, for often the writers define their positions with reference to other contexts and frequently with reference to other contributors. So A. S. P. Woodhouse's defense of genetic criticism refers to Cleanth Brooks; Brooks offers a reading of a Wordsworth poem to illustrate his formalist case; E. D. Hirsch seizes on Brooks's reading to argue the primacy of authorial meaning; and Monroe Beardsley uses the same example to try to refute Hirsch. Similarly, Louise Rosenblatt reviews the formal–genetic debate with specific reference to Brooks and Hirsch as she sets forth her rationale for reader-oriented criticism; Norman Holland, in the same context, defines his position with reference to Wolfgang Iser and other reader-response critics; both A. D. Nuttall and Bernard Paris reassert the claims of mimetic criticism in the face of formal and intertextual challenges; Northrop Frye explains how he developed an intertextual emphasis to supply the deficiencies of other contexts; Jonathan Culler extends that argument in overtly structuralist terms; and Jacques Derrida deconstructs structuralism, ushering in what is sometimes called a "poststructural" era.

In these and other ways the dialogue is carried on from essay to essay and from context to context. As a result, although the chief purpose of the book is to introduce the perennial issues of literary interpretation, the reader who works through the contexts in their order of presentation will get a sense of how the focus of interest on these issues has shifted from midcentury to the present. But despite this shifting focus, we should remember that the underlying issues are indeed perennial, and since every reading is necessarily an interpretation, every reader has an important stake in the arguments. These are contexts *for* criticism, ways of reading, and I hope that users of this book will not merely follow the dialogue but actively join it, adopting each perspective in turn, applying it to particular works, comparing it with other approaches, and deciding what use they can make of it. The book is designed to invite this participation.

Acknowledgments

A number of people have helped to make this book. When the work was in its formative stages, the National Endowment for the Humanities gave me a chance to participate in a Summer Seminar in Critical Theory under the leadership of Herbert Lindenberger at Stanford University. My students in several sections of "Modern Approaches to Literature" and in two Senior Honors Seminars showed what kind of book was needed and allowed me to test versions of the text on a live audience. Hans Guth and Herbert Lindenberger read early drafts of the manuscript; Douglas Keesey read the final draft; and all offered many helpful suggestions. Other helpful reviewers were Linda Austin, Oklahoma State University; Daniel D. Fineman, Occidental College; Jean Hall, California State University at Fullerton; Lee T. Lemon, University of Nebraska at Lincoln; Raymond N. MacKenzie, Mankato State University; Darrel Mansell, Dartmouth College; and Leonard Orr, University of Notre Dame. The book has also benefited from the skillful copyediting of Linda Purrington and from the attentions of C. Lansing Hays and the cooperative staff at Mayfield Publishing Company. Finally, a special word of thanks is due my wife, Phyllis, for listening so long and so patiently.

Contexts for Criticism

A Constructive Prologue

Some are bewilder'd in the Maze of Schools.

Pope, *Essay on Criticism*

Why study literary criticism? Even to students of literature the answer is not always clear, for I have heard students announce that they make it a principle to ignore "criticism," by which term they mean everything from the popular book review to the scholarly tome, and sometimes this attitude is encouraged by their instructors. No doubt the purpose of this principled ignorance is to keep "interpretation" from coming between the reader and the text. Critics, in this view, are specialists whose concerns are remote from the reader's interests, or may even threaten those interests. For the belief is widespread that the reader should confront the work with no preconceptions and should achieve thereby an authentic, unmediated response.

But in fact there can be no unmediated response. In the first place, every reader must bring to a text at least a basic understanding of the work's language and therefore must bring as well an extensive range of cultural experience that "understanding the language" presupposes. Only the reader who knew no English at all could have a truly unmediated response to a work in that language. In the second place, every reader must bring not only a knowledge of language but also a set of expectations about "literature" that will cause the reader to emphasize, to value, even to perceive some features of the work rather than others.

In short, we must always read in some way, for every reading is an active process of making sense, an interpretation. And since "literary criticism" may be briefly defined as the art of interpreting literature, every reading is an act of criticism and every reader is a critic. Perhaps the best argument, then, for the study of literary criticism is the realization that critics are not "other people." To read literature at all is to practice some type of criticism, to read in some way and not in some other. No reader has a choice about this. The only choice is to decide what kind of critic one will be, a critic who remains unaware of his or her own critical assumptions, or one who has chosen a way of reading with full knowledge that it is a way of reading and after some careful study of the alternatives.

But how can such a study be most usefully conducted? If every reader is a critic, then the kinds of criticism must be many and various, and certainly the names for the types or "schools" of criticism are bewildering in their number and diversity. We hear of moralists, humanists, and esthetes, of historians, antihistorians, and perspectivists, of Marxists and existentialists, Freudians and feminists, structuralists and deconstructionists, old New Critics and new New Critics. The list of labels can be extended to depressing lengths. To confuse matters further, these terms are not all built on the same principle. Some indicate a critic's philosophical assumptions, his or her view of the world or of the mind; some announce allegiance to a particular discipline or to a particular ideology; some suggest an interest or lack of interest in historical background or social concerns or biographical information. Small wonder that books attempting to survey the field of literary criticism offer a perplexing variety of labels and organizing schemes. And any number of these might be valid for descriptive purposes.

Most, however, are not very helpful for systematic study. To devise a usable grammar for this Babel, we need a conceptual scheme that will include the many types of literary criticism and at the same time separate the competing voices in a way that will help us make useful comparisons. Our categories, then, must be parallel and not so multiple that they add to the confusion. The idea of critical contexts offers such a scheme. Consider the different answers

that might be given to the deceptively simple question "Why is there a gravedigger's scene in *Hamlet?*" One type of critic will immediately translate this question to a causal context and explain that the stage traditions, or the presence of a similar scene in the source plays, or the audience's demand for a favorite clown would motivate Shakespeare to write the scene, and so sufficiently answer the question. A different critic in the same context will argue that the scene is designed to reveal further Hamlet's melancholy *adust*, especially that form deriving from sanguine humor, since his grave levity, his jesting with death, would be recognized by the Elizabethan playgoer as a standard symptom of that malady.

Operating in a different context, another critic will explain the scene in terms of its effects, pointing out that the comic interlude temporarily relieves, if only finally to heighten, the emotional tension in the audience. This is "why" the scene is in the play. Yet another critic will interpret our question as a call to explain how the scene fits with other parts of the play, how its diction, imagery, and action serve to develop the coherent structure we call *Hamlet*. And still a different critic will understand the question as a request to account for the scene on some imitative principle. Directing our vision to the world of experience, this critic will remind us that the comic and the tragic are often inextricably mixed in life, and will praise the genius of Shakespeare for furnishing richer and truer representations than those found in the more monotonic Greek or French tragedies.

These answers do not exhaust the possibilities, but they reveal an important point about the process of interpretation: the first and crucial step in that process is to decide from what perspective or angle of vision we will view the work. To put it another way, we must decide in what context the work should be placed. Since each answer to our *Hamlet* question implies the choice of a different context, we get the impression—an impression we often get from critical debates—that the respondents are not really answering the same question, are not really debating the issue. This impression is understandable, but it points up the fact that the central issue in criticism is precisely the choice of context. Each of these answers represents an implied argument that the context the interpreter has selected is the most useful, relevant, or illuminating context.

To study criticism systematically, we need to make these arguments explicit. And we need a conceptual scheme or organizing metaphor that will help us define, analyze, and compare the various contexts within which all particular interpretations are made. The scheme I use in this book may be visualized in the form of the accompanying diagram.

Because the essential critical act involves the interpretation of a particular literary work, it is natural that the work in question should hold the central place in the diagram. The symmetrical arrangement of the various "contexts" around that work is, of course, perfectly arbitrary and is designed, like the diagram itself,

simply to help us think systematically about literary criticism. As presented here, a vertical axis unites the author and the audience and represents the basic communication line. Meanings, some semanticists are fond of saying, are in people, not in words, and many theories of interpretation are based on the belief that we must look either to the author (the sender of the words), or to the audience (the receivers), if we are to understand the meaning of the literary text. The types of criticism that see the author's conscious and unconscious intentions and, beyond these, his or her entire social, political, and intellectual milieu as the determiners of the poem's meaning are necessarily concerned to investigate the causal contexts of the work and are appropriately labeled "genetic" approaches. Other forms of criticism pursue the line in the opposite direction and focus on the work's ef-

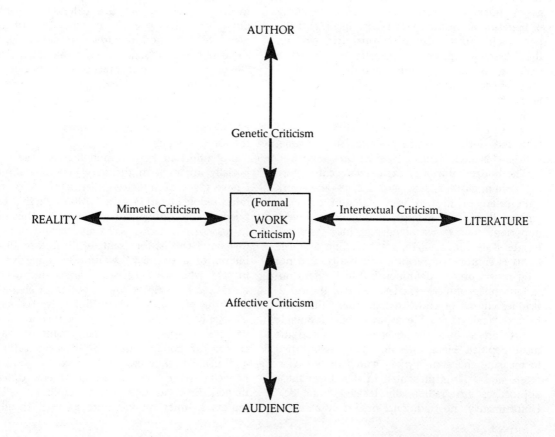

fects rather than on its causes. Critics who adopt these approaches may argue that the study of causes is beyond our reach or merely beside the point, but they agree that the real "meaning" of literature results from the interaction of audience and work. For these critics, then, the reactions of the audience form the important context for the study of literary meaning, and they may be classed together as "affective" critics.

In the view of another group of critics, this tendency to look either to the author or to the audience causes us to overlook the very thing that unites them—the literary work itself. In the language of the communication model, these critics urge us to pay less attention to senders and receivers and more attention to poems, for they believe that meanings are, in fact, in words, and especially in the arrangement of words. In practice, their efforts are devoted largely to demonstrating the poem's coherence by showing how its various parts are integrated to create a complex but artistically unified whole. On their assumptions, the primary context for the study of literature is the completed work itself, and the parenthetical placement of "formal criticism" on the diagram represents the attempt of these critics to isolate the work from the other contexts, especially those labeled "genetic" and "affective." Because they want to show how the various parts interrelate to create the complete poem, these critics are particularly concerned with the "form" of literary works, and "formal criticism" is a widely used label for this context.

The horizontal axis of the diagram cuts across the communication line and locates the work with reference to two very different contexts. One of these is that large, ill-defined, yet very important context we somewhat helplessly call *life*, or *truth*, or, as here, *reality*. None of these terms is entirely satisfactory, and the context not only resists precise definition but also offers notorious philosophical puzzles. Despite these difficulties, forms of criticism that orient the work toward "reality" or "life as experienced outside of art" are at once the most venerable and the most popular. Since they are chiefly concerned to measure the accuracy or "truth" of the characters and actions presented in literature, these approaches are traditionally labeled "mimetic." Unfortunately, no traditional or widely accepted

label exists for those kinds of criticism that direct our attention away from reality and place the work instead in the context of literature as a whole. Because these approaches stress the artifice or conventionality of all literature and argue that any work must be understood by analogy with other works that employ similar conventions, I have called such approaches "intertextual" criticism.

Additional explanations for these and other terms are developed in the introductions to the separate chapters. But the matter of terminology deserves some further comment here. First, we must face the troublesome fact that English has no synonym for the awkward "literary work"; consequently the word *poem* must do double duty, denoting sometimes a verse composition and sometimes any work of literature in verse or prose. In this book I follow the usual practice and occasionally use *poem* in the general sense. So *Hamlet*, for example, and *Heart of Darkness*, are poems as well as *Lycidas*, and "poetics" is the theory of "poetry" in this extended meaning. But I use "literary work" or "literary structure" when the situation requires the more cumbersome but less ambiguous term; and often I use "literary text," since in practice most of our concern is with the printed page, although we should remember that some poems have existed for centuries in purely oral form and that recitations or dramatic performances are not quite the same thing as "texts."

My effort to keep terminology simple is especially apparent in the very general definition I have given of "literary criticism" as "the art of interpreting literary works." Although this fairly bristles with ambiguities, attempts at this point to narrow our terms will only expand our confusions. There is, for example, no leak-proof definition of a "literary" work. The adjective fits most of what we call lyrics, dramas, and fictional narratives in verse or prose, but what else it fits is matter of endless debate. Similarly, "criticism" is usually thought to have both theoretical and practical aspects, as the arrangement of the essays in this book assumes, but it is often difficult and usually unnecessary to trace the fine line between them, or to assign them different names. So I include under "criticism" all attempts to interpret literature as well as all arguments about how this can best be accomplished, however specific or general, *ad hoc* or theoretical. In the last analysis, clarity and precision may lie down easily together, but in this introductory text, which is far from the last analysis, I have tried to keep the distinctions few and functional. After the basic issues have become clear, further refinements can be made. Provisionally, then, "literary works" will mean what we usually mean by that phrase—that is, plays, lyrics, narratives, and things that resemble them—and attempts to interpret these are forms of "literary criticism."

The diagram of critical contexts and the conceptual map it supplies are also offered provisionally, not as the only valid way to classify types of criticism, but as a way that can help us understand some of the fundamental problems of interpretation. One result of this contextual organization is that critics who are usually classed together because they share an ideology or a set of beliefs may be separated in this scheme according to the context in which they operate. So a Freudian critic who investigates an author's unconscious motivations is practicing a form of genetic criticism, while a Freudian critic studying a reader's reactions is, in this plan, an affectivist. And since Freudian psychoanalysis claims to interpret human behavior in general, it also provides a mimetic model by which the truth or "realism" of a literary character's behavior can be measured. Any other fully developed psychological theory will pattern similarly, as will any criticism grounded in a philosophical, religious, or political position like the Marxist, the feminist, the Thomist, the existentialist, and so forth. By cutting across these kinds of classifications, this book's contextual organization pushes to the background questions about the validity of these larger theories, and focuses attention instead on the basic interpretive problems central to all forms of literary criticism. Whatever the critic's political or philosophical position, he or she will have to decide questions of literary meaning within one of the contexts we will be exploring.

The neatly symmetrical diagram is designed to aid that exploration. But such a spatial metaphor can be misleading if we forget that the diagram maps only the main terminals and not the often twisty routes that traffic between them. In practice, a single critic, sometimes in a single essay, may operate in two or more of these contexts. Furthermore, the contexts themselves tend to shade into each other as we move from their central to their peripheral concerns. Nevertheless, as the diagram may serve to remind us, the central position of each context represents a particular way of looking at literary meaning. As we try out these different perspectives and come to see what each may and may not show us, we can learn something important about the art of reading literature. This is our goal; and the justification for this simplified scheme is that it can help us think more clearly about the fundamental issues of interpretation.

This goal has guided my organization in other ways as well. The book is divided into five chapters, each dealing with a separate critical context. Each chapter opens with an introductory essay that explains the basic assumptions and interests of the critics represented in that section. This essay traces briefly the role the context has played in the history of criticism, and it offers an assessment of its place and strength within the contemporary scene. But the main purpose of each prefatory essay is to show how those who adopt this perspective approach the literary work, what kinds of questions they ask, and what kinds of answers they offer.

After this general orientation, each section presents three "theoretical" essays by well-known critics who are themselves committed to this approach. As readers try to come to terms with these wide-ranging and often polemical discussions, they should find that their understanding of the issues is considerably aided by the three "application" essays that conclude each section. Since we may at least provisionally assume that the proof of a critical theory is its ability to somehow illuminate a literary work, readers must be continually testing any theory against the literature they know. Unfortunately, in most collections of critical essays they will face a random accumulation of references to a bewildering number and variety of works, many of which they may not have read well, or recently, or at all. And even those readers who manage to sort through the various examples may still complain that the arguments are difficult to compare because the theories are not brought to bear on the same literary texts. The inclusion of the application essays is designed to aid such comparison. So, after the theoretical essays that explain and defend aspects of the general approach, often with references to many and various examples, each section contains three essays that apply some version of this approach to three famous literary works: *Hamlet*, *Lycidas*, and *Heart of Darkness*.

Because these works are widely studied, chances are good that many readers will be already familiar with them. Because they are few and relatively brief, they can be read and reread along with the critical essays. And because they represent different literary forms and were written in different periods, they furnish useful test cases for theories that claim to apply to literature of all types and times. Finally, each work is extraordinarily rich and complex, and each has inspired a large body of critical commentary representing the several different perspectives. Thus, as readers see each theory applied to works they know well, they will be able to understand more fully what that approach can accomplish. Equally to the point, as they see the different approaches applied to the *same* works, they will be able to estimate more accurately their relative strengths and possible uses.

The arrangement of the contexts themselves is designed to facilitate these comparisons. Readers who work through the chapters in sequence will have some sense of a developing dialogue as they move from the genetic focus to the formal, the affective, the intertextual, and the deconstructive. (The mimetic focus cannot be so easily fixed in the sequence.) To be sure, this sense of development must remain rather hazy because none of these contexts ever completely displaces another, and each has many current proponents who offer rejoinders to earlier objections. So the arguments in the essays move back and forth in time. Nonetheless, and with many qualifications, the order of the chapters roughly follows the general development, or drift, of literary criticism in the twentieth century, especially in the English-speaking countries. And this geographical distinction is worth remarking. Most of the essays reprinted here were written originally in English, and the perspective of this book is essentially Anglo-American. Continental influences—and these are particularly strong at present—are acknowledged primarily as their impact is felt in the English-speaking world. If this dialogue were restaged from a European perspective, the chronology and the emphases would be different. But the basic questions, and the fundamental issues of interpretation, would be the same. These are what we want to get at. And since some selection is necessary, it seems to me that, for most readers of this book, the Anglo-American perspective offers the most direct way to get at them.

I have chosen a contemporary focus for the same reason. The "applications" included here are mainly of recent vintage, for I want to stress the point that although each of these contexts has a rich history, none is merely a historical curiosity; on the contrary, each is the basis for some vital contemporary criticism. At the same time, I have sought to include clear and forceful examples of each approach, and I have occasionally selected an earlier essay that met these criteria better than more recent examples. Similar concerns have controlled my choice of the "theoretical" essays. For the most part I have reprinted fairly recent writings, since these can take into account current refinements and objections and reflect more directly the contemporary debate on these perennial issues. But we should always remember that these *are* perennial issues, and I have not hesitated to include an older essay if it seemed to set forth the basic arguments and assumptions more clearly and more provocatively. Without clarity, we seldom think well; without provocation, we seldom think at all.

In fact, I am convinced that the reader who is provoked enough to enter actively into these debates will gain the most from this book. Throughout this introduction I have talked about "perspectives" and "approaches," and the book itself describes and illustrates different critical "contexts." It will be easy for the reader to assume that each context must have a special but limited validity and that the best literary criticism must be an eclectic combination of all contexts. Such a conclusion has some points to recommend it. It is consistent with the complexity of literature and with the diversity of critical practice; it acknowledges the fact that it is difficult to apply "outside" objections in some useful way to internally consistent systems; and it allows the eclectic critic to adopt an inclusive and tolerant, rather than an exclusive and combative, rhetorical stance. Besides, elementary logic suggests that no one of these contexts is likely to offer all the important truths about a literary work.

But by the same logic it is also unlikely that all contexts should offer equally valid or useful insights. To put it another way, while we may agree that there is no complete, definitive, and absolutely correct interpretation of a poem, it does not necessarily follow that there are no better or worse interpretations, interpretations more or less complete, more or less accurate, more or less approximating a "best" reading. At any rate, most of the writers included here will argue that their perspective offers a better way to read, and since all readers must confront the same problems of interpretation, all readers have a real stake in these arguments. If you are to come to an informed decision about them, you will need to analyze them carefully, compare them closely, and test them against specific literary works. This book is designed to make these operations easier. As my title is meant to suggest, these are contexts *for* criticism. Since to read at all is to read from one or another of these perspectives, the informed reader should at least know which he or she has chosen, and why.

Suggestions for Further Reading

For historical background, M. C. Beardsley's *Aesthetics from Classical Greece to the Present: A Short History* (1966) and W. K. Wimsatt and Cleanth Brooks's *Literary Criticism: A Short History* (1957) are helpful one-volume surveys. René Wellek's *A History of Modern Criticism* (4 vols., 1955–1965) is the most comprehensive history of Western critical theory from 1750 to 1900. A very selective list of the many more specialized histories, roughly in order of the period treated, includes G. M. A. Grube, *The Greek and Roman Critics* (1965), D. A. Russell, *Criticism in Antiquity* (1981), B. Weinberg, *A History of Literary Criticism in the Italian Renaissance* (2 vols., 1961), B. Hathaway, *The Age of Criticism: The Late Renaissance in Italy* (1962), E. R. Marks, *The Poetics of Reason* (1968), M. H. Abrams, *The Mirror and the Lamp* (1953). For the present century, Wellek's two-volume continuation of his *History* (1986) treats British and American criticism to about 1950. S. E. Hyman, *The Armed Vision* (rev. ed., 1955), Walter Sutton, *Modern American Criticism* (1963), and Lee Lemon, *The Partial Critics* (1965), cover some of the same territory. Wayne Booth, *Critical Understanding* (1979), Gerald Graff, *Literature Against Itself* (1979), Frank Lentricchia, *After the New Criticism* (1981), and Terry Eagleton, *Literary Theory: An Introduction* (1983), discuss more recent trends. For the parodist's vision of sanity in bedlam, try Frederick Crews, *The Pooh Perplex* (1965), and Herbert Lindenberger, *Saul's Fall* (1979).

Chapter One

Genetic Criticism: Author as Context

In ev'ry Work regard the *Writer's End*,
Since none can compass more than they
    Intend.

Pope, Essay on Criticism

Poems are caused by people. On this plausible premise the genetic critics ground their argument and approach. Most models of verbal communication posit a speaker or writer and an audience. From the author's point of view, the problem is to communicate meaning as effectively as possible; from the audience's perspective, the task is to interpret that meaning as accurately as possible. To ask what a poem means is, on this view, to ask what the author meant when he or she created it.

The model is familiar enough from everyday experience. We overhear a snatch of conversation—"At three o'clock, then"—and we wonder who is to do what and where at three o'clock. Or we're baffled by the command "Bring it here" when the referent of "it" is not clear. In each case we apply to the source to discover the meaning. "Bring what here?" we ask, or "What is to happen at three?" And so with the many examples of imperfect communication: the cryptic telegram ("ship sails back"), the short note you scribbled to yourself a week ago ("see Svoboda") and now no longer comprehend. Of course, the telegram and the note may present more challenging problems. If the sender has left no address or if repeated interrogation of the memory elicits no information about Svoboda, then you may give up and say you don't know what the telegram or the note means. That such messages meant something to the minds that formulated them, we don't doubt—but since we don't have access to those minds, we feel we can't uncover that meaning. And this is so even in the case where the mind is one's own.

The point to notice about these familiar examples is the automatic assumption that to speak of meaning or communication at all is to imply a meaning or communicating mind. And it is to imply, further, that the real meaning of any utterance is in the mind of its author at the time of the utterance. Now, since a poem is, in nearly every instance, the product of a human mind, it would seem natural to take the same approach to poetic meaning. It is true that poems are verbal constructs vastly more sophisticated and complicated than these examples. It is also true that direct consultation with the author is usually difficult. This difficulty arises partly because writers tend to be reticent, evasive, or even deceptive when discussing the "meaning" of their works and partly because they are, very often, simply dead. Here the telegram is the closer analogy. But the puzzling note provides a parallel, too. For even if authors were willing to discuss their intentions, two factors would prevent them giving the definitive interpretation. In the first place, they would have to talk about what they meant at some point in the past—yesterday, last year, a decade ago. In the second place, we may not wish to limit "meaning" to conscious intention, and authors are seldom in a position to tell us what they may have unconsciously meant.

Nonetheless, a mind had caused the poem to exist, had consciously or unconsciously meant something in forming the work, and since it is the task of criticism to discover as fully as possible the meaning of the poem, this can best be done by understanding as fully as possible the mind that created it. Although we may never know completely or precisely everything that Shakespeare meant in *Hamlet*, only to the extent that we can approximate his meaning can we claim to know what the play "means." We may suggest, and critics have suggested, dozens of interpretations for Milton's "two-handed en-

gine"; but each interpretation is a plausible "meaning" only to the degree we are convinced that Milton may have "meant" it. The genetic critic, then, provides a clear, if at first glance a rather odd, answer to the old question "What does the poem imitate?" It imitates, says this critic, the poem in the mind of the creator at the moment of composition. Therefore, in terms of our scheme the chief context for the study of poems is the relationship between the poet and his or her work, between the cause and the effect. And the task of the genetic critic is to find out everything possible about the mind of the poet in order to discover what that mind meant in any particular poem.

It is important to conceive the task in this way, because genetic critics have often shown little interest in defining carefully their assumptions and procedures, and they have sometimes lost sight of the critical object of their studies. Thus, a book advertised as a "critical" biography may offer a wealth of details about an author's life but may apply very few of these details to an interpretation of particular poems. Or such a book may spend more time using the evidence of the poems to illuminate an author's life (many "biographies" of Shakespeare are necessarily of this type) than the other way around. Indeed, these contrary lines of argument always risk getting so thoroughly tangled that we are left with a mere tautology. In that case, the whole argument fails. As for using literary works to tell us about the author's life, we need not here inquire into the legitimacy of this procedure as biography. It simply isn't a form of literary criticism at all. Our concern is only with those studies or parts of studies that move from the author to the work. For the task of the genetic *critic*, to repeat, is to understand the mind of the author in order to better interpret the creations of that mind.

Even thus limited, the job of the genetic critic is formidable. To understand the poet's mind at the time of the poem's creation means, in practice, to assemble and interpret any and all documents that may throw light on that mind, and these can be numerous. The author's letters and his or her library will be relevant certainly, earlier and later works probably, laundry lists possibly. Then there are the recorded comments of those who knew the author well or casually or hardly at all. As we approach our own time, the number of available documents pertaining to a writer may become very large, and for a contemporary author the enterprising biographer can supplement the written record with direct interviews.

Conversely, as we move back in time, the amount of information about authors rapidly diminishes; we know little about Marlowe, less about Virgil, nothing at all about "Homer." This state of affairs is naturally lamented by genetic critics who consider it axiomatic that if we had more information about, say, Shakespeare's schooling or Chaucer's reading or Sophocles' religious views, we would be better able to understand their writings. But the lack of specifically biographical information does not fatally handicap genetic criticism. We may have no documentary evidence about Shakespeare's school days, but we can find out a good deal about what was studied and how in the schools available to someone of his age and station. We may not know exactly what Chaucer read, but we can discover what most educated people of his time were reading. We can never know with any precision what Sophocles' religious views were, but we can learn something about the forms of worship practiced in his day, what was considered orthodox, what not.

By this logic the inquiry widens to include a great deal more than the strictly biographical. For the genetic critic, after all, is by definition a student of causes, and if a poem is the product of an author and the author is the product of an age, then nothing less than a full understanding of that age—the author's entire political, social, and intellectual milieu—is required if we are to fully understand that author's art. And, paradoxically, the need for this kind of information seems to grow as the author is more distant from us and the biographical information more scant. This explains why, although the known facts of Shakespeare's life will barely fill a page, the books about his life can easily fill a shelf. Add to these the many books treating Elizabethan religion, politics, economics, science, and all the other elements that make up the "life" of the "time," from sweeping generalizations about "world views" to the minutiae of numerology

and pneumatology, and you have a sizable library.

And so with every writer and his or her "age." To be sure, not all these studies are examples of genetic criticism strictly defined; some don't even pretend to be. Just as a biography, even of a literary figure, can exist as biography and make no claim to supply interpretations of poems, so a study of Elizabethan psychology or seventeenth-century religious controversy or Victorian legal reforms may be written simply to cast light on that subject, and may use literary texts as part of its evidence, without making any claim to the status of literary criticism. In practice, however, most biographies of writers and most period studies with a literary cast do make such claims, at least implicitly. When we are offered an investigation of the sources of Blake's religious thought, of the background of the Battle of the Books, of the inadequacies of Keats's philosophy or Dryden's wife, we naturally expect that the investigator will get around to telling us something interpretive about poems. Frequently this expectation is disappointed. A great number of such studies are apparently offered on the theory that if an understanding of the age will lead to an understanding of poems, the scholar need only brighten a particular corner of the subject.

But this observation simply notes again the failure of many genetic studies to keep a clear critical focus; it does not, in itself, undercut the genetic position. And of course many genetic studies do make specific references to literary works and do attempt to relate knowledge of an author's life and period to an understanding of his or her works. It is with these that we are concerned, and their number and variety are imposing. Studies of the author's life and social milieu, the philosophic currents of the age, and the history of his or her ideas, continue to multiply, continue to be the focus of much classroom instruction, continue to form the bulk of what is generally called "literary study."

This state of affairs is so familiar in the last quarter of the twentieth century that we may be a little startled to reflect that the immense industry devoted to genetic study is a relatively recent phenomenon. While the genetic context has been the most heavily cultivated one in the past century, in the previous twenty-three it was the least. Aristotle, for instance, showed a lively interest in most of the contexts I have diagrammed, but he saw no reason for criticism to be much concerned with the maker of poems, and with few exceptions critics agreed with him on this point until well into the eighteenth century. So, despite the apparently axiomatic nature of the argument for genetic criticism, and despite its prominence in bibliographies and classroom instruction, the emphasis on the author and the period, on the circumstances of the poem's composition, is distinctly modern. This emphasis seems to have come about largely as a result of two different but mutually reinforcing influences. The first was a gradual shift in the conception of a poem from something that reflected or imitated nature to something that reflected or expressed an individual, a unique mind. This shift, which had its chronological center somewhere near the beginning of the nineteenth century, was bound to focus attention on the life of the author, a kind of attention, not coincidentally, that some writers of the period seemed to invite. The second influence, which also had its roots in the eighteenth century but which did not become dominant until the nineteenth, was the sense of the *pastness* of the past, the idea that each "age" has different assumptions and different values, and hence that the art of any period can be understood only by someone specially trained to understand those assumptions and values.

These two ideas, then, one stressing the individuality of the poet, the other the individuality of the age, combined in the nineteenth century to turn literary study toward the biographical and the historical. And when, very late in the century, the graduate study of literature came into being, first in Germany, then in the United States and England, that study developed as a variation of the "scientific historicism" that dominated most academic disciplines at the time. Here the poetic value of a work might be assumed, could even occasionally be discussed in a warm "appreciation," but such discussions were "after hours," so to speak, and hopelessly "impressionistic." Real scholarship was concerned with the facts—that is to say, with the historical facts. And again this empha-

sis meant that at the inception of modern literary study on the academic level, the chief concern was with the circumstances of the poem's composition.

Thus, in the early decades of the twentieth century, genetic criticism—the approach to the poem through the study of the life and times of its author—reigned virtually unchallenged in the universities. The genetic approach dealt in facts and required "research," like any solid academic discipline. It investigated the causes of things—something else that marked it as a legitimate field of study. And if, though few as yet raised the objection, the approach had no way to distinguish a poem from any other verbal construct, this inability was not necessarily a defect; any document could tell us something about the author or the age that produced it, and that knowledge in turn could be reflected back to illuminate any document. For the study of "literature," sometimes defined as anything written, was in its grandest conception nothing less than the study of cultural history. But even when more narrowly conceived as an inquiry whose end was the understanding of poems, the genetic approach had academic respectability: it was concerned with objective data; it employed "scholarship," and—not least important—it provided an easily understood and widely accepted scheme for organizing literary study.

Given the assumptions of genetic criticism, the proper context for such study was clearly the causal context. *Paradise Lost* may be an epic, *Lycidas* a pastoral elegy, and *Samson Agonistes* a drama, but to the genetic critic the fact of overriding importance is that they are all poems by John Milton. So the author, the most obvious cause of poems, becomes the first organizing focus of literary study. As one result, we have hundreds of books describing the lives and works of major and not-so-major writers, and no English curriculum is considered complete if it lacks separate courses devoted to, at the very least, Chaucer, Shakespeare, and Milton. But the writer, according to these same assumptions, is the product of an age, and that assumption suggests another causal principle: we should study the "Renaissance" writers together, and the "Victorians," the "Romantics," the "Augustans," and so on. The different sources implicit in these labels and the notoriously shifty boundaries between such "ages" may suggest that the problems of periodicity have never been fully resolved. But these difficulties are minor. The logic of genetic criticism demands some period arrangement, just as the concern with causes further suggests that, as far as practical, we should study the writers within each period and the periods themselves in chronological order. Causes, after all, work through time and only in one direction.

In fact, despite the powerful and in some ways successful challenges to the dominance of genetic criticism, the genetic categories of author, period, nation, and chronological sequence, which are essentially the categories employed by Hippolyte Taine in the nineteenth century, remain nearly the only categories used to organize literary study in American universities. This conservatism shows partly the strength of the genetic position, partly that the other contexts, even where they have supplanted that position, have been unable to supply any alternative organizing schemes. As a consequence, the organization of literary study often shows a genetic basis even when some other forms of criticism are being practiced.

But genetic criticism continues to be much more than a framework for other kinds of studies. Many scholars accept all or part of the causal argument, teach comfortably within the period organization, and publish books and essays about the historical backgrounds of poems and authors. Biographical studies flourish, some employing the analytical tools of Freud and his followers and rivals to get at the author's unconscious meanings, others content to concentrate on more conscious and more fully documented intentions. And studies of the writer's "age," of the various aspects of the cultural milieu, continue to be published in large numbers.

Nevertheless, in contrast to the earlier decades of the century, the genetic approaches now no longer monopolize literary study. Other contexts are also heavily cultivated, and the story of their challenge to the genetic supremacy is a central chapter in the history of twentieth-century criticism. We need not rehearse here all the details of that chapter. It will be enough to sketch a few of the challengers' arguments to provide a context for the essays that follow. Some of these arguments are aimed at the geneticist's methods and some at the genetic conception of literary criticism. As for the first, because there is no single "school" of genetic criticism, challengers who try a piecemeal attack soon find they are battling a hydra. Arguments against, say, psychoanalytic interpretations, do not necessarily engage economic determinists, and attacks on both may be viewed with equanimity by advocates of "sociological" criticism. But in so far as these or any other genetic approaches claim to interpret poems, they are claiming that a study of causes tells us something useful about effects, and to question this central assumption is to question all forms of genetic criticism.

When the matter is stated this abstractly, we may remember that strong logical objections to the very concept of causality are at least as old as Hume, and they apply with particular force to causal explanations of "effects" as complicated as poems. Of course, literary studies seldom claim anything more than a fair degree of probability or plausibility, so it would be pointless to try to hold them to the absolute standards of pure logic. But granting that probability or plausibility is the best that can be achieved in any attempt to interpret poems, the objectors argue that even on these grounds the genetic position is difficult to defend. Where a particular model of the human psyche is assumed or where an established hierarchy of compelling causes is stipulated, as in some Freudian or Marxist readings, we will be inclined to accept the specific argument to the extent that we have already accepted the general model. But where such systematic faiths are not directly invoked—and they are not, in the vast majority of studies—the causal connections are likely on examination to look rather blurred. We may be ready to agree, for example, that Stephen Crane's style owes something to his training and experience as a journalist, until we reflect that some journalists write novels in a very different style and, furthermore, that some authors who write in a similar style are not journalists. Then we begin to wonder what kind of "causal" statement we have been given.

This is a simple example, but it illustrates the

objectors' point that the more we examine any relationship between an author's life and work, the more difficult it is to establish firm causal connections. Some writers lived in poverty and wrote about it; some lived in it and didn't. Some writers led apparently happy lives and described harrowing experiences; some suffered terrible personal losses and wrote lighthearted farces. Some wrote both kinds of works almost simultaneously. There are writers who had tortured relationships with their fathers and who wrote haunting allegories about harsh and inscrutable deities. Others had tortured relationships with their fathers and wrote very different kinds of books. Some writers even managed to get on tolerably well with their fathers. To be sure, concepts such as repression, displacement, and sublimation will account for all these relationships—and for any others. But the very ease of the procedure makes it suspect.

On the one hand, then, it seems unreasonable to deny that the crucial experiences in a writer's life must leave some mark on his or her character and thought. On the other hand, it is often difficult to use specific pieces of biographical information to explain the meaning of a literary work. And information about the writer's period is similarly problematic. Even if we could discover what many or most Elizabethans believed about ghosts, and even if it turned out that they believed much the same things, we still wouldn't necessarily know what Shakespeare thought about the subject or what he might have meant in *Hamlet*, unless, that is, we were willing to assume that Shakespeare was a typical Elizabethan or that he expressed only typical beliefs in his plays. Such assumptions do seem to underlie many investigations of the writer's political, social, or intellectual milieu, but the assumptions are seldom clearly stated, and when they are, they look somewhat questionable. If the "age" does in fact make the writer, then we must admit that it sometimes makes writers very different from their contemporaries. Furthermore, close examination generally shows that a historical "period" is fully as complex, unpredictable, and contradictory as the individuals it comprises. As it happens, different Elizabethans believed wildly different

things about ghosts. So here again we face a dilemma. On the one side we have the plausible assumption that authors will be affected by the intellectual currents and social conditions that surround them. As we have noted, most literary study is organized on this assumption. On the other side, we have the argument that it is seldom easy in practice to make firm connections between (1) a knowledge of these currents and conditions and (2) the attitudes held by particular authors or—and this is not always the same thing—the attitudes expressed in particular poems.

By such arguments the objectors have sought to show that causal links between the period, the poet, and the poem are much more elusive, much more difficult to establish, than many genetic critics were willing to admit, and that to demonstrate them would require much more rigor and finesse than many genetic studies were wont to show, if indeed they could be demonstrated at all. Most genetic critics today would probably admit that their task is more problematic than it had once appeared, that it demands not only wide knowledge but interpretive delicacy and tact. Naturally they would not agree that their difficulties are inherently insoluble or that the causal links can never be plausibly demonstrated.

A more radical challenge to genetic criticism does not trouble to deny the possibility of the genetic task but denies instead its relevance. The entire genetic model, so this argument runs, is misleading. Poems are not like scribbled notes or ambiguous telegrams; nor are they like any other documents. They are very special verbal constructs that use language in a special way, and they do not relate to their authors the way other documents do. Formal critics have pursued this line of argument most vigorously, an argument based on a particular conception of a poem. For the formalist, such features as the tensive balance between different parts, the unity controlling a diversity of elements, and the resultant ambiguity, paradox, and irony are the defining features of poems. These characteristics separate poems from other verbal constructs, and it is with these that criticism must deal. Thus it follows, in this view, that a study of the circumstances of the poem's composition, no matter how carefully conducted, can never tell us much about these features and so can never lead to *critical* interpretation. The geneticists' tendency to treat the poem like any other kind of document, their failure to conceive of poetry as a special use of language, deflects attention to nonessential, "unpoetic" factors, and when geneticists do provide interpretations, they are likely to be reductive. That is, even if we could discover precisely what the poem meant to its author or its original audience, we still would not have discovered the full range of the "legitimate" meanings of the poem. In short, the "real" poem, in this argument, is not the poem in the author's mind at the moment of creation, so there is little point in searching for that mind or that moment.

We will leave to another section the discussion of the ways a poem may be thought to exist independently of its author or period. Here we simply note that such a conception undermines the foundation of all forms of genetic criticism. At the same time, by urging a definition of a poem that is also a description of a "good" poem, the formalist reminds us that it is difficult to develop a convincing theory of poetic value on strictly genetic lines. Although values of a kind are apparently implied in many genetic studies—this work is worth our attention because it is so thoroughly Jamesian, so typical of the Restoration, or so representative of the Victorian concern with evolution—most often such reasons are advanced, if they are directly advanced at all, to justify the study of minor or second-rate works. And obviously a poem might just as easily be valued for the opposite reasons, for its lack of typicality. More to the point, the typicality of acknowledged masterpieces is seldom discussed, and we would think it odd if someone were to try to persuade us that *Oedipus Rex* or *King Lear* were valuable simply because they were, or were not, "representative" Greek or Elizabethan plays.

Closely related to estimates of typicality but more promising as a basis for value is the argument of the historical relativist that our judgment of poems should be guided by period standards. The poet aimed to excel under the terms

and conditions of the times, and it is unfair to try his or her work by a different court. To judge accurately a medieval fabliau or an eighteenth-century satire, a Romantic ode or a Victorian novel, we have to condition ourselves to think and feel as their intended audiences did. This position seems defensible, and has the further advantage of appealing to our sympathetic imagination. In practice, though, the advice often doesn't hold in the crucial cases. We are inclined to say that the "Miller's Tale" or *Gulliver's Travels*, "Ode on a Grecian Urn" or *Middlemarch*, are simply great works, and we probably feel little need to add that they were great by the standards of their own periods. Then too, it is easy to find examples of works we value highly, like Melville's novels or Blake's poems, which were largely unappreciated by their first audiences. And, from the other side, a check of publishing records from the eighteenth century to this week's bestseller list indicates that popular taste has rather consistently run toward what most serious students of literature would call the ephemeral and the second-rate. Historical relativists may object that they are really urging us to think like a discriminating Elizabethan playgoer, a perceptive Victorian reader. But this objection seems to beg the question.

The basic communication model suggests yet another value scheme. Every utterance is an attempt to express something, an idea, a feeling, a set of facts, and is successful to the extent that it effectively communicates what it set out to communicate. A poem, then, would be good if it achieved what its author intended. This approach, too, seems promising. Surely it is pointless to complain about the presence of a chorus in a play by Aeschylus or about the absence of one in a play by Ibsen, to object that Donne's meter lacks the regularity of Pope's or that *Ulysses* is not structured like *Tom Jones*. It is foolish to condemn a work for lacking features the author never intended to supply. But in these and similar instances the argument is not really genetic. The evidence for "intention" is simply our understanding of the work itself. The procedure becomes genetic only when the evidence for what was intended, consciously or otherwise, is sought elsewhere, in letters, diaries, recorded conversations, in assumptions about what the "age" demanded or understood; in other words, only when "intention" is conceivably different from the achieved poem and independently knowable.

In such cases, we could compare what the author did with what he or she intended to do. But even this comparison might not give us a firm basis for judging poetic excellence. For example, if coherence is a value and a poem is judged incoherent, it is a weak defense of the poem to claim that it was meant to be incoherent. For similar reasons, apparent value terms such as "sincerity" or "authenticity," in so far as they refer to an alignment of achievement and intention, are of little help. A mawkish sonnet remains mawkish even if it perfectly expresses the sentiment of its creator, and a puerile satire is none the less puerile for accurately reflecting its author's mind. Indeed, the more the subject is examined, the clearer it becomes that the study of intention provides little basis for evaluating poems. If the ghost of Chaucer were to appear to us and swear that he saw nothing funny or ironic in the "Nun's Priest's Tale," we would have to revise our estimate, not of the poem, but of the critical acumen of Chaucer's ghost.

The difficulty of establishing a genetic basis of value is one more deficiency charged against genetic criticism, and it might be added to the other and more serious objections: that genetic criticism claims to establish causal links difficult or impossible to demonstrate, and that such links are, even if demonstrable, irrelevant to the critical task. This combination of arguments has spurred many critics to develop other contexts for analyzing and evaluating poems, with the result that today genetic approaches no longer dominate literary study to the extent that they once did. But the fact that genetic criticism continues to thrive shows that large numbers of critics do not find these objections overwhelming. For them, the failure to provide a genetic scheme for evaluating poems is probably the least troublesome charge. Not all critics are convinced that judging poems is a major part of the business of criticism and, in any event, it seems axiomatic that the full understanding of a poem must precede any sound evaluation of it. To the

extent genetic critics can claim to provide at least part of that understanding, they can concede their lack of value theory with a shrug.

It is, of course, exactly their ability to contribute to our understanding of poems that is questioned in the other objections. As to the inherent difficulty of their task, here again the geneticists can grant the point. We need, they argue, more and better information, more refined methodology, and more careful application. If psychoanalytical criticism has often been clumsy, the remedy is not to abandon psychoanalysis but to apply it with more care and tact. If generalizations about, say, the "neoclassical" concern with restraint and reason are too simplistic or inaccurate to throw much light on writers such as Swift or Gay, the cure is not to abandon studies of the period but to pursue them with more intensity and rigor.

More radical objections that genetic studies, no matter how carefully conducted, are doomed to fail in the nature of the case, are more difficult to address. To answer them directly, critics must step outside their own frame of reference far enough to examine and defend their most basic assumptions. If such defenders were rare when genetic studies were—and perhaps because they were—the only firmly established kinds of literary study, they are more plentiful now that strong rivals have entered the field. On the one side, these defenders stand opposed to the ahistorical view that we *should* read each poem as if it were essentially anonymous and contemporary, a verbal object to be understood by the public norms of language and judged by universal standards. On the other side, paradoxically, they confront the radically historical view that we *must* read each poem as if it were contemporary with us, for no matter how we try to transport ourselves to other places and periods, we inevitably carry our cultural perspective with us and remain twentieth-century readers. The radical historicist, in other words, applies the genetic notion of historical relativism with a vengeance, and in such a way as to undercut the geneticist's program. For if we can never lay aside our cultural blinders, then we are forced to read as the ahistorical critics say we should.

Against this odd alliance of forces, the genetic theorists continue to maintain that we can, with much care and labor, reach an understanding of other periods at least approximating that of the poem's original and intended audience. On this point they find the radical position simply too sweeping to be logically supportable. And furthermore, they argue, we should labor to gain such understanding. For these critics, the communication model remains the fundamental model, and it follows that to speak of meaning in any determinate sense is to speak of an author's meaning. Other contexts, they grant, can tell us what a work *may* mean, but only their own can tell us what it *does* mean. Without the knowledge of an author's character and culture that genetic studies supply, there can be no useful check on the often "impressionistic," "anachronistic," "overly ingenious," and otherwise "irresponsible" interpretations that critics operating in other contexts are apt to produce. In short, only the genetic context, they claim, can offer a stable meaning for "meaning."

Suggestions for Further Reading

Because this context includes many and diverse approaches, about all one can do is cite representative examples of some of the different kinds of "genetic" criticism. At the center, of course, is the very popular "critical biography." The form is discussed in Leon Edel, *Literary Biography* (1957), and it may be sampled in such exemplary works as Edel on Henry James (1953–1972), Edgar Johnson on Charles Dickens (1952), and Richard Ellmann on James Joyce (rev. ed., 1982). See also Ellmann's *Golden Codgers: Biographical Speculations* (1973). Sigmund Freud, *On Creativity and the Unconscious* (1958), shows some of the master's ideas; Frederick Crews, *Out of My System* (1975), shows a recent critic's evaluation and use of Freud's concepts. If the author's life is the center of genetic studies, the

elastic boundaries of his or her "times" or "milieu" form the circumference. The once-popular *Zeitgeist* or "spirit of the age" study is illustrated in E. M. W. Tillyard's famous *The Elizabethan World Picture* (1943); Eleanor Prosser, *Hamlet and Revenge* (2nd ed., 1971), shows how a scholar's wide reading in one aspect of a period can be focused to challenge our usual interpretations of a literary work. A classic example of source tracing is John L. Lowes, *The Road to Xanadu* (1927); an equally classic instance of the "history of ideas" approach is A. O. Lovejoy, *The Great Chain of Being* (1936). Both of these methods overlap a good deal with intertextual criticism, though they are based on quite different assumptions about the locus of literary meaning. Raymond Williams, *Culture and Society, 1780–1950*, employs a "sociohistorical" approach. See also Jeffrey Sammons, *Literary Sociology and Practical Criticism: An Inquiry* (1977). Because Marxist critics have often been centrally concerned with genetic questions, this diverse group may be cited here. Some representative texts are Georg Lukács, *The Historical Novel* (1937), David Craig, ed., *Marxists on Literature* (1975), Terry Eagleton, *Marxism and Literary Criticism* (1976), Fredric Jameson, *The Political Unconscious* (1981), and Michael Ryan, *Marxism and Deconstruction* (1982). Two recent attempts to formulate the internal dynamics of literary history are W. J. Bate, *The Burden of the Past and the English Poet* (1970), and Harold Bloom, *The Anxiety of Influence* (1973). E. D. Hirsch, *Validity in Interpretation* (1967), advances arguments for regarding the author as the ultimate source of meaning. Some of these arguments are further developed in P. D. Juhl, *Interpretation: An Essay in the Philosophy of Literary Criticism* (1980). Essays on both sides of this issue have been gathered in D. Newton-DeMolina, ed., *On Literary Intention* (1976).

Theory

The Historical Criticism of Milton

A. S. P. Woodhouse

In "The Historical Criticism of Milton," A. S. P. Woodhouse offers "a definition and defence of Historical Criticism," under which term he includes most critical procedures this book calls "genetic." He begins his defense, which has been prompted by the writings of the New Critics or formalists, by granting that historical research is not quite the same thing as historical criticism—the application of research to the interpretation of a work or an author. Having cleared the ground, he goes on to list the areas in which this kind of application can make significant contributions to our understanding, using Milton's poetry as the exemplary case. In the process, he repeats some of the most important, and most contested, claims for genetic criticism. Central to these is the claim that a knowledge of authors' "extra-aesthetic experiences," of their lives outside their poetry, can be a crucial aid to our interpretation of their poems. Moving beyond strictly biographical information, Woodhouse argues that "Milton's thought as thought is very much 'of an age' and hence susceptible only of historical elucidation"—that is to say, elucidation only by those who have carefully studied Milton's complex intellectual and religious milieu. While he grants that a great poem in some mysterious way transcends the time of its creation, he insists that it also remains rooted in that time. To try to read it without reference to its age is not to escape historical relativism but to fall into another form of it: to exchange the blinders of the poet's milieu for the blinders of our own. In brief compass, then, Woodhouse temperately but insistently asserts many of the chief claims of genetic criticism.

Reprinted by permission of the Modern Language Association of America from *PMLA* 66 (1951): 1033–44. Copyright © 1951 by the Modern Language Association of America.

As I UNDERSTAND THE ASSIGNMENT GIVEN TO ME, it is to suggest a definition and defence of Historical Criticism as applied to Milton, while Mr. Brooks is to tell us how the New Criticism (as it is called) would deal with the poet. So short a time has elapsed since Mr. Eliot took down the sign reading "No Thoroughfare," and directing an elaborate detour around Milton, that Mr. Brooks enjoys, I imagine, a freedom from embarrassing examples, which I can only envy. Again, he has at command a growing body of theory; for the New Critics have been concerned to provide their own dialectic, whereas historical students of literature have tended to work by a silent instinct of accumulation like the bee. Obviously, no one can hope to supply in a thirty-minute paper a theory of Historical Criticism though I shall try to set down a few points toward the formation of such a theory. Nor is it any part of my purpose to attack the New Criticism in its theory or practice. First, because I do not know enough about it, being indeed somewhat in the case of Lord Monboddo. ("Have you read my last book?" asked Lord Kames. "No, my lord," said Monboddo; "I can't read as fast as you can write.") But secondly (and seriously) because we have had enough, I think, of mutual recrimination, and it is time for each side to make plain, without polemics, what it can do for the elucidation of Milton, in the hope that students who care more for literature than for labels may find something of use to them in both schools. For criticism, of whatever school, is a means, not an end; and the test to be applied to it is purely pragmatic: Does it or does it not throw new light on, or minister to an understanding of, the work or the author under examination? By that test alone it must stand or fall.

I will commence by drawing a distinction between historical criticism and historical research. The latter is concerned with the amassing and ordering of historical facts; the former, with an application of the results to the interpretation of a work or an author, which is the proper business of all criticism. In practice, of course, the two activities are often fruitfully combined, but the distinction is nevertheless valid and necessary. With historical research as such I shall not be directly concerned. But since it is clearly instrumental to historical criticism, its utility will inevitably follow from the utility of historical criticism if that is established.

Now, the common possession of all schools of criticism is the text; and where they differ is in the method which they adopt in interpreting this common possession. It is the boast of the New Criticism that it concentrates all its attention upon the text and applies to it a purely aesthetic analysis, waiving every extraneous consideration. And this we may concede to be admirable, so far as it goes. But the really difficult questions remain: What considerations are indeed extraneous, or rather, what considerations are really germane? And how far does aesthetic pattern, the object of analysis, itself involve materials which are utilized by the poetic process, but in no sense originated by it? To these questions we shall return; for they are fundamental. Meanwhile we must notice the common indictment of the Historical Critic, that he allows a consideration of sources and analogues, and of historical influences generally, to distract his attention from the text. This, in so far as it is true, is an example of human weakness, and no necessary concomitant of historical method; for the very object with which the historical data are brought forward is the elucidation of the text. But finally, under the heading of text, it is to be observed that Historical Criticism (though not every historical critic) is concerned with the text in a way in which the New Criticism is not. The establishment of the true text is the business, not merely of historical research, but of historical criticism: it demands an application of the results of historical research to this particular problem, by the critical intelligence. Of the work in progress by Professor Harris Fletcher and others, I am not competent to speak in detail. I do not know whether it has yet resulted in deter-

minations of comparable critical importance to those reached in the very different problem of Shakespeare's text—determinations like Professor Dover Wilson's that what Hamlet really said was, "O that this too, too *sullied* flesh would melt." Whether it has or not, no one will deny that the establishment of the true text is an essential task, without which neither historical elucidation nor aesthetic analysis can proceed with safety. Here, then, is the first department of Historical Criticism, and its first claim to be regarded as indispensable. It alone can supply the text on which the New Criticism desires to focus all its attention.

With the text established, a wide field of investigation and crucial decision opens out. The starting point is the text of the individual poems, but the sum of the decisions reached should yield a critical estimate of Milton the poet. So far (if I am not mistaken) the New Criticism has largely confined itself to the individual poem (and to the shorter and more purely lyric examples thereof) and has looked on, not to the character of the particular poet, but rather to the nature of poetry in general, as its larger objective. Herein it differs sharply from Historical Criticism, whose procedure is to examine all the author's poems, of whatever length and kind, and thus to advance from the individual poem (the primary concern of all criticism) to the whole body of his work. Let us compromise by taking as our starting point a poem of middle length and remind ourselves how Historical Criticism would deal—indeed has dealt—with *Samson Agonistes*.

Now, it is perfectly possible to attempt an analysis of the aesthetic pattern of *Samson Agonistes*, and to such an analysis every critic must come. The question is whether or not the analysis shall be undertaken in the light of certain historical facts. *Samson Agonistes* is Milton's deliberate effort to write a classical tragedy on a Hebrew-Christian subject (that is, an Old Testament subject as interpreted by Christianity); and to the Historical Critic this fact immediately suggests two considerations as by no means extraneous: "Milton's Debt to Greek Tragedy in *Samson Agonistes*" (to adopt the actual title of Professor W. R. Parker's book), and "Milton's Samson and the Christian Tradition" (to adopt the title of Professor F. M. Krouse's). The latter makes us aware of the various choices in interpretation and emphasis which previous commentary had placed at Milton's disposal; the former fixes our attention on his detailed imitation of the Greek tragic form. Neither seeks to lead us away from Milton's text, but at most to postpone our consideration of it till the relevant information is acquired. And both entail at the end, and indeed during the whole process, an effort of critical interpretation. It is interpretation undertaken from a particular point of view, and so can hardly even pretend to finality. But if the history of criticism demonstrates anything it is that "final interpretations" are an illusion. Criticism cannot escape from the general rhythm of human thought which prescribes its passage from thesis to antithesis to synthesis, which is itself a new thesis. Every "final interpretation" turns out to be the last but one. In certain ways the critical efforts of Parker and Krouse correct each other, simply by virtue of their different points of view. The correction of former critics is a role often assigned to Historical Criticism— particularly of course the correction of the daydreams of the Impressionist—and it is a role assumed with some degree of zest. It should not, however, be mistaken for the primary role. Historical Criticism is not merely negative in function. If it can correct errors, it can also suggest new and fruitful ways of looking at the poem under examination. Two of these are illustrated in the books to which we have referred.

There are doubtless other relevant considerations. Besides the poem, the subject, and the traditional form, there is also the poet. It was *Milton* who undertook to write a classical tragedy on the Hebrew-Christian subject of Samson, and we know a good deal about this man Milton beside the fact, never to be forgotten, that he was a poet. Upon those who would dismiss as irrelevant every consideration of Milton the man, his extra-aesthetic experience, the drama of his own life, a heavy burden of proof must rest. Now here, confessedly, we are on ground doubly debatable; for many Historical Critics draw back from the assumed presence of Milton in his works, as the "autobiographical fallacy" or the "personal heresy." The reaction against Mas-

son's heavy-handed interpretation, and particularly his reading of *Samson Agonistes* as concealed autobiography and political allegory, is understandable enough, and no doubt salutary. But that Milton's state of mind when he undertook the tragedy had no bearing upon the work which he produced remains a proposition far more difficult to establish than is its opposite. It is interesting to notice how much Professors Hanford and Parker, in their recent writings on *Samson*, have modified their former position; and yet more significant to observe how this issue of quite fundamental importance has been brought up again for debate in connection with the effort of Professor Parker, Professor A. H. Gilbert, and others, to determine a highly controversial matter of fact, namely, the date at which *Samson Agonistes* was probably written. This is very often the way of Historical Criticism: it attacks a question of fact and finds itself confronted by a question of interpretation. The remaining problems of chronology are unlikely now to be solved by a new discovery of external evidence (that is, simply by a process of historical research). They are much more likely to demand the weighing of internal evidence (that is, an exercise of historical criticism). It would be patently absurd to consider all the evidence except that afforded by the poem itself. But to read the internal evidence aright the critic must know the whole body of his author's work. He must be able to compare the undated poem with every other, and especially with those whose dates are known; he must have formed to himself a clear notion of the probable pattern of the poet's career, and be alert to see where in that pattern the updated poem finds its most natural place; and only in relation to the poet's practice in his other poems can the critical question with which we started be answered, namely, the degree to which, not *any* poet's, but *this* poet's, extra-aesthetic experience enters into his poetry. A tentative answer to that question is essential before one can determine the nature and limits of the internal evidence with which one has to deal. In the light of Milton's practice in other poems, is it more probable that the inescapable parallels between Milton's Samson and Milton himself after the Restoration are conscious and dependent on the poet's situation and state of mind when he wrote, or that they are merely coincidental and without value as evidence?

But the answer given to this question has implications far beyond the problem of the date of *Samson Agonistes*. The question may serve therefore to conduct us to some further observations on Historical Criticism as it applies to other poems; and first, to an observation on method. The degree to which Milton's extra-aesthetic experience enters into his poems is a question which can be approached only by means of hypothesis. That it enters in its plentitude, that it enters not at all, that it enters in certain degree and under certain conditions: each of these is an hypothesis, and to be subjected to the appropriate tests. Does the hypothesis run counter to any known evidence? Does it, then, cover all the phenomena? Is it the simplest hypothesis that will do so? The answer to these questions will dictate its acceptance, its abandonment, or its modification. Every time the hypothesis satisfactorily explains a poem, and every time it is found to have provided in advance for new evidence as this appears, the hypothesis has in effect received experimental verification. Every historical critic must form, for example, some hypothetical scheme of Milton's early development. I had the advantage (if I may be pardoned one personal reference) of forming mine with Dr. E. M. W. Tillyard's important argument on the date of *L'Allegro* and *Il Penseroso* before me, but Professor Parker's equally important argument on the date of the sonnet "How soon hath Time" came later. To find the hypothetical pattern fortified by his conclusion was to verify the hypothesis, and also, I think, to add an argument in favour of the conclusion itself. Hypothesis, then, is an indispensable instrument of Historical Criticism.

I have indicated that there is some dispute among historical critics as to the degree, and the manner, in which Milton's extra-aesthetic experience, including his thought, enters into his various poems. The results are worth examining.

Those who deny that such experience enters into his poetry at all, greatly restrict the range of Historical Criticism (as did Mr. Stoll in his treatment of Shakespeare). They reduce it to a consideration of the poems with reference to their genres and to the traditional patterns and conventions which Milton adopted, with perhaps some attention to the intellectual commonplaces of the age, but with none to Milton's more individual and distinctive ideas. That illuminating criticism may be achieved on this narrow basis need not be denied. It is illustrated, for example, in Mr. B. Rajan's admirable *Paradise Lost and the Seventeenth-Century Reader*. But such criticism, by restricting itself virtually to aesthetic analysis, approaches as near as Historical Criticism well may to the concerns and methods of the New Criticism. As a device for isolating certain features of Milton's poetry this is legitimate enough. It becomes dangerous only when erected into a dogma, whose effect is to prejudge the character and the historical relations of his poetry; and when it seeks to rule out as irrelevant all those studies of Milton's life and thought, and of his religious and intellectual background,[1] which, existing in their own right, may still claim to be heard before we pass final judgment on the poet—before, indeed, we can pretend fully to understand any one of his poems.

On this, as on other subjects, Historical Criticism should, it seems, preserve an open mind, till the facts suggest an hypothesis to be tested and, in the light of this testing, to be accepted, rejected or modified. The denial of any important relation between Milton's extra-aesthetic experience and a particular poem is a perfectly possible outcome of this process. For example, it seems evident that *Arcades* neither embodies nor even finds its starting point in any important extra-aesthetic experience intellectual or emotional. It takes its rise simply from the invitation to provide the text for a simple entertainment in honour of the Dowager Countess of Derby and from Milton's election of the masque form and the pastoral note. *Arcades* is a pure, and a singularly effective, example of aesthetic patterning, entirely adequate to its occasion and purpose, and carrying no overtones from Milton's life unless for a moment in the exquisite "Nymphs and shepherds dance no more." This view of the poem can be verified in different ways, and among others by observing the use to which Milton puts a favourite image, that of the music of the spheres. Whenever this image occurs elsewhere it bears an ethical and religious reference and becomes the vehicle of Milton's youthful idealism. The one exception is *Arcades:* there it is bent solely to the purpose of compliment and achieves a purely aesthetic effect with none of the overtones that it habitually carries. So much for *Arcades.* But nothing could justify an historical critic in a blanket denial of relation between Milton's poetry as a whole and his extra-aesthetic experience save an examination of his work poem by poem, undertaken with a full knowledge of his life, thought, and background. Such an examination would presently entail a comparison of *Arcades* and *Comus,* and this could not fail to bring home to the critic the wide difference between them, first in general effect, and then, on more detailed perusal, in argument and image, and in the extent to which the character of the poem can be accounted for by its occasion and avowed purpose, and by the genre in which Milton has chosen to work. Whatever is not to be accounted for by these considerations must seek its explanation elsewhere, and here the hypothesis of a relation to Milton's extra-aesthetic experience presents itself. We need go no farther. For indeed the assertion that Milton's poetry in general bears no ascertainable relation to his extra-aesthetic experience is not a result of such painstaking examination at all. It is a dogma, an assumption respecting the nature of poetry, which the critic is applying or misapplying to Milton.

Now, a sense of poetry as something *sui generis* is as necessary to the Historical Critic as to any other, and if he lacks this sense he had better betake himself to some other occupation; for he will reduce poetry to a mere document and a document whose language he cannot read. But what does the proposition, that poetry is *sui generis,* mean? It certainly does not mean that all poems are alike; for that is a notion dissipated by half an hour with any anthology, or by the simple confronting of *Arcades* and *Comus.* Poems are endlessly various. But they have certain qualities in common, two of which we may specify. First, whatever the subject, the poem develops it by means of—that is, under the form

of—an aesthetic pattern. And, secondly, whatever its starting point in extra-aesthetic experience, the poem is never a mere record of that experience. On the contrary, it is the realization of a new experience; or (to put it in another way) the poem *is* the experience which it records. And it is with this experience—this poem—that the critic *qua* critic is concerned, an experience of which the aesthetic pattern holds the key.

But when these common characteristics of poetry *qua* poetry are recognized, there still remains the vast difference between poem and poem, and between one poet and another. And the differentiating qualities are as much a part of the poem, or the body of poetry, as are the common characteristics. With these differentiating qualities, the Historical Critic is likewise concerned; and he is not content merely to observe them: he wants to know why they are there. Why is *Comus* so different from *Arcades,* or *Lycidas* from the *Epitaphium Damonis*? Why is *Paradise Lost* so different from the *Aeneid,* or *Samson Agonistes* from *Oedipus at Colonus*? Why do Milton's poems in their effect add up to something so different from Spenser's, or Donne's, or Dryden's, or Wordsworth's? No one, I suppose, will deny that these are important questions or that they fall legitimately within the critic's field of inquiry. For to recognize that complete and final answers are impossible is no reason for discarding such partial answers as can be found. And no one will imagine that these answers can be reached by any other method than the historical or without constant reference to Milton's text. One brief example will suffice. No doubt *Paradise Lost* differs from the *Aeneid* because one was written by Milton, the other by Virgil. But the answer in that form is unmanageable and unproductive—is, in fact, no answer at all. The question requires to be broken down into its parts, and of these some are certainly answerable. It is obvious, for example, that an important difference depends upon Milton's Christian subject-matter, and his Christian attitude, which entail marked adaptations of the traditional epic form; so that we are led back immediately from the poem's pattern to its subject-matter, and from the subject-matter to the poet's belief or thought, in order to account for differences in pattern and effect. This is the sort of question that can be dealt with by the Historical Critic, and by no one else.

Apart, however, from the comparative study, Historical Criticism has a vast field of inquiry open to it. *Paradise Lost* is not only a classical epic (and thus comparable with the *Aeneid*): it is also a Christian theodicy (whose avowed purpose is to "assert Eternal Providence And justify the ways of God to men") and a philosophical poem (with a view of man and of the cosmic order to present). In these aspects also it takes its place in history, and is fully understandable only in relation to history.

Though as an activity poetry is indeed *sui generis*, the particular view which the poet takes of the nature and end of poetry, and especially of his own poetry, has an immense effect on what he writes. But his view of poetry depends in part on his view of life. Behind every philosophy of art there lies a philosophy of life. In a poet like Milton who consistently asserts or assumes the closset relation between his art and life, every shaping experience, every idea embraced, will, or at least may, have its bearing on his poetry. For example, why was Milton able to adopt with such singular literalness the idea that the Christian poet was indeed inspired? Because he read the conventional idea of the inspired poet in the light of the Christian conviction, reinforced by the Reformation, that every believer is inspired. Why did he not proceed to the romantic conclusion that learning, thought, and conscious artistry are, then, superfluous, are even an impediment? Because he also inherited the Renaissance tradition of learned poetry and conscious art, because (like his fellows) he incorporated the Roman ideal of the orator in his conception of the poet, and because he adopted the Platonic view of reason, which made the flash of intuitive insight the result and the reward of patient thought, not something opposed to it. By his whole conception of poetry, with its ethical and religious as well as aesthetic end, Milton is led to embody in many of his poems his most searching thoughts and his profoundest convictions. It is not by their form alone, any more than by their content alone, that these poems seek "to imbreed and cherish . . . the seeds of virtue, to allay the perturbations of the mind, and set the affections in right tune." But indeed the dichotomy and the problem are of our making, not Milton's, as every historical student knows or may come to know.

Thus Milton's thought enters deeply into his poetry. The cosmology of the *De Doctrina Christiana* is (by grace of the epic tradition) embodied in *Paradise Lost* and adapted to the purpose of the poem. The doctrine of free will is central in Milton's reading of the action and in his whole effort to justify the ways of God to men, and thus is doubly essential to the poem. His view of the nature and function of Christ, argued at length in the *De Doctrina*, shapes and colours the two poems in which he is a central figure. In *Paradise Regained* this very question is the poem's secondary theme—until the end, when it becomes primary. And that this transition might be effected Milton chose the order of temptations in St. Luke. Thus the theological content conditions the pattern of the poem. And this is characteristic of Milton. Whatever may be said of some other poets, Milton's aesthetic patterns rely on a foundation, or rather perhaps a framework, of conceptual thought, and they cannot be elucidated without reference to it. This is already true in the Nativity Ode, and it is still true in *Paradise Regained*. Milton's thought as thought is very much "of an age," and hence susceptible only of historical elucidation. Somehow it is transmuted into poetry which is "for all time." It is for the critic to explain as best he can how this miracle is performed.

Mr. Cleanth Brooks has complained[2] that for Professor Maurice Kelley, in *This Great Argument*, "the problem of exegesis is almost amusingly simple." In the *De Doctrina* you discover what Milton's ideas were: you then explain *Paradise Lost*, that "tangled and difficult poetic document, by means of the explicit prose statement." But, Mr. Brooks continues, Mr. Kelley's argument rests on two assumptions: first, "that the Milton who wrote the *Christian Doctrine* was precisely and at all points the same man who composed *Paradise Lost*" (and this assumption Mr. Brooks surprisingly concedes); secondly, it involves "the further and much more dangerous assumption that Milton was able to say in *Paradise Lost* exactly what he intended to say, and that what he supposed he had put into the poem is actually to be found there" (and this assumption Mr. Brooks peremptorily denies).

Now, I am equally astonished at the concession of the first assumption and the denial of the second. For it seems to me that to deny to Milton a knowledge of what he was doing in *Paradise Lost* and, after it was written, a knowledge of what he had done, runs counter to all the evidence of self-possession and deliberation as distinguishing marks of Milton, which the long study of his artistry has accumulated. It appears, further, to open the way for every aberration of romantic criticism. But to me it seems equally clear that the Milton who wrote *De Doctrina* was *not* the same as the Milton who composed *Paradise Lost*. The one was Milton the thinker and controversialist; the other, Milton the thinker *and poet*. In this statement, I am not committing myself to that most absurd of dichotomies—the one adopted by Hilaire Belloc in what must surely be (among many strong competitors) the worst book on Milton ever written. I do not mean that the thinker and the poet bear no relation to each other. Far from it. I am simply recognizing the indubitable fact that poetry differs from prose, and thought in poetry from thought in prose. In the more controversial parts of the *De Doctrina* Milton is arguing a case; much of his effort goes to demolishing the case of his opponents, and the animation of the work has much in common with that of Milton's other controversial prose. His concern is with theology—not with religious, and certainly not with aesthetic, experience. He fits his thought to a theological scheme, not to a vision of existence. But in the two epics argument gives place to vision, and negation to affirmation—to an affirmation, that is, of the residuum of positive faith by which Milton lived. In the *De Doctrina* Milton argues the case for monism (I will not call it materialism). In *Paradise Lost* he embodies the doctrine in his vision of creation. In the *De Doctrina* he argues the case for an Arian or semi-Arian view of Christ. In *Paradise Lost* he realizes, and makes us realize, how entirely for him this view is compatible with the impulse of worship:

> Hail, Son of God, Saviour of Men, thy Name
> Shall be the copious matter of my song
> Henceforth, and never shall my harp thy
>   praise
> Forget, nor from thy Father's praise disjoin.

Paradise Regained is the fulfillment of this promise, and there (as we have said) the secondary theme of Christ's divinity becomes at the end primary, when, abating nothing of his Arianism, the poet reaffirms the doctrine (and fulfils the promise) of *Paradise Lost*:

> True Image of the Father, whether throned
> In the bosom of bliss and light of light
> Conceiving, or remote from Heaven, en-
>   shrined
> In earthly tabernacle and human form—

everywhere and always, the Son is the true Image of the Father. And Milton, I infer, was enabled, not to reach this position, but to realize its full implications, by the aid of poetry. For whatever his limitations, he has this indispensable mark of the religious poet: his aesthetic experience and his religious are not two things, but one. And the poem is not a record of experience: it *is* the experience. It is not a record of thought: it is compacted of those

>   thoughts that voluntary move
> Harmonious numbers,

and that reach full realization only in them.

Poetry, it seems clear, has two aspects, a temporal and a permanent. It is the reproach of Historical Criticism that it is sunk in the temporal and in the relativism that pertains thereto; and sometimes no doubt the charge is well founded. But one does not get rid of the temporal by ignoring it; and to pretend to do so often means no more than the introduction of a new relativism: one reads the poem in relation to one's own age instead of to the poet's. Milton has suffered and Donne has benefited by this new and usually concealed relativism. But to speak of a temporal aspect of poetry, and a permanent, is not sufficiently precise. It is the miracle of poetry that it makes of the temporal something permanent. And if one would understand how this is done, and even in some instances be sure that it is done, one must know the temporal conditions in which it is essayed.

The contemporary audience always enjoys two advantages: an intuitive and comprehensive grasp of the potentialities and limits of the genre in which the poet is working, so that it does not ask for the impossible, and an immediate recognition of the frame of reference within which his ideas move. Much of the misunderstanding of *Comus* springs from a failure to grasp the potentialities and limits of the masque form (with which confessedly Milton takes great liberties) and of Spenserian allegory. Much misunderstanding also arises from a failure to recognize the distinction and the relation of the two orders of nature and of grace, which furnish the poem's frame of reference. The sense of these things three centuries have almost completely destroyed, and they can be restored only by painful historical study. But, when restored, they do not merely serve to correct errors of interpretation or to crowd out the false assumptions which will always fill the vacuum when true assumptions are lacking: they also give us a new vantage point from which to attempt our analysis of the poem's pattern. For the function of Historical Criticism is not simply to act as a corrective: it can suggest new and productive ways of looking at the poem.

And this, as it seems to me, holds the best promise of some alliance between Historical Criticism and the New Criticism. They need each other. Certainly we historical critics have something to learn from the method of analysis employed by the New Criticism: from the method, for example, of Mr. Brooks's essay on *L'Allegro* and *Il Penseroso*.[3] Perhaps too, the New Critics may sometimes gather suggestions from the findings of Historical Criticism. No doubt we shall continue to disagree, and our remarks about each other will have a certain tonic bitterness. But we are all, I assume, concerned with truth, if not with finality. And I cannot help recalling two principles which Newman invoked in another and more solemn context: "Truth cannot contradict truth"; but "truth often seems to contradict truth." And the inference surely is obvious: that we should be patient one with another.

Notes

This paper was read before the Milton Group of the Modern Language Association of America on 28 December 1950. It was followed by a paper on "Milton and Critical Reestimates" by Cleanth Brooks.

1. Those of William Haller, Arthur Barker, Merritt Y. Hughes, Arnold Williams, and a host of others.

2. In his "Criticism and Literary History," *Sewanee Rev.*, LV (1947), 199–222.

3. "The Light Symbolism in 'L'Allegro–Il Penseroso,'" in *The Well Wrought Urn* (1947), pp. 47–61. I remarked above, "Whatever may be said of other poets, Milton's aesthetic patterns rely on a foundation, or rather perhaps a framework, of conceptual thought, and they cannot be elucidated without reference to it." This suggests a reservation which must not be overlooked. The method of analysis employed by the New Criticism appears to consist in a frontal attack on the imagery of the poem, with little or no attention to its theme as presented in action or argument. Applied to imagist verse, this method, corresponding to the intention of the poet, will yield whatever is to be discovered. Applied to poetry such as Milton's, it will, by itself, yield only results which, however valuable, are secondary and supplemental. This limitation, as it seems to me, is illustrated both in Mr. Brooks's essay on *L'Allegro* and *Il Penseroso* and in the part of his paper dealing with the image of "the *fruit* of the tree of Knowledge" in *Paradise Lost*. For, Dr. Tillyard to the contrary notwithstanding, the theme of *L'Allegro* and *Il Penseroso* is not day and night, but two contrasting ways of life, or two moods, as the titles indicate; day and night enter the poems because of the temporal sequence in which Milton has found his structural pattern; the images of light and darkness do not reveal the theme, but they support and supplement it. And so with "the *fruit* of the tree of Knowledge": everything that Mr. Brooks says of it may well be true, and (if true) illuminating. (Indeed an historical critic would find confirmation in Bacon's "philosophy of fruits," with which Milton must have been familiar.) But the suggestions conveyed by this image—one among many—are secondary and supplemental to Milton's theme of the Fall and his central interpretation thereof. The role of imagery in Milton would appear to be twofold: to *support* the main theme presented in action or argument, but also to *supplement* it by other and not inconsistent suggestions, and thereby to give the poem that density and richness of suggestion which differentiates it from any mere summary of its theme, as revealed through action, argument, or structural pattern. When this relation is recognized, the technique of the New Criticism in exploring Milton's imagery seems to me of the highest value, and exemplary.

Theory

Objective Interpretation

E. D. Hirsch, Jr.

The central purpose of E. D. Hirsch's "Objective Interpretation," which was written in 1960, when genetic approaches had been under heavy formalist attack for at least three decades, is to make the search for the author's meaning once again the main business of literary study, and to provide for that study a closely argued rationale that will allow it to stand as "a corporate enterprise and a progressive discipline." In making his case, Hirsch directly disputes the contention of formal and intertextual critics that the "public norms of language" are sufficient to establish the meaning of a text without reference to the author's probable intentions. Examining the Cleanth Brooks–F. W. Bateson controversy over the meaning of a Wordsworth poem, Hirsch seeks to show that such "public norms" can support different, and even totally opposed, interpretations. While he grants the relevance of most formalist criteria for meaning, including the central criterion of "coherence," Hirsch argues that "coherence" is not an absolute quality. It depends on the context the interpreter has invoked, and for an interpretation to be valid "it is necessary to establish that the context invoked is the most probable context" [author's emphasis]. And to establish this, we need to know all we can about the intender of the meaning. Thus, although Hirsch explicitly distinguishes between the "speaking subject" and the biographical person, he sets forth a clear rationale for much genetic criticism. Unless we assume an author whose probable meaning we can recover, he claims, "meaning" itself can have no stable sense, "interpretation" cannot be objective, and literary commentary is in danger of becoming a subjective and relativistic babble.

THE FACT THAT THE TERM "CRITICISM" HAS NOW come to designate all commentary on textual meaning reflects a general acceptance of the doctrine that description and evaluation are inseparable in literary study. In any serious confrontation of literature it would be futile, of course, to attempt a rigorous banishment of all evaluative judgment, but this fact does not give us the license to misunderstand or misinterpret our texts. It does not entitle us to use the text as the basis for an exercise in "creativity" or to submit as serious textual commentary a disguised argument for a particular ethical, cultural, or aesthetic viewpoint. Nor is criticism's chief concern—the present relevance of a text—a strictly necessary aspect of textual commentary. That same kind of theory which argues the inseparability of description and evaluation also argues that a text's meaning is simply its meaning "to us, today." Both kinds of argument support the idea that interpretation is criticism and vice versa. But there is clearly a sense in which we can neither evaluate a text nor determine what it means "to us, today" until we have correctly apprehended what it means. Understanding (and therefore interpretation, in the strict sense of the word) is both logically and psychologically prior to what is generally called criticism. It is true that this distinction between understanding and evaluation cannot always show itself in the finished work of criticism—nor, perhaps, should it—but a general grasp and acceptance of the distinction might help correct some of the most serious faults of current criticism (its subjectivism and relativism) and might even make it plausible to think of literary study as a corporate enterprise and a progressive discipline.

No one would deny, of course, that the more important issue is not the status of literary study as a discipline but the vitality of literature—especially of older literature—in the world at

large. The critic is right to think that the text
should speak to *us*. The point which needs to
be grasped clearly by the critic is that a text cannot be made to speak to us until what it says
has been understood. This is not an argument
in favor of historicism as against criticism—it is
simply a brute ontological fact. Textual meaning
is not a naked given like a physical object. The
text is first of all a conventional representation
like a musical score, and what the score represents may be construed correctly or incorrectly.
The literary text (in spite of semi-mystical claims
made for its uniqueness) does not have a special
ontological status which somehow absolves the
reader from the demands universally imposed
by all linguistic texts of every description. Nothing, that is, can give a conventional representation the status of an immediate given. The text
of a poem, for example, has to be construed by
the critic before it becomes a poem for him.
Then it is, no doubt, an artifact with special
characteristics. But before the critic construes the
poem it is for him no artifact at all, and if he
construes it wrongly, he will subsequently be
talking about the wrong artifact, not the one
represented by the text. If criticism is to be objective in any significant sense, it must be
founded on a self-critical construction of textual
meaning, which is to say, on objective interpretation.

•   •   •

[In the section of the essay omitted here, Hirsch
draws a distinction between the "meaning" of a
text, "in and for itself," and the "significance"
that can be given to that meaning when it is
related to something else, like contemporary issues, our present concerns, and so forth.
"Meaning," which is relatively stable and unchanging through time, is the object of "interpretation"; "significance," which may change
from reader to reader and from period to period,
is the object of "criticism." Interpretation of textual meaning, then, is the logically prior task
and the foundation for all criticism. But to what
extent is "textual meaning" the same thing as
"authorial meaning"? On this crucial question,
Hirsch parts company with the New Critics.
—ED.]

Determinateness of Textual Meaning

In the previous section I defined textual meaning as the "verbal intention" of the author, and
this argues implicitly that hermeneutics must
stress a reconstruction of the author's aims and
attitudes in order to evolve guides and norms
for construing the meaning of his text. It is frequently argued, however, that the textual meaning has nothing to do with the author's mind,
but only with his verbal achievement, that the
object of interpretation is not the author but his
text. This plausible argument assumes, of
course, that the text automatically has a meaning simply because it represents an unalterable
sequence of words. It assumes that the meaning
of a word sequence is directly imposed by the
public norms of language, that the text as a
"piece of language" is a public object whose
character is defined by public norms.[1] This view
is in one respect sound, since textual meaning
must conform to public norms if it is in any
sense to be verbal (i.e., sharable) meaning; on
no account may the interpreter permit his probing into the author's mind to raise private
associations (experience) to the level of public
implications (content).

However, this basically sound argument remains one-sided. For even though verbal meaning must conform to public linguistic norms
(these are highly tolerant, of course), no mere
sequence of words can represent an actual verbal meaning with reference to public norms
alone. Referred to these alone, the text's meaning remains indeterminate. This is true even of
the simplest declarative sentence like "My car
ran out of gas" (did my Pullman dash from a
cloud of Argon?). The fact that no one would
radically misinterpret such a sentence simply indicates that its frequency is high enough to give
its usual meaning the apparent status of an immediate given. But this apparent immediacy obscures a complex process of adjudications
among meaning-possibilities. Under the public
norms of language alone no such adjudications
can occur, since the array of possibilities presents a face of blank indifference. The array of
possibilities only begins to become a more selective system of *probabilities* when, instead of

confronting merely a word sequence, we also posit a speaker who very likely means something. Then and only then does the most usual sense of the word sequence become the most probable or "obvious" sense. The point holds true a fortiori, of course, when we confront less obvious word sequences like those found in poetry. A careful exposition of this point may be found in the first volume of Cassirer's *Philosophy of Symbolic Forms*, which is largely devoted to a demonstration that verbal meaning arises from the "reciprocal determination" of public linguistic possibilities and subjective specifications of those possibilities.[2] Just as language constitutes and colors subjectivity, so does subjectivity color language. The author's or speaker's subjective act is *formally* necessary to verbal meaning, and any theory which tries to dispense with the author as specifier of meaning by asserting that textual meaning is purely objectively determined finds itself chasing will-o'-the-wisps. The burden of this section is, then, an attack on the view that a text is a "piece of language" and a defense of the notion that a text represents the determinate verbal meaning of the author.

One of the consequences arising from the view that a text is a piece of language—a purely public object—is the impossibility of defining in principle the nature of a correct interpretation. This is the same impasse which results from the theory that a text leads a life of its own, and indeed, the two notions are corollaries since any "piece of language" must have a changing meaning when the changing public norms of language are viewed as the only ones which determine the sense of the text. It is therefore not surprising to find that Wellek subscribes implicitly to the text-as-language theory. The text is viewed as representing not a determinate meaning, but rather a system of meaning-potentials specified not by a meaner but by the vital potency of language itself. Wellek acutely perceives the danger of the view: "Thus the system of norms is growing and changing and will remain, in some sense, always incompletely and imperfectly realized. But this dynamic conception does not mean mere subjectivism and relativism. All the different points of view are by no means equally right. It will always be possible to determine which point of view grasps

the subject most thoroughly and deeply. A hierarchy of viewpoints, a criticism of the grasp of norms, is implied in the concept of the adequacy of interpretation."[3] The danger of the view is, of course, precisely that it opens the door to subjectivism and relativism, since linguistic norms may be invoked to support any verbally possible meaning. Furthermore, it is not clear how one may criticize a grasp of norms which will not stand still.

Wellek's brief comment on the problem involved in defining and testing correctness in interpretation is representative of a widespread conviction among literary critics that the most correct interpretation is the most "inclusive" one. Indeed, the view is so widely accepted that Wellek did not need to defend his version of it (which he calls "Perspectivism") at length. The notion behind the theory is reflected by such phrases as "always incompletely and imperfectly realized" and "grasps the subject most thoroughly." This notion is simply that no single interpretation can exhaust the rich system of meaning-potentialities represented by the text. *Ergo* every plausible reading which remains within public linguistic norms is a correct reading so far as it goes, but each reading is inevitably partial since it cannot realize all the potentialities of the text. The guiding principle in criticism, therefore, is that of the inclusive interpretation. The most "adequate" construction is the one which gives the fullest coherent account of all the text's potential meanings.[4]

Inclusivism is desirable as a position which induces a readiness to consider the results of others, but, aside from promoting an estimable tolerance, it has little theoretical value. For although its aim is to reconcile different plausible readings in an ideal, comprehensive interpretation, it cannot, in fact, either reconcile different readings or choose between them. As a normative ideal, or principle of correctness, it is useless. This point may be illustrated by citing two expert readings of a well-known poem by Wordsworth. I shall first quote the poem and then quote excerpts from two published exegeses in order to demonstrate the kind of impasse which inclusivism always provokes when it attempts to reconcile interpretations, and, incidentally, to demonstrate the very kind of interpretive problem which calls for a guiding principle:

> A slumber did my spirit seal;
>   I had no human fears:
> She seemed a thing that could not feel
>   The touch of earthly years.
>
> No motion has she now, no force;
>   She neither hears nor sees;
> Rolled round in earth's diurnal course,
>   With rocks, and stones, and trees.

Here are excerpts from two commentaries on the final lines of the poem; the first is by Cleanth Brooks, the second by F. W. Bateson:

> 1. [The poet] attempts to suggest something of the lover's agonized shock at the loved one's present lack of motion—of his response to her utter and horrible inertness. . . . Part of the effect, of course, resides in the fact that a dead lifelessness is suggested more sharply by an object's being whirled about by something else than by an image of the object in repose. But there are other matters which are at work here: the sense of the girl's falling back into the clutter of things, companioned by things chained like a tree to one particular spot, or by things completely inanimate like rocks and stones. . . . [She] is caught up helplessly into the empty whirl of the earth which measures and makes time. She is touched by and held by earthly time in its most powerful and horrible image.

> 2. The final impression the poem leaves is not of two contrasting moods, but of a single mood mounting to a climax in the pantheistic magnificence of the last two lines. . . . The vague living-Lucy of this poem is opposed to the grander dead-Lucy who has become involved in the sublime processes of nature. We put the poem down satisfied, because its last two lines succeed in effecting a reconciliation between the two philosophies or social attitudes. Lucy is actually more alive now that she is dead, because she is now a part of the life of Nature, and not just a human "thing."[5]

Now, if we grant, as I think we must, that both the cited interpretations are permitted by the text, the problem for the inclusivist is to reconcile the two readings.

Three modes of reconciliation are available to the inclusivist: (1) Brooks's reading includes Bateson's; it shows that any affirmative suggestions in the poem are negated by the bitterly ironical portrayal of the inert girl being whirled around by what Bateson calls the "sublime processes of Nature." (2) Bateson's reading includes Brooks's; the ironic contrast between the active, seemingly immortal girl and the passive, inert and dead girl is overcome by a final unqualified affirmation of immortality. (3) Each of the readings is partially right, but they must be fused to supplement one another. The very fact that the critics differ suggests that the meaning is essentially ambiguous. The emotion expressed is ambivalent, and comprises both bitter regret and affirmation. The third mode of reconciliation is the one most often employed, and is probably, in this case, the most satisfactory. A fourth type of resolution, which would insist that Brooks is right and Bateson wrong (or vice versa) is not available to the inclusivist, since the text, as language, renders both readings plausible.

Close examination, however, reveals that none of the three modes of argument manages to reconcile or fuse the two different readings. Mode (1), for example, insists that Brooks's reading comprehends Bateson's, but although it is conceivable that Brooks implies all the meanings which Bateson has perceived, Brooks also implies a *pattern of emphasis* which cannot be reconciled with Bateson's reading. While Bateson construes a primary emphasis on life and affirmation, Brooks emphasizes deadness and inertness. No amount of manipulation can reconcile these divergent emphases, since one pattern of emphasis irrevocably excludes other patterns, and, since emphasis is always crucial to meaning, the two constructions of meanings rigorously exclude one another. Precisely the same strictures hold, of course, for the argument that Bateson's reading comprehends that of Brooks. Nor can mode (3) escape with impunity. Although it seems to preserve a stress both on negation and on affirmation, thereby coalescing the two readings, it actually excludes both readings, and labels them not simply partial, but wrong. For if the poem gives equal stress to bitter irony and to affirmation, then any construction which places a primary stress on either meaning is simply incorrect.

The general principle implied by my analysis is very simple. The sub-meanings of a text are not blocks which can be brought together additively. Since verbal (and any other) meaning is a *structure* of component meanings, interpretation has not done its job when it simply enumerates what the component meanings are. The interpreter must also determine their probable structure, and particularly their structure of emphases. Relative emphasis is not only crucial to meaning (perhaps it is the most crucial and problematical element of all), it is also highly restrictive; it excludes alternatives. It may be asserted as a general rule that whenever a reader confronts two interpretations which impose different emphases on similar meaning components, at least one of the interpretations must be wrong. They cannot be reconciled.

By insisting that verbal meaning always exhibits a determinate structure of emphases, I do not, however, imply that a poem or any other text must be unambiguous. It is perfectly possible, for example, that Wordsworth's poem ambiguously implies both bitter irony and positive affirmation. Such complex emotions are commonly expressed in poetry, but if that is the kind of meaning the text represents Brooks and Bateson would be wrong to emphasize one emotion at the expense of the other. Ambiguity or, for that matter, vagueness is not the same as indeterminateness. This is the crux of the issue. To say that verbal meaning is determinate is not to exclude complexities of meaning but only to insist that a text's meaning is what it is and not a hundred other things. Taken in this sense, a vague or ambiguous text is just as determinate as a logical proposition; it means what it means and nothing else. This is true even if one argues that a text could display shifting emphases like those Sunday supplement magic squares which first seem to jut out and then to jut in. With texts of this character (if any exist), one need only say that the emphases shift, and must not, therefore, be construed statically. Any static construction would simply be wrong. The fundamental flaw in the "theory of the most inclusive interpretation" is that it overlooks the problem of emphasis. Since different patterns of emphasis *exclude* one another, inclusivism is neither a genuine norm nor an adequate guiding principle for establishing an interpretation.

But aside from the fact that inclusivism cannot do its appointed job, there are more fundamental reasons for rejecting it and all other interpretive ideals based on the conception that a text represents a system of meaning-possibilities. No one would deny that for the interpreter the text is at first the source of numerous possible interpretations. The very nature of language is such that a particular sequence of words can represent several different meanings (that is why public norms alone are insufficient in textual interpretation). But to say that a text *might* represent several structures of meaning does not imply that it does in fact represent all the meanings which a particular word sequence can legally convey. Is there not an obvious distinction between what a text might mean and what it does mean? According to accepted linguistic theory, it is far more accurate to say that a written composition is not a mere locus of verbal possibilities, but, rather, a record (made possible by the invention of writing) of a verbal actuality. The interpreter's job is to reconstruct a determinate actual meaning, not a mere system of possibilities. Indeed, if the text *represented* a system of possibilities, interpretation would be impossible, since no actual reading could correspond to a mere system of possibilities. Furthermore, if the text is conceived to represent all the *actual* structures of meaning permissible within the public norms of language, then no single construction (with its exclusivist pattern of emphases) could be correct, and any legitimate construction would be just as incorrect as any other. When a text is conceived as a piece of language, a familiar and all too common anarchy follows. But, aside from its unfortunate consequences, the theory contradicts a widely accepted principle in linguistics. I refer to Saussure's distinction between *langue* and *parole*.

Saussure defined *langue* as the system of linguistic possibilities shared by a speech community at a given point in time.[6] This system of possibilities contains two distinguishable levels. The first consists of habits, engrams, prohibitions, and the like derived from past linguistic usage; these are the "virtualities" of the *langue*. Based on these virtualities, there are, in addition, sharable meaning-possibilities which have never before been actualized; these are the "potentialities." The two types of meaning-possibilities taken together constitute the *langue* which the speech community draws upon. But this system of possibilities must be distinguished from the actual verbal utterances of individuals who draw upon it. These actual utterances are called *paroles;* they are *uses* of language, and actualize some (but never all) of the meaning-possibilities constituting the *langue.*

Saussure's distinction pinpoints the issue: does a text represent a segment of *langue* (as modern theorists hold) or a *parole?* A simple test suffices to provide the answer. If the text is composed of sentences it represents *parole,* which is to say the determinate verbal meaning of a member of the speech community. *Langue* contains words and sentence-forming principles, but it contains no sentences. It may be represented in writing only by isolated words in disconnection. (*Wörter* as opposed to *Worte*). A *parole,* on the other hand, is always composed of sentences, an assertion corroborated by the firmly established principle that the sentence is the fundamental unit of speech.[7] Of course, there are numerous elliptical and one-word sentences, but wherever it can be correctly inferred that a text represents sentences and not simply isolated words, it may also be inferred that the text represents *parole,* which is to say, actual, determinate verbal meaning.

The point is nicely illustrated in a dictionary definition. The letters in boldface at the head of the definition represent the word as *langue,* with all its rich meaning-possibilities. But under one of the sub-headings, in an illustrative sentence, those same letters represent the words as *parole,* as a particular, selective actualization from *langue.* In yet another illustrative sentence, under another sub-heading, the very same word represents a different selective actualization. Of course, many sentences, especially those found in poetry, actualize far more possibilities than illustrative sentences in a dictionary. Any pun, for example, realizes simultaneously at least two divergent meaning-possibilities. But the pun is nevertheless an actualization from *langue* and not a mere system of meaning-possibilities.

The *langue–parole* distinction, besides affirming the determinateness of textual meaning, also clarifies the special problems posed by revised and interpolated texts. With a revised text, com-posed over a long period of time (*Faust,* for example) how are we to construe the *unrevised* portions? Should we assume that they still mean what they meant originally or that they took on a new meaning when the rest of the text was altered or expanded? With compiled or interpolated texts, like many books of the Bible, should we assume that sentences from varied provenances retain their original meanings, or that these heterogeneous elements have become integral components of a new total meaning? In terms of Saussure's distinction, the question becomes: should we consider the text to represent a compilation of divers *paroles* or a new unitary *parole* "respoken" by the new author or editor? I submit that there can be no definitive answer to the question, except in relation to a specific scholarly or aesthetic purpose, for in reality the question is not, "How are we to interpret the text?" but, "*Which* text are we to interpret?" Is it to be the heterogeneous compilation of past *paroles,* each to be separately considered, or the new, homogeneous *parole?* Both may be represented by the written score. The only problem is to choose, and having chosen, rigorously to refrain from confusing or in any way identifying the two quite different and separate "texts" with one another. Without solving any concrete problems, then, Saussure's distinction nevertheless confirms the critic's right in most cases to regard his text as representing a single *parole.*

Another problem which Saussure's distinction clarifies is that posed by the bungled text, where the author aimed to convey a meaning which his words do not convey to others in the speech community. One sometimes confronts the problem in a freshman essay. In such a case, the question is, does the text mean what the author wanted it to mean or does it mean what the speech community at large takes it to mean? Much attention has been devoted to this problem ever since the publication in 1946 of Wimsatt's and Beardsley's essay on "The Intentional Fallacy."[8] In that essay the position was taken (albeit modified by certain qualifications) that the text, being public, means what the speech community takes it to mean. This position is, in an ethical sense, right (and language, being social, has a strong ethical aspect): if the author has bungled so badly that his utterance will be misconstrued, then it serves him right when folk misunderstand him. However, put in linguistic terms, the position becomes unsatisfactory. It implies that the meaning represented by the text is not the *parole* of an author, but rather the *parole* of "the speech community." But since only individuals utter *paroles,* a *parole* of the speech community is a non-existent, or what the Germans call an *Unding.* A text can represent only the *parole* of a speaker or author, which is another way of saying that meaning requires a meaner.

However, it is not necessary that an author's text represent the *parole* he desired to convey. It is frequently the case, when an author has bungled, that his text represents no *parole* at all. Indeed there are but two alternatives: either the text represents the author's verbal meaning or it represents no *determinate* verbal meaning at all. Sometimes, of course, it is impossible to detect that the author has bungled, and in that case, even though his text does not represent verbal meaning, we shall go on misconstruing the text as though it did, and no one will be the wiser. But with most bungles we are aware of a disjunction between the author's words and his probable meaning. Eliot, for example, chided Poe for saying "My most immemorial year," when Poe "meant" his most *memorable* year.[9] Now we all agree that Poe did not mean what speakers of English generally meant by the word "immemorial"—and so the word cannot have the usual meaning. (An author cannot mean what he does not mean.) The only question, then, is: does the word mean more or less what we convey by "never-to-be-forgotten" or does it mean nothing at all? Has Poe so violated linguistic norms that we must deny his utterance verbal meaning or "content"?

The question probably cannot be answered by fiat. But since Poe's meaning is generally understood, and since the single criteria for verbal meaning is communicability, I am inclined to describe Poe's meaning as verbal.[10] I tend to side with the Poes and Malaprops of the world, for the norms of language remain far more tolerant than dictionaries and critics like Eliot suggest. On the other hand, every member of the speech community, and especially the critic, has a duty to avoid and condemn sloppiness and needless ambiguity in the use of language, simply in order to preserve the effectiveness of the *langue* itself. Moreover, there must be a dividing line between verbal meanings and those meanings which we half-divine by a supra-linguistic exercise of imagination. There must be a dividing line between Poe's successful disregard of normal usage and the incommunicable word sequences of a bad freshman essay. However, that dividing line is not between the author's meaning and the reader's, but rather between the author's *parole* and no *parole* at all.

Of course, theoretical principles cannot directly solve the interpreter's problem. It is one thing to insist that a text represents the determinate verbal meaning of an author, but it is quite another to discover what that meaning is. The very same text could represent numerous different *paroles,* as any ironic sentence discloses ("That's a *bright* idea!?" or "That's a bright *idea!*"). But it should be of some practical consequence for the interpreter to know that he does have a precisely defined task, namely to discover the author's meaning. It is therefore not only sound but necessary for the interpreter to inquire, "What in all probability did the author mean? Is the pattern of emphases I construe the author's pattern?" But it is both incorrect and futile to inquire, "What does the language of the text say?" That question can have no determinate answer.

Verification

Since the meaning represented by a text is that of another, the interpreter can never be certain that his reading is correct. He knows furthermore that the norms of *langue* by themselves are far too broad to specify the particular meanings and emphases represented by the text, that these particular meanings were specified by particular kinds of subjective acts on the part of the author, and that these acts, as such, remain inaccessible. A less self-critical reader, on the other hand, approaches solipsism if he assumes that the text represents a perspicuous meaning simply because it represents an unalterable sequence of words. For if this "perspicuous" meaning is not verified in some way, it will simply be the interpreter's own meaning, exhibiting the connotations and emphases which he himself imposes. Of course, the reader must realize verbal meaning by his own subjective acts (no one can do that for him), but if he remembers that his job is to construe the author's meaning, he will attempt to exclude his own predispositions and to impose those of the author. But no one can establish another's meaning with certainty. The interpreter's goal is simply this: to show that a given reading is more probable than others. In hermeneutics, verification is a process of establishing relative probabilities.

To establish a reading as probable it is first necessary to show, with reference to the norms of language, that it is possible. This is the criterion of *legitimacy:* the reading must be permissible within the public norms of the *langue* in which the text was composed. The second criterion is that of *correspondence:* the reading must account for each linguistic component in the text. Whenever a reading arbitrarily ignores linguistic components or inadequately accounts for them, the reading may be presumed improbable. The third criterion is that of *generic appropriateness:* if the text follows the conventions of a scientific essay, for example, it is inappropriate to construe the kind of allusive meaning found in casual conversation.[11] But when these three preliminary criteria have been satisfied, there remains a fourth criterion which gives significance to all the rest, the criterion of plausibility or *coherence*. The three preliminary norms usually permit several readings, and this is by definition the case when a text is problematical. Faced with alternatives, the interpreter chooses the reading which best meets the criterion of coherence. Indeed, even when the text is not problematical, coherence remains the decisive criterion, since the meaning is "obvious" only because it "makes sense." I wish, therefore, to focus attention on the criterion of coherence, and shall take for granted the demands of legitimacy, correspondence, and generic appropriateness. I shall try to show that verification by the criterion of coherence, and ultimately, therefore, verification in general, implies a reconstruction of relevant aspects in the author's outlook. My point may be summarized in the paradox that objectivity in textual interpretation requires explicit reference to the speaker's subjectivity.

The paradox reflects the peculiar nature of coherence, which is not an absolute, but a dependent quality. The laws of coherence are variable; they depend upon the nature of the total meaning under consideration. Two meanings ("dark" and "bright," for example) which cohere in one context may not cohere in another.[12] "Dark with excessive bright" makes excellent sense in *Paradise Lost*, but if a reader found the phrase in a textbook on plant pathology, he would assume that he confronted a misprint for "Dark with excessive blight." Coherence depends on the context, and it is helpful to recall our definition of "context": it is a sense of the whole meaning, constituted of explicit partial meanings plus a horizon of expectations and probabilities. One meaning coheres with another because it is typical or probable with reference to the whole (coherence is thus the first cousin of implication). The criterion of coherence can be invoked only with reference to a particular context, and this context may be inferred only by positing the author's "horizon," his disposition toward a particular type of meaning. This conclusion requires elaboration.

The fact that coherence is a dependent quality leads to an unavoidable circularity in the process of interpretation. The interpreter posits meanings for the words and word-sequences he confronts, and, at the same time, he has to posit a whole meaning or context in reference to which the sub-meanings cohere with one another. The procedure is thoroughly circular; the context is derived from the sub-meanings and the sub-meanings are specified and rendered coherent with reference to the context. This circularity makes it very difficult to convince a reader to alter his construction, as every teacher knows. Many a self-willed student continues to insist that his reading is just as plausible as his instructor's, and, very often, the student is justified; his reading does make good sense. Often, the only thing at fault with the student's reading is that it is probably wrong, not that it is incoherent. The student persists in his opinion precisely because his construction *is* coherent and self-sustaining. In such a case he is wrong because he has misconstrued the context or sense of the whole. In this respect, the student's hardheadedness is not different from that of all self-convinced interpreters. Our readings are too plausible to be relinquished. If we have a distorted sense of the text's whole meaning, the harder we look at it the more certainly we shall find our distorted construction confirmed.

Since the quality of coherence depends upon the context inferred, there is no absolute standard of coherence by which we can adjudicate between different coherent readings. Verification by coherence implies therefore a verification of the *grounds* on which the reading is coherent. *It is necessary to establish that the context invoked is the most probable context.* Only then, in relation to an established context, can we judge that one reading is more coherent than another. Ultimately, therefore, we have to posit the most probable horizon for the text, and it is possible to do this only if we posit the author's typical outlook, the typical associations and expectations which form in part the context of his utterance. This is not only the single way we can test the relative coherence of a reading, but is also the only way to avoid pure circularity in making sense of the text.

An essential task in the process of verification is, therefore, a deliberate reconstruction of the author's subjective stance to the extent that this stance is relevant to the text at hand.[13] The importance of such psychological reconstruction may be exemplified in adjudicating between different readings of Wordsworth's "A Slumber Did My Spirit Seal." The interpretations of Brooks and Bateson, different as they are, remain equally coherent and self-sustaining. The implications which Brooks construes cohere beautifully with the explicit meanings of the poem within the context which Brooks adumbrates. The same may be said of Bateson's reading. The best way to show that one reading is more plausible and coherent than the other is to show that one context is more probable than the other. The problem of adjudicating between Bateson and Brooks is therefore, implicitly, the problem every interpreter must face when he tries to verify his reading. He must establish the most probable context.

Now when the *homme moyen sensuel* confronts bereavement such as that which Wordsworth's poem explicitly presents he adumbrates, typi-

cally, a horizon including sorrow and inconsolability. These are for him components in the very meaning of bereavement. Sorrow and inconsolability cannot fail to be associated with death when the loved one, formerly so active and alive, is imagined as lying in the earth, helpless, dumb, inert, insentient. And, since there is no hint of life in heaven but only of bodily death, the comforts of Christianity lie beyond the poem's horizon. Affirmations too deep for tears, like those Bateson insists on, simply do not cohere with the poem's explicit meanings; they do not belong to the context. Brook's reading, therefore, with its emphasis on inconsolability and bitter irony, is clearly justified not only by the text but by reference to universal human attitudes and feelings.

But the trouble with such a reading is apparent to most Wordsworthians. The poet is not an *homme moyen sensuel;* his characteristic attitudes are somewhat pantheistic. Instead of regarding rocks and stones and trees merely as inert objects, he probably regarded them in 1799 as deeply alive, as part of the immortal life of nature. Physical death he felt to be a return to the source of life, a new kind of participation in nature's "revolving immortality." From everything we know of Wordsworth's typical attitudes during the period in which he composed the poem, inconsolability and bitter irony do not belong in its horizon. I think, however, that Bateson overstates his case, and that he fails to emphasize properly the negative implications in the poem ("No motion has she now, no force"). He overlooks the poet's reticence, his distinct unwillingness to express any unqualified evaluation of his experience. Bateson, I would say, has not paid enough attention to the criterion of correspondence. Nevertheless, in spite of this, and in spite of the apparent implausibility of Bateson's reading, it remains, I think, somewhat more probable than that of Brooks. His procedure is also more objective. For even if he had botched his job thoroughly and had produced a less probable reading than that of Brooks, his method would remain fundamentally sound. Instead of projecting his own attitudes (Bateson is presumably not a pantheist) and instead of positing a "universal matrix" of human attitudes (there is none), he has tried to reconstruct the author's probable attitudes so far as these are relevant in specifying the poem's meaning. It is still possible, of course, that Brooks is right and Bateson wrong. A poet's typical attitudes do not always apply to a particular poem, although Wordsworth is, in a given period, more consistent than most poets. Be that as it may, we shall never be *certain* what any writer means, and since Bateson grounds his interpretation in a conscious construction of the poet's outlook, his reading must be deemed the more probable one until the uncovering of some presently unknown data makes a different construction of the poet's stance appear more valid.

Bateson's procedure is appropriate to all texts, including anonymous ones. On the surface, it would seem impossible to invoke the author's probable outlook when the author remains unknown, but in this limiting case the interpreter simply makes his psychological reconstruction on the basis of fewer data. For even with anonymous texts it is crucial to posit not simply some author or other, but a *particular* subjective stance in reference to which the construed context is rendered probable. That is why it is important to date anonymous texts. The interpreter needs all the clues he can muster with regard not only to the text's *langue* and genre, but also to the cultural and personal attitudes the author might be expected to bring to bear in specifying his verbal meanings. In this sense, all texts, including anonymous ones, are "attributed." The objective interpreter simply tries to make his attribution explicit, so that the grounds for his reading are frankly acknowledged. This opens the way to progressive accuracy in interpretation, since it is possible, then, to test the assumptions behind a reading as well as the coherence of the reading itself.

The fact that anonymous texts may be successfully interpreted does not, however, lead to the conclusion that all texts should be treated as anonymous ones, that they should, so to say, speak for themselves. I have already argued that no text speaks for itself, and that every construed text is necessarily "attributed." These points suggest strongly that it is unsound to insist on deriving all inferences from the "text itself." When we date an anonymous text, for example, we apply knowledge gained from a wide variety of sources which we correlate with data derived from the text. This extrinsic data is not, however, read *into* the text. On the contrary, it is used to *verify* that which we read out of it. The extrinsic information has ultimately a purely verificative function.

The same thing is true of information relating to the author's subjective stance. No matter what the source of this information may be, whether it be the text alone or the text in conjunction with other data, this information is *extrinsic* to verbal meaning as such. Strictly speaking, the author's subjective stance is not part of his verbal meaning even when he explicitly discusses his feelings and attitudes. This is Husserl's point again. The "intentional object" represented by a text is different from the "intentional acts" which realize it. When the interpreter posits the author's stance, he sympathetically re-enacts the author's "intentional acts," but although this imaginative act is necessary for realizing meaning, it must be distinguished from meaning as such. In no sense does the text *represent* the author's subjective stance: the intepreter simply adopts a stance in order to make sense of the text, and, if he is self-critical, he tries to verify his interpretation by showing his adopted stance to be, in all probability, the author's.

Of course, the text at hand is the safest source of clues to the author's outlook, since men do adopt different attitudes on different occasions. However, even though the text itself should be the primary source of clues and must always be the final authority, the interpreter should make an effort to go beyond his text wherever possible, since this is the only way he can avoid a vicious circularity. The harder one looks at a text from an incorrect stance, the more convincing the incorrect construction becomes. Inferences about the author's stance are sometimes difficult enough to make even when all relevant data are brought to bear, and it is self-defeating to make the inferential process more difficult than it need be. Since these inferences are ultimately extrinsic, there is no virtue in deriving them from the text alone. One must not confuse the result of a construction (the inter-preter's understanding of the text's *Sinn*)* either with the *process* of construction or with a vali-dation of that process. The *Sinn* must be rep-resented by and limited by the text alone, but the process of construction and validation in-volve psychological reconstruction and should therefore be based on all the data available.

Not only the criterion of coherence but all the other criteria used in verifying interpretations must be applied with reference to a psycholog-ical reconstruction. The criterion of legitimacy, for example, must be related to a speaking sub-ject, since it is the author's *langue*, as an internal possession, and not the interpreter's, which de-fines the range of meaning-possibilities a text can represent. The criterion of correspondence has force and significance only because we pre-sume that the author meant something by each of the linguistic components he employed. And the criterion of generic appropriateness is rele-vant only so far as generic conventions are pos-sessed and accepted by the author. The fact that these criteria all refer ultimately to a psycholog-ical construction is hardly surprising when we recall that to verify a text is simply to establish that the author probably meant what we con-strue his text to mean. The interpreter's primary task is to reproduce in himself the author's "logic," his attitudes, his cultural givens, in short his world. For even though the process of verification is highly complex and difficult, the ultimate verificative principle is very simple: the imaginative reconstruction of the speaking sub-ject.[14]

The speaking subject is not, however, iden-tical with the subjectivity of the author as an actual historical person; it corresponds, rather, to a very limited and special aspect of the au-thor's total subjectivity; it is, so to speak, that "part" of the author which specifies or deter-mines verbal meaning.[15] This distinction is quite apparent in the case of a lie. When I wish to deceive, my secret awareness that I am lying is irrelevant to the verbal meaning of my utter-ance. The only correct interpretation of my lie is, paradoxically, to view it as being a true state-ment, since this is the only correct construction of my "verbal intention." Indeed it is only when my listener has *understood* my meaning (pre-sented as true) that he can *judge* it to be a lie. Since I adopted a truth-telling stance, the verbal meaning of my utterance would be precisely the same, whether I was deliberately lying or suf-fering from the erroneous conviction that my statement was true. In other words, an author may adopt a stance which differs from his deep-est attitudes in the same way that an interpreter must almost always adopt a stance different from his own.[16] But for the process of interpre-tation, the author's private experiences are ir-relevant. The only relevant aspect of subjectivity is that which determines verbal meaning, or, in Husserl's terms, "content."

In a sense all poets are, of course, liars, and to some extent all speakers are, but the delib-erate lie, spoken to deceive, is a borderline case. In most verbal utterances the speaker's public stance is not totally foreign to his private atti-tudes. Even in those cases where the speaker deliberately assumes a role, this mimetic stance is usually not the final determinant of his mean-ing. In a play, for example, the total meaning of an utterance is not the "intentional object" of the dramatic character; that meaning is simply a component in the more complex "intention" of the dramatist. The speaker himself is spoken. The best description of these receding levels of subjectivity was provided by the scholastic phi-losophers in their distinction between "first in-tention," "second intention," and so on. Irony, for example, always entails a comprehension of two contrasting stances ("intentional levels") by a third and final complex "intention." The "speaking subject" may be defined as the final and most comprehensive level of awareness de-terminative of verbal meaning. In the case of a lie the speaking subject assumes that he tells the truth, while the actual subject retains a private awareness of his deception. Similarly, many speakers retain in their isolated privacy a self-conscious awareness of their verbal meaning, an awareness which may agree or disagree, ap-prove or disapprove, but which does not partic-ipate in determining their verbal meaning. To

---

Sinn: The work's unchanging "textual meaning," as opposed to the various types of "significance" that might be given to that meaning. —ED.

interpretation, this level of awareness is as ir-relevant as it is inaccessible. In construing and verifying verbal meaning, only the speaking subject counts.

A separate exposition would be required to discuss the problems of psychological recon-struction. I have here simply tried to forestall the current objections to extrinsic biographical and historical information by pointing, on the one hand, to the exigencies of verification, and, on the other, to the distinction between a speak-ing subject and a "biographical" person. I shall be satisfied if this part of my discussion, incom-plete as it must be, will help revive the half-forgotten truism that interpretation is the con-struction of *another's* meaning. A slight shift in the way we speak about texts would be highly salutary. It is natural to speak not of what a text says, but of what an author means, and this more natural locution is the more accurate one. Furthermore, to speak in this way implies a readiness (not notably apparent in recent criti-cism) to put forth a whole-hearted and self-crit-ical effort at the primary level of criticism—the level of understanding.

Notes

1. The phrase, "piece of language," comes from the first paragraph of William Empson's *Seven Types of Ambiguity*, 3rd ed. (New York, 1955). It is typical of the critical school Empson founded.

2. *Vol. I. Language*, trans. R. Manheim (New Ha-ven, 1953). It is ironic that Cassirer's work should be used to support the notion that a text speaks for itself. The realm of language is autonomous for Cassirer only in the sense that it follows an inde-pendent development which is reciprocally deter-mined by objective *and* subjective factors. See pp. 69, 178, 213, 249–250, et passim.

3. René Wellek and Austin Warren, *Theory of Lit-erature*, 3rd ed. (New York, 1956), p. 144.

4. Every interpretation is necessarily incomplete in the sense that it fails to explicate all a text's impli-cations. But this kind of incomplete interpretation may still carry an absolutely correct system of em-phases and an accurate sense of the whole mean-ing. This kind of incompleteness is radically dif-ferent from that postulated by the inclusivists, for whom a sense of the whole means a grasp of the

various possible meanings which a text can plau-sibly represent.

5. Cleanth Brooks, "Irony as a Principle of Struc-ture," in M. D. Zabel, ed., *Literary Opinion in Amer-ica*, 2nd ed. (New York, 1951), p. 736. F. W. Bate-son, *English Poetry. A Critical Introduction* (London, 1950), p. 33 and pp. 80–81.

6. This is the "synchronic" as opposed to the "dia-chronic" sense of the term. See Ferdinand de Saus-sure, *Cours de linguistique générale* (Paris, 1931). Use-ful discussions may be found in Stephen Ullman, *The Principles of Semantics* (Glasgow, 1951), and W. v. Wartburg, *Einführung in die Problematik und Meth-odik der Sprachwissenschaft* (Halle, 1943).

7. See, for example, Cassirer, p. 304.

8. *Sewanee Review*, 54, 1946. Reprinted in W. K. Wimsatt, Jr., *The Verbal Icon* (Lexington, Ky., 1954).

9. T. S. Eliot, "From Poe to Valéry," *Hudson Re-view*, 2, 1949, p. 232.

10. The word is, in fact, quite effective. It conveys the sense of "memorable" by the component "memorial," and the sense of "never-to-be-forgot-ten" by the negative prefix. The difference between this and Jabberwocky words is that it appears to be a standard word occurring in a context of standard words. Perhaps Eliot is right to scold Poe, but he cannot properly insist that the word lacks a deter-minate verbal meaning.

11. This third criterion is, however, highly pre-sumptive, since the interpreter may easily mistake the text's genre.

12. Exceptions to this are the syncategorematic meanings (color and extention, for example) which cohere by necessity regardless of the context.

13. The reader may feel that I have telescoped a number of steps here. The author's verbal meaning or "verbal intention" is the object of complex "in-tentional acts." To reproduce this meaning it is nec-essary for the interpreter to engage in "intentional acts" belonging to the same species as those of the author. (Two different "intentional acts" belong to the same species when they "intend" the same "in-tentional object.") That is why the issue of "stance" arises. The interpreter needs to adopt sympathet-ically the author's stance (his disposition to engage in particular kinds of "intentional acts") so that he can "intend" with some degree of probability the same "intentional objects" as the author. This is es-pecially clear in the case of *implicit* verbal meaning, where the interpreter's realization of the author's stance determines the text's horizon.

14. Here I purposefully display my sympathies

with Dilthey's concepts, *Sichhineinfühlen* and *Verstehen*. In fact, my whole argument may be regarded as an attempt to ground some of Dilthey's hermeneutic principles in Husserl's epistemology and Saussure's linguistics.

15. Spranger aptly calls this the "cultural subject." See Eduard Spranger, "Zur Theorie des Verstehens und zur geisteswissenschaftlichen Psychologie" in *Festschrift Johannes Volkelt zum 70. Geburtstag* (Munich, 1918), p. 369. It should be clear that I am here in essential agreement with the American anti-intentionalists (term used in the ordinary sense). I think they are right to exclude private associations from verbal meaning. But it is of some practical consequence to insist that verbal meaning is that aspect of an author's meaning which is interpersonally communic*able*. For this implies that his verbal meaning is that which, under linguistic norms, one *can* understand, even if one must sometimes work hard to do so.

16. Charles Bally calls this "dédoublement de la personalité." See his *Linguistique générale et linguistique française*, 2nd ed. (Bern, 1944), p. 37.

Literature and History

Terry Eagleton

Since Marxism in most of its many forms is grounded on a view of history, it is not surprising that Marxist literary critics should often adopt a genetic approach. In the first chapter of his Marxism and Literature, *Terry Eagleton asserts that critical explanation should mean grasping literary form, styles, and meanings "as the products of a particular history." In opposition, then, to those critics who claim that great literature transcends the circumstances of its creation, the Marxist critic is apt to stress its ties to those circumstances. Furthermore, Eagleton argues, the Marxist critic has a "revolutionary idea of history" that calls attention to the work's relationship to the "ideology" of its age. Eagleton defines ideology here as the "way men live out their roles in class-society, the values, ideas and images which tie them to their social functions and so prevent them from having a true knowledge of society as a whole." Ideology, in this sense, is something like a "false consciousness," a set of illusions, and Eagleton stresses his point that the literary work's relation to the ideology of its age is likely to be much more complicated than the "vulgar Marxist" will generally allow, neither simply supporting that ideology nor directly challenging it. Pointing to the work of the French Marxist critics Louis Althusser and Pierre Macherey, Eagleton calls for a truly "scientific" criticism that would "seek to explain the literary work in terms of the ideological structure of which it is part, yet which it transforms in its art."*

Marx, Engels and Criticism

If Karl Marx and Frederick Engels are better known for their political and economic rather than literary writings, this is not in the least because they regarded literature as insignificant. It is true, as Leon Trotsky remarked in *Literature and Revolution* (1924), that "there are many people in this world who think as revolutionists and feel as philistines"; but Marx and Engels were not of this number. The writings of Karl Marx, himself the youthful author of lyric poetry, a fragment of verse-drama and an unfinished comic novel much influenced by Laurence Sterne, are laced with literary concepts and allusions; he wrote a sizeable unpublished manuscript on art and religion, and planned a journal of dramatic criticism, a full-length study of Balzac and a treatise on aesthetics. Art and literature were part of the very air Marx breathed, as a formidably cultured German intellectual in the great classical tradition of his society. His acquaintance with literature, from Sophocles to the Spanish novel, Lucretius to potboiling English fiction, was staggering in its scope; the German workers' circle he founded in Brussels devoted an evening a week to discussing the arts, and Marx himself was an inveterate theatre-goer, declaimer of poetry, devourer of every species of literary art from Augustan prose to industrial ballads. He described his own works in a letter to Engels as forming an "artistic whole," and was scrupulously sensitive to questions of literary style, not least his own; his very first pieces of journalism argued for freedom of artistic expression. Moreover, the pressure of aesthetic concepts can be detected behind some of the most crucial categories of economic thought he employs in his mature work.[1]

Even so, Marx and Engels had rather more important tasks on their hands than the formation of a complete aesthetic theory. Their comments on art and literature are scattered and fragmentary, glancing allusions rather than developed positions.[2] This is one reason why Marxist criticism involves more than merely restating cases set out by the "sociology of literature." The sociology of literature concerns itself chiefly with what might be called the means of literary production, distribution and exchange in a particular society—how books are published, the social composition of their authors and audiences, levels of literacy, the social determinants of "taste." It also examines literary texts for their "sociological" relevance, raiding literary works to abstract from them themes of interest to the social historian. There has been some excellent work in this field,[3] and it forms one aspect of Marxist criticism as a whole; but taken by itself it is neither particularly Marxist nor particularly critical. It is, indeed, for the most part a suitably tamed, degutted version of Marxist criticism, appropriate for Western consumption.

Marxist criticism is not merely a "sociology of literature," concerned with how novels get published and whether they mention the working class. Its aim is to *explain* the literary work more fully; and this means a sensitive attention to its forms, styles and meanings.[4] But it also means grasping those forms, styles and meanings as the products of a particular history. The painter Henri Matisse once remarked that all art bears the imprint of its historical epoch, but that great art is that in which this imprint is most deeply marked. Most students of literature are taught otherwise: the greatest art is that which timelessly transcends its historical conditions. Marxist criticism has much to say on this issue, but the "historical" analysis of literature did not of course begin with Marxism. Many thinkers before Marx had tried to account for literary works in terms of the history which produced them;[5] and one of these, the German idealist philosopher G. W. F. Hegel, had a profound influence on Marx's own aesthetic thought. The originality of Marxist criticism, then, lies not in its historical approach to literature, but in its revolutionary understanding of history itself.

Base and Superstructure

The seeds of that revolutionary understanding are planted in a famous passage in Marx and Engels's *The German Ideology* (1845–6):

> The production of ideas, concepts and consciousness is first of all directly interwoven with the material intercourse of man, the language of real life. Conceiving, thinking, the spiritual intercourse of men, appear here as the direct efflux of men's material behaviour . . . we do not proceed from what men say, imagine, conceive, nor from men as described, thought of, imagined, conceived, in order to arrive at corporeal man; rather we proceed from the really active man . . . Consciousness does not determine life: life determines consciousness.

A fuller statement of what this means can be found in the Preface to *A Contribution to the Critique of Political Economy* (1859):

> In the social production of their life, men enter into definite relations that are indispensable and independent of their will, *relations of production* which correspond to a definite stage of development of their material productive *forces*. The sum total of these relations of production constitutes the economic structure of society, the real foundation, on which rises a legal and political superstructure and to which correspond definite forms of social consciousness. The mode of production of material life conditions the social, political and intellectual life process in general. It is not the consciousness of men that determines their being, but on the contrary, their social being that determines their consciousness.

The social relations between men, in other words, are bound up with the way they produce their material life. Certain "productive forces"—say, the organisation of labour in the middle ages—involve the social relations of villein to lord we know as feudalism. At a later stage, the development of new modes of productive organisation is based on a changed set of social relations—this time between the capitalist class who owns those means of production, and the proletarian class whose labour-power the capitalist buys for profit. Taken together, these "forces" and "relations" of production form what Marx calls "the economic structure of society," or what is more commonly known by Marxism as the economic "base" or "infrastructure." From this economic base, in every period, emerges a "superstructure"—certain forms of law and politics, a certain kind of state, whose essential function is to legitimate the power of the social class which owns the means of economic production. But the superstructure contains more than this: it also consists of certain "definite forms of social consciousness" (political, religious, ethical, aesthetic and so on), which is what Marxism designates as *ideology*. The function of ideology, also, is to legitimate the power of the ruling class in society; in the last analysis, the dominant ideas of a society are the ideas of its ruling class.[6]

Art, then, is for Marxism part of the "superstructure" of society. It is (with qualifications we shall make later) part of a society's ideology—an element in that complex structure of social perception which ensures that the situation in which one social class has power over the others is either seen by most members of the society as "natural," or not seen at all. To understand literature, then, means understanding the total social process of which it is part. As the Russian Marxist critic Georgy Plekhanov put it: "The social mentality of an age is conditioned by that age's social relations. This is nowhere quite as evident as in the history of art and literature."[7] Literary works are not mysteriously inspired, or explicable simply in terms of their author's psychology. They are forms of perception, particular ways of seeing the world; and as such they have a relation to that dominant way of seeing the world which is the "social mentality" or ideology of an age. That ideology, in turn, is the product of the concrete social relations into which men enter at a particular time and place; it is the way those class-relations are experienced, legitimized and perpetuated. Moreover, men are not free to choose their social relations; they are constrained into them by material necessity—by the nature and stage of development of their mode of economic production.

To understand *King Lear, The Dunciad* or *Ulysses* is therefore to do more than interpret their symbolism, study their literary history and add footnotes about sociological facts which enter into them. It is first of all to understand the complex, indirect relations between those works and the ideological worlds they inhabit—relations which emerge not just in "themes" and "preoccupations," but in style, rhythm, image, quality and (as we shall see later) *form*. But we do not understand ideology either unless we grasp the part it plays in the society as a whole—how it consists of a definite, historically relative structure of perception which underpins the power of a particular social class. This is not an easy task, since an ideology is never a simple reflection of a ruling class's ideas; on the contrary, it is always a complex phenomenon, which may incorporate conflicting, even contradictory, views of the world. To understand an ideology, we must analyse the precise relations between different classes in a society; and to do that means grasping where those classes stand in relation to the mode of production.

All this may seem a tall order to the student of literature who thought he was merely required to discuss plot and characterization. It may seem a confusion of literary criticism with disciplines like politics and economics which ought to be kept separate. But it is, nonetheless, essential for the fullest explanation of any work of literature. Take, for example, the great Placido Gulf scene in Conrad's *Nostromo*. To evaluate the fine artistic force of this episode, as Decoud and Nostromo are isolated in utter darkness on the slowly sinking lighter, involves us in subtly placing the scene within the imaginative vision of the novel as a whole. The radical pessimism of that vision (and to grasp it fully we must, of course, relate *Nostromo* to the rest of Conrad's fiction) cannot simply be accounted for in terms of "psychological" factors in Conrad himself; for individual psychology is also a *social* product. The pessimism of Conrad's world view is rather a unique transformation into art of an ideological pessimism rife in his period—a sense of history as futile and cyclical, of individuals as impenetrable and solitary, of human values as relativistic and irrational, which marks a drastic crisis in the ideology of the Western bourgeois class to which Conrad allied himself. There were good reasons for that ideological crisis, in the history of imperialist capitalism throughout this period. Conrad did not, of course, merely anonymously reflect that history in his fiction; every writer is individually placed in society, responding to a general history from his own particular standpoint, making sense of it in his own concrete terms. But it is not difficult to see how Conrad's personal standing, as an "aristocratic" Polish exile deeply committed to English conservatism, intensified for him the crisis of English bourgeois ideology.[8]

It is also possible to see in these terms why that scene in the Placido Gulf should be artistically fine. To write well is more than a matter of "style"; it also means having at one's disposal an ideological perspective which can penetrate to the realities of men's experience in a certain situation. This is certainly what the Placido Gulf scene does; and it can do it, not just because its author happens to have an excellent prose-style, but because his historical situation allows him access to such insights. Whether those insights are in political terms "progressive" or "reactionary" (Conrad's are certainly the latter) is not the point—anymore than it is to the point that most of the agreed major writers of the twentieth century—Yeats, Eliot, Pound, Lawrence—are political conservatives who each had truck with fascism. Marxist criticism, rather than apologising for that fact, explains it—sees that, in the absence of genuinely revolutionary art, only a radical conservatism, hostile like Marxism to the withered values of liberal bourgeois society, could produce the most significant literature.

Literature and Superstructure

It would be a mistake to imply that Marxist criticism moves mechanically from "text" to "ideology" to "social relations" to "productive forces." It is concerned, rather, with the *unity* of these "levels" of society. Literature may be part of the superstructure, but it is not merely the passive reflection of the economic base. Engels makes this clear, in a letter to Joseph Bloch in 1890:

> According to the materialist conception of history, the determining element in history is *ultimately* the production and reproduction in real life. More than this neither Marx nor I have ever asserted. If therefore somebody twists this into the statement that the economic element is the *only* determining one, he transforms it into a meaningless, abstract and absurd phrase. The economic situation is the basis, but the various

elements of the superstructure—political forms of the class struggle and its consequences, constitutions established by the victorious class after a successful battle, etc.—forms of law—and then even the reflexes of all these actual struggles in the brains of the combatants: political, legal, and philosophical theories, religious ideas and their further development into systems of dogma— also exercise their influence upon the course of the historical struggles and in many cases preponderate in determining their *form*.

Engels wants to deny that there is any mechanical, one-to-one correspondence between base and superstructure; elements of the superstructure constantly react back upon and influence the economic base. The materialist theory of history denies that art can *in itself* change the course of history; but it insists that art can be an active element in such change. Indeed, when Marx came to consider the relation between base and superstructure, it was art which he selected as an instance of the complexity and indirectness of that relationship:

> In the case of the arts, it is well known that certain periods of their flowering are out of all proportion to the general development of society, hence also to the material foundation, the skeletal structure, as it were, of its organisation. For example, the Greeks compared to the moderns or also Shakespeare. It is even recognised that certain forms of art, e.g. the epic, can no longer be produced in their world epoch-making, classical stature as soon as the production of art, as such, begins; that is, that certain significant forms within the realm of the arts are possible only at an undeveloped stage of artistic development. If this is the case with the relation between different kinds of art within the realm of art, it is already less puzzling that it is the case in the relation of the entire realm to the general development of society. The difficulty consists only in the general formulation of these contradictions. As soon as they have been specified, they are already clarified.[9]

Marx is considering here what he calls "the unequal relationship of the development of material production . . . to artistic production." It does not follow that the greatest artistic achievements depend upon the highest development of the productive forces, as the example of the Greeks, who produced major art in an economically undeveloped society, clearly evidences.

Certain major artistic forms like the epic are only *possible* in an undeveloped society. Why then, Marx goes on to ask, do we still respond to such forms, given our historical distance from them?

> But the difficulty lies not in understanding that the Greek arts and epic are bound up with certain forms of social development. The difficulty is that they still afford us artistic pleasure and that in a certain respect they count as a norm and as an unattainable model.

Why does Greek art still give us aesthetic pleasure? The answer which Marx goes on to provide has been universally lambasted by unsympathetic commentators as lamely inept:

> A man cannot become a child again, or he becomes childish. But does he not find joy in the child's naiveté, and must he himself not strive to reproduce its truth at a higher stage? Does not the true character of each epoch come alive in the nature of its children? Why should not the historic childhood of humanity, its most beautiful unfolding, as a stage never to return, exercise an eternal charm? There are unruly children and precocious children. Many of the old peoples belong in this category. The Greeks were normal children. The charm of their art for us is not in contradiction to the undeveloped stage of society on which it grew. [It] is its result, rather, and is inextricably bound up, rather, with the fact that the unripe social conditions under which it arose, and could alone rise, can never return.

So our liking for Greek art is a nostalgic lapse back into childhood—a piece of unmaterialist sentimentalism which hostile critics have gladly pounced on. But the passage can only be treated thus if it is rudely ripped from the context to which it belongs—the draft manuscripts of 1857, known today as the *Grundrisse*. Once returned to that context, the meaning becomes instantly apparent. The Greeks, Marx is arguing, were able to produce major art not *in spite of* but *because of* the undeveloped state of their society. In ancient societies, which have not yet undergone the fragmenting "division of labour" known to capitalism, the overwhelming of "quality" by "quantity" which results from commodity-production and the restless, continual development of the productive forces, a certain "measure" or harmony can be achieved between man and Nature—a harmony precisely dependent upon the *limited* nature of Greek society. The "childlike" world of the Greeks is attractive because it thrives within certain measured limits—measures and limits which are brutally overridden by bourgeois society in its limitless demand to produce and consume. Historically, it is essential that this constricted society should be broken up as the productive forces expand beyond its frontiers; but when Marx speaks of "striv[ing] to reproduce its truth at a higher stage," he is clearly speaking of the communist society of the future, where unlimited resources will serve an unlimitedly developing man.[10]

Two questions, then, emerge from Marx's formulations in the *Grundrisse*. The first concerns the relation between "base" and "superstructure"; the second concerns our own relation in the present with past art. To take the second question first: how can it be that we moderns still find aesthetic appeal in the cultural products of past, vastly different societies? In a sense, the answer Marx gives is no different from the answer to the question: How is it that we moderns still respond to the exploits of, say, Spartacus? We respond to Spartacus or Greek sculpture because our own history links us to those ancient societies; we find in them an undeveloped phase of the forces which condition us. Moreover, we find in those ancient societies a primitive image of "measure" between man and Nature which capitalist society necessarily destroys, and which socialist society can reproduce at an incomparably higher level. We ought, in other words, to think of "history" in wider terms than our own contemporary history. To ask how Dickens relates to history is not just to ask how he relates to Victorian England, for that society was itself the product of a long history which includes men like Shakespeare and Milton. It is a curiously narrowed view of history which defines it merely as the "contemporary moment" and relegates all else to the "universal." One answer to the problem of past and present is suggested by Bertolt Brecht, who argues that "we need to develop the historical sense . . . into a real sensual delight. When our theatres perform plays of other periods they like to annihilate distance, fill in the gap, gloss over the differences. But what comes then of our delight in comparisons, in distance, in dissimilarity—which is at the same time a delight in what is close and proper to ourselves?[11]

The other problem posed by the *Grundrisse* is the relation between base and superstructure. Marx is clear that these two aspects of society do not form a *symmetrical* relationship, dancing a harmonious minuet hand-in-hand throughout history. Each element of a society's superstructure—art, law, politics, religion—has its own tempo of development, its own internal evolution, which is not reducible to a mere expression of the class struggle or the state of the economy. Art, as Trotsky comments, has "a very high degree of autonomy"; it is not tied in any simple one-to-one way to the mode of production. And yet Marxism claims too that, in the last analysis, art is determined by that mode of production. How are we to explain this apparent discrepancy?

Let us take a concrete literary example. A "vulgar Marxist" case about T. S. Eliot's *The Waste Land* might be that the poem is directly determined by ideological and economic factors—by the spiritual emptiness and exhaustion of bourgeois ideology which springs from that crisis of imperialist capitalism known as the First World War. This is to explain the poem as an immediate "reflection" of those conditions; but it clearly fails to take into account a whole series of "levels" which "mediate" between the text itself and capitalist economy. It says nothing, for instance, about the social situation of Eliot himself—a writer living an ambiguous relationship with English society, as an "aristocratic" American expatriate who became a glorified City clerk and yet identified deeply with the conservative-traditionalist, rather than bourgeois-commercialist, elements of English ideology. It says nothing about that ideology's more general forms—nothing of its structure, content, internal complexity, and how all these are produced by the extremely complex class-relations of English society at the time. It is silent about the form and language of *The Waste Land*—about why Eliot, despite his extreme political conservatism, was an *avant-garde* poet who selected certain "progressive" experimental techniques from the history of literary forms available to him, and on what ideological basis he did this. We learn nothing from this approach about the social conditions which gave rise at the time to certain forms of "spirituality," part-Christian, part-Buddhist, which the poem draws on; or of what role a certain kind of bourgeois anthropology (Fraser) and bourgeois philosophy (F. H. Bradley's idealism) used by the poem fulfilled in the ideological formation of the period. We are unilluminated about Eliot's social position as an artist, part of a self-consciously erudite, experimental élite with particular modes of publication (the small press, the little magazine) at their disposal; or about the kind of audience which that implied, and its effect on the poem's style and devices. We remain ignorant about the relation between the poem and the aesthetic theories associated with it—of what role that aesthetic plays in the ideology of the time, and how it shapes the construction of the poem itself.

Any complete understanding of *The Waste Land* would need to take these (and other) factors into account. It is not a matter of *reducing* the poem to the state of contemporary capitalism; but neither is it a matter of introducing so many judicious complications that anything as crude as capitalism may to all intents and purposes be forgotten. On the contrary: all of the elements I have enumerated (the author's class-position, ideological forms and their relation to literary forms, "spirituality" and philosophy, techniques of literary production, aesthetic theory) are directly relevant to the base/superstructure model. What Marxist criticism looks for is the unique *conjuncture* of these elements which we know as *The Waste Land*.[12] No one of these elements can be conflated with another: each has its own relative independence. *The Waste Land* can indeed be explained as a poem which springs from a crisis of bourgeois ideology, but it has no simple correspondence with that crisis or with the political and economic conditions which produced it. (As a poem, it does not of course *know itself* as a product of a particular ideological crisis, for if it did it would cease to exist. It needs to translate that crisis into "universal" terms—to grasp it as part of an unchanging human condition, shared alike by ancient Egyptians and modern man.) *The Waste Land's* relation to the real history of its time, then, is highly *mediated*; and in this it is like all works of art.

Literature and Ideology

Frederick Engels remarks in *Ludwig Feuerbach and the End of Classical German Philosophy* (1888) that art is far richer and more "opaque" than political and economic theory because it is less purely ideological. It is important here to grasp the precise meaning for Marxism of "ideology." Ideology is not in the first place a set of doctrines; it signifies the way men live out their roles in class-society, the values, ideas and images which tie them to their social functions and so prevent them from a true knowledge of society as a whole. In this sense *The Waste Land* is ideological: it shows a man making sense of his experience in ways that prohibit a true understanding of his society, ways that are consequently false. All art springs from an ideological conception of the world; there is no such thing, Plekhanov comments, as a work of art entirely devoid of ideological content. But Engels' remark suggests that art has a more complex relationship to ideology than law and political theory, which rather more transparently embody the interests of a ruling class. The question, then, is what relationship art has to ideology.

This is not an easy question to answer. Two extreme, opposite positions are possible here. One is that literature is *nothing but* ideology in a certain artistic form—that works of literature are just expressions of the ideologies of their time. They are prisoners of "false consciousness," unable to reach beyond it to arrive at the truth. It is a position characteristic of much "vulgar Marxist" criticism, which tends to see literary works merely as reflections of dominant ideologies. As such, it is unable to explain, for one thing, why so much literature actually *challenges* the ideological assumptions of its time. The opposite case seizes on the fact that so much literature challenges the ideology it confronts, and makes this part of the definition of literary art itself. Authentic art, as Ernst Fischer argues in his significantly entitled *Art Against Ideology* (1969), always transcends the ideological limits of its time, yielding us insight into the realities which ideology hides from view.

Both of these cases seem to me too simple. A more subtle (although still incomplete) account of the relationship between literature and

ideology is provided by the French Marxist theorist Louis Althusser.[13] Althusser argues that art cannot be reduced to ideology: it has, rather, a particular *relationship* to it. Ideology signifies the imaginary ways in which men experience the real world, which is, of course, the kind of experience literature gives us too—what it feels like to live in particular conditions, rather than a conceptual analysis of those conditions. However, art does more than just passively reflect that experience. It is held within ideology, but also manages to distance itself from it, to the point where it permits us to "feel" and "perceive" the ideology from which it springs. In doing this, art does not enable us to *know* the truth which ideology conceals, since for Althusser "knowledge" in the strict sense means *scientific* knowledge—the kind of knowledge of, say, capitalism which Marx's *Capital* rather than Dickens's *Hard Times* allows us. The difference between science and art is not that they deal with different objects, but that they deal with the same objects in different ways. Science gives us conceptual knowledge of a situation; art gives us the experience of that situation, which is equivalent to ideology. But by doing this, it allows us to "see" the nature of that ideology, and thus begins to move us towards that full understanding of ideology which is scientific knowledge.

How literature can do this is more fully developed by one of Althusser's colleagues, Pierre Macherey. In his *Pour une Théorie de la Production Littéraire* (1966), Macherey distinguishes between what he terms "illusion" (meaning, essentially, ideology), and "fiction." Illusion—the ordinary ideological experience of men—is the material on which the writer goes to work; but in working on it he transforms it into something different, lends it a shape and structure. It is by giving ideology a determinate form, fixing it within certain fictional limits, that art is able to distance itself from it, thus revealing to us the limits of that ideology. In doing this, Macherey claims, art contributes to our deliverance from the ideological illusion.

I find the comments of both Althusser and Macherey at crucial points ambiguous and obscure; but the relation they propose between literature and ideology is nonetheless deeply suggestive. Ideology, for both critics, is more than an amorphous body of free-floating images and ideas; in any society it has a certain structural coherence. Because it possesses such relative coherence, it can be the object of scientific analysis; and since literary texts "belong" to ideology, they too can be the object of such scientific analysis. A scientific criticism would seek to explain the literary work in terms of the ideological structure of which it is part, yet which it transforms in its art: it would search out the principle which both ties the work to ideology and distances it from it.

Notes

1. See M. Lifshitz, *The Philosophy of Art of Karl Marx* (London, 1973). For a naively prejudiced but reasonably informative account of Marx and Engel's literary interests, see P. Demetz, *Marx, Engels and the Poets* (Chicago, 1967).

2. See Karl Marx and Frederick Engels, *On Literature and Art* (New York, 1973), for a compendium of these comments.

3. See especially L. Shücking, *The Sociology of Literary Taste* (London, 1944); R. Escarpit, *The Sociology of Literature* (London, 1971); R. D. Altick, *The English Common Reader* (Chicago, 1957); and R. Williams, *The Long Revolution* (London, 1961). Representative recent works have been D. Laurenson and A. Swingewood, *The Sociology of Literature* (London, 1972), and M. Bradbury, *The Social Context of English Literature* (Oxford, 1971). For an account of Raymond Williams's important work, see my article in *New Left Review* 95 (January–February, 1976).

4. Much non-Marxist criticism would reject a term like "explanation," feeling that it violates the "mystery" of literature. I use it here because I agree with Pierre Macherey, in his *Pour une Théorie de la Pro-*
duction Littéraire (Paris, 1966), that the task of the critic is not to "interpret" but to "explain." For Macherey, "interpretation" of a text means revising or correcting it in accordance with some ideal norm of what it should be; it consists, that is to say, in refusing the text *as it is*. Interpretative criticism merely "redoubles" the text, modifying and elaborating it for easier consumption. In saying *more* about the work, it succeeds in saying *less*.

5. See especially Vico's *The New Science* (1725); Madame de Staël, *Of Literature and Social Institutions* (1800); H. Taine, *History of English Literature* (1863).

6. This, inevitably, is a considerably over-simplified account. For a full analysis, see N. Poulantzas, *Political Power and Social Classes* (London, 1973).

7. Quoted in the preface to Henri Arvon's *Marxist Aesthetics* (Ithaca, 1970).

8. On the question of how a writer's personal history interlocks with the history of his time, see J.-P. Sartre, *The Search for a Method* (London, 1963).

9. Introduction to the *Grundrisse* (Harmondsworth, 1973).

10. See Stanley Mitchell's essay on Marx in Hall and Walton (eds.), *Situating Marx* (London, 1972).

11. Appendices to the "Short Organum on the Theatre," in J. Willett (ed.), *Brecht on Theatre: The Development of an Aesthetic* (London, 1964).

12. To put the issue in more complex theoretical terms: the influence of the economic "base" on *The Waste Land* is evident not in a direct way, but in the fact that it is the economic base which in the last instance determines the state of development of each element of the superstructure (religious, philosophical and so on) which went into its making, and moreover determines the structural interrelations between those elements, of which the poem is a particular conjuncture.

13. In his "Letter on Art in reply to André Daspre," in *Lenin and Philosophy* (London, 1971). See also the following essay on the abstract painter Cremonini.

Application

Spirit of Health or Goblin Damned?

Eleanor Prosser

The claims of historical scholarship are most strongly asserted when the historical critic offers not simply to support but radically to revise our usual interpretation of a major work. Eleanor Prosser's Hamlet and Revenge *is a case in point. She argues that if we could see the play as its original, intended audience saw it, with their assumptions and their ability to interpret the clues Shakespeare has provided, we would see that Hamlet's willingness to accept the ghost's commands and undertake the mission of revenge is a fatal error that will lead him not to tragic heroism but to ruin and damnation. Unfortunately, in many respects we do not share Elizabethan assumptions and, even more disabling, she claims, we have been misled by centuries of often faulty scholarship and inaccurate staging. As a result, we are conditioned to equate Hamlet's understanding of his predicament with Shakespeare's and to seriously misinterpret the play. The only remedy, Prosser argues, is to offer better historical scholarship, to equip the modern audience with the knowledge that will allow us to see the play as Shakespeare's intended audience had seen it. While no brief excerpts from her book-length, scene-by-scene reading can fully convey the effect of her presentation, nor the learning that supports it, the following selections from her discussion of Act I and the business of the ghost will give a clear sense of her line, and style, of argument.*

Reprinted from Eleanor Prosser, *Hamlet and Revenge*, 2nd ed., pp. 118–23, 133–43, with the permission of the publishers, Stanford University Press. © 1967, 1971 by the Board of Trustees of the Leland Stanford Junior University. Notes have been renumbered.

THE STUDY OF ELIZABETHAN GHOST LORE DOES not contradict our intuitive response to the first scene of *Hamlet*. It indicates that modern uneasiness may closely approximate the response of Shakespeare's audience. The play frankly invited both Protestants and Catholics to test the Ghost according to their religious beliefs and then presented them with recognizable warnings of danger.

No one in the first scene gives any indication of believing the Ghost to be the true soul of the dead King. The point of view is Protestant. Horatio, Marcellus, and Bernardo all consistently refer to the apparition as "it": not as the soul of the King himself, but as a spirit whose identity is in doubt. When Marcellus asks if this "thing" has appeared, his diction suggests not contemptuous levity but the cautious Protestant's awareness that the Ghost cannot be the actual King.[1] It is an unknown, the nature of which is still to be determined. Similarly, Horatio's "Stay, illusion" is not an echo of his earlier skepticism but the correct response of a wary Protestant. The Ghost is, indeed, an "illusion." The point at issue is what kind of illusion.

In its first minute on stage, the Ghost reveals that something is seriously wrong. What is the purpose of its first appearance? It merely enters and leaves. Little is established that could not be included in the second appearance. The usual explanation is that its first entrance is a shrewd bit of theatrical trickery intended to catch the audience's attention. The episode does much more than that. It firmly establishes one point: this Ghost is forced to leave when Heaven is invoked. Horatio follows the warnings of religion. He charges the Ghost in the name of Heaven to identify itself, and it took no pious scholar to know that only demons would be "chased" by the invocation of God. The first episode reaches its climax as the Ghost is "of-fended" and stalks away, leaving Horatio pale and trembling.

A minor detail in this episode may also be a hint that this is a demon who usurps the form of the dead King. The Ghost "would be spoke to," and Horatio, as a scholar, is urged to question it. In my judgment, this fact has been faultily glossed. It is generally held that ghosts could not speak until they were spoken to, although the only corroborating evidence seems to be a remark about Samuel Johnson in the eighteenth century.[2] The Elizabethan belief appears to have been specifically related to the problem of identifying an evil spirit. A false spirit might speak first, in which case one should be even more cautious. The informed Christian would speak before being spoken to, conjuring the spirit in the name of God to reveal its nature: if good, by speaking; if bad, by leaving. In other words, the fact that "it would be spoke to" does not prove that Bernardo believes it is a true ghost. Moreover, the fact that a scholar is urged to address it may mean that Marcellus fears it is a demon. Since Francis Douce, editors have repeated his assertion that ghosts had to be addressed in Latin. On the contrary, the evidence most frequently cited indicates something quite different. In Fletcher's *The Night-Walker*, Coachman Toby says:

Let's call the butler up, for he speaks Latine,
And that will daunt the devil.   (II.i)[3]

Exactly. Latin was the language used in the rite of exorcism. No writer claimed that good spirits must be so addressed. If Marcellus is appealing to Horatio to use Latin, he is fearful that the Ghost may be a demon.[4] More probably, however, Marcellus simply believes that a scholar is better equipped to address a doubtful spirit with safety. He is terrified, and with good reason.

The physical appearance of the Ghost may also suggest that it is suspect. As Catholics believed and Protestants had heard, Purgatory souls and good spirits both were "of sweet and amiable aspect," moved only by grace and charity. This ghost frowns as did the dead King once when he was angry with the Polacks. Moreover, Purgatory souls and good spirits are both spirits of peace. Many have noted the curious fact that the Ghost is in arms, bearing a truncheon as it moves with martial stalk. This is surely not the typical stage ghost described in the Induction to *A Warning for Fair Women* as "Lapt in some foul sheet or a leather pilch." It is conceivable that the costume is intended to lend awe, or to create a figure acceptable to a man of Hamlet's intelligence, or to portend some danger to the State. But it is also possible that Shakespeare's audience believed that armed spirits were demonic. Virgil had explained such apparitions as souls who still embraced the goods and appetites that had dominated them in life, but Le Loyer disagreed. Military garb proved that they were not souls but "devils who took the clothes and even the arms" of the men whose form they assumed.[5] I have found no indication that this belief was widespread, but it does suggest a possible association.

The second appearance of the Ghost reinforces the threat. Horatio, in an act of considerable courage, resolves to step into the path of the Ghost: "I'll cross it, though it blast me." The context makes it impossible that Shakespeare meant Horatio to make the sign of the cross. Horatio's point of view has been consistently Protestant, as shown by his repeated assumption that the Ghost is an "illusion," a spirit "usurping" the form of the dead King. Moreover, the stage direction in Q_2—"It spreads his armes"—probably refers to Horatio's movements in intercepting the Ghost's path. It does not describe the Catholic gesture, nor could it indicate any meaningful action by the Ghost. For three centuries, the direction apparently was assumed to mean that Horatio blocked the Ghost's path. Discussing Fechter's production of *Hamlet* in 1870, Kate Field expressed her delight at a new piece of business: "Heretofore Horatios have senselessly *crossed the Ghost's path*, as if such a step would stay its progress. Not so with Fechter, whose Horatio makes the sign of the cross, at which the Ghost stops, as a Catholic ghost should. Once interpreted thus, intelligence exclaims 'of course'; and yet Horatios have been crossing the stage for three hundred years!"[6] The witness of three centuries of stage tradition is not to be discounted.

Horatio's movement into the Ghost's path is, of course, not a senseless attempt to stop it. It is a determined challenge to a spirit that may be demonic, that may "blast" him with emanations of hellfire. Catholics believed the sign of the cross to be absolute protection against evil spirits, but Horatio realizes that his movement places him in danger. His courage is apparent when we note the Elizabethan belief that "crossing" the path of a specter made one subject to its malignant influence.[7] Modern directors too often have both Horatio and Hamlet cross themselves. To the Catholic, any spirit surviving such a test would necessarily be a spirit of grace, and it would hence be illogical for both Horatio and Hamlet to continue to doubt the Ghost even after it has withstood the most stringent Catholic test.[8]

A wise scholar, Horatio addresses the Ghost as both Protestants and Catholics advised. He does not question it. He charges it to speak, but only if it is a good spirit come upon some mission of grace. This time, it will be recalled, Horatio has not invoked Heaven, and the Ghost is about to speak when it is suddenly arrested by the crow of the cock. Modern editors who place the notation "Cock crows" in the middle of Horatio's speech create a misleading impression. In Q_2, the only version to indicate the sound effect, it appears opposite Horatio's last line. The Ghost is meant to react as suddenly to the voice of the cock as it did to Horatio's invocation of Heaven.

There can be little doubt that Shakespeare's audience was acquainted with the symbolic meaning of the cock. An ancient belief—found in traditional Jewish writings and later made specifically Christian by such writers as Prudentius and St. Ambrose—held that roving demons scattered in fear at cockcrow, and Le Loyer specially related the belief to his discussion of demons appearing as dead souls.[9] The Witches' Sabbath customarily began at midnight and lasted until cockcrow, at which time Satan fled terrified. As the herald of the day, the cock is the voice of light and thus of grace; in banishing night, he banishes darkness and sin. Thus Christian tradition held that cocks crowed all night at the Nativity and again at the Resurrec-

tion. More specifically, the cock symbolized the voice of Christ when it called Peter to repent, a belief reflected in the familiar weathervane cock on church steeples.[10]

After Horatio and Marcellus comment on the Ghost's sudden disappearance, even a modern audience should understand the significance of such a response to cockcrow. The Ghost "started like a guilty thing/Upon a fearful summons," and Horatio is reminded that only "extravagant and erring spirits" are banished by the herald of the sun. Good spirits, as we noted earlier, can appear at any time. Marcellus agrees and notes that evil spirits are dispelled during Advent by the night-long crowing of the cock. Modern producers make a serious mistake when they cut Marcellus's speech, for it does much more than merely "give a religious background to the supernatural happenings."[11] As H. D. F. Kitto notes, it gives "the logical and dynamic centre of the whole play. We are in the presence of evil."[12]

The first scene thus serves several important functions. It establishes that the Ghost is not a hallucination. It establishes that something is rotten in the state of Denmark. It establishes suspense. It establishes the Christian framework. But, above all, it establishes that the Ghost is probably malignant. The first four purposes could have been served by one appearance of the Ghost in a scene half the length, but the fifth required that the audience recognize a suspicious pattern. Many members of the audience would probably have been alerted when the Ghost vanished at the invocation of Heaven, but some might have missed the full significance of such a swift action. When the Ghost vanishes a second time for an equally suspicious reason, the inference is unavoidable.

I do not mean to suggest that the Ghost is established as unquestionably demonic by the end of the first scene. It is an awe-inspiring figure of regal majesty whom a loving son will, understandably, be inclined to credit. When the Ghost and Hamlet meet, we will be seeing through Hamlet's eyes and might easily overlook hints of danger. In the first scene, however, we are not yet emotionally involved. While we are still fairly objective, Shakespeare plants several clear warnings that this "guilty thing" is a creature that must be tested with extreme caution, and tested by the teachings of the Church.

Of which church? Of both? Shakespeare wisely drew from both Catholic and Protestant beliefs in order to encourage the widest possible response. Though the characters are consistently Protestant in their viewpoint, nothing is said that would alienate the Catholic. He too believed in the need for discerning between good and evil spirits. Moreover, one small hint would allow the Catholic to consider the possibility that the Ghost might be a Purgatory soul: Horatio's request that it speak if anything may do it "ease." The suggestion that the living might ease the suffering of the dead is so subtle that it would pass a rigorous Anglican censor, but it suffices. When the Ghost next appeared, every member of Shakespeare's audience would probably be prepared to test it according to the beliefs of his own faith.[13]

•   •   •

Now, at last [in Act I, Scene v], the Ghost speaks. And now we face the first serious possibility that it may indeed be the departed soul of Hamlet's father, returned from Purgatory, where he is "doomed for a certain term" to "fast" in "sulphurous and tormenting flames" until his "foul crimes . . . are burnt and purged away."[14] Very well, let us shift our perspective, as many in Shakespeare's audience may have done, and test it on its chosen grounds—test it, that is, by Catholic doctrine.

What is the mission of the Ghost? Even before it announces its identity, we are warned: it comes to command revenge. Its first long speech is skillfully adapted to its mission. It appeals to Hamlet's love and grief, relentlessly aggravating the son's anguish by describing the pains of Purgatory. Note that it does not state one specific fact, though literature abounded with useful details. It announces that it is forbidden to tell such secrets to mortal men, and then proceeds to create an even more horrifying impression than any description would. Of course Purgatory ghosts were under no such proscription. One of their purposes in returning was to make man understand the specific pains they were suffering, and thus their mission required them to give as much graphic detail as possible.[15] Why does this Ghost rely on the ghastly inference, the harrowing hint? It is skillfully arousing Hamlet's imagination, working entirely on his emotions. The speech builds to a compelling climax in "If thou didst ever thy dear father love—" What loving son could possibly remain calm? As Lady Macbeth knows, the most irresistible of human arguments is the question "Don't you love me?" With this preparation, it is no wonder that Hamlet leaps at the first word of murder:

> Haste me to know't, that I, with wings as
>   swift
> As meditation or the thoughts of love,
> May sweep to my revenge.

And the Ghost comments, "I find thee apt." That laconic observation is the first of several grim ironies in the Ghost's exhortation. Can Shakespeare have overlooked the clash of Hamlet's gentle metaphor with his violent meaning?[16] His mind is "out of joint," as he strains with passionate eagerness for confirmation of what he has already half suspected. He is, indeed, "apt," and at this moment, while Hamlet is taut, every sense alert, the Ghost plants an idea that later gives rise to the tragic dilemma:

> And duller shouldst thou be than the fat
>   weed
> That roots itself in ease on Lethe wharf
> Wouldst thou not stir in this.

Its hearer is now ready, and now the Ghost reveals the identity of the murdering "serpent." Hamlet leaps: "O my prophetic soul!/My uncle!" It is clear that, like Macbeth, he had but awaited confirmation of an idea dictated by his own desires.

If we read the Ghost's long speech without preconceptions, we should be struck by its almost exclusive reliance on sensual imagery. Like Iago, it paints a series of obscene pictures and then insistently highlights the very images that Hamlet had tried to blot out in his early soliloquy: "that incestuous, that adulterate beast . . . shameful lust . . . lewdness . . . sate itself in a celestial bed . . . prey on garbage." Hamlet had known that for his own sanity he must not visualize that bed, but the Ghost rivets his eyes upon it. The culminating exhortation is not to purge the "royal throne of Denmark." It forces Hamlet again to peer into the horror that sickens him:

> Let not the royal bed of Denmark be
> A couch for luxury and damned incest.

Can this be a divine agent on a mission of health and consolation?

Moreover, if a pious son should immediately recognize that swift revenge was a "sacred duty," why does the Ghost find it necessary to present an extended, revolting description of the poisoning? Again its appeal is entirely to the senses. This Ghost is not appealing to Hamlet's love of virtue; it is not arousing his determination to serve the justice of God. It is doing everything possible to arouse nausea and loathing.

This Ghost cannot be a penitent soul from Purgatory. It says it is, but are we intended to believe it? It does, to be sure, speak of its agony at dying without the sacraments, but the reference serves as one more detail to intensify Hamlet's pain. Moreover, a subtle hint has been planted that is to bear terrible fruit in the Prayer Scene. The Ghost's attitude toward its suffering is also telling. Does it humbly confess its sins, acknowledging the justice of its punishment? On the contrary, it "groans" and "complains" of the agony resulting from its being unfairly deprived of final sacraments. For centuries editors have tried to give "O, horrible! O, horrible! most horrible!" to Hamlet on the grounds that the reaction ill befits a spirit of grace. So it does. A Purgatorial penitent would be a loving figure of consolation, but the Ghost that Shakespeare created dwells on the horror of its pains. The exclamation is a logical climax to the extended assault on Hamlet's emotions.

At that cry of horror, when Hamlet's agony is at a peak, the Ghost gives him the tragic burden: "If thou hast nature in thee. . . . Revenge. . . ." Nothing in the scene suggests that a divine minister is appealing to Hamlet's "nature" as a creature made in God's image whose role is to fulfill His commandments.[17] Nor does the usual explanation suffice—that the Ghost is appealing to Hamlet's "nature" as an obedient and loving son. Throughout the speech it has been appealing to Hamlet's "nature" as an instinctive creature of passions and appetites—

"fallen nature," the theologian would say. Thus its challenge to Hamlet to prove his "nature" by committing murder is the same type of challenge heard in Lady Macbeth's "Are you a man?" That this is the issue as Hamlet himself is later to understand it will become clear in "To be or not to be." The Ghost, then, fails the test that every member of Shakespeare's audience undoubtedly would have recognized as the crucial one, a failure that scholars have been trying to rationalize for two centuries: its command violates Christian teaching.

Does the Ghost, in fact, pass any of the religious tests? Well, it appears as a man, not a hop-toad, and no one mentions that it smells of sulphur. On every other test, it fails. Is it humble? How is it conceivable, it asks, that Gertrude could "decline/Upon a wretch whose natural gifts were poor/To those of mine." (Characteristically, it draws our attention to the physical.) Is it in a charitable state? It is thoroughly vindictive, seething in its own hatred and aggravating Hamlet's loathing. Is its voice sweet, soft, musical, and soothing, or "terrible and full of reproach"? The actor who intones these lines with melodious grace is deaf to the meanings of words. Does it carefully refrain from charging others with sin? Its mission is to condemn Claudius. Does it beg Hamlet's prayers: It says "remember *me*."

Some critics have tried to explain these unsettling facts as further proof that the Ghost is from Purgatory on the grounds that his anger, vindictiveness, and sensuality merely indicate that he has not yet been sufficiently purged. This argument will not do. The purpose of Purgatory is not to reform a sinner but to erase the debt of punishment incurred by past sins that were repented before death. As Thomas More emphasizes, in Purgatory no soul can be angry, for all are in a state of grace.

But, it will be objected, the Ghost urges Christian forbearance for Gertrude. Admitted. But that is what we are warned the Devil will do: in order to disguise himself as an angel of light, he will, like Richard III, "clothe [his] naked villany" "with a piece of scripture" (I.iii.334–38). Catholics and Protestants both agreed that the mere repetition of Christian doctrine proved nothing. Both warned that we must be alert to the speaker's ultimate purpose. Let us note the context:

> If thou hast nature in thee, bear it not;
> Let not the royal bed of Denmark be
> A couch for luxury and damned incest.
> But, howsoever thou pursuest this act,
> Taint not thy mind, nor let thy soul contrive
> Against thy mother aught: leave her to
>   heaven. . . .

The lines are brutally ironic. "Taint not thy mind"? For over fifty lines, the Ghost has done everything possible to taint Hamlet's mind with lacerating grief, sexual nausea, hatred, and fury. It has just focused its appeal on the lewd picture that Hamlet knows can most corrupt him—and at this, it says, "Taint not thy mind"! One is reminded of Iago's consummate trickery: working Othello up to a screaming pitch and then remonstrating, "Tush, forget it. It probably means nothing."

And then: "leave her to heaven." The irony is surely the clue. Why Gertrude but not Claudius? The implication may not be immediately obvious when we see the play; we have been trapped along with Hamlet by our emotions. But if Shakespeare did not intend the irony, why did he so closely echo the familiar language of Christian exhortation—"leave them to heaven"?

Even though we have been caught up in the emotions of the scene, Hamlet's reaction when the Ghost vanishes should jolt us:

> O all you host of heaven! O earth! what else?
> And shall I couple hell? O, fie!

He is not merely adding a third power to his invocation of Heaven and earth. The word "couple" may here, as so often in Shakespeare, have a sexual connotation, reflecting the success of the Ghost's insidious method: shall Hamlet join himself to Hell? Even in his distraction, he again raises the dreadful possibility. But the moment of perspective is fleeting as the rush of emotion leads him to embrace the image of his father:

> Remember thee!
> Yea, from the table of my memory
> I'll wipe away all trivial fond records,
> All saws of books, all forms, all pressures
>   past,
> That youth and observation copied there;
> And thy commandment all alone shall live
> Within the book and volume of my brain.

"Taint not thy mind"? He will wipe away all precepts, all codes, all that he has learned from books and experience. He does not say that he will erase all petty ideas in order to concentrate on his duty to his father. "Thy commandment *all alone* shall live/Within the book and volume of my brain." And that commandment is to exact revenge. So committed, he fixes his mind on his victim, furiously focusing on the image of the "smiling, damned villain."[18] When Horatio and Marcellus enter, he is hysterical with excitement.[19]

It may not be amiss to touch briefly on two counter-theories that have gained growing support during the last few years. Several critics have recognized that Shakespeare could not have intended a spirit of health, released from Purgatory by divine will, to corrupt his son by commanding blood revenge. Thus one theory has evolved that the Ghost commands Hamlet to bring Claudius to public justice, not to murder him. A related theory reads "Taint not thy mind" to mean that Hamlet, though he is to kill Claudius, is to do so in the spirit befitting a minister of God. Most of the critics holding these views believe that Hamlet fulfills the Ghost's demand, but several see Hamlet's tragedy as arising from the fact that he either misunderstands or disobeys the Ghost.[20] I can find no warrant in the play for believing that the Ghost is on a divine mission. Not once does the Ghost suggest that its command to revenge is the will of God. Not once does it suggest that its command—"Revenge his foul and most unnatural murder"—means anything other than what Hamlet takes it to mean: brutal, unqualified murder in direct retaliation. Any doubt is eliminated when Hamlet is told to pursue revenge in any way he chooses so long as he leaves Gertrude to Heaven. By implication, Claudius is not to be punished by Heaven. The Ghost treats Hamlet as if he were a private agent who is to act out of purely personal motives. "Remember me," says the Ghost, not "Cleanse Denmark in the name of God." Of course Hamlet may, in later scenes, qualify the command in his own mind. But in the first act, the Ghost is presented as malign.

The curious cellarage scene enforces this impression. We can probably never know exactly how Shakespeare's audience responded to the scene, much less exactly what Shakespeare intended. The repeated shifting of ground in order to swear suggests a specific convention, but a study of stage tradition helps little. The only direct echo occurs in a late comedy, which provides no guide to its meaning.[21] As Nevill Coghill has noted, however, three of Hamlet's lines, together with his actions and those of the Ghost, provide several clues.[22] The significant sequence is as follows:

> (The Ghost cries from under the stage.)
> Ah, ha, boy! say'st thou so? art thou there, truepenny?
> (Hamlet shifts ground; the Ghost shifts and cries again.)
> Hic et ubique? then we'll shift our ground.
> (Hamlet shifts; the Ghost shifts and cries again.)
> Well said, old mole! canst work i' the earth so fast?
> A worthy pioner! Once more remove, good friends.
> (Hamlet shifts.)

The clearest clue lies in the third line. We have noted that demons were believed to frequent mines, and Hamlet echoes this belief when he hails the "old mole" as a "worthy pioner" that works in the earth. That Hamlet is mockingly addressing an assumed demon seems likely when we find Toby Belch referring to the Devil as a "foul collier" (*Twelfth Night*, III.iv.130).

This clue illuminates the other two lines. When the voice first sounds below the stage, Hamlet is startled. Two readings of his question are possible. "Art *thou* there, truepenny?" would imply "So it's you who are down there." "Art thou *there?*" would imply "So that's where you are." Viewed in context, the line thus suggests, "So you *are* the Devil!" The Ghost is, of course, speaking from beneath the stage, the familiar abode in Elizabethan drama of demons, furies, and damned souls. Only a "goblin damn'd" speaks from the abyss of Hell. In *The Malcontent* [John Marston, 1604], Malevole greets Mendoza with "Illo, ho ho ho, arte thou there old true penny?" (III.iii). It is significant that the line is a deliberate echo: Malevole is addressing a devilish villain. Although the OED defines "true-

penny" as a trusty person, the word also seems to have been used as a term of scorn. Hamlet's mocking tone, his almost taunting familiarity, could not be directed toward a spirit of health from Purgatory. Moreover, "hic et ubique" cannot refer to an "honest ghost," for only God and the Devil can be both here and everywhere at the same time. "*Then*," Hamlet says, "we'll shift our ground." For obvious reasons, he must try to get away from the voice.

Whether or not this interpretation is accurate in all details, of one thing we can be sure: throughout the cellarage scene, the Ghost is acting like a devil. Scholars have been driven to fantastic lengths to explain this unavoidable fact. We read that Shakespeare is tricking his audience by stopping for a playful parody; the printer is tricking the reader by including a scene from the old "Ur-Hamlet"; the Ghost is tricking Hamlet; Hamlet is tricking the Ghost; Hamlet and the Ghost together are tricking the two amazed observers. The most popular explanation is the last: that Hamlet and the Ghost both pretend the voice is a devil to mislead Horatio and Marcellus. How could the audience be expected to know this? It is just as misled. And what motive could both Hamlet and a good Purgatorial spirit have for making Horatio and Marcellus think their Prince is in league with the Devil? "To terrify them into silence" is an inadequate answer. There is one logical explanation. Shakespeare made the Ghost act like a devil because he wanted his audience to notice that it acts like a devil.

It is true that Hamlet refers to St. Patrick, the "keeper of Purgatory," and that he tells Horatio "It is an honest ghost"; but can these two facts cancel all our other impressions? The oath by St. Patrick may suggest Hamlet's belief in the Ghost as a spirit from Purgatory, but it may just as well suggest that the Ghost has come to rid Denmark of a "serpent," even as St. Patrick had banished snakes from Ireland. And even though Hamlet does for the moment accept the Ghost as "honest," when he calms down he will be less sure.

Many readers, I would expect, have long been objecting, "But how is such an interpretation possible when it conflicts with our instinctive impression of the Ghost?" I believe that this interpretation is the only one that corresponds to our instinctive impressions—or would be, if we were free to react naturally, without the misleading preconceptions fostered by critical and theatrical tradition. We have already dealt with the faulty assumptions of scholarship, but let us now consider the Ghost as it usually appears on the stage. Of course, it may not appear at all. We may see nothing but a green light that fades in and out on cue. If it does appear, typically it is, in Robert Speaight's delightful phrase, "got up like the arch-Druid of Stonehenge."[23] Because of atmospheric lighting, costume, and make-up, we rarely detect any recognizable human features. Rarely do we see a vigorous, warlike figure of martial stalk and frowning aspect, much less a terrifying "thing" which reacts suddenly and suspiciously to Horatio's invocation of Heaven. When "offended," it usually turns sedately and moves with funereal dignity to the nearest exit. Rarely do we see a noticeable reaction to the crow of the cock, much less the threatening start of a guilty thing upon a fearful summons. In fact, Marcellus's speech on the significance of the Ghost's sudden exit is usually cut.

The 1964 Gielgud-Burton production in New York was typical. The Ghost did not appear. It was a mere shadow on the backdrop, a disembodied voice filtered through an echo chamber. All the lines were exquisitely sung in the quavering tones of a dying saint. All of them, that is, except those that were too flagrantly sickening or obscene. These—the description of the poisoning and the picture of lust preying on garbage—were cut. In modern productions, are we ever really terrified or shocked by what the Ghost says and the way he says it? The actor is usually cast for his resonant voice and he knows it. Traditionally he chants the lines in mellifluous tones of melancholy tenderness—all the lines, including those of agony, pride, disgust, hatred, and urgency. Of course the actor is but following critical tradition, which emphasizes the Ghost's deep "glowing" love for Hamlet and his heartfelt compassion for Gertrude. But what is there in the play to justify this interpretation? One of the most striking facts about this supposed spirit of Hamlet's father is that he utters not one word of love for his son. The Ghost's appeal is directed to Hamlet's love for his father.

Moreover, the command to leave Gertrude to Heaven is not framed in words of compassion, as it could have been. She is to be left to the thorns that will prick and sting her. The picture of Gertrude that we see through the Ghost's eyes is that of a hypocrite who has been led by lust to prey on garbage. Rarely, however, does a modern audience even hear the crucial lines, for the descriptions of the poisoning and the bed of filth are usually cut.

In my judgment, a production following Shakespeare's every clue would create the same response in us today as I have suggested it did in the original audience. If we heard the terrible human passions in the Ghost's voice and saw them in its face, if we were startled by its sudden recoil at Horatio's invocation of Heaven, if we were made aware of the significance of the cock—if, in short, we could once see the Ghost that Shakespeare created, would we not instinctively sense that we were in the presence of evil?

Throughout the preceding analysis, I have, of course, often viewed the action from a dispassionate perspective no audience can reach so long as it remains an audience. Although I have tried to maintain awareness of this fact, in emphasizing the Ghost's malignity I may have created a misconception. I am not suggesting that we are consciously aware of the Ghost's true nature or that we want Hamlet to ignore its terrible revelations. During a good production, we rarely make objective judgments. When Hamlet is on stage, we enter his world, seeing much as he sees, feeling much as he feels. But not completely. I have stressed the many warnings of evil to suggest that our response to the Ghost is too complicated to be accounted for solely by the fact that we identify with Hamlet.

The audience cannot meet the Ghost for the first time with Hamlet in the fourth scene. We have seen things that Hamlet does not see. The first Ghost Scene created a series of impressions that will necessarily color, if only slightly, our response to the second. And throughout the opening scene, the Ghost is consistently suspect. Later, however, ambiguities begin to appear. In the first scene, Horatio had said that the Ghost was frowning as "in an angry parle"; now, in the third, he tells Hamlet that it had "a countenance more in sorrow than in anger." In the fourth scene, the Ghost is addressed as a mouldering corpse from the grave, but it speaks as a suffering soul from Purgatory. It cries for revenge against Claudius, but pleads for forbearance with Gertrude. Each of these details can be harmonized into a consistent interpretation, but only by hindsight. In the theater, Shakespeare keeps shifting our point of view. Our response is further complicated by Hamlet's own shifting perspective. He defies damnation; he weeps for his dead father; he plays games with a devil; he affirms that the Ghost is "honest." We have been asked to test the Ghost, but we have not been allowed an easy answer.

Given the perspective of the entire play, we can discern a probability; but in the fleeting perspective of the dramatic moment, we find only questions. If we could unequivocally pronounce the Ghost a demon and its command a damnable temptation, the tragedy would be destroyed.[24] We cannot, and as a result are caught up in Hamlet's dilemma. The warnings have not made us pull back and condemn his vow to take revenge; they have made us aware of the intolerable alternatives he faces. He says he will go pray, but he will not be the man we want him to be if prayer is his only recourse. Somehow, in some way, we surely want him to act. To retreat into patience would be to acquiesce in the evil. But, as both Hamlet and the audience now know, to act may be to couple Hell.

Notes

1. Q_1 and F_1 give the line to Marcellus, Q_2 to Horatio. We need not give the line to Horatio on the grounds that Marcellus believes in ghosts and would not discount the apparition by calling it a "thing," whereas Horatio is skeptical of all ghosts until he sees one. Even after he has the witness of his own eyes, Horatio—like Marcellus and Bernardo—continues to treat the Ghost as "it," as a doubtful "thing." Either character could speak the given question, though I feel it better befits Marcellus. Horatio is mildly amused, quietly detached, for the first few moments. It is Marcellus who is eager for the latest news so that he can prove the apparition was not "all in his mind."

2. Tom Tyers, in describing Johnson, said, "Sir, you are like a ghost; you never speak till you are spoken to." *Boswell's Life of Johnson*, ed. George

Birkbeck Hill, rev. L. F. Powell (Oxford, 1934), Vol. III, 307.

3. *The Works of Francis Beaumont and John Fletcher* (Cambridge, Engl., 1905–1912), Vol. VII.

4. My own feeling is that the audience would not have time to stop and make this connection. The scene goes too quickly and, of course, Horatio speaks English. S. A. Blackmore, S.J., *The Riddles of Hamlet* (Boston, 1917), p. 88.

5. Pierre Le Loyer, *IIII Livres des Spectres* (Angers, France, 1568), IV, 303–4.

6. Quoted by Arthur Colby Sprague in *Shakespeare and the Actors* (Cambridge, Mass., 1944), p. 132. Italics in the original.

7. Blakeway noted this belief, citing a story in Lodge's *Illustrations of British History*. The Earl of Derby had supposedly been bewitched because a spirit had "twice crossed him swiftly." *Variorum Hamlet*, ed. Horace Howard Furness (New York, 1877), I, 21.

8. Le Loyer, IV, 300.

9. *Ibid.*, II, 489. Cf. Le Loyer, *A Treatise*, fol. 32^v.

10. Montague Summers, *The History of Witchcraft and Demonology* (London, 1926), pp. 117–18; Christopher Devlin, *Hamlet's Divinity and Other Essays* (Carbondale, Ill., 1963), p. 31; Roy W. Battenhouse, "The Ghost in *Hamlet*: A Catholic 'Linchpin'?" *Studies in Philology* 48 (1951), 180–81; Blackmore, *The Riddles of Hamlet*, pp. 96–97. Catholic scholars believe that the cock-crown Hymn of St. Ambrose in the Liturgy for Sunday Lauds finds clear echo in the play: "The herald of the morning sounds, and calls out the sun ray. Wakened by him the day-star frees the sky from darkness: at his note the troops of prowling outlaws (*Hoc omnis erronum cohors*) forsake their baleful course." Father Devlin suggests that "extravagant and erring" looks like an etymological rendering of the Latin words *erro, erronis*, meaning "a lawless vagabond" (p. 31).

11. J. Dover Wilson, *What Happens in Hamlet*, 3rd ed. (Cambridge, Eng., 1961), p. 67.

12. H. D. F. Kitto, *Form and Meaning in Drama* (London, 1959), p. 255.

13. J. Dover Wilson's analysis of the first scene has gained such widespread acceptance that it may be pertinent to note the objections raised by this study. He finds several different attitudes toward the Ghost expressed by the "four witnesses": Bernardo is the simple soldier, guided by superstition; Marcellus is the officer, vacillating between pre-Reformation superstition and Protestant belief; Hamlet is the student of the Protestant Lavater; Horatio en-

ters a disciple of the skeptic Scot, but is converted to the position of Lavater (*What Happens in Hamlet*, pp. 66–75). As I read the evidence, all four characters respond in exactly the same manner. Until Horatio actually sees the Ghost, he quite sensibly suspects that it is a hallucination. Lavater and all knowledgeable Christians began with this assumption until they had proof to the contrary. Without the witness of his own eyes, even a plain soldier like Bernardo would probably have ridiculed such a report. Once Horatio has seen the Ghost, he, Marcellus, and Bernardo respond in exactly the same way. To all of them, the Ghost is a "thing," an "illusion," an "it" that is "like the dead King." Not one of them believes it is the dead King himself. By the end of the scene, both Marcellus and Horatio believe the apparition is malignant, and nothing Bernardo says indicates a different view. Hamlet's response will be discussed in the ensuing pages. Here be it noted that his frame of reference is the same, even though he does not first assume the Ghost to be a hallucination. He has sufficient proof of its reality in the report of Horatio, a man whose judgment he can trust.

14. Battenhouse suggests that the Ghost's description of its abode is not intended to suggest Purgatory. Citing Dante, he argues that Purgatory was envisioned as a place of angels and music and beauty, and thus that the Ghost's description of fire and horror is to be recognized as a picture of pagan hell ("The Ghost in Hamlet," pp. 185–89). I sympathize with Professor Battenhouse's awareness that the Ghost cannot possibly be a Christian spirit of grace, but the fact seems unavoidable that the Ghost uses details that would suggest Purgatory to the Elizabethan, even as they do to the modern. Sir Thomas More's description of Purgatory in the *Supplication of Souls* (1529, trans. 1557—ed. Sister Mary Thecla, S.C., Westminster, Md., 1950) includes no songs of angels. It is a place of "sights unpleasant and loathsome," a place of tormenting flames surpassing in heat any fires known on earth. The Ghost's reference to "fasting" in fires until his "foul crimes" are "purged away," his reference to the final sacraments, and the familiar details of fire and pain make it certain that both Catholics and Protestants would have recognized that he was at least claiming to be a Purgatory soul.

15. More, *The Supplication of Souls*, pp. 171, 178–80. It is for this reason, More explains, that he speaks of the "head" and "hands" of disembodied souls. In order to make mortals realize the pains of suffering souls, he must explain in humanly understandable terms. One also wonders about the odd

statement that the Ghost can walk only at night. True Purgatory spirits can appear at any time.

16. "As so often in Shakespeare, the metaphors undo the logic and tell the truth over its head." Harold Goddard, *The Meaning of Shakespeare* (Chicago, 1951), p. 349.

17. John F. Danby's discussion of the two meanings of "nature" is illuminating. On the one hand, "to follow nature" might mean to conform to one's role in the divine pattern ordained by God; on the other hand, it might mean to follow one's instincts. Danby clarifies the distinction by referring to the former as Hooker's sense of the word and to the latter as Hobbes's. (*Shakespeare's Doctrine of Nature*, London, 1949, pp. 15–53.) The Ghost's appeal has usually been interpreted in Hooker's sense: "If you have any filial feelings, obey your duty as a son." Since, however, "to follow nature" in this sense means to act by the dictates of disciplined reason, "to *have* nature" suggests that the word is used in Hobbes's sense. The Ghost seems to be appealing to something innate, something instinctive.

18. The stage tradition that has Hamlet yank out his tables and frantically write down Claudius's villainy lest he forget it has always seemed unwise to me. The action strongly suggests that he has gone mad. The most effective interpretation I have seen was by a Hamlet who jabbed the picture into his brain with a rigid finger. This seems to me Shakespeare's meaning. Hamlet has said he will clear the "table of [his] memory" and put the Ghost's command in "the book and volume of [his] brain." The imagery indicates that the "tables" are not in his pocket but in his mind.

19. The preceding analysis has been anticipated in certain respects by J. Middleton Murry, *Shakespeare* (New York, 1936), G. Wilson Knight, *The Wheel of Fire*, rev. ed. (London, 1948), Paul N. Siegel, *Shakespearean Tragedy and the Elizabethan Compromise* (New York, 1957), and Goddard. It is most closely paralleled by L. C. Knights, *An Approach to "Hamlet"* (Stanford, Calif., 1961), pp. 45–46 and *passim*, and H. S. Wilson, *On the Design of Shakespearian Tragedy* (Toronto, 1957), pp. 41–45.

20. These views have been fully developed by Fredson Bowers, *Elizabethan Revenge Tragedy, 1587–1642* (Princeton, 1940), G. R. Elliott, *Scourge and Minister* (Durham, N.C., 1951), and Irving Ribner, *Patterns in Shakespearean Tragedy* (New York, 1960).

21. The echo occurs in Fletcher's *The Woman's Prize*, V.iii. In *Antonio's Revenge*, III.ii, the voices of the dead Andrugio and Feliche as well as that of the living Pandulpho echo Antonio's words "from

above and beneath." The scene is a clear parallel but it does not include the device of shifting ground. Joseph Quincy Adams suggests that a clue may be found in the Chester *Processus Prophetarum.* Balaam, prevented by God from cursing the children of Israel, three times shifts his ground at the suggestion of Balak in an attempt to defy God's commandment. "Some Notes on Hamlet," *Modern Language Notes,* XXVIII (1913), 40.

22. *Shakespeare's Professional Skills* (Cambridge, Eng., 1964), pp. 9–16. Throughout, Professor Coghill provides many insights arising from his intimate knowledge of the theater.

23. "The Old Vic and Stratford-upon-Avon, 1960–61," *Shakespeare Quarterly,* XII (1961), 439.

24. Although my study has challenged a few of Robert West's premises, it fully supports his conclusions on the dramatic function of the Ghost's ambiguity. See *Shakespeare and the Outer Mystery* (Lexington, Ky., 1968), pp. 63–66.

Application

Lycidas and Self-Education

William R. Parker

Although many readers have viewed Lycidas *as an "impersonal" poem, a brilliant exercise in the elaborate conventions of the pastoral elegy, for William R. Parker the poem is "one of the most autobiographical of all Milton's minor works," and the conventions of the genre are seen as a safeguard, a "medium for the expression of emotion too personal for direct, unrestrained utterance." Milton's life, then, will provide the primary context for understanding the poem, and Parker offers to read it in the light of biographical information. Thus, when he remarks of lines 64–69, for example, that they "must be read in their context," he clearly considers that "context" here requires no further specification; it can only refer to the author's personal situation at the time of composition. Parker is, of course, quite aware of the many other approaches to the poem, and he agrees that they can tell us much that is useful. But he feels that these other approaches can never really account for the power of the poem, for in the last analysis, he claims, that power derives from the fact that the poem "records . . . a crucial and complicated spiritual experience, deeply personal and profoundly felt." And only the biographical critic can provide us with the information we need to understand that personal experience.*

Lycidas, IN THE TRINITY MANUSCRIPT VERSION, was evidently complete in November, for the poem there was once headed "Novemb: 1637" (later cancelled). To understand why this pastoral elegy was composed, why the long silence was at last broken, and why *Lycidas* is one of the most autobiographical of all Milton's minor verses, it is necessary to know, not only the specific event, but also the state of mind that prompted the form and content of the poem. This state of mind held in anxious suspension all the happenings of the year 1637.

The subject of *Lycidas* is premature death and the questions this raises about dedication and preparation—for the ministry and for poetry.[1] The pastoral form, which has so much and so needlessly disturbed a few literal-minded critics, is not to be explained altogether as an appropriate dress for elegy. It was that, in Milton's time, but it was also a convenient medium for the expression of emotion too personal for direct, unrestrained utterance. The long and learned convention of the pastoral elegy served to *objectify* feeling. It dignified while it comforted. It provided a sense of ritual, of public ceremony, for the soul-searching which Milton intended for his poem. He would speak, not as himself, but rather, in a dramatic lyric, as a nameless shepherd who, all one day, celebrated and lamented the death of a fellow poet-priest. This rural singer would, quite naturally, turn from the honoured dead to the problems of those left behind—the mystery of untimely death, the pointlessness of the dedicated life in a cosmos that permits such seeming injustice. To emphasize the universality of these questions, the poem would end with a reminder that it reported the thoughts and emotions of someone else.

And so, thus safeguarded, Milton begins *Lycidas* self-consciously. He is painfully aware of the unproductive years since *Comus*, of his yet incomplete preparation. Furthermore, he had meant to write no more poetry until his muse had matured. Still, King had died prematurely The laurel, myrtle, and ivy—ancient symbols of triumphant verse and immortality—must again have their unripe berries disturbed:

> Yet once more, O ye laurels, and once more,
> Ye myrtles brown, with ivy never sere,
> I come to pluck your berries harsh and crude,
> And with forced fingers rude
> Shatter your leaves before the mellowing year.
> Bitter constraint, and sad occasion dear,
> Compels me to disturb your season due:
> For Lycidas is dead, dead ere his prime,
> Young Lycidas, and hath not left his peer.
> Who would not sing for Lycidas? He knew
> Himself to sing, and build the lofty rime.
> He must not float upon his watery bier
> Unwept, and welter to the parching wind
> Without the meed of some melodious tear.

Fourteen lines of verbal music, solemn yet subtly varied. The magic lies chiefly in tonal harmony. All that Milton had learned of repetition, effective alliteration, and particularly, assonance, is here employed. The fourth line is appropriately tense and restricted. Two lines are left unrimed, but throughout the passage the "sere . . . tear" sound repeats like an insistent knell. Never send to know for whom the bell tolls; it tolls for John Milton.

He makes this clear enough in his conventional invocation of the muses. The parallel between Edward King and himself is foremost in his mind:

> Begin then, sisters of the sacred well
> That from beneath the seat of Jove doth
>   spring,
> Begin, and somewhat loudly sweep the string.
> Hence with denial vain, and coy excuse;
> So may some gentle muse
> With lucky words favour my destined urn,
> And as he passes, turn
> And bid fair peace be to my sable shroud.
> For we were nursed upon the self-same hill,
> Fed the same flock, by fountain, shade, and rill.
>   (15–24)

The "hill" upon which they were both nursed was, of course, Cambridge, their Alma Mater. The artificial language and pretty symbolism of the pastoral are not, it must be understood, intended to disguise or deceive. Instead, they serve to *generalize* the specific and actual; they bring the solace of tradition to present sorrows. We need not inquire closely what university activities were meant by

> Together both, ere the high lawns appeared
> Under the opening eyelids of the morn,
> We drove afield, and both together heard
> What time the gray-fly winds her sultry horn,
> Battening our flocks with the fresh dews of
>   night,
> Oft till the star that rose, at evening, bright,
> Toward heaven's descent had sloped his wes-
>   tering wheel.
> Meanwhile the rural ditties were not mute;
> Tempered to the oaten flute
> Rough satyrs danced, and fauns with cloven
>   heel
> From the glad sound would not be absent
>   long,
> And old Damaetas loved to hear our song.
>   (25–36)

It is enough if we realize that Milton and King— like countless young poet shepherds before them—had lived the same kind of life, had enjoyed interests in common. King is not an individual in this context, nor is Milton; together they are poets in what had once seemed a friendly world. The vague language does not rob the passage of meaning; on the contrary, it links Milton's experience with the experiences of Moschus and Theocritus and Virgil. If we could identify "old Damaetas" with a definite person at Cambridge,[2] the spell might be broken.

The pastoral tradition was both learned and artificial, but simplicity was its essence. Because this paradox was not always understood, few people had succeeded in naturalizing the tradition in English. Milton, however, realized that pastoral simplicity went beyond the mention of flocks and fauns and rural ditties; he dared to express the age-old sense of loss in language plain and repetitious:

> But O the heavy change, now thou art gone,
> Now thou art gone, and never must return!
> Thee, shepherd, thee the woods and desert
>   caves,
> With wild thyme and the gadding vine
>   o'ergrown,
> And all their echoes mourn. . . .   (37–41)

Echoes, indeed. Abandoned nature laments the departed poet, and the nymphs, absent from the scene of the tragedy, know that they would have been useless. This fact reminds Milton of one of his favourite stories, the myth of Orpheus:

What could the Muse herself that Orpheus
    bore,
The Muse herself, for her enchanting son
Whom universal nature did lament,
When by the rout that made the hideous roar
His gory visage down the stream was sent,
Down the swift Hebrus to the Lesbian shore.
                                                    (58–63)

Poets die suddenly, and the spirits that watch over poets are powerless to help. It happened to King; it could happen to Milton.

"Live, laugh, make the most of youth and the hours as they pass," Diodati had said to him. "Why persist in hanging over books and studies all day and all night?"[3] There was once a convincing answer to this teasing question, but the death of King gave the whole problem new significance:

Alas, what boots it with uncessant care
To tend the homely, slighted shepherd's trade
And strictly meditate the thankless muse?
Were it not better done, as others use,
To sport with Amaryllis in the shade,
Or with the tangles of Neaera's hair?   (64–69)

These lines must be read in their context. The sudden death of Lycidas "ere his prime" causes Milton to wonder seriously whether it is better "To scorn delights, and live laborious days" (72). Amaryllis and Neaera do not, as has been suggested, personify love poetry (or loss of chastity); they personify, as Milton tells us, "delights." The problem stated poetically in this passage is not one of "serious" verse opposed to light verse (or virtue compared with its loss); it is a questioning of the Horton period of studious preparation, as contrasted with the pleasant way of life that "others use." Milton is thinking of happy people like Diodati, not contemporary poets like Lovelace and Suckling. The muse is "thankless" because, as the reference to Orpheus was meant to illustrate, she can do nothing to ward off death by way of rewarding her devotee. The "shepherd's trade," which involves "uncessant care," is primarily the clerical life, but secondarily Milton's five long years at Hammersmith and Horton, as the little words

"homely" and "slighted" also tell us. He is here writing about himself alone, not about King; and he is questioning the validity of the course he had chosen to steer.

Why so much emphasis upon preparation? Analysing his own ambitions, he finds a not very satisfactory answer:

Fame is the spur that the clear spirit doth
    raise
(That last infirmity of noble mind)
To scorn delights, and live laborious days.
                                                    (70–72)

Had he not confided to Diodati his dreams of immortality? Edward King, too, must have hoped for fame,

But the fair guerdon when we hope to find
And think to burst out into sudden blaze,
Comes the blind fury with the abhorred
    shears
And slits the thin-spun life.   (73–76)

The word "we" brings King back into the picture, and Milton is reminded of heavenly rewards. But the emotional movement is broken as narrative suddenly interrupts the monologue, Apollo addressing the poet personally and reproachfully:

Fame is no plant that grows on mortal soil,
Nor in the glistering foil
Set off to the world, nor in broad rumour lies,
But lives and spreads aloft by those pure eyes
And perfect witness of all-judging Jove;
As he pronounces lastly on each deed,
Of so much fame in heaven expect thy meed.
                                                    (78–84)

The Renaissance desire for fame is strong in Milton,[4] but fresh reflection has made him realize again that the good man must work, primarily, for God's approval. Here is discovery of old truth, leading to new humility. And here, after eighty-four lines, the poem might have ended.

But the prime question—"Alas, what boots it . . . ?"—had been intellectually, not emotionally, answered. There was no doubting of heavenly rewards, but there was also no doubting the loneliness and tedium of preparation, all of which might lead to nothing. Moreover, the tragic death of King had brought still other matters to Milton's mind. There were, for example, the mysterious circumstances of his drowning:

The air was calm, and on the level brine
Sleek Panope and all her sisters played.
It was that fatal and perfidious bark . . .

(98–100)

Or, at least, so Hippotades is made to testify in the poem, placing the blame on man, not nature. Father Camus, symbolizing the University,[5] comes next and briefly mourns his "dearest pledge." Then Milton introduces a subject nearer his heart. Like himself, King had intended to enter the Church, which, at a time like this, could ill afford to lose men of integrity and learning. Among the mourners, therefore, "last came, and last did go" St. Peter. As founder of the Christian Church (and as the biblical denouncer of false teachers), he had stern words to speak:

How well could I have spared for thee, young
    swain,
Enow of such as for their bellies' sake
Creep, and intrude, and climb into the fold!
Of other care they little reckoning make
Than how to scramble at the shearers' feast
And shove away the worthy bidden guest.

(113–18)

Here, it must be understood, Milton's use of pastoral imagery leans upon another tradition, the Christian conception of the Good Shepherd and His sheep. The transition (aided by any recollection of Virgil's fourth Eclogue) is easy and natural, but the reader must be alert to one considerable difference. In the purely *literary* convention the imagery is purposefully vague; in Christian usage the imagery is definite and distinct. Was not Milton himself a "worthy bidden guest" who had been "Church-outed by the prelates"? He means every word of his condemnation of unworthy pastors:

Blind mouths! that scarce themselves know
    how to hold
A sheep-hook, or have learned aught else the
    least
That to the faithful herdsman's art belongs!
What recks it them? What need they? They
    are sped;
And when they list, their lean and flashy
    songs
Grate on their scrannel pipes of wretched
    straw.
The hungry sheep look up, and are not fed,

But swollen with wind, and the rank mist
    they draw,
Rot inwardly, and foul contagion spread;
Besides what the grim wolf with privy paw
Daily devours apace, and nothing said.[6]   (119–29)

The violence of this indictment is signalled by "Blind mouths," one of the most startling and unforgettable epithets in the language; and it is underlined by the flesh-crawling harshness of "Grate on their scrannel pipes of wretched straw." Reading this line aloud, one should remember John Aubrey's observation that Milton, when satirical, "pronounced the letter R very hard."[7]

Eight years later, in publishing his minor poems, Milton added a note to *Lycidas*, calling his reader's attention to the fact that in 1637 he foretold "the ruin of our corrupted clergy then in their height." He referred to the concluding couplet of the speech given St. Peter:

But that two-handed engine at the door
Stands ready to smite once, and smite no more.

(130–1)

Countless interpretations have been proposed for this terrible and mysterious symbol of divine retribution,[8] including "the axe of God's reformation" (a figure used in Milton's first pamphlet, four years after *Lycidas*)[9] and the two-handed avenging sword of Michael in *Paradise Lost*. It is not, of course, necessary to make the lines mean something definite, for their intention is clear enough and their ambiguity is effective. The death of King aroused him to denounce the corrupt clergy and gave him, later, the satisfaction of feeling like a prophet. In *Ad Patrem* he had stressed the prophetic quality of poetry, and here was an illustration which may even have convinced his father.

Although the pastoral tradition offered some precedent, the nineteen-line speech of St. Peter was a deliberate digression. To compensate for it, to restore the normal mood of pastoral, Milton added next a twenty-line catalogue of colourful flowers, beginning self-consciously:

Return, Alpheus; the dread voice is past
That shrunk thy streams. Return, Sicilian
    muse,
And call the vales and bid them hither cast
Their bells and flowerets of a thousand hues.

(132–5)

The flower passage (in the composition of the poem, a happy afterthought) is a pretty artifice that succeeds in its purpose; it contains some of the most musical and richly allusive lines in the entire poem. But Milton has to conclude, as well as begin, with an apology:

> For so, to interpose a little ease,
> Let our frail thoughts dally with false surmise.
> Ay me! whilst thee the shores and sounding
>   seas
> Wash far away . . .   (152–5)

The flowers are strewn on the thoughts of readers, not on "the laureate hearse" of the drowned Lycidas, whose body was never recovered.

We are ready now for the emotional and spiritual confirmation of the earlier idea of heavenly reward. The poet-shepherd was also a priest-shepherd. We have passed through questioning, and indignation, and assurance of divine justice. We have been comforted with beauty. Our hearts are ready for belief.

> Weep no more, woeful shepherds, weep no
>   more,
> For Lycidas your sorrow is not dead,
> Sunk though he be beneath the watery floor;
> So sinks the day-star in the ocean bed,
> And yet anon repairs his drooping head,
> And tricks his beams, and with new-spangled
>   ore
> Flames in the forehead of the morning sky.
>   (165–71)

Immortality, the reward of the dedicated, is the theme; and the music lifts impellingly to express it:

> So Lycidas sunk low, but mounted high
> Through the dear might of Him that walked
>   the waves,
> Where other groves, and other streams along,
> With nectar pure his oozy locks he laves
> And hears the unexpressive nuptial song
> In the blest kingdoms meek of joy and love.
> There entertain him all the saints above
> In solemn troops and sweet societies
> That sing, and singing in their glory move,
> And wipe the tears forever from his eyes.
>   (172–81)

The apocalyptic promise again. We have met it before in Milton's poetry; it is nothing new in his thought; but we find it now, more elo-quently, more convincingly phrased than ever, rising to the rescue of faith.

Lycidas begins and ends with Milton's own problem, as artist and as human being. The last verse-paragraph is a stanza of *ottava rima*, a quiet and personal coda, in which the poet reflects on the experience which his verse records. The monologue concluded, he turns, finally, to simple narrative, offering perspective on all that has been said. It had been a grey and still morning, suiting the mood of elegy. The obscure singer had dared to introduce a variety of strains, enlivening the pastoral with questions. In a world of lengthening shadows the sun had at last gone down, down over the Irish Sea. But the sun would rise again, and tomorrow would be another day.

> Thus sang the uncouth swain to the oaks and
>   rills,
> While the still morn went out with sandals
>   grey;
> He touched the tender stops of various quills,
> With eager thought warbling his Doric lay;
> And now the sun had stretched out all the
>   hills,
> And now was dropped into the western bay.
> At last he rose, and twitched his mantle blue;
> Tomorrow to fresh woods, and pastures new.
>   (186–93)

The epilogue serves a triple purpose: it leaves the reader refreshed, Lycidas rewarded in heaven, and Milton, the poet-priest-shepherd, facing the future with confidence. What were the "fresh woods, and pastures new"? In general, they were the world of human society, the active world, which the poet, his Horton days nearing an end, was now ready to rejoin.

More immediately and specifically, they were to prove the woods and pastures of sunny Italy. So far as we know, Milton did not take lodgings in one of the Inns of Court, as he had told Diodati he might. The lawsuit against his father was finally dropped, on 1 February 1638, and a few months later Milton was off to the Continent. It is not unlikely that he had in mind his own travels by water when he said of Lycidas:

> Henceforth thou art the genius of the shore,
> In thy large recompense, and shalt be good
> To all that wander in that perilous flood.
>   (183–5)

This idea was conventional enough and, strictly

speaking, the lines make King a local god of the Irish Sea, but the additional "recompense" may have been suggested to Milton—as so much else in the poem was—by his own plans. He intended to visit Sicily, where the pastoral tradition had been born.

Of all Milton's minor poems *Lycidas* has inspired the most superlatives. It has been called, and largely accepted as, the greatest touchstone of poetic appreciation in the English language.[10] To praise it again is to light a candle at noon. Yet candles have sometimes been lit at noon and carried gratefully into dark corners; in a naughty world one can be too timid with tapers. Let me, therefore, venture a few additional comments on *Lycidas*.

For this poem there are several well-marked avenues of appreciation.[11] The one until recently most travelled by critics and editors is perhaps the least inviting to the layman. Critics and editors, possessing a comfortable awareness of literary history, like to regard *Lycidas* as an English triumph in its European genre—a remarkably successful effort to naturalize the pastoral elegy. Knowing Milton's humanistic interest in forms, in *kinds* of poetry, they dwell upon details of the pastoral convention, and ask us to admire the many parallels to be found between *Lycidas* and poems by Theocritus, Moschus (or whoever wrote the *Lament for Bion*), Virgil, Petrarch, Mantuan, and Spenser. Seen from this point of view, *Lycidas* becomes a masterpiece of scholarship wedded to art; and undoubtedly it is. The *scholarly* excellence of Milton's elegy can be appreciated, and marvelled at, by anyone with the interest and patience to study the pastoral tradition.[12] Not incidentally, the scholarly excellence of his poem meant a good deal to Milton; it is not to be dismissed as a pedantic concern. *Lycidas* is a lament for "a learned friend"; it proclaims that its primary context is European literature.

A second avenue of appreciation also involves a knowledge of literary history. *Lycidas* has been fascinating to critics because it embodies a poetical paradox. Faithfully following one of the most artificial of all verse conventions, it is nevertheless one of the most profoundly *original* poems in the language. No close model or "source" has ever been found for it. Nothing could be more unreal, or more commonplace, than its basic imaginative assumptions—that student friends are shepherds, that university life is tending a flock, that poems are made on pipes and flutes. On the other hand, nothing could be more unconventional than the art-form in which these pleasant fictions are developed. *Lycidas* is not only unique and conspicuous among the thirty-six poems in the memorial volume to King; it is unique in the verse of its age. Its musical paragraphs, its irregular lines, its amazing mixture of assonance and unrimed lines and irregular rimes—although they doubtless owe something to Milton's reading of Italian poetry[13]—are yet the product of original genius. They would seem eccentric and unforgivable if they were not so successful. They were successful because Milton had experimented with most of them in his earlier verse, and now, putting them together, he knew exactly what he was doing.

This suggests another excellence of Milton's poem which the reader may appreciate without benefit of history. Unless one is disposed to excuse anything if only precedent can be found for it, analysis of *Lycidas* reveals many discordant elements. The monody is supposed to be about Edward King, but is chiefly about Milton. The tone is supposed to be pastoral and pagan, but St. Peter and Christ appear along with Apollo and Jove. Amidst the fauns and flowers is a long attack on the corruption of the English clergy. The nymphs are scolded for not aiding Lycidas, and are then exonerated. Flowers are lovingly gathered for the hearse of Lycidas, although no hearse exists. The poem begins as a monologue, but is several times interrupted by straight narrative. It so happens, however—and the reader can test the fact for himself—that none of these things matters in the least when the poem is felt in its totality. They are successfully, if audaciously, blended. With verbal music as a catalytic agent, they undergo a chemical change, and have separate existence only in analysis like this. They will bother no one who takes the trouble to read *Lycidas* through, aloud.

Of all Milton's minor poems, *Lycidas* has the noblest harmonies. It is metrically and musically *right*. The rhythms are subtly varied; and tonal harmony flows from the separate line through the verse-paragraph, from the paragraph through the poem as a whole. Look closely at almost any point and it will become apparent why *Lycidas* is one of the most musically satisfying poems in English. The "singing strings" effect which we noticed in the *Vacation Exercise* is used even more successfully near the close of the elegy:

There entertain him all the saints above
In solemn troops and sweet societies
That sing, and singing in their glory move,
And wipe the tears forever from his eyes.

(178–81)

The obvious device of alliteration is deftly joined to tonal harmony in dozens of memorable lines: "Sleek Panope with all her sisters played" (99). Milton avoids, however, pushing alliteration to Swinburnian excess, as one of the most often misquoted lines in English poetry attests. Readers have a tendency to substitute "fields" for "woods" in "Tomorrow to fresh woods, and pastures new." It is instructive to consider *why* Milton refused alliteration here. A little reflection will show that he emphasizes the words "fresh" and "new"—an emphasis which "fresh fields" would have weakened. Alliteration is Milton's servant in *Lycidas*, never his master. The musical effects are controlled, not only by a careful ear, but also by an artist's mind.

It is necessary to re-emphasize the music of *Lycidas* because a good deal of modern criticism has emphasized other features—the affective connotations of its words and phrases, the extraordinary richness and complexity of its imagery, particularly the archetypal imagery of death and rebirth. The poem's flowers and other vegetation have now been carefully catalogued for us; its water—from the melodious (salty?) tear to the Irish Sea itself—has all been analysed in a critical retort to literal-minded interpretation. The extremes of this generally stimulating explication have even given us Jung-Lycides, a new Adonis (nowhere alluded to in Milton's poem), a dying god celebrated in a fertility ritual of cyclical rhythms of nature.

In our enthusiasm for rich imagery, and miraculous harmonies, we must not forget that this poem records, not an idea, not a mood, not even an emotion, but a crucial and complicated spiritual experience, deeply personal and pro-

foundly felt. In the last analysis, this is the secret of the sustained tone, the artistic fusion of divers elements. *Lycidas* is a masterpiece because its author, in writing it, mastered a situation. Milton gives us a new sense of mortality ("the thin-spun life"), couched in memorable phrases. He captures in words the finality of death, the hopelessness of retrospect ("for what could that have done?"), the helplessness of loss. His poem ends on a tone of deep tenderness, modulated with infinite skill to a tone of quiet acceptance. When Sara Milton died, in April of 1637, her grieving son composed no elegy which has survived. But seven months later, thinking about the death of an old acquaintance, writing for a Cambridge miscellany and using the comfortable language of a long tradition, the son of Sara found that he could put on paper his sorrow, his fears, his tenderness, his faith.

Notes

1. Cf. E. M. W. Tillyard: "The real subject is the resolving of those fears [of premature death] (and of his bitter scorn of the clergy) into an exalted state of mental calm" (*Milton*, London, 1930, p. 82). David Daiches calls the subject "man in his creative capacity, as Christian humanist poet-priest" (*Milton*, London, 1957, p. 76).

2. William Chappell (so Newton, 1752), Robert Gell, and Joseph Mead have been suggested. See the caveat by E. S. de Beer, "Milton's Old Damætas," *Notes and Queries*, CXCIV (1949), 336–7.

3. *The Life Records of John Milton*, compiled by J. Milton French (New Brunswick, N.J., 1949–58), I, 105; *The Works of John Milton*, ed. Frank A. Patterson et al. (New York, 1931–38), XII, 294 (hereafter cited as "Columbia ed."). The letter is undated.

4. See Merritt Y. Hughes, "Milton and the Sense of Glory," *Philological Quarterly*, XXVIII (October 1949), 107–24.

5. Joseph Mead wrote from Christ's College, 1 March 1623: "Our orators fathered the old legend of Cantaber" (*Court and Times of James I*, II. 370).

6. In the summer of 1636 George Conn had come as papal agent to the Queen's court. He was so successful in proselytizing among court ladies that in October 1637 Laud was compelled to protest. On 20 December there was a proclamation against Ro-

man Catholics. For an interesting, somewhat unorthodox interpretation of this passage in *Lycidas*, see E. S. de Beer, "St. Peter in 'Lycidas,' " *Review of English Studies*, XXIII (January 1947), 60–63.

7. *The Early Lives of Milton*, ed. Helen Darbisher (London, 1932), p. 6. In the Commonplace Book, during the Horton years, Milton noted Canto 7 of the *Inferno* and commented: "Dante openly censures the avarice of the clergy," (*Complete Works of John Milton*, ed. Don M. Wolfe et al. [New Haven, 1953], p. 366; Columbia ed., XVIII. 131).

8. There is a convenient summary in C. A. Patrides, ed. *Milton's "Lycidas": The Tradition and the Poem* (New York, 1961), pp. 240–1.

9. *Of Reformation*, III. 47.

10. By Tennyson. Cf. Thomas Warton, ed. *Poems* (1785), p. 34: "He who wishes to know whether he has a true taste for Poetry or not, should consider, whether he is highly delighted or not with the perusal of Milton's *Lycidas*."

11. There has been, however, an extraordinary diversity of interpretation since 1930. See, for example, the differing views of fifteen critics in the collection edited by Patrides (note 8, above). One of them, M. H. Abrams, finds five discriminable "types" of *Lycidas*—and then adds a sixth (pp. 212–31).

12. On *Lycidas* and the pastoral tradition, see W. B. Austin, "Milton's *Lycidas* and Two Latin Elegies [*Adonis* and *Elegia*] by Giles Fletcher, the Elder" *Studies in Philology*, XLIV (1947), 41–55; Sir Edmund Chambers, "The English Pastoral," in *Sir Thomas Wyatt and Some Collected Studies* (London, 1933), pp. 146–80; Walter W. Greg, *Pastoral Poetry and Pastoral Drama* (London, 1906); James Holly Hanford, "The Pastoral Elegy and Milton's *Lycidas*," *PMLA*, XXV (1910), 403–47; Thomas P. Harrison, Jr., ed., *The Pastoral Elegy* (Austin, Texas, 1939), pp. 1–24; and George Norlin, "The Conventions of the Pastoral Elegy," *AJP*, xxxii (1911), 294–312.

13. On *Lycidas* and Italian poetry, see F. T. Prince, *The Italian Element in Milton's Verse* (Oxford, 1954), pp. 71–88, and Gretchen L. Finney, "A Musical Background for *Lycidas*," *Huntington Library Quarterly*, xv (1952), 325–50. Comparing Milton and Cowley, Francis Peck thought that in the irregular riming of *Lycidas* Milton attempted "to give us, though secretly, a poetical image or draught of the mathematical canon of music" (*New Memoirs*, London, 1740, p. 32). This suggestion may be worth exploring.

Application

Conrad: Ideology and Literary Form

Terry Eagleton

Terry Eagleton ends his discussion of "Literature and History" by calling for a "scientific" criticism that would explain the complex relationship between a work and the ideological structure of which it is a part. In Criticism and Ideology, *he shows us what such criticism might look like. Drawing on but modifying ideas developed by Pierre Macherey and other continental Marxists, Eagleton explores the connections between ideology and literary form in several nineteenth-century English writers. His discussion of Conrad, which uses* Heart of Darkness *as a central text, sees the "fatal disjuncture between fact and value, ideal and reality, matter and spirit, Nature and consciousness which pervades Conrad's work" as a product of the contradictions in "the imperialist character of the English capitalism he served." It is Eagleton's task to reveal how these contradictions are implicit not only in the ideas of the novels but in their form, for "it is not a matter of Conrad's forms 'expressing' an ideology; it is rather a question of the ideological contradictions which his literary forms inevitably produce." Ultimately, Eagleton finds the absence at the center of* Heart of Darkness *characteristic of all Conrad's work. "The need for value, and the recognition of its utter vacuity: it is here that the deepest contradiction of Conrad's enterprise, one integral to the imperialist ideology he shared, stands revealed."*

WITH THE ENTRY INTO THE ENGLISH LITERARY arena of Joseph Conrad, Polish exile and merchant seaman, we witness the emergence of a peculiarly *overdetermined* instance of the conflict between Romantic individualism and social organicism which I have traced in the work of George Eliot. Conrad's conservative patriot father became a nationalist rebel against the Russian domination of Poland—an exiled and imprisoned pan-Slavic mystic, from whom Conrad inherited a belief in his subjugated fatherland as a corporate body ("an organic living thing"[1]) with a messianic sense of its historical destiny. Yet this Romantic idealist heritage was in conflict with the pragmatic conservative realism which Conrad imbibed from his mother's family, the landowning Bobrowskis, who advocated a cautious constitutionalism and a stern renunciation of the Romantic ego. The Polish nobility to which Conrad belonged were divided: the aristocracy was effectively incorporated into the Russian ruling class, leaving landed gentry like the Bobrowskis and Conrad's own family to devise ways of throwing off the imperial yoke. Aspiring to national independence, but deprived of their social hegemony by Russian imperialism, they were hesitant in embracing the one "extreme" means—revolution—by which this could be achieved. Poland for Conrad thus came to symbolise an ideal fusion of national corporateness and liberal enlightenment; it was a "spontaneous unity," yet, with its "almost exaggerated respect for individual rights," allied itself with European liberalism against Slav "fanaticism."[2]

Conrad's self-imposed exile from Poland, as seaman and artist, flamboyantly affirms his freedom from an intolerably claustrophobic imperialism. Yet at the same time both art and the merchant service recreate the organic unity which had been brutally splintered in Poland. The ship is an organic community which, with its hierarchical structure of stable functions, curtails subversive individualism and the anarchic imagination. But, like Poland, it also represents a form of collective isolation threatened by alien forces, and so—especially for an officer socially removed from the crew—pitches the individual into lonely, testing confrontation with his own problematic identity. Art, similarly, symbolises the supreme autonomy of a personal imagination free from repressive rules; but it is also an organic whole which demands the abnegation of the individual ego. English society itself offered Conrad an ideal resolution of the conflicting ideological imperatives he inherited from his Polish context; it became a welcome enclave for the conservative émigré in flight from European political turbulence.[3] Its tolerant, pragmatic individualism united with the organic, Romantic nationalist heritage of the merchant service to provide Conrad with precisely the ideological conjuncture he sought. England, Conrad believes, is "the only barrier to the pressure of infernal doctrines born in continental backslums";[4] its settled, hierarchic traditionalism is a bastion against that "fraternity [which] tends to weaken the national sentiment, the preservation of which is my concern."[5] Conrad's entry into English letters, then, is far from the inruption of an "alien" ideology into English history, the intrusion into the native social formation of a "class-subject" produced by foreign forces. His expatriate status is relevant only as one among several possible modes of contradictory unity with the dominant native ideology. "Expatriatism" is not a "totalisation" of Conrad's individual position as "subject" within either Polish or English society; it is, rather, a set of objective ideological relations occupied by the historical subject Joseph Conrad, one determined in the last instance by the internal articulations of the native ideology.

As Avron Fleishmann has argued,[6] Conrad directly inherits the organicist tradition of nineteenth-century Romantic humanism. His positive values, incarnate above all in the virile solidarity of the ship's crew, are the reactionary Carlylean imperatives of work, duty, fidelity and stoical submission—values which bind men spontaneously to the social whole. Yet his fiction, with its recurrent motif of the divided self, is also shot through with a guilty, lawless Romantic individualism which struggles to subject itself to communal discipline. Conrad's social organicism, in other words, is united with an extreme, sometimes solipsistic individualism—a metaphysical scepticism as to the objective nature of social values, a distrust of ideals as the irrational reflexes of egoism and illusion, a view of human societies as essentially "criminal" organisations of selfish interests, a deep-rooted subjectivism which sees the world as desperately enigmatic, a sense of history as cyclical or absurd.

This ideological conjuncture in Conrad's texts is determined in the last instance by the imperialist character of the English capitalism he served; and it is overdetermined by his Polish experience, with its conflict of organicist idealism and political disillusionment. Nineteenth-century imperialism demanded the production of a corporate, messianic, idealist ideology; but it demanded this at precisely the point where mid-Victorian faith in progress was being eroded into pessimism, subjectivism and irrationalism by (in the last instance) the very economic depression which catalysed the intensified exploitation of the Empire. Imperialism threw into embarrassing exposure the discrepancy between its Romantic ideals and sordid material practice; it also bred an awareness of cultural relativism at precisely the point where the absolute cultural hegemony of the imperialist nations needed to be affirmed. The fatal disjuncture between fact and value, ideal and reality, matter and spirit, Nature and consciousness which pervades Conrad's work is a product of these contradictions.

Conrad's contemptuous rejection of humanitarianism springs in part from a recognition of the imperialist exploitation it rationalises. Yet while denouncing crudely unidealistic forms of imperialism, he is ideologically constrained to discover in the British variant a saving "idea"— a Romantic commitment to the welding of politically amorphous tribal societies into truly "organic" units. His onslaught upon nakedly exploitative Belgian or American imperialism is at root that of the traditionalist English conservative radically distrustful of bourgeois "material-ism" and "commercialism." It is only when such activity is graced by an organic ideal, as in the merchant service, that the contradiction be-tween his own Romantic nationalism, and the brutal realities of colonialism, can be "resolved." Conrad neither believes in the cultural superi-ority of the colonialist nations, nor rejects im-perialism outright. The "message" of *Heart of Darkness* is that Western civilisation is at base as barbarous as African society—a viewpoint which disturbs imperialist assumptions to the precise degree that it reinforces them.

This conflict between organic solidarity and skeptical individualism is mediated in Conrad's aesthetic. He writes of the artist as snatching "a passing phase of life" and showing its vibration, colour and form in an effort to evoke "the latent feeling of fellowship with all creation—and the subtle but invincible conviction of solidarity that knits together the loneliness of innumerable hearts. . . ."[7] The ideological function of art is to affirm human solidarity against disintegrative individualism; yet to characterise its materials as vibrant and ephemeral ironically underscores the individualist impressionism which is to be ideologically overcome. For Conrad, art consists in a scrupulous refinement of recalcitrant lan-guage into concrete image and expressive nu-ance; for him, as for Henry James, the novel constitutes a cunningly fashioned organic unity, which in turn implies a redefinition of the writer as fastidious Flaubertian *worker* of his text. (Writ-ing, he once commented, is a form of *action*.) Yet in redefining the writer as a worker, *fin-de-siècle* aestheticism severs him at the same moment from a social context. The author is a worker, but his product no longer has an assured audi-ence. The confident mid-Victorian pact between producer and consumer has partly collapsed— a collapse reflected in the increasingly problem-atic status of the writer's productive means, lan-guage itself. The author must intensively "work" his text precisely because he can no longer rely on 'ordinary language' as a nexus with his consumers, trapped as he is within an ideology which views human communication it-self as no more than transiently consoling illu-sion. Indeed, Dickens is perhaps the last his-torical point at which sheer verbal exuberance

has not come to signify writing-as-object—*écri-ture*, in Roland Barthes's sense of the term.[8] Conrad's calculated linguistic colourfulness of-fers a significant contrast. The text must be sub-tly structured into complex unity, but it is what it fails to articulate which matters most—the restlessly allusive suggestions which leave its meanings multiple, ambiguous and unachieved, the merely "adjectival" hints of meaning which F. R. Leavis correctly identifies in *Heart of Dark-ness*.[9] The work, that is to say, is at once organ-ically closed and verbally open-ended; images must be clearly etched, but "Every image floats uncertainly in a sea of doubt . . . in an unex-plored universe of incertitudes."[10] Conrad pro-ceeds in this letter to Edward Garnett, to ques-tion the very reality of the *reader*, coupling the formal question of how to write with the prob-lem of his own precarious status as literary pro-ducer. What Conrad does, in effect, is to com-bine a Romantic aesthetic with a "productive" one. The end of art is to penetrate the phenom-enal world to reveal its elusive essence; yet this task, which as it stands is a mere commonplace of idealist aesthetics, requires a crippling amount of sweated labour. Fiction struggles con-stantly to deny its own artifice, to present itself as "natural" and translucent; yet this effort must always be self-defeating. The artist, like Marlow, constantly betrays the truth in his attempt to convey it more precisely.

It is, indeed, with the discovery of Marlow as a narrative device that Conrad is able to "solve" the question of how to write. For the ploy of the narrator allows the epistemological problem of how to communicate the real to be incorporated into the formal structures of the text itself. Writing a story, discovering a form, becomes for Conrad paradigmatic of the epis-temological difficulties which beset him; to con-struct a narrative is to construct a moral order. But that order is condemned to be as precarious and provisional as the act of writing itself—a fragile and perilous enterprise, ceaselessly con-structed and deconstructed as that adventure into the unknown which is narrative unfolds its course. In working his fiction, then, the writer is shaping a vacuum, sculpting a void. Work for Conrad is a self-sacrificial sharing in the social totality, but like Kurtz's labours in *Heart of Dark-*

ness merely exposes one's estrangement from the eternally elusive Nature which is to be reduced to order. Aesthetic form must vanquish the inchoate, as imperialism strives to subdue the "disorganisation" of tribal society to "rational" structure; yet such ordering always contains its own negation.

Each of Conrad's novels, indeed, is alive with such a subversive negation of its organic unity. Ideological dissonances emerge in his fiction not, as with Dickens, in an exploitation of open-ended, internally discrepant forms, but in the calculative organisation of interlacing patterns around a central absence. At the centre of each of Conrad's works is a resonant silence: the unfathomable enigma of Kurtz, Jim and Nostromo, the dark, brooding passivity of James Wait in *The Nigger of the Narcissus*, the stolid opacity of McWhirr in *Typhoon*, the eternal crypticness of the "Russian soul" in *Under Western Eyes*, the unseen bomb-explosion and mystical silence of the idiot Stevie in *The Secret Agent*, Heyst's non-existent treasure in *Victory*.[11] These absences are determinate—they demarcate the gaps and limits of the Conradian ideology, represent the "hollows" scooped out by a collision or exclusion of meanings.

The elusiveness of Lord Jim, for example—one produced by the novel's densely-layered narrative technique—is essentially that of the cypher to which Jim is reduced by the mutual cancellation of two contradictory perspectives on him. He can be seen at once as Romantic colonialist, strenuously shaping his own destiny, and as the inexorably determined plaything of a mechanistic cosmos. A similar mutual cancellation inheres in the formal structure of *Under Western Eyes*, where the heroic but "fanatical" Russian soul, and the humane but humdrum empiricism of the English narrator, put each other continually into question in a spiral of overlapping ironies. The sturdy silence of McWhirr embodies the ineffable values of the organicist tradition, values of dogged fidelity and unreflective heroism which can be shown but not said. The brooding passivity of James Wait, conversely, signifies an anarchic dissolution of social order too metaphysically deep-seated to be articulable. The heart of darkness in the story of that title is imperialism itself, which, since it

can be figured only as farcical fantasy and metaphysical evil, must necessarily remain obscure; but it is also the African societies which imperialism plunders, societies which appear, in imperialist fashion, as baffling enigmas. The bomb-explosion in *The Secret Agent*, like Jim's jump from his ship, cannot be directly presented: it suggests a kind of cataclysmic transformation, an unpredictable "leap" in an organically evolving Nature, which the novel's conservative ideology can accommodate only as impenetrable mystery. The absent centre of *Nostromo* is in part Nostromo himself, but also the silver of which he is the agent—the inert, opaque matter around which the human action frenetically swirls. As the determining structure of which the novel's characters are the bearers (the true protagonist of the book, as Conrad commented), the silver is the unifying principle of the entire action; but since that action has for Conrad no coherent historical intelligibility, it is a principle which must of necessity be dramatically absent. It is precisely in these absent centres, which "hollow" rather than scatter and fragment the organic forms of Conrad's fiction, that the relations of that fiction to its ideological context is laid bare.

"It is evident," Conrad wrote to Garnett, "that my fate is to be descriptive, and descriptive only. There are things I *must* leave alone."[12] This, precisely, is Conrad's major problem of form, determined by—and determining—the ideological matrix in which his writing is set. For it is not a matter of Conrad's forms "expressing" an ideology; it is rather a question of the ideological contradictions which his literary forms inevitably produce. The characteristic Conradian work is an exotic tale of *action*, richly and concretely rendered, on whose margins play a set of sceptical questions about the very reality of action itself. The tale or yarn "foregrounds" action as solid and unproblematic; it assumes the unimpeachable realities of history, character, the objective world. Yet these assumptions are simultaneously thrown into radical doubt by the penumbra of spectral meanings which surround the narrative, crossing and blurring its contours. If the narrative is reduced to a yarn, those crucial meanings dissolve; if the meanings are directly probed, it is the narrative which evaporates. What unifies dramatic action and "metaphysical" intimation is mood: the exoticism of the one matches the esotericism of the other. In working the *genre* of the adventure story, then, Conrad "produces" his own ideology in a determinate form. The adventure story gives rise to a simple, solid specificity of action, which is in turn confronted with its corrosive negation—haunted like the ship *Narcissus* or *The Secret Sharer* with the ghost it must exorcise if the narrative is to survive. Such survival is for Conrad ideologically as well as artistically essential: faith, work and duty must not be allowed to yield to scepticism if the supreme fiction of social order is to be sustained. It is for this reason that Conrad the pessimist insists that the artist's task is not to convey moral nihilism, but to cherish undying hope.[13] Yet that hope can never be anything other than ambiguous. The naturalistic form of *The Secret Agent* thickens and reifies the material world to a point where its revolutionary destruction seems naturally unthinkable; yet this very thickening lends men and objects an air of grotesque mystery which merges with the book's fear of the anarchic unknown.

If such "metaphysical materialism" is needed to confirm the naturalness of the given, it also banishes that realm of subjectivity which is an equally necessary protest against bourgeois positivism. Within a dispassionately deadlocked world, then, violent change (Winnie), motion (Verloc), spiritual vision (Stevie) must insist on thrusting themselves into the text, if only in mysterious ways. Stevie's silence is that of the "mystical" which can be shown but not stated; the text *speaks* its contradictions, rather than speaks of them. Its discourse is circled by the abyss on whose brink the nihilist Professor is continually poised—the Professor, who, wired up for instant self-consignment to eternity, is thus a graphic image of the text itself. For *The Secret Agent* is able to reveal the truth of itself only by that ceaseless process of "self-detonation" which is irony. Only by the revolutionary act of negating its every proposition and reconstructing itself *ex nihilo* could it articulate the real; yet this, it knows, is impossible, for it is doomed to work with discourses riddled with ideological contradiction—or, as the novel itself

would say, condemned to the eternal inauthenticity of language. But the work cannot allow itself to disappear down the abyss of the unspeakable, allowing its propositions to be retrospectively cancelled, leaving itself with absolutely nothing to say. If it resembles the Wittgenstein of the *Tractatus Logico-Philosophicus* in its commitment to the transcendent, it must also mime the Wittgenstein of *Philosophical Investigations* in its consecration of that vast, stalemated "game" which is society. Value, identified with a despised humanitarianism of which anarchist dreams are an even more degenerate extension, is thus forced beyond the frontiers of the world, exiled beyond articulation. Yet precisely because of this, everything seems to be left exactly as it was; and this provides the text with a kind of resolution, or, better, with the illusion of one. The world, as with the *Tractatus*, just is "everything that is the case"; and in this sense there is no need for a resolution *because there is nothing, it seems, to resolve*. Stalemated games are in one way unachieved, in another way complete; the world goes on, and this is at once the question, and the answer, of the text. The need for value, and the recognition of its utter vacuity: it is here that the deepest contradiction of Conrad's enterprise, one integral to the imperialist ideology he shared, stands revealed.

Notes

1. Joseph Conrad. *Notes on Life and Letters* (London, 1921), p. 157.

2. Joseph Conrad. *A Personal Record* (London, 1921), p. xii.

3. See Perry Anderson, "Components of the National Culture," *New Left Review* 50, July/August 1968, for an analysis of the conservative "white emigration" into England crucially relevant to Conrad, Henry James and T. S. Eliot. See also my own *Exiles and Emigrés* (London, 1970).

4. *Life and Letters*, ed. G. J. Aubry (New York, 1927), p. 84.

5. Ibid., p. 269.

6. *Conrad's Politics* (Baltimore, 1967), Chapter III.

7. Preface to *The Nigger of the Narcissus* (London, 1921), p. viii.

8. See *Writing Degree Zero* (London, 1967). This

contradiction comes to a head in "modernism," where (as with Joyce) a scrupulously precise refinement of meaning paradoxically transforms the work into a self-regarding linguistic object radically closed to its audience, defying them in the act of apparently communicating more exactly.

9. *The Great Tradition* (Harmondsworth, 1962), p. 198.

10. *Letters from Conrad,* ed. Edward Garnett (London, 1927), p. 153.

11. It is perhaps worth interpolating that the most striking Victorian example of the absent-centred work is *In Memoriam.* The absent centre around which the poem broods and hovers is the blank left by the death of Arthur Hallam, which fragments the poem formally into a series of brief meditations. But the absence is an ideologically determinate one, since the poem is not primarily about Hallam's death, but about the whole spectrum of ideological anxieties and insecurities (science, rationalism, loss of faith, fear of revolution) which that blankness brings into blurred focus. Hallam is the empty space congregated with these almost inarticulable anxieties. The melancholy of the poem (c.f. Freud: melancholy is grief without an object) reflects the fact that it is ideologically prohibited from knowing precisely why it is sad; it is a classic document of bourgeois ideological insecurity which can only obliquely know itself as such, displacing its anxieties to the personal figure of Hallam.

12. *Letters from Conrad,* p. 94.

13. *Notes on Life and Letters.*

Chapter Two

Formal Criticism: Poem as Context

'Tis not a *Lip*, or *Eye*, we Beauty call,
But the joint Force and full *Result* of all.

Pope, *Essay on Criticism*

The genetic critic argues that if we want to understand poems we should look to their causes. To the same end, the affective critic maintains we should look to their effects. For the formal critic, both of these views tend to overlook the poem itself, the central object that unites authors and readers and that offers the basis for an "objective" study of poetic art free from the entangling difficulties and irrelevancies of author and reader psychology. If it is the business of criticism to understand *poems*, argues the formalist, then that business is best conducted by cutting away these secondary contexts and concentrating attention on the poetic object itself.

This argument tells us something about the way Anglo-American criticism has developed in our century. A simplified sketch of this development might well begin with the formalist challenge to the established dominance of genetic criticism. It would trace the gradual progress of that challenge as the formalist arguments found converts and the formalists themselves found prestigious academic positions. It might mark the 1950s as the apogee of the movement. This decade saw the formal approach established on nearly equal footing with historical studies in many graduate schools, and on more than equal footing in several critical journals. Even more telling, perhaps, the decade saw formal criticism also well established in hundreds of undergraduate classes in literature. If the sketch were then continued to the present day, it would show the last twenty or so years dominated by attempts to challenge in turn the new formalist orthodoxy. The beleaguered affective and genetic approaches have found new defenders while other theorists have labored to revise formal methodology on formal principles and still others have argued that we must go "beyond" formalism in new directions.

In other words, the formal context holds a central position in the development of modern Anglo-American criticism. To chart that development from the seminal suggestions in the early writings of I. A. Richards and T. S. Eliot (though neither should be called simply a "formalist") through the important theoretical essays of such critics as John Crowe Ransom and Allen Tate to the widely influential critiques and textbooks by Cleanth Brooks and Robert Penn Warren and the inclusive and systematic theorizing of Austin Warren, René Wellek, and W. K. Wimsatt is to name a number of the most important figures in twentieth-century criticism. To recount the debates between these writers and others who were often or essentially "formalists," such as R. P. Blackmur, Kenneth Burke, Yvor Winters, and the "Chicago Critics" led by R. S. Crane, Richard McKeon, and Elder Olson, is to name still more.

At the same time, it would be misleading to suggest that formal criticism represents a new or peculiarly modern approach. This approach is at least as old as Aristotle, who asserted a basic formal axiom when he declared that skill in the use of metaphor was the true mark of poetic genius, and when Aristotle showed how his six tragic elements should relate to each other, how they must work together to achieve the ideal tragedy, he was performing a formal analysis. A more frequently cited father figure is Coleridge, who defined a poem as that species of composition that "proposes to itself such delight from the whole as is compatible with the distinct gratification from each component part," and who provided a very influential phrasing of formal principles when he declared that the poetic imagination revealed itself "in the

balance or reconciliation of opposite or discordant qualities: of sameness, with difference; of the general, with the concrete; the idea, with the image; the individual, with the representative . . . a more than usual state of emotion, with more than usual order" (*Biographia Literaria*, 1817). Indeed, whenever the critic looks closely at the artistic design and devices of poems, whenever theory stresses the unity or coherence of the work of art, formal concepts are involved. In this sense, it is correct to say that the formal approach has been an important part of literary criticism from Aristotle's time to our own.

But only in our own time has the approach attained a well-developed theoretical base, and only in our own time has it achieved such popularity that it has become the central position against which other theories have had to define themselves. Since this popularity is sometimes obscured by the fact that not all analyses I here call "formal" are presented under that name, it will be useful to examine briefly some alternative labels, for each reveals something about the formalist's chief concerns.

The "New Criticism" is one of these labels, though one of the least helpful. The phrase was employed by John Crowe Ransom to refer to the work of such writers as Richards, Eliot, and others in the 1920s, but it was soon used to describe Ransom's own approach and that of his followers, and it has remained in the critical lexicon ever since to denote, and sometimes to dismiss, any formal analysis. The term was of doubtful value even when Ransom used it, and now that formal theories have been the center of critical discussion for the past four decades, the word "new" has taken on a distinctly ironic cast. The only thing to be said in its favor is that it reminds us that modern formalism developed first outside the established academic hierarchy and in opposition to the prevailing genetic approaches. Since defenders of a position often define that position with reference to the most conspicuous opposition, this point is worth remembering.

A better descriptive term is "objective" criticism. The phrase is potentially misleading, since it may call to mind a kind of scientific detachment or a dispassionate, methodical approach very far from the critic's actual purpose or practice. But the virtue of the term "objective" is that it stresses the "objectness" of the poem. The status of the poem as an "object," as something that exists independently of its creator and independently of any of its readers, is a key concept in formal theory. This concept implies, on the one hand, that we can have access to the poem quite apart from the mind of its creator or the circumstances of its creation and, on the other, that any reader's interpretation can be measured against and corrected by the "objective" standard of the poem itself, even if that reader should happen to be the author.

This view of the poem as independent "object," then, frees the formalist from the chief difficulties of the genetic and affective contexts. When Ransom advertised for an "ontological" critic, he was asking for "objective" criticism in this sense. But the conception of the "objectness" of the poem has further implications. Poetry is a verbal art, which means that we must apprehend it first as a process while our eyes move down the page or the syllables fall on the ear. But the formal emphasis on the wholeness of the poem, on its "structure," on its "organic unity," on its "patterns" of images or motifs, inevitably suggests a spatial rather than a temporal mode of perception. This emphasis is apparent in the very titles of such famous formalist works as Cleanth Brooks's *The Well Wrought Urn* or W. K. Wimsatt's *The Verbal Icon*, and it is implied in the formalist's belief that through many careful readings we can come to see the poetic object steadily and to see it *whole*.

This concern for the wholeness of the poetic object is an important characteristic of formalism, for the goal of formal analysis is to show how the various elements in the poem fit together, how the parts cohere to produce the whole and how our understanding of the whole conditions our understanding of the parts. Such an analysis illustrates the central formal axiom that the primary context for the understanding of any part of the poem is the poem itself. Consider, as a brief example, the opening lines of William Blake's short poem "London": "I wander through each charter'd street / Near where the charter'd Thames does flow." (The complete poem appears in Jonathan Culler's essay in the Intertextual section.) Suppose we want to discover the meaning of the word "charter'd" in these lines. A large dictionary will give us several possible meanings for the word. A historical dictionary will give us the range of meanings generally known to Blake's contemporaries. A study of all of Blake's writings will tell us the various ways he used the word on other occasions. But none of these, says the formalist, will tell us exactly what the word means in the lines in question. Only a full understanding of their immediate context—that is, of the poem itself—will tell us that.

Thus, of the several recorded meanings of "charter'd," only some will fit the particular context that is this poem. But contextual pressures, and particularly in poetry, can create meanings as well as eliminate them. Whatever a "charter'd Thames" may mean in, say, nautical terms, when the phrase appears in juxtaposition with "charter'd streets" and with the thickly clustered imagery of bondage, restraint, and repression developed throughout the poem, it takes on a sinister resonance far beyond any recorded legal or cartographic sense. Such is the power of context to create connotations, overtones, implications, in brief, "meanings" beyond those cited in even the largest dictionaries. And the principle applies to all elements in the poem. What is the meaning of an image, a motif, a symbol, of a character or a pattern or a scene? In each case we must see how the element fits into its context, how it functions in the poem. To investigate these relationships and the meanings they produce is the chief task of formal analysis.

"Formal criticism," then, is an accurate label for this context, as well as the most popular one. For when we consider the formalists' quarrel with the genetic and affective approaches, their conception of the objective status of the poem, and their insistence that the context formed by the poem itself is the ultimate determiner of meaning, we see that their main concern is always with the unique verbal construct before them, with these particular words in this particular order. To put it another way, formalists refuse to separate form from content.

Other types of criticism fail, they argue, because they make that separation. Thus, the psychoanalytic critic or the myth critic, who may locate a poem's appeal in the latent content or underlying patterns it shares with other poems and with our dreams, is apt to overlook those specifically formal features that set poems apart from dreams and one poem apart from another. And biographical critics, in their concern with causes, are equally likely to ignore poetic form. Representatives of these other schools may regard this charge as minor as long as they can still claim to increase our understanding the poem's meaning. But the formalists won't accept this separation. There is, they insist, no poetic meaning apart from poetic form.

This is the fundamental principle of formal criticism, and it leads directly to the formalist's famous distrust of the "paraphrase" on the grounds that too many readers are inclined to confuse the poem's paraphrasable content with its "meaning," an inclination encouraged, the formalist would argue, by other critical approaches. In reaction, formal critics are inclined to reverse the emphasis and locate poetic meaning in what can't be paraphrased. The goal of their analyses is to get us back to the poem itself, to show how it differs from the paraphrase, to point out those formal elements that make it a poem, and that particular poem, and not some other thing. By pointing to these formal elements, the formalist undertakes to show us not so much *what* the poem means, as "meaning" is usually understood in discursive contexts, but *how* it means. In large and complex structures such as *Hamlet*, for instance, one critic may demonstrate a consistent image pattern, a second may remark the fitting of speech to character, a third may illuminate structural parallels, a fourth call attention to repeated motifs, and so on. In each case, the goal is to send the reader back to the play better equipped to see all the elements working together to create a verbal structure at once richly complex and highly coherent. Readers whose vision is thus armed will see that *how* a poem means is the same thing as *what* it means. They will understand that form is meaning.

Form is also value, the formalists argue. For we should value a thing for what it does essentially and always, not for what it does incidentally and occasionally. A poem may or may not heal or reveal its author's psychic wounds; it may or may not depict accurately the social or political conditions of its time; it may or may not do all or any of the many things that nonpoetic constructs do. But to be a poem at all, say the formalists, it must be a verbal structure possessing a high degree of complexity and coherence. Since it is the purpose of formal analysis to explicate these very qualities, we can understand the formalists' contention that such explication is in itself a demonstration of the poem's value as well as of its meaning.

This is a cogent argument, and it has persuaded many. The formalists claim to deal directly with poems and in poetic terms. They detach the poem from what they consider secondary contexts in order to concentrate on the poem itself, and they undertake to illuminate both poetic meaning and poetic value by the same kind of analysis. Even critics who remain skeptical are likely to concede that the formalist argument has had the salutary effect of forcing all types of critics to look more carefully at poems and to try to explain more fully the relevance of any information they offer about them. The formal approach also places interpreters in a somewhat different relationship to their audience. Whereas the genetic critics, for example, usually appear as experts who are supplying information obtained through months or years of research into an author's life or times, formal critics appear to be simply pointing to features or patterns in the poem that we might have overlooked. They seem to claim no special expertise beyond well-developed powers of observation and a sharpened sense of what to look for. And we can all play the game. We test their reading against the poem and accept, reject, or modify that reading as our own understanding of the text demands. Indeed, we *must* all play the game, for the analysis never substitutes for the poem. The critics can only tell us where to look and what to look for; we have to see for ourselves.

In a way, then, and in spite of the formalists' belief that we can and should approach a "best" reading, formal theory appears to democratize literary criticism. And this may in part account for the popularity of formal analysis as a classroom technique at many levels of instruction. At any rate, there seems to be in theory no reason why the untrained reader equipped only with a sharp eye and a large dictionary should not explicate a given poem as well as the most experienced critic. That in practice the untrained reader can seldom do this is a phenomenon for which formal theory offers no clear explanation.

And here we touch on one of the perennial objections to the formal approach. The formal analysis, so this argument runs, is often better than formal theory because that analysis is actually based on knowledge imported from other contexts. In other words, the claim is that the formalists do not in practice really isolate the poem. A more forceful form of this objection, as we have seen, insists that they dare not isolate it, and especially not from the genetic context, because the idea of authorial meaning provides the only valid check against misinterpretation. Without it, the poem becomes either a truly closed system impervious to analysis, or an isolated verbal object open to any number of equally coherent readings but providing no valid way to choose among them. To this, the formal critics reply that we can and should establish what the poem "means" apart from what the author might have "meant," and that the public nature of language and our knowledge of its norms and conventions guarantee the validity of this distinction. At this point the intertextual critics enter the debate, insisting that to talk of norms and conventions does indeed circumvent the genetic context, but only by placing the poem in the larger context of literature as a whole. This line of argument will be developed in another chapter. Here we simply note that the concept of the poem as an object of determinate meaning existing apart from author or audience remains a central, and much contested, concept in formal criticism.

The formal theory of poetic value is also much contested. That formal analysis is designed to demonstrate the degree of complexity and coherence a poem possesses is clear; that such an analysis is therefore a demonstration of value can follow only if we are willing to accept complexity and coherence as the appropriate value terms. Some readers are reluctant to do so, and one frequent charge against formal criticism is that it ignores direct and simple literary works to concentrate instead on those special kinds of poems that allow considerable scope for critical ingenuity. Furthermore, even if it can be demonstrated that "tension," "irony," "paradox," or "ambiguity" are qualities of even apparently simple poems, it is still not clear why such forms of "complexity" as these should be considered valuable.

Now I. A. Richards, as we will see, had also been concerned to demonstrate the complexity and coherence of poems, and Richards was a strong influence on formal criticism. But Richards has grounded these terms in his affective theory of value. The complex poem is better than the simple poem because it appeals to a greater number of our desires and aversions. And a coherent poem is better than an incoherent poem because in organizing its diverse elements it also organizes the reader's psyche. In this way, Richards furnished a cogent defense of complexity and coherence as value terms on strictly affective grounds. But many formal critics, while not necessarily denying that poems have the potential to do something like this for certain readers, rejected the entire affective approach as largely irrelevant. The poem, they argued, is not your experience or my experience; it is only a potential cause of experiences, and the adequacy of any subjective response must be tested against the "objective" poem itself. This argument eliminates some of the problems that trouble affective theories, but it also eliminates the affective defense of complexity and coherence as poetic values.

Indeed, as long as the poem is supposed to exist in isolation from other contexts, it is difficult to see how the formal critic can find a basis for any value scheme at all. But in practice most formalists do not really isolate the poem so completely. Part of the difficulty is simply a matter of rhetorical emphasis. Developing their views in opposition to the once more popular genetic and affective approaches, the formalists often insisted on the separateness of the poetic "object," but they chiefly meant its separateness from those particular contexts, from its possible causes or its possible effects. Some objectors, taking them literally, have charged that the formalists advocate "art for art's sake," that they wish to isolate the poem from "life," from "human significance." But this charge reveals a serious misunderstanding of the formalist position as it has been explained and applied by its leading advocates in this century. Far from urging the poem's isolation from experience outside art, Anglo-American formal theory has usually insisted that the real function of poetry is to tell us the truth about that experience.

At the same time, the formalists, like many other modern critics, were unwilling to concede that the "scientific" model for truth is the only or the most adequate model. To be sure, the scientific picture of the world possesses a kind of truth. But the very nature of scientific inquiry dictates that this picture will be highly abstract and skeletal. The atomic physicist's conception of my desk, for example, which tells me that the desk is mainly space, or a time–space event, may well be true, but it doesn't appear to describe the knuckle-rapping, shin-barking solidity that is my experience of the desk. The world presented in literature seems to have more of this kind of concreteness. It describes more nearly the world as we experience it. It puts flesh on the scientist's skeletal picture and gives us, in Ransom's phrase, the "world's body."

And it does more. By presenting complex characters in complex situations, it offers us a world of actions with emotional and moral significance. For the poem, through the magic of the concrete symbol, mediates between the abstract world of the philosophic and moral precept and the solid but chaotic world of felt experience. It provides for the first a specific illustration, for the second, a significant form. If the poem is, as Aristotle said, a more philosophical thing than history, it is also, as he did not say, a more concrete thing than philosophy. Philosophy, like science, tends toward the abstract and the systematic. But these qualities are achieved only by simplification; life as we experience it remains multifaceted and contradictory. And poetry offers to deal with, to assimilate, all of it: Desdemona and Iago, Falstaff and Hotspur, Edgar and Edmund. This is why good poems must be "multivalent," "ambiguous," "paradoxical," and all the other things formal critics say they are, because these are the salient characteristics of the life poems seek to describe. These are all forms of complexity, and the good poem is complex because, more than any other kind of discourse, it deals faithfully with our complex experience of the world. It tells us the truth about that experience.

In other words, many formal critics ultimately ground their value theory in the mimetic or "imitative" context. And they do this so consistently that we might properly speak of the "formal-mimetic" critic. This phrase is rather awkward and hardly anyone uses it, but it has the virtue of being reasonably accurate, and its use would remind us that the formalists actually make very large claims for poetry. It might also remind us that very few critics are really "pure" formalists, perhaps for the simple reason that the poem "in itself" supplies no base for a theory of value. The mimetic context, on the contrary, offers the oldest and most popular value criterion, the appeal to truth. Of course, this criterion is not without its own difficulties, and it will be the business of another section to explore some of these. Here we should simply notice that if the formal critics are seldom "pure" formalists, neither are they "pure" mimeticists. Their concern for poetic form remains the defining feature of their criticism and the mainstay of their claim that their type of analysis is centrally relevant to poetry.

Now, since the term *form* seems to refer most directly to such elements as rhythm and repetition, to those patterns and structural devices that chiefly provide the poem's coherence, the formal critic is faced with a rather puzzling problem. Complexity, we saw, can be justified as a value on mimetic grounds. The complex poem is "congruent" with reality as we experience it and therefore "true." But it is not clear that "coherence" can be similarly explained. For many readers, in fact, reality as we experience it seems conspicuously to lack satisfactory design, to lack precisely that formal coherence we find in the poem. To be sure, in some philosophical systems—Plato's for one, and perhaps Aristotle's—there is no ultimate conflict between coherence or formal order and congruence or imitative accuracy, but the number of contemporary readers deeply committed to these or similar systems is small. For many of us, the claims of congruence are not easily reconciled with those of coherence. And while we may wish to assent to the argument that art, by selecting and arranging the material of ordinary experience, gives that material extraordinary intensity and significance, our empirical premises lead us to suspect that any selecting and arranging is necessarily a kind of falsification, a diminution of complexity, and that therefore coherence is a value different from and opposed to congruence.

It is this apparently polar opposition that causes our perplexity. As certain features of a prose narrative, for example, move toward the pole of congruence, as the characters and their actions take on the endless complication and apparent randomness of people and actions outside of art, our sense of shape and point diminishes. Only chaos truly mirrors chaos. But as we move toward the opposite pole, as the characters become simpler, the actions more directed, the plot more symmetrical, our sense of the incongruity of life and art increases. Perhaps the magic of great poetry lies in its ability to have it both ways, to reconcile the apparently rival claims of coherence and congruence in the same way it is said to combine the concrete and the universal. As W. K. Wimsatt, one of the most influential formal theorists, has put it, "poetry is that type of verbal structure where truth of reference or correspondence reaches a maximum degree of fusion with truth of coherence—or where external and internal relations are intimately mutual reflections" (*The Verbal Icon*, p. 149). Perhaps so. Yet it is difficult to avoid the feeling that formal criticism insists finally on two opposing principles of value—the mimetic principle of congruence and the formal principle of coherence—and that these are not easily reconcilable under one theory of value.

And this problem leads to a further difficulty, a difficulty inherent in the term *form* itself. We use this term in a number of senses, two of which are of particular interest here. When formal critics speak of *form*, they mean nearly everything about the poem, these particular words in this particular order. In this sense, every poem is a unique form. But we also speak of form when we say this poem is a sonnet, a villanelle, a rondeau, or when, with less precision but more significance, we describe a work as a satire or a tragedy, an epic or a pastoral. That is, we also use the term *form* to suggest that this particular poem is a certain kind of poem.

These two senses of *form*, then, are really quite different. One stresses the singularity or uniqueness of the poem, the other calls attention to features it shares with similar poems. The "formal" critics are very much concerned with form in the first sense, very little with form in the second. Indeed, they are often impatient with discussions of genre, feeling that the distinctions such discussions seek to draw are problematic, arbitrary, and generally irrelevant. Studies that attempt to show that *Hamlet* is or is not a "real" tragedy, that *Paradise Lost* is or is not a "true" epic, reveal more, the formalists think, about definitions than they do about poems. And like all "irrelevant" contexts, such studies distract our attention from the unique form that is the particular poem in question. So, for many formal critics, classifications such as "tragic novel" or "pastoral elegy" are similar to the genetic categories "a Conrad novel" or "a seventeenth-century poem." Formalists may find it convenient to use the phrases, but they have little use for the contexts these terms imply. Formalists feel their task is to explicate the unique verbal object before them, and the poem, whether others call it tragic or comic, elegiac or satiric, will be good to the extent that it possesses a high degree of complexity and coherence. On these grounds, a good poem, regardless of its period or type, is simply a good poem, and the judgment needs no historic or generic qualification.

As we have seen, this "absolute" standard of value is ultimately grounded in the mimetic context. The more complex poem is better because it more adequately "imitates" complex reality. But can we account for poetic form on this ground? As long as we think primarily of the characters or plots of "realistic" plays or novels, we might be inclined to feel that these forms present imitations of human actions. And in a sense even a lyric poem is a small drama. The speaker is a character who undergoes emotional changes as the "plot" of the poem moves from mood to mood, from statement to counterstatement, from problem to solution. So even a Petrarchan sonnet may be said to possess character and plot and to imitate action. On the other hand, it also possesses an octave, a sestet, and five iambic feet per line, and in these respects it imitates nothing in the world at all—except other Petrarchan sonnets. Working back, then, from this point, we may be moved to argue that even the most "realistic" novel has a degree of conventionality and stylization, in short, a formal order that causes it to resemble more nearly a sonnet than it does the apparent formlessness of experience outside of art. It most resembles, of course, other "realistic" novels. In this way the opposition between congruence and coherence returns to haunt the key term *form* and makes it very difficult to account for literary form on mimetic grounds. Thus, to push the point to its paradoxical conclusion, to the extent that they have developed their evaluative principles on those grounds, the "formal" critics can deal with nearly everything in the poem except its "form."

Here again formal practice has often been more flexible than its supporting theory, and admittedly I am highlighting only one of the several senses of the word *form*. But it is an important sense, and the failure of formal theory to account for the formal principles of literature must be considered a deficiency. As we will see later, the intertextual critics offer to make good precisely this deficiency. But to do so, they must abandon some of the central tenets of the formalist position. So the debate between these two critical schools centers around their different conceptions of literary form. Meanwhile, many genetic and affective critics remain unconvinced by the formalists' attempts to isolate the poem from its historic causes or its particular effects. And, to repeat, there is the central problem within formal theory of how to reconcile the conflicting claims of coherence and congruence, formal unity and imitative fidelity. So the formalists, holding their central position, find themselves open to objections from all sides. And the objectors have become more numerous in the past two decades as the formalist argument, having been so successfully established, has increasingly become the position against which other contexts must define themselves.

In part, these challenges are simply the price of success, and they remind us that, in our own century, the formal context is central historically as well as conceptually. Thus, while the formalists sometimes claim that other perspectives are often irrelevant to the main business of crit-

icism, their own position is largely immune to that charge. Objectors may find formal theory flawed, limited, and ultimately inadequate, but they can't seriously claim that the formalists' concentration on the poem is irrelevant. In fact, even the most committed opponent will probably admit that the formalists' abiding concern with the poem—with these particular words and the specific pattern they make—has taught critics of all persuasions the value of close, careful reading. Furthermore, and despite the very real difficulties in formal theory, many "revisionists" have discovered that it is one thing to point out some problems with the formalists' key concepts, but quite another thing to try to do without them. The most basic of these concepts is, of course, the formalists' insistence that poetic form and poetic meaning are inseparable, are, in fact, one and the same thing, and that all relevant criticism must start from this principle. This concept will inevitably lead critics into some puzzling theoretical difficulties. But it also promises to lead them toward the central mysteries of the art of poetry. This promise is the fundamental reason why formal criticism, under its various labels and adaptations, continues to thrive.

Suggestions for Further Reading

Formal criticism in its Anglo-American versions (still often called "New Criticism") is displayed in a group of central texts: William Empson, *Seven Types of Ambiguity* (rev. ed., 1947), John Crowe Ransom, *The World's Body* (1938), Cleanth Brooks, *The Well Wrought Urn* (1947), René Wellek and Austin Warren, *Theory of Literature* (3rd ed., 1956), and W. K. Wimsatt, Jr., *The Verbal Icon* (1954). Critics who share many of the formalists' basic assumptions include Kenneth Burke, *The Philosophy of Literary Form* (1941), R. P. Blackmur, *Language as Gesture* (1952), and the "Chicago" or "neo-Aristotelian" group represented by R. S. Crane, ed., *Critics and Criticism* (1952), and Wayne Booth, *The Rhetoric of Fiction* (rev. ed., 1982). Some recent attempts to restate and defend the formalist position are Monroe Beardsley, *The Possibility of Criticism* (1970), John Ellis, *The Theory of Literary Criticism* (1974), and Murray Krieger, *Theory of Criticism* (1976). Krieger's *The New Apologists for Poetry* (1956) is a sympathetic and insightful analysis of main-line Anglo-American formalism. Victor Erlich, *Russian Formalism* (2nd ed., 1965), describes the sometimes similar but largely unrelated Russian movement. Some of the key essays in that movement are translated in Lee Lemon and Marion Reis, *Russian Formalist Criticism* (1965).

Theory

Irony as a Principle of Structure

Cleanth Brooks

Cleanth Brooks has been one of the leading figures in Anglo-American formal criticism, and his essay "Irony as a Principle of Structure" illustrates several of the formalists' key ideas. One of these is the insistence that poetry is radically metaphorical—its meaning is bound to the particular, the concrete, and no paraphrase can carry the same meaning. Another key idea is that the parts of a good poem are "organically" related, so each part can have meaning only within the "context" of the work as a whole. As Brooks examines the contextual pressures exerted in a few short poems, he discovers that in each case these pressures produce a kind of "irony," and this is the mark of a mature or complex vision that takes in more than the simple or single vision. Good poetry, then, is congruent with experience (complex, ironic) but, at the same time, unified and "coherent"; it is "a poetry which does not leave out what is apparently hostile to its dominant tone and which, because it is able to fuse the irrelevant and discordant, has come to terms with itself and is invulnerable to irony."

ONE CAN SUM UP MODERN POETIC TECHNIQUE BY calling it the rediscovery of metaphor and the full commitment to metaphor. The poet can legitimately step out into the universal only by first going through the narrow door of the particular. The poet does not select an abstract theme and then embellish it with concrete details. On the contrary, he must establish the details, must abide by the details, and through his realization of the details attain to whatever general meaning he can attain. The meaning must issue from the particulars; it must not seem to be arbitrarily forced upon the particulars. Thus, our conventional habits of language have to be reversed when we come to deal with poetry. For here it is the tail that wags the dog. Better still, here it is the tail of the kite—the tail that makes the kite fly—the tail that renders the kite more than a frame of paper blown crazily down the wind.

The tail of the kite, it is true, seems to negate the kite's function: it weights down something made to rise; and in the same way, the concrete particulars with which the poet loads himself seem to deny the universal to which he aspires. The poet wants to "say" something. Why, then, doesn't he say it directly and forthrightly? Why is he willing to say it only through his metaphors? Through his metaphors, he risks saying it partially and obscurely, and risks not saying it at all. But the risk must be taken, for direct statement leads to abstraction and threatens to take us out of poetry altogether.

The commitment to metaphor thus implies, with respect to general theme, a principle of indirection. With respect to particular images and statements, it implies a principle of organic relationship. That is, the poem is not a collection of beautiful or "poetic" images. If there really existed objects which were somehow intrinsically "poetic," still the mere assemblage of these would not give us a poem. For in that case, one might arrange bouquets of these poetic images and thus create poems by formula. But the elements of a poem are related to each other, not as blossoms juxtaposed in a bouquet, but as the blossoms are related to the other parts of a growing plant. The beauty of the poem is the flowering of the whole plant, and needs the stalk, the leaf, and the hidden roots.

If this figure seems somewhat highflown, let us borrow an analogy from another art: the poem is like a little drama. The total effect proceeds from all elements in the drama, and in a good poem, as in a good drama, there is no waste motion and there are no superfluous parts.

In coming to see that the parts of a poem are related to each other organically, and related to the total theme indirectly, we have come to see the importance of *context*. The memorable verses in poetry—even those which seem somehow intrinsically "poetic"—show on inspection that they derive their poetic quality from their relation to a particular context. We may, it is true, be tempted to say that Shakespeare's "Ripeness is all" is poetic because it is a sublime thought, or because it possesses simple eloquence; but that is to forget the context in which the passage appears. The proof that this is so becomes obvious when we contemplate such unpoetic lines as "vitality is all," "serenity is all," "maturity is all,"—statements whose philosophical import in the abstract is about as defensible as that of "ripeness is all." Indeed, the commonplace word "never" repeated five times becomes one of the most poignant lines in *Lear*, but it becomes so because of the supporting context. Even the "meaning" of any particular item is modified by the context. For what is said is said in a particular situation and by a particular dramatic character.

The last instances adduced can be most properly regarded as instances of "loading" from the context. The context endows the particular word or image or statement with significance. Images so charged become symbols; statements so charged become dramatic utterances. But there is another way in which to look at the impact of the context upon the part. The part is modified by the pressure of the context.

Now the *obvious* warping of a statement by the context we characterize as "ironical." To take the simplest instance, we say "this is a fine state of affairs," and in certain contexts the statement means quite the opposite of what it purports to say literally. This is sarcasm, the most obvious kind of irony. Here a complete reversal of meaning is effected: effected by the context, and pointed, probably, by the tone of voice. But the modification can be most important even though it falls far short of sarcastic reversal, and it need not be underlined by the tone of voice at all. The tone of irony can be effected by the skillful disposition of the context. Gray's *Elegy* will furnish an obvious example.

> Can storied urn or animated bust
> Back to its mansion call the fleeting breath?
> Can Honour's voice provoke the silent dust,
> Or Flatt'ry soothe the dull cold ear of death?

In its context, the question is obviously rhetorical. The answer has been implied in the characterization of the breath as fleeting and of the ear of death as dull and cold. The form is that of a question, but the manner in which the question has been asked shows that it is no true question at all.

These are obvious instances of irony, and even on this level, much more poetry is ironical than the reader may be disposed to think. Many of Hardy's poems and nearly all of Housman's, for example, reveal irony quite as definite and overt as this. Lest these examples, however, seem to specialize irony in the direction of the sardonic, the reader ought to be reminded that irony, even in its obvious and conventionally recognized forms, comprises a wide variety of modes: tragic irony, self-irony, playful, arch, mocking, or gentle irony, etc. The body of poetry which may be said to contain irony in the ordinary senses of the term stretches from *Lear*, on the one hand, to "Cupid and Campaspe Played," on the other.

What indeed would be a statement wholly devoid of an ironic potential—a statement that did not show any qualification of the context? One is forced to offer statements like "Two plus two equals four," or "The square on the hypotenuse of a right triangle is equal to the sum of the squares on the two sides." The meaning of these statements is unqualified by any context; if they are true, they are equally true in any possible context.[1] These statements are properly abstract, and their terms are pure denotations. (If "two" or "four" actually happened to have connotations for the fancifully minded, the connotations would be quite irrelevant: they do not participate in the meaningful structure of the statement.)

But connotations are important in poetry and do enter significantly into the structure of meaning which is the poem. Moreover, I should claim also—as a corollary of the foregoing proposition—that poems never contain abstract statements. That is, any "statement" made in the poem bears the pressure of the context and has its meaning modified by the context. In other words, the statements made—including those which appear to be philosophical generalizations—are to be read as if they were speeches in a drama. Their relevance, their propriety, their rhetorical force, even their meaning, cannot be divorced from the context in which they are imbedded.

The principle I state may seem a very obvious one, but I think that it is nonetheless very important. It may throw some light upon the importance of the term *irony* in modern criticism. As one who has certainly tended to overuse the term *irony* and perhaps, on occasion, has abused the term, I am closely concerned here. But I want to make quite clear what that concern is: it is not to justify the term *irony* as such, but rather to indicate why modern critics are so often tempted to use it. We have doubtless stretched the term too much, but it has been almost the only term available by which to point to a general and important aspect of poetry.

Consider this example: The speaker in Matthew Arnold's "Dover Beach" states that the world, "which seems to lie before us like a land of dreams . . . hath really neither joy nor love nor light. . . ." For some readers the statement will seem an obvious truism. (The hero of a typical Hemingway short story or novel, for example, will say this, though of course in a rather different idiom.) For other readers, however, the statement will seem false, or at least highly questionable. In any case, if we try to "prove" the proposition, we shall raise some very per-

plexing metaphysical questions, and in doing so, we shall certainly also move away from the problems of the poem and, finally, from a justification of the poem. For the lines are to be justified in the poem in terms of the context: the speaker is standing beside his loved one, looking out of the window on the calm sea, listening to the long withdrawing roar of the ebbing tide, and aware of the beautiful delusion of moonlight which "blanches" the whole scene. The "truth" of the statement, and of the poem itself, in which it is imbedded, will be validated, not by a majority report of the association of sociologists, or a committee of physical scientists, or of a congress of metaphysicians who are willing to stamp the statement as proved. How is the statement to be validated? We shall probably not be able to do better than to apply T. S. Eliot's test: does the statement seem to be that which the mind of the reader can accept as coherent, mature, and founded on the facts of experience? But when we raise such a question, we are driven to consider the poem as drama. We raise such further questions as these: Does the speaker seem carried away with his own emotions? Does he seem to oversimplify the situation? Or does he, on the other hand, seem to have won to a kind of detachment and objectivity? In other words, we are forced to raise the question as to whether the statement grows properly out of a context; whether it acknowledges the pressures of the context; whether it is "ironical"—or merely callow, glib, and sentimental.

I have suggested elsewhere that the poem which meets Eliot's test comes to the same thing as I. A. Richards' "poetry of synthesis"—that is, a poetry which does not leave out what is apparently hostile to its dominant tone, and which, because it is able to fuse the irrelevant and discordant, has come to terms with itself and is invulnerable to irony. Irony, then, in this further sense, is not only an acknowledgment of the pressures of a context. Invulnerability to irony is the stability of a context in which the internal pressures balance and mutually support each other. The stability is like that of the arch: the very forces which are calculated to drag the stones to the ground actually provide the principle of support—a principle in which thrust and counterthrust become the means of stability.

In many poems the pressures of the context emerge in obvious ironies. Marvell's "To His Coy Mistress" or Raleigh's "Nymph's Reply" or even Gray's "Elegy" reveal themselves as ironical, even to readers who use irony strictly in the conventional sense.

But can other poems be subsumed under this general principle, and do they show a comparable basic structure? The test case would seem to be presented by the lyric, and particularly the simple lyric. Consider, for example, one of Shakespeare's songs:

Who is Silvia: what is she
    That all our swains commend her?
Holy, fair, and wise is she;
    The heavens such grace did lend her,
That she might admired be.

Is she kind as she is fair?
    For beauty lives with kindness.
Love doth to her eyes repair,
    To help him of his blindness
And, being help'd, inhabits there.

Then to Silvia let us sing,
    That Silvia is excelling;
She excels each mortal thing
    Upon the dull earth dwelling:
To her let us garlands bring.

On one level the song attempts to answer the question "Who is Silvia?" and the answer given makes her something of an angel and something of a goddess. She excels each mortal thing "Upon the dull earth dwelling." Silvia herself, of course, dwells upon that dull earth, though it is presumably her own brightness which makes it dull by comparison. (The dull earth, for example, yields bright garlands, which the swains are bringing to her.) Why does she excel each mortal thing? Because of her virtues ("Holy, fair, and wise is she"), and these are a celestial gift. She is heaven's darling ("The heavens such grace did lend her").

Grace, I suppose, refers to grace of movement, and some readers will insist that we leave it at that. But since Silvia's other virtues include holiness and wisdom, and since her grace has been lent from above, I do not think that we can quite shut out the theological overtones. Shakespeare's audience would have found it even more difficult to do so. At any rate, it is interesting to see what happens if we are aware of these overtones. We get a delightful richness, and we also get something very close to irony.

The motive for the bestowal of grace—that she might admired be—is oddly untheological. But what follows is odder still, for the love that "doth to her eyes repair" is not, as we might expect, Christian "charity" but the little pagan god Cupid ("Love doth to her eyes repair, / To help him of his blindness.") But if Cupid lives in her eyes, then the second line of the stanza takes on another layer of meaning. "For beauty lives with kindness" becomes not merely a kind of charming platitude—actually often denied in human experience. (The Petrarchan lover, for example, as Shakespeare well knew, frequently found a beautiful and *cruel* mistress.) The second line, in this context, means also that the love god lives with the kind Silvia, and indeed has taken these eyes that sparkle with kindness for his own.

Is the mixture of pagan myth and Christian theology, then, an unthinking confusion into which the poet has blundered, or is it something wittily combined? It is certainly not a confusion, and if blundered into unconsciously, it is a happy mistake. But I do not mean to press the issue of the poet's self-consciousness (and with it, the implication of a kind of playful irony). Suffice it to say that the song is charming and delightful, and that the mingling of elements is proper to a poem which is a deft and light-fingered attempt to suggest the quality of divinity with which lovers perennially endow maidens who are finally mortal. The touch is light, there is a lyric grace, but the tone is complex, nonetheless.

I shall be prepared, however, to have this last example thrown out of court since Shakespeare, for all his universality, was a contemporary of the metaphysical poets, and may have incorporated more of their ironic complexity than is necessary or normal. One can draw more innocent and therefore more convincing examples from Wordsworth's Lucy poems.

She dwelt among the untrodden ways
    Beside the springs of Dove,

A maid whom there were none to praise
 And very few to love;

A violet by a mossy stone
 Half hidden from the eye!
Fair as a star, when only one
 Is shining in the sky.

She lived unknown, and few could know
 When Lucy ceased to be;
But she is in her grave, and, oh,
 The difference to me.

Which is Lucy really like—the violet or the star? The context in general seems to support the violet comparison. The violet, beautiful but almost unnoticed, already half hidden from the eye, is now, as the poem ends, completely hidden in its grave, with none but the poet to grieve for its loss. The star comparison may seem only vaguely relevant—a conventional and here a somewhat anomalous compliment. Actually, it is not difficult to justify the star comparison: to her lover's eyes, she is the solitary star. She has no rivals, nor would the idea of rivalry, in her unselfconscious simplicity, occur to her.

The violet and the star thus balance each other and between themselves define the situation: Lucy was, from the viewpoint of the great world, unnoticed, shy, modest, and half hidden from the eye, but from the standpoint of her lover, she is the single star, completely dominating that world, not arrogantly like the sun, but sweetly and modestly, like the star. The implicit contrast is that so often developed ironically by John Donne in his poems where the lovers, who amount to nothing in the eyes of the world, become, in their own eyes, each the other's world—as in "The Good-Morrow," where their love makes "one little room an everywhere," or as in "The Canonization," where the lovers drive into the mirrors of each other's eyes the "towns, countries, courts"—which make up the great world; and thus find that world in themselves. It is easy to imagine how Donne would have exploited the contrast between the violet and the star, accentuating it, developing the irony, showing how the violet was really like its antithesis, the star, etc.

Now one does not want to enter an Act of Uniformity against the poets. Wordsworth is en-

titled to his method of simple juxtaposition with no underscoring of the ironical contrast. But it is worth noting that the contrast with its ironic potential is there in his poem. It is there in nearly all of Wordsworth's successful lyrics. It is certainly to be found in "A slumber did my spirit seal."

A slumber did my spirit seal;
 I had no human fears:
She seemed a thing that could not feel
 The touch of earthly years.

No motion has she now, no force;
 She neither hears nor sees,
Rolled round in earth's diurnal course,
 With rocks, and stones, and trees.

The lover's insensitivity to the claims of mortality is interpreted as a lethargy of spirit—a strange slumber. Thus the "human fears" that he lacked are apparently the fears normal to human beings. But the phrase has a certain pliability. It could mean fears *for* the loved one as a mortal human being; and the lines that follow tend to warp the phrase in this direction: it does not occur to the lover that he needs to fear for one who cannot be touched by "earthly years." We need not argue that Wordsworth is consciously using a witty device, a purposed ambiguity; nor need we conclude that he is confused. It is enough to see that Wordsworth has developed, quite "normally," let us say, a context calculated to pull "human fears" in opposed directions, and that the slightest pressure of attention on the part of the reader precipitates an ironical effect.

As we move into the second stanza, the potential irony almost becomes overt. If the slumber has sealed the lover's spirit, a slumber, immersed in which he thought it impossible that his loved one could perish, so too a slumber has now definitely sealed *her* spirit: "No motion has she now, no force; / She neither hears nor sees." It is evident that it is her unnatural slumber that has waked him out of his. It is curious to speculate on what Donne or Marvell would have made of this.

Wordsworth, however, still does not choose to exploit the contrast as such. Instead, he attempts to suggest something of the lover's agonized shock at the loved one's present lack of motion—of his response to her utter and horrible inertness. And how shall he suggest this? He chooses to suggest it, not by saying that she lies as quiet as marble or as a lump of clay; on the contrary, he attempts to suggest it by imagining her in violent motion—violent, but imposed motion, the same motion indeed which the very stones share, whirled about as they are in earth's diurnal course. Why does the image convey so powerfully the sense of something inert and helpless? Part of the effect, of course, resides in the fact that a dead lifelessness is suggested more sharply by an object's being whirled about by something else than by an image of the object in repose. But there are other matters which are at work here: the sense of the girl's falling back into the clutter of things, companioned by things chained like a tree to one particular spot, or by things completely inanimate, like rocks and stones. Here, of course, the concluding figure leans upon the suggestion made in the first stanza, that the girl once seemed something not subject to earthly limitations at all. But surely, the image of the whirl itself is important in its suggestion of something meaningless—motion that mechanically repeats itself. And there is one further element: the girl, who to her lover seemed a thing that could not feel the touch of earthly years, is caught up helplessly into the empty whirl of the earth which measures and makes time. She is touched by and held by earthly time in its most powerful and horrible image. The last figure thus seems to me to summarize the poem—to offer to almost every facet of meaning suggested in the earlier lines a concurring and resolving image which meets and accepts and reduces each item to its place in the total unity.

Wordsworth, as we have observed above, does not choose to point up specifically the ironical contrast between the speaker's former slumber and the loved one's present slumber. But there is one ironical contrast which he does stress: this is the contrast between the two senses in which the girl becomes insulated against the "touch of earthly years." In the first stanza, she "could not feel / The touch of earthly years" because she seemed divine and immortal. But in the second stanza, now in her grave, she still does not "feel the touch of earthly

years," for, like the rocks and stones, she feels nothing at all. It is true that Wordsworth does not repeat the verb "feels"; instead he writes "She neither *hears* nor *sees*." But the contrast, though not commented upon directly by any device of verbal wit, is there nonetheless, and is bound to make itself felt in any sensitive reading of the poem. The statement of the first stanza has been literally realized in the second, but its meaning has been ironically reversed.

Ought we, then, to apply the term *ironical* to Wordsworth's poem? Not necessarily. I am trying to account for my temptation to call such a poem ironical—not to justify my yielding to the temptation—least of all to insist that others so transgress. Moreover, Wordsworth's poem seems to me admirable, and I entertain no notion that it might have been more admirable still had John Donne written it rather than William Wordsworth. I shall be content if I can make a much more modest point: namely, that since both Wordsworth and Donne are poets, their work has at basis a similar structure, and that the dynamic structure—the pattern of thrust and counterthrust—which we associate with Donne has its counterpart in Wordsworth. In the work of both men, the relation between part and part is organic, which means that each part modifies and is modified by the whole.

Yet to intimate that there are potential ironies in Wordsworth's lyric may seem to distort it. After all, is it not simple and spontaneous? With these terms we encounter two of the critical catchwords of the nineteenth century, even as *ironical* is in danger of becoming a catchword of our own period. Are the terms *simple* and *ironical* mutually exclusive? What after all do we mean by *simple* or by *spontaneous*? We may mean that the poem came to the poet easily and even spontaneously: very complex poems may—indeed have—come just this way. Or the poem may seem in its effect on the reader a simple and spontaneous utterance: some poems of great complexity possess this quality. What is likely to cause trouble here is the intrusion of a special theory of composition. It is fairly represented as an intrusion since a theory as to how a poem is written is being allowed to dictate to us how the poem is to be read. There is no harm in thinking of Wordsworth's poem as simple and spontaneous unless these terms deny complexities that actually exist in the poem, and unless they justify us in reading the poem with only half our minds. A slumber ought not to seal the *reader's* spirit as he reads this poem, or any other poem.

I have argued that irony, taken as the acknowledgment of the pressures of context, is to be found in poetry of every period and even in simple lyrical poetry. But in the poetry of our own time, this pressure reveals itself strikingly. A great deal of modern poetry does use irony as its special and perhaps its characteristic strategy. For this there are reasons, and compelling reasons. To cite only a few of these reasons: there is the breakdown of a common symbolism; there is the general scepticism as to universals; not least important, there is the depletion and corruption of the very language itself, by advertising and by the mass produced arts of radio, the moving picture, and pulp fiction. The modern poet has the task of rehabilitating a tired and drained language so that it can convey meanings once more with force and with exactitude. This task of qualifying and modifying language is perennial; but it is imposed on the modern poet as a burden. Those critics who attribute the use of ironic techniques to the poet's own bloodless sophistication and tired scepticism would be better advised to refer these vices to his potential readers, a public corrupted by Hollywood and the Book of the Month Club. For the modern poet is not addressing simple primitives but a public sophisticated by commercial art.

At any rate, to the honor of the modern poet be it said that he has frequently succeeded in using his ironic techniques to win through to clarity and passion. Randall Jarrell's "Eighth Air Force" represents a success of this sort.

> If, in an odd angle of the hutment,
> A puppy laps the water from a can
> Of flowers, and the drunk sergeant shaving
> Whistles *O Paradiso!*—shall I say that man
> Is not as men have said: a wolf to man?
>
> The other murderers troop in yawning;
> Three of them play Pitch, one sleeps, and one
> Lies counting missions, lies there sweating
> Till even his heart beats: One; One; One.
> *O murderers!* . . . Still, this is how it's done:

> This is a war. . . . But since these play, before
>   they die,
> Like puppies with their puppy; since, a man,
> I did as these have done, but did not die—
> I will content the people as I can
> And give up these to them: Behold the man!
>
> I have suffered, in a dream, because of him
> Many things; for this last saviour, man,
> I have lied as I lie now. But what is lying?
> Men wash their hands, in blood, as best they can:
>   I find no fault in this just man.

There are no superfluous parts, no dead or empty details. The airmen in their hutment are casual enough and honest enough to be convincing. The raw building is domesticated: there are the flowers in water from which the mascot, a puppy, laps. There is the drunken sergeant, whistling an opera aria as he shaves. These "murderers," as the poet is casually to call the airmen in the next stanza, display a touching regard for the human values. How, then, can one say that man is a wolf to man, since these men "play before they die, like puppies with their puppy." But the casual presence of the puppy in the hutment allows us to take the stanza both ways, for the dog is a kind of tamed and domesticated wolf, and his presence may prove on the contrary that the hutment is the wolf den. After all, the timber wolf plays with its puppies.

The second stanza takes the theme to a perfectly explicit conclusion. If three of the men play pitch, and one is asleep, at least one man is awake and counts himself and his companions murderers. But his unvoiced cry "O murderers" is met, countered, and dismissed with the next two lines: ". . . Still this is how it's done: / This is a war. . . ."

The note of casuistry and cynical apology prepares for a brilliant and rich resolving image, the image of Pontius Pilate, which is announced specifically in the third stanza:

> I will content the people as I can
> And give up these to them: behold the man!

Yet if Pilate, as he is first presented, is a jesting Pilate, who asks "What is truth?" it is a bitter and grieving Pilate who concludes the poem. It is the integrity of Man himself that is at stake. Is man a cruel animal, a wolf, or is he the last savior, the Christ of our secular religion of humanity?

The Pontius Pilate metaphor, as the poet uses it, becomes a device for tremendous concentration. For the speaker (presumably the young airman who cried "O murderers") is himself the confessed murderer under judgment, and also the Pilate who judges, and, at least as a representative of man, the savior whom the mob would condemn. He is even Pilate's better nature, his wife, for the lines "I have suffered, in a dream, because of him,/ Many things" is merely a rearrangement of Matthew 27:19, the speech of Pilate's wife to her husband. But this last item is more than a reminiscence of the scriptural scene. It reinforces the speaker's present dilemma. The modern has had high hopes for man; are the hopes merely a dream? Is man incorrigible, merely a cruel beast? The speaker's present torture springs from that hope and from his reluctance to dismiss it as an empty dream. This Pilate is even harder-pressed than was the Roman magistrate. For he must convince himself of this last savior's innocence. But he has lied for him before. He will lie for him now.

Men wash their hands, in blood, as best they
    can:
I find no fault in this just man.

What is the meaning of "Men wash their hands, in blood, as best they can"? It can mean: Since my own hands are bloody, I have no right to condemn the rest. It can mean: I know that man can love justice, even though his hands are bloody, for there is blood on mine. It can mean: Men are essentially decent: they try to keep their hands clean even if they have only blood in which to wash them.

None of these meanings cancels out the others. All are relevant, and each meaning contributes to the total meaning. Indeed, there is not a facet of significance which does not receive illumination from the figure.

Some of Jarrell's weaker poems seem weak to me because they lean too heavily upon this concept of the goodness of man. In some of them, his approach to the theme is too direct. But in this poem, the affirmation of man's essential justness by a Pilate who contents the people as he washes his hands in blood seems to me to supply every qualification that is required. The sense of self-guilt, the yearning to believe in man's justness, the

knowledge of the difficulty of so believing—all work to render accurately and dramatically the total situation.

It is easy at this point to misapprehend the function of irony. We can say that Jarrell's irony pares his theme down to acceptable dimensions. The theme of man's goodness has here been so qualified that the poet himself does not really believe in it. But this is not what I am trying to say. We do not ask a poet to bring his poem into line with our personal beliefs—still less to flatter our personal beliefs. What we do ask is that the poem dramatize the situation so accurately, so honestly, with such fidelity to the total situation that it is no longer a question of our beliefs, but of our participaton in the poetic experience. At his best, Jarrell manages to bring us, by an act of imagination, to the most penetrating insight. Participating in that insight, we doubtless become better citizens. (One of the "uses" of poetry, I should agree, is to make us better citizens.) But poetry is not the eloquent rendition of the citizen's creed. It is not even the accurate rendition of his creed. Poetry must carry us beyond the abstract creed into the very matrix out of which, and from which, our creeds are abstracted. That is what "The Eighth Air Force" does. That is what, I am convinced, all good poetry does.

For the theme in a genuine poem does not confront us as abstraction—that is, as one man's generalization from the relevant particulars. Finding its proper symbol, defined and refined by the participating metaphors, the theme becomes a part of the reality in which we live—an insight, rooted in and growing out of concrete experience, many-sided, three-dimensional. Even the resistance to generalization has its part in this process—even the drag of the particulars away from the universal—even the tension of opposing themes—play their parts. The kite properly loaded, tension maintained along the kite string, rises steadily *against* the thrust of the wind.

Note

1. This is not to say, of course, that such statements are not related to a particular "universe of discourse." They are indeed, as are all statements of whatever kind. But I distinguish here between "context" and

"universe of discourse." "Two plus two equals four" is not dependent on a special dramatic context in the way in which a "statement" made in a poem is. Compare "two plus two equals four" and the same "statement" as contained in Housman's poem:

—To think that two and two are four
  And neither five nor three
The heart of man has long been sore
  And long 'tis like to be.

The Structure of the Concrete Universal

W. K. Wimsatt, Jr.

W. K. Wimsatt, one of the foremost theoreticians of formal criticism, here examines a question that has long interested philosophers of literature: "how a work of literature can be either more individual (unique) or more universal than other kinds of writing, or how it can combine the individual and the universal more than other kinds." A good formalist, Wimsatt finds the heart of the mystery in the idea of metaphor—"the structure most characteristic of concentrated poetry." And, like Cleanth Brooks, he concludes that the good poem will take in more of experience than the weak poem will: "The unity and maturity of good poems are two sides of the same thing. The kind of unity which we look for and find in poetry is attained only through a degree of complexity in design which itself involves maturity and richness." Having located the value of poetry in its form, Wimsatt argues that studies of authors, readers, and literary periods are simply off the point, for only an "objective" criticism carefully focused on the "form" of the verbal object can hope to tell us much about the meaning and value of poetry.

THE CENTRAL ARGUMENT OF THIS ESSAY, CONcerning what I shall call the "concrete universal," proceeds from the observation that literary theorists have from early times to the present persisted in making statements which in their contexts seem to mean that a work of literary art is in some peculiar sense a very individual thing or a very universal thing or both. What that paradox can mean, or what important fact behind the paradox has been discerned by such various critics as Aristotle, Plotinus, Hegel, and Ransom, it will be the purpose of the essay to inquire, and by the inquiry to discuss not only a significant feature of metaphysical poetics from Aristotle to the present day but the relation between metaphysical poetics and more practical and specific rhetorical analysis. In the brief historical survey which forms one part of this essay it will not be my purpose to suggest that any of these writers meant exactly what I shall mean in later parts where I describe the structure of poetry. Yet throughout the essay I shall proceed on the theory not only that men have at different times used the same terms and have meant differently, but that they have sometimes used different terms and have meant the same or somewhat the same. In other words, I assume that there is continuity in the problems of criticism, and that a person who studies poetry today has a legitimate interest in what Plato said about poetry.

The view of common terms and their relations to classes of things from which I shall start is roughly that which one may read in the logic of J. S. Mill, a view which is not much different from the semantic view of today and for most purposes not much different from the Aristotelian and scholastic view. Mill speaks of the word and its denotation and connotation (the term, referent and reference, the sign, denotatum and designatum[1] of more recent terminologies). The denotation is the *it*, the individual thing or the aggregate of things to which the term may refer; the connotation is the *what*, the quality or classification inferred for the it, or implicitly predicated by the application of the term or the giving of the name.* One main difference between all modern positivistic, nominalistic, and semantic systems and the scholastic and classical systems is that the older ones stress the similarity of the individuals denoted by the common term and hence the real universality of meaning, while the modern systems stress the differences in the individuals, the constant flux even of each individual in time and space and its kinetic structure, and hence infer only an approximate or nominal universality of meaning and a convenience rather than a truth in the use of general terms. A further difference lies in the view of how the individual is related to the various connotations of terms which may be applied to it. That is, to the question: What is it? the older writers seem to hold there is but one (essentially right) answer, while the moderns accept as many answers as there are classes to which the individual may be assigned (an indefinite number). The older writers speak of a proper essence or whatness of the individual, a quality which in some cases at least is that designated by the class name most commonly applied to the individual: a bench is a bench, essentially a bench, accidentally a heavy wooden object or something covered with green paint. "When we say *what* it is," observes Aristotle, "we do not say 'white,' or 'hot,' or 'three cubits long,' but 'a man' or 'a god.' "[2] And this view is also a habit scarcely avoidable in our own daily thinking, especially when we think of living things or of artifacts, things made by us or our fellows for a purpose. What is it? Bench, we think, is an adequate answer. An assemblage of sticks painted green, we consider freakish.

---

*The terms "denotation" and "connotation" are commonly and loosely used by literary critics to distinguish the dictionary meaning of a term (denotation) from the vaguer aura of suggestion (connotation). Both these are parts of the connotation in the logical sense.

II

Whether or not one believes in universals, one may see the persistence in literary criticism of a theory that poetry presents the concrete and the universal, or the individual and the universal, or an object which in a mysterious and special way is both highly general and highly particular. The doctrine is implicit in Aristotle's two statements that poetry imitates action and that poetry tends to express the universal. It is implicit again at the end of the classic period in the mystic doctrine of Plotinus, who in his later writing on beauty reverses the Platonic objection that art does not know the ultimate reality of the forms. Plotinus arrives at the view that the artist by a kind of bypass of the inferior natural productions of the world soul reaches straight to the forms that lie behind in the divine intelligence.[3] Another version of the classic theory, with affinities for Plotinus, lies in the scholastic phrase *resplendentia formae*.

Cicero's account of how Zeuxis painted an ideal Helen from the five most beautiful virgins of Crotona is a typical development of Aristotelian theory, in effect the familiar neoclassic theory found in Du Fresnoy's *Art of Painting*, in the writings of Johnson, especially in the tulip passage in *Rasselas*, and in the *Discourses* and *Idlers* of Reynolds. The business of the poet is not to number the streaks of the tulip; it is to give us not the individual, but the species. The same thing is stated in a more complicated way by Kant in telling how the imagination constructs the "aesthetical normal Idea":

> It is the image for the whole race, which floats among all the variously different intuitions of individuals, which nature takes as archetype in her productions of the same species, but which seems not to be fully reached in any individual case.[4]

And Hegel's account is as follows:

> The work of art is not only for the sensuous apprehension as sensuous object, but its position is of such a kind that as sensuous it is at the same time essentially addressed to the *mind*.[5]

> In comparison with the show or semblance of immediate sensuous existence or of historical narrative, the artistic semblance has the advan-

tage that in itself it points beyond self, and refers us away from itself to something spiritual
which it is meant to bring before the mind's
eye. . . . The hard rind of nature and the common world give the mind more trouble in breaking through to the idea than do the products of
art.[6]

The excellence of Shakespeare, says Coleridge,
consists in a "union and interpenetration of the
universal and particular." In one terminology or
another this idea of a concrete universal is found
in most metaphysical aesthetic of the eighteenth
and nineteenth centuries.

A modern literary critic, John Crowe Ransom, speaks of the argument of a poem (the universal) and a local texture or tissue of concrete
irrelevance. Another literary critic, Allen Tate,
manipulating the logical terms "extension" and
"intension," has arrived at the concept of "tension" in poetry. "Extension," as logicians use the
word, is the range of individuals denoted by a
term (denotation); "intension" is the total of
qualities connoted (connotation). In the ordinary
or logical use of the terms, extension and intension are of inverse relationship—the wider the
one, the shallower the other. A poem, says Tate,
as I interpret him, is a verbal structure which in
some peculiar way has both a wide extension
and a deep intension.

Not all these theories of the concrete universal lay equal stress on the two sides of the paradox, and it seems indicative of the vitality of
the theory and of the truth implicit in it that the
two sides have been capable of exaggeration into
antithetic schools and theories of poetry. For Du
Fresnoy, Johnson, and Reynolds poetry and
painting give the universal; the less said about
the particulars the better. This is the neoclassic
theory, the illustrations of which we seek in
Pope's *Essay on Man* or in Johnson's *Ramblers*,
where the ideas are moral and general and concerned with "nature," "one clear, unchanged,
and universal light." The opposite theory had
notable expression in England, a few years before Johnson wrote *Rasselas*, in Joseph Warton's
Essay on Pope:

A minute and particular enumeration of circumstances judiciously selected, is what chiefly dis-
criminates poetry from history, and renders the

former, for that reason, a more close and faithful
representation of nature than the latter.

And Blake's marginal criticism of Reynolds was:
"THIS Man was Hired to Depress art." "To Generalize is to be an Idiot. To Particularize is the
Alone Distinction of Merit. General Knowledges
are those Knowledges that Idiots possess." "Sacrifice the Parts: What becomes of the whole?"
The line from Warton's *Essay* to Croce's *Aesthetic*
seems a straight and obvious one, from Thom-
son's specific descriptions of flowers to the individual act of intuition-expression which is
art—its opposite and enemy being the concept
or generality.[7] The two views of art (two that can
be held by different theorists about the same
works of art) may be startlingly contrasted in the
following passages about fictitious character—
one a well known statement by Johnson, the
other by the philosopher of the *élan vital*.

[Shakespeare's] characters are not modified by
the customs of particular places, unpractised by
the rest of the world; by the peculiarities of studies or professions, which can operate but upon
small numbers; or by the accidents of transient
fashions or temporary opinions: they are the
genuine progeny of common humanity, such as
the world will always supply, and observation
will always find. His persons act and speak by
the influence of those general passions and principles by which all minds are agitated, and the
whole system of life is continued in motion. In
the writings of other poets a character is too often an individual; in those of Shakespeare it is
commonly a species.

Hence it follows that art always aims at what
is *individual*. What the artist fixes on his canvas
is something he has seen at a certain spot, on a
certain day, at a certain hour, with a colouring
that will never be seen again. What the poet
sings of is a certain mood which was his, and
his alone, and which will never return. . . .
Nothing could be more unique than the character of Hamlet. Though he may resemble other
men in some respects, it is clearly not on that
account that he interests us most.[8]

Other critics, notably the most ancient and the
most modern, have tried to hold the extremes
together. Neither of the extremes gives a good
account of art and each leads out of art. The
theory of particularity leads to individuality and

originality (Edward Young was another eighteenth century Crocean), then to the idiosyncratic and the unintelligible and to the psychology of the author, which is not in the work of art and is not a standard for judgment. The theory of universality as it appears in Johnson and Reynolds leads to platitude and to a standard of material objectivity, the average tulip, the average human form, some sort of average.[9]

III

"Just representations of general nature," said Johnson, and it ought to be noted, though it perhaps rarely is, that two kinds of generality are involved, as indeed they are in the whole neoclassic theory of generality. There is the generality of logic or classification, of the more general as opposed to the more specific, "essential" generality, one might say. And there is the generality of literal truth to nature, "existential" generality. The assumption of neoclassic theory seems to be that these two must coincide. As a matter of fact they may and often do, but need not. Thus: "purple cow" is a more general (less specific) term and concept than "tan cow with a broken horn," yet the latter is more general or true to nature. We have, in short, realism or fantasy, and in either there may be various degrees of the specific or the general. We have *A Journal of the Plague Year* and *The Rambler, Gulliver's Travels* and *Rasselas*. The fact that there are a greater number of "vicissitudes" and "miscarriages" (favorite *Rambler* events) in human experience than plagues at London, that there are more tan cows than tan cows with broken horns, makes it true in a sense that a greater degree of essential generality involves a greater degree of existential. But in this sense the most generally reliable concept is simply that of "being."

The question is how a work of literature can be either more individual (unique) or more universal than other kinds of writing, or how it can combine the individual and the universal more than other kinds. Every description in words, so far as it is a direct description ("The barn is red and square") is a generalization. That is the nature of words. There are no individuals conveyed in words but only more or less specific

generalizations, so that Johnson is right, though we have to ask him what degree of verbal generality makes art, and whether "tulip" is a better or more important generality than "tulip with ten streaks," or whether "beauty" is not in fact a much more impressive generality than "tulip." On the other hand, one cannot deny that in some sense there are more tulips in poetry than pure abstracted beauty. So that Bergson is right too; only we shall have to ask him what degree of specificity in verbal description makes art. And he can never claim complete verbal specificity or individuality, even for Hamlet.

If he could, if a work of literary art could be looked on as an artifact or concrete physical work, the paradox for the student of universals would return from the opposite direction even more forcibly—as it does in fact for theorists of graphic art. If Reynolds' picture "The Age of Innocence" presents a species or universal, what species does it present? Not an Aristotelian essence—"man," or "humanity," nor even a more specific kind of being such as "womanhood." For then the picture would present the same universal as Reynolds' portrait of Mrs. Siddons as "The Tragic Muse," and all differences between "The Age of Innocence" and "The Tragic Muse" would be aesthetically irrelevent. Does the picture then present girlhood, or barefoot girlhood, or barefoot girlhood in a white dress against a gloomy background? All three are equally valid universals (despite the fact that makeshift phrases are required to express two of them), and all three are presented by the picture. Or is it the title which tells us what universal is presented, "The Age of Innocence," and without the title should we not know the universal? The question will be: What in the individual work of art demands that we attribute to it one universal rather than another?

We may answer that for poetry it is the generalizing power of words already mentioned, and go on to decide that what distinguishes poetry from scientific or logical discourse is a degree of irrelevant concreteness in descriptive details. This is in effect what Ransom says in his doctrine of argument and local irrelevance, but it seems doubtful if the doctrine is not a version of the theory of ornamental metaphor. The argument, says Ransom, is the prose or scientific meaning, what the poem has in common with other kinds of writing. The irrelevance is a texture of concreteness which does not contribute anything to the argument but is somehow enjoyable or valuable for its own sake, the vehicle of a metaphor which one boards heedless of where it runs, whether crosstown or downtown—just for the ride. So Ransom nurses and refines the argument, and on one page he makes the remark that the poet searches for "suitability" in his particular phrases, and by suitability Ransom means "the propriety which consists in their denoting the particularity which really belongs to the logical object."[10] But the difference between "propriety" and relevance in such a context is not easy to see. And relevance is logic. The fact is that all concrete illustration has about it something of the irrelevant. An apple falling from a tree illustrates gravity, but apple and tree are irrelevant to the pure theory of gravity. It may be that what happens in a poem is that the apple and the tree are somehow made more than usually relevant.

Such a theory, not that of Johnson and Reynolds, not that of Warton and Bergson, not quite that of Ransom, is what I would suggest—yet less as a novelty than as something already widely implicit in recent poetical analyses and exegeses, in those of Empson, for instance, Tate, Blackmur, or Brooks. If a work of literature is not in a simple sense either more individual or more universal than other kinds of writing, it may yet be such an individual or such a complex of meaning that it has a special relation to the world of universals. Some acute remarks on this subject were made by Ruskin in a chapter of *Modern Painters* neglected today perhaps because of its distasteful ingredient of "noble emotion." Poetry, says Ruskin in criticizing Reynolds' *Idlers*, is not distinguished from history by the omission of details, nor for that matter by the mere addition of details. "There must be something either in the nature of the details themselves, or the method of using them, which invests them with poetical power." Their nature, one may add, as assumed through their relation to one another, a relation which may also be called the method of using them. The poetic character of details consists not in what they say directly and explicitly (as if roses and moonlight were poetic) but in what by their arrangement they *show* implicitly.

IV

"One," observes Ben Jonson, thinking of literature, "is considerable two waies: either, as it is only separate, and by it self: or as being compos'd of many parts it beginnes to be one as those parts grow or are wrought together."[11] A literary work of art is a complex of detail (an artifact, if we may be allowed that metaphor for what is only a verbal object), a composition so complicated of human values that its interpretation is dictated by the understanding of it, and so complicated as to seem in the highest degree individual—a concrete universal. We are accustomed to being told, for example, that what makes a character in fiction or drama vital is a certain fullness or rotundity: that the character has many sides. Thus E. M. Forster:

> We may divide characters into flat and round. Flat characters were called "humours" in the seventeenth century, and are sometimes called types, and sometimes caricatures. In their purest form, they are constructed round a single idea or quality: when there is more than one factor in them, we get the beginning of the curve towards the round. The really flat character can be expressed in one sentence such as "I never will desert Mr. Micawber."

It remains to be said, however, that the many traits of the round character (if indeed it is one character and not a hodgepodge) are harmonized or unified, and that if this is so, then all the traits are chosen by a principle, just as are the traits of the flat character. Yet it cannot be that the difference between the round and flat character is simply numerical; the difference cannot be merely that the presiding principle is illustrated by more examples in the round character. Something further must be supposed—a special interrelation in the traits of the round character. Bobadil is an example of the *miles gloriosus*, a flat humour. He swears by "The foot of Pharaoh," takes tobacco, borrows money from his landlady, is found lying on a bench fully dressed with a hangover, brags about his feats at the siege of Strigonium, beats Cob, a poor water carrier, and so on. It is possible that he has numerically as many traits as Falstaff, one of the most vital of all characters. But one of the differences between Falstaff and Bobadil is that the things Falstaff says are funny; the things Bobadil says are not. Compared to Falstaff, Bobadil is unconscious, an opaque butt. There is the vitality of consciousness in Falstaff. And further there is the crowning complexity of self-consciousness. The fact that Morgann could devote a book to arguing that Falstaff is not a coward, that lately Professor Wilson has argued that at Gadshill Falstaff may exhibit " 'all the common symptoms of the malady' of cowardice" and at the same time persuade the audience that he has " 'never once lost his self-possession,' " the fact that one can conceive that Falstaff in the Gadshill running-away scene really knows that his assailants are the Prince and Poins—all this shows that in Falstaff there is a kind of interrelation among his attributes, his cowardice, his wit, his debauchery, his presumption, that makes them in a special way an organic harmony. He is a rounded character not only in the sense that he is gross (a fact which may have tempted critics to speak of a rounded character) or in the sense that he is a bigger bundle of attributes, stuffed more full, than Bobadil or Ralph Roister Doister; but in the sense that his attributes make a circuit and connection. A kind of awareness of self (a high and human characteristic), with a pleasure in the fact, is perhaps the central principle which instead of simplifying the attributes gives each one a special function in the whole, a double or reflex value. Falstaff or such a character of self-conscious "infinite variety"* as Cleopatra are concrete universals because they have no class names, only their own proper ones, yet are structures of such precise variety and centrality that each demands a special interpretation in the realm of human values.

---

*I do not mean that self-consciousness is the only principle of complexity in character, yet a considerable degree of it would appear to be a requisite for poetic interest.

Character is one type of concrete universal; there are other types, as many perhaps as the central terms of criticism; but most can be learned I believe by examination of metaphor—the structure most characteristic of concentrated poetry. The language of poets, said Shelley, "is vitally metaphorical: that is, it marks the before unapprehended relations of things and perpetuates their apprehension." Wordsworth spoke of the abstracting and modifying powers of the imagination. Aristotle said that the greatest thing was the use of metaphor, because it meant an eye for resemblances. Even the simplest form of metaphor or simile ("My love is like a red, red rose") presents us with a special and creative, in fact a concrete, kind of abstraction different from that of science. For behind a metaphor lies a resemblance between two classes, and hence a more general third class. This class is unnamed and most likely remains unnamed and is apprehended only through the metaphor. It is a new conception for which there is no other expression. Keats discovering Homer is like a traveler in the realms of gold, like an astronomer who discovers a planet, like Cortez gazing at the Pacific. The title of the sonnet, "On First Looking into Chapman's Homer," seems to furnish not so much the subject of the poem as a fourth member of a central metaphor, the real subject of the poem being an abstraction, a certain kind of thrill in discovering, for which there is no name and no other description, only the four members of the metaphor pointing, as to the center of their pattern. The point of the poem seems to lie outside both vehicle and tenor.

To take a more complicated instance, Wordsworth's "Solitary Reaper" has the same basic metaphorical structure, the girl alone reaping and singing, and the two bird images, the nightingale in Arabian sands and the cuckoo among the Hebrides, the three figures serving the parallel or metaphorical function of bringing out the abstraction of loneliness, remoteness, mysterious charm in the singing. But there is also a kind of third-dimensional significance, in the fact that one bird is far out in the northern sea, the other far off in southern sands, a fact which is not part of the comparison between the birds and the girl. By an implication cutting across the plane of logic of the metaphor, the girl and the two birds suggest extension in space, universality, and world communion—an effect supported by other details of the poem such as the overflowing of the vale profound, the mystery of the Erse song, the bearing of the song away in the witness' heart, the past and future themes which the girl may be singing. Thus a central abstraction is created, of communion, telepathy in solitude, the prophetic soul of the wide world dreaming on things to come—an abstraction which is the effect not wholly of the metaphor elaborated logically (in a metaphysical way) but of a working on two axes, by association rather than by logic, by a three-dimensional complexity of structure.

To take yet a third instance, metaphoric structure may appear where we are less likely to realize it explicitly—in poetic narratives, for example, elliptically concealed in the more obvious narrative outlines. "I can bring you," writes Max Eastman, "examples of diction that is metrical but not metaphoric—a great part of the popular ballads, for example—and you can hardly deny that they too are poetic." But the best story poems may be analyzed, I believe, as metaphors without expressed tenors, as symbols which speak for themselves. "La Belle Dame Sans Merci," for example (if a literary ballad may be taken), is about a knight, by profession a man of action, but sensitive, like the lily and the rose, and about a faery lady with wild, wild eyes. At a more abstract level, it is about the loss of self in the mysterious lure of beauty—whether women, poetry, or poppy. It sings the irretrievable departure from practical normality (the squirrel's granary is full), the wan isolation after ecstasy. Each reader will experience the poem at his own level of experience or at several. A good story poem is like a stone thrown into a pond, into our minds, where ever widening concentric circles of meaning go out—and this because of the structure of the story.

"A poem should not mean but be." It is an epigram worth quoting in every essay on poetry. And the poet "nothing affirmeth, and therefore never lieth." "Sit quidvis," said Horace, "simplex dumtaxat et unum." It seems almost the reverse of the truth. "Complex dumtaxat et unum"* would be better. Every real poem is a complex poem, and only in virtue of its complexity does it have artistic unity. A newspaper poem by Edgar Guest† does not have this kind of unity, but only the unity of an abstractly stated sentiment.

The principle is expressed by Aristotle when he says that beauty is based on unity in variety, and by Coleridge when he says that "The Beautiful, contemplated in its essentials, that is, in *kind* and not in *degree*, is that in which the *many*, still seen as many becomes one," and that a work of art is "rich in proportion to the variety of parts which it holds in unity."

V

It is usually easier to show how poetry works than to show why anyone should want it to work in a given way. Rhetorical analysis of poetry has always tended to separate from evaluation, technique from worth. The structure of poems as concrete and universal is the principle by which the critic can try to keep the two together. If it be granted that the "subject matter" of poetry is in a broad sense the moral realm, human actions as good or bad, with all their associated feelings, all the thought and imagination that goes with happiness and suffering (if poetry submits "the shews of

---

*First Latin phrase, "Let each thing be only simple and a unit"; second Latin phrase, "Only complex and a unit."—ED.

†A reader whose judgment I esteem tells me that such a name appears in a serious discussion of poetics anomalously and in bad taste. I have allowed it to remain (in preference to some more dignified name of mediocrity) precisely because I wish to insist on the existence of badness in poetry and so to establish an antithetic point of reference for the discussion of goodness. Relativistic argument often creates an illusion in its own favor by moving steadily in a realm of great and nearly great art. See, for example, George Boas, *A Primer for Critics* (Baltimore, 1937), where a cartoon by Daumier appears toward the end as a startling approach to the vulgar. The purpose of my essay is not judicial but theoretical, that is, not to exhibit original discoveries in taste, but to show the relationship between examples acknowledged to lie in the realms of the good and the bad.

things to the desires of the Mind"), then the rhetorical structure of the concrete universal, the complexity and unity of the poem, is also its maturity or sophistication of richness or depth, and hence its value. Complexity of form is sophistication of content. The unity and maturity of good poems are two sides of the same thing. The kind of unity which we look for and find in poetry is attained only through a degree of complexity in design which itself involves maturity and richness. For a visual diagram of the metaphysics of poetry one might write vertically the word complexity, a column, and give it a head with Janus faces, one looking in the rhetorical direction, unity, and the other in the axiological, maturity.

A final point to be made is that a criticism of structure and of value is an objective criticism. It rests on facts of human psychology (as that a man may love a woman so well as to give up empires), facts, which though psychological, yet are so well acknowledged as to lie in the realm of what may be called public psychology—a realm which one should distinguish from the private realm of the author's psychology and from the equally private realm of the individual reader's psychology (the vivid pictures which poetry or stories are supposed to create in the imagination, or the venerable action of catharsis—all that poetry is said to *do* rather than to *be*). Such a criticism, again, is objective and absolute, as distinguished from the relative criticism of idiom and period. I mean that this criticism will notice that Pope is different from Shakespeare, but will notice even more attentively that Shakespeare is different from Taylor the Water Poet and Pope different from Sir Richard Blackmore. Such a criticism will be interested to analyze the latter two differences and see what these differences have in common and what Shakespeare and Pope have in common, and it will not despair of describing that similarity (that formula or character of great poetry) even though the terms be abstract and difficult. Or, if we are told that there is no universal agreement about what is good—that Pope has not been steadily held in esteem, that Shakespeare has been considered a barbarian, the objective analyst of structures can at least say (and it seems much to say) that he is describing a class of poems, those which through a peculiar complexity possess unity and maturity and in a special way can be called both individual and universal. Among all recorded

"poems," this class is of a relative rarity, and further this class will be found in an impressive way to coincide with those poems which have by some body of critics, some age of educated readers, been called great.

The function of the objective critic is by approximate descriptions of poems, or multiple restatements of their meaning, to aid other readers to come to an intuitive and full realization of poems themselves and hence to know good poems and distinguish them from bad ones. It is of course impossible to tell all about a poem in other words. Croce tells us, as we should expect him to, of the "impossibility of ever rendering in logical terms the full effect of any poetry or of other artistic work." "Criticism, nevertheless," he tells us, "performs its own office, which is to discern and to point out exactly where lies the poetical motive and to formulate the divisions which aid in distinguishing what is proper to every work."[12] The situation is something like this: In each poem there is something (an individual intuition—or a concept) which can never be expressed in other terms. It is like the square root of two or like pi, which cannot be expressed by rational numbers, but only as their *limit*. Criticism of poetry is like 1.414 . . . or 3.1416 . . . , not all it would be, yet all that can be had and very useful.

Notes

1. Charles W. Morris, "Esthetics and the Theory of Signs," in *Journal of Unified Science*, VIII (1939), 131–50.

2. *Metaphysics*, VII (Z), 1 (1028). Cp. Mortimer J. Adler, *The Problem of Species* (New York, 1940), 24–25.

3. "The arts are not to be slighted on the ground that they create by imitation of natural objects; for, to begin with, these natural objects are themselves imitations; then, we must recognize that they give no bare reproduction of the thing seen but go back to the ideas from which Nature itself derives." *Enneads*, V, viii, 1, *Plotinus–The Fifth Ennead*, Stephen MacKenna, tr. (London, 1926), 74.

4. *Kant's Critique of Judgment*, J. H. Bernard, tr. (London, 1931), 88–89.

5. *The Introduction to Hegel's Philosophy of Fine Art*, Bernard Bosanquet, tr. (London, 1886), 67. Cp. Walter T. Stace, *The Meaning of Beauty* (London, 1929), 41.

6. *The Introduction to Hegel's Philosophy of Fine Art*, 16. Cp. pp. 72–78, 133–37.

7. It is true that Croce has protested: "Ce qu'on démontre comme inconciliable avec le principe de la pure intuition, ce n'est pas l'universalité, mais la valeur intellectualiste et transcendante donnée dans l'art à l'universalité, sous la forme de l'allegorie ou du symbole." "Le Caractère de Totalité de l'Expression Artistique," in *Bréviaire d'Esthétique*, Georges Bourgin, tr. (Paris, 1923), 170. But the main drift of Croce's aesthetic, in being against conceptualization, is radically against the universal.

8. Henri Bergson, *Laughter, An Essay on the Meaning of the Comic* (New York, 1928), 161–62.

9. Roger Fry in his Introduction to Reynolds' *Third Discourse* argues that the species presented in painting are not those of the natural, but those of the social world, as king, knight, beggar. *Discourses*, Roger Fry, ed. (London, 1905), 46. And a modern critic of sculpture, R. H. Wilenski, offers what is perhaps the last retreat of the doctrine of universals in visual art: not man, flower, or animal but the forms of life analogous in (that is, common to) man, flower, and animal are abstracted and presented pure in sculptural art. R. H. Wilenski, *The Meaning of Modern Sculpture* (London, 1939), 159–60.

10. *The New Criticism* (Norfolk, 1941), 315. Maritain, coming from a different direction, arrives at somewhat the same poser. "If it pleases a futurist to paint a lady with only one eye, or a quarter of an eye, nobody denies him such a right: all one is entitled to require—and here is the whole problem—is that the quarter eye is all the lady needs *in the given case.*" *Art and Scholasticism* (New York, 1937), 28. Here indeed is the whole problem. Aristotle said, "Not to know that a hind has no horns is a less serious matter than to paint it inartistically." *Poetics*, XXV, 5.

11. *Discoveries*, Maurice Castelain, ed. (Paris, 1906), 139. Jonson translates from Heinsius.

12. *Ariosto, Shakespeare and Corneille* (London, 1920), 146–47.

Textual Meaning and Authorial Meaning

Monroe C. Beardsley

In 1946 Monroe Beardsley and W. K. Wimsatt published "The Intentional Fallacy," an essay that attacked the very basis of genetic criticism by arguing that an author's intended meaning was not the same thing as the poem's meaning. This essay has become one of the most famous modern critical statements, and one of the most contested. Here, more than twenty years later, Beardsley discusses one of the chief contestants, E. D. Hirsch's Validity in Interpretation (1967), a book that included Hirsch's "Objective Interpretation" and expanded the arguments of that earlier essay. Fundamentally, Beardsley seeks to establish the difference between "textual meaning" and "authorial meaning," for unless a literary text has a determinate meaning independent of what its author may have intended it to mean, formal criticism lacks a firm foundation. Conversely, if the case for a stable and independent textual meaning can be made, formal criticism becomes not only possible but necessary, for in a poem, as the formalist defines it, the textual meaning is the only meaning that matters.

"IT IS A TASK FOR THE HISTORIAN OF CULTURE," Hirsch begins his first chapter, "to explain why there has been in the past four decades a heavy and largely victorious assault on the sensible belief that a text means what its author meant" (p. 1).* The prior task, of course, is to show that the belief is sensible, if that can be done. This belief, the burden of Hirsch's chapter, is what I want to challenge. It is basic to the whole book; it is subversive of many widespread assumptions. It is therefore important to examine.

The Hirsch thesis can conveniently be referred to as the Identity Thesis: that what a literary work means is identical to what its author meant in composing it. A text has "to represent *somebody's* meaning"—and who has a better claim than the author to be "the determiner of the text's meaning" (p. 3)? Hirsch insists upon "the determinant power of the authorial will that is required in order to make the [linguistic] signs represent *something*" (p. 68).

The issue over the Identity Thesis must be very sharply and clearly posed. The question is not whether the text's meaning and the author's meaning can coincide—i.e., be very similar. Certainly they can. The question is not whether the text's meaning is often adequate evidence of the author's meaning. Certainly it often is. The question is whether they are one and the same thing. If they are, it follows, as Hirsch argues, that when the literary interpreter interprets a text, what he is really doing is discovering what the author meant in composing it. And from that proposition follow various consequences about the kinds of evidence that are relevant to

---

---

*Page numbers in parentheses refer to E. D. Hirsch, Jr., *Validity in Interpretation* (New Haven, Conn.: Yale University Press, 1967).—ED.

interpretation and decisive in validating (i.e., confirming) an interpretation.

I

As I make them out, Hirsch gives two arguments for identifying textual meaning with authorial meaning. Both have a reductio-ad-absurdum form. Both raise fundamental questions.

The first argument can be summarized in this way: If textual meaning is not identical to authorial meaning, then there is no ("determinate") textual meaning—which is absurd.

The steps in the argument are these:

Almost any word sequence can, under the conventions of language, legitimately represent more than one complex of meaning. A word sequence means nothing in particular until somebody either means something by it or understands something from it (p. 4).

A determinate verbal meaning requires a determining will. Meaning is not made determinate simply by virtue of its being represented by a determinate sequence of words. Obviously any brief word sequence could represent quite different complexes of verbal meaning, and the same is true of long word sequences, though it is less obvious. . . . Unless one particular complex of meaning is *willed* (no matter how "rich" or "various" it might be), there would be no distinction between what an author does mean by a word sequence and what he could mean by it. Determinacy of verbal meaning requires an act of will (pp. 46–47).

Hence Hirsch's "provisional" definition of "verbal meaning" (i.e., the meaning of a text):

Verbal meaning is whatever someone has willed to convey by a particular sequence of linguistic signs and which can be conveyed (shared) by means of those linguistic signs (p. 31).

The statement that "Almost any word sequence can, under the conventions of language, legitimately represent more than one complex of meaning" is Hirsch's postulate of the "indeterminacy" of possible meaning. And the first thing to be said about it, I think, is that it is a considerable exaggeration.[1]

One kind of extreme case might be a button found in the street, reading "Vote for Senator Kennedy." Shorn of any larger context, this text provides no way of determining which of the two Senators it refers to. So we can say it has two possible referents, but no actual one. A great many comparatively short and colloquial texts and utterances may be indeterminate in one respect or another—though none of them can be indeterminate in *all* respects, and therefore every one of them can at least be partially interpreted without any information about is authorial meaning. But surely we can find plenty of counterexamples to the indeterminacy postulate. Take one of Hirsch's own examples: a man's remark, "Nothing pleases me so much as the Third Symphony of Beethoven" (p. 48). No doubt we can think of a lot of questions that his single remark does not answer. But what is indeterminate about it? Hirsch suggests that it is indeterminate because the speaker's friend can reply, "Does it please you more than a swim in the sea on a hot day?" Of course, the friend is interested in discovering what the man was trying to say, or thought he had said: whether he was mentally comparing the symphony with other musical compositions, other works of art, or pleasures in general. But clearly the friend is not asking for a removal of any indeterminacy in the original remark. (Indeed, the remark must be pretty determinate, or we could not see that it is flatly self-contradictory—since *something* must please the speaker as much as the *Eroica*, namely the *Eroica* itself.) The friend is in fact asking for further information about the speaker's attitude. The original remark is less *informative* than if the speaker had said: "No other symphony pleases me as much as Beethoven's Third," but it is no less *determinate*.

There is always, of course, the familiar phenomenon of ambiguity. But the more complicated a text, the more difficult it becomes (in general) to devise two disparate and incompatible readings that are equally faithful to it. Hirsch denies this. His main example in the text, Donne's "Valediction: Forbidding Mourning," does not convince me. The other main example, which originally appeared in his *PMLA* article, . . . is the Lucy poem, "A slumber did my spirit seal." It is an interesting case, and deserves discussion. Hirsch quotes two irreconcilable interpretations: (1) Cleanth Brooks' view that "[the poet] attempts to suggest something of the lover's agonized shock at the loved one's present lack of motion—of his response to her utter and horrible inertness;" and (2) F. W. Bateson's view that "the final impression the poem leaves is not of two contrasting moods, but of a single mood mounting to a climax in the pantheistic magnificence of the last two lines." Hirsch claims that "both the cited interpretations are permitted by the text" (p. 228). Thus the only way to resolving the issue is for the interpreter to turn to the "stance" of the author, noting the biographical fact that in 1799 Wordsworth was a pantheist (pp. 239–40). Then he will decide that the meaning of the poem is (approximately) what Bateson ascribes to it.

Now, it seems to me that if in fact the two interpretations were equally coherent with the text, we would simply have to say that the poem is radically ambiguous. But the case is contrived. For Brooks' reading is (uncharacteristically) distorted. "Part of the effect," he says, "resides in the fact that a dead lifelessness is suggested more sharply by an object's being whirled about by something else . . ." But Lucy is not whirled, she is "rolled." Brooks speaks of "the girl's falling back into the clutter of things"—but trees do not make a clutter, and they are not "lifeless." He simply substitutes words with connotations quite absent from the poem, and builds his "horrible image" out of them. Lucy has indeed "become involved in the sublime processes of nature," as Bateson says: she is more than the "thing" she was.

So I would argue that this text is not indeterminate on the crucial points, and can be interpreted without recourse to the author's "stance." But if Hirsch cannot make his postulate of (practically) universal indeterminacy stick in this chosen example, it seems fair to conclude that examples of radically indeterminate poems are not all that easy to come by.

But even if they were, as I have said, we would simply have to call them ambiguous. And an ambiguous text doesn't become any less ambiguous just because its author *wills* one of the possible meanings. Will as he will, he cannot will away ambiguity. There is, in fact, something odd about the notion of "willing" a meaning. It's almost as though we could order someone to

"Say 'cat' and mean *dog*." Can one do that? How does one do it? True, I can say, "Vote for Senator Kennedy!" and be thinking of Edward Kennedy, when I could have uttered the same words and thought of Robert Kennedy. But if I say "Kennedy" and think of Edward Kennedy, do I thereby make "Kennedy" in that utterance mean *Edward Kennedy*? That seems quite impossible.

The fundamental error, as I see it, in Hirsch's account of verbal meaning is summed up in his statement, quoted above, that "A determinate verbal meaning requires a determining will." My position is, rather, that texts acquire determinate meaning through the interactions of their words without the intervention of an authorial will. If the determinate meaning of a text is produced by the transformation of possible meanings into an actual meaning, this transformation is generated by the possibilities (the Leibnizian compossibilities) themselves; it neither requires nor can be helped by an authorial act of will.

Hirsch's second argument may be summarized in this way: If textual meaning is not identical to authorial meaning, then there can be no standards of "validity" in interpretation—which is absurd.

One of the main themes of Hirsch's book is that interpretations can be "genuine knowledge" (p. viii), that they can be true or false, well-confirmed ("validated") or disconfirmed. In this issue, I am completely on his side. Like him, I would seek a theory of literary interpretation that makes interpretation a legitimate cognitive enterprise. But I deny the consequences that he immediately draws:

> For, once the author had been ruthlessly banished as the determiner of his text's meaning, it very gradually appeared that no adequate principle existed for judging the validity of an interpretation. By an inner necessity the study of "what a text says" became the study of what it says to an individual critic (p. 3).

> To banish the original author as the determiner of meaning was to reject the only compelling normative principle that could lend validity to an interpretation (p. 15).

I hold that there is no such "inner necessity" and that we are not limited to Hirsch's two alternatives: either that a valid interpretation is one that corresponds to the authorial meaning or that there is no distinction between a valid and an invalid interpretation.

Evidently the constructive answer to Hirsch's second argument would be a detailed exhibition of a third alternative: an interpretive procedure that is neither intentionalistic nor relativistic. Instead, and less ambitiously, I propose merely to call up reminders of some familiar propositions which, together, could be developed into a satisfactory rebuttal.

First, to go back for a moment to Hirsch's definition of "verbal meaning": if we leave out the element of "will," which has nothing to do with verbal meaning, we are left with "a particular sequence of linguistic signs" and a meaning "which can be conveyed (shared) by means of those linguistic signs." This suggests a recognition of the true nature of verbal meaning: that it consists in a capacity or potentiality of some kind. However, the definition is far from coming to grips with the nature of that capacity or its conditions. Roughly speaking, to know the meaning of a word is to know how to use it in the performance of linguistic acts: in such acts as asserting, promising, threatening, commanding. And to know how to use it is to be able to use it in accordance with rules that govern its use in a certain speech community. So the first point is that some sort of rule-governed behavior is essential to the very existence of meaning, and therefore one broad condition of valid interpretation is that it be in accordance with the rules governing the words that are being interpreted.

Second, once we learn rules of language use, we have all we need for interpreting at least the plain meaning of an indefinite number of utterances, without inquiring into anyone else's acts of will—in the same way we can discover (without asking) that four people at a table are playing bridge, if we know the rules of that game and observe the way they proceed. I don't understand why Hirsch attacks "the so-called intentional fallacy and, more generally, the doctrine of semantic autonomy" as resting on "the concept of a public consensus" (p. 12), and adds that "the idea of a public meaning sponsored not by the author's intention but by a public consensus is based upon a fundamental error of observation and logic" (p. 13). If the idea is that every reader of every poem will immediately agree, of course there is no such "public consensus." But there is no common language at all unless people are playing the same "language game" according to many of the same rules: as that "cow" is the name of an animal, that promises refer to future actions, that "Hello" is a greeting, not a farewell, etc. And the concerted following of such rules builds "public meanings."

Third, the crux of the validity problem (it seems to me) comes when so much has been conceded, and we consider just those subtle poetic meanings that give rise to the conflicts of interpretation (e.g., the pantheism in Wordsworth, if it is indeed contained in the connotations of words like "rolled round in earth's diurnal course"). For it can be claimed that here the rules run out—that everything beyond syntax and dictionary senses is subjective. This is the line where the battle for "validity in interpretation" is to be fought. And two things are wanted in my view. (1) We need to show how the rough account of meaning just given can be extended to such poetic meanings as the connotations of "rolled," so that these meanings will not be relegated to the category of "psychological associations." (2) We need to show how in interpreting a metaphor (say), we are constrained by rules of procedure that are widely followed, though unverbalized, so that the question whether we are following these rules correctly or incorrectly can be raised—and answered, within certain limits. All this would not reduce literary interpretation to anything like cost accounting, of course; it would, however, give it the sort of cognitive status that Hirsch is after.

II

The Identity Thesis can be conclusively disproved by the following three arguments.

1. Some texts that have been formed without the agency of an author, and hence without authorial meaning, nevertheless have a meaning, and can be interpreted. For example, certain

kinds of verbal mistake: the following comes from the Portland *Oregonian*, by way of the *New Yorker:*

> "It showed that there is at least one officer on the Portland police force who had not seen Officer Olsen drunk," Apley quietly observed.
>
> In contrast to Apley, Jensen argued like a man filled with righteous indigestion.

Here there *is* no "authorial will," since the final phrase is inadvertent; yet the phrase is very intelligible. When Hart Crane wrote "Thy Nazarene and tender eyes," a printer's error transformed it into "Thy Nazarene and tinder eyes"; but Crane let the accident version stand as better.[2] Then there are poems composed by computers:

> While life reached evilly through empty faces
>   While space flowed slowly o'er idle bodies
> And stars flowed evilly on vast men
>   No passion smiled.[3]

Here one might claim that there is something like a hovering "authorial will," expressed in the instructions of the programmer; but the instructions were general, and the poem is a particular new composition of words. It has meaning, but nothing was meant by anyone.

There are textual meanings without authorial meanings. Therefore textual meaning is not identical to authorial meaning.

2. The meaning of a text can change after its author has died. But the author cannot change his meaning after he has died. Therefore, the textual meaning is not identical to the authorial meaning.

I do not know how to make the force of this argument any plainer. Hirsch, in purporting to reply to it, states the argument in a confused form ("The meaning of a text changes—even for the author," p. 6), so that his refutation becomes question-begging. "When critics speak of changes in meaning, they are usually referring to changes in significance" (p. 9), says Hirsch, appealing to one of his favorite distinctions. Not so. The *OED* furnishes an abundance of evidence that individual words and idioms acquire new meanings and lose old meanings as time passes; these changes can in turn produce changes of meaning in sentences in which the words appear. I cite, as example, these lines

from Mark Akenside, *The Pleasures of Imagination* (II, 311–313), referring to "the Sovereign Spirit of the world":

> Yet, by immense benignity inclin'd
> To spread about him that primeval joy
> Which fill'd himself, he rais'd his plastic arm . . .

I say that "plastic arm" has acquired a new meaning in the twentieth century, and this is now its dominant one (though the older one is not dead). Consequently the line in which it occurs has also acquired a new meaning.

We are forced, then, to distinguish between what these lines meant in 1744 and what they mean in 1968. Of course we can inquire into both meanings, if we will; but the point is that they are two distinct inquiries. And if today's textual meaning of the line cannot be identified with any authorial meaning, it follows that textual meanings are not the same thing as authorial meanings.

3. A text can have meanings that its author is not aware of. Therefore, it can have meanings that its author did not intend. Therefore, textual meaning is not identical to authorial meaning.

Again, Hirsch purports to deal with this sort of argument, but states it in a confused and conveniently self-refuting form: "The author often does not know what he means" (p. 19). But my argument is that the author often does not know what his *work* means, and, therefore, the work's meaning is not the same thing as his meaning.

I suppose it is not necessary to give examples to support my first premise, especially as Hirsch concedes that it is true. He himself gives the example (p. 21) of a critic pointing out to an author that he had emphasized a similarity by parallel construction. "What this example illustrates," he says, "is that there are usually components of an author's intended meaning that he is not conscious of." Thus it is my second proposition that he denies:

> It is not possible to mean what one does not mean, though it is very possible to mean what one is not conscious of meaning. That is the entire issue in the argument based on authorial ignorance. That a man may not be conscious of all that he means is no more remarkable than that he may not be conscious of all that he does (p. 22).

This analogy gives the case away. If the psychological act of "meaning" something (supposing that there is such a psychological act) were like the overt physical act of *doing* something, then it *would* be possible (logically speaking) to mean unconsciously. The only way one can mean something unconsciously is to say something that (textually) means something one is not aware of.

In order to identify authorial meaning and textual meaning, Hirsch is compelled to extend the former to include some dubious entities. Indeed he shifts his position uneasily in the course of a key paragraph (p. 22). First he says there can be unconscious meanings. Then he is reminded of his own repeated view that "meaning is an affair of consciousness," so he says "there is a difference between consciousness and self-consciousness." This suggests another position: that the author in the above example was somehow conscious of his similarity-emphasis, but not *self*-conscious. Unsatisfied with this, Hirsch immediately introduces a "distinction between attended and unattended meanings": the author *meant* his similarity-emphasis, but somehow neglected to attend to it until the critic pointed it out.

All these verbal maneuvers are unconvincing. Meaning (in the psychological sense) *is* an "affair of consciousness," and those textual meanings the author was not aware of—has never been aware of—could not have been intended by him. Therefore they cannot be identified with authorial meanings.

The same problem returns in Hirsch's second chapter, where he discusses "implications" of texts. The problem is what to do about the numerous suggestions and intimations that a text may have, quite independently of what its author has "willed to convey" by it. You may recall what Senator Dodd of Connecticut said to the senators who investigated the tax-free personal funds he obtained from four "testimonial dinners" that were advertised as political fund-raising events: "If there is anything more common to Connecticut than nutmeg it is testimonial affairs, and they go on there every week." He certainly did not *will* to suggest that his testimonial dinners were as phony as the celebrated wooden nutmegs sold by the old Yankee peddlers, who thus gave Connecticut its nickname. But that's what he did suggest. Hirsch's solution of the problem is not the simple and sensible one of admitting that textual meaning can go beyond authorial meaning; instead, he tries to stretch the concept of *will* far enough so that whatever the text *does* mean can be said to be "willed" by the author—however unwittingly.

Hirsch defends his extended notion of will with ingenuity. But consider his main argument.

"It is possible," says Hirsch, "to will an et cetera without in the least being aware of all the individual members that belong to it" (p. 49). True enough. But is it relevant? I can ask someone to bring me all the books on the top shelf without knowing the names of any of the books. But then I have not asked for any particular book. Suppose *Huckleberry Finn* is on the top shelf and is brought to me—that doesn't mean that I asked for *Huckleberry Finn*. Similarly, I can agree to stand behind all of the implications of my poem, without knowing what the implications are. But if my poem turns out to have a particular implication that I was not aware of, it does not follow that I willed that particular implication. Whatever is unwitting is unwilled.

III

Though textual meaning is not reducible to authorial meaning, it does not automatically follow that the rest of Hirsch's enterprise is misguided. If these were identical, then certainly the task of the literary interpreter would be to get at the authorial meaning. If they are not identical, it follows that there are two distinct interpretation-tasks or inquiries: (1) to discover the textual meaning, and (2) to discover the authorial meaning. But Hirsch could still maintain that the proper function of the literary interpreter is the latter, even if it is not the only function that he *can* perform.

I do not, of course, want to deny that there are many practical occasions on which an interpreter's task is precisely to try to discover authorial meaning: what the writer or speaker had in mind and wanted us (in Hirsch's term) to "share." If there is a difficulty in reading a will or a love-letter, or in grasping an oral promise or instruction, our primary concern is with authorial meaning. So if there is ambiguity or the possibility of misspeaking, we want to correct it, if we can. To do this, we may avail ourselves of such evidence as fuller explanations by the author himself, if we can find him; and information about his actions (as when the testator's intentions about a particular beneficiary are not plain, but his probable intentions may be supported by information about his previous behavior toward that person).

All this seems beyond dispute. But I hold that the case is different when we turn to *literary* interpretation. The proper task of the literary interpreter is to interpret textual meaning. I support this claim by two arguments, one drawn from considerations of inductive logic, the other from aesthetic considerations.

The first argument involves the well-known dispute about the "accessibility" of the author. Hirsch discusses this question in his own way, and his main point is unobjectionable: there are no sound grounds for general skepticism. Certainly, in many cases, textual meaning is adequate evidence of authorial meaning: once we have understood what the *text* means, we can legitimately infer that that is what the *author* meant—because he presumably could read what he had written, and he had the power to alter or cancel it. But there is a special and important sense in which the authors of many literary texts are not accessible: they cannot be appealed to *independently* of the text in order to settle *disputes* about interpretation. Therefore, if the literary interpreter's proper task were to get at authorial meaning, and if (as Hirsch holds) this involves choosing among alternative interpretations, there would be many literary works that could not be interpreted, since no evidence independent of the text is available. But all literary works can be interpreted, at least to some extent—even those that are utterly anonymous. Therefore, the interpretation of a literary work is not the discovery of authorial meaning.

This becomes evident when we consider the conditions under which authorial meaning can be determined. In the case of the *Eroica*-admirer mentioned above, we can say to him, "You're talking loosely. Surely you don't want to say what you've just said, so explain yourself further." Such words cannot be addressed to Milton or Shakespeare. If two interpreters come up with different interpretations of a poem they can compare their interpretations, and test them against the poem. But they can seldom compare their interpretations with the author's own interpretation of his work, for few such authorial interpretations exist. It is in this sense that the literary authorial meaning is often "inaccessible." Not always, of course: living poets can still be written to, and may reply. Romantic poets have left behind no dearth of evidence of their feelings and attitudes on several subjects, and this can legitimately be used to support inferences about *authorial* meaning in disputed cases. But for authorial meaning in numerous cases, no evidence besides the work itself can be forthcoming. That is one of the reasons why I conclude that the *general* and *essential* task of the literary interpreter cannot be the discovery of authorial meaning.

The foregoing argument is not conclusive, of course. One could still maintain that even where there is no independent evidence of authorial meaning—no recourse but the text itself—the literary interpreter is properly concerned with the textual meaning not for its own sake, but only for the authorial meaning it discloses. With or without independent evidence of it, authorial meaning remains the proper object of literary interpretation. I hope my second argument will dispose of this view.

What is the primary purpose of literary interpretation? It is, I would say, to help readers approach literary works from the aesthetic point of view, i.e., with an interest in actualizing their aesthetic value. The work is an object, capable (presumably) of affording aesthetic satisfaction. The problem is to know what is there to be responded to; and the literary interpreter helps us to discern what is there, so that we can respond to it more fully.

Now the aesthetic value in which we take an interest (when our interest is aesthetic) is something that arises out of the ingredients of the poem itself: the ways its verbal parts—its words and sentences—work together to make something fresh and novel emerge. The poem, the verbal structure and texture, has to work on us. It works by manipulating our understanding of parts to make us experience a whole that contains something not in the parts. The individual words, in combination, make suddenly a metaphor, and language means something there that is meant nowhere else. The names and verbs strung together concresce into a story, with dramatic tensions and resolutions. Regional qualities play on the surface—wit, or tenderness, or elation. Themes and theses rear up to be contemplated.

It is the language of the poem, with its meanings, that does this work upon us. It is the language which is the object of our attention, and which we finally want to understand—with the help, where needed, of the literary interpreter. It is not his proper task, then (I argue), to draw our attention off to the psychological or biographical states of the author—as would be suitable if we were approaching the work from a historical point of view—but to keep our eye on the textual meaning. For it is there that the aesthetic process occurs.

This second argument is somewhat condensed and no doubt it takes for granted quite a few assumptions about art and aesthetics (some of which I have defended in turn elsewhere[4]). But even if this argument, too, is inconclusive, I hope it points in the right direction. Mainly, I want to show that if we once pose the question, Which of the two meanings is the proper object of literary interpretation? this can be satisfactorily answered only by considering the function of literary interpretation, the nature of literature, and the nature of aesthetic value.

I confess to qualms about the stiffness and formality of my purported demonstration. Why can we not, it might be asked, supplement textual meaning with touches of authorial meaning, when the latter enriches the former? Sometimes a fact about the author, of which the text itself gives not the slightest hint, adds something aesthetically valuable to the work, if we are permitted to take it as part of the work. Why not, then, admit it? For example, suppose we discovered that Donne's "Valediction" was written for his wife, and was in fact presented to her on some particular occasion. There is no clear indication in the text that the speaker is addressing his wife (only the suggestion that their "joys" have a sacred sanction, and the reference to "home"). But suppose we find the poem better if, on the biographical warrant, we add this meaning to the poem and say that the speaker and his beloved are married. What would be the harm in this?

It seems to me that there might in many cases (I don't insist on this one) be no harm, and the importation might be allowable. But notice what we would be doing: we would be stretching the weak intimations in the text to make them reveal the speaker as a spouse. We would be using the biographical fact not *qua* evidence of authorial meaning, but as an aid in reading something into the work. A tight, complex poem can probably absorb a certain amount of this kind of construction or reconstruction. And, after all, the boundaries of textual meaning are not all that sharp. Some things are definitely said in the poem, and cannot be overlooked; others are suggested, as we find on careful reading; others are gently hinted, and whatever methods of literary interpretation we use, we can never establish them decisively as "in" or "out." Therefore whatever comes from without, but yet can be taken as an extension of what is surely in, may be admissible. It merely makes a larger whole.

But this concession will not justify extensive borrowings from biography. Suppose we read a dull poem, and then its author tells us that he meant it to be ironic. We can try to read it as ironic—try to import the irony from authorial meaning into textual meaning. And no doubt, as Hirsch would say, our willingness to cooperate may lead us to find clues to irony in the text itself. But if the alleged irony remains unsupported by the text, even after further analysis, then it cannot be experienced as a quality *of the poem*. It is as if the poem merely told us it was ironic, but did not succeed in *being* ironic. We would still not be enjoying irony aesthetically—any more than we would be enjoying drama aesthetically if we watched two actors sit quietly on a stage holding up placards stating that they hate each other. The point of the slogan "Back to the text" is that there is where the gold is.

Notes

1. George Dickie, in his review of Hirsch's book in the *Journal of Aesthetics and Art Criticism*, suggests

that Hirsch is in danger of an infinite regress. For if (nearly) every text is indeterminate, and its indeterminacy can be removed only by another text (say, a statement by the author), which is in turn indeterminate, etc.—then how is interpretation possible? But if interpretation must in the end rest on some "semantically autonomous" utterance, why can't that be the poem itself?

2. I owe this example to my colleague, Samuel Hynes.

3. Wilbur Cross, "Machine Miltons," *New York Times Magazine*, December 4, 1966, p. 59.

4. *Aesthetics* (New York, 1958); "On the Creation of Art," in *Aesthetic Inquiry*, ed. Beardsley and Schueller (Belmont, California, 1967).

Application

Historical Criticism and the Interpretation of Shakespeare

Robert Ornstein

Despite the similarity of their titles, Ornstein's emphasis is almost the reverse of Woodhouse's. While Woodhouse praises the ability of historical criticism to correct misreadings, Ornstein notes that the historical perspective is quite as apt to produce them. Claiming that our moral apprehension of drama is "an aesthetic experience which depends upon the immediately created impression of character, thought, and action," Ornstein argues that this experience will override any contradicting evidence that scholarship may adduce. In his analysis of the Closet scene in Hamlet, *he undertakes to show how Shakespeare manages to transvalue actions that, to an "objective" and "rational" view, must show a "brutal callousness." He finds the answer in Shakespeare's ability to make us identify with Hamlet. This is, of course, exactly what Eleanor Prosser complains of, and Ornstein's essay looks like a direct counterstatement to Prosser's argument, though it was actually written some years earlier. "We accept the morality of blood revenge instantaneously and unquestioningly because Hamlet the idealist does," declares Ornstein. "Indeed, nothing that we learn about Renaissance attitudes toward revenge can alter that assumption." Ultimately, Ornstein argues that the apparent opposition between scholarly fact and aesthetic impression is a false opposition, for "the refined, disciplined aesthetic impression* is *the fact upon which the interpretation of Shakespeare must ultimately rest; that is to say, all scholarly evidence outside the text of the play is related to it by inferences which must themselves be supported by aesthetic impressions." In other words, though we are inclined to assume that our critical interpretations can be built on scholarly*

Reprinted by permission from *Shakespeare Quarterly* 10 (1959): 3–9. Copyright © 1959 by the Shakespeare Association of America, Inc.

facts, in reality what we will accept as relevant fact depends on our critical interpretations, that is, on our reading of artistic intention that is "fully realized in the play and can be grasped only from the play."

THERE IS NO DOUBT THAT SHAKESPEARE SCHOLarship has advanced far beyond the Romantic criticism which confused literature and life. Yet it is possible that future generations will in their turn smile at the naïveté of some of our Shakespeare studies, particularly those concerned with the ethics of the plays. In recent decades the definition of Shakespeare's moral attitudes has been viewed as a problem in the history of ideas that can be solved by the accumulation of objective factual evidence. At best such an approach oversimplifies a complex aesthetic problem; at worst it ignores the essential realities of dramatic art. Professor E. E. Stoll suggested some years ago that we cannot intelligently discuss Shakespeare's characters unless we understand how the impression of character is created in poetic drama. I would suggest, in addition, that we cannot accurately interpret Shakespeare's moral intention unless we understand how moral judgments are translated into the artifice of poetic drama and apprehended by an audience.

It has been too frequently assumed that the moral interpretation of Shakespeare is the province of the scholarly researcher, who relates the thought and action of a play to the commonplace political, moral, and religious beliefs of the Elizabethan age. But the same assumptions about a dramatist and his cultural milieu which lead scholars to interpret Shakespeare by means of La Primaudaye, Charron, and Coeffeteau should lead us to interpret *A Streetcar Named Desire* by reference to Norman Vincent Peale, a latter-day ethical psychologist no less influential than his Renaissance counterparts. To be sure, Dr. Peale sheds some light on the tragedy of Blanche Du Bois: she has no mustard seeds, no "Attitude of Gratitude"; she might possibly have been saved had she been more of a positive thinker. We would not be surprised, moreover, to find striking similarities between Mitch's views on marriage and motherhood and those of Dr. Peale. Still we must insist that Tennessee Williams' view of life is not Dr. Peale's. We must distinguish between popular and intellectual levels of thought when discussing the cultural milieu of any dramatist. And we must recognize the difference between a moral intuition expressed in art and the traditional platitudes of systematized ethics.

That scholarly research enriches our understanding of Shakespeare is undeniable; that it affords a unique revelation of the meaning of the plays is debatable. The very nature of Elizabethan dramaturgy—the immediate plunge into dramatic action—demands that the moral apprehension of character be immediate. Motivation may be complex, subterranean, even inscrutable. The psychological depths of a character like Iago may be dark indeed; but we penetrate to that darkness in a very few moments. In their moral natures the characters of Shakespearian tragedy are infinitely more transparent than the men and women we live among.

The art that creates this moral transparency is not easily analyzed, but it is an art—a mastery of language and of living speech, not a mastery of philosophy or theology. We apprehend a philosopher's moral vision intellectually, a dramatist's aesthetically. In the most prurient love scenes of Fletcher's plays, for example, there is no rational confusion of moral values. We do not accuse Fletcher of tampering with moral categories but of failing to translate a rhetorical morality into the presentation of character. We are *told* that adultery is evil but it appears attractive; we listen to moral sentiments even while our erotic impulses are aroused. Fletcher illustrates (negatively, of course) the fact that the moral apprehension of drama is an aesthetic experience which depends upon the immediately created impression of character, thought, and action. In other words, the moral judgment in art

must be translated into qualitative, affective terms; it must communicate an almost sensuous awareness of the beauty of virtue and the sordidness of vice. Biblical and theological allusions may deepen this immediate "sensuous" impression of character in action, but they cannot substitute for it if the drama is to live upon the stage.

The difference between Shakespeare and Fletcher is not that between an objective and an objectional dramatist but between one who appeals to and refines our deepest moral intuitions and one who places theatrical effect above moral perception. Although Shakespeare does not use his art to propagandize, although he does not pattern experience according to rigid formulae, he nevertheless imposes immediately on his audience's sensibility a particular moral criticism of life. In the great tragedies almost every line is calculated to elicit a specific emotional response—to shape a particular moral judgment. But the art that elicits and shapes that judgment is so sophisticated that it hides itself. We *seem* to know the moral nature of Goneril or Iago intuitively. Moreover Shakespeare's moral vision is so humane that it accords always with the empirical truths of human experience; through his eyes we see life clearly and whole.

If we turn to the Closet scene in *Hamlet*, we can see the extent to which Shakespeare's poetic and dramatic art shapes our moral responses. Consider the evidence objectively and rationally: An overwrought, passionate youth, bent upon revenge, strikes out in a blind fury at someone hidden behind the arras. He *hopes* that it will be the King, but he has no assurance that it will be, especially since he left Claudius at prayer in the preceding scene. Hamlet does not intend to kill Polonius, but at the moment he does not seem too much concerned about whom he may kill, and the preceding dialogue would lead us to believe that without Polonius' intervention he might possibly have killed his own mother. When he sees his error he is not stricken with remorse; instead he quips sardonically about Polonius' "policy," lectures to his mother on *her* guilt, and finally with a brutal callousness lugs the guts off the stage. Why do we not think of Hamlet then and thereafter as a murderer who, giving rein to his passions, dyed his hand indelibly in an innocent (or relatively innocent) man's blood? The answer is that the murder of Polonius does not disturb us because it does not disturb Hamlet; it is not near our conscience because it is not near his.

Here is a paradox that illuminates the difference between literature and life. In the ordinary world a criminal's remorse softens a spectator's condemnation while callousness and indifference to a criminal act seem chilling signs of unregeneracy. But in drama a guilty conscience may have an almost opposite effect on the spectator because conscience damns: it is the internalized moral chorus through which the dramatist and his audience contemplate the moral significance of a criminal act. It was convenient for Shakespeare that Elizabethans believed that most criminals suffer pangs of remorse, but that conventional belief does not explain the artistic function of conscience in Shakespearian tragedy. For example, the coldblooded treachery by which Richard III murders his brother should arouse a deeper moral revulsion than Macbeth's tormented and anguished decision to kill Duncan. However, just the reverse is true. The very loathing with which Macbeth contemplates his crime burns his guilt into our consciousness, while Richard's high-spirited lack of conscience temporarily suspends moral judgment and allows a moral holiday in which we can momentarily enjoy his outwitting of those who would play the same deadly, amoral game. When a pattern of retribution begins to impose itself on Richard's successes, then the signs of gnawing conscience in Richard and his henchmen dissipate the mood of melodramatic farce and engage a deeper moral response to Richard's villainy.

To return to the Closet scene, I would suggest that were Hamlet more sensitive about Polonius' death we would think the worse of him. The very accusation of his conscience would brand him a murderer in our eyes. But as the scene stands, instead of contemplating his guilt in killing Polonius, Hamlet shifts his mother's attention (and our own) away from his act to Gertrude's guilt in marrying Claudius. Because the moral significance of Hamlet's act is not contemplated, we feel no bizarre incongruity when he lectures to Gertrude on ethics while Polonius' body lies at his feet. Nor do we smile sardoni-

cally when in the midst of his moral exhortation Hamlet begs forgiveness for his virtue.

I do not mean that in this crucial scene Shakespeare juggles our moral responses or that he preserves our sympathy with Hamlet by avoiding condemnation of what should be condemned. I mean rather that our moral response to this scene is a complex aesthetic experience that is influenced by the total artifice of the play. What is not near Hamlet's conscience is not near our own because he is our moral interpreter. He is the voice of ethical sensibiltiy in a sophisticated, courtly milieu; his bitter asides, which penetrate Claudius' façade of kingly virtue and propriety, initiate, so to speak, the moral action of the play. And throughout the play our identification with Hamlet's moral vision is such that we hate what he hates, admire what he admires. As centuries of Shakespeare criticism reveal, we accuse Hamlet primarily of what he accuses himself: namely, his slowness to revenge. And we accept the morality of blood revenge instantaneously and unquestioningly because Hamlet the idealist does. Indeed, nothing that we can learn about Renaissance attitudes towards revenge can alter that acceptance.

Our moral impression of Hamlet's character derives primarily from what he says rather than what he does. It is an almost intuitive awareness of the beauty, depth, and refinement of his moral nature, upon which is thrust a savage burden of revenge and of disillusion. If Shakespeare's characters are illusions created by dramatic artifice, then what we love in Hamlet is an illusion within an illusion: i.e., the suggestion of Hamlet's former self, the Hamlet whom Ophelia remembers and who poignantly reappears in the conversations with Horatio, particularly those just before the catastrophe. Through his consummate artistry Shakespeare creates within us a sympathy with Hamlet which becomes almost an act of faith—a confidence in the untouched and untouchable core of his spiritual nature. This act of faith, renewed by the great speeches throughout the play, allows us to accept Hamlet's brutality towards Ophelia, his reaction to Polonius' death, his savage refusal to kill Claudius at prayer, and his Machiavellian delight in disposing of Rosencrantz and Guildenstern. Without the memory of the great soliloquies which preceded it, our impression of the Closet scene would be vastly different. And, in fact, to attempt to define Hamlet's character by weighing his motives and actions against any system of Renaissance thought is to stage *Hamlet* morally without the Prince of Denmark: i.e., without the felt impression of Hamlet's moral nature which is created by poetic nuance.

Equally important in shaping our reaction to the Closet scene is our response to Polonius. So far as a rational moral judgment of Hamlet's "crime" is concerned, it does not matter who besides Claudius was behind the arras. Yet the audience's reaction would be vastly different if, let us say, Ophelia were the eavesdropper. Believing the worst of her, Hamlet might as callously dismiss her death, but from that moment the audience would part moral company with him. Polonius is, of course, more expendable. While we may not share Hamlet's cynical contempt, we cannot escape feeling that the foolish, doting, prying old man received the just wages of a dupe and spy; he did find it dangerous to be too busy.

Even the moralistic critic derives some satisfaction in seeing Polonius hoist with his own petard; and yet nothing which the ancient Councilor does warrants death—indeed, if eavesdropping be a mortal offense, God help the wicked! Although he snoops, pries, and carries out Claudius' plans, it is without evil purpose; there is absolutely no suggestion that he acts except for the general (and his personal) good in discovering the cause of Hamlet's melancholy. He is as ignorant of Claudius' crimes as are the bystanders who are bewildered by the final slaughter. Our "satisfaction" with Polonius' death, then, must lie outside the realm of moral philosophy; and strictly speaking it is not moral at all. By legal obligation the good citizen must inform on his neighbors' misdemeanors, but who does not despise the informer whether he is outside or within the law? To society and even to the law, the devious means are repugnant, however moral the intention. A deeply engrained "folk" morality (built up, I imagine, through centuries of police oppression) cherishes openness, candor, and directness; we realize that no

man is safe and no life secure in an atmosphere of mutual suspicion and distrust.

Thus the audience feels quite rightly that Polonius does not belong behind the arras. But one could quote a dozen Renaissance moral and political authorities who insist that a high Minister of State, entrusted with the security and well-being of a nation, has the right (nay, the duty) to go about the law, to spy and use suspect means to achieve a worthwhile end. Consider the long controversy over the Duke in *Measure for Measure*. The many essays on the play reveal that some very respectable critics see the Duke as a snooper, a meddler in other men's lives, a well-intentioned official who resorts to repugnant stratagems to achieve a moral goal. Scholars insist that this impression is mistaken and unhistorical; they quote Renaissance political, moral, and religious treatises to demonstrate that the Duke has a perfect justification for his deeds and that a Renaissance audience would not have been disturbed by what seems devious or sordid to a modern reader. Perhaps so, but let us be consistent in our criticism. If our moral judgment of the Duke is to be based, not on the immediate impression of his character but on the weight of Renaissance commonplace opinion, then the same should be true of our judgment of Polonius. Or, conversely, if a mass of carefully selected Renaissance opinions cannot obliterate our distaste for Polonius' policy, then it cannot obliterate a similar response to the Duke's policy.

I do not mean to identify Polonius and the Duke. Our response to Vincentio is far more complex because he plays a more significant and many-sided role. And if it is true, as critics argue, that the action of *Measure for Measure* proceeds on an allegorical as well as realistic level, then our apprehension of the Duke's dramatic role must be different from that of Polonius. But we cannot escape from the immediate impression of the Duke's character by defining his role analogically. The symbolic vision which allegory embodies in art cannot dictate our response to the immediate realities of life or to the image of life presented on a stage; it can only build upon that response, illuminating the shared qualities of "thing" and idea—the analogical relationships between character and concept—which allow the mind to move freely between the realistic and symbolic levels of action. When the mind of the audience cannot move freely in this way because the analogical relationships are obscurely, ingeniously, or casuistically contrived, then the allegory is decadent. When the symbolic vision seeks to identify the devious and the Divine, then the allegory is immoral.

Consider another instructive parallel, this time between Hamlet and Othello. We are told that Othello is damned to everlasting torments because he murdered innocence and did not, according to strict theology, repent. If so, what shall we say of Hamlet? He does not strangle Ophelia, but he shocks and torments her, humiliates her before the Court, suggests that she is and treats her like a whore, murders her father and thus drives her insane. Othello's crimes against Desdemona have at least the extenuating circumstance of Iago's diabolical malice. Hamlet's brutality towards Ophelia is the product of his own hypersensitive imagination and the sexual nausea produced by the shock of his mother's infidelity. At her funeral he shouts melodramatically that he loved her but offers no apology for his treatment of her and recognizes no guilt. How shall Othello be damned and flights of angels sing Hamlet to his rest?[1]

Needless to say, we feel that the endings of *Hamlet* and *Othello* are inevitable and "right." This is so, not because we can by scholarly documentation "prove" that Hamlet was inspired always by moral or religious motives and that Othello fell beyond repentance, but because Shakespeare emphasizes the unsullied core of Hamlet's goodness (the exquisite moral sensibility temporarily o'erthrown) while he emphasizes the degradation of Othello's noble spirit. He shapes different judgments of character by creating different artistic perspectives. Like Polonius, Ophelia is a minor character; Hamlet's "crimes" against her are placed in proportion and overshadowed by the larger moral action of the play. Desdemona is the heroine; Othello's crime against her *is* the moral action of the play.

To put it differently, in *Hamlet* and *Othello* as in *Lear* Shakespeare presents heroes who are sinned against as well as sinning, who may be pitied as victims and condemned as wrongdoers. He is interested in dramatic situations which although unambiguous admit diametrically opposite moral emphases. In *Othello* his emphasis is upon the brutality of the destructive impulse. As we watch the unsuspecting Desdemona prepare for bed, our hearts steel against sympathy for the "abused" Othello. After this knowledge of Desdemona's purity, innocence, and love, what forgiveness for Othello? But without altering either his characterizations or the incidents of his fable, Shakespeare might have created a very different judgment of Othello's deed. Were the scene mentioned above eliminated, were the focus in the last scenes shifted to Iago's sin (to the crime against Othello's innocence) we might accept as inevitable and "right" a very different final impression; we might look upon the tormented Othello as one who deserves more pity than blame. A theological gloss of Othello's last speeches cannot tell us how to judge Othello nor can we discover by this means the particular moral emphasis which Shakespeare creates through the total design of his play. One doubts, moreover, that the mystery of Hamlet's "innocence" can be solved either by Renaissance theology or moral philosophy. The codes which govern society cannot easily admit what an audience knows during a performance of *Hamlet:* namely, that a man's spirit may be superior not only to his fate but even to his own acts.

Thus while scholarship can make the interpretation of Shakespeare more scientific, it cannot make of interpretation a science based upon factual information. The dichotomy of scholarly fact and aesthetic impression is finally misleading because the refined, disciplined aesthetic impression *is* the fact upon which the interpretation of Shakespeare must ultimately rest; that is to say, all scholarly evidence outside the text of a play is related to it by inferences which must themselves be supported by aesthetic impressions.[2] The attempt of historical criticism to recapture (in so far as it is possible) Shakespeare's own artistic intention is, or should be, the goal of all responsible criticism. But we must insist that that intention is fully realized in the play and can be grasped only from the play. A study of Renaissance thought may guide us to what is central in Shakespeare's drama; it may tell us why Shakespeare's vision of life is what it is. But we can apprehend his vision only as aesthetic experience. When the long history of Shakespeare studies indicates that certain characterizations are ambiguous, scholarly information cannot erase those ambiguities, for they arise either from detached, ironic, or ambivalent conceptions of character or from failures to translate univocal judgments into effective artifice. To announce that Ulysses' speech on order and degree is a great statement of Elizabethan commonplaces is merely to accent the irony of its dramatic context and to define more sharply the problem which the critical faculty alone can solve.

There will always be a welcome variety in the interpretation of Shakespeare. And there will always be eccentric interpretations, but they will not long withstand the assault of common sense, the sensitive and scrupulous examination of the text, and the insistence that Shakespeare's art is dramatic in intention—created for theatrical performance. Historical criticism has, of course, eliminated eccentric interpretations, but it has also, in some respects, fostered them by substituting completely unliterary standards for the traditional standards of critical perceptivity. We need now to redefine what is eccentric in interpretation by first redefining the legitimate criteria of critical judgment and the proper relationship between scholarship and criticism in Shakespeare studies. Only through the cooperation of scholarship and criticism will we arrive at an understanding of Shakespeare's art that precludes the dogmatism of the learned and the uninformed.

Notes

1. I do not argue that Horatio's exquisite farewell to his Prince proves the blessed state of Hamlet's immortal soul. On the contrary, unless a character were literally God's spy he would scarcely have authoritative knowledge of the Divine Judgment. We cannot dogmatize about the function of imagery drawn from popular religious beliefs in Shakespeare's plays, but we can demand consistency in critical methods. If the imagery of hell in Othello's last speeches indicates his damnation, then the apocalyptic references at the end of *Lear* ("Is this the promised end?/Or image of that *horror?*" [my italics]) must indicate a failure of belief in Providential Order, a sense of cosmic dissolution and disillusion.

2. How shall we decide which of the Elizabethan views of melancholy are relevant to Shakespeare's portrait of Hamlet? Certainly not every obscure and contradictory Elizabethan opinion is part of the background of the play. If we are not to stress coincidental parallels or make erroneous assumptions about Shakespeare's beliefs, the selection of scholarly evidence must be an act of critical judgment. A scholar must begin with a conception of Hamlet's character if he is to find the contemporary thought which underlay Shakespeare's dramatic portrait. Thus while scholarly documentation validates a critical impression, that documentation will be apposite and illuminating only if based upon a sensitive and perceptive reading of the text.

Moreover, unless we are to assume that Shakespeare was incapable of original insights into human nature, we cannot say that an interpretation of character is mistaken because we cannot find sanction for it in Elizabethan treatises on moral philosophy or psychology. The Romantic notion that Hamlet loses his will to action in thought may be mistaken (I think it is mistaken), but it is not mistaken simply because Elizabethan courtiers were (or were supposed to be) men of action as well as thought. Beaumont and Fletcher's Amintor and Philaster are proof that the Romantic conception of Hamlet was plausible to the Elizabethan artistic mind, if not to the compiler of courtesy books.

Application

Lycidas as Pastiche

Eugene Nassar

The formalist's concept of unity in diversity is a central concern in Eugene Nassar's reading of Lycidas. *He complains that other readers have tried to force upon the poem a unity of their own devising because they have started from preconceived ideas about "archetypes," or about Milton's religious beliefs, or about the form of the "pastoral." In this complaint he displays the formalists' distrust of generic or genetic categories because they fear these may distort our view of the unique verbal form we are trying to read. The formalists' corrective is to accept what "scholarship" has to offer, but to keep the focus sharply on the poem before us, for, as Nassar insists, "the soul of a successful poem is in its uniqueness, its contextual pattern, its complex of attitudes which is like no other; and criticism's job, which begins where scholarship leaves off, is to react to and articulate this uniqueness."*

I WAS RATHER CAVALIER IN MY REMARKS ON *Lycidas* and other works in the last chapter [Chapter 1 of original source]. I want now . . . to try to buttress those remarks. It is the premise of [this essay] that the literary work of art creates as one reads a psychological state (a complex of attitudes, the book's "tone") which can be articulated in precise and sensitive criticism.[1] This articulation is the primary aim of the critic. I have not found despite the voluminous bibliography what I feel is the unique tone, the complex of attitudes of *Lycidas*, convincingly articulated, though I do feel that that tone communicates itself to readers.[*]

To call *Lycidas* a pastiche may seem needlessly extreme, but the word serves in two ways: (1) I feel it comes closer than others to describing the structural principles in the poem, and (2) I hope it dislodges a bit some fixed ideas about the poem, such as those which focus it as conventional or archetypal in its pattern and those which see a sort of rigid logic or rigorous dialectic progressing through it.[2]

The poem, it seems to me, has no direction (nor does it need any) save that of the forward and backward movement of the mind of the Christian poet as it flops and jumps and starts, engaged in a meditation upon last things and using conventional pastorale machinery for that meditation. That machinery has some traditional sequences just as Christian apologetics has some traditional answers to conventional eschatolog-

---

*See *Milton's Lycidas: The Tradition and the Poem* (1961); excellently edited by C. A. Patrides, a collection of the best *Lycidas* essays, with a fine annotated bibliography. Scott Elledge's *Milton's Lycidas* (1966), contains substantial scholarly apparatus: poems in the pastoral tradition, contemporary remarks on elegy, biographical and historical material, and selections from commentary on the poem.

---

ical problems, but we have in *Lycidas* a very bold mind breaking patterns and returning to them at will, and finally eschewing any pattern save the fidelity to the emotional fluctuations of its own brooding.[3] The drama of this mind in action is intensely moving; its twists and turns, its a-logical transitions demonstrate a flow more psychological than conventional. The poem is quite personal and unique in its handling of conventional materials, and yet its psychological fluctuations are typical of all men's broodings. The poem is magnificent and continuous, but not because of the traditional recipes or apologetics contained in it.

To be more specific, one is not reading the poem at all, as far as I am concerned, unless one finds maddening and fascinating (not conventional) the reason the poet's mind moves, say, from the two-handed engine which kills the wicked wolf, to the flower passage, then from the flowers to the vision of the floating corpse, and then most importantly from the corpse to the exulting "weep no more, woeful shepherds." Each movement is part of a drama of the mind and it is Milton's drama, not a conventional pastoral or mythic or dialectic flow (though within each of the mind's movements are used conventional figurations to pose an attitude).

With immense impetuosity, Milton rushes in the first eighty-four lines through various responses towards death and the artistic task before him and ends with a resolution (Phoebus's) which is patently a Christian sort of answer. One feels that Milton has that answer all through the poem, Saint Peter's and the swain's being variations of it. There is little dialectic progress in the poem and no dialectic interest generated. What is interesting, what we want to know, is why Phoebus breaks in at half-line in line 76, or why Milton twice in the poem brings in his answers or resolutions only to apologize, both in line 87 ("That strain I heard was of a higher mood/But now my Oat proceeds") and in line 132 ("Return *Alpheus*, the dread voice is past,/That shrunk thy streams"), for thus breaking convention and logic. Further, why does Camus come as the third of four visitors—what is the logic of his appearing then rather than ear-

lier? Or, why does Milton break impulsively in, at lines 100–2, on Hippotade's disclaimer of blame with his own (ambiguous) answer as to where the blame lies? And then why Camus after the interruption? The abrupt transitions from image to image all through this poem seem really to come out of the logic of the emotional, not the rational life, or literary reflex.

The answers I have to offer to the questions I have posed about the poem (and so many more could be asked) are perhaps no more important than the fact that with this poem (as with so many major poems) "criticism" has not handled very often or very well the obvious large internal questions. We do no good for the young man in love with Literature by the passing off of good scholarship as good criticism.

Is not the triple assertion of the Christian answer which separate passages of lyric sadness and tragic vision expressive dramatically of a mind struggling not to doubt (rather than of various three-part patterns given us, whether Hegelian, vegetal, or rhetorical)? Are not the quick shifts in voice, imagery, and point of view expressive dramatically of a mind that will not rest in doubt (rather than of Milton's desire, as some scholars would lead one to think, to weight the poem with allusions from his reading and patterns from his models)? The poem bristles with such questions:

Alas! What boots it with incessant care 64
To tend the homely slighted Shepherds trade,
And strictly meditate the thankles Muse,
Were it not better don as others use,
To sport with *Amaryllis* in the shade,
Or with the tangles of Naera's hair?
Fame is the spur that the clear spirit doth raise 70
(That last infirmity of Noble mind)
To scorn delights, and live laborious dayes;
But the fair Guerdon when we hope to find,
And think to burst out into sudden blaze,
Comes the blind *Fury* with th' abhorred shears, 75
And slits the thin spun life. But not the praise,
Phoebus repli'ed, and touch'd my trembling ears;
Fame is no plant that grows on mortal soil,
Nor in the glistering foil
Set off to th' world, nor in broad rumour lies, 80
But lives and spreds aloft by those pure eyes,
And perfet witnes of all-judging *Jove*;
As he pronounces lastly on each deed,
Of so much fame in Heav'n expect thy meed. 84

Who is it that answers the question ending in line 69? Is not the line expressive of the mind of the poet turning back swiftly on itself? Line 71 twists in a different direction; the mind turns again in this rapid sequence in line 73. The "But" of line 76 represents another turn, this time towards a calming resolution of the whole sequence. The resolution is accompanied (or accomplished) by a switch of voice (poet to Phoebus) and tense (present to past), by theological violence (Jove all-judging, and in Heaven) and by apparent structural illogic (a resolution of sorts come too early). What is truly astounding in this short passage from a short poem is its audacity, its tone of independence from traditional controls and the vivid impression it gives of a mind in action, of a dynamic, swift, rather undirected movement, of a flow with the impelling forces more emotional than rational.

Let us examine further the mind-flow of the poet. Neptune asks the question of lines 91–2, and Hippotades brings the answer that the natural elements had nothing to do with the young man's death. The poet breaks in then with an air of impatience and anger; the style changes from reportorial to editorial, and the meaning of the answer is hard to fathom:

It was that fatall and perfidious Bark   100
Built in th' eclipse, and rigg'd with curses dark,
That sunk so low that sacred head of thine.   102

The suggestions are of an evil Nemesis (more like Satan than Atropos). There is in the lines anguish that the sacred could fall thus to the power of evil.[4] The same ubiquity in divine justice is the first subject for the apparently helpless Saint Peter ("How well could I have spared for thee, young swain/Anow of such as for their bellies sake. . . ."). Why then separate passages developing a major attitude of the poem with the Camus lines?

Next Camus, reverend Sire, went footing slow, 103
His Mantle hairy, and his Bonnet sedge,
Inwrought with figures dim, and on the edge
Like to that sanguine flower inscrib'd with woe.
Ah! Who hath reft (quoth he) my dearest
          pledge?   107

Milton in the face of Nemesis and death apparently felt more poignantly the loss of life, as figured in Cambridge and camaraderie, than he

felt the necessity to enter immediately into Christian apologetics concerning cosmic justice. Saint Peter's mind, like Milton's, is more on earth than on heaven, and full of pity and indignation. In his concluding lines we have another drama of a mind jumping rapidly from pity to anger to resolution:

The hungry Sheep look up, and are not fed,
But swoln with wind, and the rank mist
          they draw,   125
Rot inwardly, and foul contagion spread:
Besides what the grim Woolf with privy paw
Daily devours apace, and nothing sed,
But that two-handed engine at the door,   130
Stands ready to smite once, and smite no more.

The last two lines (whatever the "two-handed engine" refers to) are a resolution of the same sort as those of the Phoebus and the "Weep no more" passages: that is, all else does not logically lead up to them. They are not more important than other lines of other passages; they are *part*, the consoling part, of the whole complex of attitudes of the brooding mind of the poet. The impulse to make these assertions of transcendence the *raison d'etre* of the other attitudes in the poem is what lies behind many of the patterns that have been drawn for *Lycidas*. For however subtly done, many of the recent *Lycidas* essays tend to downgrade the attitudes in passages between Phoebus and Saint Peter, and between Saint Peter and the "Weep no more" (whereas older criticism often focused on the St. Peter passage as a "digression"). The flower passage, for instance, is called the "prologue" or beginning of a "third act" or "movement," or an interlude, a diversion, a stock item of pastoral elegy, or its own excuse—anything but a rendering of an attitude in the mind of the poet toward the problem of death of equal intensity to all the others. The theory has been that the passage must be "leading up" logically or rhetorically to something else to have real relevance. But if the whole is seen as a magnificent rendering of a mind in irresolution and conflict, then all this terribly misleading talk of "resolution," with its implications of purposeful progress, comes to be off the mark. The flower passage seems simply and most movingly an attempt of the spirit to submerge its fears and terrors in the beauty of nature. That it is necessary after Saint Peter's speech signifies that the poet's spirit is not ready for consolation. That that spirit can slip so easily (in line 154) into the blackest vision of the whole poem, that of Lycidas sinking beneath the waves with the archangel helpless, is symptomatic of the brooding spirit's inability to be consoled by the world's frail beauty. The immediate leap then into apotheosis from the deepest and darkest spiritual state in the poem is the farthest thing from a resolution of all the attitudes of the poem; it is rather an obvious rejection of most of them.[5]

The leap has been dramatically prepared for. It is absolutely convincing that that mercurial "insubordinate" mind we have found everywhere in the poem would in the moment of deepest depression demand the highest exultation, that consolation would be acceptable only after the widest, deepest exploration of the alternative attitudes. What is unconvincing is the explaining away of the leap or any other effect in the poem by the laying on of pre-cut patterns, whether they be mythic patterns of death and rebirth or patterns out of literary tradition where, say, pastoral grief goes from bad to worse to better.[6] Richard P. Adams, in his "The Archetypal Pattern of Death and Rebirth in Lycidas," presents the archetypal pattern that often appears in pastoral elegy:

> The emotional pattern of the poem consists of a twofold movement. First it goes from the announcement of the friend's death downward through various expressions of sorrow to despair; then comfort is offered, and the sequence reverses itself until the conclusion is reached in heavenly joy. It is the conventional pattern of pastoral elegy, at least from the time of Virgil, and it is at the same time the pattern of Milton's feeling about death at the time he wrote Lycidas. (Patrides, pp. 121–2)*

This no more accounts for the unique drama and pattern of Lycidas than to say with Thomas Gradgrind that a horse is a "graminivorous quadruped." It is not that such patterns do not have some validity and interest, but that operating critically with them dulls the senses to the

unique drama of the individual artist working out his expressive forms. Where else in mythic or pastoral patterns does the intensest moment of darkness provoke immediately the brightest moment of light? And if one finds a model, one can obviously never find the moment prepared for as it is in this unique context which dramatizes the tremulous psychology of the brooding poet. The unique context is the poem, its greatness is in the unique, continuous context, not in its somewhat sameness to other poems of the same genre.

The poet "touched the tender stops of various quills/with eager thought warbling his Doric lay." The "lay" expresses his "eager" ("impatient," "biting," "impetuous") thoughts, the various quills represent the various postures or attitudes his thoughts lead him to. The poem ends in diminuendo (186–93) because it is but a dramatization of a meditative mind, not a philosophic or any other sort of dialectic. He picked up one pipe, made music with it, put it down and played another. This is the quality of pastiche, though here of immensely significant pastiche. Milton has caught his own mind in action as it adopts various attitudes towards death. The continuity of the poem is in the completely convincing rendering of the dynamics, the shifting attitudes, of that mind. The switch in the last eight lines from first to third person is quite continuous with the tone of the whole poem as the poet here assumes an attitude of separation from the brooding self he must leave in order to go on living.

This is how I see the poem—patternless, save for the pattern of mind flow of an immensely well-read and sensitive man who has felt the patterns in works of the artists and thinkers of the past and manipulates these patterns at will. This seems to me to be a modest statement of the true formal dynamics of Lycidas. Most of the recent Lycidas essays insist on finding in the poem far more complex or rigid patterns, whether traditional, or mythic (unconsciously there), or dialectical. I would briefly note a few of these comments.

The following is from Arthur Barker on the "three movements" of Lycidas:

---

*C. A. Patrides, ed. Milton's Lycidas: The Tradition and the Poem (New York, 1961).—ED.

The first movement laments Lycidas the poet-shepherd; its problem, the possible frustrations of disciplined poetic ambition by early death, is resolved by the assurance, "Of so much fame in heaven expect they meed." The second laments Lycidas as priest-shepherd; its problem, the frustration of a sincere shepherd in a corrupt church, is resolved by Saint Peter's reference to the "two-handed engine" of divine retribution. The third concludes with the apotheosis, a convention introduced by Virgil in *Eclogue V* but significantly handled by Milton. He sees the poet-priest-shepherd worshiping the Lamb with those saints "in solemn troops" who sing the "unexpressive nuptial song" of the fourteenth chapter of Revelation. The apotheosis thus not only provides the final reassurance but unites the themes of the preceding movements in the ultimate reward of the true poet-priest. (Patrides, p. 126)

The analysis has the appearance of logical neatness, which hides the fact that it attributes in the poem no organic relation to the three movements save that poet and priest together get their eternal reward. By focusing on what is really mere description of the rhetorical figurations Milton uses, rather than the flow of emotions in the poet-shepherd which impel the figurations, Barker sacrifices our sense of the emotional continuity of the poem to satisfy our appetite for pat logical order.

The lust for rhetorical order and/or logical continuity is what is behind formulations such as this of Jon Lawrey:

We may however take an additional step toward reconciling the supposedly antagonistic modes of statement in *Lycidas* by considering the poem as in part a dialectical process, in the Hegelian sense: the initial dogmatic proposition (thesis) is opposed by a skeptical second (antithesis); from their encounter there arises a third statement, one of mystic certainty (synthesis). Within *Lycidas*, the major subject of this process is poetry itself. The timeless, serene, and objective attitudes of pastoral, impassioned only in formal artistic imitation of loss, are opposed by the skeptical affronts of death, temporal corruption, and several failures of consolation, all of which are impassioned in and through actual experience. However, each of these two modes of awareness or response is found to be incomplete in the course of the work and a consummate statement,

greater than either but partaking of both, gradually evolves. (*PMLA*, Vol. 77, p. 27)

Or this of Rosemond Tuve:

. . . not only is the poem a structure of cumulative, not contrasted, insights into the meaning of life and death, but also there is yet to come the vision of the nuptial union of the soul with the source of love, a third vision of judgement. Moreover, though it is notable that symbols are chosen at these three crucial points to convey great fundamental oppositions like growth and destruction, life and nothingness, union and sundering, fruition and annihilation, there is also the whole continuing web of the poem with its living and tender sense of imperishable sweetness in all moving and growing things. (Patrides, p. 172)

Or this of M. H. Abrams:

The movement of *Lycidas* . . . is patently from despair through a series of insights to triumphant joy. We can put it this way: read literally, the elegy proper opens with the statement "Lycidas is dead, dead ere his prime"; it concludes with the flatly opposing statement "Lycidas your sorrow is *not* dead." Everything that intervenes has been planned to constitute a plausible sequence of thoughts and insights that will finally convert a logical contradiction into a lyric reversal by the anagnorisis, the discovery, that for a worthy Christian poet-priest a seeming defeat by death is actually an immortal triumph. (Patrides, p. 226)

What bothers me with these statements and others about *Lycidas* is the implication that all detail in the poem is constantly building or working toward resolution—the implications, that is, of "dialectic," or "cumulative," or "evolving"— statements which tend to falsify the integrity or quality of the doubt in the poem. The Christian Union of the dualism of life *is* the basis for Milton's *theology*, but what the *poem* renders is not the dialectic but a poet struggling in a very human way to maintain the dialectic. It is not (as the above statements imply) as if the poet-shepherd of the poem need pass through a process of discovery of the Christian answers; the "Weep no more" answer would be impossible in the poem if the poet were not a Christian long before the poem begins. The poet is not discovering Christianity, but attempting to keep his faith in it.

The feeling that one has read a poem when one has come to know the patterns of the genus to which it belongs, or the mythic pattern into which it falls, or the packaging of ideas it contains, or the sources or traditions or historical context for any or all of these is the scholar's false paradise. There is partial critical paralysis when the interested reader has not assimilated such information, but there is total critical paralysis when he rests with this information. The soul of a successful poem is in its uniqueness, its contextual pattern, its complex of attitudes which is like no other; and criticism's job, which begins where scholarship leaves off, is to react to and articulate this uniqueness. The sort of questions this essay asked about the uniqueness of *Lycidas* are not the sort to be answered by literary comparisons and analogies to other poets or poems or other disciplines. The body of attitudes that impel *Lycidas* has an emotional continuity created by the dramatization of a mind not at ease, one which will impose no final formal ordering (hence "pastiche") on its intractable fluctuations. This articulation of response to the poem answers with more accuracy I feel, the critical questions I have posed, and accounts better for the reader's sense of the continuity in *Lycidas*, than the highly patterned paradigms that have been so often drawn in the literature on the poem.

Notes

1. Cf. René Wellek's chapter on "The Mode of Existence of a Literary Work of Art" in his *Theory of Literature* for a discussion of the objective existence of what are called "norms" in the literary work (what I call a "normative tone" in chap. Ten, "The Critical Act"). W. K. Wimsatt, Jr., and Monroe Beardsley postulate this common psychological state in the conclusion of their essay "The Affective Fallacy":

> Poetry is a way of fixing emotions or making them more permanently perceptible when objects have undergone a functional change from culture to culture, or when as simple facts of history they have lost emotive value with loss of immediacy. . . . A structure of emotive objects so complex and so reliable as to have been taken for great poetry by any past age will never, it seems safe to say, so wane with the waning of human

culture as not to be recoverable at least by a willing student. (*The Verbal Icon*, 1954, pp. 38–9)

This objective structure of emotions (or tone) is distinguished in the essay from emotions inspired in the reader not by the text but by extrinsic personal considerations.

2. The remarks to follow concerning the structure of *Lycidas* have perhaps a Burkean tinge in method and approach. "Qualitative progression" is Burke's term for the emotional flow I find informing *Lycidas*.

3. Cf. John Crowe Ransom's summation in his essay "A Poem Nearly Anonymous": "Milton's bold play with the forms of discourse constitutes simply one more item in his general insubordinacy" (in C. A. Patrides, ed., *Milton's "Lycidas": The Tradition and the Poem* [New York: 1961], p. 80). Also interestingly, in the eighteenth century, Richard Hurd, "There is a very original air in it, though it is full of classical imitations"; and in the nineteenth, William Hazlitt, "A certain tender gloom overspreads it, a wayward abstraction, a forgetfulness of his subject in the serious reflections that arise out of it. The gusts of passion come and go like the sounds of music borne on the wind . . .", (Scott Elledge, ed., *Milton's "Lycidas"* [New York, 1966], pp. 228, 232).

4. Michael Lloyd (in *Modern Language Notes*, LXXV, pp. 103–8) takes an opposite tack to those few critics who attempt to explicate the lines. He asserts that the bark is man's fallen, perfidious body. The eclipse is the Fall, the curse is mortality—again the Christian answer to the problem of Death. I find this dubious (it accuses King of the human frailties, which the poem avoids doing elsewhere). But if this *were* Milton's intent for the lines, it would be just another example of the abruptness and pastiche-like quality of the mind flow of the poet.

5. Compare Hopkins' similar leap in "Heraclitean Fire" (which I discuss in chapter Three):

> . . . all is in an enormous dark
> Drowned, O pity and indignation! Manshape,
>   that shone
> Sheer off, disseveral, a star, death blots black
>   out; nor mark
>   Is any of him at all so stark
> But vastness blurs and time beats level. Enough!
>   the Resurrection,
> A heart's-clarion! Away grief's gasping.

6. Wayne Shumaker in his "Flowerets and Sounding Seas" and M. H. Abrams in his "Five Types of Lycidas" do handle the problem of the abrupt transitions in *Lycidas* which I have focused on. Shu-

maker, quite rightly I feel, labels the structural movement "affective," "not logically but emotionally inductive" and shakes up fixed ideas effectively by calling the "leap" discussed above "a natural emotional rhythm, illustrated in the abnormal level by the familiar manic-depressive pattern" (Patrides, p. 127). Abrams' essay is masterful in pulling together all the strands of *Lycidas* criticism, but I find unconvincing his argument that Saint Peter's speech plants the final "resolution" in the shepherd's mind (the implications of the speech being released by an associative link between Lycidas floating on the water and Christ walking on it, see pp. 228–9, Patrides).

Conrad: The Imaged Style

Wilfred S. Dowden

The formalist's contention that the "soul" of a successful poem is a "contextual pattern," with its suggestion of a spatial metaphor, is a contention most easily illustrated with reference to a lyric poem. But formal criticism has discovered the same kind of image patterns in complex plays, like Hamlet, *and in well-structured prose narratives like* Heart of Darkness. *In fact, the first narrator's remark in the novel that Marlow's yarns did not have a "direct simplicity," for to Marlow "the meaning of an episode was not inside like a kernel but outside, enveloping the tale which brought it out only as a glow brings out a haze," might be taken as an invitation to read the novel with particular attention to style, tone, and image. Wilfred Dowden is one of those who have accepted that invitation, and this selection from his book on Conrad's "imaged style" shows how a formalist reading of prose narrative can help us see the ways imagery functions to reveal theme.*

Reprinted by permission from Wilfred S. Dowden, *Joseph Conrad: The Imaged Style*, pp. 71–83. Copyright © 1970 by Vanderbilt University Press. Notes have been renumbered.

IN "HEART OF DARKNESS," CONRAD MAKES USE OF contrasts in light and dark imagery to develop a threefold theme, each aspect of which is inherent in the ambiguity of the title. There is the heart of the darkness in which the narrator (Marlow) tells his story. There is also the heart of the great continent into which Marlow journeys, a land largely unexplored and still commonly thought of as the "Dark Continent." One important part of this aspect of Conrad's theme is the narrator's journey toward the darkness of savagery. When he finally reaches the heart of the Dark Continent, he is at the heart of the darkness of a primitive society. This primitivism is symbolized by the infrequent, shadowy appearance of the natives whom Marlow encounters on his freshwater voyage. They are seen fleetingly through the breaks in the foliage of the dense jungle. The natives, therefore, are always dimly seen, never in complete darkness, yet never in the bright sunlight, which, in spite of its joyless intensity, cannot penetrate the deep shade of the jungle which is their home.

Of still more significance to Conrad's narrative is the third aspect of the theme, and this one is suggested by the first two. As the darkness deepens about the narrator and his listeners, Marlow proceeds farther, in his story, up the muddy, glistening river toward the heart of the Dark Continent; and he moves deeper into the mystery of Kurtz. The shadowy, mysterious nature of Kurtz, and of humanity, which he comes to symbolize, is a darkness which also deepens as Marlow approaches his destination. At first, there is only a reference to this remarkable man. When Marlow finally meets Kurtz, "several weeks later and a thousand miles farther," the figure of the man takes on reality; Kurtz is no longer an unknown person, about whom people speak but say nothing which gives a clue to the mystery surrounding him. He is at last flesh and blood, but the reality behind the veil of flesh becomes more shadowy as Marlow becomes better acquainted with the outer man. The savagery which surrounds Kurtz has appealed to some primitive, evil instinct in his nature, and the "deep damnation" of his response is darker than savagery itself. He has moved into realms where men like Marlow, ordinary, "normal" men who dwell in the sunlight of civilization (however thin the cultural veneer may be), cannot follow. Marlow perceives his degradation and has a vague understanding of its import; Marlow's audience cannot comprehend it, but listens "for the sentence, for the word, that would give . . . the clue to the faint uneasiness inspired by this narrative . . ." (p. 83).* The narrator has arrived at the heart of the darkness which surrounds a lost soul just as he has arrived at the heart of the darkness of the Dark Continent; but he is alien to both regions; and, in the end, the river bears him away from those things which he has perceived but has not fully comprehended.

The theme of this narrative, therefore, is developed on three levels, each of which is supported by the central image of contrasts in light and darkness. There is the contrasting light and deepening darkness of the physical setting in which the narrative is told; there is the contrast of the light on the river up which the steamer moves with the darkness of the bordering jungle, as Marlow and his companions travel toward the heart of the Dark Continent; and there is the contrast of the light in which men like Marlow move with the darkness which surrounds Kurtz and, potentially, every man, since, in the thematic development of the story, Kurtz represents the ultimate possibility of degradation in mankind. This last aspect of the theme is the heart of Conrad's "Heart of Darkness," and the first two aspects form the matrix for it.

Conrad begins the narrative by describing the brilliance of the evening on which Marlow and his friends meet:

The day was ending in a serenity of still and exquisite brilliance. The water shone pacifically; the sky, without a speck, was a benign immensity of unstained light; the very mist on the Essex marshes was like a gauzy and radiant fabric, hung from the wooded rises inland, and draping the low shores in diaphanous folds. (p. 46)

The serenity and brilliance of the late afternoon is broken by a peculiar gloom to the west, which is "brooding over the upper reaches" and becomes "more somber every minute, as if angered by the approach of the sun" (p. 46). Thus, the tone of the narrative and its framework too are set at this moment. The brooding gloom to the west presages the coming of night in which the narrative is told; and it also foretells the indecisiveness of Marlow's journey into the Congo and the spiritual gloom and darkness in the heart of Kurtz. As the sun approaches this peculiar gloom in the west, it changes from a glowing white to a dull red, "without rays and without heat." Even the brilliance of the sun seems "to go out," to be "stricken to death" by that gloom which is "brooding over a crowd of men" (p. 46), as if this gloom were always ready to close about man and turn what is brightest in his nature and his surroundings into darkness.

As the sun goes down, the river becomes tranquil and rests at the close of day, leading "to the uttermost ends of the earth" (p. 47). We move, therefore, from the familiar to the unfamiliar, from the light of the known to the darkness of the unknown. Lights appear on the shore and penetrate the dusk surrounding the little group of men on the ship. Lights appear everywhere—the strong light of Chapman's lighthouse, moving lights of ships in the stream, "a great stir of lights going up and going down" (p. 48). These lights in the deepening dusk make a cheerful sight, but their cheerfulness is offset by the scene farther west, where "on the upper reaches the place of the monstrous town was still marked ominously on the sky, a brooding gloom in sunshine, a lurid glare under the stars" (p. 48). This peculiar brooding gloom impresses itself on the senses and prompts Marlow to begin his story:

" 'And this also,' said Marlow suddenly, 'has been one of the dark places of the earth' " (p. 48). As he talks, the traffic of the great city goes

---

*Page numbers in parentheses refer to Conrad's *Works*, 20 vols. (London and Edinburgh: John Grant, 1925). —ED.

"on in the deepening night upon the sleepless river" (p. 51). As he begins his journey into the "heart of darkness," the shadows deepen and night falls, as if nature were lending verisimilitude to his tale.

The somber, ominous gloom in the west, which is juxtaposed to the lights of the city and harbor, seems to symbolize to Marlow the entire effect which his remarkable freshwater voyage had upon him. What happened to him there, at the "farthest point of navigation and the culminating point of [his] experience," seems to "throw a kind of light on everything about [him]—and into [his] thoughts. It was somber enough, too—and pitiful—not extraordinary in any way—not very clear either. . . . And yet it seemed to throw a kind of light" (p. 51).

As Marlow describes his experience—the meeting with the owner of the Company, the journey up the muddy river, the sight of the emaciated natives lying in the gloomy shade of the first outstation, and the climactic, yet indecisive meeting with Kurtz—as his boat penetrates farther into the heart of the Dark Continent, and as he goes deeper into the mystery of Kurtz, the voyager is given proportionately deeper insight into humanity, into a darkness which is ready to break through the thin curtain of culture that separates civilized man from his primitive brothers. Marlow's experience throws a "kind of light" on the innermost workings of the human heart, and what he sees there is "not very clear" but pitiful and somber.

Marlow begins his narrative by describing his visit to the city, which always reminded him of a whited sepulcher. His purpose is to secure a position as the skipper of a riverboat in Africa. Upon his arrival, the mystery through which he is to move immediately surrounds him. His first stop is at the headquarters of the Company. The gloomy appearance of the street outside; the dim, somber rooms and offices inside; and the humorless, dark-clad figures of the women,[1] clerk, and owner (all of which have been prefigured by the "brooding gloom" setting of the framework) foretell the nature of Marlow's coming adventure and leaves him with a sensation of impending disaster.

As he proceeds toward Africa, the narrator becomes conscious of the sun, which burns fiercely down upon the white beach as it moves slowly by. The bright ferocity of the sun is accentuated by the contrasting dark green of the jungle, "so dark-green as to be almost black" (p. 60). There is no joy or comfort in the light of the sun or the dark shade of the jungle. This contrast is central to Marlow's description of the scene at the first of the company stations, which the riverboat reaches as it makes its way up the muddy river. He sees the station first at a moment when its devastation is drowned in blinding sunlight. He climbs the hill toward the buildings, passes a stack of rusty rails, and notes on the left a clump of trees which make a shady spot in the blinding glare. Underneath "dark things seemed to stir feebly" (p. 64). A chain gang passes him, toiling up the hill, driven by a grinning guard. He turns and makes for the trees, intending to remain in the shade until the chain gang is out of sight. Suddenly, he has a premonition of what is to come:

> . . . I foresaw that in the blinding sunshine of that land I would become acquainted with a flabby, pretending, weak-eyed devil of a rapacious and pitiless folly. How insidious he could be, too, I was only to find out several months later and a thousand miles farther. For a moment I stood appalled, as though·by a warning. Finally I descended the hill, obliquely, towards the trees I had seen. (p. 65)

The "rapacious and pitiless folly" is mankind at its depth, as symbolized by Kurtz, and it is significant that this scene of inhabited devastation, drenched in blinding and comfortless sunlight, should forewarn Marlow of the human degradation which he was to see.

He continues to walk toward the shade.

> At last I got under the trees. My purpose was to stroll into the shade for a moment; but no sooner within than it seemed to me I had stepped into the gloomy circle of some Inferno. . . .
>
> Black shapes crouched, lay, sat between the trees leaning against the trunks, clinging to the earth, half coming out, half effaced within the dim light, in all the attitudes of pain, abandonment, and despair. . . . And this was the place where some of the helpers had withdrawn to die.
>
> They were dying slowly—it was very clear. They were not enemies, they were not criminals,

they were nothing earthly now,—nothing but black shadows of disease and starvation, lying confusedly in the greenish gloom. . . . While I stood horror-struck, one of these creatures rose to his hands and knees, and went off on all-fours towards the river to drink. He lapped out of his hand, then sat up in the sunlight, crossing his shins in front of him, and after a time let his woolly head fall on his breastbone. (pp. 66–67)[2]

Throughout this scene, contrasts of light and dark are used to emphasize its horror. Another example is the bit of white worsted tied about the neck of one of the poor creatures. Marlow is unable to understand the reason for its being there. "Why? Where did he get it? Was it a badge—an ornament—a charm—a propitiatory act? Was there any idea at all connected with it? It looked startling round his black neck, this bit of white thread from beyond the seas" (p. 67).

A sharper contrast in light and dark, and consequently a deeper insight into the heart of man betrayed by the surface aspects of civilization, is emphasized when Marlow meets the clerk of the Company, as the former leaves the depressing sight in the shade of the trees and walks up the hill toward the buildings. This man is first seen by Marlow in the bright sunlight. He is dressed in unexpected splendor—high collar, white cuffs, snowy trousers, light alpaca jacket, clear necktie, and varnished boots—all glittering and shining in contrast to the miserable black men in their dim shade. "In the great demoralization of the land he kept up his appearance" (p. 68). His inhumanity is symbolized by the white and brilliant perfection of his dress, which contrasts sharply with the surrounding devastation and the misery of the black men who creep about in the gloom of the trees. It is also symbolized by the condition of his books, which are in "apple-pie order." The callousness which underlies this meticulous outward manifestation of his culture is emphasized by the irony of his greatest accomplishment: he had taught one of the native women, who "had a distaste for the work," to starch and iron his snowy white shirts. He is sensitive only to the amenities of the civilization of which he is a part and is conscious of the sufferings of the natives only when their noise disturbs his concentration on his books. Thus, he exhibits no sympathy for the

dying man who is brought to the station and placed outside his window. In his strict adherence to superficialities, he is isolated from the rest of mankind; his humanity is forgotten in the process of keeping up appearances in the great demoralization of the land.

The miserable state of the natives, emphatically brought to the attention of the reader by the contrasting brightness of the sunlight and the whiteness of the clothing of the fanatically attired clerk, is also prophetic of the degradation of Kurtz, whose name Marlow first hears spoken by the clerk. He is unable to grasp the true nature of Kurtz, however, and can get from the man only the statement that Kurtz "will go far, very far" (p. 70). The agent becomes a part of the shadow-peopled mystery of the Dark Continent.

The sun, too, is a symbol of the obscurity and ambiguity in which Marlow finds himself. It burns without comforting, as the shade of the forest darkens the world without giving any real relief from the ferocity of the sun. The sun, brilliant as it is, fails to penetrate a white fog which settles over the river. When the mist lifts, Marlow is conscious of the forest, the matted jungle, and "the blazing little ball of the sun hanging over it . . ." (p. 101). The sun can penetrate the fog and the matted jungle no more easily than Marlow can penetrate the darkness of Africa and the mystery of Kurtz, who is as shadowy and indistinct a figure to Marlow as the dismal, starving black men in the dim shade of the trees at the first station.

The sun also emphasizes the inscrutable nature of the natives who attack the steamer (on orders from Kurtz, as it later turns out). They are seen fleetingly as they run through the infrequent open spaces in the jungle, places which the sun can penetrate. They become as shadowy as the jungle they inhabit and are seen intermittently and vaguely, like figures in a dream. They are almost always in the darkness of the jungle, never for long in the bright sunlight. They are "vague forms of men" who run "bent double, leaping, gliding, distinct, incomplete, evanescent" (p. 111).

When Kurtz is first seen, borne by a group of natives wading waist deep in weeds, he is reminiscent of the dying creatures of the dilapidated station at which the steamer stopped early in the voyage. He is emaciated, long, ungainly, horribly sick. As Marlow listens to him talk, the speaker is engulfed in gloom—he is only a voice speaking from the oppressive dimness about him—a voice speaking from a ruined hovel fronted by a row of stakes with human heads drying on them, while Marlow's companions on the steamer are yet in the sunlight.

Kurtz's degraded condition is made abundantly clear to Marlow in a climactic scene which occurs before the narrator and his companions (the "pilgrims") begin their voyage out of the Congo. Marlow has just been told by the Russian about Kurtz's attempt to forestall the coming of the steamer by ordering the natives to attack it. When he awakes, shortly after midnight, Marlow goes out into the night and looks about, seeing the glow of native campfires, "where Mr. Kurtz's adorers were keeping their uneasy vigil" (p. 140). Kurtz has left his bed in the ship's cabin, and Marlow begins to follow his trail through the tall grass toward the camp of the natives. Marlow comes upon him as he is crawling toward the fires, and as Kurtz rises, "unsteady, long, pale, indistinct, like a vapor exhaled by the earth" (p. 142), he appears as shadowy, as nebulous, as mysterious as the jungle itself. Marlow cannot "appeal to anything high or low" in the man because Kurtz is no longer of this world—he has isolated himself in his own incredible, exalted degradation.

Kurtz and the fantastically dressed clerk of the first station are, in a sense, kindred beings. They have both succeeded in isolating themselves from mankind, in kicking themselves "loose of the earth" (p. 144). Kurtz has accomplished this end by casting aside that which is most noble in his culture, by allowing the primitive, evil instincts to respond to the savagery around him; and he has succeeded in going beyond mere savagery. His evil is something that cannot exist in sunlight. The clerk, too, has cast aside the noble aspects of his culture, but instead of substituting the darkness of primitivism, he has taken refuge in the superficialities of civilization, symbolized by the glittering whiteness of his attire and the apple-pie order of his books, which are kept in top shape at the expense of sympathy for the suffering natives connected with his station.

Kurtz's callous isolation becomes further apparent as the magnificent native woman stands on the shore extending her bare arms over the water toward the riverboat, which bears the near-dead agent away from the scene of his triumph and degradation. He is isolated from her as surely as he is isolated from his "intended" at home. His own extreme and incredible debasement makes it impossible for him to communicate with another mortal.

The river bears the voyagers out of the Heart of Darkness faster than it bore them in, and the life of Kurtz, whom Marlow is taking out, seems to ebb as fast as the stream. Marlow has at last dissolved the outward mystery of Kurtz. He knows the man, the emaciated, sickly body of Kurtz; and he knows that the brute deep within the man has responded to the savagery of his surroundings—has been awakened and has responded with a completeness that has caused Kurtz to kick himself loose of the earth, to cast himself into the darkness of complete isolation. As the voice from this emaciated form flows from the pilot house of the steamer, Marlow sees into "the barren darkness of his heart. . . . But both the diabolic love and the unearthly hate . . . fought for the possession of that soul satiated with primitive emotions, avid of lying fame, of sham distinction, of all the appearances of success and power" (pp. 147–148). Toward the end of his life, Kurtz recognizes his own failure. At last, his being is laid bare in all its pride, ruthless power, craven terror, and darkness. The voice comes as a whisper, repeating the words, "The horror! The horror!" (p. 149).

Marlow's task is not over, however. There is still Kurtz's "intended" to see—to face with the burden of the knowledge of Kurtz's extreme degradation. She, too, is a shadowy figure, dressed in black, seen in the dusk. As Marlow speaks to her the room darkens and "only her forehead, smooth and white, remained illumined by the unextinguishable light of belief and love" (p. 158). Like everything else associated with the man, she is a dim, almost spectral figure. As Marlow listens to her she becomes, like Kurtz, only a voice, which seems "to have the accompaniment of all the other sounds, full of mystery, desolation, and sorrow . . . the whisper of a voice speaking from beyond the threshold of an eternal darkness" (p. 159).

This girl has been anticipated by the tragic figure of the native woman who stretches her bare arms over the water toward the departing steamer, just as the emaciated Kurtz is prefigured by the dying natives in the deep shade of the Company station. The girl, like the native woman, "put out her arms as if after a retreating figure, stretching them black and with clasped pale hands across the fading and narrow sheen of the window" (p. 160). The girl and the native woman are also kindred spirits, because each has lost the man who could not trust or be trusted by any other human being.

In the end, Marlow cannot tell this woman the truth about Kurtz. His last words, says Marlow, were the young woman's name. To tell her what he actually said "would have been too dark—too dark altogether" (p. 162), would have opened the bleakness of his heart to her view; and she would have known the depths to which he had sunk.

Looked at strictly from the point of view of plot structure, Marlow's visit to Kurtz's "intended" seems anti-climactic. It is necessary, I think, in order to present fully the narrator's own importance in the story, for it is at this point that we learn of the insight Marlow gained in his encounter with Kurtz. It seems also clear that Marlow is not fully aware of the meaning of his journey until he comes face to face with the girl. Thus, it seems to him best to leave her with illusions which are an integral part of her culture, for they furnish a necessary, if feeble restraint.

The girl would also have seen something more sinister than Kurtz's degradation, for she would have seen that which Kurtz perceived even before he reached the debased state in which Marlow found him. Kurtz expressed his perception in a painting which he left at one of the stations before he went into the center of Africa. This painting was a "sketch in oils, on a panel, representing a woman, draped and blindfolded, carrying a lighted torch. The background was sombre—almost black. The movement of

the woman was stately, and the effect of the torch-light on the face was sinister" (p. 79).[3] Significantly, Marlow sees this painting in the light of a single candle. The sketch only increases the mystery of Kurtz, and prompts Marlow to make further inquiries about the agent. When the darkness surrounding Kurtz is partially dispelled, however, the reader (and perhaps Marlow) sees what Kurtz intended the painting to mean: it symbolizes mankind, groping blindly through the darkness of his existence, seeking his way with what light civilization can offer. But this light also emphasizes the sombre, sinister nature of man, just as the fierce sunlight beating down on the starving native, as he creeps from the shade of the trees, emphasizes his abased state. In a sense, it betrays man, as it betrays the white clerk, who mistakenly identifies its superficial, dazzling whiteness with reality. To Kurtz, however, the light illuminates that which is most sinister in the heart of man; it enables him to see perhaps too clearly how sheer the protective curtain of civilization really is. Kurtz knows of the blackness which is at the heart of humanity; he knows the depths to which man is capable of sinking; he knows that the light of civilization cannot penetrate this darkness, that it can only emphasize its sinister pervasiveness; and worst of all, he knows that he turned away from this feeble light, so that he was enveloped in the darkness which is at the heart of every man. He has, in the end, "pronounced a judgment upon the adventures of his soul on this earth" (p. 150). Kurtz is a remarkable man because he perceives this darkness, and since Marlow has vicariously partaken of Kurtz's revelation, he is the only person associated with the agent who can come near to penetrating the meaning of Kurtz's summing up: "The horror! the horror!" He can understand the meaning of Kurtz's stare as the man lay dying—a stare "that could not see the flame of the candle, but was wide enough to embrace the whole universe, piercing enough to penetrate all the hearts that beat in the darkness" (p. 151). To explain all this to Kurtz's fiancée would be "too dark—too dark altogether." Only he who has "peeped over the edge" (p. 151) himself can understand it in all its horror.

On several occasions, Marlow speaks of "a choice of nightmares" or "the nightmare of my choice" (pp. 138, 141). To a man of Marlow's temperament (reflecting perhaps the ambivalence in that of his creator), the individualistic and (initially, at least) the idealistic Kurtz is a much more attractive figure than the white clerk or the avaricious "pilgrims." Nevertheless, his statement that Kurtz is a "remarkable man" refers neither to the agent's idealism and individualism nor to the "nightmare" of his own choice between decadent civilization (the clerk and "pilgrims") and idealistic isolation turned to near-primeval power (Kurtz). He is deeply impressed by Kurtz's remarkable perception and by what he had learned by having "peeped over the edge," himself: every man is capable of descending to the depths reached by the clerk, "pilgrims," and Kurtz.

Marlow finishes his tale, and a silence falls upon the group of men on the ship. Perhaps they had also "peeped over the edge" and had learned something of the revelation which came so forcibly to Kurtz. This seems to be implied in Conrad's conclusion to "Heart of Darkness," in which he focuses the reader's attention again on these friends who hear Marlow's tale, thus completing the framework to his narrative. As they gaze westward, they are conscious that "the offing was barred by a black bank of clouds, and the tranquil waterway leading to the uttermost ends of the earth flowed sombre under an overcast sky—seemed to lead into the heart of an immense darkness" (p. 162). One might compare Marlow to Coleridge's Ancient Mariner and the audience in "Heart of Darkness" to the Wedding Guest, who became "a sadder and a wiser man." Marlow gains insight through partial involvement in Kurtz's story; the audience gains partial insight vicariously through Marlow's narration.

Notes

1. The black-clad women are usually identified with the Fates of classical literature. For a suggestion that they may be more precisely identified with two figures in the "cave of nymphs" passage in Book XIII of the *Odyssey*, see G. M. Harper, "Conrad's Knitters and Homer's Cave of Nymphs," *English Language Notes* I (1963): 53–57.

2. See Lillian Feder, "Marlow's Descent into Hell," *Nineteenth-Century Fiction* IX (1954–55): 280–292. Miss Feder calls attention to the similarity of this and other passages in "Heart of Darkness" to the "descent into Hell" tradition of the classical epic. See also Robert O. Evans, "Conrad's Underworld," *Modern Fiction Series* II (1956): 56–62.

3. Compare this painting with the marble statue of a sightless woman holding a cluster of lights in "The Return." *Cf.* also the scene in *The Rescue* when Edith Travers holds at arm's length the torch which has been unceremoniously thrust into her hand.

Chapter Three

Affective Criticism: Audience as Context

Which, without passing thro' the *Judgment*, gains
The *Heart*, and all its End *at once* attains.

Pope, *Essay on Criticism*

While the genetic critics ground their approach on the firm fact that poems have authors, the affective critics claim the equally solid basis that they also have audiences. By starting at this end of the communication line, they avoid most of the difficulties that trouble genetic criticism. Certainly, a poem is caused to exist at a particular moment in time, but it continues to exist long after its causes have vanished. Authors grow old and die, and the circumstances surrounding the poem's creation soon slip away into the irrevocable past. But the poem, a foster child of slow time, remains for us in the perpetual present.

For the affective critic is most often concerned with the present audience. There are, it should be noted, audience-oriented critics with a historical bent who study the reception of poems over time. And there have long been studies focused on a poem's original audience. But many of these latter investigations seem to be special forms of genetic criticism that assume if we could learn to think like the intended audience we could better grasp the intended meaning. Most affective critics, however, are less concerned with authors and much more concerned with the responses of readers, especially current readers. The poem exists now. It affects us now. These, they claim, are the crucial facts, and any relevant criticism must be built on them.

Not only do poems exist independently of their authors, they are almost always valued independently of their original contexts. Even genetic criticism must start from this point. Milton's biography has received more attention than Cowley's because we have judged Milton's poems, not his life, to be more important than Cowley's. We may try to become Elizabethans to understand *Hamlet;* we do not read *Hamlet* to become Elizabethans. That is, we must first respond to the power of poems before we trouble to investigate their causes, and we do not cease to respond if that investigation proves futile. What is that power, and what is the nature of our response to it? What happens when we read a novel, hear a poem, see a play? What is this interaction between audience and work without which that work would have no meaningful existence and certainly no value? The study of these questions, says the affective critic, is the chief business of literary criticism.

But before we consider what such study entails, we need to make some distinctions. Everyone agrees that we are affected by literature—delighted, disturbed, sometimes even instructed. Concern with the effects of art in a broad sense is as old as Aristophanes and as recent as the latest censorship case; and the long-playing debate about the moral and educative value of poetry has occasionally produced an attack, like Plato's, or a defense, like Shelley's, which are important documents in the history of literary criticism as an intellectual discipline. But only very occasionally. Similarly, the sort of affectiveness found in numerous impressionistic essays that tell us how the critic felt while reading may seldom contribute directly to our general understanding of literature. In other words, while a good deal of the talk about literature has always been loosely affective, significant attempts to develop a consistent theory along these lines have been few, and most of these are quite modern.

There is, of course, the long and strong "rhetorical" tradition, which includes Aristotle, Horace, Cicero, Quintilian, and their legions of followers in Renaissance and post-Renaissance

Europe. Certainly the language of this tradition is heavily "affective," stressing the ways authors can persuade or otherwise work upon their audiences. But in practice the rhetorical approach, especially when it was applied to poetry and drama, concentrated on the formal arrangement of elements within the work. It was assumed that these arrangements would produce certain effects, but little attempt was made to demonstrate this assumption or to study the responses of actual audiences. Consequently, the real heirs of this tradition have been the modern formalists who found they could often use the well-developed terminology of the rhetoricians in their analyses while paying scant attention to the study of audience response.

But such study has become the focus of several other schools of modern criticism, and especially of those based on some form of psychology, for the very conception of the reader–poem context invites a psychological investigation. In fact, probably as many different affective approaches exist as different kinds of psychology. Experimental psychologists, for example, have wired readers to galvanometers, with sometimes hilarious results, and some other schools of psychology have appeared only slightly less clumsy when they have tried to deal with the subtleties of poetry. But two forms of modern psychology have seemed to hold a special promise to illuminate our reactions to literature. One form is Freudian psychoanalysis. The poem, like the dream, has its manifest and latent content. Like the dream, it works for the reader's psyche. And like the dream, it yields its real meaning only to the critic trained in the proper psychoanalytical technique. Until quite recently, though, the affective uses of Freudian psychology have been less fully developed than the genetic or mimetic uses.

The theories of Carl Jung, on the other hand, have been most frequently employed in the affective context to account for the power of poetry. Jung's model of the different facets of the human psyche, his idea of the "collective unconscious," and above all his conceptions of "symbol" and "archetype" have seemed to many critics directly applicable to literary experience, and Jungian ideas have strongly influenced a number of studies usually classed under the label "myth criticism." Such studies often show as well the influence of such mythographers as G. S. Frazer, Gilbert Murray, and Joseph Campbell. As this diversity of influences suggests, "myth criticism" is not a single approach or a unified school, and in terms of the organization of this book "myth critics" can be found in most of our contexts. But they are found most often in the affective context for, whether they base their readings on Jung or on some other model of the human psyche, they agree that the power of literature chiefly resides in its presentation of special symbols, characters, and patterns of action to which we respond at the deepest levels of our being.

Great literature, in their view, is not great because it possesses complex verbal texture, realistic characters, fidelity to historical fact, or formal symmetry. A poem can have all these qualities and still be second-rate. Conversely, it can be marred by textual lacunae, as is the *Oresteia,* or by structural flaws, as is *Moby Dick,* and still succeed brilliantly. For in the imagery and characters of great works, in the green gardens and wintery wastelands, in the questing heroes and menacing villains, and in the archetypal patterns of their actions that form analogies to rites of spring and rites of passage, to cycles of death and rebirth, we recognize, usually at some subconscious level, the images and actions that haunt our dreams and that form the substance of our psychic lives. Here, too, as in the Freudian model, the poem is seen to have levels of meaning, a surface level available to formal or rhetorical analysis and a deeper level that can be explained by those armed with the insights of a particular psychological theory. And the psyches of unarmed readers have corresponding levels. Such readers may believe they are responding to the surface level, but they are really being affected by the underlying patterns of archetypal symbolism.

But not all sophisticated forms of affective criticism depend on a type of depth psychology. In the third decade of this century, I. A. Richards, whose bent was empirical and behavioristic, developed an influential line of affective criticism, a line that included a fully argued theory of affective value. Since the strengths and the weaknesses of Richard's theory are in many respects representative, it will be worthwhile to examine his argument. Richards, an esthetician, psychologist, and pioneering semanticist as well as a man very well read in ancient and modern literature, differed from many twentieth-century critics in his willingness to concede that the scientific or positivistic conception of truth is correct. Science provides accurate statements about the world; poems supply only "pseudo-statements." At the outset, then, Richards abandoned the traditional mimetic justifications for literature. With equal nonchalance, he abandoned the genetic researches so vigorously pursued by historical critics. The study of the circumstances of the poem's creation is simply not very relevant.

We are left, then, with some artfully constructed "pseudo-statements" and their readers. This may not look like a very promising basis for a defense of poetry. But people, Richards reminds us, do not live by scientific truth alone. Indeed, we live very little by it. Human beings are essentially bundles of desires and aversions, of "appetencies," to use Richards's term. Our lives consist of trying to satisfy as many of these appetencies as we can. And this task is not simple. The universe seldom seems designed to suit our purposes, other people's desires frequently contend with ours, and—perhaps most troublesome—our own appetencies often conflict with each other.

Yet our psychic health depends entirely on our ability to harmonize and satisfy these appetencies. The desire for truth is only one appetency, and in awarding its satisfaction to science Richards was not awarding so much as it might seem. For people have many other needs, one of the most important of which is a need to construct a vision of the world in which we can feel at home. Religion used to supply this vision, but since we moderns have largely lost our religious beliefs without losing the wants they used to satisfy, it will fall to poetry to fill their place, just as Matthew Arnold had predicted. More accurately, we now see from this perspective that religion, myth, and poetry are functionally the same thing. They are all imaginative constructs. The mistake was to think of them as offering "truth" in the scientific sense. The real purpose of art is to answer the human need for an intelligible and satisfying vision of the universe and our place within it and to answer as well our many other psychic wants, few of which can be met by scientific truth or the brute facts of experience. And poetry, because it operates through language, the most potent and flexible artistic medium, can encompass the greatest part of our psychic life, can appeal to and harmonize the greatest number of our appetencies. Poetry is art *par excellence.*

One advantage of Richards's view is that it offers to account for all features of the literary work. As we noticed, Jungian and Freudian attempts to explain the power of poems sometimes produce analyses that strip away the verbal texture and rhetorical structure of the work to reveal its underlying patterns, its embodiment of the dream or the myth that carries its true appeal. This focus on the latent content opens both methods to the charge that they are reductive, that they fail to deal with the art of poetry, and that, in their search for the mythic patterns or psychological mechanisms that inform many poems, such methods ignore the unique poem before them. If the oedipal conflict is the heart of *Hamlet,* in what ways does Shakespeare's play differ from an analyst's case history? If all tragedies embody the death–rebirth cycle, then why does *King Lear* affect us more strongly than *Alcestis* does, and why is a performance of *Oedipus Rex* more powerful than a summary of its plot? These charges do not apply to Richards's approach. The orderly structure and rich verbal texture of literary works, their networks of images and motifs, their symmetrical designs, their tricks and tropes, their rhythms and rhymes are not decorative excrescences—they are in themselves important sources of our satisfaction. For art, to repeat, appeals to many of our appetencies. Poetry allows us the chance to experience, and to experience more fully, more of life's possibilities than our nonverbal existence ordinarily affords, and a great poem, like *Hamlet,* is great because it deals with a wider range of human experiences than does a lesser poem. This is why "complexity" is a value in art; the complex poem appeals to more appetencies than a simple poem does.

But complexity is only part of the effect. In ordinary existence, appetencies are often in conflict. In art, however, the formal unity of the artistic structure arranges and contains this complexity; it subdues even the painful and the ugly; it holds the disparate elements in a tensive balance; and it offers not the chaotic fragment but the harmonious whole. The more we look at *Hamlet,* the more we see that all its elements from the smallest to the largest, all its special and local effects, are working together. It takes in much more than a carefully wrought sonnet, but it is just as superbly organized, in fact, more superbly because there is more to organize. And when we read a great poem, as so many of our desires and aversions are brought skillfully into play, they are also brought—as they almost never are in experiences outside of art—into harmonious balance. The harmony in the poem becomes a harmony in the reader's psyche. This is why human beings need poetry. It is indispensable to our psychic health.

Thus, Richards constructs an ambitious and cogent defense of art on affective grounds. Unlike some other affective approaches, his does not require that we separate form from content or buried meaning from surface meaning. On the contrary, it stresses the importance of the uniquely poetic devices. It promises to deal with both the complexity and the coherence of poems, and it accounts for each in terms of a fully articulated affective theory of value. Having explained his theory in *Principles of Literary Criticism* (1925), Richard went on to study the actual responses of readers in *Practical Criticism* (1929). He gave some Cambridge students several short poems that he felt varied widely in poetic quality. To eliminate any interference from preconditioned effects, he deleted all references to authors and dates, and he asked the students to read the poems as often as they wished and to write down their reactions and evaluations. The widely disparate readings that resulted seemed to Richards to indicate that most people are poor readers of poetry. And this, for him, was a serious deficiency. So Richards set about arranging, classifying, and analyzing the various ways his readers' responses had gone awry, and in the process he supplied his own often subtle and informed analyses of the same poems. Ironically, his analytical techniques were to be widely imitated in the next decades by many formalist critics who raised, at the same time, serious questions about his underlying affective theory.

Because the problems they pointed to can be found in many types of criticism that deal with audience response, they are worth examining at this juncture. The first and fundamental problem is to decide exactly whose response we are going to talk about. It is easy to speak in general terms about what "people" do, about the behavior of "audiences" or the reactions of "readers," but as Richards's research showed, and as a moment's reflection will confirm, different people react very differently to the "same" poem. Some see superficiality where others find profundity; some praise uplifting sentiments where others complain of cliches; some discover coherence where others see only chaos.

Is there any way to tell which of several responses is the best one? Richards thought there was, for he classified the various ways his respondents had deviated from the "right" or "more adequate" reading. And to illustrate what that better reading was, he appealed to "the poem itself." He pointed out what the words meant, how the sentiments expressed in the poem were or were not appropriate to the fictive speaker and situation, how the imagery developed consistently or inconsistently, how the parts fit or failed to fit together. In short, claims the formalist critic, Richards furnished a formal analysis, an analysis not of readers but of texts. Without this or some other standard, no way exists to decide if one response is better than another. In fact, without some standard there appears to be no alternative to complete relativism. For if, as many affective theorists argue, the poem truly exists only when it is apprehended, then we seem to be driven toward the conclusion that there are as many *Hamlets* as there are readers of *Hamlet*. More accurately, there are as many *Hamlets* as there are readings, for our responses change from year to year, or even from day to day.

So this variability gives rise to one set of problems: How can the affective critics avoid the conclusion, and the total relativism it entails, that a new poem is created with every reading? How can they establish a standard to measure the adequacy of any particular reading without assuming the stability of the text and importing that standard from some other context—in other words, without grounding meaning in the text, or the author, or the structure of language? And if affective critics do import a standard from some other context, how can they keep the discussion from shifting to that context, thus leaving behind as irrelevant the whole question of the reponses of actual readers? In short, how can they talk *critically* about the poem–audience relationship?

These questions pose problems, of course, only so long as the "better" interpretation is seen, as it usually has been seen, as the goal of literary criticism. For some reader-response critics, this goal is neither attainable nor even especially desirable. And they contend that our responses to literature are in themselves a subject of sufficient psychological interest as to require no further justification. Without disputing this contention, we should at least notice that the work of these critics differs in some important ways from that produced by critics working in other contexts. When genetic critics, for example, offer us information about the author's life or intellectual background, they are claiming that this information will alter our understanding of poems, that it will confirm or eliminate certain interpretations. When formal critics point to a cluster of images or a pattern of motifs, they are claiming to show us something important that we may have overlooked, something that, now that we see it, will allow us to better understand and evaluate the poem. So they, too, are offering to confirm or eliminate readings. Affective critics who abandon this normative function (and certainly not all affective critics do abandon it) are simply not performing a parallel function. The claim to describe or even to explain the reactions of specific readers is a very different thing from the claim to supply insights that will alter or correct reactions. In each case, the critics stand in quite a different relationship to the reader and the poem. Not until the affectivists go beyond the description and analysis of actual readings and begin to tell us how and why we should respond do their statements really parallel those of critics in other contexts. And at exactly this point, of course, the critics encounter the first problem we discussed:

how can they find, in the affective context, a normative standard for measuring the adequacy of any reading?

Some serious conceptual problems, then, face critics who work in this context. Even so, the audience response seems to many critics so obviously central to the business of literature that the affective context has remained one of criticism's perennial interests. And at the moment that interest is flourishing. Symposia, sections of professional meetings, journal articles, and book-length studies devoted to exploring aspects of the affective context have appeared with increasing frequency in the past decade. These works go under various labels—"phenomenological criticism," "speech act criticism," "transactive criticism," "subjective criticism," and "rhetorical criticism," to name a few—but the most popular name is "reader-response" criticism, and in one sense that term fits some current approaches a little better than "affective" criticism, for several of these approaches give the reader such a dominant role in the transaction that "affective" seems a label too suggestive of passivity. In fact, though, critics operating in this context differ on this very point. They are all concerned, of course, with the interaction between the audience and the literary work, but they differ in the way they distribute their interest between these two poles, some keeping their focus near the text and only occasionally nodding toward actual readers, others concentrating on the responses of specific readers while paying scant attention to the text as a separable entity. Since this brief introduction can cite only a few representative examples of contemporary affective or reader-response criticism, it will be helpful to think of our exemplary critics as occupying a series of points along the imaginary line connecting the work and the reader.

Louise Rosenblatt, for instance, has a position near the textual terminus of that line. Although she has long argued that contemporary critical theory has given too little attention to the role of the reader, she is wary of "aggressively subjective" approaches that analyze responses but not texts, and she often remarks the need to distinguish "relevant" from "irrelevant" responses. Nevertheless, her "transactional" theory puts her well within the affective context. In her terminology, a "text" may exist independently of a reader, but a "poem" exists only when a reader "compenetrates" a text, that is, when he or she chooses to read it "aesthetically." Whether that choice is entirely free is not quite clear since Rosenblatt implies that some texts have features that invite an aesthetic reading and others—a newspaper article, for example—have features that do not. But this very ambiguity is consistent with her view that both the nature of the text and the nature of the reader determine the "poem as event," which is the "transaction" in her transactional theory.

A little further down the line, but still very much toward the textual end, we reach the position of Wolfgang Iser, a German critic whose work is well known in the United States. Iser shares with many other continental critics a strong interest in phenomenology, a philosophy that stresses the perceiver's role in any perception and that insists that it is difficult or impossible to separate the thing known from the mind that knows it. Other European critics who share these assumptions include Roman Ingarden, Gaston Bachelard, and the "Geneva Critics" or "Critics of Consciousness," as they are sometimes called, of whom the best known to English readers is Georges Poulet. But whereas Bachelard, for example, is willing to follow at great length a train of personal associations set in motion by an image in the text, and whereas Poulet is often struggling to merge his "consciousness" with the "consciousness" of the author as that consciousness is revealed not only in a particular work but in everything the author has written, Iser's uses of phenomenology keep him much closer to the text. From another direction, although he has ties with the movement, he distances himself from the practitioners of "reception aesthetics," a line of inquiry employed by some German scholars who study the history of a text's reception. Iser's concern is not with "actual readers"; he is interested, instead, in the "implied reader," a reader who "embodies all those predispositions necessary for a literary work to exercise its effect—predispositions laid down, not by an empirical outside reality, but by the text itself. Consequently, the implied reader as a concept has its roots firmly planted in the structure of the text; he is a construct and in no way to be identified with any real reader" (*The Act of Reading*, 1976, p. 34).

Clearly, then, Iser wants to stay near the textual pole of our diagram. But he keeps a distance between himself and the formalist position as well. There can be no single best meaning that all readings must strive to approximate. The idea of a single meaning is not only at odds with Iser's phenomenological assumptions, but it is equally inconsistent with his view of our experience of literature and of the value of that experience. Much of that value lies exactly in the "indeterminacy" of the text. The text, for Iser, doesn't "contain" the meaning of the poem. Rather, we must "assemble" that meaning from the perspectives the texts provides. In a complex novel such as Joyce's *Ulysses*, these perspectives are so many and varied that reconstructing the novel's meaning is like reconstructing reality itself. And our reconstructions always remain various because they always depend more on what the reader brings to the text than the formalist's model allows. It is true, and here Iser would agree with the intertextual critic, that what the "implied reader" brings to the text is a knowledge of the appropriate conventions or codes that allow him or her to decode the poem. But here again Iser would insist on the poem's ability to transcend the code, to violate the conventions. It does so by presenting readers with "gaps" or "blanks" that they must bridge; in the process they have to construct, from the conventions they bring, new and unconventional meanings. So the text does offer a broad base of determinate meaning, as the formalist argues, and the "implied reader" brings to it a knowledge of the relevant conventions, as the intertextual critic claims, but the "poem itself" exists only in the interaction of the text and the implied reader, and the meaning that results is reducible neither to the conventions the reader has brought nor to the text.

Iser's position, then, allows for more "openness" in the text and more variability in our responses than critics operating in other contexts will usually admit. Equally to the point, Iser finds the value of literature largely in those "gaps" in the text that force the readers to transcend the received codes as they construct, from their interaction with the text, new meanings. We should remember, though, that this value is most available to the "implied reader." Actual readers, who may lack the implied reader's mastery of the appropriate conventions and who may overlook important textual cues, will be more likely to misinterpret the text and produce readings outside Iser's vaguely defined but certainly fairly narrow range of permissible "meanings."

A very different emphasis appears in the work of Norman Holland, who usually operates at a considerable distance from the textual end of our line. More accurately, he has operated at different distances over the years as his focus has moved ever closer to an exclusive concentration on the responses of actual readers. In his 1964 book *Psychoanalysis and Shakespeare*, Holland applied to Shakespeare's plays the terms and concepts of Freudian analysis. While he granted the usefulness of these concepts in the genetic and mimetic contexts, he thought their application in the affective context held the greatest potential for literary criticism, a potential that, aside from a few studies such as the pioneering work of S. O. Lesser, had remained largely unexplored. Holland continued to explore that potential with reference to a variety of texts in *The Dynamics of Literary Response* (1968). Here the text itself was seen as embodying various fantasies and their transformations. Readers "participate" in these to the extent that their own psychic imperatives allow, and to this extent the poem can "work" for them.

In his later writings, though, Holland has been more impressed by the reader's share in the transaction. In *Poems in Persons* (1973), in *5 Readers Reading* (1975), and in several later essays, he has argued that an individual reader's psychic needs—more specifically, his or her "identity theme"—dictates that reader's perception of the text:

> By means of such adaptive structures as he has been able to match in the story, he will transform the fantasy content, which he has created from the materials of the story his defenses admitted, into some literary point or theme or in-

terpretation. . . . He will, finally, render the fantasy he has synthesized as an intellectual content that is characteristic—and pleasing—for him (5 *Readers Reading*, pp. 121–22).

By now the reader's share in the transaction has become almost total, and we are very close to the view that a new poem is created with every reading. If two or more readers should happen to agree about an interpretation, this agreement could only arise because their "identity themes" were so similar to begin with that they created very similar poems as they read. All that remains, then, is to study readers reading.

Holland is not alarmed by this conclusion, but he is occasionally nagged by the difficulty of talking about a largely one-sided transaction. "The literary text may be only so many marks on a page—at most a matrix of psychological possibilities for its readers. Nevertheless only some possibilities truly fit the matrix" (5 *Readers*, p. 12). This comment suggests that the text does set some boundaries to interpretation. But as soon as we try to measure these boundaries, the problem returns from the other direction. "A reader reads something, certainly, but if one cannot separate his 'subjective' response from its 'objective' basis, there seems no way to find out what that 'something' is in any impersonal sense. It is visible only in the psychological process the reader creates in himself by means of the literary work" (5 *Readers*, p. 40). But neither is there any compelling need to find out what that "something" is, for the focus of study now is precisely this psychological process. As we study readers reading and see the various defenses and adaptations they adopt as they confront the text, we can hope to learn something about defenses and adaptations in general—our own and others'—in all kinds of situations.

Although we seem at this point to be very near the reader's end of the line, we are not quite near enough to suit David Bleich. While Bleich agrees in most respects with Holland's emphases (though not necessarily with his Freudian terminology), he complains that Holland's refusal to distinguish between the "objective" and the "subjective" merely confuses the argument, and he suspects that Holland is really trying to find his way back to "objectivity." In Bleich's view, criticism has labored too

long on the mistaken assumption that the poem can be profitably considered as an "object" independent of the perceiving "subject":

> The assumption derived from the objective paradigm that all observers have the same perceptual response to a symbolic object creates the illusion that the object is real and that its meaning must reside in it. The assumption of the subjective paradigm is that collective similarity of response can be determined only by each individual's announcement of his response and subsequent communally motivated negotiative comparison. . . . The response must therefore be the starting point for the study of the aesthetic experience (*Subjective Criticism*, 1978, p. 98).

What the end point of such a study must be is not so clear. It could not, of course, be a progressively brighter illumination of the text, since this goal is ruled out from the start by Bleich's epistemology. But presumably "communally motivated negotiative comparison" could throw light on our motives and strategies for reading. By honestly and tolerantly exchanging information about our responses to literature, we might begin to understand our own psyches and this self-knowledge, for Bleich, is the larger and more important goal, for "each person's most urgent motivations are to understand himself" (*Subjective Criticism*, p. 298).

Finally, then, though Bleich endorses no particular school of psychology, he shares with Holland a basically psychological emphasis, and also a nearly exclusive focus on the responses of actual readers. Assuming, as both critics do, that the poem as independent object is beyond our reach, they argue with some force that no other focus is really available. Even so, the wary reader may feel inclined to wonder why their extreme scepticism about our ability to understand poetic objects should seem so noticeably relaxed when it comes to our ability to understand perceiving subjects. For in such studies, readers must become, in turn, perceived objects, and objects quite as complex as poems.

A last representative critic, and one who threatens to undermine my scheme of placing affective critics at neat intervals on the line between text and reader, is Stanley Fish. When Fish first displayed his "affective stylistics," his position seemed to be somewhere near Iser's.

Like most recent affectivists, he was rebelling against the formalist's doctrine that the poem "in itself" provided an objective standard of meaning, but he was rebelling more strongly against the formalists' view of the poem as a static object, something to be grasped as a whole. Instead, he argued, we really experience the poem as a sequence of effects. Analyzing *Paradise Lost* and several other seventeenth-century poems on this premise, Fish sought to show how the poem worked on the reader, setting up a pattern of responses or a set of expectations that it later violated or undercut. Our experience of the poem was sequential and dynamic. The focus here was clearly on the reader, but Fish was careful to point out that he had in mind a specially qualified reader, someone trained, as Fish himself was, in the conventions of seventeenth-century poetry. Such a figure is rather like Iser's "implied reader," the reader the text seems to require.

But as Fish continued to explore the problems of interpretation, he came to feel it was really inaccurate to speak of the text as directing the reader's response. It would be more precise to say that the reader creates the poem in the very act of perceiving it, and what we call "interpretation" is a more elaborate process of creation in which the formal features the reader claims to "find" in the text are "(illegitimately) assigned the responsibility for producing the interpretation which in fact produced them" (*Is There a Text in This Class?*, p. 163). Fish is willing to push this argument to its logical conclusion: each reading is a new creation and the poem that results is the creature of whatever "interpretive strategies" the reader has employed. The poem "in itself" has quite disappeared.

What, then, is the interpreter interpreting? "I cannot answer that question," Fish admits, "but neither, I would claim, can anyone else." The illusion that we are reading the "same" poem seems to derive support from the fact that many readers can agree about the text's meaning, and even more support from the fact that some readers will allow their readings of a poem to be "corrected." But this support is itself illusory, argues Fish. Readers can agree when they are members of the same "interpretive community"; that is, when they share the same "interpretive

strategies." And when readings are "corrected," they are simply brought into line with those agreed-upon strategies, not with the poem "itself." In Fish's latest view, then, his own "affective stylistics," a way of reading that would place him nearer the textual end of our line than either Holland or Bleich, is simply one more arbitrarily chosen method, a method no more authorized by his theory than any other.

Fish's concept of interpretive communities has far-reaching implications, some of which we will consider in a later section. Most affective critics, though, continue to hold that they have very sound reasons for placing their focus where they do, and they are willing to argue that the nature of the poem, the nature of readers, or both combined dictate where the critics' emphasis should be if they are going to do justice to the literary experience. They differ, as we have seen, in their placement of that emphasis. While no affective critic gives the text the autonomy that the formal critic would give it, some affectivists do see the text as considerably restricting the range of readings they will accept. So these critics must construct some hypothetical reader whose responses will be in conformity with the text's clues, and they show, consequently, little interest in the responses of actual readers. Other affective critics largely reverse this emphasis. We must start with the responses of actual readers, they argue, because that is all we can directly discover. So they complain that the first group is often practicing a type of disguised formalism and giving the text an illusory "objectivity" and an indefensible degree of control over the reader. The first group, in turn, complains that the second, while showing us what some readers do, can never show us what they should do. So the various kinds of affective critics find much to argue about. But they agree on one main point: since the "poem" exists only when the reader (however defined) encounters the text, literary criticism must focus on that encounter.

Suggestions for Further Reading

The range of contemporary reader-response criticism can be sampled in collections made by Susan Suleiman and Inge Crosman, eds., *The*

Reader in the Text (1980), and Jane Tompkins, ed., *Reader-Response Criticism* (1980); both contain useful introductions and full bibliographies. Since many "myth critics," and especially those influenced by Jung, are more concerned with literature's effect on the reader than with other contexts, they may be classed under this heading. John B. Vickery, ed., *Myth and Literature* (1966), provides the most convenient collection of essays on this large topic. Some representative books are Carl Jung, *Psyche and Symbol* (1958), Maud Bodkin, *Archetypal Patterns in Poetry* (1934), Joseph Campbell, *The Hero with a Thousand Faces* (1949), and Richard Chase, *Quest for Myth* (1949). I. A. Richards, in *Principles of Literary Criticism* (1925), makes a pioneering twentieth-century attempt to construct an affective poetics. Simon O. Lesser, in *Fiction and the Unconscious* (1957), offers one of the first books to systematically apply Freudian concepts to explain reader response. Norman Holland has continued work in that direction in *The Dynamics of Literary Response* (1968) and, more radically, in *5 Readers Reading* (1975). Versions of continental phenomenological approaches are represented by Gaston Bachelard in *The Poetics of Reverie* (1960); by the Geneva critics, handily described by Sarah Lawall in *Critics of Consciousness* (1968); and by Wolfgang Iser in *The Act of Reading* (1976). Stanley Fish, in *Self-Consuming Artifacts* (1972), and Louise Rosenblatt, in *The Reader, The Text, The Poem* (1978), use reader-oriented approaches that still see the text as largely controlling the reader's response. Near the opposite pole is David Bleich's *Subjective Criticism* (1978), where the subject is the main object.

Theory

The Quest for "The Poem Itself"

Louise M. Rosenblatt

In her book The Reader, The Text, The Poem, *Louise Rosenblatt offers a "transactional" theory of the reading experience in which the reader and the text may exist separately but the "poem" comes into being only when the reader and the text "compenetrate." In the chapter reprinted here, Rosenblatt reviews the debates between the formal and genetic critics, debates that often found the formalists invoking "the poem itself" as the ultimate ground of meaning, and that usually found both sides ignoring the responses of the reader. Focusing on E. D. Hirsch's replay of the Brooks–Bateson argument over Wordsworth's "Slumber," she awards some points to both sides before providing her own reconciliation of opposites, one that promises to take into account the reader's share in the transaction and to explain in what ways different interpretations can still be valid interpretations. In the process, she furnishes a compact summary of the positions many contemporary reader-response critics are reacting against, as well as a succinct rationale for the renewed interest in the role of the reader.*

THE DOMINANT CRITICAL CLIMATE OF THE MID-century, it is usually pointed out, was largely shaped by reaction, on the one hand against the academic preoccupation with literary history, and on the other hand against romantic impressionism. A third influence often cited is the prestige of objective scientific modes of thought. All of these militated against recognition of the important role of the reader. A reaction, in turn, against the hegemony of the New Critics has now gained momentum. Yet resistance to emphasis on the reader's role still persists. In this chapter, I shall deal with two major current views of the nature of the literary work that rule out the transactional emphasis.

Excessive concern with the history of literature or with literature as an expression of biographical and social factors, the New Critics claimed, led to neglect of literature as an art. Building on one facet of I. A. Richard's work, they did much to rescue the poem as a work of art from earlier confusions with the poem either as a biographical document or as a document in intellectual and social history. A mark of twentieth-century criticism thus became depreciation of such approaches to literature and development of the technique of "close reading" of the work as an autonomous entity. The extraordinary success of some of the critical works and textbooks presenting this general approach established it as practically an unquestioned orthodoxy, if not for whole generations of readers emerging from our schools and colleges, certainly for those trained as specialists in literature.

The reaction against romantic impressionism fostered the ideal of an impersonal or objective criticism. Impressionist critics were charged with forgetting "the poem itself" as they pursued the adventures of their souls among masterpieces.

Walter Pater, seeking to make of his own criticism a work of art, became (with only partial justice, I believe) the exemplar of the reader too preoccupied with his own emotions to remain faithful to the literary work. As so often happens, the reaction produced an equally extreme counter position—emphasis on something called "the work itself," treated as if it were an object whose parts could be analyzed without reference to the maker or the reader.

This trend in criticism undoubtedly paralleled, and was reinforced by, the ideal of the "impersonality" of the poet to which T. S. Eliot brought so much prestige. Spurning romantic self-expression, he declared poetry to be "not a turning loose of emotion, but an escape from emotion; it is not the expression of personality, but an escape from personality."[1] Thus, the literary work is seen as existing apart from the immediate circumstances in the poet's personal life that gave rise to it.

Eliot's famous phrase "the objective correlative"—despite the rather confused concepts associated with it, or perhaps because of its ambiguities*—also undoubtedly strengthened the view of the literary work as something existing in isolation. Eliot's definition of his key term does imply the presence of a reader, since the adequacy of the objective correlative depends on what it can evoke: "The only way of expressing emotion in the form of art is by finding an 'objective correlative'; in other words a set of objects, a situation, a chain of events which shall be the formula of that particular emotion; such that when the external facts, which must terminate in sensory experience, are given, the emotion is immediately evoked."[2] In this phrasing, however, the implied reader seems passively to wait for the signal or formula for a particular and already completely determined emotion. This is an oversimplification not only of the reader's response to a highly complex work like *Hamlet* but even to a simpler one—say, a lyric about life "under the greenwood tree." Even this, we have seen, requires the reader's active contribution. The danger of this formulation is the general assumption that the more uniform and automatic the response to an image or a scene, the better it is as an "objective correlative" and the better the work. This would reduce literature, at worst, to a series of automatic signals, like traffic lights, and, at best, to a collection of static symbols or emblems.

Eliot's basic contention is, rather, that, whatever the author's personal emotion, he must rely on the text to embody it. Reacting against the romantic emphasis on the poet's self-expression, Eliot is actually concerned with communication, and—a point in harmony with the transactional theory—he equates this with finding "a set of objects, a situation, a chain of events," that will enable *the reader* to produce the desired emotions. These were not the emphases generally drawn from the much-cited concept of the objective correlative, however. Freed from romantic identification with the biography and day-to-day personality of the author, the work, it seemed, existed objectively, impersonally, autonomously.

By analogy and example, evidently, rather than as the result of a clearly developed theory, the notion of the impersonality of the literary work of art was paralleled by the ideal of an impersonal, objective criticism. This tended to focus on explication, elaborate formal analysis, and discussion of the technique of the poem, viewed as an autonomous object. The author having been eliminated, the reader, too, was expected to approximate the impersonal transparency of the scientist.

Theory of Literature, by René Wellek and Austin Warren, published in 1949, contributed probably the clearest and most influential theoretical framework for concentration on "the poem itself," as against its study as a document in literary or social history. This work did much to provide a scholarly basis for consideration of major problems of critical theory. Yet, dominated by the notion of something nonpersonal,

---

*In "Hamlet and His Problems," Eliot uses the term in two ways. Part of the time he is discussing whether the situation and facts presented in the play justify Hamlet's emotions as expressed in the play. But Eliot primarily raises the question whether the total play is an adequate "objective correlative" for the author's emotions. Eliot argues that the difficulty of interpreting the play demonstrates its inadequacy in relation to Shakespeare's confused generating emotions.

something apart from particular readers, which "is" the poem, their book has undoubtedly reinforced a narrow view of literary objectivity and a reluctance to recognize the contribution of the reader. Aware of the philosophical difficulties implicit in this problem, Wellek and Warren survey the various positions concerning the nature of the poem, and in their famous chapter 12 develop a sophisticated theory to support their view of "the mode of existence of the poem." Their arguments present in a more developed form what in the writings of their contemporaries is often merely arbitrary dictum or unquestioned assumption.

In the following statement, Wellek and Warren at first glance might seem to be attacking the position developed in the preceding chapters. But they set up as their target an extreme, even caricatured, version of the approach to the poem as embodied in unique evocations: "The view that the mental experience of a reader is the poem itself leads to the absurd conclusion that a poem is non-existent unless experienced and that it is recreated in every experience. There would thus not be one *Divine Comedy* but as many Divine Comedies as there are and were and will be readers. We end in complete scepticism and anarchy and arrive at the vicious maxim of *de gustibus non est disputandum.*"[3] One of the fallacies illustrated by this excerpt is the assumption that the title of a work or the term "the poem itself" must necessarily refer to an entity. Critical practice and literary pedagogy are frequently confused by this assumption. "The real poem," "the true poem," "the novel as it really is," "the genuine novel," "the poem itself," such phrases constantly invoked in *Theory of Literature* and other critical discussions, beg the question concerning whether there is indeed any single thing to which such a term might point. Thus, instead of the first sentence in the above excerpt, the problem should be phrased: "Given the fact that a poem is re-created each time it is read, can we validly speak of anything as being 'the poem itself'?"

The statement by Wellek and Warren illustrates another current confusion—the assumption that recognition of the reader's activity in evoking the poem inevitably implies that any reading is as valid as any other. Any such view

would of course lead to critical chaos. *But nothing in my insistence on the reader's activity necessitates such a conclusion.*

It is hard to liberate ourselves from the notion that the poem is something either entirely mental or entirely external to readers. "The poem" cannot be equated solely with *either* the text *or* the experience of a reader. Something encapsuled in a reader's mind without relevance to a text may be a wonderful fantasy, but the term "poem" or "literary work," in transactional terminology, would not be applicable to such a "mental experience" any more than to an entity apart from a reader. As soon as "poem" is understood to refer to the relationship between a reader and a text, the threatened critical anarchy does not follow; this and the following chapter will show that the basis exists for orderly and systematic criticism.

What each reader makes of the text is, indeed, *for him* the poem, in the sense that this is his only direct perception of it. No one else can read it for him. He may learn indirectly about others' experiences with the text; he may come to see that his own was confused or impoverished, and he may then be stimulated to attempt to call forth from the text a better poem. But this he must do himself, and only what he himself experiences in relation to the text is—again let us underline—*for him*, the work.

This point is frequently glossed over, evidently out of fear that it will lead to an assertion of brash literary egalitarianism. The solution is, rather, to face the uniquely personal character of literary experience, and then to discover how in this situation critical discrimination and sound criteria of interpretation can be achieved.

•   •   •

Wellek and Warren's effort to maintain the autonomy of "the work itself" apart from author and readers, does not succeed theoretically. Yet for at least a generation such arguments satisfied those who sought a rationalization for a formalistic criticism. In the recent reaction against the narrowness of the New Criticism, the historical and biographical approaches are being newly defended. Ironically, however, Wellek and Warren and the New Critics are being attacked for being too flexible in their view of the identity of the work, for conceding too much to the reader! For example, E. D. Hirsch, in his impressive *Validity in Interpretation*, not only insists on the identity of the work but condemns the New Critics for their "banishment of the author."[4] Since Hirsch is even more stringent than Wellek and Warren in his rejection of the reader, I shall briefly sketch some of his arguments and especially cite some of his applications. My main purpose is to make clear what the transactional view offers that is lost in concentration either on the hypostatized poem or on the author.

Hirsch also accepts the fact of the openness of the text, the fact that the same sequence of words can sponsor different meanings. But he rejects as leading only to critical confusion the idea that there can be more than one "correct" interpretation of the text. When the author wrote the text, he "meant" something by it; that must be the sole acceptable meaning. "For if the meaning of a text is not the author's then no interpretation can possibly correspond to *the* meaning of the text, since the text can have no determinate or determinable meaning" (p. 5). His purpose is to develop principles that will counteract skepticism concerning the "conception of absolutely valid interpretation" (p. viii).

Hirsch deplores the effects of the famous essay by W. K. Wimsatt and Monroe Beardsley, "the Intentional Fallacy," with its reminder of the distinction between an author's intention and his actual accomplishment in the text.[5] Agreeing that we "cannot get inside" the author's head and can never be certain of his intended meaning, Hirsch nevertheless argues that "common sense" tells us that author's meaning is the only universally acceptable norm. If genuine certainty in interpretation is impossible, the "aim of the discipline must be to reach a consensus, on the basis of what is known, that correct understanding of the author's meaning has *probably* been reached" (p. 17). This, of course, reflects a highly admirable scientific approach to knowledge in which valid conclusions are drawn on the basis of the available evidence and revised as new evidence emerges. If Hirsch settles on the question, what did the author mean to convey? as the *only* acceptable question, it is evidently because it lends itself to such a method. This search for correctness of the kind that, for example, we desire in interpreting a scientific formula or a logical statement, is precisely what ultimately vitiates much that is insightful in Hirsch's discussion.

Of course, Hirsch cannot, we have seen, completely ignore the fact of the readers' experiential evocation of the work. His method is to relegate it to a theoretical limbo, as self-confirmatory imaginative guesswork,* which then must be scientifically tested against all the relevant knowledge available. The real work of arriving at the author's meaning is seen in the process of validation, which can be carried on "in the light of day" (p. 206). This sets up an arbitrary break between the process of shaping what I call an experienced meaning, and the process of critical validation.

In the course of scientific discovery, the scientist often proceeds by intuition and imagination to arrive at an idea or hypothesis which he then must test by evidence and logical principles.[6] The scientist retains and reports only the logical and evidential proof; the prior intuitive creative process is taken for granted. Hirsch seems to want to do the same thing for the literary work of art—and in stressing so much the logical processes of validation he has forgotten the essential difference between science and art. In dismissing the creative evocation of the poem as mere imaginative guesswork, Hirsch has thrown out the experienced work of art and retained only the scholarly apparatus.

•   •   •

---

*Northrop Frye, in *Anatomy of Criticism* (Princeton, N.J.: Princeton University Press, 1957), similarly dismisses the actual evocation of literary works to the limbo of "history of taste" (pp. 9–10). In his effort to develop a pseudoscientific taxonomy of literature, he sets up for his treatment of literature that model of the physicist analyzing nature. (Frye shows himself very much out of touch with contemporary philosophy of science, which would have shown him that the physicist's "nature" is no more completely "out there" than is our transactionally understood literary work.)

Concentration on extrinsic evidence concerning the author's meaning unfortunately tends to lead to neglect of the poem or novel or play as primarily a work of art. (The New Critics were correct in this contention, although their solution, the fiction of a supposedly autonomous work, had its own unfortunate limitations.) In adjudicating between two contradictory interpretations of a text by Wordsworth, Hirsch exemplifies the way in which such disregard of the aesthetic event comes about (pp. 227 ff.).

A slumber did my spirit seal;
    I had no human fears:
She seemed a thing that could not feel
    The touch of earthly years.

No motion has she now, no force;
    She neither hears nor sees;
Rolled round in earth's diurnal course,
    With rocks, and stones, and trees.

Hirsch presents excerpts from commentaries on the last two lines of this poem. The first is by Cleanth Brooks.

[The poet] attempts to suggest something of the lover's agonized shock at the loved one's present lack of motion—of his response to her utter and horrible inertness. . . . Part of the effect, of course, resides in the fact that a dead lifelessness is suggested more sharply by an object's being whirled about by something else than by an image of the object in repose. But there are other matters which are at work here: the sense of the girl's falling back into the clutter of things, companioned by things chained like a tree to one particular spot, or by things completely inanimate like rocks and stones. . . . [She] is caught up helplessly into the empty whirl of the earth which measures and makes time. She is touched by and held by earthly time in its most powerful and horrible image.

The second excerpt is from F. W. Bateson.

The final impression the poem leaves is not of two contrasting moods, but of a single mood mounting to a climax in the pantheistic magnificence of the last two lines. . . . The vague living-Lucy of this poem is opposed to the grander dead-Lucy who has become involved in the sublime processes of nature. We put the poem down satisfied, because its last two lines succeed in effecting a reconciliation between the two phi-losophies or social attitudes. Lucy is actually more alive now that she is dead, because she is now a part of the life of Nature, and not just a human "thing."

Somewhat too generously, in the light of his later comments on Bateson, Hirsch grants that "both the cited interpretations are permitted by the text." He proceeds to demonstrate that it is not possible validly to reconcile or fuse the two as somehow inherent in the ambiguity of the text. He then repeats his argument that the text can mean only what its author intended. Hence he argues from extratextual knowledge about the author: that is, that Wordsworth's "characteristic attitudes are somewhat pantheistic. Instead of regarding rocks and stones and trees as inert objects, he probably regarded them in 1799 as deeply alive." Hirsch is forced to concede, however, that "Bateson fails to emphasize the negative implications in the poem. He overlooks the poet's reticence, his distinct unwillingness to express any unqualified evaluation of his experience." Yet Hirsch concludes: "*Nevertheless, in spite of this, and in spite of the apparent implausibility of Bateson's reading*, it remains, I think, somewhat more probable than that of Brooks." (Italics added.)

Hirsch recognizes (rather belatedly) that "a poet's typical attitudes do not always apply to a particular poem." Why, then, can he not recognize that even a pantheist might undergo the initial shock of realizing the absence in death of the usual physical attributes of the live being? And why should Wordsworth not have recaptured that traumatic moment in a poem? Later, of course, he might find consolation in a pantheistic view of death, to be expressed in other poems. Nevertheless, Hirsch insists that Bateson's reading (despite its acknowledged failure to do justice to the negative aspect of the text) is more "probable" because he grounds it in external "data" concerning the poet's typical outlook. How far removed this is from any actual experienced meaning derived from the verbal stimuli! The impact of the exact words of the total text has been overshadowed, thrust aside, in the preoccupation with extrinsic information about the author. Arriving at an interpretation thus becomes an exercise in the logic of evidence. The essentiality of both reader and text is ignored.

Even if a letter were discovered tomorrow, in which Wordsworth stated his intention to express a consolatory pantheistic view of death in this poem, we should still have to ask: does the total text permit the evocation of such a poem? Would we not have to point out that the words of this text focus our attention on a mistaken lack of "human fears" of death and on death as an inert state, sans energy, motion, sight, or hearing? There is nothing *in the text* to arouse the feeling that rocks and stones and trees are "deeply alive, part of the immortal life of nature." On the contrary, their being "rolled round in earth's diurnal course" reinforces the link with the effect of inertness produced by the first lines of the stanza, so that even the trees are assimilated to the inert immobility of stones and rocks. If Wordsworth "meant" an optimistic, pantheistic poem, he did not provide a text that enables a reader not already a pantheist to evoke such a meaning. Other Wordsworthian texts, such as "Lines, Written above Tintern Abbey" or "The Prelude" do enable the reader to participate in pantheistic attitudes.

Brooks's interpretation, as Hirsch admits even while rejecting it, does greater justice to the negative emphasis of the text. Yet we must not forget that this, too, is Brooks's particular experience with the text. He infuses a quality, especially indicated through his repeated use of "horrible," that other readers may not elicit from the text. For example, I tend rather to feel, not horror, but an almost stunned realization of the brute fact of lifelessness. If we free ourselves from the obsession with a single correct reading, whether of the autonomous "poem itself" or of the author's meaning, we can recognize that such differences between what readers make of a text can validly exist. And extrinsic evidence can help us to differentiate the author's probably intended "meaning" from the meanings nevertheless validly derived from the text by contemporary or later readers.

•   •   •

Thus, I am ready to accept Hirsch's criteria of validity as *one* possible basis for evaluating a reading. As a student of comparative literature, I frequently read to discover the probable meaning of a text for the author and his contemporaries. My reading, then, should be judged in terms of the extent to which I have been able to limit myself to the horizon of the author and his age.

I am even ready to say that in most readings we seek the belief that a process of communication is going on, that one is participating in something that reflects the author's intention. And especially if our experience has been vivid or stirring, we may wish to ascertain what manner of temperament, life-situation, social or intellectual or philosophic environment, gave rise to this work. Especially if it is a text of the past, we may wish to discover to what degree our experience differs from that of the author's contemporaries. All of the approaches of the literary historian become potentially relevant—textual study, semantic history, literary, biographical, and other types of history. All of these may aid the reader to limit himself to the horizon of the author and his time.

Such acceptance of the traditional approach to the work as primarily the expression of a particular person, time and place, however, should first of all be qualified by an awareness of, and vigilant guarding against, the dangers of the absolutistic concern with the author's "meaning." We need to recognize the uncertainty of being able to duplicate the author's mentality or that of his contemporaries. Hence the danger of either unconsciously or, like Hirsch, consciously substituting knowledge *about* the author and his times in place of an actual aesthetic engagement with the text. The text thus becomes a document in the author's biography, a weak one at that, requiring support from more direct biographic and historical sources.

First and foremost, the priority of the lived-through relationship with the text should be maintained. Anything, any knowledge, that may help us to such participation is to be valued. With that clearly in mind, we can welcome any "background knowledge" that may enhance our ability to validly organize the experience generated by the text. Hence we can reject the notion of the intentional fallacy to the extent that knowledge of the author's intentions may alert us to textual clues that might have been overlooked.

To object to the monolithic views of Hirsch is not to reject the author but to recognize the complexity of the relationship between reader and author. Hirsch would lead us to make of the poem merely the starting point for a scholarly investigation. Rather, we need to keep our priorities clear. Whatever knowledge or insight we might gain by nonaesthetic means will be valued if it enhances the work-as-experienced. Anything else can be valued as biography, as literary history, as social documentation; but these will not be confused with or substituted for the literary experience.

Interest in the author's intention is not the only justification for reading a text. As in the cases of Blake's or Wordsworth's poems discussed above, other criteria of adequacy may be acceptable. A reader of the twentieth century may bring to these poems or to a Shakespeare play, be it *Hamlet* or *Coriolanus*, a "world" that enables him to evoke an experience whose intensity, complexity, subtlety, and human range can be judged to be an acceptable reading of the text, that is, to activate the actual words of the text and not to impose meanings for which the text offers no valid basis. Here, the criteria of adequacy are implicit in such words as intensity, complexity, subtlety, human range. Again, I am aware that such a reading may not meet the criterion limiting us to what we know of Elizabethan attitudes or beliefs, yet by the second yardstick the twentieth-century reading may rate higher. Often, but not necessarily always, the two sets of criteria may be satisfied by the same reading.

•   • •

Those who bring a particular systematic ideology to the text especially need to weigh the effect on their criteria of validity. For example, early Christian exegetes read the Old Testament with the underlying assumption that the only acceptable interpretations were ones that made every part of the Old Testament a prefiguring of the New Testament. Only interpretations that, say, make Adam a foreshadowing of Jesus would be acceptable. A Jewish theologian who

might argue that his interpretaion did greater justice to the text would make little impression: the essential differences would reside in their standards of validity by which to evaluate the theologians' various interpretations, as well as their own. Those who apply a Freudian or a Marxist ideology to their readings are also usually introducing very special criteria of validity of interpretation.

It is sometimes maintained that readers tend to agree on the work and to differ only on matters of detail.* This impression—which is by no means generally supported by the evidence—is largely due to the fact that discussion of a text tends to be carried on among people sharing a common cultural climate. Within the setting of a particular time, culture, and social milieu, a group of readers or critics can bring a sufficiently similar experience to the text to be able to arrive at fairly homogeneous readings. And when they have in common a set of criteria of what constitutes a sound reading, they can then rank the various interpretations and agree on some "hierarchy of viewpoints." Despite the inevitable uniqueness of each life, readers under such circumstances may have acquired the language under similar conditions, had a similar literary training, read the same books, participated in the same social milieu, and acquired similar ethical and aesthetic values. Such a body of readers may thus be able to communicate easily with one another about their still, to some extent, diverse individual responses to a text. They may also be able to come to a common judgment about which reading seems most satisfactory. But always this judgment will be in terms of particular linguistic, semantic, metaphysical factors appropriate to a particular time and place *and* a particular—more or less coherent—set of criteria for an adequate reading.

Actually, since the discusson of a reading of a particular work tends to be carried on among

---

*See Wayne C. Booth, "Preserving the Exemplar," *Critical Inquiry* 3, 3 (1977), 412. Unanimous amusement at Mr. Collins's proposal to Elizabeth Bennet requires that Austen's readers share certain cultural assumptions, e.g., that marriage proposals should be couched in romantic terms.

people within a particular cultural context, the text as "control" or "norm" usually seems to them to be paramount. The readers point toward the set of symbols as they seek to compare what the words called forth for them. The adequacy or inadequacy of a reading can be demonstrated by indicating the parts of the text which have been ignored, or which have not been woven into the rest of the semantic structure built on the text. The readers sharing a similar "background" take for granted their commonly held assumptions. Yet, as we have seen, even within the same general cultural situation, differences in what the reader brings to the text and differences in criteria of adequacy will make possible different though equally "acceptable" readings.

In the aesthetic orientation, the reader probably selects, out of many potential systems of limitations, an arc within which he seeks to synthesize all of the aspects of reference and feeling that the text evokes in him. He brings to this also a particular set of criteria for evaluating the soundness of his own performance. The more self-aware the reader, the more he will feel it necessary to critically scrutinize his own evocation of "the poem" as a transaction between himself and the text.

To speak of the text as a constraint rather than a norm or "system of norms" suggests a relationship rather than a fixed standard. Instead of functioning as a rigid mould, the text is seen to serve as a pattern which the reader must to some extent create even as he is guided by it. The text presents limits or controls; the personality and culture brought by the reader constitute another type of limitation on the resultant synthesis, the lived-through work of art.

The reader's attention constantly vibrates between the pole of the text and the pole of his own responses to it. The transactional view of the "mode of existence" of the literary work thus liberates us from absolutist rejection of the reader, preserves the importance of the text, and permits a dynamic view of the text as an opportunity for ever new individual readings, yet readings that can be responsibly self-aware and disciplined.

Notes

1. T. S. Eliot, *Selected Essays*, new ed. (New York: Harcourt, Brace, 1950), p. 11.

2. Eliot, pp. 124–25.

3. René Wellek and Austin Warren, *Theory of Literature*, 3d ed. (New York: Harcourt, Brace and World, 1956), p. 146. All further references to this work appear in the text.

4. (New Haven, Conn.: Yale University Press, 1967), p. 1. All further references to this work appear in the text.

5. In W. K. Wimsatt, Jr., *The Verbal Icon* (New York: Noonday Press, 1958), pp. 5–18.

6. Banesh Hoffmann, *Albert Einstein* (New York: Viking, 1972); Marston Morse, "Mathematics, the Arts, and Freedom," *Thought*, 34 (Spring 1959); Norwood Russell Hanson, *Patterns of Discovery* (Cambridge University Press, 1958); Henri Poincaré, *The Foundations of Science*, tr. G. B. Halstead (New York: Science Press, 1913), chap. 9, "Science and Hypothesis"; Anthony Storr, *The Dynamics of Creation* (New York: Athenaeum, 1972), p. 67; Thomas S. Kuhn, *The Structure of Scientific Revolutions*, 2d ed. (University of Chicago Press, 1970); Stephen E. Toulmin, *Human Understanding* (Princeton University Press, 1972).

Theory

Interaction Between Text and Reader

Wolfgang Iser

Like Louise Rosenblatt, Wolfgang Iser proposes a phenomenological theory of reading that stresses the role of the perceiver in perception and that locates the poem in the interaction between text and reader. In this view, the text is always incomplete; it presents a series of gaps or blanks that the reader will need to bridge as he or she "actualizes" the text. As Iser has elsewhere explained it, the text offers not the aesthetic experience itself, but a set of instructions for creating that experience. This explanation seems to leave room for some variability in our responses, and "indeterminacy" is one of Iser's key terms. Yet Iser's emphasis finally is more on the instructions than it is on the variability. The reader he speaks of is the "implied reader," that reader who can bridge the gaps in the text and reconcile its diverse perspectives according to the instructions the text itself provides. His idea of the reader, then, is quite close to Rosenblatt's, and quite different from Norman Holland's.

CENTRAL TO THE READING OF EVERY LITERARY work is the interaction between its structure and its recipient. This is why the phenomenological theory of art has emphatically drawn attention to the fact that the study of a literary work should concern not only the actual text but also, and in equal measure, the actions involved in responding to that text. The text itself simply offers "schematized aspects"[1] through which the aesthetic object of the work can be produced.

From this we may conclude that the literary work has two poles, which we might call the artistic and the aesthetic: the artistic pole is the author's text, and the aesthetic is the realization accomplished by the reader. In view of this polarity, it is clear that the work itself cannot be identical with the text or with its actualization but must be situated somewhere between the two. It must inevitably be virtual in character, as it cannot be reduced to the reality of the text or to the subjectivity of the reader, and it is from this virtuality that it derives its dynamism. As the reader passes through the various perspectives offered by the text, and relates the different views and patterns to one another, he sets the work in motion, and so sets himself in motion, too.

If the virtual position of the work is between text and reader, its actualization is clearly the result of an interaction between the two, and so exclusive concentration on either the author's techniques or the reader's psychology will tell us little about the reading process itself. This is not to deny the vital importance of each of the two poles—it is simply that if one loses sight of the relationship, one loses sight of the virtual work. Despite its uses, separate analysis would only be conclusive if the relationship were that of transmitter and receiver, for this would presuppose a common code, ensuring accurate

Reprinted from Susan R. Suleiman and Inge Crosman, eds., *The Reader in the Text: Essays on Audience and Interpretation.* Copyright © 1980 by Princeton University Press. Pages 106–19 reprinted with permission of Princeton University Press.

communication since the message would only be traveling one way. In literary works, however, the message is transmitted in two ways, in that the reader "receives" it by composing it. There is no common code—at best one could say that a common code may arise in the course of the process. Starting out from this assumption, we must search for structures that will enable us to describe basic conditions of interaction, for only then shall we be able to gain some insight into the potential effects inherent in the work.

It is difficult to describe this interaction, not least because literary criticism has very little to go on in the way of guidelines, and, of course, the two partners in the communication process, namely, the text and the reader, are far easier to analyze than is the event that takes place between them. However, there are discernible conditions that govern interaction generally, and some of these will certainly apply to the special reader–text relationship. The differences and similarities may become clear if we briefly examine types of interaction that have emerged from psychoanalytical research into the structure of communication. The finds of the *Tavistock School* will serve us as a model in order to move the problem into focus.[2]

In assessing interpersonal relationships R. D. Laing writes: "I may not actually be able to see myself as others see me, but I am constantly supposing them to be seeing me in particular ways, and I am constantly acting in the light of the actual or supposed attitudes, opinions, needs, and so on the other has in respect of me."[3] Now, the views that others have of me cannot be called "pure" perception; they are the result of interpretation. And this need for interpretation arises from the structure of interpersonal experience. We have experience of one another insofar as we know one another's conduct; but we have no experience of how others experience us.

In his book, *The Politics of Experience*, Laing pursues this line of thought by saying: "*your experience of me is invisible to me and my experience of you is invisible to you. I cannot experience your experience. You cannot experience my experience. We are both invisible men. All men are invisible to one another. Experience is man's in-*

visibility to man."[4] It is this invisibility, however, that forms the basis of interpersonal relations—a basis which Laing calls "no-thing."[5] "That which is really 'between' cannot be named by any things that come between. The between is itself no-thing."[6] In all our interpersonal relations we build upon this "no-thing," for we react as if we knew how our partners experienced us; we continually form views of their views, and then act as if our views of their views were realities. Contact therefore depends upon our continually filling in a central gap in our experience. Thus, dyadic and dynamic interaction comes about only because we are unable to experience how we experience one another, which in turn proves to be a propellant to interaction. Out of this fact arises the basic need for interpretation, which regulates the whole process of interaction. As we cannot perceive without preconception, each percept, in turn, only makes sense to us if it is processed, for pure perception is quite impossible. Hence dyadic interaction is not given by nature but arises out of an interpretative activity, which will contain a view of others and, unavoidably, an image of ourselves.

An obvious and major difference between reading and all forms of social interaction is the fact that with reading there is no *face-to-face-situation*.[7] A text cannot adapt itself to each reader it comes into contact with. The partners in dyadic interaction can ask each other questions in order to ascertain how far their images have bridged the gap of the inexperienceability of one another's experiences. The reader, however, can never learn from the text how accurate or inaccurate are his views of it. Furthermore, dyadic interaction serves specific purposes, so that the interaction always has a regulative context, which often serves as a *tertium comparationis*. There is no such frame of reference governing the text–reader relationship; on the contrary, the codes which might regulate this interaction are fragmented in the text, and must first be reassembled or, in most cases, restructured before any frame of reference *can* be established. Here, then, in conditions and intention, we find two basic differences between the text–reader relationship and the dyadic interaction between social partners.

Now, it is the very lack of ascertainability and

defined intention that brings about the text–reader interaction, and here there is a vital link with dyadic interaction. Social communication, as we have seen, arises out of the fact that people cannot experience how others experience them, and not out of the common situation or out of the conventions that join both partners together. The situations and conventions regulate the manner in which gaps are filled, but the gaps in turn arise out of the inexperienceability and, consequently, function as a basic inducement to communication. Similarly, it is the gaps, the fundamental asymmetry between text and reader, that give rise to communication in the reading process; the lack of a common situation and a common frame of reference corresponds to the "no-thing," which brings about the interaction between persons. Asymmetry and the "no-thing" are all different forms of an indeterminate, constitutive blank, which underlies all processes of interaction. With dyadic interaction, the imbalance is removed by the establishment of pragmatic connections resulting in an action, which is why the preconditions are always clearly defined in relation to situations and common frames of reference. The imbalance between text and reader, however, is undefined, and it is this very indeterminacy that increases the variety of communication possible.

Now, if communication between text and reader is to be successful, clearly the reader's activity must also be controlled in some way by the text. The control cannot be as specific as in a *face-to-face situation*, equally it cannot be as determinate as a social code, which regulates social interaction. However, the guiding devices operative in the reading process have to initiate communication and to control it. This control cannot be understood as a tangible entity occurring independently of the process of communication. Although exercised *by* the text, it is not *in* the text. This is well illustrated by a comment Virginia Woolf made on the novels of Jane Austen:

> Jane Austen is thus a mistress of much deeper emotion than appears upon the surface. She stimulates us to supply what is not there. What she offers is, apparently, a trifle, yet is composed of something that expands in the reader's mind and endows with the most enduring form of life scenes which are outwardly trivial. Always

> the stress is laid upon character. . . . The turns and twists of the dialogue keep us on the tenterhooks of suspense. Our attention is half upon the present moment, half upon the future. . . . Here, indeed, in this unfinished and in the main inferior story, are all the elements of Jane Austen's greatness.[8]

What is missing from the apparently trivial scenes, the gaps arising out of the dialogue—this is what stimulates the reader into filling the blanks with projections. He is drawn into the events and made to supply what is meant from what is not said. What is said only appears to take on significance as a reference to what is not said; it is the implications and not the statements that give shape and weight to the meaning. But as the unsaid comes to life in the reader's imagination, so the said "expands" to take on greater significance than might have been supposed: even trivial scenes can seem surprisingly profound. The "enduring form of life" which Virginia Woolf speaks of is not manifested on the printed page; it is a product arising out of the interaction between text and reader.

Communication in literature, then, is a process set in motion and regulated, not by a given code, but by a mutually restrictive and magnifying interaction between the explicit and the implicit, between revelation and concealment. What is concealed spurs the reader into action, but this action is also controlled by what is revealed; the explicit in its turn is transformed when the implicit has been brought to light. Whenever the reader bridges the gaps, communication begins. The gaps function as a kind of pivot on which the whole text–reader relationship revolves. Hence, the structured blanks of the text stimulate the process of ideation to be performed by the reader on terms set by the text. There is, however, another place in the textual system where text and reader converge, and that is marked by the various types of negation which arise in the course of the reading. Blanks and negations both control the process of communication in their own different ways: the blanks leave open the connection between textual perspectives, and so spur the reader into coordinating these perpectives and patterns—in other words, they induce the reader to perform basic operations *within* the text. The various types of negation invoke familiar and determinate elements or knowledge only to cancel them out. What is cancelled, however, remains in view, and thus brings about modifications in the reader's attitude toward what is familiar or determinate—in other words, he is guided to adopt a position *in relation* to the text.

In order to spotlight the communication process we shall confine our consideration to how the blanks trigger off and simultaneously control the reader's activity. Blanks indicate that the different segments and patterns of the text are to be connected even though the text itself does not say so. They are the unseen joints of the text, and as they mark off schemata and textual perspectives from one another, they simultaneously prompt acts of ideation on the reader's part. Consequently when the schemata and perspectives have been linked together, the blanks "disappear."

If we are to grasp the unseen structure that regulates but does not formulate the connection or even the meaning, we must bear in mind the various forms in which the textual segments are presented to the reader's viewpoint in the reading process. Their most elementary form is to be seen on the level of the story. The threads of the plot are suddenly broken off, or continued in unexpected directions. One narrative section centers on a particular character and is then continued by the abrupt introduction of new characters. These sudden changes are often denoted by new chapters and so are clearly distinguished; the object of this distinction, however, is not separation so much as a tacit invitation to find the missing link. Furthermore, in each articulated reading moment, only segments of textual perspectives are present to the reader's wandering viewpoint.

In order to become fully aware of the implication, we must bear in mind that a narrative text, for instance, is composed of a variety of perspectives, which outline the author's view and also provide access to what the reader is meant to visualize. As a rule, there are four main perspectives in narration: those of the narrator, the characters, the plot, and the fictitious reader. Although these may differ in order of importance, none of them on its own is identical to the meaning of the text, which is to be

brought about by their constant intertwining through the reader in the reading process. An increase in the number of blanks is bound to occur through the frequent subdivisions of each of the textual perspectives; thus the narrator's perspective is often split into that of the implied author's set against that of the author as narrator. The hero's perspective may be set against that of the minor characters. The fictitious reader's perspective may be divided between the explicit position ascribed to him and the implicit attitude he must adopt to that position.

As the reader's wandering viewpoint travels between all these segments, its constant switching during the time flow of reading intertwines them, thus bringing forth a network of perspectives, within which each perspective opens a view not only of others, but also of the intended imaginary object. Hence no single textual perspective can be equated with this imaginary object, of which it forms only one aspect. The object itself is a product of interconnection, the structuring of which is to a great extent regulated and controlled by blanks.

In order to explain this operation, we shall first give a schematic description of how the blanks function, and then we shall try to illustrate this function with an example. In the time flow of reading, segments of the various perspectives move into focus and are set off against preceding segments. Thus the segments of characters, narrator, plot, and fictitious reader perspectives are not only marshaled into a graduated sequence but are also transformed into reciprocal reflectors. The blank as an empty space between segments enables them to be joined together, thus constituting a field of vision for the wandering viewpoint. A referential field is always formed when there are at least two positions related to and influencing one another—it is the minimal organizational unit in all processes of comprehension,[9] and it is also the basic organizational unit of the wandering viewpoint.

The first structural quality of the blank, then, is that it makes possible the organization of a referential field of interacting textual segments projecting themselves one upon another. Now, the segments present in the field are structurally of equal value, and the fact that they are brought together highlights their affinities and their differences. This relationship gives rise to a tension that has to be resolved, for, as Arnheim has observed in a more general context: "It is one of the functions of the third dimension to come to the rescue when things get uncomfortable in the second."[10] The third dimension comes about when the segments of the referential field are given a common framework, which allows the reader to relate affinities and differences and so to grasp the patterns underlying the connections. But this framework is also a blank, which requires an act of ideation in order to be filled. It is as if the blank in the field of the reader's viewpoint had changed its position. It began as the empty space between perspective segments, indicating their connectability, and so organizing them into projections of reciprocal influence. But with the establishment of this connectability the blank, as the unformulated framework of these interacting segments, now enables the reader to produce a determinate relationship between them. We may infer already from this change in position that the blank exercises significant control over all the operations that occur within the referential field of the wandering viewpoint.

Now we come to the third and most decisive function of the blank. Once the segments have been connected and a determinate relationship established, a referential field is formed which constitutes a particular reading moment, and which in turn has a discernible structure. The grouping of segments within the referential field comes about, as we have seen, by making the viewpoint switch between the perspective segments. The segment on which the viewpoint focuses in each particular moment becomes the background against which the next segment takes on its actuality, and so on. Whenever a segment becomes a theme, the previous one must lose its thematic relevance[11] and be turned into a marginal, thematically vacant position, which can be and usually is occupied by the reader so that he may focus on the new thematic segment.

In this connection it might be more appropriate to designate the marginal or horizontal position as a vacancy and not as a blank; blanks refer to suspended connectability in the text, va-

cancies refer to nonthematic segments within the referential field of the wandering viewpoint. Vacancies, then, are important guiding devices for building up the aesthetic object, because they condition the reader's view of the new theme, which in turn conditions his view of previous themes. These modifications, however, are not formulated in the text—they are to be implemented by the reader's ideational activity. And so these vacancies enable the reader to combine segments into a field by reciprocal modification, to form positions from those fields, and then to adapt each position to its successor and predecessors in a process that ultimately transforms the textual perspectives, through a whole range of alternating themes and background relationships, into the aesthetic object of the text.

Let us turn now to an example in order to illustrate the operations sparked off and governed by the vacancies in the referential field of the wandering viewpoint. For this reason we shall have a brief look at Fielding's *Tom Jones* and again, in particular, at the characters' perspective: that of the hero and that of the minor characters. Fielding's aim of depicting human nature is fulfilled by way of a repertoire that incorporates the prevailing norms of eighteenth-century thought systems and social systems and represents them as governing the conduct of the most important characters. In general, these norms are arranged in more or less explicitly contrasting patterns; Allworthy (*benevolence*) is set against Squire Western (*ruling passion*); the same applies to the two pedagogues, Square (*the eternal fitness of things*) and Thwackum (*the human mind as a sink of iniquity*), who in turn are also contrasted with Allworthy and so forth.

Thus in the individual situations, the hero is linked up with the norms of latitudinarian morality, orthodox theology, deistic philosophy, eighteenth-century anthropology, and eighteenth-century aristocracy. Contrasts and discrepancies within the perspective of the characters give rise to the missing links, which enable the hero and the norms to shed light upon one another, and through which the individual situations may combine into a referential field. The hero's conduct cannot be subsumed under the norms, and through the sequence of situations the norms shrink to a rei-fied manifestation of human nature. This, how-ever, is already an observation which the reader must make for himself, because such syntheses are rarely given in the text, even though they are prefigured in the theme-and-background structure. The discrepancies continually arising between the perspectives of hero and minor characters bring about a series of changing po-sitions, with each theme losing its relevance but remaining in the background to influence and condition its successor. Whenever the hero vi-olates the norms—as he does most of the time—the resultant situation may be judged in one or two different ways: either the norm appears as a drastic reduction of human nature, in which case we view the theme from the standpoint of the hero, or the violation shows the imperfec-tions of human nature, in which case it is the norm that conditions our view.

In both cases, we have the same structure of interacting positions being transformed into a determinate meaning. For those characters that represent a norm—in particular Allworthy, Squire Western, Square, and Thwackum—hu-man nature is defined in terms of one principle, so that all those possibilities which are not in harmony with the principle are given a negative slant. But when the negated possibilities exert their influence upon the course of events, and so show up the limitations of the principle con-cerned, the norms begin to appear in a different light. The apparently negative aspects of human nature fight back, as it were, against the prin-ciple itself and cast doubt upon it in proportion to its limitations.

In this way, the negation of other possibilities by the norm in question gives rise to a virtual diversification of human nature, which takes on a definite form to the extent that the norm is revealed as a restriction on human nature. The reader's attention is now fixed, not upon what the norms represent, but upon what their rep-resentation excludes, and so the aesthetic ob-ject—which is the whole spectrum of human na-ture—begins to arise out of what is adumbrated by the negated possibilities. In this way, the function of the norms themselves has changed: they no longer represent the social regulators prevalent in the thought systems of the eigh-teenth century, but instead they indicate the amount of human experience which they sup-press because, as rigid principles, they cannot tolerate any modifications.

Transformations of this kind take place whenever the norms are the foregrounded theme and the perspective of the hero remains the background conditioning the reader's view-point. But whenever the hero becomes the theme, and the norms of the minor characters shape the viewpoint, his well-intentioned spon-taneity turns into the depravity of an impulsive nature. Thus the positon of the hero is also transformed, for it is no longer the standpoint from which we are to judge the norms; instead we see that even the best of intentions may come to nought if they are not guided by *cir-cumspection*, and spontaneity must be controlled by *prudence*[12] if it is to allow a possibility of self-preservation.

The transformations brought about by the theme-and-background interaction are closely connected with the changing position of the va-cancy within the referential field. Once a theme has been grasped, conditioned by the marginal position of the preceding segment, a feedback is bound to occur, thus retroactively modifying the shaping influence of the reader's viewpoint. This reciprocal transformation is hermeneutic by nature, even though we may not be aware of the processes of interpretation resulting from the switching and reciprocal conditioning of our viewpoints. In this sense, the vacancy trans-forms the referential field of the moving view-point into a self-regulating structure, which proves to be one of the most important links in the interaction between text and reader, and which prevents the reciprocal transformation of textual segments from being arbitrary.

To sum up, then, the blank in the fictional text induces and guides the reader's constitutive activity. As a suspension of connectability be-tween textual perspective and perspective seg-ments, it marks the need for an equivalence, thus transforming the segments into reciprocal projections, which in turn organize the reader's wandering viewpoint as a referential field. The tension that occurs within the field between het-erogeneous perspective segments is resolved by the theme-and-background structure, which makes the viewpoint focus on one segment as the theme, to be grasped from the thematically vacant position now occupied by the reader as his standpoint. Thematically vacant positions remain present in the background against which new themes occur; they condition and influence those themes and are also retroactively influenced by them, for as each theme recedes into the background of its successor, the vacancy shifts, allowing for a reciprocal transformation to take place. As the vacancy is structured by the sequence of positions in the time flow of reading, the reader's viewpoint cannot proceed arbitrarily; the thematically vacant position always acts as the angle from which a selective interpretation is to be made.

Two points need to be emphasized: (1) we have described the structure of the blank in an abstract, somewhat idealized way in order to explain the pivot on which the interaction between text and reader turns; (2) the blank has different structural qualities, which appear to dovetail. The reader fills in the blank in the text, thereby bringing about a referential field; the blank arising in turn out of the referential field is filled in by way of the theme-and-background structure; and the vacancy arising from juxtaposed themes and backgrounds is occupied by the reader's standpoint, from which the various reciprocal transformations lead to the emergence of the aesthetic object. The structural qualities outlined make the blank shift, so that the changing positions of the empty space mark out a definite need for determination, which the constitutive activity of the reader is to fulfill. In this sense, the shifting blank maps out the path along which the wandering viewpoint is to travel, guided by the self-regulatory sequence in which the structural qualities of the blank interlock.

Now we are in a position to qualify more precisely what is actually meant by reader participation in the text. If the blank is largely responsible for the activities described, then participation means that the reader is not simply called upon to "internalize" the positions given in the text, but he is induced to make them act upon and so transform each other, as a result of which the aesthetic object begins to emerge. The structure of the blank organizes this participation, revealing simultaneously the intimate connection between this structure and the reading subject. This interconnection completely conforms to a remark made by Piaget: "In a word, the subject is there and alive, because the basic quality of each structure is the structuring process itself."[13] The blank in the fictional text appears to be a paradigmatic structure; its function consists in initiating structured operations in the reader, the execution of which transmits the reciprocal interaction of textural positions into consciousness. The shifting blank is responsible for a sequence of colliding images, which condition each other in the time flow of reading. The discarded image imprints itself on its successor, even though the latter is meant to resolve the deficiencies of the former. In this respect the images hang together in a sequence, and it is by this sequence that the meaning of the text comes alive in the reader's imagination.

Notes

This essay contains a few ideas which are dealt with more comprehensively in my book *The Act of Reading: A Theory of Aesthetic Response* (The Johns Hopkins University Press: Baltimore, 1978).

1. See Roman Ingarden, *The Literary Work of Art*, trans. George G. Grabowicz (Evanston, Ill., 1973), pp. 276ff.

2. R. D. Laing, H. Phillipson, A. R. Lee, *Interpersonal Perception: A Theory and a Method of Research* (New York, 1966).

3. Ibid., p. 4.

4. Laing, *The Politics of Experience* (Harmondsworth, 1968), p. 16. Laing's italics.

5. Ibid., p. 34.

6. Ibid.

7. See also E. Goffman, *Interaction Ritual: Essays on Face-to-Face Behavior* (New York, 1967).

8. Virginia Woolf, *The Common Reader: First Series* (London, 1957), p. 174. In this context, it is well worth considering Virginia Woolf's comments on the composition of her own fictional characters. She remarks in her diary: "I'm thinking furiously about Reading and Writing. I have no time to describe my plans. I should say a good deal about *The Hours* and my discovery: how I dig out beautiful caves behind my characters: I think that gives exactly what I want; humanity, humour, depth. The idea is that the caves shall connect and each comes

to daylight at the present moment." *A Writer's Diary: Being Extracts from the Diary of Virginia Woolf,* ed. Leonard Woolf (London, 1953), p. 60. The suggestive effect of the "beautiful caves" is continued in her work through what she leaves out. On this subject, T. S. Eliot once observed: "Her observation, which operates in a continuous way, implies a vast and sustained work of organization. She does not illumine with sudden bright flashes but diffuses a soft and placid light. Instead of looking for the primitive, she looks rather for the civilized, the highly civilized, where nevertheless something is found to be *left out.* And this something is deliberately left out, by what could be called a moral effort of the will. And, being left out, this something is, in a sense, in a melancholy sense, present." "T. S. Eliot 'Places' Virginia Woolf for French Readers," in *Virginia Woolf: The Critical Heritage,* ed. Robin Majumdar and Allen McLaurin (London, 1975), p. 192.

9. See Aron Gurwitsch, *The Field of Consciousness* (Pittsburgh, 1964), pp. 309–75.

10. Rudolf Arnheim, *Toward a Psychology of Art* (Berkeley and Los Angeles, 1967), p. 239.

11. For a discussion of the problem of changing relevance and abandoned thematic relevance, see Alfred Schütz, *Das Problem der Relevanz,* trans. A. v. Baeyer (Frankfurt am Main, 1970), pp. 104ff., 145ff.

12. See Henry Fielding, *Tom Jones,* III.7 and XVIII, Chapter the Last (London, 1962), pp. 92, 427.

13. Jean Piaget, *Der Strukturalismus,* trans. L. Häfliger (Olten, 1973), p. 134.

The Miller's Wife and the Professors: Questions About the Transactive Theory of Reading

Norman Holland

In contrast to Wolfgang Iser, who puts much of his emphasis on the ways the text controls the implied reader's responses, Norman Holland is more concerned with the ways actual readers control the text. Thus, while Iser offers a reader-response theory that explains why we should have similar reactions to the same text, Holland offers one that explains why we very often do not. Basing his literary theory on a psychoanalytic view of readers rather than on a phenomenological view of reading, Holland claims that each reader will impose his or her individual "identity theme" on the text, to a large extent recreating that text in the reader's image. And this process can be illustrated, Holland argues, even when the readers are professional literary analysts. This argument naturally raises questions about the relative weight of "subjective" and "objective" data, about the possibility of "misreadings," and about the need to account for a reader's changing interpretations, questions that Holland undertakes to answer as he sets forth his own "transactive" theory of reading and defines his position with reference to several other reader-response critics.

Reprinted by permission from *New Literary History* 17 (1986): pp. 423–47. Copyright © 1986 by The Johns Hopkins University Press.

THE SCENE: SPRING AT A LARGE MIDWESTERN UNIversity. 10:15 A.M. A seminar room. Around the long table and in outer rows of seats are gathered a score or so of professorial-looking types from the English department, some senior, some junior. About a quarter are women, some of them, it turns out, faculty wives. They have assembled for a "Working Teachshop" by the Visiting Fireman.

It is the morning after the lecture and party the night before. People are gearing up for the day or, having taught 9:00s, gearing down. Those seated at the table are holding photocopies of a poem. As they banter, they seem to be approaching the morning's exercise in a spirit of curiosity. Let's play the VF's game and see what happens.

The VF himself, neatly dressed if slightly hung over, sits in the middle of one long side. He speaks in a friendly but hesitant voice, feeling his way with this group, new to him. He begins by reading the poem aloud:

The Mill

The miller's wife had waited long,
   The tea was cold, the fire was dead;
And there might yet be nothing wrong
   In how he went and what he said;
"There are no millers any more,"
   Was all that she had heard him say;
And he had lingered at the door
   So long that it seemed yesterday.

Sick with fear that had no form
   She knew that she was there at last;
And in the mill there was a warm
   And mealy fragrance of the past.
What else there was would only seem
   To say again what he had meant;

And what was hanging from a beam
   Would not have heeded where she went.

And if she thought it followed her,
   She may have reasoned in the dark
That one way of the few there were
   Would hide her and would leave no
      mark:
Black water, smooth above the weir
   Like starry velvet in the night,
Though ruffled once, would soon appear
   The same as ever to the sight.

"The Mill" is by Edwin Arlington Robinson, 1920. This morning's consensus is: Not a great poem, but good. One senior man in American literature gravely opines that Robinson is "much underrated."

The VF remarks that he picked this particular poem because part of his lecture the night before dealt with Robert Frost's comments on it. He therefore thought the assembled company might find this poem a useful starting point. This morning, as advertised, he would like to consider how one might apply the theoretical ideas developed in the lecture (the transactive theory of reading, identity theory, feedback networks, cognitive psychology, the architecture of the brain) to something more practical, the teaching of literature. Would the professors be so kind as to fill in answers to the following five questions?

Actually, of course, the VF has a hidden agenda. As he goes to and fro on the earth, from campus to campus, explaining his devilish ideas about reading, he gets the same questions over and over. Last night's lecture was no exception. Three questions, in particular, always arise:

Doesn't this make every reading totally subjective, so that any one reading is as good as any other?

In teaching what do you do about misreadings?

Don't people change their readings? I know I read *Huckleberry Finn* differently now from the way I did when I was a child.

In answer, the VF has stated his views, his transactive theory of reading, many times. Although there are (obviously!) shared elements in the reading situation, we can represent someone's reading a poem or a story as a personal transac-

tion—as an expression of character or identity. The VF is not abandoning the text or techniques of interpretation or the social situation within which interpretation takes place. He is not saying that a reading is not *also* a function of these things. Quite the contrary! he says. He is simply claiming that we *can* understand someone's reading as a function of personal identity.[1]

Sadly, however, the VF feels deep down inside him that no matter how clearly he says these, by now, to him, palpable truths, he will hear these same questions over and over again. To elicit them and discuss them and perhaps even lay to rest these recurring questions he has put together some materials for a workshop for professors of literature. If he coalesces several occasions on which he got groups of professors to work on his materials, he comes up with the scene with which this article began.

Meanwhile, back in that seminar room, the VF, ever hopeful, hands out questionnaires. He promises to hand out his own answers in exchange for their candor, but even so, the professors assembled around the seminar table are a little reluctant, a little shy, a little tested in their professional mettle.

1. To what does the clause "what was hanging from a beam" refer? _____
_____

2. To what does the clause "What else there was" refer? _____
_____

3. What is the most important single word in the poem? _____
Why? _____

4. What does the miller's wife look like (features, build, clothing, etc.)? _____
_____

5. Whom does she remind you of, and why?
_____

The questions artfully span a gamut from the most "objective" to the most "subjective." That is, question 1 asks a grammatical question which I think most professional readers would agree has one "right" and various "wrong" answers.

Question 2 looks like 1, but there probably is no definitely right answer. Still, some answers would be clearly wrong ("the wife," say) while a number of others would be acceptable and, in that sense, "right." I had in mind here Stanley Fish's concept of an "interpretive community." When we ask a grammatical question of a poem, we apply the procedures and conventions of the community of university readers, professors, and students to answer it. We use "interpretive strategies" that we learned from an "interpretive community." These, says Fish, "enable," "constitute," "make available" such ideas as a clause's referring to something.[2] Would the professors' answers demonstrate Fish's claim?

Question 3 asks for a more freely imaginative response. There are no "wrong" answers except (I suppose) words that do not occur in "The Mill." I took the question from David Bleich's book on "subjective" pedagogy in which the author says an answer to this question "begins in complete subjectivity and is then transformed into judgments that appear to be objective."[3]

Question 4 asks for even more projection, since the poem does not describe the wife at all. I wrote this question hoping to test Wolfgang Iser's model of response in which the text leaves gaps (here, the wife's appearance) which the reader feels impelled to fill.[4]

Question 5 admits a wholly personal response. That is, anyone would comprehend a description answering 4 (thin, gaunt, even "like an Eskimo"), but no one else in the room but the answerer could understand some of the answers possible for 5: my mother-in-law; a woman I saw once. Thus 5 calls for a "very subjective" and 1 for a "very objective" answer, and indeed the responses came out accordingly.

Most readers gave the "right" answer to question 1:

The miller

the miller's body

The miller's corpse

the miller

THE DEAD MILLER

refers to a new subj. serving as gr. subj. of verb "could not have heeded." serves as antecedent of "it"—applies to hanged miller.

Inevitably, there were a few who arrived at special results:

fear or the fear of what the future holds

I have no idea.

Seems something dead, fearful, underscoring her fright.

Question 2, allowing more leeway, elicited more varied answers and varied wordings:

THE DEAD MILLER

Again it is referentially the hanged body of No. 1.

This also refers to the hanging body of the miller.

Various possibilities: Hanged miller—smell of hanged miller (bowels loosening, etc.—in contrast to pleasant "fragrance"), what was "there" beside the fear, finally given form—the scene & situation—

Maybe those who said in answer to 2 the miller's body (incorrect, in my reading) had some sort of carryover from question 1. They tended to use more language in answering question 2, possibly expressing uncertainty about their answers.

Some people wrote down what seems to me, at least, the "right" answer, namely, other things that embody the miller's outmoded craft:

The other reminders in the mill of the dead occupation.

Everything in the mill that reminds the wife of the Miller's life & that Millers are now unnecessary.

Still others suggested vague fears or futures or failures:

"what else there was" refers to "what he had meant" and "what was hanging from the beam." The referents are nonspecific and what floats around is the phantom of fear, or doubt or distrust—something that has no form.

It refers to that "something" that pervades the room, fills it with suspense. Not knowing what that something is is half the reason for its powerful effect.

It refers to the *non*-reassuring aspects of the mill—what speaks to her fears (of the future), not to her knowledge of the past. Fear directs itself toward the future.

Questions 1 and 2 should surely evoke the effects of Stanley Fish's interpretive communities. And they do. Clearly the professors were drawing on a common store of syntactic knowledge and shared principles of reading. On the other hand, there was no great unanimity. The idea of interpretive communities may be necessary, but it is not sufficient to explain these responses.

Question 3 elicited (as I had expected) a wide variety of answers:

> dead. is right at beginning of poem & puts weight on everything that follows

> "dead." It suggests what happens.

> fear: Because of her first phrase "There are no millers anymore" which is, it appears, the point of her fear of economic downfall. Such things as yesterday, past, linger

> Fear. It colors all responses to her encounters in the mill

> hanging   Because he's hanging (the miller) in a society that no longer needs him.

> hanging—everything in the poem seems to hang, be suspended, the wife waiting, the miller, no need, the dead miller, hope etc.

Some said there was *no* most important word, leaving the question blank or fussing with it:

> There isn't one.   To answer, though: dead so much death, everywhere—no more millers (other words seem to say again what it had meant).

> I'm uncomfortable choosing—each word seems to be dependent on the others. "There" is used many times in different ways—as a place—as a nonplace—The poem draws attention to *place* (The Mill) as determining action.

Others showed remarkable ingenuity:

> Same.   The irony that there are no millers anymore—and yet no change, no mark, everything still appears the same.

> what   brings reader in

> "No"   that which *is* disappears; connects to "nothing," "no millers," "no form," would not, "no mark."

> MIL   The assonant found in "meal" & "miller"—it ties the entire poem together—especially in "mealy fragrance"

> mealy?   pleasant, warm ground-down grain, devastated people, "mealy-mouthedness" of the probably—uncomplaining wife to the miller, & miller to anyone who might have heard or understood

> yet   she does not know—yet—and so the poem hangs in the moment before knowing, when she suspects, doesn't know, doesn't want to believe

And, of course, there was a joker. The most important word? " 'Hangs.' It jars you."

Surely one could say with Bleich that these answers begin in subjectivity and end in objectivity, but does that statement do more than describe what is taking place? Surely these answers are, finally, "subjective," yet they make various "objective" appeals to the poem. There must be more helpful metaphors than "begins" and "ends" for developing the relation.

Asked in question 4 to project visually, some hesitated, agreed to make an image, but insisted they did not know for sure:

> I remember nothing of her appearance. She seems an image—abstract—of domesticity.

> She is not described at all, of course, and the poem seems to convey a sense of formlessness. There is a sense of evasion, of dimly making out the forms and outlines of things. Yet I see her as a heavy set woman, with a pale face, broad features, a woman who has worked hard all her life.

> No clue in poem—probably small, plain, calico & gingham—anything but velvet

Others tried to reason an image into being:

> ? young?

> She is *probably* short, as she must look up at the beam where he is hanging

> Apron (tea). White face in fear, Hands red

with hard work. Slightly overweight = the diet of poor people who eat a lot of starch.

Some simply went ahead and described her:

Older woman, motherly, has known hard time

apron, thin, long hands & fingers, gaunt cheeks

Slightly over-weight, plain, middle-aged woman—wearing work clothes (housedress)

like a fat Russian peasant-woman in late middle-age

Others resorted to pictures and analogies:

not described—we are free to create our own image—I see a Brueghel.

Like a weaker version of the woman in Grant Wood's "American Gothic"

Several possibilities: the mother in the Katzenjammer Kids strip (older, obese/sturdy/hard-farm working immigrant with apron)—in this case suicide results of economy, or Nastasia Kinsky (grey peasant dress unbuttoned at the top showing inner breast & chest wall, hair seductively falling over left eye, pushed back, falls again)—then suicide due to jealousy, etc.

The variability in these pictures suggests to me a number of things about Iser's model. For one thing, Iser writes as though the bulk of the response were controlled by the poem and the reader simply fills in some inessential gaps. The poems these people describe, however, are *so* different (Grant Wood, Brueghel, thin, fat) that the balance seems rather the other way. Also, the answers to questions 1 and 2 suggest that, even in simple grammatical matters, readers are not constrained or limited. Third, it is not clear to me that readers are "impelled" to fill in gaps. Several of these professors simply refused.

To the last and most projective question of the five, there were the predictable blanks and responses like

no one

I can't think of anyone right now

—Can't think of a literary character just now

As in that last response, most of these professors of literature assumed, more or less automatically, that what was called for was a literary association, and most provided one. Some were predictable, others quite ingenious:

Chaucer—connotations of famous Miller?

The Wife in "Death of a Salesman"

Tristan, Romeo

Women in the Death of the Hired Man, Hedda Gabler

the old peasant woman whose shoes Heidegger writes about in "The Origin of Art"—because she seems to have been totally and unreflectively absorbed in her work (or her husband's) until the event which precipitates the poem occurs. Then, she is incapable of going on.

Others did what I had hoped for the purposes of my demonstration:

An old woman I saw once.

My grandmother—because she was old world & full of care & overworked

My Aunt Betty, who discovered her husband dead on his workshop floor

A former girlfriend, a timorous and dependent person, who gave meaning to her own life by identification with others—an identification with me I couldn't tolerate in the end.

They recalled figures entirely personal to themselves, people no one else in the room would know—except for

She does not remind me of anyone I know. In her fear that something may have happened to hurt a loved one, she reminds me of me.

Others turned to works of art or places, personal recollections but not entirely personal:

Woman figure in Dorothea Lange's depression photo. Sense of being lost, bereft, nowhere, empty.

Any Iowa farmer's wife, perhaps from a photo in the depression, black & white

I saw many working women in England who had that stoical air about them; they were worn by life, not very "well cared for" but still cheery and tough.

She's probably like that only without much fight left in her. Her ending seems so quiet and undramatic—just a bowing to the inevitable.

Finally others *imagined* a person to be reminded of:

She reminds me of someone who someone wants taking a less active role—content to let things happen "They also serve who stand & wait" She is unaffected by what's happening & partly paying no attention

And, of course, there was a joker. "Whom does she remind you of?" "The miller."

So far, we have been looking at answers by many different people to one question. Although these are skilled professional readers, although they are part of an interpretive community—American university teachers of literature—although most are drawing on an essentially similar "New Critical" training, their answers vary all over the place. Question 1 has "right" and "wrong" answers, but after that, responses go every which way.[5]

When we look at many answers to single questions, we can trace some rather vague patterns, but the whole picture is rather a jumble. We can get more coherence, however, if, instead of comparing everyone's answer to one question, we look at one person's answers to all five questions. For example:

1. body hanging there

2. the only thing that was left was his found body—

3.   fear   gives feeling of dread

4.   no idea—housewife—heavy set; placid air of waiting—doesn't pay much attention Keeps on with her

5.   She reminds me of someone who someone wants taking a less active role—content to let things happen "They also serve who stand & wait" She is unaffected by what's happening & partly paying no attention

In these five answers by someone I'll call Professor One, I can read back from the last to the first and perceive a pattern. Answer 5 has a mistake: the repeated "someone," as if the final clause could stand alone, "Someone wants taking a less active role," as if the final clause could apply to Professor One herself as well as to the miller's wife. (Evidently she felt rushed—see 4.) To 5, the most projective of the questions, the one that allows most room, for individual feelings and associations, she speaks of someone "less active," who only stands and waits, who is partly paying no attention.

I see the same theme in her answer to question 4: placid, waiting, not paying attention. Again, as though what Professor One was saying applied equally to the miller's wife and to herself, she does not finish her last clause in 4. Perhaps she as well as the miller's wife is not paying attention. Perhaps she has identified herself with the wife.

In 3, she names "fear" as the most important word because it "gives feeling of dread." Again the phrasing is both passive and vague: the word *does something* to One, something vague. It "gives feeling." The verbs in 2 are exaggeratedly passive: "The only thing that was left was his found body." Finally, in 1, "body hanging there," we get a "correct" answer to this "objective" question, but stated so as to emphasize the theme of passivity ("hanging") and vagueness ("there") that I find more obvious in her longer, more projective responses.

In tracing these themes, of course, I am primarily talking about her responses, only secondarily, inferentially about her. The distinction is essential, for two reasons. First, one cannot infer from One's writing alone what the relation is between her responses and her personality. The passivity I see in this specimen of her writing might be an overreaction by an intensely active person, or it might be a special frame of mind for reading, or it might simply be the result of the party the night before. Second, my reading of her response is as much a function of my identity as her reading of the poem is of hers. My conclusions, like hers, express me as well as what I am reading. Hence, what I am describing is a mutual interpretation. She reads the poem and the poem, so to speak, reads her. I read her response and her response, so to speak, reads me. My reading is my attempt to represent that systematically elusive process in words.

Possibly these interrelations will become clearer if we contrast One's reading with Professor Two's set of five responses:

1. refers to a new subj. serving as gr. subj. of verb "could not have heeded." serves as antecedent of "it"—applies to hanged miller.

2. 2d attribution of something in the mill—1st thing being "fragrance"

3.

4. Unspecified—yet implied she follows, by drowning, her husband's departure by hanging.

5. Tristan, Romeo

Two is reluctant to project at all: he leaves 3 blank and insists in 4 that the wife's looks are "Unspecified." He makes up the lack by a process of inference which he attributes to the poem: the poem "implied" she drowned. Similarly, in 5, he pointed out by way of explanation, Tristan and Romeo fit in a sort of logical way. Each is a literary figure who dies in a double suicide or mutual love-death. His appeal to logic and observable behavior (as in 4) outweighed the woman's sex: very few respondents to 5 were reminded of men by the miller's *wife*.

The wife reminded him of literary figures, Tristan and Romeo, and he showed in 1 and 2 a similar focus on language (at the expense of the physical world). In 1 he spelled out a grammatical answer to a grammatical question exactly, almost fussily. In 2 he provided a grammatical answer—two grammatical answers—to a question that most people answered by an appeal to the events. In 4 he phrased the distressing facts of the poem in tangled euphemisms, "departure" for death or suicide, "follows" for the second death. From merely these brief responses, I can phrase a pair of themes that will unify Two's responses for me: displacement to logic, language, or demonstrable, surface behavior; conversely, a reluctance to imagine what is not directly observable.

Young Professor Three was unusual in being witty:

1. The husband (miller) who has hanged himself. Poem draws attention to, depicts the

transformation of person → object ("it" followed her); woman submerged beneath water, which then heals itself.

2. Various possibilities: Hanged miller—smell of hanged miller (bowels loosening, etc.—in contrast to pleasant "fragrance"), what was "there" beside the fear, finally given form—the scene & situation—

3. I'm uncomfortable choosing—each word seems to be dependent on the others. "There" is used many times in different ways—as a place—as a non-place—The poem draws attention to *place* (The Mill) as determining action.

4. We don't know; the poem doesn't tell us. Wet.

5. The miller.

She, too, is reluctant to project in 4 and 5. Her jokes in 4 and 5 serve as an evasion of the imagining the questionnaire asked her for. Her jokes take us, like Professor Two's focus on language, somewhat stubbornly back to what is demonstrable and obvious. Other themes: smells (2), body wastes (2) being "wet" (2,4), autonomy and dependency both for herself and for the words (3), persons as inanimate objects (1) and vice versa (1), delivering a precise and "professional" reading of the poem even if not called for (1). A psychoanalytic critic might well call this cluster of themes of self-rule and rule by others, obsessional, or, in a bodily terminology, "anal" themes. That is, to make a unity of this reading, I draw (from *my* interpretive community) psychoanalytic accounts of the kind of conflict parents and children have over who is autonomous and who is dependent. Whose rules will be followed, particularly about delivering from one's body something that may or may not be a living part of oneself? Possibly that question applies to Professor Three's relation to this questionnaire as much as to the two-year-old on the potty.

I will call the next reader Professor Four, although I am not sure whether this woman was a professor or a graduate student.

1. fear or the fear of what the future holds

2. millers who are no more.

3. fear: Because of her first phrase "There are no millers anymore" which is, it appears, the point of her fear of economic downfall. Such things as yesterday, past, linger

4. Older woman, motherly, has known hard times

5. poverty of a woman on the brink of it.

The themes that come across to me are fear—the word occurs four times—loss, and deprivation of poverty, specifically in an economic sense (2,3,4,5). In her metaphors, the future is a container that holds something to fear (1). Poverty is a pit one can fall into (5). She gives graphic versions of psychosocial deprivation from a "primary caretaker." I would call the container and pit symbols for what Four calls "motherly." The ultimate fear (in psychoanalytic theory) is annihilation at the hands of such a failing caretaker, and Four repeats that threat twice (2,3): one is no more, and she attributes the phrase to the wife. What defense Four expresses against this fear seems to be simply to face the danger, as the analysts might say, counterphobically: to fear the future, to know hard times, to be on the brink. If the choice is fight or flight, Four says fight: accept the fear and live with it.

The dominant motif in Professor Five's responses is also fear, but with a somewhat different tone:

1. The miller's wife's fears of her husband's suicide: she sees him *as if* hung

2.   It refers to the *non*-reassuring aspects of the mill—what speaks to her fears (of the future), not to her knowledge of the past. Fear directs itself toward the future.

3.   "Dead"
The "dead" fire suggests the failures—and fears—which haunt the poem.

4. I remember nothing of her appearance. She seems an image—abstract—of domesticity.

5.   She does not remind me of anyone I know. In her fear that something may have happened to hurt a loved one, she reminds me of me.

Five's last, candid answer suggests how his whole set of responses may reflect his own anxiety, leading to his error in the "objective" question, 1. The other answers suggest he may have a characteristic way of speaking about that fear: saying it applies to the unknown rather than the known, a kind of denial. The miller is only "as if" hung (1). Something "may have happened" (5). Fears apply to the necessarily unreadable future (2) and to abstractions, the "*non*-reassuring aspects" of a mill (2), or the "nothing" of an abstract image of domesticity (4). Five moves from relatively concrete images—"mill," "fire"—to abstractions—fear, failure, domesticity, future. The hanged man is only "as if" hung. He thus wards off literal fear: "She does not remind me of anyone I know." But he does make a mistake in 1.

Professor Six's responses somewhat resemble Five's:

1. The miller

2. His absence

3.   "No"
That which *is* disappears; connects to "nothing," "no millers," "no form," would not, "no mark."

4. apron, thin, long hands & fingers, gaunt cheeks

5.   Woman figure in Dorothea Lange's depression photo. Sense of being lost, bereft, nowhere, empty.

If Five was defending against anxiety, Six was warding off a sense of absence, emptiness, or depression, as she (like Five) frankly says in her last response. She chooses "no" for the most important word, coupling it with phrasings of absence. In 2 she speaks of absence directly, and in 4 she imagines thinness and gauntness and, first of all, an apron obscuring the woman's body. In 1, perhaps one can find a significance in her speaking of "the miller" who is absent instead of "the miller's body" which is present.

In short, if I look at all the answers by one person, I can trace a theme or themes that permeate all five:

Professor One: being passive and vague

Professor Two: displacement to language

Professor Three: "anal" themes

Professor Four: loss from a mother

Professor Five: fear of loss, displacement to the unknown

Professor Six: depression at absence; painful acceptance

If these themes permeate *all* of one person's answers, then they have entered into the answer to 1 just as much as the answer to 5. In other words, identical answers can be based on very different underlying concerns.[6] If we were to judge by the answers to questions 1 and 2 alone, we might very well say most of the professors were reading the same text in more or less the same way. We might conclude the text was constraining or limiting their responses. We might say they were applying the canons of an interpretive community. We might say they were constrained another way, by the workshop we were all engaged in.

Having the answers to questions 3–5 as well, though, we can see that they were reading the same text in very different ways. Some were concerned with realism, some with logic, some with language, some with literary form. Some were concerned with fear, others with loss, and others with deprivation.

Question 1 asked an "objective" question with "right" and "wrong" answers. The "right" answers all look more or less alike. Since question 5 asked each person to imagine or remember in a very personal way, people's answers to question 5 look very different. Behind the answers to both 1 and 5, however, is the same personal process, although it may be visible only in the answers to question 5 (or 4 or 3), and invisible in the answers to question 1 (or visible only as capitals or lower case or such slight differences in phrasing as "the miller," "the miller's body," "the miller's corpse," and so on). The "objective" and "subjective" answers draw on the same internal process in which themes of interest or concern to the answering professors shaped the way they worked with the text which was the same for all of them. *Both objective and subjective responses emerge from a process in which subjectivity shapes objectivity.*

The transactive theory of reading models this process as a person, with a certain identity, *using* (as an artist or a craftsman uses) the poem and the various codes, strategies, and settings to achieve a reading that *feels right*. For example, Professor Three was concerned with the relationship between person and thing. Her interest enabled her to *use* familiar interpretive techniques to read the poem as transforming persons to objects, for example, to understand the phrase "would soon appear/The same as ever to the sight" as "heals itself." Persons becoming objects also reflected some aspects of her personality or identity (as I read it). Her overall concern guided her use of shared techniques toward a particular reading that felt "right" to her. She was using the techniques many critics share with her, but using them to suit her unique identity. In the same way, Professor Six used them to suit her unique identity. In the same way, Professor Six used a critic's skill with ambiguity to manage his anxiety. Professor Two used a displacement to language that many critics would applaud, and he used it to serve his defensive needs as well as to interpret the poem. And so do we all.

I suggest that we all, as readers, use shared techniques to serve highly personal, even idiosyncratic, ends. We put hypotheses out from ourselves into the text. Indeed, the psychologists tell us this is the way we see and hear any chunk of the world.[7] Then we perceive *and feel* a return from the text. The poem seems delightful, pleasing, anxiey-arousing, incoherent, frustrating, satisfying, or whatever. Both emotionally and cognitively, then, both as a whole and part by part, we *feel* the poem responding to the hypotheses we bring to it.

For example, a VF hands us a questionnaire. It asks, "To what does the clause 'what was hanging from a beam' refer?" Those who have agreed to fill in the blanks approach the poem with hypotheses about grammar and antecedents. Within those hypotheses, the text enables us to arrive at some image of the miller's body which feels (emotionally and cognitively) like a satisfactory response to the VF's question. "To what does the clause 'What else there was' refer?" Here, the text does not give so clear a feedback to our hypotheses, and we respond differently. To some of us, flour bags and mice felt "right," to others the miller's body, and so on.

In other words, "The Mill," did not, on its own initiative, so to speak, cause what we saw. "The Mill" did not "constrain" a certain response among these professors. Rather, what the poem "did" depended on what we asked it to do. That in turn depended on what we brought to it: what questions, what expectation, what prejudices, what stock responses, what trust, what codes and rules. "The Mill" made a certain reading easy or difficult relative to the hypotheses *we* brought, hypotheses (in this instance) from the VF's questionnaire. If we had not been looking for antecedents for "what," we would not have seen the text the way we did.

That spring morning, the VF supplied the hypotheses. In the more usual situation, we supply our own. We may derive them from what we have been taught, from our culture (our "interpretive community"), or from the situation in which we find ourselves (a classroom, for example, or a theater). We may simply invent our own expectations for a poem. We always hypothesize, however, for that is the way we perceive not only poems and stories but everything. Hence, we perceive the text *only* as it responds to the hypotheses we bring to bear. The text can only affect our recreation reactively, the way the transparency of watercolors affects what a painter can do.

According to the transactive theory, then, reading is a creative process in which (one might say) subjectivity questions objectivity, thereby enabling objectivity to respond to and shape subjectivity. But that appealing paradox, obviously, does not provide a precise phrasing. We can imagine the reading of "The Mill" more rigorously, as a processing of information described by a feedback diagram (see Fig. 1).

While the appeal to a feedback model makes more precise various philosophical ways of stating the process (as dialectical, for example, or as deconstructive, perhaps), it has the further advantage of linking this account of reading to Piaget's idea of development, to theories of artificial intelligence, to brain physiology, to cognitive science, and to various psychological accounts of perception, symbolization, and memory.

In thinking through this picture (my students call it the "lima bean diagram") and the results of the questionnaire, however, it is essential to keep in mind a rather formal threefold definition of identity.[8] Identity is ARC—agency, representation, and consequence. That is, a person's identity is what initiates the feedback loops which are the

way we sense and act on not only poems, but everything. In that sense, identity is an *agency:* it puts out hypotheses from our bodies into the world. The world (or a text) in turn gives back answers to those hypotheses, in a form which is ultimately sensory, and the way we feel about those answers determines the success or failure of the hypotheses. Identity is also therefore the cumulating *consequence* of those perceptions and actions. We are the history of what we have experienced. Finally, however, and this is most important, identity is somebody's *representation* of that identity, just as a history is not just events but somebody's narrative of those events. In representing identity, I have urged the use of a theme and variations which I find most telling. Identity then becomes *the history of an identity theme and its variations.*

Evidently, if Professor Two's reading of "The Mill" is a function of his identity, my reading of Professor Two's identity and its recreation in his reading of the poem is a function of mine. In effect, the lima bean diagram is itself the loop in somebody else's lima bean diagram. If this is a schematic of Professor Two responding to "The Mill," one has to imagine another identity (mine) over to one side of this one hypothesizing this process of Two's and forming a narrative of it (see Fig. 2).

To use this concept of identity effectively, one has to keep all three components of this definition in mind at once, particularly the third. Omitting one or another leads to the common misunderstandings of the theory. In particular, if one neglects the idea of identity as representation, the concept becomes excessively deterministic. Unless one remembers identity is ARC, all three, the theory says that we have identity themes imposed on us in early childhood and we can never ever change them.[9]

Thus, one finds people asking: "Don't people change their readings? I know I read *Huckleberry Finn* differently now from the way I did when I was a child." Yes, of course people change their readings, and it would be the task of a person phrasing an identity to represent those changes. That would involve showing *both* the sameness *and* the differences in someone's readings of *Huckleberry Finn*, since one recognizes difference against a pattern of sameness and sameness against a flow of differences. Putting these samenesses and dif-

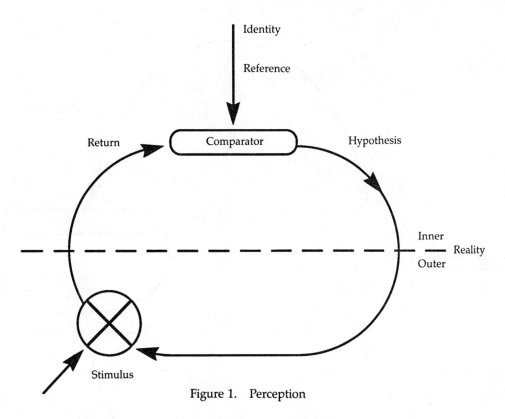

Figure 1.   Perception

ferences into words neither causes nor limits them. It is not the phraser who can affect an AC-identity but the person with an AC-identity who can affect its phrasing (R).

For theories of reading, a feedback model is useful because it provides for *both* the reader's expression of self *and* the reader's use of semantic codes, taught techniques, interpretive communities, or, in general, the social, cultural, interpersonal, or transpersonal features of reading. One is not forced to such extreme claims as, "My language is not mine, just as my unconscious is not mine."[10]

Identity (loosely, "the subjective") enters the feedback loop in at least four different ways. First, identity was the agent. Each professor adapted from my questionnaire the hypotheses with which to approach the poem, doing so in as individual a style as they would later write their answers. Second, the poem did not simply "return" an answer. Each of us *heard* an answer, and we heard it with our own set of ears, our own linguistic usage, our own inner sentences, and all the rest. That is, we

heard the questionnaire, and we heard "The Mill" answer the questions we asked of it—both in the idiom of our identities.

Third, what sounded "right" or satisfying or incoherent to each of us in the poem's answers to those hypotheses depended on the standards each of us applied. What seems coherent to you may not seem coherent to me. What pleases passive Professor One may not please fearful Professor Five. What suits Four as an answer to question 1 may not suit Two's more finely honed sense of grammar. All these criteria in turn are aspects of personality.

More precisely, they are the kinds of things we think about when we put someone's identity into words. When I say "fearful Professor Five," I am phrasing *my* reading of his standards for apprehending loss and anxiety, inferring them from the answers he wrote down and phrasing them in the light of my own standards and hypotheses. Hence we need to imagine another identity in the lima bean diagram, one who is representing the identity of the reader under discussion.

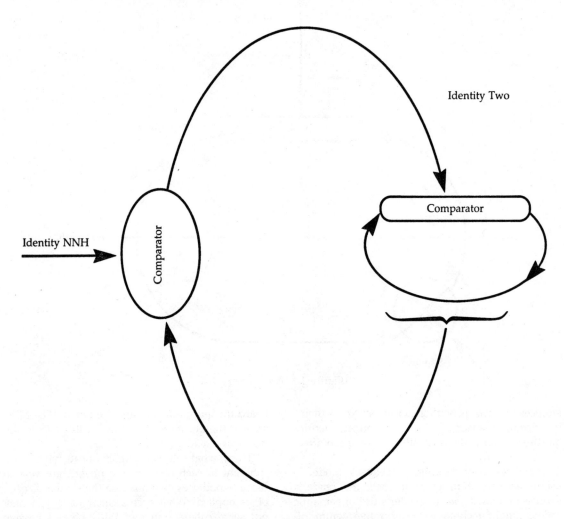

Figure 2.   Perception of an Identity

Identity thus enters the feedback picture in at least four points. Identity frames the hypotheses, identity hears the return, and identity *feels* the discrepancy between that return and one's inner standards. Finally, *my* identity phrases the identity which does these things. Moreover, to avoid confusion, it is important to distinguish between different kinds of hypotheses an identity can put out into the text. Some are physiological. How fast can my eyes scan this novel? How fast can I absorb it? How much of the wording of this poem can I remember as I start the next page? How will the page division affect my reading? The answers to such

questions would appear at the bottom of the feedback picture. They affect the answers the reader gets from his hypothesis in quite literal, physical ways.

Other hypotheses make use of cultural or semiotic codes. I intend "code" in the strict sense: a rule that makes a message possible.[11] I mean letters of the alphabet, numbers, grammar, dictionary meanings, and other things which have relatively fixed significations to all people in a given culture. For example, I see an *A* as an *A*. It would be very difficult for me to interpret it any other way. Indeed I learned this code so young and used it so often it would be well-nigh impossible for me to unlearn it. I could live for fifty years in Ulan Bator, reading nothing but Khalkha Mongol, and still, if I saw *A*, I would very likely think *A*.

Such codes are indispensable, enabling and constraining almost in the same sense as our bodies. We put them as hypotheses into the poem in order to read words, construe sentences, and arrive at meanings, and we do so automatically. The whole process is so fast and unconscious, we scarcely notice it unless we are dealing with a strange language. The only such code the questionnaire overtly used was syntax, in questions 1 and 2.

The other codes a professor uses to read a poem are of an entirely different order. We have seen our six readers seek unity in the poem ("each word . . . dependent on the others"). We have seen professors resist the idea of imagining either the look of the miller's wife or a private association to her. They are, I take it, tacitly following a rule: stick to the words on the page. I hear professors reaching for themes that go far beyond the immediate story of the poem, themes like irony, love–death, social determinism (Four), or negativity (Six).

Any one reader uses both kinds of rules, semiotic codes and interpretive canons, putting them out as hypotheses into the poem. The two kinds of rules are quite different, however. One can put aside a search for unity and start deconstructing as easily as one can drop the Odd Fellows and join the Elks.[12] One cannot so easily abandon seeing *A* as *A* or thinking in terms of subject–verb. One kind of rule, the interpretive canon, is chosen. The other, the cultural or semiotic code, is learned willy-nilly and can hardly be unlearned.

The "subjective" individual—an identity—puts forth these "objective" codes as hypotheses with which to read the text. The text in turn rewards some hypotheses and defeats others. As a result, the person senses both a cognitive and an emotional return from the text. The poem may feel delightful, moderately pleasing, anxiety-arousing, incoherent, frustrating—whatever. These sensations come about as we readers compare the return we get from the text without inner standards for, perhaps, coherence, complexity, unity, or intensity. These inner standards are in turn functions of any one reader's personality or, better, identity. They

may, of course, be learned. We first apply them as the hypotheses we put forward (but those hypotheses may also be our use of convention, an interpretive community, a semiotic code, or even our physiology). We apply these standards to judge the return our hypotheses yield. These standards provide the language—the terms of the contract, so to speak—in which we hear the return from the text.

In short, a person—an identity—*uses* hypotheses with which to sense the poem. The poem responds to those hypotheses, and the individual *feels* whether it is a favorable or unfavorable response and so closes the loop, preparatory to sending another hypothesis out around it. This is the model that has been so closely questioned.[13]

"Doesn't all this make every reading totally subjective, so that any one reading is as good as any other?" That is the one question people most commonly ask me. What I can answer, on the basis of the identity-cum-feedback model, is that every reading inextricably combines subjective and objective aspects to the point where those words cease to be useful terms with which to address the problem. Merely to use those words is to assume that one could separate reading into subjective and objective parts, as though one could separate the process of painting into one part from the medium and another part from the artist, or a hammering into part from the carpenter and part from the hammer.

The metaphor hidden in "totally" raises the problem. It assumes that a reading can be "totally" or "more" or "less" subjective, as though it were addable parts. By my feedback picture, I am suggesting that we need to think of identity as *using, working with, building on, creating from* various hypotheses projected into the world. The world and the hypotheses are, in a manner of speaking, "objective." One cannot separate them from the hypothesizer and perceiver, however, any more than in a sculpture one can sort out the sculptor's subjectivity from the objectivity of the bronze.

One would quite lose sight of the process of sculpting by asserting this sculpture is less subjective than that. It is equally falsifying to assume that a reading could be totally subjective or more subjective than another reading, as the question does. Hence, there is no way to answer such a question. Properly, I am not saying all readings are equally or totally or even partially subjective. I am claiming that one cannot characterize readings as subjective or objective at all.[14]

The next most common question follows from the first. "In teaching, what do you do about mis-readings?" Or sometimes, "If all readings are 'sub-jective,' what's the good of teaching reading?" One purpose of the identity-and-feedback model is pre-cisely to enable us to sort out what we *are* doing when we teach people how to read. That was the reason I addressed a group of professors with it. That is, the model enables us to get beyond the old opposition of objective and subjective, and ask ourselves more tellingly what we are doing by any given classroom move. For example, some teach-ing consists simply of exposing the student to the world of letters: "Read Chapters 20–30 of *A Tale of Two Cities* by Wednesday." In terms of the model, that move simply places students in contact with what is labeled "Outer Reality." We expect the stu-dents to use the hypotheses they already have for addressing a text, the ability to put shapes together to form letters, letters to form words, words to form sentences, sentences to form plot, characters, setting—and so on. If one goes further, if one poses (in the manner of many textbooks) "Study Questions," one provides the student with ready-made hypotheses to try out on that (as did my questionnaire).

Just as a beginning reader learns how to use hypotheses to find the sound or meaning of an unknown word, so a more sophisticated reader learns how to use hypotheses to interpret a whole text. Higher level teaching tries to provide the stu-dent with hypotheses with which to address *any* text or, even better, the ability to hypothesize hy-potheses which will give the best return from this particular text.

In general, then, the familiar modes of teaching literature address the *hypotheses* a student brings to a text, hypotheses like: You will be able to read the poem as referring to more than its ostensible sub-ject (the obsolescence of millers). You will be able to shape the poem into a unity. Once you have done so, you will not be able to find an unnec-essary word in this poem. Any changes you make in details will change the whole, probably for the worse. You will probably be able to find an irony crosscutting the poem, complicating it ("velvet," for example). You will probably be able to find a

reference in the poem to its own creation; often such a reference will seem to deconstruct or cut across the ostensible sense of the poem.

At any given moment a teacher may be giving a student hypotheses or hypotheses for finding hy-potheses or may be carrying a hypothesis through its testing to sense the return. All these are familiar strategies in teaching. All use the students' re-sponses but seek a homogeneity of response. Typ-ically this kind of teaching uses only those re-sponses that can be generalized, shared, or otherwise made available to all the students. Like question 1 in the Visiting Fireman's questionnaire, they look objective because one is providing a pig-ment or a canvas for the picture of the poem the reader will paint. In fact, however, the identity of the artist will govern the use made of the hypoth-esis the teacher gives. Ultimately, whether the hy-pothesis is used at all or whether any given ap-plication feels right will depend on the response of the reader—his or her identity.

In recent years, another kind of response-cen-tered teaching has grown up which addresses the nature of the reading process itself instead of some particular hypotheses associated with one or an-other school of criticism. Such teaching strives to make explicit the experience—the feelings—the student has in addition to or instead of the in-terpretive strategies. In terms of the model, the teacher does not talk about the hypotheses coming out of the right side of the student "comparator," so much as the "return" on the left. He asks stu-dents to be aware specifically of how a given return *feels* (as opposed to "fits"). The teacher may (but need not) go further and explore how a given hy-pothesis or return fits the identity of the reader in question so far as it has appeared in the class-room.[15] In terms of the model, this is a process quite distinct from examining the right and wrong applications of hypotheses.

In my experience, the two kinds of teaching are essentially independent (except that they cast one teacher in contrary roles, permissive and correc-tive). The familiar teaching of how-to-read-litera-ture, by addressing the hypotheses by which one reads, directs attention away from the person ap-plying the hypotheses. Reader-response teaching addresses the person as an applier of hypotheses, how that person feels, and what that person says when those hypotheses are applied. Hence reader-response teaching points away from a critique of the hypotheses themselves or the ways they are applied.

I cannot find any reason, however, why two teachers or even one could not apply both methods as they seemed appropriate. One could do the regular teaching only, as most teachers do. One could concentrate on responses only, as reader-response teachers do. Or one could consider the response as a function of both the person and the hypotheses chosen and applied. In that sense, a misreading would correspond to a wrong hypothesis or a wrong application of a right hypothesis. But it is not true that the transactive model of reading eliminates the idea of a misreading. It does ask, however, that the one who proclaims a misreading make the rule or context explicit that makes the reading a misreading. Too often teachers take it for granted—as part of a residual belief, I think, that modes of reading are self-evident, not to be questioned, eternal verities, linguistic competences, objective.

By contrast, the psychological theory of identity and the transactive model of reading let us tell a more coherent story of reading. I believe that, using these theories, we have obtained good evidence, both from these workshops on "The Mill" and earlier work with individual readers, for the proposition that each of us reads a poem or a story as a personal transaction. We, as individuals with individual styles, create literary experiences within those styles. In doing so, we *use* the text. We *use* the methods we have learned in school. We *use* the classroom or reading room or theater or learned conference in which we are responding. We *use* the canons of the interpretive community to which we have allied ourselves. And in reading, in using all these things, we recreate our personal identities (understood as the agency, consequence, and representation—ARC—of our own continuity in time).

It is too simple to say texts impose meanings or control responses. It is too simple to say there is a subjective part of reading and an objective part. Rather, we need to understand the text, the interpersonal situation, or the rules for reading, as all interacting with a self in a feedback (like a painter's pigments) *in which the self is the active, creative element.* The interpretive community, the armchair or theater or classroom, even the text itself, affect our

recreation only *reactively*, the way a chisel acts back on a carpenter's plans or as bronze both enables and limits a sculptor. The text, the rules, the codes are like musical instruments with which we play variations on our identity themes.[16]

In short, reading is an art like any other art. It has its medium, its techniques, its failures, and its successes. Above all, it has its mysteries. The three questions with which I began, however, are not among them.

Notes

1. I have expounded these theories through all too many years and stages of development. See *Poems in Persons: An Introduction to the Psychoanalysis of Literature* (New York, 1973); *5 Readers Reading* (New Haven, 1975); and *Laughing: A Psychology of Humor* (Ithaca, 1982).

2. Stanley Fish, *Is There a Text in This Class? The Authority of Interpretive Communities* (Cambridge, Mass., 1980), pp. 357, 338, 366, and passim.

3. David Bleich, *Readings and Feelings: An Introduction to Subjective Criticism* (Urbana, Ill., 1975), p. 49.

4. Wolfgang Iser, *The Act of Reading: A Theory of Aesthetic Response* (Baltimore, 1978).

5. In designing my questions, I now realize I had met some objections raised by Jonathan Culler to my work at an English Institute panel on reading. See his "Prolegomena to a Theory of Reading," in *The Reader in the Text: Essays on Audience and Interpretation*, ed. Susan R. Suleiman and Inge Crosman (Princeton, 1980), pp. 46–66, esp. pp. 53–56. He objected to studying reading through the free associations of undergraduate readers on the grounds they were not competent, that the search for free associations will hide the agreement of "ninety-three out of a hundred" readers, and so on. Here, the readers are professors, committed to professional techniques in reading. The occasion was public, not a private interview. The questions pointed to the text rather than seeking associations "away" from the text. I believe this article shows that the conclusions of *5 Readers Reading* hold in this situation, *pace* Culler, as well as for undergraduate free associations.

6. Obviously, realizing this more complex process is important in basing psychological or literary research on questionnaires. The same answer may not express the same underlying process at all. If one is simply counting deodorant users or Democrats, that may not matter. If one is studying reading, it may matter very much. For example, I think my caveat is important

for using such valuable survey work as the IEA (International Association for the Evaluation of Educational Achievement) data bank or the 3rd National Assessment of Reading and Literature. See Alan C. Purves, "Using the IEA Data Bank for Research in Reading and Response to Literature," *Research in the Teaching of English*, 12 (1978), 289–96 and Anthony R. Petrosky, "The 3rd National Assessment of Reading and Literature Versus Norm- and Criterion-Referenced Testing," Paper presented at the Annual Meeting of the International Reading Association, May 1–5, Houston, 1978, ERIC Document No. 159599.

7. A brief, lucid, and authoritative introduction to modern perceptual theory is Edwin Land's "Our 'Polar Partnership' with the World Around Us," *Harvard Magazine*, 80 (1978), 23–26.

8. I have spelled out this concept of identity in detail most recently in my *Laughing: A Psychology of Humor*, chs. 9 and 11.

9. For instance, David Bleich can claim that with this theory "the idea of novelty loses its meaning altogether." See *Subjective Criticism* (Baltimore, 1978), p. 121. The theory, however, claims no more than that *one can trace* a consistent pattern in a person's behavior beginning in early childhood. Obviously, neither one's ability to trace nor a mere consistency implies that novelty drops out of human experience.

10. Culler, "Prolegomena," p. 56. One might ask with Freud, "Whose is it then?" "Unless the content of the dream . . . is inspired by alien spirits, it is a part of my own being." Sigmund Freud, "Moral responsibility for the Content of Dreams," from "Some Additional Notes on Dream-Interpretation as a Whole" (1925), in *The Standard Edition of the Complete Psychological Works of Sigmund Freud*, tr. and ed. James Strachey et al. (London, 1961), XIX, 133.

11. I find conceptual difficulties in the loose sense of "code" some semioticians use. They announce what is no more than a personal interpretation as a code. In this sense, the famous Dorothea Lange photograph of the Depression farm wife to which several readers referred would be a "code" for poverty, obsolescence, or depression. Why not a code for the oppression of women? For aprons? For thinness? A code in this sense simply decrees a single, universal meaning for what is patently variable.

12. Jonathan Culler, however, has called these interpretive rules, the conventional procedures of teachers of literature today, "literary competence," analogizing to Chomsky's idea of grammatical competence. His metaphor equates the deliberate, studied practice of a small group of people in universities with the syntactic rules an entire speech community is born into, acquires almost intuitively, without study, as children, and continues to live by. See Culler's "Literary Competence," in *Reader-Response Criticism: From Formalism to Post-Structuralism*, ed. Jane P. Tompkins (Baltimore, 1980), pp. 101–17, esp. 108–15.

13. The model, I find, bears some similarity to the "three worlds" hypothesis derived from studies of the brain by Sir Karl Popper and Sir John Eccles. Basically, World 2 (self-conscious mind), acting through World 3 (mental products such as language, arts, or theories), governs and is governed by World 1 (physical reality). See Karl Popper and John C. Eccles, *The Self and Its Brain* (Berlin and New York, 1977).

14. Working from a different point in the transactions, the interpretive community or cultural code, Stanley Fish comes to the same conclusion. See *Is There a Text in This Class?*, pp. 332, 336.

15. I have discussed this procedure as a Delphi ("know thyself") seminar. See Norman N. Holland (with Murray M. Schwartz), "The Delphi Seminar," *College English*, 36 (1975), 789–800; Norman N. Holland, "Transactive Teaching: Cordelia's Death," *College English*, 39 (1977), 276–85; and Norman N. Holland (with the members of English 692, Colloquium in Psychoanalytic Criticism), "Poem Opening: An Invitation to Transactive Criticism," *College English*, 40 (1978), 2–16.

16. You could, of course, in the manner of some deconstructionists, choose to read this feedback upside down. You could say *we* are the instruments on which the poem, the rules of interpretation, or the semiotic codes play out variations on *their* identities. That seems, however, a perversely difficult way of thinking about human perception.

Application

Hamlet—My Greatest Creation

Norman Holland

In "The Miller's Wife and the Professors," Norman Holland argues that each reader recreates the text according to his or her "identity theme," and he analyzes the responses of several readers to illustrate his case. In "Hamlet—My Greatest Creation," he shows us how the process works by analyzing his own responses. Far from trying to refute the charge often leveled against affective criticism—namely, that it entails the relativistic view that there must be as many Hamlets *as there are readers of* Hamlet—*Holland accepts this as his starting assumption. Examining five lines from this vast play, he shows how the techniques of close reading, the careful attention to sound, shape, and syntax (Holland was trained as a formalist critic and has, he notes, a psychological affinity for formal analysis), can be combined with a psychoanalytic orientation focused on the reader's response to give an account of the reading process.*

Reprinted by permission of John Wiley & Sons, Inc., from the *Journal of the American Academy of Psychoanalysis* 3 (1975): 419–27. Copyright © 1975 by John Wiley & Sons.

YOU MUST THINK, THAT BY MY TITLE, I HAVE gone beyond even chutzpah to downright blasphemy. Chutzpah, that would be like the sign I used to pass on the old Yiddish theatre in New York when I was a boy. In big letters, *Hamlet*. In smaller letters, By William Shakespeare. And in the biggest letters of all, Translated and Improved by Moishe Schwartz. But I'm going even farther than the great Moishe Schwartz. I'm claiming I don't just improve *Hamlet*, I create it. And I fully expect Shakespeare to hurl down, from whatever Elysium he now inhabits, a sonnet shattering me into fourteen pieces where I stand.

Before he does that, I would like to explain what I mean. We used to say purely and simply that Shakespeare created the tragedy *Hamlet*. That is, he wrote down certain words which contained certain ideas, characters, themes, and even unconscious fantasies and defense mechanisms. That is what we mean when we say a text has a certain "content"—the text is a container. This is *Hamlet* as cocktail shaker into which Shakespeare has poured a lovely, cool, exhilarating, and slightly befuddling content.

But if Shakespeare put a certain content into the play, what content did he put in? If he created *Hamlet*, which *Hamlet* did he create? In the three and three-quarters centuries since the play was first produced, we have seen at least three very different versions of the hero and therefore of the play. So far as we can tell, the seventeenth and eighteenth centuries, closest to Shakespeare himself, thought of Hamlet as a young man of great expectation, promise, and vivacity, a Renaissance prince. The nineteenth century enjoyed Goethe's Hamlet, a willowy, delicate, poetic man incapable of committing the revenge his father demands. And, of course, in our own century we have had Hamlet with an oedipus complex. It isn't just that each century has had its own Hamlet the Prince and *Hamlet* the play. If you look at the volumes upon volumes of commentary on this tragedy, you will realize that, finally, each person has his own *Hamlet*. I find, also, that the *Hamlet* I am talking about today is different from the *Hamlet* I wrote about in, say, 1964 or 1966 or 1961. The play changes even for the same person over his lifetime. If *Hamlet* is a container, it is a magician's cocktail shaker from which one can pour at will martinis, daiquiris, coca-cola, and vanilla milkshakes. The idea of *Hamlet* as having a fixed content just won't do.

What then did Shakespeare create? When we use the word "create" in the sense of being creative, we mean at least two related, but different, things. We mean that the creator creates some physical thing: he makes a movie, embodying it in so many yards of film; he composes a quartet which can be recorded on a paper or disc; he writes a play which can be acted or written down. At the same time we imply that he is able to involve other people in what he has created. When other people are given a chance to see his movie, or hear his quartet, or watch his play, they don't turn their backs—they participate in the aesthetic experience made possible by the artist's creation. Think for a moment about the phrase "failure of creativity." We can mean by it that someone simply stops producing. We can mean equally well that he continues to produce, but that it just doesn't click anymore—people don't take to it. Somehow he's lost the knack. That knack is what Freud called the writer's "innermost secret." As he said, "The essential *ars poetica* lies in the technique of overcoming the feeling of repulsion in all of us which is undoubtedly connected with the barriers that rise between each single ego and the others."

At the Center* where I work, we believe we have been able to get at that technique. We have

built on Freud's writings on creativity, particularly jokes, on some of the concepts developed by the English object relations theorists, and on the identity theory of Heinz Lichtenstein. We have arrived at four quite detailed principles about the way people make experiences out of the raw materials presented to them by, for example, a writer like Shakespeare. The general principle is, in the most exact terms, identity replicates itself. Or one could use the older psychoanalytic term, character: character creates itself. We use the term identity, however, because we define it quite exactly—as the invariant one can abstract from all the ego choices that make up the life of an individual.

Perception is one of those ego choices. Each of us, as we experience not only plays and movies and novels but all of reality, uses the materials that reality gives us within our own personal style of experiencing. Thus each of us creates our own *Hamlet* from the words that Shakespeare gives us. We used to ask, "What in the text accounts for its success with readers?" Or, more precisely, "What in the text accounts for its reader's successful responses?" But we now know that that puts the question the wrong way round. What we really need to ask is, "What in the reader's responses accounts for the success of the text?" In other words, *Hamlet* is not just the words-on-the-page, but, rather, a combination of things in the play with our own ways of assimilating reality. To understand *Hamlet*, we need to begin by understanding our own reactions to the play.

Hamlet is a huge play, Shakespeare's longest. An uncut performance takes from five to six hours. To tell you my reactions to all of it would take weeks, but I can tell you about my five favorite lines from the thirty-nine hundred or so that make up the tragedy as a whole. They are:

O, what a rogue and peasant slave am I (2.2.550)

What's Hecuba to him, or he to Hecuba,
That he should weep for her?   (2.2.559–60)

How all occasions do inform against me
And spur my dull revenge!   (4.4.32–33)

What do these lines permit me to do which is so satisfying?

---

*The Center for the Psychological Study of the Arts, State University of New York at Buffalo. Norman Holland is now Milbauer Professor of English, University of Florida.—ED.

To answer that question, I have to talk not just about the lines, but about me. Let me tell you a few things about myself, things, by the way, that I said in print before I ever became involved with trying to explain my pleasure at these five lines from *Hamlet*. I have "a passionate desire to know about the insides of things with an equally strong feeling that one is, finally, safer on the outside." The core of my identity involves "preserving a sense of self and securing self-esteem by gaining power over relations between things, in particular, mastering them by knowing or seeing them from outside rather than being actually in the relationships." You can see how being a critic of films and drama has fitted my identity, particularly in the modern mode of formal, linguistic analysis. "I *like* examining the verbal surface of a text, looking particularly for an 'organic unity' in the way the parts all come together."

Now, when I turn back to those five favorite lines, I am puzzled to notice that each of them lacks, rather than has, the tight kind of organic unity I prize. Each of them has a little something unnecessary in it, a kind of padding, if you will. "O, what a rogue and peasant slave am I!" Why not, "O, what a rogue am I!" or, "O, what a peasant slave am I"? It could just as well be, "What's Hecuba to him that he should weep for her?" Or, "What's he to Hecuba that he should weep for her?" But Shakespeare does it both ways. When I read, "How all occasions do inform against me and spur my dull revenge!," the second phrase seems superfluous. It dangles at the end of the sentence which could just as well be simply, "How all occasions do inform against me." Or, "How all occasions spur my dull revenge!" But Shakespeare gives us both.

Interestingly, it is just this quality in Shakespeare's writing which his friend, Ben Jonson, singled out as his principal fault.

I remember . . . the players have often mentioned it as an honor to Shakespeare, that in his writing, whatsoever he penned, he never blotted out a line. My answer hath been, "Would he had blotted a thousand!" Which they thought a malevolent speech. I had not told posterity this, but for their ignorance, who choose that circumstance to commend their friend by, where in he most faulted. . . . He flowed with that facility, that sometime it was necessary he should be stopped. . . . Many times he fell into those things, could not escape laughter.

It's amusing that Jonson of all people should complain of this quality in Shakespeare's writing, for Jonson is perhaps the finest example in our literature of an obsessional writer, a man excessively careful about what he would let flow out onto the paper. Another identity creating his own Shakespeare.

Shakespeare was just the opposite of Jonson. Often, he seems to have in excess that quality the Renaissance called *copia* (copy), a fullness of expression. But he does not simply pad his lines. Rather, the extra words permit subtleties and complexities. Consider the single line, "O, what a rogue and peasant slave am I!" "Rogue" could be a noun, but it could also be an adjective modifying "slave," as "peasant" seems to be. A rogue slave. A peasant slave. By the same token "peasant" could also be either an adjective modifying "slave" or a noun, thereby making "slave" the final noun in a series of three, the final and most terrible of the three: "O, what a rogue and peasant—slave!—am I." Because of the extra phrase, I find myself preconsciously following out alternative possibilities and structures within the line.

Thus, for example, first I imagine the player looking toward Hecuba. I see the queen through his eyes but then on the phrase, "or he to Hecuba," I find myself looking the other way from Hecuba to the player. And then the two possibilities are resolved in the final clause, "that he should weep for her."

The third line introduces two complicated and somewhat inconsistent images. At first it seems as though occasions inform against Hamlet like spies reporting to some superior—his father perhaps. Then the second clause suggests his revenge is like a dull horse that has to be spurred to get into action. One of the images has to do with words or information; the other treats a word, "revenge," as though it were something concrete.

I find that my favorite lines make it possible for me to create and explore several grammatical and semantic possibilities within a single thought. They are, in effect, the opposite of denial. They suggest and even ask me to follow out all kinds of complexities and alternate possibilities. So, even if Shakespeare's individual lines do not let me find the tight, organic unity I seek, they do let me master the insides, as it were, of the sentence by understanding verbal and imagistic complexities. I can stand outside the sentence, so to speak, and explore relations within it.

Further, these alternatives take a recurring form or shape. Consider the line "O, what a rogue and peasant slave am I!" It begins with the long vowel O and ends with the long vowel I. The complexities are all in between, as the words "and peasant" bounce off grammatical structure against rhythmical pattern. The same thing happens in the second passage. The sentence begins with the regular foot, "What's Hec-" and then goes into the complexities both in grammar and in sound associated with Hecuba, coming out in the absolutely regular third clause, "That he should weep for her." Just like "And spur my dull revenge!" That sentence, too, begins with the open and regular, "How all" and then becomes involved in the complexities of rhythm and meaning in "occasions" and "inform against."

In short, these sentences begin with a simplicity, move into something full of alternatives and complexities, and come around to a simplicity again. This is, of course, the pattern of the tragedy as a whole. On seeing the ghost, Hamlet resolves purely and simply to set the times right. As you know, we then go into three long and involved acts in which he does anything but. He does not return to his task of revenge until the final scene of the play when he accepts his destiny. "If it be now, 'tis not to come; if it be not to come, it will be now; if it be not now, yet it will come. The readiness is all."

> There's a divinity that shapes our ends,
> Rough-hew them how we will.

Could I not say then that I find in each of these lines the combination of risking and security I enjoy in the tragedy as a whole? They make it possible for me to explore alternatives, but, finally, from their regularity and completion and endstops, I can make a mastery of those alternatives. There is, if not a divinity that shapes their ends, at least a sense for me of regularity and order.

My five favorite lines suggest still another source of my pleasure. All three of these sentences take an external event and make it reflect upon the speaker or, in the Hecuba line, the player whom Hamlet later in this soliloquy will in turn refer to himself. Each one of these sentences creates a situation in which events in the external world acquire their meaning by providing an occasion for an essentially separate and observing Hamlet to reflect upon himself. This is just what Shakespearean plays do for critics like me. But Hamlet does not simply ingest experience. He makes it refer to himself and then from it he creates words, the magnificent speeches that we all admire. Here, too, these three sentences exemplify a pattern that runs all through the play. The very first time we see Hamlet, he appears at Claudius's court in his suits of inky black and watches the goings on, scarcely speaking to Claudius at all, replying to his mother only to point to "that within which passes show." Then, when the rest have left the stage, he lets it all out in the magnificent soliloquy, "O, that this too too sullied flesh would melt." Throughout the play he does the same: after the ghost speaks to him, after Rosencrantz and Guildenstern try to get information out of him, after he watches the players, after he watches the play within the play, after he sees Fortinbras's army. An event outside him becomes focused on him, and then he turns it into words. Sometimes he gives these words in soliloquy, sometimes he speaks fully to Horatio or his mother. But in all cases the pattern is the same: the whole of external reality, love, statecraft, life and death, heaven and hell, all seemed focused upon Hamlet, and from them all he fashions not revenge, but words.

The greatness of *Hamlet* is not the plot alone, nor the character, but the way the thousands, or tens of thousands, of details make it possible for me to explore possibilities and yet master them, to escape reality and yet, in a way, master it, too, by turning it into words.

Notice, too, that all three of these favorite sentences are attacks on a person, two on Hamlet himself, one on his surrogate, the actor. They denigrate—I am a rogue and peasant slave. Or they dehumanize—my revenge is a horse; occasions are spies, Hecuba is something to him—what? Yet this killing anger of Hamlet's is turned inward from its real object—his parents. It feels to me as though Hamlet can tolerate his anger toward them better than their anger toward him. They angry at me? No, it is I who am angry at them. Have they left something undone? No, it is I who have left something undone. In effect, by what he does say, Hamlet tells me what he cannot say. My parents are angry at me. My parents are indifferent to me. They value me as a word or a thing.

Thus, Hamlet uses words to build up substitutes for a world of personal relations, particularly the relations among parents and children, and still more particularly between fathers and sons. It is as though, if there were that personal relation, if there were no words, parents would be violent toward their children or would neglect them. Is this a glimpse at the source of Shakespeare's creativity—a young boy able to substitute words for what he could not tolerate in his relation toward his parents, their violence toward him or their indifference? Perhaps. Perhaps a violence and indifference he imagined as he heard them at night in that doorless bedroom.

At any rate, if words substitute for parental violence or indifference toward a child, then at those points in the play where words are suppressed, violence and parental self-preoccupation should come through. The Ghost's refusing to speak to Horatio and Marcellus, is an example of such an occasion. They "offer it the show of violence." The ghost refuses to tell Hamlet about its purgatory: "I could a tale unfold whose lightest word/Would harrow up thy soul, freeze thy young blood,/Make thy two eyes like stars start from their spheres . . ." (Act I, Scene V). And somehow the very silence is worse than what could be told. When Hamlet swears his comrades to silence, the ghost menaces them from beneath the stage. When Polonius forbids Ophelia to "give words or talk with the Lord Hamlet," he is using her for his own advancement. Hamlet's breaking off his "To be or not to be" soliloquy ("Soft you now,/The fair Ophelia") leads

to his brutal rejection of her. Claudius's prayers lead only to an indifferent heaven. When Hamlet swears his mother to silence, she asks, "What shall I do?" and he replies in these words:

> Not this, by no means, that I bid you do:
> Let the bloat King tempt you again to bed,
> Pinch wanton on your cheek, call you his mouse,
> And let him, for a pair of reechy kisses,
> Or paddling in your neck with his damned fingers,
> Make you to ravel all this matter out . . .
> (3.3.181–86)

Is this the violence and indifference that Hamlet and Shakespeare and I share a fear of—the parents loving each other and not me? Certainly it is the first thing Hamlet complains of in his first soliloquy:

> That it should come to this:
> But two months dead, nay, not so much, not two,
> So excellent a king, that was to this
> Hyperion to a satyr . . .

—That is, a sun god beaming down perhaps on his "son," as against a creature of lust and lechery.

> Hyperion to a satyr, so loving to my mother
> That he might not beteem the winds of heaven
> Visit her face too roughly.   (1.2.137–142)

> Why, she would hang on him
> As if increase of appetite had grown
> By what it fed on; and yet within a month—
> Let me not think on't; frailty, thy name is woman—
> A little month, or ere those shoes were old
> With which she followed my poor father's body . . .

—and those shoes I find suggestive—she married.

> O, most wicked speed, to post
> With such dexterity to incestuous sheets!

Not in the wind and sunlight now, but in bed. And then Hamlet ends,

> But break my heart, for I must hold my tongue.
> (1.2.143–59)

It is as though, when one cannot speak, one is left only the alternatives of an inner sickness, an "imposthume" "That inward breaks and shows no cause without/Why the man dies," or else the explosion into action which ends the play.

Words in this tragedy are, for me certainly and perhaps also for Hamlet and Shakespeare, a kind of potential space in which I can create alternatives and possibilities instead of being faced with violent action or parental indifference. We have sampled but five, yet there are nearly four thousand lines, each one of which, to some degree, allows me to use words to work out alternatives and so control my very deep fears. I fear that parents or parent-figures will be angry at me—I would rather be angry at them. I fear that they will ignore me—I would rather ignore them. Although I enjoy risking these possibilities, I want, finally, to have them controlled as easily as one can control words. All

it takes is a line of verse or a phrase as regular in scansion as "That he should weep for her" or "And spur my dull revenge."

Hamlet has been described as a "great neurotic," a term whose meaning I'm not sure of. I am sure, however, that Hamlet allows me a great countertransference. And that is the secret of the greatness of this tragedy and, finally, of all great works of art: they permit us to become creators ourselves.

Note

Presented at the meeting of the American Academy of Psychoanalysis, Beverly Hills, California, May 1975.

Application

Lycidas and the Reader's Response

William E. Cain

Starting with a nod to Stanley Fish's "affective sty-listics," William E. Cain produces a reader-response analysis closer to Iser's model than to Holland's. The reader here is an ideal construct, someone well informed about the conventions of the pastoral and the devices of seventeenth-century poetry and some-one able to follow the clues of Milton's text as well as any formal critic. But this reader will see the poem not as a static pattern but as a dynamic pro-cess designed to move the reader, at times, even to false surmises and momentary confusions. The ideal reader, in short, will let the text play on him or her as the author intended it should. By carefully ex-amining the text and the reactions of other informed readers (those, for example, who have published commentaries on the poem), the critic can bring us closer to the ideal reading. Yet the term play *also implies some flexibility in the process, an element of indeterminacy in the text that allows for some ir-reducible variation in response. And the wise critic will not try to impose a determinate meaning where the poem offers none.*

Reprinted by permission from the *Dalhousie Review* 58 (1978): 272–84. Copyright © 1978 by the Dalhousie University Press.

I. Pastoral and the Reader

Recent critical work on "Lycidas" includes a number of first-rate analyses, particularly those written by Tuve, Rajan, Friedman, and Brisman; and it might even be argued that these readings imply a critical consensus.[1] But there remain several passages which confuse or trouble critics, or about which they have said relatively little. I will assume (borrowing terms discussed by Stanley E. Fish)[2] that these debates and omis-sions help to clarify important features of our response to the poem: the reader's response to "Lycidas" continually develops and structures it-self from line to line; and the history of the re-sponses of different readers can be found in the critical work. For "Lycidas" our expectations about the pastoral genre are crucial in forming and in understanding our experience of the poem; and (as critics) we enjoy the advantage in this instance of having Milton's first version of "Lycidas" in the Trinity manuscript, which high-lights his effort to re-work the genre and guide our response to its conventions.

The section of the poem which begins "Where were ye nymphs?" offers a useful point of departure, since it is, first, a conventional in-gredient of pastoral, and second, a passage which Milton revised. It opens with a question:

Where were ye nymphs when the remorseless
    deep
Clos'd o'er the head of your lov'd Lycidas?
                                        (50–51)[3]

The reader's response proceeds from his ac-knowledgement of the pastoral convention, for which Rosemond Tuve provides this fine de-scription:

Because it is so familiar an echo, his "Where were ye nymphs?" can and does carry all its old weight of a sympathy that extends throughout the great frame, and that connects natural powers specifically with poets. We accepted the sympathy when we recognized the genre, for it is perhaps the greatest and most moving conception pastoral has borne down the ages.[4]

As Tuve points out, these two lines continue the speaker's (and also the reader's) attempt to account for Lycidas's death. Because the pastoral setting usually connotes a sympathetic order in nature, the reader is prompted to form expectations about what will follow the appeal to the nymphs. Perhaps, for example, circumstances somehow prevented them from performing their duties; regrettably (for Lycidas and for us) the nymphs were elsewhere, but, if present, they surely would have led a successful rescue mission.[5] The reader is next presented with a series of rejected possibilities:

> For neither were ye playing on the steep,
> Where your old Bards, the famous Druids lie,
> Nor on the shaggy top of Mona high,
> Nor yet where Deva spreads her wizard stream.
>
> (52–54)

The failure to this point to locate the nymphs pressures the reader to discover where in fact they were; and it further encourages him to realize the consolation that will follow the pinpointing of that location—that there is, after all, a rational explanation for the nymphs' failure. The next line reveals this desire for an explanation more fully, but leaves unanswered the previous question of "Where were ye nymphs?": "Ay me! I fondly dream!" (55). The reader is stripped of his hope that the nymphs' location can (and will) be specified; but he still appears headed for some reassurance. "Where?" remains an unanswered question, but at least the nymphs' serviceable role is intact. The reference to "fondly" dream likely implies the speaker's affection for his drowned friend; but "fondly" also suggests—and I think this meaning is impossible to discount—"foolishly" and without reason.[6] The next line seems about to grant the expected consolation: "Had ye been there—." But it is instead unremittingly denied: "Had ye been there—for what could that have done?" (56). The preceding lines create expectations about an action whose efficacy is finally discredited. Even if the nymphs *were* present at the

site (still unspecified) of Lycidas's death, their presence wouldn't have made any difference.

The speaker next alludes to Calliope and Orpheus, enabling the reader to view the situation from a mythological perspective:

> What could the Muse herself that Orpheus bore,
> The Muse herself, for her enchanting son
> Whom universal nature did lament,
> When by the rout that made the hideous roar,
> His gory visage down the stream was sent,
> Down the swift Hebrus to the Lesbian shore?
>
> (57–62)

The figure of Orpheus, as Caroline Mayerson notes, embraces a range of associations: the musician and poet, the representative of civilized society, and even, in some exegetical circles, the type of Christ.[7] But these all suggest reasons why Orpheus *should* have been rescued; and the death of this famous mythic and allegorical personage even more grimly reinforces the absence of a sympathetic order in nature. The new question of these lines ("What could the Muse?") follows upon two earlier ones: "Where were ye nymphs" and "For what could that have done?" But the withholding of consolation is now intensified. "Before the question is completed," Leslie Brisman perceptively explains, "nature is described with the words 'did lament'; the chance to do something is over, in the past tense."[8] Not only efficacious action, but *all* action, is denied as a possibility; and the reader's expectations, deflected a few moments ago ("For what could that have done?") are now undercut more severely. As Brisman observes, "the reader is caught in the anticipation of the event and is shocked in reading the next lines to find it is already over."[9] But still more can be said. Before at least the reader was presented with a verb: "have done"; action may have been deprived of its efficacy, but the nature of the action was at least considered, if only to be set aside. Now the reader is even deprived of a verb. He likely expects to read: "What could the Muse herself . . . *have done?*"; but the verb does not arrive, and the reader is left suspended, waiting for the description of action which fails to be forthcoming. Not only pastoral conventions, but now even syntax, fail to function properly.

Milton's revisions of the Orpheus passage clearly intimate his intention to undermine his

reader's desire for action.[10] In the Trinity manuscript, Milton wrote *"might* lament," rather than
"did lament." To leave the verb in the condi-
tional would have kept open alternatives: perhaps sometime in the future "universal nature"
might extend its sympathy to Orpheus. But "did
lament" closes down this option by placing the
action, as Brisman remarks, "in the past tense";
this possibility is now unavailable, because it
has been performed already. Milton also originally wrote "divine head," later correcting it to
read "gory visage." The earlier version ascribed
to Orpheus the noble and reverential aura summarized in Mayerson's essay. But the revision
emphasizes death-deformed features (the "gory
visage") rather than divine attributes. The
reader is not allowed to glimpse the image of
what Orpheus was in life, but is instead forced
to visualize the change brought about by his
death.

Roy Daniells notes in relation to the Orpheus
passage that "the window on this vision of
ghastly dismemberment instantly shuts. A meditation of fame ensues."[11] His judgment may
seem at first to support Wilson Knight's well-
known belief that "Lycidas" lacks "unity," and
stands only as "an accumulation of magnificent
fragments."[12] But both critics' reservations point
interestingly to the poem's effect here (and elsewhere) on its readers: its refusal to provide
smooth formal transitions, and its denial of comforting answers to the questions which pastoral
raises. The reader comes upon a question
("Where were ye nymphs?"), expects an answer
to unfold, fails to receive it, and is left with still
more questions.[13]

The next question arises from the speaker's
complaint that he is not rewarded for his activity:

> Alas! What boots it with uncessant care
> To tend the homely slighted Shepherd's trade,
> And strictly meditate the thankless Muse? (63–66)

He employs the pastoral fiction to protest the
failure of his tasks to meet with fair compen-
sation. Of what use are pastoral commonplaces
when they prove unable to bring about the rescue of Lycidas, or to console those who remain
for the fact of his death? The alternative is
tempting:

> Were it not better done as others use,
> To sport with Amaryllis in the shade,
> Or with the tangles of Neaera's hair?   (67–69)

The speaker has outlined two modes of conduct:
his present and unsatisfying "trade," and the
pleasant pastimes enjoyed by others. Which, the
reader is invited to ask, will be judged preferable? How will the speaker adjudicate between
conflicting vocations? But the anticipated choice
is left unclear:

> Fame is the spur that the clear spirit doth raise
> (That last infirmity of Noble mind)
> To scorn delights and live laborious days. (70–72)

As Merritt Hughes reminds us in a textual note,
Milton's reference to "fame" as a motive for virtuous action expresses a Renaissance commonplace. But its authority again fails to reassure the
reader. The first line appears to suggest that the
speaker has decided in favor of the shepherd's
"trade"; he bears up under trial for the eventual
reward of "fame." But the reader's assent to this
traditional notion barely survives into the next
line. "Fame," whose worth was unquestioned a
moment ago, is now declared an "infirmity." It
may be desirable, but is inappropriate for the
truly virtuous. The force of these lines can be
better appreciated if the single line in parenthesis is omitted:

> Fame is the spur that the clear spirit doth raise
> To scorn delights and live laborious days.

Here the run-on line offers a smooth transition;
and the commonplace is untainted by any suggestion of its inadequacy. In the poem "fame"
is assigned an ambiguous status; at best it stimulates good conduct, but for the wrong reasons.

Perhaps the reader presumes at this point
that the speaker will clarify his position on
"fame" in a different way: "The desire for fame
leads to this hard labor, but look how worthwhile are the results." And the pressure to resolve this issue is all the greater for the reader,
because of his desire to understand why "fame"
must be judged dismayingly as an "infirmity."
But the poem denies the issuance of "fame" by
taking a vicious turn:

> But the fair Guerdon when we hope to find,
> And think to burst out into sudden blaze,
> Comes the blind Fury with th'abhorred shears,
> And slits the thin-spun life.   (73–76)

Not only is "fame" an "infirmity," and therefore an improper motive for virtuous conduct; it is also a reward which never arrives—to hope so is to be self-deceived. This realization is forced on the reader by the sudden appearance of "comes" in line 75. After the reader negotiates the first two lines, he likely assumes that "comes" belongs with "the fair Guerdon"; that is, he proceeds from "hope to find" to "think to burst out" to "comes," expecting to discover that the reward "comes" (say) only at the end of life, when it is too late to be truly enjoyed. But the truth is presented more cruelly. "Comes" is an activity not associated with "the fair Guerdon," but with "the blind Fury." The Fury's presence in the line (linked with "comes") is designed to startle the reader; it is quite unexpected, and interrupts both "the meditation on fame" and the effort to maintain the usual syntactical order. The reader who hopes for direct action now receives it, as the Fury "slits" the threads of men's lives. B. Rajan nicely describes this effect:

> The word "slit" placed with almost malignant accuracy in the halting march of the monosyllabic line, is potent in evoking a calculating power of destruction, all the more challenging because it is driven by blindness.[14]

Pastoral sympathy and positive action (labor which ends in deserved fame) are ruthlessly denied.

The reference to "blindness" is, as the Variorum editors explain, Milton's addition, and suggests that the action is not only vicious, but indiscriminate. Yet, as the editors also mention, it is difficult to determine why Milton refers at all to "Fury" when he should (of course) mean "Fate." They are right, I think, to observe that Milton isn't guilty of "confusing Atropos, the third of the Fates, with the Furies." What he achieves by the substitution is continued surprise and disorientation of the reader. The editors duly note that "the function of Furies is always the avenger of crime"; but they add that, while Milton does present a "Fury," it is "not of course as an avenger of crime." This effort to distinguish Milton's usage from what is "always" true elsewhere makes it all the more likely to form part of the reader's response—he must work to redefine and somehow reorganize the roles of these mythological figures.

The rest of the line appears to mark a recovery: "But not the praise"[15] (76). The speaker seems about to declare that, despite death, the laborer's fame survives: he will be remembered. But the reader quickly finds out that it is "Phoebus" who speaks: "But not the praise,/Phoebus replied, and touch'd my tremblng ears" (77–78). The "voice," as Brisman comments, undergoes "a correction";[16] and the reader fails at first to perceive the identity of the new speaker. Phoebus redefines "fame":

> Fame is no plant that grows on mortal soil,
> Nor in the glistening foil
> Set off to th' world, nor in broad rumor lies,
> But lives and spreads aloft by those pure eyes
> And perfect witness of all judging Jove;
> As he pronounces lastly on each deed,
> Of so much fame in Heav'n expect thy meed.
>
> (78–84)

The reader now learns that the pastoral terms to which both he and the speaker have assented offer no source of fame or (immediate) consolation: if fame lives on at all, it does so in ways not accounted for by pursuits on "mortal soil." The "But" in the fourth line may (once again) connote to the reader the sense that at last truth—delivered authoritatively—will arrive. The answer may be harsh, but negative options (what "fame" is *not*) have been eliminated, and a full definition appears imminent. At first glance the answer seems conventional—the promise of a heavenly reward; and the fulfillment of the convention indicates a notable step forward in the reader's search for justice and order. Yet this Christian consolation is articulated by pagan deities. Brooks and Hardy comment helpfully:

> The shock of transition from pagan to Christian is being cushioned by the poet's having one of the classic gods proclaim in effect that his "Kingdom is not of this world." But "cushioned" really overstates the case. Milton obviously wants us to feel some kind of clash. . . .[17]

They are correct not only to point to the "shock" of the transition, but also to concede that "cushioned" overstates the case. Rather than "cushioned," I would propose "reinforced." This disjunction between pagan and Christian disorients the reader—it is as though Christ in *Paradise Regained* were to speak of the primacy of the classics. Rosemond Tuve's claim that the pagan and Christian elements are not incompatible may miss the point. She writes: "This is not a matter of 'Christian' and 'Pagan' but of direction and indirection, of a less or more figurative functioning in the language. Both are Christian."[18] Even if Tuve is right, the lines remain problematical, the speaker and reader are again told to "expect" an action, and by way of a rather pat rhyme: "deed/meed." Expectations about fame are not resolved, but simply postponed.

II. Some Specific Problems

The Variorum editors term the question "Who or what is 'the two-handed engine'?" the "most debated crux in Milton"; and they spend some twenty pages listing various readings, debating alternatives, and choosing finally to return the issue to the reader: "It is the reader's privilege to make his own choice or to offer a new one, if that is possible." The most recent proposal has been made by Karl Felsen, who maintains that the "two-handed engine" is the scales of the Last Judgment. He explains:

> Let the engine be a single uncomplicated easily recognizable one—the scales in other words— which may have to do the smiting figuratively, but certainly gains in violence and swiftness in that the sword is poised over it. In other words the scales can share in the virtues of the sword simply because of proximity without an actual closer combining of the two images.[19]

Felsen's "single," "uncomplicated," and "easily recognizable" reading will not resolve the debate, and his phrasing—"let the engine be"— seems more an appeal than a solution. As Northrop Frye once remarked, "there are forty-odd answers"—there are now even more—and "none of them completely satisfactory."[20] But to add (as does Frye) that this critical confusion doesn't much matter—"the fact that they are not wholly satisfactory hardly seems to be important"—argues against the evidence to the contrary compiled by the Variorum editors and supplemented by Felsen and others.

The identity of the "two-handed engine" is only part of the story. What does it do? And when, and to whom, is it going to do it? David Daiches alludes to these issues when he states that, whatever the "two-handed engine" is, it indicates that "retribution is certain through a device which suggests purposive action on the part of society."[21] Of course "certain" implies the magnitude of the problem: When is *that*? Rosemond Tuve, perhaps referring to Daiches, argues that "it seems difficult to press the image, as many critics do, to answer the question 'when will it'?"[22] But readers *do* "press the image" in this way, and to claim otherwise is to ignore their collective testimony.

As the variety and range of the critical work imply, the lines on the "two-handed engine" beg more questions than they answer:

> But that two-handed engine at the door
> Stands ready to smite once, and smite no more.
>
> (130–131)

The reader's hopes for "retribution" depend upon knowing the precise referents for the image—a knowledge which is withheld. This indefiniteness is crucial to the effect: reassurance seems far away when the reader cannot determine how the action will come about (how? and by whose hands?). The reader is not only deprived of the *kind* of action, but left waiting for it to occur: it stands "ready to smite once," but doesn't. Perhaps the reader expects that "once" will be pinpointed as the line continues; or perhaps he assumes that the next part of the line will describe those upon whom the "two-handed engine" will execute its business.[23] But there is finally no assurance given that good and evil men will receive their just rewards; and there is no precise naming of who or what will "smite" when (and if) the time arrives. In one sense the action occurs even before it happens— a disturbing paradox which becomes clearer with the next phrase: "and smites no more." At first the action seems *about* to take place ("stands ready to smite once"), and then it appears *already* to have taken place ("and smite no more"). Instead of finding out when that "once" will be, the reader discovers "no more": time runs out even before it begins.

The much-admired flower passage follows:

> Bring the rathe primrose that forsaken dies,
> The tufted Crow-toe, and pale Jessamine,
> The white Pink, and the Pansy freakt with jet,
> The glowing violet,
> The musk-rose, and the well-attir'd Woodbine,

With cowslips wan that hang the pensive head,
And every flower that sad embroidery wears:
Bid Amaranthus all his beauty shed,
And Daffadillies fill their cups with tears.

(142–150)

Tillyard notes the "incredible beauty" of this passage;[24] and Wilson Knight comments on its "Spenserian fluidity" and "luscious music."[25] But its beauties are complicated by the word "bring," which again raises questions about action and agency (when? where?). The next line describes the action to be performed, but doesn't locate it specifically: "To strew the Laureate Hearse where Lycid lies" (151). "Where" and for what purposes Lycidas "lies" are exactly the questions that the reader has been unable to answer. The shortcomings of the whole procedure strike home in the next lines:

For so to interpose a little ease,
Let our frail thought dally with false surmise.

(152–153)

The reader is now dismayed to learn that this "luscious music" occurs as part of the speaker's deliberate self-deception: the request to "bring" flowers is no more than a "false surmise."

What follows is far from heartening:

Ay me! Whilst thee the shores and sounding
        seas
Wash far away, where'er thy bones are hurl'd,
Whether beyond the stormy Hebrides,
Where thou perhaps under the whelming tide
Visit'st the bottom of the monstrous world;
Or whether thou to our moist vows denied,
Sleep'st by the fable of Bellerus old,
Where the great vision of the guarded Mount
Looks toward Namancos and Bayona's hold.

(154–162)

This new panoramic perspective begins again the effort to find Lycidas. But the "shores" and "sounding seas," rather than cooperate to return the body, conspire to "wash" it "far away"; and the phrase "where'er thy bones are hurl'd" even more firmly denies a beneficent nature—Lycidas's body could be anywhere. Milton's revisions are again suggestive. The first version of the poem had "floods" instead of "shores"; the final version implies that the land (as well as the sea) works to prevent the body's return. And Milton's decision to replace (in the first version) "the humming tide" with "the whelming tide"

connotes an additional violence and intensity: nature not only denies pastoral appeals for sympathy, but actively fights against them.

The "great vision" referred to in these lines has been fully glossed by the Variorum editors; they carefully discuss matters of distance, location, function—everything, in other words, that we do *not* know about Lycidas. The next line presents the famous petition: "Look homeward angel now, and melt with ruth" (163). Most commentators are confident that the Angel addressed is St. Michael, but others argue for Lycidas himself. Yet let us assume—though the dispute about identity helps to make my point—that the Angel *is* St. Michael. How comforting is the request that he "look homeward"? The editors record their uneasiness by noting the "sudden shift in attention from Lycidas"; and, while they add that this "need not trouble us," their disclaimer only heightens the necessity for an explanation. The Angel "looks" (away from Lycidas) and "melts" with pity (that is, if the speaker's petition is granted), but he doesn't *do* anything. Instead a new request is made: "And, O ye Dolphins, waft the hapless youth" (164). The action presented here ("waft") is pathetically weak and inadequate: "Waft" where? From where? What are its points of reference and relation to Lycidas? Is he merely "hapless," unfortunate, the victim of bad luck? The allusion to the dolphins is equally disconcerting. The Variorum editors' list of probable and possible references divides basically into two groups. One includes the story of Melicertes, whose drowned body was returned to shore by a dolphin; others in this group similarly refer to returns of dead figures. The second, however, emphasizes rescues of still-living figures, such as Arion, whom dolphins carried safely to shore. The reader therefore confronts an allusion capable of what seems to be mutually exclusive interpretations: the return of a dead figure or a successful rescue. The availability of a great deal of evidence on both sides makes problematical the reader's efforts to privilege one over the other. Or perhaps the reader feels that the context precisely *does* warrant an allusion which implies (since Lycidas is dead) the return of a dead figure. Then he would be faced with the bitter reminder of that second group of allusions, which refer to those (unlike Lycidas) who are still alive, and none of which are applicable here.

The real transition in the reader's experience comes about in the next lines: "Weep no more, woeful shepherds, weep no more" (165). While this is of course another convention—one "widely accepted" by both classical and Christian writers—the presence of the convention hardly accounts for the reader's surprise. My term "transition" is in fact misleading because there isn't any "transition" in the poem's formal argument. The movement is, as Donald Friedman finely explains, experiential rather than formal:

> It is crucial that we realize that Milton forbids us to feel that we understand how the swain has come to this knowledge of the truth. The transformation he undergoes has nothing to do, in the poem, with a logical or sequential argument or demonstration; nothing he is told, nothing he hears, can account for his grasp of the new truth he promulgates to the listening shepherds.[26]

This leap to faith is not confined to the speaker, but extends to the reader, for him to affirm or deny:

> For Lycidas your sorrow is not dead,
> Sunk though he be beneath the wat'ry floor.
> (165–166)

The first line pressures the reader to select one of two possible interpretations:

1. That Lycidas, the object of your "sorrow" (the word "sorrow" would be in apposition to Lycidas) is not dead after all; he lives.

2. That the *sorrow* you feel for Lycidas is not dead; you should feel disturbed by the demand to "weep no more," since your sorrows continue.[27]

The reader may bear witness to the truth, testifying that Lycidas "is not dead," whatever the evidence to the contrary. Or else he may reject that faith as unwarranted by the external evidence. (Of course that the speaker's faith *is* unwarranted by the evidence is exactly the point.) The next line tears the reader's choice: "Sunk though he be beneath the wat'ry floor" (167). The literal truth is that Lycidas has drowned, and that his body lies somewhere beneath the

"wat'ry floor." For the reader who has rested on the literal details the literal truth remains the whole truth, a bitter temporal reality. But to the reader who has affirmed his faith, the literal is there only to be transcended by a higher truth, a new interpretive rule which sweeps aside the evidence of the phenomenal world.[28] What the reader of "Lycidas" finally takes away as consolation depends upon how he sees—whether he rests on literal facts, or creates new ones.

Notes

I would like here to thank my friend Jackie Miller for her helpful comments on an earlier version of this essay.

1. Rosemond Tuve, *Images and Themes in Five Poems by Milton* (Cambridge: Harvard University Press, 1962), pp. 73–111; B. Rajan, *The Lofty Rhyme* (London: Routledge & Kegan Paul, 1970), pp. 45–55; Donald Friedman, " 'Lycidas': The Swain's Paideia," *Milton Studies III*, ed. James D. Simmonds (University of Pittsburgh Press, 1971), pp. 3–34; and Leslie Brisman, *Milton's Poetry of Choice and Its Romantic Heirs* (Cornell University Press, 1973). Throughout this essay I shall also make extensive use of the admirable *Variorum Commentary on the Poems of John Milton*, vol. II, part two, ed. A. S. P. Woodhouse and Douglas Bush (New York: Columbia University Press, 1972).

2. Professor Fish's most recent exposition of his theoretical views occurs in "Interpreting the *Variorum*," *Critical Inquiry* 2 (1976), pp. 465–485.

3. All quotations will be taken from *John Milton: Complete Poems and Major Prose*, ed. Merritt Y. Hughes (New York: The Odyssey Press, 1957).

4. Tuve, p. 97. Useful background studies of the pastoral convention are provided by James Holly Hanford, "The Pastoral Elegy and Milton's 'Lycidas,' " 1910, rpt. in *Milton's "Lycidas": The Tradition and the Poem*, ed. C. A. Patrides (New York: Holt, Rinehart & Winston, Inc., 1961), pp. 27–55; and by Paul Alpers, "The Eclogue Tradition and the Nature of Pastoral," *College English* 34 (1972), pp. 352–371. Alpers observes that "in fact *all* the elements of 'Lycidas' are traditional in pastoral" (p. 367). Cf. also on this point Hanford, *A Milton Handbook* (New York: Appleton-Century-Crofts, 1970), pp. 134–140, at p. 136; and also Jon S. Lawry, *The Shadow of Heaven: Matter and Stance in Milton's Poetry* (Cornell University Press, 1968), pp. 105, 108.

5. Cleanth Brooks and J. E. Hardy, in "Essays in

Analysis: 'Lycidas,' " 1951, rpt. in Patrides, op. cit., pp. 136–152, helpfully testify to the reader's expectations here: "On the day of Lycidas's death the nymphs were not playing where one would have expected them to play. The speaker knows this—because, had they been there, they would surely have tried to save Lycidas" (p. 141).

6. This reading is supported by the *Variorum* editors.

7. Caroline Mayerson, "The Orpheus Image in 'Lycidas,' " *PMLA* LXIV (1949), pp. 189–207. She notes in summary that Orpheus was seen as "a revered musician-poet-prophet-teacher who had sung of God and creation, whose songs had affected man and beast, stock and stone, even the inhabitants of Hades. His music and his teachings had contributed to the establishment of a harmonious and civilized society. His musical skill, his power over nature, and his premature death kept alive his historic association with the pastoral elegy. To the Christian world, his personality and his accomplishments invited comparison with those of other venerated prophets, both heathen (the Druids, among others) and sacred (Christ). Finally, for a society traditionally inclined to allegorical interpretation, Orpheus became a symbol of human wisdom directed to social ends, the civilizing force which renews itself, despite periodic destruction" (p. 198).

8. Brisman, p. 250.

9. *Ibid.*

10. Commentary on Milton's revisions is provided by J. B. Leishman, *Milton's Minor Poems* (University of Pittsburgh Press, 1969), pp. 246–343, at pp. 291ff.; and by Rajan, pp. 47, 52. Cf. also C. F. Stone, "Milton's Self-Concerns and Manuscript Revisions in 'Lycidas,' " *MLN* 83 (1968), pp. 867–881. Patrides' list of 'corrigenda' and textual notes in his edition of the poem, op. cit., pp. 10–11, 233–236, is also helpful.

11. Roy Daniells, *Milton, Mannerism, and Baroque* (University of Toronto Press, 1963), pp. 37–50, at p. 39.

12. G. Wilson Knight, *Poets of Action* (London: Methuen & Co., Ltd., 1967), p. 28.

13. As my analysis suggests, I agree with Friedman that "the attitude of questioning" is "at the heart of the poem" (p. 5).

14. Rajan, p. 50.

15. Here I follow Alpers' suggestion that the quotation marks, as printed in Hughes' edition, be omitted. Alpers points out that these are modern additions, not part of Milton's original text. (cf. p. 367).

16. Brisman, p. 220.

17. Brooks and Hardy, p. 144.

18. Tuve, p. 76.

19. Karl Felsen, "The 'Two-Handed Engine,' A Balanced View," *Milton Quarterly* 9 (1975), pp. 6–14, at p. 10.

20. Northrop Frye, "Literature as Context: Milton's 'Lycidas,' " in *Fables of Identity* (New York: Harcourt, Brace and World, Inc., 1963), pp. 119–129, at p. 124.

21. David Daiches, from *A Study of Literature*, 1948, excerpted in Patrides, op. cit., pp. 101–119, at p. 115.

22. Tuve, p. 77.

23. R. W. French, in his fine essay "Voice and Structure in 'Lycidas,' " *TSLL* XII (1970), pp. 15–25, seems to be the only critic to call attention to these possibilities (cf. pp. 22ff.).

24. E. M. W. Tillyard, *Milton* (1930; rpt. New York: Collier Books, 1967), pp. 70–74, at p. 73.

25. Knight, p. 51.

26. Friedman, p. 18; cf. also French, pp. 15, 20–21.

27. Douglas Bush, in *The Portable Milton* (1949; New York: The Viking Press, 1968), chooses to punctuate the line as follows: "For Lycidas, your sorrow, is not dead." Professor Bush tidies up the packed syntax, but I think at the expense of eliminating a crucial ambiguity.

28. The word "though" also may provide a second chance to the reader who refused the leap to faith; because it implies a contrast with the preceding line, it may prompt such a reader to reread that line and perhaps re-think his position.

Application

Joseph Conrad's Voice in *Heart of Darkness:* A Jungian Approach

Nancy McNeal

Drawing on the insights of Carl Jung, Nancy McNeal offers yet another version of affective criticism. Like the Freudian critic, the Jungian finds the poem working at a deep, usually subconscious level. But where the psychoanalytic critic will emphasize the individuality of our responses, the Jungian critic will expect to find a basic similarity in our reactions to the truly great work, that is, to the work that draws upon the archetypal images held in the "collective unconscious." On this very deep level, neither the individual "personality" of the author nor that of the reader will be especially relevant. What is relevant is that psychic reservoir of symbols or archetypes that author and audience share by virtue of their common humanity. By tapping this reservoir, the "visionary" artist puts us in contact with our deepest collective fears and desires, and this is what gives his or her work its extraordinary power.

Reprinted by permission from the *Journal of Evolutionary Psychology,* 1 (1979): 1–12. Copyright © 1979 by the Institute of Evolutionary Psychology.

Introduction

In his essay "Psychology and Literature" Jung writes that an artist "must pay dearly for the divine gift of creative fire, since he is a man upon whom a heavier burden is laid than upon ordinary mortals."[1] One might view Joseph Conrad as an author carrying the heavy burden of man's inhumanity to man. Conrad's *Heart of Darkness* embodies his literary purpose which he stated in 1879: "My task which I am trying to achieve is by the power of the written word, to make you hear, to make you feel—it is above all, to make you *see*."[2] Conrad's novella conveys a tale of atrocities to the world. However, the task of the literary critic is to discover the best possible method for interpreting the author's experience and for developing the ability to convey the "intimate immediate experience which is the final touchstone of critical theory."[3] This paper will attempt to develop the theme of *Heart of Darkness* within the framework of analytical psychology. Special reference will be made to what Jung terms the "Collective Unconscious."

Jung's Collective Unconscious

Dr. Jung first presented his essay on the Collective Unconscious in 1912; Conrad wrote *Heart of Darkness* approximately twelve years prior to this. Yet there are many amazing similarities of thought, and one wonders why Jung does not include Conrad among his list of writers who express themselves in what Jung terms the "Visionary Mode." The archetypal imagery in *Heart of Darkness* is Conrad's voice to the world. The author presents a truth "more profound and human than any modern novelist, however great, could be expected to invent."[4] According to R.

S. Crane, the archetypal interpretation holds true for literature as well as for criticism. Both are "ultimately metaphorical and symbolic," and "there are great advantages in so conceiving it."[5] According to Jung, archetypes are the mythological associations which can spring anew in every age and clime, without historical tradition of migration. They are indeed the contents of the Collective Unconscious. The archetype or primordial image is the psychic apprehension of the object. Jung states: "It is his art that explains the artist and not the insufficiencies and conflicts of his personality."[6] Thus, the major concern in Jungian literary criticism is the psychological significance of the work of art. An effective Jungian interpretation should therefore bring about effects fraught with meaning which would then lead to an understanding of the subject matter.[7] Jung's key hypothesis, revolving around archetypes, emphasizes a certain kind of art on a collective level comparable with the function of "private" symbols in individual psychology. An archetypal image "derives its existence from the hinterland of man's mind—that suggests the abyss of time separating us from pre-human ages, or evokes a super-human world of contrasting light and darkness. It is a primordial experience which surpasses man's understanding, and to which he is therefore in danger of succumbing."[8] This disturbing vision of monstrous happenings exceeds the grasp of human feeling and comprehension and makes demands upon the powers of the artist which are different from the experiences of the conscious.

The Archetypal Journey in *Heart of Darkness*

In *Heart of Darkness* Conrad offers imagery of an archetypal nature in connection with the personality of Kurtz, who represents the evil aspect of unconscious primitivism, i.e., the shadow, latent in all humanity. Thus Marlow, Conrad's spokesman in *Heart of Darkness* refers to the lower reaches of the sea where it is easy for a man "to evoke the great spirit of the past."[9] The beginning of this journey into the darkest part of Africa is, psychologically speaking, man's quest to come to terms with the psychic sub-

stratum. Marlow must first raise his steamship sunk in the mucky river from the primordial element; but, Kurtz's subsequent death is the symbolical return to this primal source when Marlow buries him in the mud of Africa. The cycle is completed as Marlow returns to the Thames which Conrad describes as "the tranquil waterway leading to the uttermost ends of the earth, . . . under an overcast sky . . . into the heart of an immense darkness" (p. 79).

These primordial experiences rend the curtain upon which civilization painted the picture of an ordered world, and they allow a glimpse into the unfathomed abyss of what has not yet become. These visions are of another world, of the beginning of things before the age of man or of the unborn generations of the future.[10] These visions also reflect the creative spontaneity of the writer, i.e., his visionary mode, in which an intention "beyond his comprehension"[11] is representative of a *participation mystique*. This is corroborated by Shelley, who, with reference to the visionary mode, states: "a great poem expresses truth concerning man and nature which the poet himself does not fully understand, and which is discerned by the reader of succeeding ages in such degree as their peculiar relations enable them to apprehend."[12]

In *Heart of Darkness* Conrad unknowingly dips into this well of the Collective Unconscious and brings to surface archetypes which present themselves to the conscious mind as ideas or images. Conrad's archetype of primordial evil not only depicts the sinister forces which exist in the phylogenetic memory of the past, but it also reflects the contemporary and possible future manifestation of this subliminal horror. The shocking experience which Conrad produces in *Heart of Darkness*, mainly through the character Kurtz, might be considered indicative of Jung's assumption that "the contents of the collective unconscious are not only the residues of archaic, specifically human modes of functioning, but also the residues of functions from man's animal ancestry, whose duration in time was infinitely greater than the relatively brief epoch of specifically human existence."[13] Conrad extends this archaic mode of functioning within the collective unconscious to the future as well, when he states: "there is all the past as well as the future in man's mind" (p. 36). The *summum bonum* of psychological clarification lies in the ability to raise the contents of the psychic substratum to the conscious level, an act which one might consider analogous to Marlow's raising his ship from the water. The visionary artist uses archetypes; archetypes are to the psyche "what an instinct is to the body."[14]

Primordial imagery or archetypes of primitivism prevail throughout *Heart of Darkness*; indeed, the title itself is symbolic. Further, this imagery operates upon a dualistic level. The journey Marlow makes into the deepest area of the jungle is a symbolic archetypal journey or quest into man's unconscious. The jungle represents the undifferentiated stage of human evolution, devoid of "any clear idea of time" (p. 41). But this pristine setting in *Heart of Darkness* represents primal unity as well as creativity. William Blake writes in "Jerusalem": "The primeval State of Man was Wisdom, Art and Science." On this level the primitives are in harmony with nature and their environment. Indeed, in Conrad's work the primitives are more "civilized" than the white pilgrims aboard Marlow's ship, who enjoy firing into the jungle with no apparent purpose; whereas, the starving cannibals also on board do not attack the other passengers, even though they outnumber them. Judging from the cruel practices of the white tradesmen during the era of Western imperialism, the term "cannibalism" appears in a very ambivalent light, indeed. Further, the darkness of the jungle is in sharp dialectical contrast to Brussels, which as Marlow states, always makes him "think of a whited sepulchre" (p. 9). One senses beneath the respectable veneer of civilization an archaic primitivism, not in terms of unity, but in terms of archaic, archetypal evil.

Conrad presents this primitivism extant in contemporary man through the "shadow" representing the dark side, the primitive animal instincts which man inherited in his phylogenetic evolution from the lower forms of life. Obviously, socially reprehensible thoughts and feelings repressed in the unconscious enter the sphere of consciousness from this shadow, i.e., the personal unconscious. Thus, the shadow is "also the opposite of whatever the individual has emphasized in his ego-consciousness or actual living."[15] These ancestral experiences, echoes of prehistoric world events, or "racial" memories inherited in the brain structure, in the form of "primordial images" called archetypes contain large quantities of emotion which some aspect of an individual's life situation may elicit. In *Heart of Darkness* Conrad emerges on the plane of consciousness to warn his readers of the horror innate and latent in mankind. By means of the jungle as the catalyst, the shadow is personified in Kurtz. Conrad writes: "All Europe contributed to the making of Kurtz" (p. 50). Kurtz represents a civilization which is disintegrating. As the shadow, Kurtz disintegrates in *Heart of Darkness* as he realizes in his final moment what had happened to him and to civilization. After his last words: "The Horror! The Horror!", he returns to the primal chthonian unity with his burial in the mud.

Conrad presents other references to the primal source throughout the novella. The station manager's uncle visiting the Congo extends "his short flipper of an arm" at the beginning of the tale; then, as mentioned above, Marlow's journey begins literally and figuratively rising from the mud and water. Later, Marlow states: "Going up that river was like travelling back to the earliest beginnings of the world" (p. 34). The deeper he penetrates into the heart of darkness the more he senses the "stillness of an implacable force brooding over an inscrutable intention" (p. 34). Marlow feels that they "were wanderers on a prehistoric earth" (p. 36).

Marlow's journey represents "The Central Archetype, The Self,"[16] or quest motif, as he searches for self unity or psychic wholeness in the Congo. His physical journey parallels the psychic quest. Thus he states: "we were too far and could not remember, because we were travelling in the night of first ages, of those ages that are gone, leaving hardly a sign—and no memories" (p. 36). Implied here is Conrad's premise that the past, present, and future lie in man's mind. Marlow dwells upon man's kinship with the "wild and passionate uproar" of the jungle. He feels that he could admit to himself that there was in one just the faintest trace of a response to the terrible frankness of that noise, a dim suspicion of there being a meaning in it which one could comprehend, because the mind of man is capable of anything, because everything is in it, all the past as well as all the future (p. 37, passim).

The selfhood Marlow searches is, however, not easy to achieve. Jung writes: "The Individual must also listen to the 'inner voice' of his unconscious, use its aspects, and cope with its darker side. He must make the moral decision, go his own way in isolation, separating himself from group convention, becoming a person in his own right."[17] This appears to be Marlow's quest, and perhaps Conrad's voice, as Marlow guides his steamship and his soul into the innermost depths of Africa. But alas! Kurtz succumbs to the jungle and achieves integration through death. This is not unusual; "the full development of the personality of the self is an achievement of heroic proportions and is not attained by the great mass of mankind."[18]

Marlow emerges as the only character in the novella who escapes the process of reification. His psyche is not affected by the jungle. Part of Marlow's salvation is his persistence in work. This is in spite of the fact that he does not particularly care for work as he initially relates: "I don't like work—no man does—but I like what is in the work—the chance to find yourself. Your own reality—for yourself, not for others—what no other man can ever know. They can only see the mere show, and never can tell what it really means" (p. 29). Work helps to save Marlow later in the tale when the jungle, representing intense primitive allure, confronts him. Marlow hears the drums and the chants from the shore, and he experiences a strange sensation, a temptation to enter the unknown, a sensation of kinship with those who inhabit the jungle. "They howled and leaped, and spun, and made horrid faces, but what thrilled you was just the thought of their humanity—like yours—the thought of your remote kinship with this wild and passionate uproar" (p. 37). He busies himself, however, with the repair of his steamship and with the supervision of his native boilerman.

But Marlow questions what he might learn if he were to go ashore, or symbolically to join in the primitivism which the jungle represents. Conrad presents this most effectively in Marlow's dialogue which is quasi a debate with his conscience: "What was there after all? Joy, fear, sorrow, devotion, valour, rage—who can tell?—but truth—truth stripped of its cloak of time" (p. 37). He goes on to explain that a man must be as "much of a man as these on the shore. He must meet that truth with his own true stuff—with his own inborn strength" (p. 37). This symbolic plunge into the darkness, representative of the Jungian shadow, reflects the horror which Kurtz voices as he dies. It is not the horror of jungle primitivism, but rather it is that evil primitivism surviving in civilized man.

Albert J. Guerard avers that *Heart of Darkness* is the most famous of Conrad's personal short novels, and that it is a *Pilgrim's Progress* for a pessimistic and psychologizing age. Further, "this autobiographical basis of the narrative is well known, and its introspective bias obvious; this is Conrad's longest journey into self."[19] Perhaps one might assume that as Conrad searches for an expression of the living nightmare he encountered in the jungle of life, he voices primordial imagery through his surrogate, Marlow. In one of his letters Conrad remarks: "to create a story, you must cultivate your poetic faculty. . . . You must search the darkest corners of your heart . . . for the image."[20] Marlow explores the spaces of the dark continent, an allusion to probing the depths of his unknown self. Conrad demonstrates through the novella and through Marlow's search for, and the achievement of truth, that only through self-knowledge can man realize the "idea" or the "illusion" which will save him from the dark powers he faces. This need of ethical recognition forces Marlow to search out his hidden affinity with Kurtz who represents his accusing conscience. Marlow's quest reflects Conrad's personal *Sturm und Drang*. Conrad later wrote in one of his letters: "what occurred in the Congo was reckless without hardihood, greedy without audacity, and cruel without courage . . . with no moral purpose at the back of it."[21] Frederick R. Karl adds further that "Marlow's experience is a nightmare for creator, narrator, and reader. The jungle, that thick verdant cover, disguises all, but most of all hides a man's real existence from himself."[22] Conversely, one might also learn the essence of life from the jungle, as Marlow does seem to achieve cognition and even transcendence.

Kurtz is the epitome of the Belgium doctor's reference to the process of reification. This writer of the seventeen-page report for the "International Society for the Suppression of Savage Customs" changes into a creature who scrawls a postscript to this report: "Exterminate all the brutes!" Thus, Kurtz, who supposedly possesses the very best talents and educaton available in Western Europe, succumbs to a mysterious shadow and presides "at certain midnight dances ending with unspeakable rites, which were offered up to him" (p. 51). Apparently, Kurtz has lived in a state of ambivalence, his benevolent attitude in his report for the "International Society" notwithstanding. One wonders if Kurtz really hates the natives as his postscript indicates, or whether he achieves primordial unity with them, while in reality he hates the civilization which has turned into a perverse jungle. Marlow muses that it is easy to do good when all the accruements and institutions of civilization surround one; however, when one faces an ultimate test such as the jungle with its unfathomable mysteries, "how can you imagine what particular region a man's untrammelled feet may take him into by the way of solitude—utter solitude without a policeman . . ." (p. 50). Marlow discovers that the ultimate defense is indeed the moral policeman of one's inner voice. Perhaps one might agree that *Heart of Darkness* is then an archetypal journey of initiation and moral education, of man's exploratory descent into primitive primordial sources. Marlow is both Conrad and all men who have taken the "night journey" into the primeval depths of their own and their racial consciousness."[23] Robert Penn Warren affirms that for Conrad "the very act of composition was a way of knowing, a way of exploration."[24]

Heart of Darkness indeed explores and presents a moving picture of personal situation ethics and of a civilization which projects fraudulent philanthropy. In contrast, nature in its primitive state is devoid of moral checks, hence visibly true and integrated. Kurtz's brief career "has been a triumph in the stripping away of all the rags of ethical self-deception with which

men fatuously seek to confront the eternal powers of darkness; and, dying, he has won a further victory in his vision of 'the horror.' "[25] Marlow understands that the white sepulchral cities of the trading companies of the world offer nothing to scale against such a revelation as Kurtz has had. Just as the black mistress of Kurtz, bedecked in the ivory so precious to this white civilization, reflects the totality of Kurtz's experience in the jungle, the modern city, totally incapable of comprehending what occurs in the primordial aspect of man's nature is buried in the humdrum of an artificial civilization.

Heart of Darkness presents a painful question to the reader as well as a warning: What exists in the unconscious of man that can so readily revert to such degradation? Perhaps it is, as Jung suggests, that civilization has never been able to totally cope with man's innate aggression. This is very apparent in the behavior of all the colonials in *Heart of Darkness* and particularly in the depiction of Kurtz, who "brings to the jungle weapons encompassing two thousand years of western civilization."[26] In the characterization of Kurtz, Conrad depicts the residuum of archetypal evil in man which represents the ever-present dialectical challenge of social morality. Kurtz's obsession with power and his greed for ivory are shocking reminders of Western colonialism. Kurtz, in fact, is the representative of the colonial traders who manipulated people for purely selfish ends, and who drove for advancement and aggrandizement without larger considerations.

Before his death Kurtz realizes, however, that the potential for goodness in mankind may be overshadowed by man's innate aggression and greed. Through the voice of Marlow, Conrad's social and moral message in *Heart of Darkness* reflects "a microcosm of the great world in which those who can, plunder those who cannot."[27] Conrad presents this by pointing at the Janus-like quality of the human psyche which is capable of "unplumbable depravity, the primal unanalysable evil, implicit in Kurtz's reversion to the jungle from the high moral sentiments of his report."[28] This jungle Kurtz reverts to, however, is also symbolic. It exists in primordial man, but it has not lost any of its terrifying acumen as man increases his technological capabilities.

Conrad's Personal Projection: The *Vis Matrix* in *Heart of Darkness*

Although literary criticism should normally view the work of art in itself, it is pertinent to discuss the background which motivated Conrad in his search for a voice or vehicle to express his experience. In 1876 King Leopold of Belgium called a conference in Brussels to examine the African situation and "to open to civilisation the only part of our globe where Christianity has not penetrated and to pierce the darkness which envelops the entire population. . . . He legally absorbed the Congo and left an unfathomable history of plunder, rape, greed, and inhumanity in the very worst possible degree."[29] Soon, however, reports began to appear from the Congo from men and women who had witnessed the atrocities, along with reports of those who did not deny having committed them. These individuals point out that they were "merely obeying orders." One report included the statement that, "in the jungle, away from the sight of men, all things are possible."[30] Some of the records relate tales of human limbs which traders brought to authorities, of hands and other parts of the body drying in the sun at the posts along the river, and of a flowerbed bordered with human skulls.

In *Heart of Darkness* Conrad offers this information to the reader particularly through Kurtz. His fence of shrunken heads, his participation in jungle rituals, and his power over the natives are the symbols of the worst aspects of colonial degradation. Kurtz's power extends beyond his deification by the natives as he enjoys the status of hero among the colonials. What he does not recognize until his death is that deception is most sinister when it becomes self-deception, and the propagandist takes his own fictions seriously.[31] Kurtz plays the role of grand manipulator; even Marlow is awed by him. In him the need for doing good and the sinister propensity of evil and aggression are juxtaposed within an unstable psychic cohabitation.

Conrad represents the artist who works in the "Visionary Mode." It is truly a unique experience of human life, replete with contents of dreams, night-time fears, and journeys to the dark recesses of the mind. With reference to this mode of writing, Jung states:

> The vision is not something derived or secondary, and it is not a symptom of something else. It is true symbolic expression—that is the expression of something existent in its own right, but imperfectly known. . . . the creative process is the unconscious animation of the archetype, and in a development and shaping of this image till the work is completed.[32]

Indeed, Conrad appears to delve into the collective unconscious which as Maud Bodkin states, contains a sense of a latent or active greater power.[33] One might conjecture further that Conrad does catch sight of the figures that people the night world. It sounds as though Jung were describing Conrad's work when he writes: "He knows that a purposiveness outreaching human ends is the life-giving secret for man; he has a presentiment of incomprehensible happenings. . . . In short, he sees something of that psychic world that strikes terror into the savage and the barbarian."[34]

Conrad's voice rising from this psychic well attempts to offer justice to the world and to illuminate man with a warning which indeed should be heard by people of all eras. His warning rises from the collective unconscious to the collective neuroses of the twentieth century. With reference to *Heart of Darkness* Frederick Karl points out that "Such an insight is timeless, but particularly appropriate for developments since 1900. For when has man tried so carefully to preserve life while also squandering it so carelessly? Conrad caught not only hypocrisy but the illogic of human behavior which tries to justify itself with precision, only to surrender to explosive inner needs."[35] The key word in Conrad's voice is "darkness," the black of the jungle. Black is conventionally representative of chaos, the mysterious, the unknown, death, evil, and perhaps for Conrad, the darkness that has enveloped the consciousness of mankind, the nightmare of human existence. He also states that the artist must descend within himself. In this lonely region of stress and strife, he may find that which is normally kept out of sight. The result of Conrad's descent into self is the voice of Marlow through whom Conrad appeals to the latent feeling of fellowship with all creation."[36] Thus, Marlow states, "for good or evil mine is the speech that cannot be silenced," since man must "meet that truth with his own true stuff,—with his own inborn strength" (p. 37). When society is ineffective, only the responsible individual counts; possibly one acquires restraint as the sum total of what one is because the "future of civilized society hangs in the balance. . . . In this respect *Heart of Darkness* is one of our archetypal existential literary documents in which all is contingency."[37]

Marlow represents an individual who achieves balance and integration in his quest. He finds the kind of order which is congruent with man's nature rather than contradictory to it.[38] Kurtz achieves integration when he realizes the terrible horror that he was a part of. He dies and returns to what Yeats terms the *Anima Mundi*. Kurtz succumbs to the lures of the jungle and is absorbed within the tellurian matrix of primitivism. Conrad illlustrates this through the black boy's unemotional statement: "Mistah Kurtz—he dead." Thus, *Heart of Darkness* is Conrad's message to our era, and admittedly, to future eras. It creates an awareness of the psychic imbalance within the human condition. The primordial experience Conrad depicts is a carryover from the abyss of prehuman ages. As Marlow relates about the jungle episode: "The essentials of this affair lay deep under the surface, beyond my reach, and beyond my power of meddling" (p. 39). Implicit, however, is Conrad's warning of the jungle which is also an attempt to raise the jungle within each and everyone to the level of conscious grasp for the sake of inner moral restraint. At the crossroads of civilization, old symbols fall by the wayside, and new ones must be substituted. The process of cultural rebirth is initiated when old, archaic symbols have been replaced by symbols that relate meaningfully to the new circumstances. True enlightenment consists, according to Conrad, in the symbolic integration of self. This is truly Joseph Conrad's appeal to man's creativity, expressed in and indigenous to the mythopoeic proclivity of the human condition.

In Sum:

Joseph Conrad's theme in *Heart of Darkness* is the necessity for man's journey into self in order to understand and cope with the potential for evil that lies within the human race. By applying Jungian archetypes and his theory of the artistic expression in the visionary mode, we can more thoroughly grasp the symbolic and universal significance of Conrad's work. Jung's theory of mythological associations manifested in the Collective Unconscious raises the reader's consciousness, making him aware of Conrad's message of primordial primitivism in man and of past conditioning in terms of archaic societal restraints. Thus, Conrad, the writer carrying the "heavier burden" achieves his task of enabling us to hear, to feel, and "above all," to "see."

Conrad's journey in *Heart of Darkness* is everyman's journey. His surrogate Marlow's ability to overcome and to transcend offers hope for humanity, if we follow our "inner voice." This is the only weapon by which man can prevent loss of control over his destructive propensity. Those who do not, may as Kurtz, the literal and figurative shadow, have to face the horrors of reification and concomitant loss of humanity.

Notes

1. Clifton Snider, "C. G. Jung's Analytical Psychology and Literary Criticism (I)," *Psychocultural Review*, 1 (1977), p. 96.

2. Robert Kimbrough, "Conrad on Life and Art," in *Joseph Conrad: Heart of Darkness: An Authoritative Text*, ed. Robert Kimbrough (New York: W. W. Norton & Co., 1963), p. 136.

3. Maud Bodkin, *Archetypal Patterns in Poetry*, 2nd ed. (New York: Vintage Books, 1961), p. 22.

4. R. S. Crane, *The Languages of Criticism and the Structure of Poetry* (1953; rpt. London: Oxford Univ. Press, 1957), p. 138.

5. Crane, p. 138.

6. Morris Philipson, *Outline of a Jungian Aesthetics* (Northwestern Univ. Press, 1963), p. 91.

7. Philipson, p. 101, passim.

8. Philipson, p. 102.

9. Robert Kimbrough, ed., *Joseph Conrad: Heart of Darkness: An Authoritative Text* (New York: W. W. Norton & Co., 1963), p. 4. All further references to this work appear in the text.

10. Philipson, pp. 106–7, passim.

11. Philipson, pp. 100–11.

12. Bodkin, p. 811.

13. Bodkin, pp. 57–8.

14. Snider, p. 103.

15. James C. Coleman, *Abnormal Psychology and Modern Life*, 3rd ed. (Glenview, Ill.: Scott, Foresman and Co., 1964), p. 741.

16. Snider, p. 103.

17. Coleman, p. 642.

18. Coleman, p. 642.

19. Albert J. Guerard, "From Life to Art," in *Joseph Conrad: Heart of Darkness: An Authoritative Text*, ed. Robert Kimbrough (New York: W. W. Norton & Co., 1963), p. 122.

20. Stewart C. Wilcox, "Conrad's 'Complicated Presentations' of Symbolic Imagery," in *Joseph Conrad: Heart of Darkness: An Authoritative Text*, ed. Robert Kimbrough (New York: W. W. Norton & Co., 1963), p. 216.

21. Guerard, p. 124.

22. Frederick R. Karl, " 'Heart of Darkness' Introduction to the Danse Macabre," in *Joseph Conrad, A Collection of Criticism*, ed. Frederick R. Karl (New York: McGraw-Hill, Inc., 1975), p. 31.

23. Wilcox, p. 212, passim.

24. Wilcox, p. 213.

25. Paul L. Wiley, "Conrad's Skein of Ironies," in *Joseph Conrad: Heart of Darkness: An Authoritative Text*, ed. Robert Kimbrough (New York: W. W. Norton & Co., 1963), p. 136.

26. Karl, p. 35.

27. Karl, p. 33.

28. Marvin Mudrick, "The Originality of Conrad," in *Joseph Conrad: Heart of Darkness: An Authoritative Text*, ed. Robert Kimbrough (New York: W. W. Norton & Co., 1963), p. 209.

29. Maurice N. Hennessy: "The Congo: A Brief History, 1876–1908," in *Joseph Conrad: Heart of Darkness: An Authoritative Text*, ed. Robert Kimbrough (New York: W. W. Norton & Co., 1963), p. 87.

30. Richard Harding Davis, "His Brother's Keeper," in *Joseph Conrad: Heart of Darkness: An Authoritative Text*, ed. Robert Kimbrough (New York: W. W. Norton & Co., 1963), p. 93.

31. Guerard, p. 122, passim.

32. Philipson, pp. 122–3.

33. Bodkin, p. 23. passim.

34. Philipson, p. 124.

35. Karl, p. 29.

36. Joseph Conrad, "To Make You See," in *Joseph Conrad: Heart of Darkness: An Authoritative Text*, ed. Robert Kimbrough (New York: W. W. Norton & Co., 1963), p. 143.

37. Karl, p. 31.

38. Eloise Knapp Hay, "The Artist of the Whole Matter," in *Joseph Conrad, A Collection of Criticism*, ed. Frederick R. Karl (New York: McGraw-Hill, Inc., 1975), p. 31, passim.

Chapter Four

Mimetic Criticism: Reality as Context

First follow NATURE, and your Judgment
   frame
By her just Standard, which is still the same
                    Pope, *Essay on Criticism*

We saw in a previous section how formal critics often come to locate at least part of the poem's value in its ability to depict accurately the world outside of art. Despite this mimetic drift, formalists still deserve their name because their approach emphasizes the fitting of the parts to the whole that produces a coherent poem. A theory that emphasizes instead the correspondence of the poem to external reality, and that makes that correspondence the ultimate standard of literary excellence, is more properly called "mimetic." This term is widely used in discussions of criticism, and it is in most respects preferable to "imitative." Although "imitation" is the usual translation of the Greek *mimesis*, the familiar English word might too easily suggest a call for a direct copy of reality. In practice, even the most naive mimeticist is likely to admit some difference between the literary work and the world it imitates, and sophisticated theories have always acknowledged the problematic nature of this relationship. The alien ring of "mimetic" might serve to keep us alert to the problems while its basic sense accurately denotes those critics who are primarily concerned to measure the poem against the external universe, to decide how far and in what ways poetry tells us the truth.

The critic who undertakes to do this joins a great tradition in Western literary criticism. Among the ancients, the idea that literature was essentially mimetic was not so much an argued conclusion as it was the unchallenged premise on which all arguments were built. And with very few exceptions that premise continued to control discussions of literature well into the eighteenth century. Even when genetic concerns began to dominate the academic study of literature, these concerns were not often seen as opposing mimetic criticism. People assumed that great literature revealed truth; this revelation justified interest in its author and the circumstances of its creation. In this respect, the academic critic and the common reader often share the same predilection, and the mimetic value terms are at once the most venerable and the most popular. For many readers, terms such as "real," "true," and "lifelike" when applied to literature are assumed to name incontestable values.

This predilection is illustrated in censorship controversies and even court cases where the prosecution is likely to argue the affective line that the work in question, in its language or the actions it portrays, has a harmful effect on its audience, while the defense may think it sufficient to respond with the mimetic argument that the work gives, nonetheless, an accurate picture of reality. After all, people say and do such things, and the author is simply reporting the facts of life. Thus, one side appeals to goodness, the other to truth. (Very seldom do such cases admit an appeal to beauty.) For mimeticists, though, truth is a higher good. And sometimes their argument wins. The famous decision that allowed James Joyce's *Ulysses* to be sold in the United States, for example, justified the work in part as an honest and accurate portrait of middle-class Dubliners at the turn of the century. Those who objected to the book's "too poignant preoccupation with sex" were reminded that Joyce's "locale was Celtic and his season Spring." Our commitment to "truth" as a value term runs deep.

This commitment is also reflected in our tendency to claim a mimetic justification for changes in literary fashions and conventions. As drama, for instance, gradually dropped the use of meter and adopted "natural" speech and carefully detailed settings and costumes to portray contemporary bourgeois characters, each development was hailed as making the drama more "realistic." Yet Chekhov, for one, looked on plays that employed all these devices as "unrealistic" in their presentation of well-made plots and of characters who could concentrate their attention on a single theme or follow the thread of a complex conversation. In the name of realism, he introduced the meandering dialogue, the "irrelevant" remark or development, and with these mimetic devices he anticipated some of the conventions of the "theater of the absurd," conventions that are in turn defended as "true to life." Similarly, techniques of modern prose fiction such as the stream of consciousness or the rigorously limited point of view have usually been explained as attempts to portray reality more accurately. That one generation's realistic device should so often be the next generation's "mere convention" might lead us to suspect the entire line of argument. But the prevalence of this line illustrates the potency of the mimetic appeal. We incline to believe that if we can claim for a device, a technique, or a whole work a "realistic" purpose, we have provided an ultimate justification.

It follows, of course, that a poem's failure on these grounds is cause for condemnation. On such mimetic principles, Plato, in history's most famous attack on poetry, banished the poet from the ideal state. Actually, Plato said several and sometimes contradictory things about poets in his various writings, and he also objected to poetry on the affective grounds that it feeds and waters the passions. But his best-known remarks occur in *Republic* X, where he attacks poetry because it gives us a false view of the world. His argument is of interest chiefly for the answers it has inspired.

In Plato's philosophy, the world most of us call "real," the world apprehended by the senses, is an imperfect manifestation of the true reality, the world of immutable ideas or forms, the Parmenidean stasis that stands behind the Heraclitean flux of the sensuous world and that can be apprehended only by the mind. The idea of the perfect circle, for example, is prior to and apart from all circles we may draw or see, and that idea is the standard against which any physical circle can be measured. Obviously, only the mind can know the idea of a circle, and the mind must know that idea independently of any drawn circle. Likewise, when we see a pencil protruding from a glass of water, our sense of sight tells us that the pencil is bent, but the mind, which understands the truth, corrects the false report. And so for all knowledge. The business of humanity is to use our reason to pierce the veil of illusion, to transcend the false reports of the senses, to escape from the shadowy knowledge of the cave and to come to know the real world of the ideal forms. What furthers that knowledge is good; what inhibits it is harmful. Poetry inhibits it.

To explain his point, Plato resorts, as he often does, to visual metaphor. We start with the idea of a bed. A kind of practical artist, the carpenter, copies the idea of the bed to produce a physical bed. This bed, though a mere "imitation" and necessarily imperfect because a translation of an idea into a physical medium, has nonetheless a practical use. But when a painter paints a picture of that bed, he or she makes an imitation of an imitation that has no practical use. Worse, by copying the physical bed, which was itself a copy of the real bed, the painter produces a work twice removed from reality and so leads us not toward the realm of true knowledge but in the opposite direction.

By this argument, one of the world's great image makers and symbol wielders banished poets from his perfect state. The paradox did not go long unnoticed, and at least as early as Plotinus we find art defended on the same Platonic grounds that Plato had used to condemn it. If a thinker can manage to escape the cave and enter the transcendent realm of pure forms, he or she can communicate what is discovered only by means of metaphor and symbol. To talk at all about such a realm, the thinker must perforce become, like Plato, a poet. Thus Shelley, in one of the best-known Platonic defenses of poetry, can claim that

Poets, or those who imagine and express this indestructible order, are not only the authors of language and of music, of dance and architecture, and statuary, and painting; they are the institutors of laws, and the founders of civil society, and the inventors of the arts of life, and the teachers, who draw into a certain propinquity with the beautiful and the true, that partial apprehension of the agencies of the invisible world which is called religion.

In other words, the artist's bed need not be a copy of the carpenter's. The artist's vision can penetrate to the ideal realm, and his or her skill can translate that vision into the artistic symbol that is, if not quite the idea itself, something that can lead us to conceive the idea. Like Keats's urn, the artist's symbol mediates between the physical world of flux and the immutable, transcendent realm. Through synesthesia and paradox it takes us past the mode of sensuous apprehension toward the unheard melodies beyond the sounded notes, the static pattern behind the frenzied action. It allows us to contemplate that realm beyond appearances where beauty and truth are indeed one and the same. This realm is the reality that art imitates and that *only* art can imitate. Thus, despite Plato's argument in the *Republic*, Platonic philosophy has most often been used to defend poetry, and specifically on mimetic grounds.

But the earliest reply to Plato had been argued on a different basis. At any rate, the *Poetics*, that curious treatise attributed to his student, Aristotle, has generally been thought to have as one of its purposes the attempt to refute Plato's charge by redefining the sense in which poetry imitates reality. *Mimesis* is Aristotle's key word, and not all he says about it in this fragmentary document seems entirely clear and consistent. But his central concepts are plain enough. Like Plato, Aristotle builds his poetics on his metaphysics, but in solider Aristotle's scheme the reality that art imitates is quite literally a different matter. "Form" is no longer something beyond the physical world. The material world we apprehend with our senses is the real world, and everything in it consists of matter that is formed in some way. This concept is easy enough to conceive if we think of manmade things like a bed, or a poem, and in fact Aristotle's concepts provide part of the basis for "formal" criticism. But when we think of the forms of living things, the forms that poems imitate rather than the forms they possess, we are apt to misunderstand. The true "form" of a living thing is that which it most characteristically is. The form of a man, for example, is best represented by a vigorous adult who has reached that stage toward which childhood develops and from which old age declines. The form of an acorn is not a small and somewhat spherical object but a full-grown, majestic oak tree.

Now there is a sense in which this true form is never realized in nature. Warping winds, poor soil, impatient lumberjacks, and a hundred other "accidents" may prevent the acorn from achieving its true form. So Aristotle develops his own split between form and appearance, and this split has important implications for his concept of mimesis. For one thing, it explains how it is possible for a mimetic art to represent men as "better than they are" or things "as they ought to be," just as a sculptor may study several models in order to "imitate" a form possessed by none of the models. More importantly, it explains how the artist must look past the accidents, the individual peculiarities, to discover the essential or characteristic form that underlies them. The artist gives us the essence of a character, a situation, an action. The artist shows us not what that person or this person did, but what such people do. In perceiving this essential form and then imitating it in the medium of his art so that we may perceive it, the poet achieves "a more philosophical and a higher thing than history: for poetry tends to express the universal, history the particular." Both the poet and the historian tell us truths, but the poet tells the more important truths.

Here is a mimetic defense of poetry as cogent as the Platonic and even more influential. Between them, these defenses provided the philosophic foundations for nearly every mimetic theory of literature until the eighteenth century, and their influence is still felt in many ways in contemporary criticism. Despite their considerable differences, the Platonic and Aristotelian views of mimesis have at least two important similarities. First, each bases its concept of poetic imitation on a well-developed philosophic system that includes a theory of the nature of the world and a theory of how that nature can be known. Clearly, any mimetic approach to poetry raises the question of what "reality" the poem is supposed to be imitating. And while

several mimetic theories have been developed to a considerable degree on appeals to common sense or to general experience—that is, without positing a specific epistemology or metaphysic—any mimetic criticism becomes more intelligible, if not more compelling, to the extent that the critic makes clear his or her view of the reality against which the poem is to be measured. Both the Platonic and the Aristotelian systems do make this clear.

And they do something even more important. Whether the poet is thought to pierce the illusory veil of sense to enter the transcendent realm of the true forms, or whether he or she is thought to penetrate the accidents of local particularity to perceive the essential and universal character of persons and actions, each system offers a view that separates appearance and reality. Consequently, each avoids a serious problem that troubles many mimetic theories. Generally, the more heavily we stress the congruence of the poem to reality, the more difficult it becomes to explain the formal coherence of the poem. But if the poem is congruent not with the shifty and chaotic world of appearance but instead with some transcendent or underlying reality, the usual tension between coherence and congruence is considerably relaxed, perhaps even dissolved. In the Platonic scheme especially, the coherence of the work of art can be explained on mimetic grounds as an imitation of the coherence of the real world of ideal forms, that realm where coherence and congruence, beauty and truth, are one and the same. In the Aristotelian view, of course, the gap between appearance and reality is not so wide. But it is wide enough to establish a concept of artistic imitation as a process that strips away the peculiar, local, and temporary to reveal the characteristic, general, and permanent; and this view also exempts the poem from any need to conform closely to the appearance of things.

When we contemplate, for example, Aristotle's favorite play, *Oedipus Tyrannus*, we notice that by the standards of circumstantial realism it is a confabulation of implausible premises, improbable coincidences, and impossible circumstances. In fact, the famous economy and symmetry of its structure are salient among the things that set it apart from the world of ordinary experience. But, Aristotle implicitly argues, precisely those same things throw into sharp relief the essential action and, hence, the essential meaning of the play. The coherence of the poem, achieved by pruning away the distracting and confusing details of life as we usually experience it, is exactly what allows us to perceive the poem's universal relevance, its correspondence to the form beneath appearances. So the Aristotelian concept of mimesis, too, is able to lessen, if it cannot entirely eliminate, the troublesome opposition between coherence and congruence, between formal unity and imitative accuracy.

Plato and Aristotle, then, present two cogent and fully developed mimetic theories of literature. But their strengths are also their weaknesses. The cogency of each theory derives mainly from the philosophic system of which it is a part, and its usefulness depends largely on the extent to which readers are willing to accept that system. For the last two hundred years, fewer and fewer readers have been willing to accept either system. Increasingly, modern thought has been dominated by what may be called a pervasive "empirical" view of reality, which says that the world apprehended by the senses, the confusing flux of felt experience, is the real world. Such a view makes it much more difficult to separate the poet's truth from the historian's, or from the psychologist's, the sociologist's, or the physical scientist's. One solution is simply to give up poetry's claims to truth and to defend it on entirely different, usually affective, grounds. I. A. Richards, we noticed, attempted to do precisely that. But this radical solution has not appealed to many of the major figures in modern criticism, and Richards's denial of the referential function of poetic language was in turn denied even by critics who accepted his analytical techniques. These critics and others vigorously asserted the truth of poetry on empirical grounds and even against the claims of empirical science, and in the process they brought about a rather startling shift of perspective.

Aristotle, we saw, argued that poetry, because it was not confined as history was to the unique acts of specific persons at particular times and places, could reveal a higher and more universal truth. Certainly the poem presents particular characters and particular actions, but these are represented in their essentials, and the purpose of artistic shaping is to reveal their general truth. Samuel Johnson, who was often a staunch mimeticist, was very much in this tradition when he had his character Imlac declare that it is not the business of poetry to "number the streaks of the tulip"; his business is rather "to examine, not the individual, but the species; to remark general properties and large appearances." Sir Joshua Reynolds, Johnson's contemporary and a famous painter, took a similar view when he claimed that the "disposition to abstractions, to generalizing and classification, is the great glory of the human mind," a remark that prompted William Blake to write in his *marginalia* on Reynolds, "To generalize is to be an idiot." Blake strikes the modern note. Many twentieth-century attempts to assert the claims of poetic truth against those of scientific truth have taken the tack we noticed in the discussion of formal criticism. Science obviously deals in "general" truths. Newton's apple and Humpty-Dumpty obey the same "laws," which can be stated in compact formulas to describe an infinite number of specific cases. But, replies the literary critic, such description is too general. It provides an even ghostlier paradigm than the Platonic forms. It is too abstract to adequately describe the heft and feel, the smell and sound and sight of the world as we actually experience it. For that we need a more concrete medium, something, if not more simple, at least more sensuous and passionate. We need poetry.

In this way the modern mimeticist comes very often to stress the solidity and particularity of the poetic symbol, the complexity and tensions of the poetic structure. In doing so, we should remember, he or she is simply putting the emphasis on the other side of the same concrete–universal coin that is the poem. Aristotle and centuries of later critics, defining poetry with reference to the historian's particularity, stressed its universality. Many modern critics, and especially those with a formalist bent, defining poetry with reference to the universality of science, have emphasized its particularity. Each emphasis is understandable. Hamlet is interesting because he is in some sense every man, but Everyman is less interesting than Hamlet.

Still, the critic who undertakes a mimetic defense of poetry on empirical grounds faces one problem that neither Aristotle nor Plato had. For he or she cannot so easily explain in what way a poem can have "universal" or general truth. It doesn't present the universally applicable scientific law; neither does it represent a statistical mean or average. And "typical" seems not quite the right term for a Falstaff or a Lear. But modern critics share with these earlier philosophers the fact that their views of the reality the poem somehow imitates gain in clarity if these views are integrated with larger systems of thought. The "psychological" critic, for example, though usually focusing attention on the author and sometimes on the audience, is also able to operate in the mimetic context, and often does. Whether a follower of Freud, Jung, Lacan, Horney, Maslow, or some other leading figure, such a critic brings to a reading of literature a fully developed theory about the way people really behave and their reasons for so doing, and this theory provides a standard by which the critic can measure the accuracy of the poet's representations. Such a critic differs from the unaffiliated amateur chiefly in that he or she claims that a chosen school of thought offers special insights into human behavior and a special vocabulary with which to talk about it. And in measuring literary works against this standard, such a critic is often pleased, but not at all surprised, to find that great poets have seen human nature in much the same way.

Freud, for instance, noticed that creative writers had anticipated many of his own discoveries. He named his famous "Oedipus complex" after a play by Sophocles, and he suggested its application to one by Shakespeare. In doing so, we should notice, he was practicing mimetic criticism, for he was claiming that these playwrights were perceptive students of reality whose intuitive grasp of human nature was later confirmed by more methodical and scientific observation. "Not I, but the poets, have discovered the unconscious." And when we respond to these poets we do so because at some level of consciousness we recognize the truth of their representations. This approach is fundamentally different from that of the genetic scholar who tells us, for example, that *Hamlet* must be understood in the light of some long-forgotten Renaissance theory of psychology that Shakespeare either accepted or assumed his audience accepted. To the mimetic critic of a psychoanalytic persuasion, there is nothing anachronistic in reading classical or Elizabethan drama in Freudian terms. The psychologist and the poet study the same nature, and the truth of their findings, not at all limited by time and place, is always referable to this same standard, "at once the source, and end, and test of art." And of science.

So any psychology, indeed, any systematic view of human behavior, can provide the basis for a mimetic criticism of literature. In our own century, one of the most influential systems of thought has been the Marxist. To be sure, Marxist critics have often analyzed the social and economic forces acting on writers, and they have frequently been very much concerned with literature's effects. But these genetic and affective concerns are often based on a mimetic criterion: the work is good to the extent that it accurately depicts the clash of class interests, the forces of economic determinism, the dialectic process of history, in brief, the social reality as the critic's particular interpretation of Marxism may conceive it.

In other words, however much they may differ among themselves, critics operating within a system of thought can account for the function of literature and measure its truth in terms of a larger framework of ideas. As we noted with reference to the Platonic and Aristotelian views, this is a potential strength, but only to the extent that we are willing to accept the whole system of thought that supports the criticism. In practice, the great majority of readers has found the mimetic standards of most systems too partial, too limited, to deal adequately with the abundance and variety of literature that the world has generally called great. What system is capacious enough to comprehend Homer's cosmology and Milton's, Dante's ethics and de Sade's, Assisi's flowers and Baudelaire's? Or, take him all in all, what system can contain Shakespeare alone? Perhaps this is why the largest number of mimetic critics—and this number would include most of us at one time or another—feel no need to claim allegiance to a particular school of thought. Apparently unaffiliated and eclectic, they appeal to empiricism in its root meaning, to our common sense and our common experience of the world, to provide the mimetic standard, and what they may lose in philosophic rigor they gain in flexibility and wider assent.

But even the most eclectic and flexible forms of mimetic criticism must encounter some basic difficulties that seem to inhere in the very nature of the problematic relationship between art and "reality," and the more firmly the criticism is based on empirical premises, the more troublesome these difficulties will be. One of these difficulties may be expressed in the form of two related questions: How does the poem, in conforming to a reality already known, give us knowledge? Or, if the reality is not already known, how can we be sure the poem does in fact conform to it? We may praise a work by remarking that it is congruent to life as we know it: this is the way things look; this is how people really behave. But it is not clear why we want to have such representations. Since we already possess the standard by which we judge them— that is, since we already know the reality imitated sufficiently well to judge the accuracy of the imitation—in what sense can we be said to learn anything from the poem?

This is not easy to answer. Aristotle's remarks that people learn by imitation and that they enjoy learning are not especially helpful, since he doesn't explain in what way people learn from artistic representations, and the example he gives muddies the waters further. Drawing on visual metaphor, he says that only those who know the original that the painter imitates can derive pleasure from the comparison; those who lack that knowledge derive what pleasure they have from some other, apparently nonmimetic, source. A better answer seems to be implicit in Aristotle's view of the poem as a special arrangement of particulars that somehow more clearly reveals their universal significance. Fra Lippo Lippi, in Browning's poem of that name, provides a well-known account of the phenomenon when he explains, again using the "realistic" painting as his example, that we look at things every day but we don't really see them

until the artist's picture calls our attention to them. Then we say, "That's the very man!" but in fact we hadn't been fully aware of the life around us until the artist taught us to see it.

This line is promising, and a critical theory could be developed at some length in this direction. But when we inquire how the artist has achieved this result, we seem to be faced with the paradox that it has been achieved by altering the very reality the artist claims to imitate. The alteration may take the form of simply selecting or rearranging details to heighten our awareness and focus our vision, but nonetheless it is, by definition, alteration. And once we start to argue that even the most "realistic" plot, the most "lifelike" characters and actions, have some degree of distortion, then on the same principles we might argue that the most elaborate plots, the most outlandish caricatures, the most fantastic fictions can be similarly justified. For they too could be called heightenings and intensifications of reality. And by such argument the so-called realistic devices and modes of literature lose their special standing. If forms such as "realistic" drama or "naturalistic" fiction achieve their ends by departing from direct imitation in at least some respects, then those same ends might be as well attained by forms such as epic, romance, pastoral, and others that depart from direct imitation in most respects. Such a line of argument does promise to account for the great variety of literature, but since it locates the special function and force of art in its power to select from, rearrange, and otherwise distort reality, it doesn't seem appropriate to call such a line mimetic.

So the question of just how an arrangement of words can be said to imitate reality remains a rather difficult question to answer, and so does the question of why we should want such imitations. And the answers are made all the more difficult when "reality" is defined in empirical terms. A related problem, how to reconcile the poem's formal coherence with its mimetic function, is also made more difficult. As we noticed, only idealistic philosophies like the Platonic can fully achieve this reconciliation. As the conception of reality becomes more empirical, the problem grows more troublesome, because any selection from the flux of felt experience and any imposition of formal pattern must to some extent lessen the poem's correspondence to empirical reality. Thus the formalist's dilemma returns now from the other side and, as we should expect, the formalist has often raised the objection against many types of mimetic criticism that they ignore the very things that make poems, poems. Whatever ideology or philosophy is used to provide the standard of "truth," none can very well account for the art of poetry, and all are inclined to separate form and meaning, to extract the paraphrasable content of the poem and to judge that as if the poem were a philosophic treatise or a religious or economic tract. And even when the mimetic critic is willing to acknowledge the formal aspects of the poem, to grant its difference from discursive argument, the mimetic context cannot itself provide the concepts that will allow an explication or account of these formal aspects. Thus, the opposition between artistic design and imitative accuracy troubles virtually all mimetic theories, and it especially troubles those with an empirical basis.

This same opposition, we noticed, puzzled formal critics, though they approached the problem from the other direction. In fact, we could locate both formal and mimetic critics somewhere on that imaginary line that connects the work of art with reality as we experience it outside of art. The difference between them is often a matter of emphasis. Mimetic critics are primarily concerned to measure the poem's congruence with reality and to judge it on that basis, but they can neither entirely overlook nor, on mimetic grounds, adequately account for the formal features of the poem that set it apart from the world of experience and from other forms of discourse. Conversely, formal critics stress the uniqueness of poetic language and the inseparability of form and content, and their analyses are designed to explicate the poem's formal coherence. Yet they usually insist as well on the referential function of poetic language, and they often find the meaning and value of the poem's "complexity" in its correspondence to the complex reality of life as we experience it. So for both the formal and the mimetic critic, despite their different starting points, coherence and

congruence are always necessary, but seldom easily reconcilable, principles.

A third problem confronting all mimetic approaches is brought into focus by a more radical objection. When formalists complain that mimetic critics cannot deal with the form of the poem, they mean by "form" these particular words in this particular order. When intertextual critics make the same complaint, they mean by "form" all the literary conventions that make up the poem. This objection is more radical because the intertextual perspective sees the poem not as an imitation of life but as an imitation of other poems. This perspective threatens, therefore, to undermine the mimetic premise entirely, to simply deny the referential function of art.

The development of this line of criticism is the subject of the next chapter. Here we shall simply note some implications of this objection. The mimetic perspective seems to bring naturally to mind narrative and dramatic structures, particularly those that offer "rounded" characters and "realistic" settings and actions and that seem to invite comparison with life outside of books. The novel, for example, is sometimes thought to be synonymous with the techniques of "circumstantial realism," and the tendency of much recent fiction to abandon these techniques has been seen by some to herald "the death of the novel." But the intertextual critic reminds us that even so-called realistic techniques are simply conventions, and he calls our attention to the myriad forms that make up the bulk of literature, the romances and pastorals, the farces and burlesques, the chameleon satire, that can infiltrate any form, and the encyclopedic work, like *Ulysses*, that can contain most. He reminds us, further, that to defend *Ulysses* as a faithful picture of middle-class Dublin life at the turn of the century in the spring of the year may be judicially useful, but it is critically myopic. And he reminds us, finally, that it is very difficult to account for the many generic conventions and their endless permutations on mimetic grounds. Yet these are the salient features of literary form, in a fundamental sense of the term, and a theory's inability to account for them must be considered a serious weakness.

Mimetic critics, then, encounter some difficult problems. On the one hand, they must face the charge of reductivism because they cannot easily cope with literary "form" in either the formal or the intertextual senses of the term. On the other hand, their own context is replete with philosophical puzzles about the relationship between verbal structures and the "reality" these structures are supposed to imitate. Although most of these problems are very old, they are made especially difficult by the prevailing modern tendency to define "reality" in empirical terms. Still, as the very hoariness of the problems indicates, their existence has never drastically diminished the popularity of the mimetic context. From Aristophanes' day to Samuel Johnson's, mimetic concerns dominated literary discussions, and these concerns have continued to play a major role in much modern criticism. Genetic critics, for example, who have some difficulty forming a theory of poetic value within their own context, are frequently willing to assume a mimetic basis for value, to agree that good literature tells the "truth" about human nature. And formal critics often gravitate toward the same position, and largely for the same reasons. Add to these the Freudians, Jungians, Marxists, Thomists, feminists, and other representatives of various philosophies, psychologies, or ideologies whose approach to literature is likely to stress the poem's relationship to "reality," and it is apparent that mimetic criticism, under a variety of names, continues to occupy much of our attention.

There are good reasons why it should. The notion that literature in some way imitates life has been an accepted axiom of Western thought from its earliest records. While critics in some of our contexts have occasionally been willing to ignore that axiom, only the intertextual critics are inclined to deny it. In other words, we are accustomed to thinking in mimetic terms. But more than habit is involved. Almost any verbal representation, particularly one in narrative or dramatic form, seems to force some kind of comparison with our nonliterary experience. Such comparison furnishes an obvious, an almost inevitable, point of reference for the viewer or reader, a standard automatically invoked whenever we remark the "consistency" of a charac-

ter's behavior or the "plausibility" of an action. In other words, our understanding of the characters and actions in poetry seems to be at least partly, and almost by reflex, a matter of reference to the mimetic context.

Further, and perhaps most importantly, there is the large question of the value of literature. As we have seen, the attraction of the mimetic context has often been strongest here. As we have also seen, poetic value is a problem in any context, and the empirical emphasis of much modern thought has made it harder in some ways to work out a theory of value on mimetic lines. Yet at the same time, this empirical bias seems to make it all the more imperative that a defense of poetry be conducted exactly on these lines. To put it simply, if we can show that literature does, in some important ways, tell us the truth about experience, then the various forms of "scientific" thought can be met on their own grounds, and the vast enterprise connected with literature, and our own intense personal interest in it, can be given an ultimate, or at least a widely accepted, justification. Only the mimetic context promises to provide such justification.

Suggestions for Further Reading

Erich Auerbach's *Mimesis: The Representation of Reality in Western Literature* (1946) is a classic text; John D. Boyd's *The Function of Mimesis and Its Decline* (2nd ed., 1980) is a history of some of the key concepts. Harry Levin, in *The Gates of Horn* (1963), Herbert Lindenberger, in *Historical Drama* (1975), and Frank Kermode, in *The Sense of an Ending* (1967), all investigate the ways in which literature can be said to "imitate" reality. George Bisztray's *Marxist Models of Literary Realism* (1978) recounts the arguments among Marxist critics about this tricky term. Other explorations of "realism" include Ian Watt, *The Rise of the Novel* (1957), J. P. Stern, *On Realism* (1973), and Kathryn Hume, *Fantasy and Mimesis* (1984). Ernest Jones's *Hamlet and Oedipus* (1949) is a famous study asserting the psychological truth of Shakespeare's character on Freudian lines; Bernard Paris, in *A Psychological Approach to Fiction* (1974), argues the case for mimeticism using a different psychological model. Although feminist critics operate in several contexts, this diverse group may be cited here, for their main challenges to other forms of criticism, and to our usual ways of thinking about society, sex, and history, are often grounded in the mimetic context. K. K. Ruthven's *Feminist Literary Studies* (1984) and Toril Moi's *Textual/Sexual Politics* (1985) give an overview of the various issues and positions covered by the term "feminist criticism." Sandra M. Gilbert and Susan Gubar's *The Madwoman in the Attic* (1979) and Elaine Showalter's *A Literature of Their Own: British Women Novelists from Bronte to Lessing* (1977) are two well-known studies. Representative essays can be found in Josephine Donovan, ed., *Feminist Literary Criticism* (1975), Mary Jacobus, ed., *Women Writing and Writing About Women* (1979), and Sally McConnell-Ginet et al., eds., *Women and Language in Literature and Society* (1980).

The Two Languages of Criticism

A. D. Nuttall

*In "The Two Languages of Criticism," A. D. Nut-
tall contrasts the "Transparent" language of mimetic critics with the "Opaque" language of critics
who would severely restrict or quite deny the mimetic reference of the work of art. When he calls
this latter group "formalists," he refers primarily to
the Continental formalists, who are more inclined to
take a markedly antimimetic position, as opposed to
Anglo-American formalists who, as we have noted,
often give the mimetic aspect of art an important
place in their theory. Yet even these "soft formalists," as Nuttall elsewhere calls them, emphasize
those features of poetic language that cause us to
look at that language, rather than through it.
Nuttall also has very much in mind what this book
calls "intertextual" critics, including structuralists
and semioticians, whose theories are often radically
antimimetic. All these are included under Nuttall's
"formalist" group, and he feels that these exponents
of the "opaque" languages of criticism have come
increasingly to dominate discussions of literature in
this century. He reminds us, though, that in the
preceding twenty-four centuries the reverse emphasis was dominant (his use of the analogy to painting to illustrate his case has a pedigree equally
long), and his chapter, like the book from which it
comes, is a vigorous defense of mimetic criticism.*

THERE ARE TWO LANGUAGES OF CRITICISM, THE
first "opaque," external, formalist, operating
outside the mechanisms of art and taking those
mechanisms as its object, the second "transparent," internal, realist, operating within the
"world" presented in the work. The first language throws upon the screen of critical consciousness all the formal devices of a work in
such a way that the eye is arrested by them.
Formal characters, in order that they should be
the more visible, are deliberately made opaque.
In the second language, formal devices are, like
windows, transparent. We shall refer to the first
mode, shortly, as the Opaque language and the
second as the Transparent language. "Opaque"
and "Transparent" are morally neutral terms.
The initial capitals mark these words as technical
terms.

The following sentences are all in the Opaque
language:

1. In the opening of *King Lear* folk-tale elements proper to narrative are infiltrated by
   a finer-grained dramatic mode.

2. In Brueghel's *Fall of Icarus,* as the eye travels from the top of the picture, the shapes
   become increasingly curved; the bottom
   third of the painting is a sort of rollicking
   march of swooping, overlapping loops.

3. In *Portrait of a Lady* James applies to human
   figures language normally reserved for artefacts; Isabel Archer is "written in a foreign
   tongue"; Daniel Touchett presents "a fine,
   ivory surface"; Henrietta Stackpole "has no
   misprints."

4. In *Hamlet* Shakespeare contrives that the
   delay should be unintelligible, because the
   principal figure functions not as an explanatory device but as a source of intellectual
   frustration.

These sentences on the other hand, are in the Transparent language:

1. Cordelia cannot bear to have her love for her father made the subject of a partly mercenary game.

2.   The ploughman may
   Have heard the splash, the forsaken cry,
   But for him it was not an important failure;
   the sun shone
   As it had to on the white legs disappearing
   into the green
   Water; and the expensive delicate ship that
   must have seen
   Something amazing, a boy falling out of the
   sky,
   Had somewhere to get to and sailed calmly
   on.
   (W. H. Auden, "Musée des Beaux Arts")[1]

3. Isabel Archer is innocent, but in quite a different way from Henrietta Stackpole.

4. Hamlet delays because, once he has cut himself off from the psychic support of human society, the central structure of his original motivation decays.

It is highly likely that to many readers of this book the first list will automatically look like "real criticism" and the second like "self-indulgent pseudo-criticism." Yet sentences of the second type have always figured in critical writing.

Each sentence in the first list makes explicit reference to the artifice of the work; it takes as its province the artist's distinctive disposition of forms, the mechanisms of representation, evocation, enchantment. There is a mild presumption that to move from such formal scrutiny into a freer discussion of that which is represented would be to leave criticism altogether. Each sentence from the second set, on the other hand, passes shamelessly into the world mimetically proposed in the work of art, and discusses elements of that world as though they were people or physical objects. Cordelia is considered, not as a sequence of harsh yet appealing chords cutting across the sombre confusion created by the Lear figure, but as a young woman in great distress. In the Opaque group explanation is generally sought in terms of what happens in other works of art, or elsewhere in the present work.

In the Transparent group no tabu exists against explaining fictitious behaviour by analogy with real-life equivalents.

Latent in the Opaque approach is a severe separation of critic and reader (or spectator). The critic knows how the conjuror does the tricks, or how the tricks fool the audience, and is thereby excluded, by his very knowingness, from the innocent delight of those who marvel and applaud. Such criticism can never submit to mimetic enchantment because to do so would be to forfeit critical understanding of the means employed. The Transparent party, on the other hand, is less afraid of submission, feeling that enchantment need involve no submersion of critical faculties, but that on the contrary without such a willingness to enter the proffered dream a great many factors essential to a just appreciation may be artificially excluded from discussion. After all its members are not in any fundamental sense fooled by the conjuror. They know perfectly well that all is done by artificial means. But at the same time they can perceive the magic as magic. They know that Ophelia is not a real woman but are willing to think of her as a possible woman. They note that Shakespeare implicitly asks them to do this, but they do more than note the request; they comply with it. They are much less aware than the Opaque party of restrictions on what they are allowed to discuss. For example, they are free to explore all the formal features which in Opaque criticism expand to fill the picture. A statement like "The ideas of women presented in this novel are inadequate," though it refers externally to the artifice of the work, is thoroughly Transparent in its acceptance of mimetic reference. Adverse criticism of the values implied by texts is normally thus. Without a prior submission to the sovereign force of mimesis, no injustice could ever have been perceived. The Opaque critic, on the other hand, can be displeased by a work, but can never dissent from it. An Opaque critic would censor all the statements in the second group; a Transparent critic would pass all the statements in the first. The Transparent critic can and will do all the things done by the Opaque critic but is willing to do other things as well.

The main thrust of the case against Transparent criticism is that it confounds art and reality. Such was the case put in L. C. Knights's celebrated essay, "How many children has Lady Macbeth?"[2] Knights damned Bradleian character-critics for speculating about Hamlet as if he were a real person; "Hamlet" is not a real man at all, but a string of poetic expressions, a constellation of images. With human beings we may legitimately indulge in inference and supposition; we may say, "She must have lived in India" or "He must have been very religious at one time"; but with dramatic characters such inference is manifestly absurd; we cannot guess at Lady Macbeth's previous life for the simple reason that she has no previous life; her being begins and ends with what Shakespeare sets down for her to say.

It is strange that so coarse a piece of reasoning should have passed for a great stroke of destructive theory. Knight's singular presumption that humane inference is inapplicable to drama is simply mistaken. When a character sits up and yawns we infer that he has been sleeping. When another character gives a certain sort of start we infer that he is guilty (readers of *Macbeth*, especially, should be aware of this). If no inferences whatever are allowed, certain negative conclusions, on the other hand, can be drawn about Hamlet. For example he has no legs. For Shakespeare never mentions them—or may we infer (*infer?*) one leg from a down-gyved stocking? This may be thought merely silly, but a large part of Knights's case really does depend on the absolute exclusion of inference. Moreover, in a curious manner, Knights's criticism suggests that he really was more than half-willing to draw the conclusion that Hamlet is not a man. Here too one is drawn to offer a consciously philistine reply, "Hamlet is a funny name for a sequence of images—sounds more like a person, a sort of Danish prince." A dramatist faced with an entire audience who austerely repressed all inferences and bayed for image-patterns might well despair. Of course Bradley never supposed for a moment that Hamlet was a real man. Knights's ill-made shaft misses both Shakespeare and Bradley, and falls on stony ground. But the stony ground, it must be confessed, received it with joy.

What remains strong in Knights's attack is his intuition that Bradleian critics occasionally carried their unverifiable surmises to ludicrous lengths. I cannot agree that the question about Lady Macbeth's children is as absurd as Knights would have had us believe, but certain of Maurice Morgann's observations on the military career of Falstaff . . . are truly foolish. But the simple test of verifiability will not serve to distinguish an absurd from a reasonable surmise. All our inferences and suppositions with regard to fictitious persons are in terms of probability, not fact. The objection to Morgann's speculations is not that Falstaff has no previous life but that Shakespeare does not give us enough clues to render Morgann's more detailed inferences probable. Knights's logical universe (like Todorov's later) was Puritan. There are facts and there are images. He is a logical Calvinist, forbidding all intercourse with the hypothetical, the merely probable.

The Transparent critic, who wonders why Cordelia cannot answer more warmly and thinks of other daughters, some of whom have lived outside the pages of books, is charged with confusing art and reality, but the charge is simply false. Where is the confusion? When Balzac sent for Dr. Bianchon (a character in one of his books) to come to his bedside, he really did confuse art and reality. If he had merely asked "What would Bianchon have said about a case like this?" no eyebrow would have been raised. The question is perfectly rational.

A whole generation was taught by Herbert Read to repress its natural engagement with mimetic painting. Delighted gazers at Edvard Munch's *House under Trees* (1905) had allowed their eyes to linger on the group of women in the foreground, so close to one another, so enigmatic, and then to be drawn into the further space, the pale wall and the trees, wintry yet with a bloom of spring in their soft extremities, and then beyond again to someone else's house, darker in the distance. Herbert Read, on the other hand, taught them, perfectly correctly, that Munch "sacrificed tone to line" and that his lines enclosed definite, powerful planes.[3] The error was to suppose that such formal analysis somehow prohibited the other way of looking and this error was repeated again and again. It became fashionable to laugh at Walter Pater's rhapsodic musings on the *Mona Lisa*[4] and John Addington Symonds's prose poem on Lorenzo dé Medici.[5]

An early consequence of this severe separation of technical ("critical") appreciation and ordinary "entranced" appreciation is an impoverishment of criticism itself. If the critic never enters the dream he remains ignorant about too much of the work. The final result may be a kind of literary teaching which crushes literary enjoyment, the natural *coitus* of reader and work endlessly *interruptus*. The student who begins to talk excitedly about Becky Sharp will suddenly find himself isolated in the seminar. Another cooler student who is careful to speak of "the Becky Sharp motif" tactfully assumes the central role in the discussion and covers the first student's confusion.

There is one other characteristic of the Opaque set of criticisms which should be noticed. They can never quite attain to pure formalism. Language has accepted (one suspects by Darwinian principle) the convenience of referring to characters in books by their fictitious names. We may remorselessly prefix such allusions with formal specifiers—"the character, Hamlet," "the motif, Becky Sharp" and so on—but there is something ponderously redundant about such scrupulousness. Language permits the bare use of the name because context renders the meaning sufficiently unambiguous. As we have seen, old-fashioned readers are in no way confused by this way of discussing fictional persons. Meanwhile the mere use of the proper name, "Becky Sharp," however we fence it about with formal impediments, propels us into the world mimetically proposed, sets our thought in terms of people rather than artistic conventions. It is very hard indeed to describe a novel without referring to the things which are described as happening in it. It is similarly hard to describe a picture without occasionally looking through the arrangement of colour as if it were a window and allowing ourselves to notice, as it might be, the face, the raised hand, the distant tower.

The most determined effort to isolate "the aesthetic emotion" was Clive Bell's *Art* (1914) with its immensely influential conception of "significant form." It was a time of violent re-

action from Victorian "story pictures," like *When Did You Last See Your Father?*, and Bell had no difficulty in rejecting, as irrelevant to the aesthetic emotion, all narrative features. Symbolic and representational features soon followed, leaving the purist formulation, "lines and colours combined in a particular way, certain forms and relations of forms."[6] Here the mimetic dimension itself becomes aesthetically tabu. Most intelligent people agreed, but not all. In the first chapter of Evelyn Waugh's *Brideshead Revisited* (1945) there is a fragmentary paragraph of remembered conversation, set in 1923, which perfectly encapsulates the resistance of the unregenerate few.

> Collins had exposed the fallacy of modern aesthetics to me: " . . . the whole argument from Significant Form stands or falls by *volume*. If you allow Cézanne to represent a third dimension on his two-dimensional canvas, then you must allow Landseer his gleam of loyalty in the spaniel's eye" . . . but it was not until Sebastian, idly turning the pages of Clive Bell's *Art* read:
> " 'Does anyone feel the same kind of emotion for a butterfly or a flower that he feels for a cathedral or a picture?' Yes. *I* do," that my eyes were opened.[7]

The natural movement of mimetic sympathy can be arrested at different levels. A man looking at a Vermeer may be told, by a mild Opaque formalist, that he may see a woman with a letter in her hand but must not speculate on her thoughts, on what has happened or is about to happen. A harder formalist may tell him that he must not see a woman, but a massively rounded monumental form enclosed by rectilinear space. A still harder formalist may forbid the inference of depth or monumental character and restrict the viewer to coloured planes and shapes. Each of these restrictions can be genuinely fruitful critically, since it turns out that art is already achieving complex and important results at all these stages. It would have been so easy to assume that all these things merely served the mimetic end. In fact in a great work of art each has its own separate flowering. Both Clive Bell and Herbert Read saw this clearly and our debt to them is incalculable. But none of the *prohibitions* is in order.

Similarly with literature: a certain sort of

Opaque critic will simply insist that we do not speculate about characters; a severer Opaque critic will begin to fret at the very term "character" (feeling that it somehow suggests an ersatz person) and will, if he is writing in the 1930s, restrict us to the images used or else, if he is writing in the 1980s, restrict us to the semasiological codes. One could imagine a further degree, which would restrict the reader to what philosophers call the actual "token," that is, to the black letters on the printed page (which would at last bring formalist literary theory to the same level as formalist art theory), but, to the literate, print is instantaneously transparent: the mind intuits the word in the token so swiftly that the formalist has no chance to insert his screen. And all words are windows. They are never *purely* formal.

It is curious that the modernist opponents of mimesis have turned to primitive art for support. In fact the primitive mask divagates from the normal human face, not only because its maker is interested in abstract form but because he or she is so confident of the mimetic element that it is taken as read. The primitive tends not to use the external language, "I am making a device," but rather runs to its opposite, Transparent extreme ("I am making a Face"). The resultant artefact is not seen as more or less *like* a face. It *is* a face.[8] Nor are we so far removed culturally as to be unaware, when confronted with such a mask, that a face is looking at us. Where there are two spots side by side and a vertical line below and a horizontal line below that, there is a face. It will look at you; it will catch and hold your eye. It does so not because of its autonomous formal beauty but because the two spots work as eyes. Similarly, in Homer's *Iliad* (vi. 273), when Hector wishes his mother to lay a gift on the knees of the statue of Athene in the temple, he says nothing about a statue, but simply asks her to "lay the robe on Athene's knees."

This primitive level of response is always operative. Indeed it can be variously manipulated by the great masters of mimesis. Rembrandt chose in his self-portraits to blaze upon the viewer from a circumambient darkness, looking straight at him. If we try critically to define the principal differences between Vermeer and Rembrandt we shall be paralysed unless we are allowed to notice that in Vermeer the subject very rarely looks out of the painting. Usually his people are preoccupied, in profile or turned away, and we are like "visual eavesdroppers." Sometimes, as we shall see in more detail later, Vermeer flirts with a stronger reciprocity; a chair may be turned towards the viewer, but no one is sitting in it; a frontal view of the face we see in profile may be tantalizingly half-visible in dim reflection elsewhere in the room. But most of the time—and quite systematically—he works against the grain of immediate or warm relationship with the viewer. His very use of light and shade reverses the normal practice of Rembrandt. Where Rembrandt illuminated the face and plunged the rest in shadow, Vermeer commonly makes his figures somewhat darker than the environment, as though he deliberately disdains any attempt to conciliate our attention or involvement. And he knows very well that all these things will merely make us watch with another sort of attention. The viewer of a Vermeer is admitted by stealth to the world of the picture. The viewer of a Rembrandt is merely overwhelmed. But all this talk is idle if we are not to allow Transparent "reading" of the picture.

Neither Plato nor Aristotle, using the term "mimesis," begins from an assumpton that art of itself has nothing to do with nature and that any possible contingent link with nature must be carefully explained. Rather, like Cassirer's tribesmen, they begin from the assumption that the artist makes a man, or a war, or a bed, and then carefully point out that it is not a real man etc., but an imitation one. Both begin from the fact that the poet is a maker. Today it is only the learned who are aware that the idea of making is implicit in the word "poet." But for the ancient Greek the word for "poet" is simply one and the same as the word for "maker": ποιητής. The notion of the poet as maker is usually congenial to formalists because the question "What does he make?" for them naturally invites an Opaque, externalist answer: he makes an epic, or he makes a song. The Greek language certainly permits this kind of answer, but it seems at least as ready to receive answers of the other kind: "The poet makes a sack of Troy." One can watch English translators flinching from the forthrightness of this. Jowett translates *Republic* 569E as follows: "the painter also creates a bed. Yes, he said, but not a real bed."[9] Where Jowett gives the august word "creates," Plato uses the ordinary word, ποιεῖ, "makes." Of course Plato, by his metaphysical theory, considers both actual, physical beds and beds in pictures to be unreal imitations of the ideal Bed, and Aristotle laboured in his *Poetics* to show that poetic imitations might serve society, by channelling off violent emotion, and at the same time might also engage with genuine probability. Thus they differ deeply. But one point on which it does not occur to either of them to raise any difficulty is the assumption that when an artist paints a picture of a bed what he does bears some relation to a physical bed. Why else, they might ask, do we call it painting a *bed?*

•   •   •

Of the two languages of criticism it is the internal, Transparent one which most obviously lets in the outer world. *Enter* the work and you walk *out*, free, into the surrounding landscape. The external, Opaque language, sticking as it does to the analysis of mechanisms and formal factors, is far more narrowly confined to a single plane. It is conceived in cool, Olympian detachment but its very aloofness leads to its confinement. Moreover, just as it cannot move freely into the proposed, hypothetical events of the book, similarly it cannot move back from the public, manifest superficies of the work to the range of human activities and emotions which give force and meaning to fictions. The door to the larger world is likewise kept firmly shut. When we say (and people say such things all the time, quite incurably) that in a given novel "the social scene is sharply observed," we break out in two directions at once: we presume that a high degree of probability is observed in the hypothesis (that is, that the characters are made to act and talk as their equivalents would in real life) and, at the same time, we imply that to secure such close correspondence is an acheivement on the part of the real author: we make a loose but irreducible claim about the circumstances of composition. And, as long as we al-

low that the universe is not really partitioned into verified truths and free-floating fictions, but on the contrary admits such things as probability and possibility, we have no ground for legislating against such luminously normal talk.

The admission of a sense of authorial achievement, of human energy and striving, is immediately consonant with our conception of art as more concerned with *connaissance* than with *savoir*. If we think the artist is trying hard to reach us we in our turn will try. *Savoir* is expressed in propositions which are either understood or not. It can be added to or extended but its essence is homogeneous. The *connaissance* of a single person or thing, on the other hand, can be deepened or intensified without any material addition to the stock of information. Such deepening is accomplished more effectively when the entire apparatus of human prehensive emotion is involved. The effect of learning that a work to which one was beginning to respond in this profoundly personal manner was composed automatically is immediately disconcerting and has practical aesthetic consequences. The stream of personal response is abruptly curtailed. The devices of obfuscation by which, as we saw, artists can energize the responses of viewers so that they win through to an enhanced intuition, work because they are "read" as human, and they are so read because in general they are known to be so. Particular cases will commonly be unverifiable but without the common presumption the entire enterprise fails.

Yet even this technique of obfuscation, still paradigmatically human for most observers, can now be produced mechanically. Gombrich shows in his *Meditations on a Hobby Horse*[10] two photographs of a sickly-smooth *Three Graces* painted in 1900, one clear and the other broken and blurred. The blurring process is mechanically obtained. Gombrich observes that nevertheless it activates our "reading" of the picture. He is right, but one can sense, even as one looks at his example, how the activation is dying away to something of minor importance. We "twig" that the blurring is inertly uniform and therefore mechanical. As soon as this happens three-quarters of the sensibility falls into quiescence. The minimal interpretation of the image goes on and for this indeed some extra energies are needed. But that is all. Thus, as an example of what happens in postimpressionist painting the photograph is oddly weak.

In *War and Peace* Tolstoy at one point describes an operatic performance:

> The floor of the stage consisted of smooth boards, at the sides was some painted cardboard representing trees, and at the back was a cloth stretched over boards. In the centre of the stage sat some girls in red bodices and white skirts. One very fat girl in a white silk dress sat apart on a low bench, to the back of which a piece of green cardboard was glued. They all sang something. When they had finished their song the girl in white went up to the prompter's box, and a man with tight silk trousers over his stout legs, and holding a plume and a dagger, went up to her and began singing, waving his arms about.[11]

This description comes at the beginning of a chapter. It feels very odd and the reader is slightly disconcerted that so "harsh" and idiosyncratic a view should be "backed" or rather simply given, by the author. In a novel of switching viewpoints, like Smollett's *Humphrey Clinker*, this would be the ostentatiously subjective perception of a particular character. In fact Tolstoy, within a few paragraphs, ascribes this view of the opera to Natasha, who is in the audience, but he has so ordered his chapter as to imply, quite simply, that she is right. The "authorial status" of the opening paragraphs is not cancelled by the later ascription of this view to a character.

The passage is a classic example of "defamiliarization," of "making it strange" as that concept is defined in the criticism of the Russian formalists. The prime purpose of "making it strange" is to induce an innocent vision, unmediated by preconceptions. Tolstoy, in effect, says to his readers, "Let us, just for once, say what a stage presentation really looks like." This enterprise is profoundly opposed, in its most immediate implications, to radical formalism. For it assumes the possibility of a "pure" objectivity. It is a curiosity of literary history that this impulse has been overlaid by successive accretions of formalist theory. One effect of isolating

the unmediated perception is to make one acutely conscious of the immense play of prior modifying categories in "ordinary" perception. Poetic language, in particular, may be seen as "negatively truthful" in the way it deliberately forces the means of expression on our attention, so that we cannot mistake them for realities which have, so to speak, been transcribed without any alteration. But to reason in this way is to forget one's original praise of that literature which successfully conveyed an unmediated vision. Sometimes the difficulty is merely evaded by an unobtrusive transference of "defamiliarization" from the objects described to the means of expression, so that the poet, in stressing the autonomous richness of words in separation from their referents, is "defamiliarizing" language itself. Thus the banner of defamiliarization is still held high and the fundamental shift of theory is suppressed.[12] Otherwise one may direct the reader's attention to the formal methods which are actually employed in the star cases of supposedly "innocent eye" description. This is the truly formalist response (exactly analogous to what Barthes did in his essay "L'Effet de réel"[13] and its immediate result is the destruction of the "innocent eye" theory. "Making it strange" is, now, not the isolation of an unmediated, unconditioned perception, but the substitution of one set of (artistic) governing conditons for the usual set. The artist may think he is giving his reader a stark, immediate reality, but the formalist critic, by turning a similar searchlight on the artist's means of expression, by making them strange, reveals the fact that he is doing no such thing.

It is at this point that the real, obstinate resistance of the Tolstoy passage begins to be apparent. At first it seemed merely a congenial example of the original, root conception of "making it strange." But Tolstoy has made matters difficult for the formalist by applying *his* technique, *within* the novel, to a work of art. The passage in question is both fiction and criticism at the same time. Thus the shift of defamiliarization from the object to the means of expression has already occurred, within the novel, wholly naturally, because in this case the means of expression are the concrete features of a theatrical performance and are thus susceptible of seemingly direct, empirical description. This ought to mean that Tolstoy has become a good formalist critic. He has learned to arrest his perceptions at the level of the means.

In fact, as is made utterly clear both by the manner of writing and by the context, Tolstoy regards the entire paragraph, not as normal critical description of art, but as a *reductio ad absurdum*. The opacity of the means is for him a simple offence. This judgement he makes as a great realist, as one who believes that art really can be natural and ought to be so. His own realism in describing the theatrical display is, by his own theory, unexceptionable. The performers give an untruthful or improbable account of a love story (if that is what it is) but he gives a truthful, or probable account of a theatrical show.

If we now try to apply to Tolstoy as artist the formalist theorem whereby supposedly "direct" accounts may themselves be resolved into formal structures, we are in danger of noticing something rather awkward, once again, for radical formalist theory. For we shall now be saying that the "cold identification of the means of expression" does not really happen in Tolstoy at all. Rather some other sort of myth (perhaps a positivist one) replaces the common myth. This may be borne, as long as its application is restricted to Tolstoy (where, indeed, it could be argued that the savagely phenomenal description of the opera is echoed, on a larger scale, in the reductive account of military conquest, both proceeding from an essentially *"faux-naïf"* metaphysic). But the implication that other "identifications of means of expression" must be subject to the same formalist solvent is not far to seek. And if that is true, the concrete critical enterprises of formalist theory are themselves subverted by the running metaphysic. We are back to the scientist who discovered an acid which would dissolve anything and went mad looking for something to put it in. Meanwhile Tolstoy, with his belief in the direct realism, is in no danger of falling into an infinite regress.

It would be pleasant to end there, with praise of the firm sanity of the greatest of all mimetic novelists. Unfortunately, one final note of reservation is necessary. The formalists are entirely right when they allege that no vision is unconditioned by prior conceptions. Tolstoy was wrong if he thought otherwise. But, if he operated with *interrogative* conceptions, with a readiness to change if the world failed to answer them, his underlying claim to realism survives. Indeed, the point can be put more simply. If some theatrical performances are like this, the passage is realistic. They are, and it is.

Notes

1. W. H. Auden, *Collected Poems*, ed. E. Mendelson, London, 1976, pp. 470–1.

2. First published in 1933, reprinted in a modified form in his *Explorations*, London, 1946, pp. 1–39. Knights later changed his mind very considerably; see his "The question of character in Shakespeare," first published in J. Garrett, ed., *More Talking of Shakespeare*, 1959, pp. 55–69.

3. Herbert Read, *Art Now* (first published 1933), London, 1960, pp. 62–3.

4. Walter Pater, *The Renaissance*, London, 1961, pp. 122–3.

5. J. A. Symonds, *The Life of Michelangelo Buonarotti*, London, 1893, vol. 2, p. 32.

6. Clive Bell, *Art*, 3rd edn., London, 1916, p. 8.

7. Evelyn Waugh, *Brideshead Revisited*, London, 1958, p. 28. Bell concedes the representation of volume on p. 27 of *Art*. His remark about butterflies and cathedrals is on pp. 12–3.

8. See Ernst Cassirer, *The Philosophy of Symbolic Forms*, trans. Ralph Mannheim, New Haven, 1953–7, vol. 2, p. 42.

9. *The Dialogues of Plato*, trans. B. Jowett, Oxford, 1875, vol. 3, p. 491.

10. London, 1963, plates 18 and 19.

11. *War and Peace*, VIII. ix, trans. Louise and Aylmer Maude, Oxford, 1942, p. 615.

12. This happens in Terence Hawkes, *Structuralism and Semiotics*, Berkeley, California, 1977, p. 63.

13. *Communications*, II (Paris, 1968), pp. 84–9.

Theory

The Uses of Psychology

Bernard Paris

Critics have often applied the concepts of modern psychological theories in the genetic context to get at the author's psyche, and in the affective context to get at the reader's. Bernard Paris argues that these theories can also be applied in the mimetic context to help us understand fictional characters, including "implied authors." Like A. D. Nuttall, Paris is fully aware of the objections to treating fictional characters as if they were real people, but he finds the arguments on the other side more persuasive, especially in the case of "realistic" novels where "representation" is the dominant mode. As his recent work on Shakespeare indicates, Paris would include certain kinds of drama here as well. Citing such proponents of realism as Erich Auerbach, Georg Lukács, and Ian Watt, Paris claims that with the great novels of psychological realism "thematic and formal analysis can't begin to do justice to the psychological portraiture which is often the greatest achievement of these works." We need, instead, a mimetic criticism deploying the insights of modern psychology. Although he later argues specifically for the uses of "third force" psychology associated with such figures as Karen Horney and Abraham Maslow, Paris presents in his opening chapter a general defense of mimetic criticism and a rationale for applying psychological theories to fictional characters "as though they were real people."

Reprinted by permission of the author from Bernard Paris, *A Psychological Approach to Fiction*, pp. 1–13, 23–27. Copyright © 1974 by Indiana University Press. A part of the chapter has been omitted, and the notes have been renumbered.

NORMAN HOLLAND FINDS IT "HARD TO SEE HOW a psychology [can] deal with a work of art *qua* work of art," and observes that in practice psychoanalytic critics "do not."[1] Psychology cannot consider works of art in themselves, he argues, because psychology as such is concerned "not with literature, but with minds" (p. 293). "Any psychological system," therefore, "must deal, not with works of art in isolation, but with works of art in relation to man's mind" (p. 151). The "three possible minds to which the psychological critic customarily refers" are the author's mind, a character's mind, and the audience's mind. It is only the study of the audience's mind, Holland feels, that can lead "to a bona-fide method; the other two tend to confusion" (p. 294). I believe that there are two kinds of minds within realistic novels that can be studied in psychological terms: they are the minds of the implied authors and the minds of the leading characters.

Holland argues that "we should use psychology on our own real and lively reactions" to the work "rather than on the characters' fictitious minds" (p. 308). He feels that character study is useful and legitimate only when it is incorporated into our analysis of the audience's mind. Then it is seen to "identify 'latent impulses' of the characters which may be considered as stimuli to or projections of latent impulses of the audience" (p. 283). Character study is not legitimate when, as in most psychological criticism, it talks "about literary characters as though they were real people" (p. 296). Holland's strongest argument in support of this position is that "Homo Fictus and Homo Dramaticus do not so much what Homo Sapiens would do in similar circumstances, but what it is necessary for them to do in the logical and meaningful realities of the works of art in which they live" (pp. 305–306). The artist "hovers between *mimesis*, making like, and *harmonia*, the almost musical ordering of the events he depicts. . . . The psychoanalytic critic of character neglects the element of *harmonia*, the symbolic conceptions that must modify the mimetic" (p. 306). Other critics of literature have learned to avoid this mistake: ". . . as a plain matter of fact, most literary critics do not—any more—treat literary characters as real people" (p. 296).[2]

Holland is participating in what W. J. Harvey calls "the retreat from character" in modern criticism, a retreat which Harvey's book, *Character and the Novel*, is intended to halt. "What has been said about character" in the past forty years, Harvey observes, "has been mainly a stock of critical commonplaces used largely to dismiss the subject in order that the critic may turn his attention to other allegedly more important and central subjects—symbolism, narrative techniques, moral vision and the like."[3] In the criticism of realistic fiction this has been especially unfortunate, for "most great novels exist to reveal and explore character" (p. 23). There are many reasons for this retreat, Harvey continues, the most important of which is the rise of the New Criticism:

> The New Criticism was centrally concerned to apply close and rigorous analytical methods to lyric poetry; it is noticeable how ill at ease its practitioners have been when they have approached the bulky, diffuse and variegated world of the novel. What we might expect is in fact the case; the new critic, when dealing with fiction, is thrown back upon an interest in imagery, symbolism or structural features which have little to do with characterization. (p. 200)

The danger that the critic of novels must now be warned against is not the neglect of *harmonia*, but the neglect of *mimesis;* for *harmonia* has had its due of late, and "a mimetic intention" was, after all, "the central concern of the novel until the end of the nineteenth century" (p. 205).

No study of character should ignore the fact that characters in fiction participate in the dramatic and thematic structures of the works in which they appear and that the meaning of their behavior is often to be understood in terms of its function within these structures. The less mimetic the fiction, the more completely will the characters be intelligible in terms of their dramatic and thematic functions; and even in

highly realistic fiction, the minor characters are to be understood more functionally than psychologically. But, as Harvey points out, the authors of the great realistic novels "display an appetite and passion for life which threatens to overwhelm the formal nature of their art" (pp. 187–188). There is in such novels "a surplus margin of gratuitous life, a sheer excess of material, a fecundity of detail and invention, a delighted submergence in experience for its own sake" (p. 188). The result is "that characterization often overflows the strict necessities of form" (p. 188). This is especially true in the characterization of the protagonists, of "those characters whose motivation and history are most fully established, who conflict and change as the story progresses . . ." (p. 56). What we attend to in the protagonist's story "is the individual, the unique and particular case. . . . We quickly feel uneasy if the protagonist is made to stand for something general and diffused; the more he *stands for* the less he *is*" (p. 67). Though such characters have their dramatic and thematic functions, they are "in a sense . . . end-products"; we often feel that "they are what the novel exists for; it exists to reveal them" (p. 56).

The retreat from character of which Harvey complains has been in part a reaction against reading plays, stories, impressionistic novels, and other tightly structured or basically symbolic works as though they were realistic fiction. This has frequently resulted, ironically, in the study of realistic novels as though they were tightly structured or basically symbolic forms. In our avoidance of what Northrop Frye would call a low-mimetic provincialism, we have often failed to do justice to the low-mimetic forms themselves.

Fortunately, the most recent trend in literary criticism has been to emphasize the qualities that distinguish the literary modes and kinds from each other. In the study of narrative art, we are learning to appreciate a variety of forms and effects; and this, in turn, is enabling us to grasp the distinctive characteristics of each form with greater precision.[4] We are coming to see, among other things, that character is central in many realistic novels and that much of the characterization in such fiction escapes dramatic and thematic analysis and can be understood only in terms of its mimetic function. A careful examination of the nature of realistic fiction as modern criticism is coming to conceive it will show that in certain cases it *is* proper to treat literary characters as real people and that only by doing so can we fully appreciate the distinctive achievement of the genre.

The diversity of aesthetic theories and of critical approaches is in part a reflection of the multiplicity of values to be found in literature and in part a product of the varying interests and temperaments with which different critics come to literature. Not all approaches are equally valid: the most satisfying kind of criticism is that which is somehow congruent with the work and which is faithful to the distribution of interests in the work itself. The approach employed here attempts to stress values which are inherently important in realistic fiction and to make these values more accessible to us than they hitherto have been.

The primary values of fiction can be described in a variety of terms; I shall classify them as mimetic, thematic, and formal. Fiction is mainly concerned with the representation, the interpretation, and the aesthetic patterning of experience.[5] In different works and in different fictional modes the distribution of emphasis varies; and in some works one of these interests may be far more important than the others. When a work concerns itself seriously with more than one of these interests, it must bring its various impulses into harmony if it is to be organically unified.

From the middle of the eighteenth to the beginning of the twentieth century, the novel attempted, by and large, to realize all of these values; but its primary impulse seems to have been the mimetic one. Henry James is reflecting not only his own taste, but the essential nature of the genre when he characterizes the novel as "a picture" and proclaims that "the only reason for the existence of a novel is that it does attempt to represent life."[6] It is not its interpretation of life or its formal perfection but its "air of reality (solidity of specification)" that James identifies as "the supreme virtue of a novel" (p. 14). Arnold Kettle distinguishes between the moral fable, which is dominated by "pattern" or "sig-

nificance" and the novel, in which "pattern" is subordinate to "life." Despite a frequently strong commitment to thematic interests, the great realists, says Kettle, "are less consciously concerned with the moral significance of life than with its surface texture. Their talent is devoted first and foremost to getting life on to the page, to conveying across to their readers the sense of what life as their characters live it really feels like."[7]

The view of realistic fiction that we are developing is confirmed by such classic works on the subject as Ian Watt's *The Rise of the Novel* and Erich Auerbach's *Mimesis*. Formal interests cannot be paramount in a genre that, as Watt describes it, "works by exhaustive presentation rather than by elegant concentration."[8] Like E. M. Forster, Watt sees "the portrayal of 'life by time' as the distinctive role which the novel has added to literature's more ancient preoccupation with portraying 'life by values' " (p. 22). The domain of the novel is the individual and his social relationships, and it tends to present its subject less in terms of ethical categories than in terms of chronological and causal sequences. The distinctive characteristics of the novel are, for Watt, its emphasis upon the particular, its circumstantial view of life, and its full and authentic reporting of experience (pp. 31–32).

To our statement that the novel's primary impulse is a mimetic one, we must add the qualification that the reality imitated is not general nature or the world of Ideas, but the concrete and temporal reality of modern empirical thought. The novel came into being in a world dominated by secularism and individualism, a world in which men were losing their belief in the supernatural and institutional bases of life. "Both the philosophical and the literary innovations," says Watt, "must be seen as parallel manifestations of a larger change—that vast transformation of Western civilization since the Renaissance which has replaced the unified world picture of the Middle Ages with another very different one—one which presents us, essentially, with a developing but unplanned aggregate of particular individuals having particular experiences at particular times and at particular places" (p. 31).

For Erich Auerbach the foundations of modern realism are, first, "the serious treatment of everyday reality, the rise of more extensive and socially inferior human groups to the position of subject matter for problematic-existential representation"; and, second, "the embedding of random persons and events in the general course of contemporary history, the fluid historical background."[9] Throughout *Mimesis* Auerbach is concerned with the contrast between the classical moralistic and the problematic existential ways of presenting reality. The distinction is basically between the representation of life in terms of fixed canons of style and of ethical categories which are a priori and static, and a stylistically mixed, ethically ambiguous portrayal which probes "the social forces underlying the facts and conditions" that it presents (p. 27). The problematic existential perception of reality, which *Mimesis* exists to celebrate, is one that is informed by the insights of Historicism. It is characterized by an awareness that "epochs and societies are not to be judged in terms of a pattern concept of what is desirable absolutely speaking but rather in every case in terms of their own premises"; by "a sense of historical dynamics, of the incomparability of historical phenomena and of their constant inner mobility"; and by a "conviction that the meaning of events cannot be grasped in abstract and general forms of cognition" (p. 391).

It is evident that in fiction employing the classical moralistic perspective, interpretation will outweigh and, indeed, govern representation, whereas in fiction written from a problematic existential point of view the mimetic impulse will be predominant. In many realistic novels, however, the classical moralistic perspective continues to exist alongside of, and often in disharmony with, the concrete, "serio-problematic" representation of life. Auerbach observes that Balzac, for example, "aspires to be a classical moralist" but that "this suits neither his style nor his temperament" (pp. 422–423). In his novels "the classically moralistic element very often gives the impression of being a foreign body." It expresses itself in the narrator's "generalized apophthegms of a moral cast," which are "sometimes witty as individual observations," but which are often "far too generalized" and are sometimes "plain 'tripe' "(p. 422).

Realism for Auerbach means essentially social realism—the presentation of events in terms of the network of historical relations in which they exist and a concern for all of the forces at work, not simply for a limited, class-determined set of causes. His distinction between the categorical and the historistic views of experience applies just as readily to the presentation of character as it does to the rendering of society, though Auerbach himself has little to say about psychological realism. Representation is the primary interest of realistic fiction, and the two chief objects of representation are character and social milieu. Some novels are profoundly concerned with both character and society; others focus primarily on social or on psychological reality. Novels in which psychological realism predominates tend to present society from the point of view of the individual; novels of social realism often take a sociological rather than a psychological view of character.

Though realistic fiction is more concerned with mimesis than it is with theme and form the latter are, nonetheless, very important elements in the majority of novels. Indeed, one of the basic problems of the novel as a genre is that it attempts to integrate impulses which are disparate and often in conflict. The problematic existential portrayal of reality defies, by its very nature, authorial attempts at analysis and judgment. The great realists see and represent far more than they can understand. And, as Northrop Frye observes, "the realistic writer soon finds that the requirements of literary form and plausible content always fight against each other."[10] Form derives from generic conventions, and ultimately from mythic patterns, which are inherently unrealistic; realistic content obeys the laws of probability, of cause and effect, and belongs to a different universe of discourse. The integration of theme, form, and mimesis is an extremely difficult task.

Critics of realistic fiction, even some of those who best understand its nature, come to it demanding formal and thematic perfections which very few novels can achieve. The novel "may have a distinctive representational technique," says Ian Watt, "but if it is to be considered a valuable literary form it must also have, like any other literary form, a structure which is a coherent expression of all its parts" (p. 104). The novel, Watt feels, must "supplement its realism of presentation with a realism of assessment." If the interpretive element is weak "we shall be wholly immersed in the reality of the characters and their actions, but whether we shall be any wiser as a result is open to question" (p. 288). Arnold Kettle recognizes that "there are writers, and great ones, whose books have more vividness than wisdom, more vitality than significance"; but he feels that "the central core of any novel is what it has to say about life." Novels with more life than pattern, or in which life and pattern are not integrated, are wanting in the quality of their perception (pp. 14–16).

It is my impression that if we come to novels expecting moral wisdom and coherent teleological structures we are usually going to be disappointed. Such expectations are frequently aroused by the works themselves, and it is natural for the reader to want them fulfilled; but the mimetic impulse that dominates most novels often works against total integration and thematic adequacy. Even so, the novel is a valuable literary form. As Watt himself says, "In the novel, more perhaps than in any other literary genre, the qualities of life can atone for the defects of art . . ." (p. 301). The novel's weaknesses are in many cases the defects of its virtues, and its virtues are very great indeed. Some novels, of course, are integrated: they are usually those in which the interpretive element either is almost nonexistent or is incorporated into the mimesis. Such novels have coherent teleological structures, but they do not provide the kind of wisdom that Kettle, Watt, and many other critics seem to be looking for.

It is because they contain highly individualized characters or extremely detailed pictures of society that many novels lack total artistic integration. In novels of psychological realism (on which we shall focus here) there is a character-creating impulse which has its own inner logic and which tends to go its own way, whatever the implied author's formal and thematic intentions may be. As critics we demand, indeed, that the central characters of realistic fiction be like real people, that they have a life of their own beyond the control of their author. The novelist, says Harvey, "must accept his charac-

ters as asserting their human individuality and uniqueness in the face of all ideology (including his own limited point of view)" (p. 25). In realistic fiction, proclaims Georg Lukács, "what matters is the picture conveyed by the work; the question to what extent this picture conforms to the views of the authors is a secondary consideration."[11] "A great realist," Lukács continues,

> . . . if the intrinsic artistic development of situations and characters he has created comes into conflict with his most cherished prejudices or even his most sacred convictions, will, without an instant's hesitation, set aside these his own prejudices and convictions and describe what he really sees, not what he would prefer to see. This ruthlessness towards their own subjective world-picture is the hall-mark of all great realists, in sharp contrast to the second-raters, who nearly always succeed in bringing their own *Weltanschauung* into "harmony" with reality. . . . (p. 11)

Lukács is chiefly concerned with the portrayal of social reality, but his observations apply also to the presentation of character:

> The characters created by the great realists, once conceived in the vision of their creator, live an independent life of their own; their comings and goings, their development, their destiny is dictated by the inner dialectic of their social and individual existence. No writer is a true realist—or even a truly good writer, if he can direct the evolution of his own characters at will. (p. 11)

The point I am trying to make has been most brilliantly developed by E. M. Forster, in his discussion of flat and round characters. "The novelist," he observes, "has a very mixed lot of ingredients to handle." He is telling a story ("life in time") which has a meaning ("life by values"). His story is "about human beings":

> The characters arrive when evoked, but full of the spirit of mutiny. For they have these numerous parallels with people like ourselves, they try to live their own lives and are consequently often engaged in treason against the main scheme of the book. They "run away," they "get out of hand": they are creations inside a creation, and often inharmonious towards it; if they are given complete freedom they kick the book to pieces, and if they are kept too sternly in check, they revenge themselves by dying, and destroy it by intestinal decay.[12]

What Forster has described here is the dilemma of the realistic novelist. If his characters are truly alive they will have a motivational life of their own and will tend to subvert the main scheme of the book. If he keeps his characters subordinated to their aesthetic and thematic functions, however, they will be lifeless puppets and his book will be flawed in a different and more serious way.

In their excellent book on narrative literature, Robert Scholes and Robert Kellogg recapitulate and refine many of our most recent insights into the nature of realistic fiction. Their division of characters into three types—aesthetic, illustrative, and mimetic—provides the best taxonomy that we have to date and offers a convenient way of formulating the thesis which I have been developing.

Characters should be understood in terms of the kind of function that they perform. Aesthetic types—"villains, ingénues, *ficelles*, choral characters, *nuntii*, and so on"—serve mainly to create formal patterns and dramatic impact. They have little inner depth or moral significance. Illustrative characters are most important in works governed by the classical moralistic perspective:

> Illustration differs from representation in narrative art in that it does not seek to reproduce actuality but to present selected aspects of the actual, essences referable for their meaning not to historical, psychological, or sociological truth but to ethical and metaphysical truth.

Illustrative characters

> . . . are concepts in anthropoid shape or fragments of the human psyche masquerading as whole human beings. Thus we are not called upon to understand their motivation as if they were whole human beings but to understand the principles they illustrate through their actions in a narrative framework. (p. 88)

Behind realistic fiction there is a strong "psychological impulse" that "tends toward the presentation of highly individualized figures who resist abstraction and generalization, and whose motivation is not susceptible to rigid ethical interpretation" (p. 101). When we encounter a fully drawn mimetic character "we are justified in asking questions about his motivation based on our knowledge of the ways in which real people are motivated" (p. 87).

There are aesthetic and illustrative types in realistic novels, of course, and in the central characters there is often a mixing of and a tension between illustrative, mimetic, and aesthetic functions. But in novels of psychological realism the main characters exist primarily as mimetic portraits whose intricacies escape the moral and symbolic meanings assigned to them. Many aspects of their characterization which are of little formal or thematic interest become very significant when we see them as manifestations of the characters' inner being, as part of the author's unfolding of character for its own sake.

The great gift of the psychological realists, then, even of the most intellectually proficient and ethically sensitive of them, is not in the interpretation but in the representation of the experience of their characters. Their characters may have important functions in the thematic and formal structures of the works in which they exist, but thematic and formal analysis cannot begin to do justice to the psychological portraiture which is often the greatest achievement of these works, and it frequently blinds us to the fact that the experience represented does not always sustain the dramatic and thematic effects for which the work is striving.

Ortega y Gasset contends that all of the

> . . . psychological knowledge accumulated in the contemporary mind . . . is to no small degree responsible for the present failure of the novel. Authors that yesterday seemed excellent appear naive today because the present reader is a much better psychologist than the old author.[13]

This is true only if we judge the old authors primarily in terms of their analyses and assessments of their characters' behavior. Given the fact that the old authors were not necessarily gifted as analysts and moralists, that their value judgments were bound to be influenced by their own neuroses, and that the psychological theories available to them were inadequate to their insights, it was inevitable that their interpretations would be inferior to their representations of experience and that the beneficiaries of a more advanced psychological science would feel superior to them. If we do justice to their representations of character, however, we will see that they were excellent psychologists indeed, and that we need all of the resources of modern knowledge to understand and appreciate their achievement.

•   •   •

The question of what kind of illumination art—or, in our case, realistic fiction—*does* supply is too large to be dealt with completely here; but it is central to our concerns, and I shall attempt to offer a partial answer. If we have realism of presentation without realism of assessment, says Ian Watt, "we shall be wholly immersed in the reality of the characters and their actions, but whether we shall be any wiser as a result is open to question" (p. 288). Immersion in the inner reality of characters provides a kind of knowledge which is not wisdom, though it may be the basis of wisdom, and which realistic fiction is especially fitted to supply. If we understand by phenomenology the formulation of "an experience of the world, a contact with the world which precedes all" judgment and explanation,[14] we can say that highly mimetic fiction gives us a phenomenological knowledge of reality. It gives us an immediate knowledge of how the world is experienced by the individual consciousness and an understanding of the inner life in its own terms. It enables us to grasp from within the phenomena which psychology and ethics treat from without.

As Wayne Booth has observed, when we read novels in which there are deep inside views "that . . . give the reader an effect of living thought and sensation" (p. 324), we tend to abandon judgment and analysis. When we are immersed in the "indomitable mental reality" (p. 323) of a character, we adopt his perspective and experience his feelings as though they were our own. This kind of experience, which is one of the great gifts of fiction, is acceptable to Booth only when the character's perspective is, in his view, an ethically acceptable one. It is very dangerous, he feels, if the character's values are destructive, for then the reader is liable to be corrupted by his identification with unhealthy attitudes. I feel that Booth has overestimated both the danger which the reader is in and the effectiveness of rhetoric as a corrective, and that

he has underestimated the value of deep inside views, though he admits that they "can be of immeasurable value in forcing us to see the human worth of a character whose actions, objectively considered, we would deplore" (p. 378). Robbe-Grillet's *The Voyeur* "does, indeed, lead us to experience intensely the sensations and emotions of a homicidal maniac. But is this," Booth asks, "really what we go to literature for?" (p. 384). My answer is, Yes.

We go to literature for many things, and not the least of them is the immediate knowledge that it gives of variously constituted human psyches. The novel makes its revelations not only through mimetic portraits of characters, but also, in many cases, through the picture that it creates of the implied author. As both Wayne Booth and Sheldon Sacks point out, when the implied author functions as interpreter, he often makes a multitude of particular judgments as his characters display their temperaments and confront their choices. This gives rise to "a much more detailed ordering of values" than we ever encounter in systematic philosophy. Even if we cannot accept the implied author's values as adequate either to his fictional world or to life outside, we have a marvellously rich portrayal of a particular kind of consciousness making ethical responses to a variety of human situations. Through the novel's rhetoric we become aware of the meaning which the characters' experience has for a mind like that of the implied author, and we enter thus into his subjective world.

What I am suggesting, then, is that if we view him as a fictional persona, as another dramatized consciousness, rather than as an authoritative source of values, the implied author, too, enlarges our knowledge of experience. What we have, in effect, is a deep inside view of *his* mind, a view which makes us phenomenologically aware of *his* experience of the world. When we see him as another consciousness, sometimes the most fascinating one in the book, it becomes more difficult to regret the technical devices by which he is revealed, even when they produce aesthetic flaws. To see him in this way we must set aside the fictional conventions which encourage us to invest him with the authority which Wayne Booth would like him to have; but it is essential to do so if we are to appreciate many great narrators whose wisdom we must question and whose obtrusiveness we must otherwise regret.

As long as we regard the implied author as a kind of God whose will we must understand but never question, it seems quite inappropriate to analyze him psychologically. His contradictions are manifestations of a higher harmony which we have not yet grasped; and his judgments, being right, require no explanation. When we see him as a dramatized consciousness whose values can be as subjective and as confused as those of an ordinary man, psychological analysis becomes a necessity.

I have tried to show by an analysis of the genre that it is often appropriate to study the characters and implied authors of realistic novels by a psychological method. In the interpretations of individual novels that will follow our discussion of Third Force psychology, I hope to demonstrate that the approach employed here helps us to appreciate some of fiction's most important values and to resolve some difficult critical problems.

I am aware, however, that the very arguments by which I have attempted to justify a psychological approach may seem to preclude it. I have argued that one of the chief interests of realistic fiction is a mimetic characterization which gives us a phenomenological grasp of experience in its immediacy and ambiguity and that the value of such characterization lies precisely in its continual resistance to the patterns by which the author has tried to shape and interpret it. It may be objected that the values of such characterization are incommensurate with any kind of analysis and that to intellectualize them is to destroy them. My reply must be that any criticism, whether it be psychological or not, is bound to operate with categories and abstractions which, if they are allowed to replace the values of literature, will destroy them. Criticism can make literature more accessible to us, but we must use it as a means to rather than as a substitute for the aesthetic encounter.

A common complaint about the psychological analysis of character is that is does violence to the literary values of fiction by reducing the novel to a case history, the character to his neurosis. We must recognize that literature and criticism belong to different universes of discourse. As Northrop Frye says, "the axiom of criticism must be, not that the poet does not know what he is talking about, but that he cannot talk about what he knows."[15] The function of criticism is to talk about what the artist knows, and to do that it must speak in the language of science and philosophy rather than in the language of art. But if we are aware of what we are doing this does not convert art into science or philosophy. Criticism points to a reality which is far more complex and of a different nature than itself; the values of which it speaks can be experienced only in the aesthetic encounter. All criticism is reductive. Psychological analysis is our best tool for talking about the intricacies of mimetic characterization. If properly conducted, it is less reductive than any other critical approach.

It is extremely valuable to bring literature and psychology together. The psychologist and the artist often know about the same areas of experience, but they comprehend them and present their knowledge in different ways. Each enlarges our awareness and satisfies our need to master reality in a way that the other cannot. The psychologist enables us to grasp certain configurations of experience analytically, categorically, and (if we accept his conceptions of health and neurosis) normatively. The novelist enables us to grasp these phenomena in other ways. Fiction lets us know what it is like to be a certain kind of person with a certain kind of destiny. Through mimetic portraits of character, novels provide us with artistic formulations of experience that are permanent, irreplaceable, and of an order quite different from the discursive formulations of systematic psychology. And, if we view him as a fictional persona, as a dramatized consciousness, the implied author, too, enlarges our knowledge of the human psyche.

Taken together, psychology and fiction give us a far more complete possession of experience than either can give by itself. Psychology helps us to talk about what the novelist knows; fiction helps us to know what the psychologist is talking about.

Notes

1. *Psychoanalysis and Shakespeare* (New York, 1966), p. 151. Whenever the source is clear, page numbers will be given parenthetically in the text.

2. There is a slight modification of Holland's position in *The Dynamics of Literary Response* (New York, 1968), Chapter 10 ("Character and Identification"): "Psychoanalytic critics regularly apply psychological concepts from the world of everyday reality to characters who exist in a wholly different kind of world—it should not work but it does" (p. 267). My contention is that it should work, and it does.

3. (Ithaca, 1965), p. 192.

4. See especially, Robert Scholes and Robert Kellogg, *The Nature of Narrative* (New York, 1966); Northrop Frye, *The Anatomy of Criticism* (Princeton, 1957); Wayne C. Booth, *The Rhetoric of Fiction* (Chicago, 1961); and Sheldon Sacks, *Fiction and the Shape of Belief* (Berkeley and Los Angeles, 1964).

5. There is an element of interpretation in all representation, of course, in that representation is not mere copying but involves artistic selection for the purpose of creating a more effective mimetic portrait. When I distinguish between representation and interpretation, I am using "interpretation" to mean analysis and judgment.

6. "The Art of Fiction," in *Myth and Method, Modern Theories of Fiction*, ed. James E. Miller, Jr. (Lincoln, 1960), pp. 24–25.

7. Arnold Kettle, *An Introduction to the English Novel* (Harper Torchbook ed.: New York, 1960), Vol. 1, p. 21.

8. (Berkeley and Los Angeles, 1965), p. 30.

9. *Mimesis, The Representation of Reality in Western Literature*, trans. by Willard Trask (Anchor Book ed.: New York, 1957), pp. 433–434.

10. "Myth, Fiction, and Displacement," in *Fables of Identity* (New York, 1963), p. 36.

11. *Studies in European Realism* (New York, 1964), p. 10.

12. *Aspects of the Novel*, (London, 1927), Chapter 4.

13. *The Dehumanization of Art* (Anchor Book ed.: Garden City, 1956), p. 92.

14. Merleau-Ponty, quoted by Herbert Spiegelberg, *The Phenomenological Movement: A Historical Introduction* (The Hague, 1960), Vol. 2, p. 416.

15. *Anatomy of Criticism*, p. 5.

The Gender Principles

Marilyn French

Feminist criticism includes several diverse groups and operates in several critical contexts. When feminist critics operate in the mimetic context, as they frequently do, they are often concerned to measure the literary work against a conception of reality that literature has traditionally distorted or denied.

Thus, as Marilyn French sets up her "gender principles" as a preface to her study of Shakespeare's works, she notes that these principles are "not necessarily identical with gender" and she grants that she is describing "conceptions" rather than direct experience. But she reminds us that it is very difficult to separate our conceptions from our experience, and that in literature female figures have almost invariably been associated exclusively with these feminine principles, an association "not without consequence on moral, political, and philosophical levels," because actual women "have been, and still are, under great pressure to conform to the image of them entertained by Western culture." One task of criticism, then, is to show the ways this culture has typically divided experience and created conceptions that, while they may be false to real experience, are "perpetuated by the conventions of our literature, art, and language."

THE WHOLE NOTION OF DIVIDING EXPERIENCE into gender principles is a "masculine" one. (This is not to say only males created and perpetuated it. The gender principles as I describe them are not necessarily identical with gender.) It is "masculine" because it originally arose as a form of control. Because it is "masculine," it is linear, which is to say it has a fixed, stipulated goal.

Because the notion is linear, the gender principles may be laid on a gamut. The poles of this gamut are masculine and feminine. At the center are qualities which are not gender-specific, which are valued in both genders. The extreme of the masculine side is the ability to kill; that of the feminine side is the ability to give birth: the two most profound of all human activities. Clustered about each pole are qualities which support the extreme.

The masculine principle, predicated on the ability to kill, is the pole of power-in-the-world. It is associated with prowess and ownership, with physical courage, assertiveness, authority, independence, and the right, rights, and legitimacy. It claims to be able to define and administer justice; and it supports law and order as an arrangement imposed and maintained by force.

Its energies are directed at making permanent, fixing the flux of experience. It exalts the individual (who wants to transcend nature and natural oblivion). It values action over feeling, thought over sensation. Its ultimate goal is transcendence of nature; its immediate goal is the attainment and maintenance of power-in-the-world, whether as force or authority. In principle, it is conceived of as a means of protecting and ensuring the continuation of the human race and its felicity.

The masculine principle is linear, temporal, and transcendent, for it aims to construct something in the world and within time that will enable the individual to transcend nature (which is cyclic), time, and mortality. The thing erected is a sort of immortality. It may be a tribe bearing the father's name, or a dynasty; it may be a noble act recorded in legend and poetry. Or an institution or tradition such as a religion, a school of thought, a school of art. Or it may be an artifact, Stevens' jar in Tennessee which imposes human significance on the impersonal and undifferentiating cycles of nature.

The masculine principle is thus profoundly threatened by and antagonistic to impulses towards acceptance of simple continuation, of present pleasure, of surrender to mortality. These impulses are associated with the feminine principle, which is identified with nature. Defying the power of nature, the masculine principle is the standard of hu(mankind), and identifies the human with the male.

The divisiveness associated by the Pythagoreans with the number *two*, the number of femaleness, may be connected with parturition. But it is certainly connected with the perception of a duality in nature. Nature has two aspects (although they are not always easily distinguishable): a benevolent (nutritive, regenerating, supportive) and a malevolent (destructive, subversive of human constructions, and more powerful than any human constructions—up until the atomic age, anyway). Because we die, nature always, inevitably vanquishes us. Human effort has always been to diminish this power, whether through belief in control of an afterlife (supranatural) or through erection of cultural traditions and artifacts that carry on our lives.

As far as I can deduce, the two aspects of nature were taken as a whole in pre-Christian thought. Identified then as now with the female, nature was a powerful lover and a powerful hater. Eve the instigator of the fall was also Eve the mother of all living; Aphrodite was a goddess of shifting weather, of the fruitfulness of spring and the withering of autumn, the goddess of sexual desire and of wedded love and fruitfulness; Kali incarnated both natural creativity and temporal destructiveness. The goddess was at least dual, and sometimes triple in her manifestations as nubile virgin, mother-whore, and wise old hag. But all those manifestations were *male* perceptions of female power. In such a conception, the feminine prin-

ciple has great power, but it is also very threatening to the "masculine" drive towards control.

The later myths of Aphrodite and Athene as having been produced by the immaculate conception of their fathers' brains or sperm are attempts to harness the powers of the feminine principle into service to the masculine. But these attempts were not notably successful. They drove female goddess-worshippers underground; the old religions were denigrated as mere magic; the goddesses gave up their names to the new gods; the character of the Erinyes was changed from agents of justice to avengers; and the father was declared the true parent of the child, the mother being merely a vessel. Zeus (power) and Apollo (light and order seen as harmony) superseded the older, more earthy deities. Flesh, body, was declared inferior to mind, and the two were perceived as antagonists inhabiting a single entity. Word was declared prime, and the nature of deity; while spirit, which is feeling, was ignored. In the beginning was the word, and the word was with God, and the word was God.

These efforts to establish a new hierarchy of value were intermittently successful until Christianity. It was the architects of the early Christian church who first understood *divide and conquer* in the moral realm. Christianity succeeded in defeating the supremacy of the feminine principle by splitting it in two. The Eve who was responsible both for the fall from unity with nature and for the continuation of the race becomes a subversive figure "redeemed" by the Mary who accepts that she is *ancilla*, ancillary, a handmaiden, only a vessel in the transmission of a male line. This split in the principle of nature, the feminine principle, still exists in our perception of actual women; there is the mother madonna, and the whore; the nourisher and the castrator.

This split in the feminine principle I call inlaw and outlaw aspects of it. The outlaw aspect retains the characteristics of femaleness described by the Pythagoreans. It is associated with darkness, chaos, flesh, the sinister, magic and above all, sexuality. It is outlaw because it is subversive, undermining of the masculine principle. It claims both poles of the gamut, the ability to give birth and the ability to kill, both of which actual females possess. Its sexuality is dynamic and nearly irresistible; it is sex as abandonment (as opposed to "masculine" sexuality, which is possession or aggression—rape) and a power like that of nature to destroy. It has no end, no goal beyond the pleasure of being. Its rebellion against the masculine principle is based not in the desire to set up controlling structures of its own, but in the desire to eradicate such structures completely. It is tremendously threatening to the masculine principle because it does not respect the constructs attendant on that principle, and because it is vital and attractive. It is vital and attractive because it contains fundamental human energy and will, and because it sees the end of life as pleasure.

Pleasure of all sorts, but especially sexual pleasure, is a threat to the masculine principle, the energies of which must be directed towards transcendent goals. Aggression and usurpation are part of the masculine principle, but beneath any "masculine" hostility is a respect for structure, hierarchy, and legitimacy: revolutions may place different people or classes or races in the chairs of power, but the chairs of power remain. Permanency is the greatest good. The outlaw feminine principle is a rebellion against any permanency except the cyclic permanence of nature. These two principles comprise a dichotomy of their own: the masculine principle, the pole of power, is the pole of the individual who dedicates his life to a suprapersonal goal; the outlaw feminine principle, the pole of sex and pleasure, is the pole of people destined for oblivion who dedicate their lives to personal satisfaction.

There is, however, a third "pole." It is the inlaw feminine principle, the benevolent aspects of nature "purified" of their malevolent side. Since most of the power resident in the feminine principle as a whole is attributed to its outlaw aspect, the inlaw feminine principle is rather wispy. Its great strengths are castrated by its scission from its other half. The inlaw feminine principle is an expression of the benevolent manifestations of nature. Founded on the ability to give birth, it includes qualities like nutritiveness, compassion, mercy, and the ability to create felicity. It requires volitional subordination, voluntary relinquishment of power-in-the-world. It is impersonal, or suprapersonal, or al-

truistic, totally: it values above all the good of the whole, the community. It exalts the community above the individual, feeling over action, sensation over thought. *It is not passive:* it actively reaches for subordination for the good of the whole and finds its pleasure in that good rather than in assertion of self.

The split in the feminine principle was designed to guarantee the subordination of the benevolent aspects of nature to the human need to transcend nature, and cast into a no-man's-land the outlaw feminine principle, which could then be destroyed without scruple. Each quality of the inlaw principle was seen as connected to, and supportive of, a quality in the masculine principle, but always as subordinate. Mercy may only temper justice; compassion may only temper authority; feeling is essential, but must defer to thought; nutritiveness must bow to power.

What developed was a value system in which the masculine principle, originally designed to be the means to protect and foster the true ends of human life, procreation and pleasure, became instead its own end. The philosophy of Jesus became the Catholic church; the ends of Christianity—volitional subordination of self to attain human harmony, meekness and tolerance as Jesus preached them—were taken over, preempted by the church which preached them, a church dedicated above all to power, control, and transcendence. And a church which has, for the past two thousand years, dominated Western thought.

Because it abjures power-in-the-world in favor of what may be called the quality of life, the feminine principle is (in both aspects) circular, atemporal, and accepting (as opposed to transcendent). It is associated with the cycles of nature, eternal recurrence, with eternity and the present moment. It does not admit the possibility of transcendence, nor the need for it. However, when it is split in two, its inlaw side is pressed into the service of transcendence. Sometimes the outlaw aspect is given a word of praise for the same act: the whore with a golden heart is its symbol.

The only way the masculine principle can control the feminine principle is by fission. In its inlaw aspect, the feminine principle which supports and nourishes the masculine principle is associated with civilization; thus, occasionally, women (identified with the feminine principle by most literature) are identified with culture, control of the animal man, and morality (seen as oppressive). At other times, the inlaw feminine principle is seen as divine, as a moral touchstone, as lifting man from his essential bestiality. The outlaw feminine principle is sometimes seen as threatening, as castrating and destroying the masculine principle; at other times, it is seen as a source of energy and force. What remains still, stable amid this fluctuation, is the masculine principle, the human image, subject to or overcoming the overwhelming "feminine" force surrounding it.[1]

The imagery associated with the feminine principle is natural imagery: the moon and the sea, menstruation and menopause, the seasons' difference and their eternal recurrence; fruitfulness; and sex. The imagery associated with the masculine principle is both natural and civilized: thunder and lightning, of the heavens or of human warfare; cities, industry, human occupation, from farming to weaving to making art, mining and fishing and governing: every form of control.

The associations of the gender principles are not without consequence, on moral, political, and philosophical levels. The masculine principle is, through most of literature, identified with males. When one is dealing with a field of males alone, only certain males possess full legitimacy: the rest are "women" to the males with rights (prerogatives). When one is dealing with a field of males and females, all males have right (prerogative). The male is the image of the human, the standard, in the moral, political, or philosophical dimension. The male is judged ethically, expected to conform to the laws laid down by other men, expected to take his place in the hierarchy of males without demur.

Females can never fully enter this dimension. They represent the nonhuman; they are superhuman (inlaw aspect) or subhuman (outlaw aspect), but they are differentiated from the human. They are judged mythically. Females may be saints and goddesses, or they may be whores and witches; they may be the martyred mother or wife, or the castrating bitch. In either case, they are seen only in relation to males and the

male (human) standard. Autonomy is impossible in females because they are not seen as human, but as parts of the dimension (nature) with or against which humans operate. They are therefore invariably seen as trying—successfully or vainly—to exert control over the male, the human.

In actuality, of course, all people manifest qualities associated with all aspects of the gender principles. However, literature, history, theology, and philosophy, all "masculine" since they all aim to erect permanencies, tend to reflect not actual experience but traditional conceptualizations of it. In fact, we cannot talk about actual experience, because we are incapable of knowing it beyond our conceptions of it—although sometimes those conceptions are shattered enough that new conceptions can enter our minds.

In literature, therefore, males act out the human role, erring and correcting, experiencing the gamut of emotion and behavior, while females act out the type, standing as static poles in human (male) experience.[2] Some forms of literature contain no human figure at all: the human is the confluence of a set of types. This is the case in allegory, and in miracle and morality plays. The difference between the human and the type is that the former has the possibility of change, and the latter does not. Types, whether archetypes or stereotypes, represent moral positions not amenable to change.

Human figures in a work are the major characters; most works contain only one. They are mobile and dynamic; they make mistakes of judgment, of values; they grow, learn, change, and fail or succeed. They possess moral excellence and moral fallibility. Their moral flexibility is what makes their experience interesting and significant. Although Antigone is the dominant figure of Sophocles' play, it is Creon who is the human figure. Antigone is absolute, static, inflexible; it is impossible to imagine her behaving in any way other than she does. She is an archetype in Creon's moral life, a symbol of a way of thinking with which he must come to terms.

Female figures may suffer unjustly, like Cordelia, Hero, and Hermione; they may inflict suffering, like Goneril, Regan, and a host of nameless or faceless or characterless female figures in Shakespeare: but their experience does not change them. There is no residue of anger or resentment in Julia, Kate, Titania, Hero, Cordelia, Desdemona, Imogen, Hermione, and others.

Male figures, on the other hand, may survive or not, but they are changed by their experience. Oedipus and Orestes must suffer through the consequences of their actions, but they are changed by that suffering and thus exemplify a human pattern. Lear and Gloucester are transformed by their experience, as are Leontes and Prince Hal and even Macbeth. That consummate villain, Edmund, has a change of heart as he lies dying, and tries—vainly—to do some good.

On the other hand, Medea, Elektra, and Clytemnestra perform actions that change their worlds, but they themselves do not change. Their actions are the inevitable consequence of their characters, and their characters are one-dimensional, they are fixed. Lady Macbeth is psychologically destroyed by her actions, but that destruction was implicit in her statements at the opening of the play, and does not change her character. Macbeth, on the other hand, grows to larger awareness, even though he also is destroyed.

Spenser's Una does not turn against Redcrosse for his abandonment of her, nor does Duessa learn from her humiliating public exposure. Spenser's characters are allegorical, and therefore types, but his male heroes, who exemplify human undertaking, do err and grow and learn. It is significant that his female hero, Britomart, does not make any serious error in her quest, and is the only knight in *The Faerie Queene* who does not require rescue by Arthur. This is not, however, because Spenser necessarily saw females as morally superior to males. It is because, according to the traditional division of experience, females *had to be* morally superior to males. Females were not permitted to err: had Britomart made the errors of Redcrosse or Guyon or Artegall or Calidore, she *could not have been* redeemed. She is the knight of chastity; had she fallen into unchastity, what could save her?

Females are inevitably bound inside the feminine principle in traditional—and even untraditional (consider Blake)—Western thought and literature. Even when female figures begin to act as human figures, in eighteenth- and nineteenth-century novels, they are tightly constricted within a type. Their problem is still to adjust to a male world, to male needs, desires, and power. Female figures have little power-in-the-world, and what power they do possess, they are likely not to use because of the onus on female power-in-the-world. When oppression moves out, guilt moves in. But not only do these figures have narrow physical and political room: they also have little moral room.

Because of the very effective split of the feminine principle created by Christianity, and because in both the actuality and the written records of the Western world, males voted themselves the economic and political power, females have been, and still are, under great pressure to conform to the image of them entertained by Western culture. Not only are they expected to fit themselves into the narrow category labeled "feminine," but they are expected to use only a fragment of their capacities—the inlaw feminine principle, the aspect that supports the dominant male establishment.

The split in the feminine principle precludes the slightest error in the females associated with it. Females are seen as untrustworthy; like Chaucer's Cressida, all women are susceptible to "slydyng." They must therefore be, like Caesar's wife, beyond reproach, beyond even suspicion. They must renounce any quality which is threatening to the more powerful masculine principle. Any error can plunge them into an abyss of darkness from which they cannot arise again. Even the rumor of an error is enough to destroy them—in literature generally, but even, sometimes, in life.

A character like Shakespeare's Prince Hal can experiment with elements of misrule (outlaw feminine principle) and return enriched to rule, right, and legitimacy. Henry V is admirable for his "feminine" qualities—his democratic movement among his men, his charming deference to his future wife. But female figures who attempt to move into the masculine principle, like Queen Margaret, Joan, Lady Macbeth, Goneril, and Regan, are condemned as fiends, witches, and devils: the most usual term applied to them is "unnatural." In Shakespeare (as well as other poets of his time), males are urged to incorporate the inlaw feminine principle, but females who attempt to incorporate the masculine principle—to exercise authority, to show physical prowess, to kill—fall inevitably into the outlaw feminine principle. It is not mere chance that St. Joan became, in Shakespeare's first tetralogy, and in popular British imagination, not only a witch but a whore, or that Jezebel, whose crime was worshipping foreign gods and influencing her husband, is remembered as a fornicatress. The door between the gender principles opens only one way.

Females may incorporate some of the capacities of the masculine principle if they do so in disguise and continue to accept the constrictions of femaleness. Thus Rosalind and Viola are able to move about in the world in male dress (something they could not do in upper-class female dress), but both are shown to cling almost lovingly to their female limitations, suffering from physical weariness, or terror at the thought of a duel. In fact, female limitations are so severe in Shakespeare's work that despite their charm and unshakable good values—or perhaps precisely because of their unshakable good values—females are rather static. They do not change: they are either utterly good or utterly evil because if they are not utterly good, they become instantly utterly evil.

Stasis of character is found in female figures throughout literature. It is impossible to imagine Circe growing old like Odysseus; Antigone as a happy pregnant wife; Dido returning stoically and with bitterness against men to her duties as governor of Carthage; Lavinia complaining that she likes Turnus better than Aeneas—as well she might. Niobe and Hecuba weep through eternity, and Helen is always young.

Because the two gender principles occupy different conceptual realms—the human and ethical versus the type and the mythical—they cannot be synthesized. They cannot be equal because they are not like. But because both principles are abstractions from universal human experience, representing urges and needs found in all of us, they desperately need synthesis. And much of the thought and literature of the past has been devoted to attempts to produce a synthesis.

The most common form of arrangement is to see the masculine principle as dominant. Its power makes it legitimate, and right and rights are its prerogatives. It accepts the feminine principle (and usually, the women associated with it) insofar as that principle is inlaw, insofar as it volitionally subordinates itself to the nourishment and support of the masculine ends of control and transcendence. In this arrangement, the outlaw feminine principle is feared and condemned. Utterly illegitimate (the inlaw aspect may borrow legitimacy from the masculine principle when it operates under a masculine aegis, but can never possess it independently), it is subversive of legitimacy. However, the masculine principle requires the energy and freedom of this pole, and therefore tolerates it in nonthreatening forms. Nonthreatening forms are those in which males maintain control; thus, sexual freedom is permitted to men in the form of concubinage or prostitution. A degree of sexual freedom in males is in fact seen as admirable (although not by late Shakespeare). But too much abandonment to sexual pleasure is deplored. The onus of sexuality is placed entirely on the women involved, who are, in almost every Western culture, looked down on as subhuman and entitled to absolutely no rights.

A more religious synthesis of the gender principles places the inlaw feminine principle above the masculine; its ends, procreation and the good of the whole, and its qualities of subordination (humility, meekness), compassion, and nutritiveness are seen as ideal. However, in this synthesis, the masculine goal of transcendence is absorbed by the inlaw feminine principle, and the realm in which it is supreme is placed beyond worldly human life, in some sort of heaven. The inlaw feminine principle is seen as divine, and the masculine principle is urged to uphold it. In this arrangement, the outlaw feminine principle is utterly beyond the pale, for men or women.

This kind of synthesis varies from religion to religion, but in Christianity, the divine element is actually a fusion of feminine and masculine qualities (always omitting the outlaw aspect). Dante's *Paradiso* fuses love (feminine) with power (masculine) to create justice which is also love. But his heaven, like the structure of the church which holds its keys, is hierarchical and legitimate. The feminine principle suffuses the power structure with love that is light, thus combining the two.

The greatest poets of the English Renaissance—Shakespeare, Spenser, and Sidney—all attempted to synthesize the gender principles in more earthly locales, in a similar way. Their visions involved male (human) figures assimilating, absorbing the qualities of the feminine principle through education and through suffering, becoming in the process good governors, good men, or not doing so, and being destroyed. Shakespeare's nightmare visions always involve the destruction of the qualities of the feminine principle by masculine abuse of power. But occasionally, as in Spenser's Bower of Bliss, or Cleopatra's Egypt, the outlaw feminine principle vanquishes the masculine, leading to indolence and shame. The attractiveness of the outlaw feminine world is probably best seen (by our biased eyes) in males like Falstaff.

These visions of synthesis are invariably visions of male figures. It is never suggested that any female figure should or could absorb the masculine qualities of power, authority, or right, or should or could claim legitimacy in her own right. But these conceptions have little to do with actual life, actual women and men. They rest on perceptions that have been forgotten by the conscious mind, but which are perpetuated by the conventions of our literature, art, and language. Men insist that the word *man* is generic, and includes women. Women know better. For centuries they have been conceptualized as static figures operating in male experience, and denied entrance into full humanity.

Notes

1. Leslie Fiedler points out that women in Shakespeare are defined as "superhuman or subhuman, divine or diabolic," and that they feel like strangers "in a culture whose notion of the human is defined by males." *The Stranger in Shakespeare* (New York, 1972), pp. 44–45.

2. Robert E. Fitch, *Shakespeare: The Perspective of Value* (Philadelphia, 1970), p. 210, remarks that women are more "normative" than men in Shakespeare, and that they are always seen as functions of men.

Application

Hamlet and Shakespeare's Division of Experience

Marilyn French

Having established her "gender principles," Marilyn French proceeds to examine Shakespeare's "division of experience" by reading his plays in terms of these principles. In the case of Hamlet, *which she calls one of the "problem" plays, she finds a central character originally given to polar thinking and absolute values who discovers he lives, as we all must, in an ambivalent and ambiguous world. Hamlet's sexual disgust and his obsessive concern with legitimacy and female chastity have been frequently noted and variously explained by a number of critics. But French is willing to go further than most in seeing Hamlet's division of experience as closely parallel to Shakespeare's own. In this play, she claims, Shakespeare "challenges, examines, probes his own ideals" and "finds them shaky and untrue to actual human life."*

Reprinted from Marilyn French, *Shakespeare's Division of Experience*, pp. 145–58. Copyright © 1981 by Marilyn French. Reprinted by permission of Summit Books, a division of Simon & Schuster, Inc. Notes have been renumbered.

THE PLAY OPENS IN MURKY LIGHT, ON A COLD BATtlement, and its first line is a question. Soon, a ghost appears, but he does not speak. He speaks to no one, throughout the play, but Hamlet. By revealing the ghost to eyes others than Hamlet's—indeed to the audience—Shakespeare establishes its objective reality, validates its existence. The presence of the skeptical, rational Horatio emphasizes that the ghost is not a figment hallucinated by a fevered mind. The ghost is as real as a ghost can be.

What is ambiguous is the import of the ghost, not just whether it is a "spirit of health or goblin damn'd," but what its message really means. Maynard Mack and Harry Levin have pointed out that the entire play occurs in an atmosphere of ambiguity, irony, and interrogation.[1] Doubt is the prevailing emotion.[2] All the major characters except Horatio are at some time or in some way acting a part: even Horatio is being careful not to show what he knows or feels.[3] All the other characters manifest inconstancy; they are continually checking up on each other—probing, eavesdropping, spying, even betraying.[4] The world of *Hamlet* is a world of incertitude.[5]

Generally, the incertitude that informs the play is attributed to some split—between seeming and being, appearance and reality; between an ideal good and a real evil; between a false ideal that is really an outmoded traditional code, and a perversion of that code; between intellect and action; between inside and outside.[6] The incertitude is sometimes seen as afflicting Hamlet alone, sometimes as the sickness that is polluting all of Denmark.[7] But the incertitude of the entire drama clusters around, flows out of the ambiguous figure of the ghost who speaks only to Hamlet. It is necessary to examine his message.

The ghost begins by telling Hamlet about

purgatorial punishments that sound more like hell. This is odd. Although he was killed without time for "reck'ning," the terrible torments he implies and describes sound severe for a man who, we are told over and again, was perfection itself—a Hyperion, a Jove, a Mars, a Mercury, a great soldier and a loving faithful husband. One wonders what he can have done to deserve such torture.

The ghost lingers on the horrible nature of the place where he now resides, and then announces, briefly, the horrible truth of the place where he used to reside: man is murderous, woman is unchaste. He dwells rather differently on these two facts, giving each a different amount of attention and a different rhetoric.

First he recounts the overall fact of the murder, and the cover story given out. In this section, he calls Claudius a *serpent*. But quickly, the focus of his attention moves elsewhere—to Claudius as an *incestuous, adulterate beast*. His treachery and "witchcraft" are damned, not because of the murder, but because of Claudius' seduction of Gertrude. And, within a few lines, the ghost is attacking not Claudius, but his queen—and with considerable self-congratulation: "what a falling-off was there" (I, v, 47). In haste, the speech moves to a passionate climax, as the ghost describes Gertrude as lewd and lustful, sated in a "celestial" bed, and declining from it to "prey on garbage" (I, v, 56, 57). This is strong language indeed. What on earth could make a bed *celestial*? And the Claudius we have seen does not seem to be garbage, nor Gertrude, a predator.

The ghost returns to his tale for five and a half lines. The remainder of this section focuses on the horrible sensation of being poisoned, and the ugly look of a poisoned body. This is the longest segment of all the ghost's speeches. In this segment, Claudius is referred to as "thy uncle," and "a brother." Nothing more. Then the ghost returns to his present condition of torment and rises to his second climax: "O horrible!" (I, v, 80).

At the opening of the ghost's dialogue with Hamlet, after his first description of hell pains, the ghost several times commands Hamlet to revenge his murder. Nevertheless, in the rest of the speech, Claudius and his act are given neg-

ligible attention. After his outburst—"O horrible!"—the ghost returns to the sexual element—*luxury* and *damned incest*. Then he forbids Hamlet to take action against Gertrude, and in moments, he departs.

This is a strange speech for a man who was deprived of life in his full vigor and power. He does order revenge against Claudius, but his real fury is directed against Gertrude and his outrage at the "pollution" of his bed, that is, the royal bed of Denmark. Although we must accept that the ghost speaks the truth, since it is confirmed in the course of the play—that Claudius seduced Gertrude and killed King Hamlet, and strongly suggested that Gertrude had an affair with Claudius while her husband was alive—it is still difficult to decipher precisely what the ghost is saying. It is difficult because his priorities are contradictory to his explicit orders. His orders are: revenge my murder; leave your mother to heaven. The priorities of his speech are: (1) and first in attention—his own sensations in the torments he is now undergoing, the ugly and unpleasant sensation and appearance of being poisoned; (2) and first in fury—Gertrude's lustful inconstancy; (3) and first in outrage—Gertrude and Claudius enjoying themselves in "his" bed. Then, more or less equal in importance or attention—the recounting of his murder, the orders of revenge and restraint, and self-praise of a rather high order.

In fact, the ghost's major priorities are identical to Hamlet's, both in his immediate response to the spirit and throughout the play. Hamlet's highest value, his primary response to experience, is to "feel" it—through sensation, emotion, or reflective thought. His response to life, then, is "feminine"—to experience it, and to articulate it (which would be masculine [a structuring] if it were expressed to others and thus became a form of action). As it is, he articulates his feeling-thoughts mainly to the audience—himself. Thus, after the ghost leaves, Hamlet devotes thirteen lines to expression of his feelings. His second priority is hatred for his mother; and he moves immediately from his own feelings to "O most pernicious woman!" (I, v, 105). Only finally does he arrive at Claudius, and calls him *villain*. Under the circumstances, it seems a weak word, and its etymology suggests the view of him Hamlet will take through-out the play: he damns Claudius not because he is evil or wicked or hateful, but because he is a diminishment of an ideal (explicitly a diminish-ment from his predecessor). Claudius is damned because he is illegitimate.

Hamlet has already given us a similar set of priorities in the first soliloquy, in I, ii. He spends ten lines describing his own emotional/intellec-tual state, which is extremely depressed, even despairing. It is not his father's death that has shaken him: he grants that only a phrase—"But two months dead" (I, ii, 138). He spends only a phrase considering the difference between Claudius and his father. He then moves to the real object of his outrage: Gertrude. He cannot bear his mother's remarriage, but it is the speed, rather than the deed itself—remarriage—that he harps on. Haste in remarriage might, in an or-dinary way, bother a person who is very con-scious of social forms, of ceremony and ritual. But Hamlet is not elsewhere shown to be such a person; it is Laertes who cares about cere-mony, and protests his father's and sister's scant burials.[8] The speed of Gertrude's remarriage vi-olates Hamlet's sensibilities because of what it betrays: sexual desire in Gertrude, desire great enough to lead *her* to ignore standard social forms. The horror and shock he feels at the fact that she can feel desire at all is evident later, in his speech to her in her chamber, but it under-lies all earlier references to the marriage. For Hamlet, sexual desire in a woman is a posting "with . . . dexterity to incestious sheets" (I, ii, 157). The phrases he uses here and elsewhere to describe sexual acts have the same ugly fas-cination of the abomination, the same fastidious revulsion, found in Iago's description of sex be-tween Desdemona and Othello, Desdemona and Cassio. The haste of the marriage suggests Ger-trude's desire existed before King Hamlet's death. Any remarriage by Gertrude shows her inconstant; hasty remarriage suggests she may also be unchaste.

And for Hamlet, there is no mean between chastity—pure, cold, and holy—and depravity in women. In addition, for Hamlet as for his ghost-father, men are divided into gods, the ce-lestial, falling off into garbage, the ideal and the perversion.[9] Hyperion lacking, the satyr ap-

pears: men and women are gods or they are beasts. For Hamlet, there is no realm of the hu-man, no masculine principle. There is the su-perhuman and the subhuman, and his cate-gories apply to both genders. Hamlet's values are thus absolutist: one must have very fixed, firm standards so to categorize human behavior. Hamlet's thinking is very *young* thinking. And the young man has suddenly been thrust by events into a situation that is not easily under-standable, and not at all manageable by absolute thinking. He, like the rest of us, lives in a world where the ideal exists, but only at moments, and only in certain areas of people's behavior. Like us, Hamlet has "declined" into an ambivalent and ambiguous world.

The second scene of the play presents the earthly dimension of the cosmic ambiguity which the ghost will later present. Claudius opens it with mixed grief for death and joy for marriage, an "auspicious and a dropping eye." He proceeds to state business with authority, in-telligence, and benevolence of manner. He is not a king debilitated by lack of assurance, intelli-gence, or corrupted by egoism. He is concerned with the welfare of his country, seeking peaceful means to secure it. He is generous to Laertes and kind to Hamlet. He maintains his equanim-ity even after Hamlet's surly response to him: "Why, 'tis a loving and a fair reply" (I, ii, 121).

In general, the world that surrounds Hamlet is as morally ambiguous as the actual world. Claudius is a good ruler; he loves his wife and is patient and kind with her difficult son. He is also a murderer and an adulterer, according to the ghost. Gertrude is a loving concerned mother, a compassionate queen, a loving wife (to Claudius, so far as we see her), who is also able to comment with force and intelligence on Polonius' tediousness and the Player Queen's protestations. She is also inconstant.

Polonius is a more complex figure than either the King or the Queen. He seems to love his children; he seems to have the welfare of the kingdom in mind. His means of action, how-ever, are totally corrupt. In I, iii, both Polonius and Laertes tell Ophelia that the words and ac-tions of Hamlet that she has taken as "holy" are mere seemings. The nature of the male is lustful and deceitful, they inform her: she must not honor her love lest she dishonor her father. She must guard her chastity closely, for men are inconstant, their blazes "giving more light than heat, extinct in both, / Even in their promise" (I, iii, 117–119). Nature itself is dangerous: "the chariest maid is prodigal enough / If she unmask her beauty to the moon" (I, iii, 36–37).

The assumptions of Ophelia's "guardians" are that females are responsible for human sexuality, but that the world is full of aggressive lecherous men out to destroy utterly desirable, utterly helpless women. Female virtue is identical with chastity; thus, Polonius, who has carefully trained his daughter to be obedient and chaste, is able to use her as a piece of bait for his spying without any sense that he has compromised her—after all, her hymen is still intact.

The viciousness that both Polonius and Laertes attribute to men underlies another scene, in which Polonius gives orders for his son to be spied upon and even slandered, sure that Laertes is engaged in some vice, and willing to defame him in order to discover a truth he believes he already knows. And Laertes, who rushes home like an obedient son to avenge his father's murder, is willing to resort to treacherous and underhanded means to accomplish it.

In a sense, *Hamlet* is a fulfillment of the Old Testament verdict that the imagination of man's heart is evil from his youth. A sense of human nature as incorrigibly vicious leads to a code enjoining self-control and assumed virtue as necessary if humankind is to live together in society. But the irrationality of paradox underlying such a set is emphasized in the family scene. In the very middle of that scene, and juxtaposed with the two men's warnings to Ophelia, occurs Polonius' sermon to his son advising proper male behavior—moderation, self-control, and calculation for effect. Yet the old man ends: "To thine own self be true." To which self? The moral schizophrenia which is the real disease of this play is capsulized in this scene.

The eavesdropping, setting of traps, and spying which are Polonius' notions of statecraft come in time, because of Hamlet's odd behavior, to characterize the entire Danish court. Rosencrantz and Guildenstern are really awed by the King and Queen, and are, like Ophelia, obedient to the proper authority. They thus sacrifice the bond of human friendship to a social propriety. So too Laertes, later, obeys Claudius' suggestions as to how to revenge the murder, and in suggesting the poisoned rapier, sacrifices the code of honor he has been trained in. Obedience to constituted authority has sometimes been seen as one of Shakespeare's articles of belief, but in this play as well as the other problem plays, such obedience leads inevitably to corruption.[10] Hamlet's sense of Claudius as illegitimate can lead us to believe that it is Claudius personally who is to blame for this, but surely the play has a more universal significance than that. It is difficult to find in Shakespeare (outside of some rather cardboard figures in the history plays) a man who is both legitimate and powerful. Except (perhaps) for Henry V, the fully legitimate figures in Shakespeare are invariably dead and haloed by memory.

And to repeat: the Claudius who opens scene ii appears as legitimate as it is possible to be. Indeed, Hamlet's response to the courteous, patient, cordial King could lead a newcomer to the play to decide that Hamlet is a sullen resentful young man hugging his own untested virtue while accusing his parents of hypocrisy, and the soliloquy which follows it could reinforce our sense of Hamlet's priggish self-righteousness. But it does not. This is not because at this point in the play we believe Hamlet's feelings or judgments to be correct, but because of the power of his outrage. It overwhelms us, we are impelled into sympathy with him because the dramatist has so magnificently articulated his anguish and his hate. G. Wilson Knight has remarked that we see Denmark largely through Hamlet's eyes, yet they may not be trustworthy.[11] It does not matter, however: Hamlet's feelings are the most powerful things in the play, and they sweep us up.

The Prince has several responses to what he sees around him. His intellectual response is to question the whole notion of legitimacy—as his creator did in the first tetralogy. At first, he questions only the legitimacy of his world, and finds everywhere hypocrisy, mere seemings. Lacking chaste constancy to guarantee male transcendence, the world falls back into mere nature, is an "unweeded garden" possessed by "things rank and gross in nature" (I, ii, 135,

136). The masculine principle, based on control and transcendence of nature, becomes a mockery in the face of an amoral, engulfing, animal nature. Since the masculine principle is the pole that attempts to deduce or impose significance on human life, the undermining of legitimacy also undermines whatever significance an age has attributed to *bios*. Without the guarantee of female chaste constancy, life loses all meaning.

The young idealist is thrown into despair by this perception. He has believed what he was taught too (like Ophelia and Laertes), that women were chaste and constant, males legitimate and noble, that both genders bent to the support and protection of the other in the face of the rough winds of heaven.

But the truth he discovers is other: no man should 'scape whipping. Thus, quickly, Hamlet's questioning of male legitimacy extends to his own. The "vicious mole of nature" infects him as well as other humans. His own flesh is—perhaps—sullied; he is rogue, slave, peasant, whore, drab, an arrant knave crawling between earth and heaven, a sinner who now believes that all humans are depraved. And this belief, conveyed to Hamlet by the ghost's information, becomes a self-fulfilling prophecy.

Hamlet harps on his major concerns throughout the play. His dialogue with Polonius in II, ii, contains three main themes: an attack on the fragility of female chaste constancy; mockery of the counsellor, who, as he is old and foolish, is illegitimate and not deserving of respect; and his desire to die. Immediately afterwards he tells Rosencrantz and Guildenstern that Denmark is a prison—a cage full of illegitimates—and moves to the theme of illegitimacy. He announces, almost with surprise, that "then are our beggars bodies, and our monarchs and outstretch'd heroes the beggars' shadows" (II, ii, 263–264). Soon afterwards, he refers to himself as a beggar.

Loss of faith in the inlaw feminine principle leads to loss of faith in male legitimacy, and thus to suspicion of male pretensions. But Hamlet's whole world is built on male pretensions. Seeing male prerogatives as pretensions, however, leads to his sense of Claudius as a diminished thing, his abuse of the old counsellor who was his father's advisor as well, and his disrespectful treatment of his mother. It leads also to his sense of himself as being weak as a peasant, wordy as a whore, as helpless as an infant to put the times in joint.

Hamlet's real hate for Claudius is not for the fact of the murder, but for his illegitimacy: Claudius is, he claims, a slave, a cutpurse, a "king of shreds and patches" (III, iv, 102). In this way, the seemingly digressive scenes with the players are central to the play. In a world where everyone is vicious, everyone is a player. What is important in such a world is *how* you play the game; Hamlet's instructions to the players are a parallel to Polonius' directions to Laertes, and to Hamlet's own orders to his mother to assume a virtue she does not possess.

The appearance of the actors is preceded by a discussion of the inconstancy and low standards of a city audience willing to take children in place of men (which Hamlet compares with the willingness of the Danes—and implicitly of his mother—to take his uncle in place of the real thing). Hamlet asks the players to perform an esoteric piece, a passage describing a situation somewhat like Hamlet's own: a man avenges his father's killing by killing the father of the man who killed him. The language, however, describes the destruction of the feminine principle—Priam is old and physically powerless; he is reverent, his head is milky; at his fall, the heavens should cry milky tears; Hecuba is constant, worn out by childbearing—by a "painted tyrant," who is momentarily paralyzed in his slaughter by an accident that "takes prisoner Pyrrhus' ear" (II, ii, 480, 477), an illusion that reminds us of the "leprous distillment" poured into the ear of Hamlet's father, paralyzing him by posseting his blood; and the poison poured in Hamlet's ear by the ghost, paralyzing him.

The relation between appearance and reality are not simple in this play—or elsewhere in Shakespeare. For the players' expressions, offering an acted despair, seem realer than Hamlet's expression of his real despair. He mistrusts everyone around him (except Horatio), but some of what occurs around him is real in some way. Ophelia is part of a trap, but she is innocent; Claudius feels guilty despite his assurance. Hamlet's "mad" seemings are as real as, or perhaps more genuine than his calmer behavior.

Certitude resides only with legitimacy, which seems to have vanished from the earth.

Challenge of the very notion of legitimacy informs Hamlet's confrontation with Claudius after his murder of Polonius, as he derisively tells the King "your fat king . . . may go a progress through the guts of a beggar" (IV, iii, 23, 30–31). And challenge of legitimacy reaches its climax in the graveyard scene, when Hamlet traces the transformation of the most legitimate of legitimates, the world's greatest conquerors, through to the loam used to stuff bungholes. He does not, in this scene, come to terms with his mortality, as much as he discards finally the entire notion of legitimacy.[12]

Nevertheless, he claims it on occasion. He uses his father's ring to seal the substituted letter Rosencrantz and Guildenstern bear with them to England; he challenges Laertes in Ophelia's grave, crying "It is I, Hamlet the Dane!" And his final act, his request that Horatio remain alive to tell his story, is another motion toward legitimacy: he cares about his name, fame, honor, immortality.[13]

This split in attitudes towards male legitimacy is of a piece with many other of Hamlet's attitudes. His language is alternately lofty or vulgar—or at least, slangy—if always eloquent.[14] His behavior alternates between rash cruelty, savage action, and gentle, melancholy reflection.[15] He vacillates between thinking he must avenge his father by killing Claudius, and wanting to avenge himself by injuring Gertrude. He frequently exhorts himself to anger against the King; but he must exhort himself to control his anger against his mother.

For, if Hamlet's primary intellectual response to the information given him by the ghost is to question legitimacy, his primary emotional response is outrage at his mother's failure in chaste constancy.[16] Hamlet passes Claudius in the chapel, missing his chance and rationalizing this with a religious "reason." But Hamlet would surely know that repentance for sins like Claudius' requires penance more substantial than prayer. He does have bloody thoughts, but they are not directed at the King. They are directed at Gertrude, and despite his attempt at control, he does physically assault her to the degree that she thinks he is about to kill her.

Within moments, he stabs Polonius, taking him for the King, although he has just seen Claudius in the chapel. It is unclear whether Hamlet is being illogical or simply unthinking: what is clear is that in his mother's closet he is emotionally fevered enough to act, furious enough to kill, and could have killed Claudius—*there*.

The central act of the play opens with a court scene involving plotting to discover Hamlet's problem by setting Ophelia out as a trap. In their encounter, Hamlet savagely attacks Ophelia. At the end of the act, he savagely attacks his mother. The central act of the play is thus framed by Hamlet's attacks on women, underscoring the centrality—and failure—of chaste constancy in Hamlet's moral universe.

Hamlet begins to attack Ophelia by suggesting that she may be chaste, but will not be for long because even his mother is not—"the time gives it proof" (III, i, 114).[17] He moves immediately to a satiric estimation of his own illegitimacy and viciousness. He ends with a scathing attack on Ophelia, and all women, as false, wanton, and able to turn men into monsters. As we have seen before, failure in one woman is projected to failure in all in Shakespeare's work. Hamlet's words and rhythms in the speeches are powerful; there is nothing in the play that can compare to these speeches in hatred except those uttered to his mother.

He attacks Gertrude more directly. Her act, he says,

> blurs the grace and blush of modesty,
> Calls virtue hypocrite, takes off the rose
> From the fair forehead of an innocent love
> And sets a blister there, makes marriage vows
> As false as dicers' oaths, O, such a deed
> As from the body of contraction plucks
> The very soul, and sweet religion makes
> A rhapsody of words. Heaven's face does glow
> O'er this solidity and compound mass
> With heated visage, as against the doom;
> Is thought-sick at the act.   (III, iv, 41–51)

Hamlet is outraged that Gertrude should feel desire at all:

> O shame, where is thy blush? Rebellious hell,
> If thou canst mutine in a matron's bones,
> To flaming youth let virtue be as wax
> And melt in her own fire. Proclaim no shame
> When the compulsive ardure gives the charge,

Since frost itself as actively doth burn,
And reason panders will. . . .
                        Nay, but to live
In the rank sweat of an enseamed bed,
Stew'd in corruption, honeying and making love
Over the nasty sty! . . .
Let the bloat king tempt you again to bed,
Pinch wanton on your cheek, call you his
    mouse,
And let him, for a pair of reechy kisses,
Or paddling in your neck with his damn'd fin-
    gers,
Make you to ravel all this matter out.
                (III, iv, 81–88; 91–94; 182–186)

Like his ghost-father, Hamlet barely mentions Claudius in this scene, and his references are diminishing rather than angry or hating: Gertrude, Hamlet says, has stepped from a man who combined the qualities of the gods, to a "mildewed ear" (III, iv, 64).

The scene with Gertrude is, on one level of the play, the climax. After Hamlet has persuaded his mother to refrain from Claudius' bed, he becomes somewhat a different person. He is openly flip and derisive to Claudius, which he has not been before. He seems to feel he has accomplished his real task, as indeed, if the ghost's words at the beginning of the play are examined carefully, he has. He accepts without demur the decision to send him to England. And upon his return, knowing Claudius sent him abroad to be killed, he goes back to the court easily, without pressure, seemingly without anxiety.

Whatever Hamlet may say to himself (and to us), there is no escaping the conclusion that Hamlet does not want to kill Claudius: Claudius the King is not important to him. Claudius the King is man dressed in a little brief authority, mere shreds and patches on a stick whose head will someday be a skull lying in the ground beside Yorick's. Like Pyrrhus, Claudius is a "painted tyrant." Hamlet is not interested in power-in-the-world. He knows legitimacy is a delusion, a pretension.

Claudius, Gertrude's husband, is another matter. The root of Hamlet's feeling about his mother's sexuality may perhaps be Oedipal jealousy, but it has been transformed into something very different. The play is full of clues to the source of his outrage as Hamlet feels it: it

lies in a sense of humankind as vicious, and of sex as disgusting, loathsome, and bestial, as a giving up of the control necessary to distinguish man from animal. Woman, the link between these two realms, must therefore renounce sexuality, and this act is *absolutely necessary* to purify, sanctify any human claims to humanness, to difference from, transcendence of the beast. A chaste constant woman would not feel desire, would do "but duty," and would firmly corset her man, and guarantee a line of legitimate males.

The placing of so much moral weight on the state of a vagina is rationally absurd, and charges of insufficient objective correlatives to Hamlet's emotional state are understandable. But chaste constancy is the cornerstone of Shakespeare's moral universe throughout his work. Hamlet's feelings are understandable only in the context of this fact, understandable perhaps only through immersion in the entire canon. For Shakespeare, without chaste constancy, nothing is real except death, because only death endures when women are not constant, and in a world of appearances, only what endures is real.

The central segment of *Hamlet* opens with the plot and the attack on Ophelia, closes with the attack on Gertrude. Between these is the visit of the players and the performance of "The Mouse-Trap." The entire spoken portion of the play-within-a-play concerns constancy, and is implicitly a reproach to inconstant women. The King insists constancy is difficult and perhaps impossible; the Queen insists it is possible and swears herself to it. Hamlet comments: "If she should break it now!" (III, ii, 224). He arranges for the play to catch the conscience of the King, he says; but that conscience, which is moved to prayer (or its attempt), seems of little interest to him once it is caught. It is rather the conscience of the Queen that Hamlet is fishing for.

The two crimes that have been committed in Denmark are murder and "incest." Both acts are permissible if performed with license—with ceremonial purification by the state operating under what are claimed to be divine sanctions (Henry VIII married his brother's legal wife). The state (or its military or judicial agents) may kill those called enemies or criminals, and may even praise its own acts. Copulation is permitted in marriage (and tolerated in men who use women who have been isolated and segregated in a special class designed precisely for this purpose—demimondaines and prostitutes). Murder is the extreme of the masculine principle; copulation is the foundation of giving birth, the extreme of the feminine principle. Of the two, copulation without sanctification, by a woman, is the worst crime. This is suggested in *Much Ado*, and is explicit in both the design and the plot of *Hamlet*. In *Measure for Measure*, the subject is debated by Angelo and Isabel. They disagree on most things, but agree on this.

Because of the importance of chaste constancy in *Hamlet*, the intellectual level (plot) of the play conflicts with the emotional level (design). The split apparent in Hamlet's sensibility and behavior is built into the very structure of the play. The linear plot—Hamlet's bond to avenge his father—is irrelevant to his real priorities. Thus, his path *is* blocked, his paralysis is real—he is uninterested in doing what he thinks he should do, and wants to do what he knows he should not do. And nothing can repair the situation. The Queen's failure in chaste constancy cannot be altered; it can be remedied, and is, although early in the play Hamlet does not conceive of ordering his mother to refrain from sex. But even so, its fatal work has been done: Gertrude's failure has inspired Claudius to kill his brother: God is dead, a creature of shreds and patches sits on the throne. And indeed, when Hamlet does finally kill Claudius, he does not kill a king, he kills an "incestious, murd'rous" man (V, ii, 325), the man who "whor'd" his mother (V, ii, 64).

On the mythic level, *Hamlet* is about a young man growing into adulthood. His memories of the past are idyllic—his father is full of both power and "divine" virtues, is a perfect synthesis of masculine and feminine principles. He is the full incarnation of the ideal and legitimate male: God, King, Father. And, like the ideal Henry V, and the ideal fathers who follow him in haunting the first tetralogy, he is dead. He exists as memory, tradition, and above all, certitude. He haunts, with knowledge of a prelapsarian virtue and certitude, the imagination of

an idealist unlucky enough to stumble on sexuality in his mother and murder in his father.

Claudius and King Hamlet have performed the same acts. Both are devoted to Gertrude and have made love to her, one after ceremonial purification, the other without it. Both have killed, one in a ceremonially purified way (war), the other independently and for himself (murder). On the mythic level, the dead King and his loving wife are the idyllic creations of childhood; the murderous King and his ardent wife are the parents the young man returns to discover after years spent away at school. The disguise convention that permits Hero to die and be resurrected is here internalized and reversed: the play opens after both funeral and wedding. The old King and his wife have died and have been resurrected in Claudius and Gertrude.

Hamlet's primary response in action to the discovery or realization that all human experience is bounded by its two most profound acts—killing and giving birth (with the implicit corollary that birth requires sexual intercourse)—is to meditate upon and feel its implications. It is because of this tendency that Hamlet is seen as sensitive, intellectual, and feminine.[18] Actually, his actions are more violent, and rasher than those of any other character. He is as malicious (to Rosencrantz and Guildenstern) as Claudius, as savage as Laertes, as given to plots (the play-within-the-play) as Polonius. And like Hamlet, the play is formally and in content divided between the gender principles.

To meditate on and consciously feel experience is "feminine." Such behavior never moves in a linear way, but occurs in clusters which may be static and are essentially associative rather than logical. Thus, the structure of *Hamlet* is at times "feminine," comedic, and seems digressive for a tragedy. There are loose connections, many delays, and full stops during the soliloquies which are devoted to Hamlet's sensations/emotions/thoughts.[19] The rigorous causal logic of action-oriented plays is lacking, as Tillyard complains.[20] Rather, the play "creates so marvelous a sense of the actual improvisation of life that we can find no simple logic in its sprawling action."[21]

In addition, the play has a more multiple focus than most of the tragedies, and resembles comedy in this. It casts attention on Polonius, his family, and servant; on Claudius with a series of characters; on Gertrude and Ophelia, as well as the protagonist. And it shows the effect, not just in behavior, action, but in feeling and thought, of a thought pattern or set that is rooted in a belief in the inherent viciousness of humankind. The series of son–father vengeances that appears in the larger play and the play within demonstrate the impossibility of right action in an illegitimate world. G. W. Knight suggests that "the question of the relative morality of Hamlet and Claudius reflects the ultimate problem of this play."[22] But that relativity embraces others too—Laertes, Fortinbras, and the female figures as well. *Hamlet*, along with *King Lear*, directly confronts the void in which we live if we permit ourselves to penetrate the carefully erected curtain of significance that normally obscures it. Incertitude about the purpose of life leads to incertitude about any code of behavior.

In this play, Shakespeare challenges, examines, probes his own ideals—male legitimacy and female chaste constancy—which, like all ideals, are based on faith rather than knowledge, and finds them shaky and untrue to actual human life, which is based on sex and killing. To do such a thing requires enormous moral courage—a willingness to cut away the foundation from under one's own feet.

Notes

1. Maynard Mack, "The World of *Hamlet*," *Yale Review* XLI (1952): 502–523; Harry Levin, *The Question of "Hamlet"* (New York, 1959).

2. Mack, "*Hamlet*."

3. Mack, "*Hamlet*," points out that all the major persons of the drama are players. This notion is developed by Ann Righter, *Shakespeare and the Idea of the Play* (London, 1964).

4. That the characters are continually checking up on each other is pointed out by Robert Heilman, "The Lear World," *English Institute Essays: 1948*, ed. D. A. Robertson, Jr. (New York, 1949).

5. Many critics have suggested this or something like it. Dover Wilson was probably the first to suggest it. Wilson, *What Happens in "Hamlet"* (Cambridge, 1935).

6. These are suggested, in order, by: Theodore Spencer, *Shakespeare and the Nature of Man* (New York, 1942); Spencer, *Nature*, and H. B. Charlton, *Shakespearian Tragedy* (Cambridge, 1948); Norman Council, *When Honour's at the Stake* (London, 1973) and E. K. Chambers, *Shakespeare* (London, 1925), as well as Patrick Cruttwell, *The Shakespearian Moment* (New York, 1955), who speaks of lost ideals; Chambers, *Shakespeare*; and Erich Heller, *The Artist's Journey Into the Interior* (New York, 1976), among others.

7. Rossiter, *Angel with Horns*, ed. Graham Storey (London, 1961), p. 179, writes that Hamlet is inclined to believe in absolute good and evil but is placed in circumstances which cause him to act as if there were no absolutes. H. D. F. Kitto sees the entire play-world as polluted: "A Classical Scholar Looks at Shakespeare," *More Talking of Shakespeare*, ed. John Garrett (London, 1959). Alice Shalvi, *The Relationship of Renaissance Concepts of Honour to Shakespeare's Problem Plays* (Salzburg, Austria, 1972), and Norman Council, *Honour*, both see Hamlet as attempting to act genuinely in the face of a society riddled with outworn and conventional moral precepts. It was Caroline Spurgeon, of course, who first pointed to the images of sickness, disease, and disfigurement. *Imagery*, p. 316.

8. This is discussed by Shalvi, p. 132.

9. James Joyce has not been taken seriously as a Shakespeare critic, despite the importance of Shakespeare the man and his creations to *Ulysses*. But, although Joyce seized on only those elements of Shakespeare that were useful to him, he was an incisive reader of the poet. The character of Stephen Dedalus is to some degree modeled on Hamlet. Stephen is paralyzed, fearing the consequences both of action and inaction; he desires above all certitude, a rational explanation of the cosmos that would provide him with a clear basis for right action. He also wants undying love, love for him alone. He sees Shakespeare's obsession with cuckoldry and money as a need to possess, to pin down; he associates Shakespeare with Shylock and with Othello. Stephen's fiction about Shakespeare is as much about himself as the playwright, but it has relevance to Shakespeare's work, particularly *Hamlet*. The young man describes Shakespeare thus: "Lover of an ideal or a perversion, like José he kills the real Carmen." Stephen too is filled with disgust for sexuality, and sees fornication as a clasping and sundering, doing "the coupler's will," and conception and gestation as being "wombed in

sin darkness." Joyce, *Ulysses* (New York, 1966), p. 212; p. 38.

10. Council, *Honour*, p. 110, discusses conventional virtue as being untrustworthy as a guide to action.

11. G. Wilson Knight, *The Wheel of Fire* (New York, 1947), p. 43.

12. Mack, *"Hamlet,"* claims that in the graveyard, Hamlet finally accepts his mortality.

13. Cruttwell, *Moment*, p. 85, points out that at the end of their lives, both Hamlet and Othello show concern with their reputations on earth.

14. Wolfgang Clemen, *The Development of Shakespeare's Imagery* (Cambridge, Mass., 1951), p. 109.

15. Robert Ornstein, *The Moral Vision of Jacobean Tragedy* (Madison, Wis., 1960), p. 235, analyzes the way the point of view of the drama allows us to accept Hamlet's brutality and cruelty without questioning it.

16. Many critics, from Boas on, have pointed out that it is "the queen's frailty" that moves Hamlet rather than the King's "villainy." Frederick Boas, *Shakspere and His Predecessors* (New York, 1896), p. 403. Tillyard discusses this situation at length: *Problem Plays,* (Toronto, 1949), pp. 22–26, as does Dover Wilson, *The Essential Shakespeare* (Cambridge, 1932), p. 119.

17. Numerous critics have suggested a connection between Hamlet's feelings about his mother and his treatment of Ophelia. Reuben Brower, *Hero and Saint* (New York, 1971), p. 263, writes of Troilus that he, "like Hamlet . . . feels that if his love is false all 'womankind,' all 'mothers,' must be so too." O. J. Campbell, however, sees in Hamlet's tirade to Ophelia (III, i) "little importance for the plot of the play," since it is "merely a familiar satiric interlude." *Shakespeare's Satire* (New York, 1943), p. 153.

18. Knight, *Wheel*, p. 307, sees Hamlet's mind as set between extremes of "extraversion and introversion, of masculine and feminine."

19. Boas, *Shakspere*, p. 389, writes that the soliloquies have little relation to the "actual progress of events" in the play. Wolfgang Clemen, *Shakespeare's Dramatic Art* (London, 1972), p. 65, finds the structure full of retarding episodes and digressions and concludes that the play is "loosely constructed."

20. Tillyard, *Problem Plays*, p. 29.

21. Ornstein, *Moral Vision*, p. 234.

22. Knight, *Wheel*, p.28.

Application

Lycidas and the Stages of Grief

Barbara C. Bell

Narrative and dramatic forms seem to invite discussion in the mimetic context; the obviously conventional pastoral elegy seems to resist it. Yet, as Barbara Bell's analysis shows, even a lyric poem can be seen as an "imitation of an action," and the uses of psychology may extend to this literary form as well. Noting that readers of various times and persuasions have testified to the power of Lycidas, *and doubting that traditional literary critics have located the source of that power, Bell looks to modern psychology to illuminate the mystery. She finds the answer in studies that show that people react to grief in clearly defined and predictable stages, stages well imitated by the action of Milton's poem. The real appeal, then, runs deeper than our grasp of literary conventions, deeper perhaps than even our religious beliefs; it is founded on the "fundamental commonality of the grief process." Since most readers must recognize that process at a subconscious level, Bell's argument operates in that space where the mimetic and affective contexts overlap, as her phrase "emotional verisimilitude" suggests. Because Milton has so perfectly represented the stages of grief, the poem "recreates for us, in us, a realistic response to loss."*

Reprinted by permission from *Literature and Psychology* 25 (1975): 166–74. Copyright © 1975 by Fairleigh Dickinson University.

"WEEP NO MORE, WOEFUL SHEPHERDS, WEEP NO more." For nearly three and a half centuries, many people have been remembering and rereading "Lycidas," Milton's elegy for Edward King, in witness to its emotional power. They have found lines in it, like the one just quoted, that carry more meaning for them than the words seem to say; yielding to the experience of the poem, they have felt deeply and unforgettably touched. Despite its basis in a classical literary genre that has become less and less familiar, its reference to a political situation that lasted only a few years, and its resolution in a Christian vision of personal immortality that is no longer widely believed, "Lycidas" has traditionally been regarded as a supremely moving expression of grief.

At once, such a statement brings to mind a whole history of controversy. " 'Lycidas' is not to be considered as the effusion of real passion. . . ." This taunt by Dr. Johnson in his *Lives of the Poets* (1779) spurred a dispute about emotion in "Lycidas" that engaged dozens of noted critics throughout the nineteenth and twentieth centuries. It has been a valuable dispute, generating much knowledge about the poem, but one point it illustrates is that critics have often felt the emotional power of "Lycidas" without being able to explain it precisely. The burden of proof has been heavy on Dr. Johnson's opponents. For them, the simple question "Why is the poem's emotional impact so strong?" still prompts consideration.

Some testimonials have been nearly mystical, like Paul More's: "I do not know how others are affected, but I can never peruse the climax of the poem without a thrill such as scarcely any other verses of the language express. . . . I am not competent to explain by what devices, what choice of words, Milton obtains his sublime effect . . . ; indeed I question whether any skill of criticism can penetrate to the heart of that mystery of the word which we call inspiration, and leave at that."[1]

Those critics who *have* attempted explanation of "Lycidas" ' emotional effect—a majority— have offered interpretations that seem limited. Several propose views that have an uncomfortable, somewhat arbitrary formality. Barker, for instance, analyzes the poem's feeling as moving through " 'three successive and perfectly controlled crescendoes,' culminating in a second triumphal resolution of tensions already half-released in their appropriate sections."[2] We wonder first, why the number three should have special magic, and second, whether emotions really do work in this way. Or when Northrop Frye sees an "ABACA" structure in the poem's feeling, likening it to a musical rondo, we appreciate the analogy but put to him the same type of questions we put to Barker.[3]

Other critics are tantalizingly general. For instance, E. M. W. Tillyard explains that the emotion in the poem moves from struggle to calm. Richard P. Adams declares, "The emotional pattern of the poem consists of a twofold movement. First it goes from the announcement of the friend's death downward through various expressions of sorrow to despair; then comfort is offered, and the sequence reverses itself until the conclusion is reached in heavenly joy." Rosemund Tuve proposes that "The ebb and flow of love and hostility in the universe is the secret of 'Lycidas' obscure and almost primitive power." A. S. P. Woodhouse refers to "the dynamic of the Christian monody, the transition from mourning to consolation. . . ."[4] Although each of these critics enriches our appreciation of the poem, the two-termed view they all share must, of necessity, be general. Lack of agreement about the intermediate terms, or failure to discriminate them, remains a problem.

Given a sense that more can be said about the emotion in "Lycidas," where can we turn? While examining criticism of the poem, I have been struck by contemporary scholars' hesitancy about applying to it some of the knowledge gained from the disciplines that investigate human emotion most directly—psychology, psychiatry and psychoanalysis.

"Lycidas" is a poem of mourning. Perhaps we can tell more precisely how it moves us if we analyze it in terms of what is now known about the general phenomenon of human grief. Within the last 15 years a fair-sized literature has accumulated on this subject, and I will try to review it here, hoping that the necessary brevity will be somewhat corrected by my references.

According to investigators, mourning is a well-structured psychological process that is experienced in much the same way by most people who suffer loss.[6] Pathology does occur, of course, but it only is analyzable because normal or "healthy" mourning can be so well defined. The first systematic investigator of grief, Erich Lindemann, stated that "Acute grief is a definite syndrome with psychological and somatic symptomatology. . . . The picture shown by persons in acute grief is remarkably uniform"; and these statements have never been challenged. A later psychiatrist has added, "I know of no other psychological illness which follows so stereotyped and predictable a course."[7]

The psychological symptomatology that Lindemann identified and others have confirmed includes the following: denial, anger, depression, and resolution. Not all writers use the same set of terms, but their basic agreement is evident, since the differing sets are roughly interchangeable. Elaboration on what the terms denote, as well as comments on the somatic symptoms of grief, will come later in the course of this paper.

Not only are these symptoms specified; their sequence is too. Denial comes first and is followed by anger, followed by depression, followed by resolution. Substages are designated at points: denial is divided into shock and refusal to accept the loss; resolution, into acceptance and relinquishment, or "decathexis." With regard to sequence, as one might guess, there is less unified opinion. The first and the last stages are completely agreed upon, but the middle two are occasionally seen to overlap or intertwine. Even this amount of variation, however, has not been crucial. Psychiatrist Elisabeth Kübler-Ross, who in her book *On Death and Dying* (New York: Macmillan, 1969) has described the stages of mourning with the greatest particularity, has not prompted refutation.

In fact, the important debate seems to have been not over the description of either symptomatology or sequence at all, but over the psychogenesis of mourning: a psychoanalytic controversy into which we, for the purposes of this paper, need not go. Rather, we can settle with confidence on a descriptive "model" for the process of mourning, based on concensus, that has four main stages and certain "sub-stages" arranged in the order given above. In this description of grief, the psychological sciences have not so much unveiled new facts, as made familiar ones more clear. To anyone who has mourned, the model seems true in the sense that it speaks of emotions we know we have had, giving us a convenient vocabulary to distinguish them and a "map" for the pattern organizing them so that we may more lucidly reflect on them in ourselves and communicate them to others.

Now we come back to "Lycidas." We want to use the tools provided by the psychological sciences to help us understand the poem's emotion better; and thereby to explain its power.

The poem begins with a sense of shock. In ll. 1–7 the elegist bursts out against an unnatural event that he hasn't expected, and certainly not planned. His sense of being taken unawares applies equally to the fact of his own untimely writing and to Edward King's death: Rosemund Tuve refers to the "wild incalculableness" of the situation. (Patrides, 184) A heightening of the shock comes with the repeated "dead, dead" in l. 8, and immediately we hear denial creeping in.[8] The phrases "ere his prime" and "Young Lycidas" imply an underlying protest, "Young people can't die!"[9] The entire first part of the poem through line l. 49 could be considered "denial," as the elegist struggles, with final success, to grant the plain fact of King's death. Ll. 10–17 illustrate a preliminary acknowledgement of it, but that is not easy to maintain, as l. 18 shows: "Hence with denial vain, and coy excuse" of course expresses most directly the elegist's dismissal of his doubts about writing, but it could also be read as his self-exhortation to stop denying King's death, for that denial fuels his reluctance to write. In ll. 23–36, the elegist relapses and, recalling what he has shared with King, seems to defy awareness of the latter's death. During this first stage of grief, a mour-

ner's preoccupation with his own mental image of the dead person is common. It is as if, in his vivid memories of togetherness, the elegist is trying to make King come alive again. A new paragraph begins, however, "But O the heavy change, now thou art gon,/Now thou art gon, and never must return!" Here, the elegist is overcoming his refusal to believe, repeating to himself "thou art gon" and securing his realization with the irrevocable "never must return!" Subsequent lines solidify his awareness of loss as he envisions places without King ("the Woods, and desert Caves," "the Willows, and the Hazle Copses green") and adds similes supporting the finality of his classmate's death. ("As killing as the Canker to the Rose/Or Taint-worm to the weanling Herds . . ./Or Frost to Flowers . . ./Such *Lycidas*, thy loss . . ."). After initial shock and attempts at refusal, he finally faces the fact of death.

Notable in the culminating line of this section is the phrase "lost to Shepherds *ear*." (Underlining mine.) Somehow, sound has departed. Sound, in the elegy's present time, is at any rate not very pleasing. We hear the elegist's amateurish first notes, the sacred sister's somewhat loud noise, and hollow echoes. The "melodious tear," it seems, is not yet singing clear. These distorted sounds in the present are strongly contrasted with the glad ones from the past of "grayfly," "ditties," "flute" and "song" in harmony. Not hearing those lovely tunes any more, we are like the bereaved person who says, "I feel numb." The loss of sound, perhaps similar to the experience we have when the speaker on our TV set goes off and we hear either nothing or odd beeps and chatters, corresponds to a major somatic symptom during the first stage of grief, the one we pass through, with the elegy, in the first four verse paragraphs.

In the next section, the elegist rages. Once denial has been overcome, the poem begins to move into statements and images at the highest pitch of emotion. "It is during the [middle stages] that the greatest degree of anguish or despair, within the limits imposed by cultural patterns, is experienced and expressed."[10] First, the elegist blames the nymphs for not doing enough to avert King's death. Then, when he realizes that the accusation is inappropriate, he complains about Fate, angrily questioning what a person's work in life is worth if it is to be so arbitrarily cut off by death, and threatening to give up all effort. That complaint, too, is answered. Next, he stages a trial, looking for someone to punish, but ending only with curses on a ship. Two angry *personae* then enter. First comes Camus, actually a figure of mixed dejection and rage. His slow pace and sigh are characteristic of depression, but he, like an angry mourner, is still looking for someone to blame. After him, much less ambiguous and more important, comes St. Peter, who gives such a withering denunciation that this section of the poem ends in a tremendous crescendo of anger.

All this accords with the mood seen by clinicians, who speak of mourners feeling "bitter, resentful, irritable and inclinded to blame [themselves] and others for death." (Parkes, 11) Guilt preoccupies some people, while the elegist, not blaming himself, seems the more eager to attack others: this variation within the norm is quite common. Nor are the fearful parts of St. Peter's vision—treachery, blind mouths, inner rot, the savage wolf, the two-handed engine—unnaturally exaggerated. Lindemann writes, "These feelings of hostility, surprising and quite inexplicable to the [mourners], disturbed them and . . . were often taken as signs of approaching insanity" (142).

During this section, the elegy's "sensorium" has aroused again, predictably, but two new somatic symptoms are reflected, distresses that are common during grief's middle stages. One is a sense of strangeness, as if the mourner were in some unknown place, seeing hallucinations. This is signaled by the dramatic appearance of characters from myth and classic or Christian fable. They appear at other points in the poem, too, of course, but nowhere in such numbers. Second is the feeling of overwhelming emptiness. The mountains are empty of nymphs, Orpheus is not whole, no reward is forthcoming for greatness, life is terribly thin, no evidence about the shipwreck can be found. Most effective of all, perhaps, since the empty feeling of grief is often physically experienced in the stomach, is the imagery in St. Peter's speech describing men bloated with air or gobbled food, hunger, intestinal rot, all extreme discomforts of a

stomach that is not satisfied—empty. Others have written about the spiritual emptiness of the corrupt clergy and their congregations that these images convey, and certainly Milton intends a symbolic meaning: I merely note that the somatic site of the emptiness, as conveyed by the literal meaning of the images, is particularly painful for the mourner during this stage of his grief. Once more, we see the extent of verisimilitude in the poem.

Rage usually burns itself with a final explosion, as happens here, and the abrupt change in l. 132 from St. Peter's speech to the next stage of grief, depression, is not surprising. For those who study mourning, important signs of depression are restlessness, aimless wandering and inability to initiate or maintain organized activity, *along with* those affects we more conventionally associate with depression: sadness, anxiety, helplessness and hopelessness. Lindemann identifies a general loss of patterns of conduct. "The activity throughout the day of the severely bereaved person shows remarkable changes" (142). During this stage, awareness of loss is most acute, for anger, although it is not quite denial, may be seen partly as a way of getting the lost person back, while in depression, hope disappears. Bowlby summarizes depression as "disorganization of personality accompanied by pain and despair" (319).

In "Lycidas," both the "floweret" and the "sounding seas" passages, despite their different moods, belong to the overall experience of depression. In the "floweret" passage, the action is manic, an odd mixture of festival gesture with sad occasion. Even the elegist admits to its craziness (l. 153), and his frankness is natural, since the depressed mourner usually does lose some of his self-esteem. The passage describes only crude action ("cast," "throw," "bring," "strew"); it has slight aim (for the ease can only be temporary); it exhibits basic weakness ("frail" and "false" are poor attributes, "daily" is a feeble action, and a "surmise" has little value); and it seems to lack inner organization. (The catalogue, for all the beautiful sense impressions it arouses, is still only a catalogue, its items having no necessary logical connections.)

The sudden interruption of a sigh and introduction of a new subject are quite characteristic—in this stage, the mood is restless. Letting his mind wander passively, almost the way King's body is carried by the waves and certainly the way depressed people feel bound by forces beyond their control, the elegist thinks of the vast ocean from North to South where King might be and prayerfully begs the minions of either God or Nature to help. He cries and imagines the angel to cry; he is anxious, for he has a vision of monsters; he leaves action up to others. Certainly in the combination of both the "floweret" and "sounding seas" passages, we see all the symptoms of depression, as the section overall leads us through the feelings of a disorganized personality, pained and despairing.

Finally, comes the last stage: resolution. "Weep no more, woeful Shepherds, weep no more." The elegist can arrive here, it seems, only after having acknowledged his ultimate helplessness in the face of death. Bowlby describes the psychic transition this way: "Since the patterns of behaviour which have grown up in interaction with the lost object or goal have ceased to be appropriate, were they to persist they would be maladaptive: only if they are broken down is it possible for new ones, adapted to new objects, to be built up. Although such disorganization is painful and carries with it the risk that satisfactory reorganization will never be achieved, it seems clear that it is an indispensable preliminary to new adaptation" (335). When acceptance does come, at the end of the other stages of grief the elegist has gone through, it is both convincing and rewarding. His emotions have evolved to a point where he can reconcile himself to death and live meaningfully because he has known grief. Again citing Bowlby, "The [last] phase completes the work of mourning and leads to a new and different state: during it a reorganization takes place, partly in connexion with the image of the lost object, partly in connexion with a new object or objects" (319–320).

For Milton, the character of the acceptance happens to be conventionally Christian, and certainly part of "Lycidas' " power lies in its sharply realized picture of Elysium, with the seductive hope of personal immortality. No mourner, no matter how unbelieving, can prevent himself from wanting to share this hope. Bowlby writes ". . . some persistence of behaviour oriented towards the lost object, who is often believed to continue his existence in another world, is the rule" (337). He goes on to say that such behavior commonly modifies through the next sub-stage of resolution, relinquishment, but his initial statement simply underlines the fact that while the Christian doctrine of immortality may be less and less approved, it has a psychological power that goes far deeper than doctrine. A mourner need not be Christian in order to share the profound emotional change that begins happening in "Lycidas" at l. 165 and concludes 20 lines later. In fact, Milton's own mention of a pagan acceptance after the Christian one ("Henceforth thou art the genius of the shore . . ."), illustrates this point. It has been called incongruous by many critics of the poem, but it can seem appropriate if we read it as reflecting the fundamental commonality of the grief process. The fact of acceptance is more important than the form acceptance takes. The main point is that most people, whatever their creed or despite a lack of one, do move into acceptance at the end of mourning, and the penultimate section of "Lycidas" parallels this natural emotional movement.

The ultimate point of resolution, according to the description of mourning, is decathexis, or relinquishment: the mourner gives up the attention he has centered on the lost person and commits himself to fashioning a new life. Seemingly cold and rejective to those who do not understand it, his turning to his own concerns is simply a demonstration that death is sure, and that everything possible has been done to meet it. Grief is self-limiting, recognizes the poem. If the mourner allows his emotions their natural evolution, the way out is as inevitable as the way in. Thus, the ottava rima at the end of "Lycidas" seems a model example of decathexis, with the elegist abruptly changing the subject to himself after having mourned fully and deeply. Now it is up to him alone to make new object choices, new relationships. "Tomorrow to fresh woods and pastures new."

If we read "Lycidas" with the tools that the psychological sciences suggest, we find a new way of explaining why this elegy's emotional impact is so powerful. It recreates for us, in us, a realistic response to loss. Its structure is in no way arbitrary, but follows what observations have shown to be the inner course of grief. At the poem's end, we find we have been emotionally fulfilled because we have moved successively through the several stages of mourning that are as natural to human beings as the fact of death itself.

An interpretation of "Lycidas" such as the one I propose obviously imposes itself on a huge amount of scholarship. In this paper, I cannot attempt satisfactorily to reconcile my reading with all the others; however, since I think a reconciliation is possible, I can sketch a few examples of how it might work.

In many cases, all that is involved is a simple change of terms, with the psychological ones justified because they form a unified set, and also because they are more "neutral." The tenor of what one might say about the "acceptance" section would not change if one switched from using the term "consolation," but the necessity for justifying Milton's Christian beliefs would.

In other cases, new solutions to old problems might appear. Take the question of the passages on fame and the corrupt clergy, both of which were termed "digressions" by early critics, not only for their length, but also for their lack of direct connection to each other or to the subject at hand, but have later been justified, thematically or formally, as integral to the poem. In terms of the reading proposed here, both of these passages are embedded in a larger section, ll. 50–131. If we view these lines as expressing the angry stage of grief, we can justify: (1) the passages' length, for we all sense that anger takes the longest time to work out; (2) their seeming unrelatedness to each other, for we are familiar with the fact that anger causes people to "go off on tangents": and (3) the apparent irrelevance of their content in an elegy, for we remember that anger also causes people to strike out wildly, attacking any source of irritation as if it were the problem's main cause. Our way of making the "digressions" integral to the poem is to see them as *emotionally* valid.

Then we might take new tacks on the familiar question of whether Milton was mourning for

Edward King or for himself. First, it is an accepted psychological fact that all mourning for other people is to some extent mourning for oneself. What in earlier years was viewed as Milton's "egotism" in "Lycidas" may now be viewed as his faithfulness to human nature. Second, one need not be surprised (and therefore forced to suspect "egotism") that Milton mourned someone he probably knew only slightly. King was a popular figure at Cambridge, symbolizing certain possibilities to his fellow students, and psychiatrists have noted that people *can* experience complete mourning over the death of a person whom they do not know intimately, but who has public significance, John F. Kennedy, Robert F. Kennedy, and Martin Luther King being the most recent tragic examples.[11] Third, and most interesting, the description of mourning that I have given in preceding pages can be supplemented somewhat by mention of "identification." Common to mourning and occurring throughout, is incorporation by the bereaved of some of the lost person's characteristics. This can be pathological, as when a mourner develops symptoms of the dying person's sickness. Much more often it is therapeutic, the mourner saying first, for instance, "X would have wanted me to make new friends," and then, "As a loving person, like X, I will find it natural to make new friends." Through identification, the mourner finds ways to recover his shaken self-esteem, gain new abilities or strengthen tentative ones.[12]

In "Lycidas," we can see a healing, strengthening identification. Milton identifies with King's youth, his unfulfilled talents, his spiritual virtue, and, most of all, with his being a poet. Much commentary has already been written about this identification, but many critics assume it is "put on": both an exaggeration of King's qualities to make Milton's own seem better, by correspondence, and an over-insistence on similarity, given the differences between the two men. Actually, these seemingly artificial features are quite natural, as identification in mourning does involve idealization and does necessitate unusual attempts to see the dead person reflected in the living. A reading such as the one offered here would propose that King's death was not a mere excuse for Milton to proclaim himself a poet, but an important contributory event in his feeling himself to *be* a poet.

What about scholars' demonstrations that the structure of "Lycidas" is taken from pastoral models? This knowledge does not necessarily contradict a view that the poem's structure follows the stages of grief. First, pastoral conventions may fit perfectly well within this emotional progression. For instance, the procession of mourners (ll. 89–131) appears in accordance with pastoral "rules." It also follows emotional "rules" since, appropriately to the stage in which they appear, the mourners are either under angry attack or are themselves angry. The two sets of "rules" are not mutually contradictory. Second, the structure of monody itself, as enunciated by ancient and Renaissance theorists, may be interpreted to follow the stages of grief, if its terms are thoroughly analyzed. Alternatively, although not quite contrarily, perhaps those departures from his models that Milton has been praised for making are just those leading in the direction of emotional verisimilitude. That is, "Lycidas" may be different from other elegies because of both the *thoroughness* with which it recapitulates the normal stages of mourning and the *depth*. As to the first point, one notes the close fit between "Lycidas" and the model for mourning in contrast to many elegies that, while moving generally from denial to resolution, fail to differentiate clearly between constituent parts of the intervening process. As to the second point, one notices Milton expressing emotions that are as extreme as possible, given cultural convention. He pushes against barriers, for instance, in writing St. Peter's speech, envisioning Lycidas' body among sea monsters, or developing the striking image of resurrection as sunrise. Such pressure to articulate different emotions seems valuable. In explaining why some people go astray from normal mourning and develop pathology, Lindemann says, "One of the big obstacles to [the 'grief work'] seems to be the fact that many [mourners] try to avoid the intense distress connected with the grief experience and to avoid the expression of emotion necessary for it" (143). The farther the poem can push in expressing emotion at each stage, the more satisfying it must seem, for unless a mourner experiences each stage of grief fully, he will not be ready for the next: neither will he be ready for a satisfying life after a loved person's death until the entire grieving process has run its course. Key to "Lycidas'" power, then, is the completeness with which it recapitulates grief, a feature that few other elegies can match, even though in cruder terms their structure may be similar.

Dr. Johnson's scorn for "Lycidas" has brought many rebuttals. Mine, since it is based on terms from outside the field of literature, is meant to suggest new possibilities in helping us better to understand—and explain—why people in all decades since 1638 have found "Lycidas" a deeply moving expression of grief.

Notes

1. "How to Read 'Lycidas,' " *Milton's "Lycidas": The Tradition and the Poem*, ed. C. A. Patrides (New York: Holt, Rinehart and Winston, 1961), p. 94.

2. Quoted by Wayne Shumaker, "Flowerets and Sounding Seas: A Study in the Affective Structure of 'Lycidas,' " *Ibid.*, p. 126.

3. "Literature as Context: Milton's 'Lycidas,' " *Ibid.*, p. 202.

4. "from *Milton,*" *Ibid.*, p. 63; "The Archetypal Pattern of Death and Rebirth in 'Lycidas,' " *Ibid.*, pp. 121–22; "Theme, Pattern, and Imagery in 'Lycidas,' " *Ibid.*, p. 188; [comment from *Milton the Poet*], *Ibid.*, p. 246.

5. The only editor I have found who makes a constant point of noting Milton's attention to emotional verisimilitude is Frank Patterson, *The Student's Milton*, rev. ed. (New York: Appleton-Century-Crofts, Inc., 1933), [Textual Notes] pp. 2, 56–60. Perhaps a reason is that people have only recently overcome cultural taboos and begun talking openly about feelings associated with death.

6. A note on definitions. In the scientific literature, a distinction is often made between "grief" and "mourning," but I do not plan to make a point of it in this paper, because I do not think it is entirely necessary for an "interdisciplinary" audience. Keep in mind throughout that "mourning" nowhere refers to social expressions of grief—funeral ceremonies and rituals of various sorts—but denotes

the emotional and physical changes an individual goes through after the death of a loved person.

7. "Symptomatology and Management of Acute Grief," *American Journal of Psychiatry*, 101 (1944), 141; C. M. Parkes, "Grief as an Illness," *New Society*, 3 (April 9, 1964), 11. (All further references to Lindemann will be to this article, and page numbers will be given in parenthesis after the quotations. Parkes's article will also be cited in the short form in the text.) Differences in mourning according to age, sex, marital situation and a number of other variables are often cited, even though some of these factors have been shown, in experiments, *not* to matter: at any rate, "standard" differences are accepted within the description of mourning proposed. Some anthropological evidence seems to show that the mourning process is invariant across cultures, although this argument has not been presented thoroughly, and, more often, cultural differences in bereavement behavior are noted. (Edmund H. Volkart with Stanley T. Michael, "Bereavement and Mental Health," *Explorations in Social Psychiatry*, eds. A. H. Leighton, J. A. Klausen, & R. N. Wilson [New York: Basic Books, 1957], pp. 281–304). Animal mourning behavior has been studied casually, and observations show a certain similarity between animals and humans that leads to some of the most fascinating considerations in the literature on mourning. John Bowlby mentions them in "Processes of Mourning," *International Journal of Psychoanalysis*, 42 (1961), 317–338. (All further references to Bowlby will be to this article, and page numbers will be given in parentheses after the quotations.) This article is, in my opinion, the clearest and most complete discussion of mourning. Since it incorporates a great deal of the literature, it is the best single source to read, although at sev-

eral points in my paper I have diverged from it. The information it provides will probably be included—and supplemented—in *Loss*, the final volume, soon to be published, of Bowlby's comprehensive series, *Attachment, Separation* and *Loss*.

8. All "Lycidas" quotations are taken from *The Works of John Milton*, ed. Frank Patterson *et al.* (New York: Columbia University Press, 1931–38), I, 76–83.

9. Even one kind of somatic distress doctors link with shock and disbelief—excessive sweating that cycles with a dried-out feeling—comes into the poem through the references to salt water and parching wind. The image of a blundering young poet with crude and disruptive fingers reminds us of another somatic symptom: lack of muscular coordination.

10. G. L. Engle, *Psychological Development in Health and Disease* (Philadelphia: W. B. Saunders, 1962), p. 275.

11. I use these examples simply because they are familiar to us, not because I think Edward King's stature equalled theirs.

12. Discussion of identification in mourning is particulary interesting, since it is the focus for much disagreement among analysts. The best summaries of the controversy are in Bowlby and in David K. Switzer, *The Dynamics of Grief* (Nashville and New York: The Abingdon Press, 1970), Chapter 2. Two classic sources are Sigmund Freud, "Mourning and Melancholia," *The Standard Edition of the Complete Psychological Works of Sigmund Freud*, ed. James Stachey et al., 24 vols. (London: Hogarth Press, 1953–74), XIV, 243–58; Melaine Klein, "Mourning and Its Relation to Manic-Depressive States," *International Journal of Psychoanalysis*, 21 (1940), 126.

Application

Truth in Conrad's Darkness

Walter J. Ong, S.J.

In what ways does the literary work relate to the world outside of literature, and how does it tell us the truth about that world? As Walter J. Ong demonstrates, with a story as complex and multilayered as Heart of Darkness *the ways can be many and various. From one perspective, the actions, characters, and setting are symbols in a psychodrama. From another perspective, these elements tie the work to the specific historical conditions of its creation. Eagleton's concern with the work's relationship to the ideology of its age stresses one aspect of this "historicity," an aspect that Ong also acknowledges. In yet another view, however, the work transcends its own time, not only by representing perennial human conflicts and concerns, but in this case by revealing "a network of human activities which have been generating certain human problems or issues, issues slowly breaking through the disguises in which at first, and necessarily, they had presented themselves to the human psyche, among them issues which we have latterly learned to label colonialism, racism, and antifeminism." On these matters, Ong claims, the story presents insights that neither Conrad nor his first readers could recognize quite as consciously as we do. In all these ways, and in others,* Heart of Darkness *tells us important truths. It is consistent with Conrad's layered ironies and paradoxical reversals that Ong should find many of these truths summed up in Marlow's lie.*

Reprinted by permission from *Mosaic* 11 (1977): 151–63. Copyright © 1977 by *Mosaic*.

I

Conrad's truth lies deep, and perhaps nowhere deeper than in *Heart of Darkness*. Many of Conrad's stories turn on the protagonist's facing up to a deep truth previously masked by a lie or a cover-up—*Lord Jim* or *The Secret Sharer* or *The Secret Agent*. Others, for example *The Nigger of the Narcissus*, center on what may or may not be a lie: the reader is not sure and, it seems, neither is the protagonist himself. But no other Conrad story deals with truth and lying more explicitly and integrally and climactically than does *Heart of Darkness*.

Nor does any other deal more integrally and profoundly with self-discovery. Confrontation of essential truth and integration of one's real self are two sides of the same coin in Conrad's stories. For Conrad truth is a kind of totality, a whole, binding together exterior and interior. The binding goes on at all levels and pitches, conscious and subconscious and unconscious, articulate and inarticulate, public and private. Moreover, confrontation and self-integration take place not in a world of mere fancy but in a world shaped by history. Any real, nonfictional human being always achieves his or her identity in a historical matrix, in a situation in a particular time and a particular place. In his fiction, however inobtrusively, Conrad abundantly registers this fact of human historicity.

Marlow's identity crisis in *Heart of Darkness* has a time, the late nineteenth century, and a locale, the Congo basin in Central Africa as recollected in England on a ship tied up at the mouth of the Thames. Marlow's world and Marlow's story exist in a network of human activities which have been generating certain human problems or issues, issues slowly breaking through the disguises in which at first, and necessarily, they had presented themselves to the human psyche, among them issues which we have latterly learned to label colonialism, racism, and antifeminism. Today these same issues have surfaced even more conspicuously in consciousness. The past decade has brought home quite explicitly and dramatically, not to say historically, how they touch the identity both of social groups and of individual persons across the globe today. Marlow's involvement in such issues, though in part veiled, is far from incidental: these were becoming more and more issues which one had somehow to face if one wanted to be a human being, and they enmesh the truth which Marlow undertakes to convey.

Marlow's involvement in these issues, especially the first two, is in fact often quite conscious, but less conscious than the present day would call for in similar circumstances. For Hegel was right: everything does become more and more explicit as history moves on. What gives Conrad's sparse story its gargantuan psychological force is the fact that it operates precisely on the front where issues previously lodged in the unconscious are moving into consciousness, where the implicit is becoming explicit, both individually and collectively. Because he operates on this front—and in many other stories besides *Heart of Darkness*, though never more actively than here—like many good, and some bad, writers and artists, Conrad can be prescient: mankind's shaping of consciousness out of the unconscious in time, which is what history ultimately deals with, can take place to some degree in Conrad's fiction before it does in real life. This is not to say that colonialism, racism, and antifeminism are exactly what *Heart of Darkness* is "about," but only that Marlow's and Conrad's truth lies deep, and that whatever the story is "about," the reader finds himself involved in such issues if he wants really to appropriate the narrative. In the present discussion of Conrad's and Marlow's truth, these issues will thus frequently surface.

II

The resolution of the story in *Heart of Darkness* is in many ways enigmatic, yet it has commonly been understood that the climactic statement about Kurtz's last words, made in Marlow's re-port to Kurtz's fiancée, Kurtz's "Intended," is essential to what the tale is "about" and that this statement was an out-and-out lie. But was it? The question will lead into the issues just mentioned—colonialism, racism, antifeminism—into them and out again.

At first blush, Marlow's final report to Kurtz's "Intended" indeed appears to be a lie, and conspicuously a lie. From Conrad's text the reader learns how Marlow tells the Intended, anxious, expectant, poised in well-gowned mourning in the lofty European drawing-room, that Kurtz's last word was her name, whereas the reader knows from Marlow's earlier account that Kurtz's last words in fact had been "The horror! The horror!" But lies come cheap and they are not essentially moving. The climactic effect of this closing incident in Marlow's tale cannot be explained in terms of a simple lapse into dishonesty on Marlow's part. If this is a lie, it is not any old lie. The effect of Marlow's reply, felt by the reader for the most part subconsciously, comes largely from the shocking equivalence which the reply establishes: Marlow has interchanged the cry "The horror! The horror!" and the name of Kurtz's fiancée—and done so without ever pronouncing her name, which he refers to only as "your name" and which consequently Marlow's hearers and Conrad's readers never do learn. The name of the Intended remains a permanent blank in the story, a blank which can only be filled in by "The horror! The horror!"

This substitution is of course exquisite irony. But at what level? In this story irony is the rule, and any interpretation risks oversimplicity. Even more than most narratives of Conrad's this one is delivered layer within layer, Conrad's own sensibility encasing Conrad's persona or narrator's voice, whose story encases Marlow's, which in turn encases Kurtz's story, itself first delivered in snatches to Marlow by a medley of exiled voices and finally distorted by the voice of the girl, projecting Kurtz in her own way.

Heart of Darkness consists of a web of voices, of cries and responses, often explicitly called to the reader's attention to establish multi-layered involvement and mystery. Kurtz first enters the story through the voices of others: Marlow muses, "He was just a voice for me" (p. 22).[1]

When Kurtz appears, his voice takes over in a world of many voices: "He was very little more than a voice. And I heard—him—it—this voice—other voices—all of them were so little more than voices" (p. 40). "You don't talk with that man [Kurtz]—you listen to him" (p. 44). "We talked of everything" (p. 46). "A deep voice [of the ailing Kurtz, at Marlow's first encounter with him] reached me faintly" (p. 50). And so on and on. Has anyone counted the times voice is mentioned in the story? "A voice! A voice! It rang deep to the very last" (p. 57). Kurtz's last recorded act is his final utterance. Kurtz is dead, Marlow goes on eating his dinner. "The voice was gone. What else had been there?" (p. 59). More than a year after Kurtz's death, asked by the girl what Kurtz's last words were, Marlow thinks of her present sorrow as coinciding in time with Kurtz's dying voice: "I saw them to-gether—I heard them together" (p. 63). Then Marlow speaks the crucial words.

At the same time, voice is not all. At points, visual impressions compete with auditory and other, or dominate the narrative. The story is set in light and dark polarities, as critics have uniformly noted. Through the closing scene especially, Marlow's encounter with Kurtz's fiancée, the reader is explicitly and repeatedly made to attend to darkness, light, dusk, luminosity, murkiness, and a host of other light–dark qualities. The title of the story flits all through the text (e.g., p. 29), but especially toward the end: "the beating of a heart—the heart of a conquering darkness" (p. 62), "panic in my heart . . . the room was growing darker . . . darkness deepened" (p. 63). With its closing words, "into the heart of an immense darkness" (p. 65), the narrative enters forever into the mystery announced by its title.

On the surface Kurtz's adventure had appeared simply enough: serving commercial interests, he goes, an extraordinarily talented and engaging European, to the then Belgian Congo, where, indulging what today might be described as an "ego trip," he deteriorates morally, "goes native," is brought back seriously ill from his station in the interior, and dies, expressing with his last words the horror of the state of soul in which he ultimately finds himself. Marlow's part appears also simple enough

on the surface: coming to the Congo, he hears of and meets Kurtz, empathizes with Kurtz's deathbed expression of horror, and lies to Kurtz's fiancée to keep her from becoming aware, uselessly, of Kurtz's moral collapse. But the echoing of voices and the constant chiaroscuro in the imagery of the narrative hint that all is not so straightforward: being a European and "going native" are both puzzling routines and at points blur with each other. It is the Thames, where Marlow and his listeners had shipped and were awaiting the turn of the tide, not the Congo, that flows at the end of the story "into the heart of an immense darkness." The Thames slips into the sea, where its waters and those of the Congo are one. The last message to the reader is that the whole business of the narrative is enigmatic. Ford Madox Ford has rehearsed how he anguished with Conrad over the exact wording of the final paragraph of this tale, a paragraph which Ford believed was the finest thing in all of Conrad's early work.[2]

Conrad's own suggested hermeneutic for dealing with the enigma of his tale is itself paradoxical, for, though a secret or a mystery or an enigma is normally inwardness, Conrad's persona—the narrator who tells about Marlow and retells Marlow's story—says that Marlow's enigmas have their explanations not within themselves but without. To Marlow, as we read at the beginning of the story, "the meaning of an episode was not inside like a kernel, but outside, enveloping the tale which brought it out only as a glow brings out a haze" (p. 3). Kurtz's Intended is in a curious way the haze outside, which the narrative illuminates. Far beyond Africa, in the lofty European drawing room, Marlow meets her when "the dusk was falling" (p. 62). Within Conrad's hermeneutic, her physical setting is an obvious analogue for her role in the narrative: she catches the glow of the tale. The figure of the Intended concentrates the meaning of Africa and of Kurtz—and, more significantly, of Marlow. For this story, as Albert Guérard has correctly pointed out, is not about Africa or Kurtz or Kurtz's fiancée, but about Marlow himself.[3]

Illuminated, the Intended is still hazy. Still, she reveals meanings—hazily. This she does chiefly because of the context of the question she puts to Marlow and because of the answer she elicits from him. And the paradox of paradoxes here—absolutely crucial in the story's depths, though unnoticed I believe by commentators thus far, perhaps because Western eyes turned to Africa have been so pitifully clouded, even Conrad's consciously controlled eyes, though his heart, his unconscious, was dead right—is that, however it may appear at the surface or just beneath the outermost wrappings, Marlow's response to her, his last recorded words to her, his assurance to her that Kurtz's final utterance was her name, at its deepest level was not a lie at all. It was in itself the starkest truth, but, in the story, veiled. By what? Almost everything, in the story and outside.

III

Throughout his story Marlow worries about lies, lies in general and lies in particular. About a third of the way into the story he talks about an earlier near-lie which Kurtz evoked from him. "I would not have gone so far as to fight for Kurtz, but I went for him near enough to a lie. You know I hate, detest, and can't bear a lie, not because I am straighter than the rest of us, but simply because it appalls me. There is a taint of death, a flavor of mortality in lies" (p. 22). In this early incident Marlow does not lie outright, but he allows the Central Station brickmaker, vaguely Kurtz's rival, to conclude falsely regarding his, Marlow's, own influence in Europe.

Two-thirds of the way through the story Marlow's detestation of lies comes up in full force again, and this time with an explicit statement that he lied at the end to Kurtz's Intended. "I laid the ghost of his gifts at last with a lie" (p. 40). The lie he rationalizes to a degree. The girl to whom he told the lie was "out of it," fittingly and compellingly. "They—the women I mean— are out of it—should be out of it. We must help them to stay in that beautiful world of their own, lest ours gets worse" (p. 40).

This sounds like male insecurity, and of course it is. The obtrusion of male insecurity, here as elsewhere through Conrad's narratives, is significant, for male insecurity is one of the most easily identifiable shadows of the uncon-

scious, which is where the action is for Marlow and Conrad, as Albert Guérard again has made exquisitely clear. Marlow's final response to the Intended, like the whole of the narrative, leads undeviatingly into the unconscious, ontogenetic (Marlow's own) and philogenetic (Europeans' or whites' generally).

Delving into the unconscious, which means lifting parts of the unconscious into consciousness, can be confounding and even terrifying, but it is also humanizing. It reveals to us some of our complexities. In this story Africa stands for the unconscious. But this means that, paradoxically, for Europeans Africa is civilizing and humanizing because it is bewildering in its special way. Conrad himself testified to the effect of his African experience on his own unconscious and consciousness: "Before the Congo I was just a mere animal."[4] (So of course was Kurtz, and so was Marlow). It is hardly surprising, and indeed is inevitable, that the journey into the unconscious involves, among other dialectics, the dialectic of masculine and feminine, in terms of which the growth of the conscious out of the unconscious can so largely be plotted. Kurtz's Intended, both as a stay-at-home European and as a woman in Marlow's (and Conrad's) almost entirely male world, cuts across the unconscious depths of the story in such a way as to climax and interpret or illuminate Marlow's grasp of the issues and of himself.

IV

To assess in Marlow's encounter with the Intended his avoidance of Kurtz's last words, we have to ask more specifically what "the horror" was that elicited Kurtz's dying outcry and how deep it went. "The horror" involved a good many interrelated things, as the wealth of critical literature has detailed. First of all, it referred to the bad features of colonialism, its avarice and exploitation and all that went with these in many Europeans, including the worst brutality. The horror included, besides, Kurtz's personal reaction to Africa, his participation in European brutality, his self-aggrandisement, but it also included, along with the repulsive features of European behavior, various repulsive features of African behavior. The brutality both of Europeans to Africans and of Africans to Africans was symbolized by the human heads which Kurtz had stuck on posts around his residence. Kurtz was involved at both ends, European and African. "All Europe contributed to the making of Kurtz," Marlow says (p. 41), and this same Kurtz had interacted with aspects of African culture because it was what it was as well as because of the way Europe had trained him.

The horror that Kurtz faced ultimately was not merely the outside, where the two cultures could be conveniently differentiated, but more devastatingly, the devious human reality, the self-deception regarding both inside and outside lodged in the interior of his own Europeo-African self. This self-deception had got him involved in the external world the way he had been involved, and it could not be purified by any amount of high-minded, idealistic rhetoric, either in his spellbinding talk with others or in his ambitious report to the International Society for the Suppression of Savage Customs, a report "vibrating with eloquence, but too high-strung," Marlow notes (p. 41). The report revealed the true state of affairs: its altruistic sentiments went up in smoke with the final outburst of hatred appended by Kurtz impulsively on his last page, an outburst, Marlow comments, "luminous and terrifying, like a flash of lightning in a serene sky: 'Exterminate all the brutes!' " (p. 42). In one of its guises "the horror" was ultimately Kurtz's earlier, deluded, narcissistic self, and the violence it had both succumbed to and wreaked because it itself contained violence.

Whether Kurtz's final avowal of the horror represented some kind of final redemption need not concern us here, though it has concerned a good many commentators on the story. Marlow describes Kurtz's avowal of horror complexly. It was "the expression of some sort of belief; it had candor, it had conviction, it had a vibrating note of revolt in its whisper, it had the appalling face of a glimpsed truth—the strange commingling of desire and hate" (p. 59). Recognition of the truth is at least initial conversion, or change, from which redemption can start. In recognizing the horror within himself, Kurtz had countered

it in some measure at least. And what Kurtz here at least began, Marlow completed. For Marlow himself had the time, as Kurtz did not, to work out and live with a changed awareness.

Though Kurtz is a real person distinct from Marlow, Marlow in a way is Kurtz and Kurtz Marlow, as critics have often observed. Marlow's story is the account of how he entered into Kurtz's experience, partly in actuality by visiting some of the same places, seeing some of the same people, and partly vicariously, empathetically. Like other Conrad characters, such as the stowaway in the captain's cabin in *The Secret Sharer*, Kurtz is an alter ego, a *Doppelgänger* of the story's protagonist, here Marlow. He is the incarnation of Marlow's Jungian shadow, the unconscious opposite or the foil of Marlow's consciously programmed self. Marlow is simultaneously repelled and attracted by Kurtz, and in Kurtz by the Africa in which Kurtz submerged himself and lost himself and at long last found himself, or at least made it possible for Marlow to find himself.

Marlow had gone to Africa for reasons which he could not fully articulate but which, Conrad signals, were certainly connected with his childhood and the process of self-discovery, of moving unconscious materials into consciousness. From his childhood he had had a passion for maps, Marlow tells his auditors (p. 5). Maps, it should be noted (for Conrad does not say this), are guides to the unknown: what is perfectly known requires no map. Marlow's childhood passion attached itself particularly to the unexplored areas indicated on maps (the most unknown unknown) and his passion had cooled as explorations had filled in the blanks (p. 5) and also as Marlow got older. He had developed a particular passion for Africa because it was to the European consciousness the least known of all large populated areas, "a place of darkness" (unknowing, the unconscious). His passion for Africa centered on Africa's "mighty big river . . . resembling an immense snake uncoiled, with its head in the sea . . . its tail lost in the depths of the land. . . . It fascinated me as a snake would a bird." (The place of the snake in the archetypal life of the unconscious and the meaning of this uncoiled, strungout uroboric figure demand more commentary than can be afforded here. From its source to its debouchement into the sea, the Congo describes the greater part of a circle, suggesting more than any other great river does, the ouroboros, the snake with its tail in its mouth.) Going to the Congo became an obsession of Marlow's after his return from some years in the East. He "could not shake off the idea," he says, "The snake had charmed me" (p. 6).

Marlow goes to Africa, "the biggest, the most blank" (p. 5) of the many then empty places on the map that he had dreamed as a boy of exploring, unconsciously expecting to encounter not only the darkness without but also the darkness within, the hidden reaches of self. The emptiness or blankness on a map has no counterpart in the external reality the map represents, for real space is not empty but full: the emptiness of the map is an emptiness in the mind, a psychic void, or darkness. Marlow's preoccupation with his own problems, which encouraged him to zero in on Africa, not surprisingly colors everything he sees, hears, or does in Africa. There Kurtz's character and actions in particular remain a blend of specifically reported or observed phenomena and of Marlow's own expectations or projections.

By far most of Marlow's contacts with Kurtz are indirect, mediated by others—in stories, in responses to his own anxious questions, in mementos or souvenirs of various sorts, including bits of personal property left by Kurtz at his death—and thus readily subject to Marlow's own interpretation, to accommodation to his own needs. Marlow did not just run across Kurtz. He zeroed in on him, as he had zeroed in on Africa. He first gets involved with Kurtz not because he has heard anything about him but because he notices "a small sketch in oils, on a panel, representing a woman, draped and blindfolded, carrying a lighted torch. The background was somber—almost black. The movement of the woman was stately, and the effect of the torch-light on the face was sinister" (p. 20). Asking who painted the picture, he is told that it was a Mr. Kurtz. And from this point on, as he was earlier "hooked" on Africa, so he is now "hooked" on Kurtz. What hooked him was

not Kurtz himself at all, but a painting of a woman, and apparently not even a distinctive painting, but rather a conventional, archetypal one, a painting of the "dark lady." Kurtz has put in his appearance—or nonappearance—properly veiled in archetypal mystery.

The meaning here, as at the end of the story, is enshrouded in a female figure. This figure is enveloped in darkness. Later, Kurtz's African mistress is seen by Marlow in the same trappings and aura. At the close of Marlow's narrative, the figure of the Intended similarly appears against a less dark background, not in daylight but in "the dusk," a feminine figure, stately, "floating towards me," no longer entirely the dark lady, but only dark-eyed with "fair hair" (pp. 62–63), seeming "surrounded by an ashy halo" and revealing "all the remaining light" in the dusk—and also in the story, for she is the outside which, as we have seen, explicates the story's inwardness. When the two figures are juxtaposed thus starkly here, the contrast between them appears heavy-handed. In the course of the story it is not so at all. Nothing is more natural than archetypes. And of course it is not at all necessary that Conrad should have adverted consciously to the contrast. He might have noted it consciously before he wrote it out (unlikely, from his own accounts of his mode of composition), or while he wrote it, or afterwards, or not at all.

From the encounter with the oil painting Marlow works his way deliberately to its painter, Kurtz, inquiring about him, avidly seizing on others' conversation about him, cherishing chance impressions, dreaming of what Kurtz will be like when he meets him. As the "grimy beetle," the river steamboat, crawls upstream, Marlow muses: "Where the pilgrims imagined it crawled to I don't know. To some place where they expected to get something. . . . For me it crawled towards Kurtz—exclusively" (p. 29). He hears rumors of Kurtz's death (p. 39), which prove false. From the harlequin Russian adventurer and others he learns of Kurtz's "unspeakable" deeds, his raids on the country for ivory, his lording it over the Africans and their apotheosis of him. He is assured by the Russian that "You can't judge Mr. Kurtz as you would an ordinary man" (p. 47). And finally he meets Kurtz, carried onto the steamboat mortally ill, looking preternaturally tall laid out on the litter, gaunt, his mouth agape—and quite unromantically bald. On the steamboat he talks to Kurtz, but he never witnesses any "unspeakable deeds" other than Kurtz's leaving his sickbed on the steamboat in an attempt, which Marlow thwarts, to join in a night tribal ritual of some sort.

Marlow interprets this attempt as something very sinister, although there appears no really clear evidence that it is so at all. Conrad does not advert explicitly to the fact, but the night is long all year round near the equator. Twelve hours of each day are without the sun—and consequently a great deal of African village social life is normally lived at night, for agricultural peoples and herdsmen need the daylight to work. Every gathering at night under such circumstances is hardly automatically sinister, even if a mask appears—yet Marlow conjecturally interprets the figure wearing antelope horns as "fiend-like" (p. 55). This is not to say that Kurtz was not at some point involved in "unspeakable deeds," but it is to say that, so far as the story tells, Marlow knew of them only at second hand and by empathetic identification with Kurtz, and that Marlow very likely exaggerated them. Marlow was fascinated by "unspeakable deeds" first, only secondly by Kurtz as an emanating source for them. From all sides, Marlow gathered loads of reports on Kurtz, but engaged in almost no direct observation of his activities. He is told by the Russian that Kurtz had ordered the attack on his steamboat by warriors who killed his helmsman. But had he? The Russian was emotionally overcharged and unreliable, and so were other informants, more or less.

Kurtz satisfied Marlow's needs so well that the line between actuality and Marlow's psychological projections becomes very thin. As Marlow goes to retrieve Kurtz when the latter is en route to the night rendezvous, the beat of the drum sounds sinister, yet, Marlow observes, "I remember I confounded the beat of the drum with the beating of my heart" (p. 54). He never betrayed to others in the party Kurtz's attempt to join the night ritual (though he had avidly

hung on the words of anyone who would detail to him Kurtz's other aberrations). "It was ordered I should never betray him—it was written I should be loyal to the nightmare of my choice. I was anxious to deal with this shadow by myself alone" (p. 54—the suggestion of a Jungian kind of awareness is evident here: as noted earlier, Kurtz is Marlow's Jungian "shadow" or nightmare). Though Kurtz is a real problem to himself, he is certainly also Marlow's problem, or better, Marlow's project.

By the time he meets Kurtz, Marlow is well on the way to acquiring an empathetic identification with Africans allied to Kurtz's own. As the steamboat moves up the river, African dancers on the shore fascinate and appall and frighten him. "They howled and leaped, and spun, and made horrid faces" (p. 29). But he feels intensely a "remote kinship with this wild and passionate uproar" (p. 29), sensing that there is in the noise "a meaning . . . which you—you so remote from the night of first ages—could comprehend" (p. 30). There is of course a great deal of projection here: descriptions of Conrad's (Marlow's) sort sound quaint today when compared with the understanding descriptions now provided by anthropologists or by non-African Christian missionaries who have totally identified with their African peoples, or by African university professors who have grown up in villages in the interior of Zaire and from childhood have experienced the feelings humanly associated with these dances. But besides projecting, Marlow is also empathizing and identifying. To find the truth in the African dance, he observes, a man "must at least be as much of a man as these on the shore" (p. 30). Africa was changing Marlow, educating him, maturing his European psyche, just as Europe was maturing the African psyche in contact with it. The closed-system paradigm for cultures favored in the past—the false paradigm of integral and isolated culture commemorated in Gibbon's vision of a Rome that "fell" by losing its (imputed, projected) integrity, that lost its soul by entering into contact with the rest of mankind—is being abandoned here in favor of an open-system paradigm. Or, in another way, consciousness is allowing the unconscious freer entry into consciousness, and even doing so rather consciously.

V

In "The horror!" Kurtz had faced the truth at last—about Europe, about Africa, and mostly about himself as he related, and belonged, to both continents. Marlow had not only faced this same truth, helped by Africa itself and also by Kurtz himself and by his own projections concerning Kurtz, but had also continued to live, as Kurtz had not, and thus had come to experience deep within himself the change which the truth had wrought. Man—not African man or European man, but mankind, all of it, men, women, children—is deep and dark and dangerous from within, and more so if a person does not recognize this fact openly. The old narcissistic threat had been met by Kurtz, and met and lived with, if not totally conquered, by Marlow—one of the lessons of maturity being that this threat is never quite conquered. How about Kurtz's Intended? Had she responded to the same threat, and if so, how?

Marlow's encounter with Kurtz's Intended reveals in her a conspicuous narcissism, understandable, but real and hardly admirable. In response to her initial remark, Marlow states that "Intimacy grows quickly out there" and adds, "I knew him as well as it is possible for one man to know another." Almost immediately, however, she rejoins that "no one knew him so well as I! I had all his noble confidence. I knew him best" (p. 63). To which Marlow echoes, wisely, "You knew him best." The girl comes back, "I am proud to know I understood him better than anyone on earth—he told me so himself." And soon, "What a loss to me—to us . . . To the world" (p. 64). In that order. Other equally self-conscious remarks follow: "He needed me! Me!" "Nobody near to understands him as I would have understood." And when Marlow tells her, "The last word he pronounced was—your name," she cries, "I knew it—I was sure" (p. 65). The self-concern is quite understandable, but it is hardly balanced with much evident concern about Kurtz himself, questions about what he underwent, his last illness—at least not as Marlow tells her story, but this is a story, not

history, and her character is fitted to the fiction and it to her.

Why did Marlow at all bring up the fact that he had heard Kurtz's last words? For it was he who brought it up. His doing so appears senseless. "Perhaps no one to hear . . . ," the girl had broken off, and Marlow filled in "To the very end," adding immediately, "I heard his very last words." And at this he "stopped in a fright." Consciously he had of course not wanted to mention the real words to her, and hence should have been on his guard against saying that he had heard them. But something in the whole situation had countered his conscious designs.

It was impossible not to think of Kurtz's last words when one was talking to this girl. For she, too, was Kurtz, as Marlow had been. She, too, had projected herself onto Kurtz, taken him to serve her needs, had in fact needed him far more than even she could believe he needed her. Deep down, Marlow would have to be profoundly concerned with what would happen if he should tell her Kurtz's exact words. They had marked the moment of truth for Kurtz. They had marked the moment of truth for Marlow and had changed his life for good. Would they do the same for the Intended? Marlow could not avoid this at least unconscious issue. If he was Kurtz and she was Kurtz, she too needed the words. Should he utter the words for their therapeutic value? Marlow had every reason to believe that the words "The horror!" would not help the girl—though perhaps some of his reasons may have related to his own male insecurity, his resentment of womanly self-possession. And so he said, "The last word he pronounced was—your name."

At first blush, this presents itself as a lie, a lack of conformity of words to truth. But in a deeper sense, it was not a lie at all, but the starkest veracity: for there is a sense, a real sense, as I hope is clear by now, in which what Kurtz said, "The horror! The horror!" was truly her name. If the horror that Kurtz faced and acknowledged was the human reality, the interior of his own self with propensity to self-deception and thus its collusion with all sorts of external insensitivity and brutality, there appeared an example of just that horror in his Intended. Of course, perhaps again we might have here a projection of Marlow's own insecurity. Maybe Kurtz's Intended was tougher than Marlow could afford to think. But her narcissism—so notable, even though under the circumstances, hardly conspicuously offensive—gives strong indication that she could not have taken the direct answer. Marlow was probably responding correctly. She had not, after all, had the good fortune to have had her horizons enlarged beyond the experiences for which her culture had directly prepared her, as both Kurtz and Marlow had had theirs enlarged by being in Africa.

And so Horror was her name: she was the unregenerate Kurtz and Marlow. Significantly, as noted here at the start, nowhere in the story is her real name mentioned. She is simply the external incarnation which sets off the interiority of the tale. For she is exterior not only to the African experience. She is also exterior to the entire arena of action in the narration, for the story is one of interior conversion, and her interior remains unchanged, untouched. Were she to go to Africa in her state of mind, she could be expected to be the feminine counterpart of the atrocious Kurtz. She is the Western consciousness without self-knowledge.

VI

The validity of this interpretation does not of course depend on Conrad's conscious intent to make Marlow's "lie" a deep truth or even on his ever being consciously aware of the possibility of this interpretation. Fully honest, or almost fully honest stories, stories which are not kitsch, speak their truths at depths which their authors never command in full consciousness. At his best, Conrad could be so deep into truth that the truth would speak for itself, though not without the exquisitely painstaking work by which the author had felt his way into the total situation. Presumably, of course, had Conrad consciously adverted to this implication of his tale—as of course he well may have—he would have agreed with it. No more than this is being claimed here for authorial involvement.

The persuasion that this deeper interpretation, perhaps present to the author only implicitly and darkly, can be made visible invites two other questions concerning related possible

implications of *Heart of Darkness*. Is it antifeminist? And is it racist? Both these questions are involved in the matter of Marlow's "lie," and they must be dealt with, as the question of the "lie" must be dealt with, on unconscious at least as much as on conscious grounds.

At the depths which Conrad reaches in this story, it would be pretty difficult to be antifeminist in any ultimate sense. At these depths, secrets tend to be bared, and whatever antifeminism appears immediately invites interpretation as a projection of insecurity, mostly male insecurity. That is to say, whatever persona or voice or behavior manifests, antifeminist sentiment evokes from the attentive reader not concurrence in antifeminism but understanding, conscious or unconscious, of that weakness in the given character which occasions the antifeminism that the character manifests. Irony becomes awesomely comprehensive at these depths: flaws even in the ultimate authorial voice appear as such, so that even the conscious intent of the author is not to be accepted uncritically.

There is no doubt that Marlow—who is not even the ultimate authorial voice, but a voice within a voice (Conrad's narrator persona) within a voice (Conrad's own)—is somewhat antifeminist, seemingly in about the way in which his age in general was: the authority of mother in childhood (and thus in adulthood, *mutatis mutandis*) was overpowering enough in the culture generally to evoke widespread defenses against femininity on the part of men and women both. Marlow's vocally condescending attitude, more or less normative for his age, toward women in general—they are "out of it"—reveals its roots when we note his obvious awe in the presence of individual female figures such as Kurtz's African mistress, or Kurtz's European Intended, or even the mere painting of the dark lady. His statement that women are "out of it" is asseveration or protestation rather than conviction. It is charged with nervous anxiety and overassertiveness. Marlow's investment in keeping women "out of it" is less in the naked truth than in his own identity. His antifeminism, which on the whole is mild enough, given its cultural setting, hints nevertheless at his own insecurity. Since this insecurity is much of what the tale is about, the antifeminism which appears in the tale is not an attitude the sensitive reader is urged to adopt but some of the evidence he is encouraged to weigh. In this sense, antifeminism is hardly advocated or promoted by the tale.

Similar strictures have to be put on any racism showing in the story. In its deepest sense, the story is not racist but antiracist. The brutality of Africans, extending even to cannibalism, is matched by the brutality of Europeans. Marlow feels a deep kinship, terrifying and exhilarating, with the wildly dancing tribesmen. His helmsman is a second-rate person compared to the cannibal crewmen, for the helmsman had become detached from his own culture without being really engrafted in another. By contrast, the nonacculturated crewmen were "men one could work with" (p. 28). Even so, the helmsman is also regarded with some respect: indeed, he, too, like Kurtz, is a kind of alter ego for Marlow—what Marlow might have been, or maybe was—that is to say, uprooted. In the long run, Africa and Africans would call for scorn in the story only on the part of those who scorn the unconscious or fear it. For in this story, as has been seen, Africa is the unconscious (as it need not be, of course, in other stories), Europe is the conscious. The story is a put-down of the conscious rather more than of the unconscious.

One of the truths conveyed in the tale is that consciousness has as many seeds of evil in it as the subconscious or the unconscious does, if not more. The unconscious is not completely to be trusted either, but when the tally is all in, the unconscious does appear in the story to have a certain edge over the conscious in at least some conspicuous ways. Insofar as she can be judged by the meager clues we are given, Kurtz's African mistress certainly comes across as a more integral person and stronger woman, more outgoing as well as more self-contained, than the European Intended. At both the conscious and the unconscious level, however, it must be finally admitted, the negative elements in Afro-European relationships are played up in this story, the many positive achievements on both sides hardly adverted to. But you cannot write about everything at once, and no one would want too much contrast in a story which conveys so strongly as this one does a definite mood. As Heidegger has observed, it is with a mood that thinking begins.

Notes

1. All page references here are to Leonard F. Dean (ed.), *Joseph Conrad's Heart of Darkness: Backgrounds and Criticism* (Englewood Cliffs, N.J., 1960).

2. Ford Madox Ford, "Conrad at Work," in Leonard F. Dean (ed.), op. cit., pp. 130–32—from Ford Madox Ford, *Portraits from Life* (Boston, 1937).

3. *Conrad the Novelist* (Cambridge, Mass., 1958), p. 33.

4. Georges Jean-Aubry, *Joseph Conrad: Life and Letters* (Garden City, N.Y., 1927), I, 141.

Chapter Five

Intertextual Criticism: Literature as Context

Be *Homer's* Works your *Study*, and *Delight*,
Read them by Day, and meditate by Night
Pope, *Essay on Criticism*

Poems do not imitate life; they imitate other poems. This is the central idea of the perspective I have labeled "intertextual criticism," a perspective that says the poem can best be understood by seeing it in the larger contexts of the linguistic and literary conventions it employs. Unless we know these, says the intertextualist, we can't know the poem at all. Not all of the many critics who have adopted this perspective consider themselves members of the same critical school, and perhaps only a few would answer to the name I have given to their approach. I can only plead that no other term would meet with greater recognition. And this is odd, because the approach itself has a history as old and as rich as any other. But this approach has never had a widely accepted label, and often has had no label at all. Northrop Frye states the case, and the problem, in his essay on *Lycidas* that appears later in this section:

> In the writing of *Lycidas* there are four creative principles of particular importance. . . . One is convention, the reshaping of the poetic material which is appropriate to this subject. Another is genre, the choosing of the appropriate form. A third is archetype, the use of appropriate, and therefore recurrently employed, images and symbols. The fourth, for which

there is no name, is the fact that the forms of literature are autonomous: that is, they do not exist outside of literature. Milton is not writing an obituary: he does not start with Edward King and his life and times, but with the conventions and archetypes that poetry requires for such a theme.

This fourth principle, "for which there is no name," includes the other three; to name it is to name the entire context. But critics have failed to agree on an appropriate label.

To supply this lack, some have tried to promote one of the other words to the status of cover term, and here again each label tells us something about the interests of this perspective. So we hear, for example, of "genre criticism," and clearly any conception of genre does fall within this context. But as a cover term, "genre criticism" has two drawbacks. First, it suggests to many minds a rigid and even hierarchic conception of discrete forms and a concern with arid distinctions parodied in Polonius's pedantic taxonomy: "tragedy, comedy, history, pastoral, pastoral-comical, historical-pastoral, tragical-historical, tragical-comical-historical-pastoral." This reaction may be prejudice, but it is strong enough to erode the usefulness of the term. More importantly, the concept "genre" is itself reducible to an indefinite number of conventions by which we recognize the various "kinds" of literature. Consequently, many critics can operate in this context without being directly concerned with "genre" in the usual sense of the word.

The word *archetype* offers another possibility, and Frye himself is often called an "archetypal" or a "myth" critic. Some justification exists for these terms if they are understood to have the special meanings Frye sometimes gives them. Unfortunately, Frye uses the term *myth* in several different senses and, even more confusing, it has long been used to label critical approaches very different from his own. *Archetype* presents similar problems. Frye's sense of "recurrently employed images and symbols" clearly fits the context I am describing here, though, like "genre," it too seems reducible to "convention." But the chief difficulty is that *archetype* inevitably suggests to many readers the very different Jungian sense of the word. The fact that Frye is

still often classed with "myth" critics or with "archetypal" critics of a Jungian persuasion shows that these labels are likely to cause confusion.

There remains, then, the basic term "convention." Archetype, in Frye's sense, and "genre" as well, are simply elaborations of this more fundamental concept. And a concern with the conventional aspects of art is indeed the characteristic feature of the criticism we are here describing. All art, in this view, is conventional, and any work of art can be understood only by those who know the conventions it employs. So it would be both accurate and appropriate to call this approach "conventional" criticism. I can think of only one disadvantage to this name: the obvious and fatal one that "conventional" criticism, like "conventional" wisdom, will be taken to mean the dull, the ordinary, the uninspired, approach to literature, and that would be neither accurate nor appropriate. Convention, nevertheless, remains the key concept. Our understanding of a particular work is an analogical process by which we measure its conformity to the linguistic and literary conventions we know. The conformity, of course, is never absolute; in this sense each work is "unique." Yet, if the work were totally unique, if it used no conventions we knew, it would be simply unintelligible. This is the primary reason I have labeled the approach to literature by way of its conventional elements an "intertextual" approach.

The term has achieved some currency, particularly in connection with the related terms "semiotics" and "structuralism," which we'll need to glance at again later in this introduction. Here we simply note that "semiotics" and "structuralism" are used to describe movements in several intellectual fields besides literary criticism. That is, they are both more and less than approaches to literature. But when structuralists or semioticians do concentrate on literature, they are primarily concerned with the conventional and self-referential aspects of the art, with literature as a system of signs. So "intertextual" is an appropriate cover term for most semiotic and structuralist, and even for most "poststructuralist," criticism.

But I use "intertextual" here in an even wider yet fairly obvious sense. While interest in structuralism and semiotics is a relatively recent phenomenon, especially among English-speaking critics, interest in "intertextual" relations, under a variety of cover terms, is very old and very widespread. In this broad sense of the term, whenever a critic focuses on the conventional elements of literature and relates the poem not to "reality" but, by analogy, to other poems, he or she is practicing "intertextual" criticism.

The term understood in this sense helps to clarify the crucial distinction between the genetic and the generic perspectives. Studies that attempt to trace the lines of literary influence converging on a particular poem have long been a staple of genetic or historical criticism. As the words "genetic" and "influence" imply, such studies seek the causes of poems and necessarily operate in chronological sequence. With a tradition as diffuse as that of the pastoral and with an author as learned as Milton, tracing the sources of a poem such as *Lycidas* becomes difficult and frustrating. The difficulty results from the vast number of parallels that exist for many features of the poem. The frustration follows from our inability to know precisely which of these parallels Milton had in mind when he wrote. But when we shift from the genetic to the intertextual perspective, the difficulty evaporates. We need to know pastoral conventions to understand *Lycidas*, and therefore we need to know other pastoral poems, but it makes little difference on this view whether we know only those pastoral poems that Milton knew. For that matter, our knowledge of later poems in the genre may be quite as helpful as our knowledge of earlier ones. Yet clearly no one would argue that Arnold's "Thyrsis," say, or Shelley's "Adonais" in any way "influenced" Milton's poem.

Similarly, our comprehension of the *Aeneid* is improved when we read it with *Paradise Lost* in mind, and our understanding of the *Iliad* is conditioned by our reading of Virgil's epic, even though the "lines of influence" in each case run in the opposite direction. And the process operates when there are no clear lines of influence at all. Thus, the question of how much Shakespeare could have known about Sophocles' drama is, on this view, less important than the reciprocal illumination that results when their plays are compared. The relationships in all these instances are not genetic but generic, not diachronic but synchronic, not causal but analogical. Robert Frost, though he probably never used the term at all, has furnished a succinct description of the intertextualist view of the reading process: "A poem is best read in the light of all the other poems ever written. We read A the better to read B (we have to start somewhere; we may get very little out of A). We read B the better to read C, C the better to read D, D the better to go back and get something out of A. Progress is not the aim, but circulation. The thing is to get among the poems where they hold each other apart in their places as the stars do" (*Selected Prose*, New York, 1966, pp. 96–97).

"Intertextual" criticism, then, is something neither new nor strange, and the idea that our understanding of literature depends on a knowledge of its conventions may often go unremarked because it goes, as we say, without saying. But quite as often, one suspects, it goes unsaid because it is *unseen*. One curious thing about conventions is that the more firmly established they are, the less likely we are to notice them. Scarcely any visitor to a museum remarks the absence of octagonal paintings, and few concert goers in the West notice departures from five-tone or quarter-tone scales. Literary critics have often displayed a similar inattention to literary convention.

Perhaps for this reason the real history of intertextual criticism is to be found in the observations and, above all, in the practice of the poets themselves. It now seems clear, for example, that the *Iliad* and the *Odyssey*, those songs of "Homer" that for us stand at the beginning of Western literature, achieved their final form only at the end of several centuries of oral heroic poetry. During these illiterate centuries, the characters, the actions, the meter, and the hundreds of formulaic phrases that make up these poems were gradually developed, refined, and transmitted from poet to poet. How much of either poem can be attributed to an individual genius is quite impossible to determine and, for the intertextualist, quite unnecessary to determine. But the image of the self-effacing lyre-smiter, the Phemios or the blind Demodokos, who must quite sincerely invoke the aid of Memory's daughters, is very much to the point. For what these bards must remember are all the other poems on the same themes and all the formulas with which they will build their own at each performance. They tell the old stories in the old way, and their success consists in doing well what many others have done before.

Traditional poets may be self-effacing, but their art is very important. That art is sometimes called the "collective memory" of the tribe, but it is really more like the tribe's collective imagination. The epic poem, under the guise of re-creating the distant past, actually creates a world of more heroic characters and more significant actions than those its hearers know from life. So the worlds of Achilles and Odysseus, far from mirroring the lives of their listeners, provide an image of greatness, an imagined standard, against which those lives can be measured. The mirror may tell us what we are; memory may tell us what we were; but only the imagination can tell us what, for better or worse, we might be. It is the function of art to provide these imagined worlds, and to the extent that artists work with the materials of this world, they must not copy but transform those materials. "All the world," said Mallarmé, "exists in order to make a book," a bit of "decadent aestheticism" anticipated many centuries earlier by Homer's Phaiakian king, who gives the poet's game away when he reminds the weeping Odysseus that the whole tragic action of Troy had been fashioned by the gods, "so that it might become a song for future generations."

Most often, however, what the artist transforms is not the raw material of life but the conventions of his or her medium. And this is why, says the intertextualist, only an absurdly small proportion of the world's literature can be accounted for on "mimetic" principles. It is not the mimetic but the conventional elements in art that enable us to understand it, and the great poets from Homer to the present have always known this. Pope pictures Virgil as closing up the barren leaves of art to turn directly to nature as the model for his Roman epic, only to discover that Homer had already produced the faithful copy. In actuality, it is very unlikely that Virgil ever contemplated any such thing; and

neither did Pope. Virgil follows Homer at every turn because he wants his readers to know that the *Aeneid* is a heroic poem, and that meant for him, as it means for us, a poem that looks like the *Iliad* and the *Odyssey*. He also follows Homer at every turn because he wants his readers to know how profoundly his vision differs from Homer's. In other words, Virgil carefully copies the Homeric poems because much of the meaning of his work depends on our marking these comparisons. And there is reason to believe that "Homer" relates to his predecessors in the same way. For precisely the same reasons, Milton takes pains to copy Homer and Virgil in *Paradise Lost* and Pope, in turn, draws on all these in *The Rape of the Lock*.

The last is, of course, a mock heroic. But from the intertextual perspective, all poems are to some degree "mock" forms. That is, it may be readily admitted that Pope's *Rape of the Lock* will not be very meaningful to anyone who doesn't understand the conventions of heroic poetry and that the reader who comes to the poem with a knowledge of the epics of Homer and Virgil and Milton is better equipped than one who brings only a knowledge of Pope's life, or of Arabella Fermor's. But a knowledge of the conventions of heroic poetry is equally indispensable, says the intertextual critic, to our understanding of the "primary" works. And this knowledge can be gained only by studying heroic poems.

And so with every other form or "genre." It can be said that Pope, like Milton, never sat down to write a poem; he always wrote some "kind" of poem. All poets must do this, the intertextualist claims, but not all poets have been equally conscious of the fact. One of the few things that makes Wordsworth's 1800 "Preface" to the *Lyrical Ballads* a truly revolutionary critical document is his inclination to talk about poetry with no reference to generic type and with little reference to convention, except for those conventions he wishes to extirpate. Somehow the term *decorum* has become attached to those conventions, and the poor reputation of the word dates from about this time. This represents a clear and symptomatic decline from the term's earlier meaning of "suitability," specifically that suiting of image, diction, style, and tone to theme and subject that Milton had in mind when he pronounced "decorum" to be "the grand masterpiece to observe," a pronouncement that makes sense only in the context of some conception of genre and convention.

The intertextual critic will point out, of course, that Wordsworth's poems, despite his critical theory, are quite as conventional as any others. But the tendency to overlook this fact is by no means limited to Wordsworth. Perhaps, as some have argued, the modern emphasis on individualism and "originality" has served to further obscure the conventional and communal elements in literature. At any rate, it is the case that until fairly recently modern critical theory has tended to play down the role of convention. Yet most readers remain at least dimly aware that many of the masterpieces of Western literature, including the works of Virgil, Dante, Chaucer, Shakespeare, and Milton, are profoundly "conventional" poems, though we may prefer to call them "highly allusive" instead; and few works require a greater knowledge of literary conventions than do such modernist masterpieces as *The Waste Land* and *Ulysses*. This interdependence is not really surprising, argues the intertextual critic, for poetry, being an art, must go on rediscovering, recreating, and recombining the conventions of that art if it is to exist at all. And poetry must continue to do so even when critical theory takes little notice of the fact and even when its readers come less and less to share similar assumptions and similar training.

This last is a serious difficulty, and for the past two hundred years, as the number of readers has increased several times over but the number trained as Pope and Milton were trained has steadily declined, poets have lamented their plight. Yeats, like Blake before him, tried to solve the problem by making of his own poems an interlocking set of images and symbols, a sounding box in which the individual poem may resonate. Eliot complained that the modern poet and his readers lacked anything like the extensive system of attitudes and symbols that Dante shared with his audience, but then proceeded to write poetry nearly as allusive as Dante's. Each solution illustrates the intertextualist's point: the poet can speak only through the conventions of poetry.

In his famous essay, "Tradition and the Individual Talent" (1917), Eliot asserted that "Honest criticism and sensitive appreciation are directed not upon the poet but upon the poetry," and the essay has been often cited as an opening shot in the formalist's battle against genetic criticism. But the formalists largely ignored, and their theory cannot easily deal with, the chief thesis of that essay in which Eliot explained that "no poet, no artist of any art, has his complete meaning alone." He urged both the poet and the critic to develop what he called a "historical sense," which "involves a perception, not only of the pastness of the past, but of its presence; the historical sense compels a man to write not merely with his own generation in his bones, but with a feeling that the whole of the literature of Europe from Homer and within it the whole of the literature of his own country has a simultaneous existence and composes a simultaneous order." While we may hesitate to call this synchronic view a "historical" sense, Eliot's vision of all the works of Western literature, not strung out in fixed sequence but arranged in some kind of conceptual space to form a context for the understanding of each poem, is precisely the vision of intertextual criticism.

From this perspective, the intertextual critic offers to explain a central fact that nearly everyone recognizes but that no other theory can adequately account for: people who have read a lot of poetry can generally interpret a given poem better than people who have not. We noticed in particular that critics operating in the formal and mimetic contexts find this phenomenon difficult to explain, and for the simple reason that these contexts have no way of dealing with literary convention. The problem goes much deeper than "allusion." In discussing formalism, I remarked that formalists sometimes appear to confront the poem armed only with their wits and a dictionary. But this remark immensely oversimplifies the case. In the first place, if the poem is in English, any reader has already more or less—and it is always more or less—mastered several systems of conventions that make up "written English." That certain marks should stand for certain sounds and that these sounds should stand for things, actions, and relationships are matters quite arbitrary and peculiar to each language. In English, for example, we depend almost exclusively on word order to signal meaning, and we are required to describe a certain spatial relationship by saying, "the cat is on the mat" rather than "the mat is on the cat." These devices are not the result of our perception of the world; they are purely conventional elements. But unless one has mastered these conventions, one cannot understand even the simplest English sentence.

Now, poems, says the analogist, present analogous cases. But to explain literary conventions by analogy to linguistic conventions somewhat clouds the issue, for a poem is in the first place a system of linguistic conventions, the "system" itself being one of the conventional elements. It differs from other utterances in the same language, the intertextual critic would argue, by also employing a number of supralinguistic conventions peculiar to or characteristic of literature. This fact explains, incidentally, why poems are and are not translatable. Linguistic conventions and the literary conventions most closely bound to them, such as meter, rhythm, and rhyme, are notoriously difficult to reproduce in another language. But devices of structure and plot, techniques of character representation, and a vast reservoir of images and symbols are conventions that most of the Western literatures, at least, have in common, and these easily cross linguistic boundaries. But, like the conventions of one's own language, they have meaning only to those who have learned them. As Eliot says in the essay cited earlier, the literary tradition "cannot be inherited, and if you want it you must obtain it by great labour."

This idea that literary conventions must be learned is a crucial point that sets intertextual critics apart from typical "myth" critics. The latter, whatever their psychological or anthropological affiliation, are generally affectivists who locate the power of poems in special patterns or symbols that have the ability to appeal directly and forcefully to our subconscious or unconscious minds. They may, like the Jungians, account for this power on the basis of some theory of inherited racial memory, or like the Freudians, they may feel that the essential similarity of human experience offers sufficient explanation. In either case they are concerned only with

certain special poetic "conventions" (though they would surely find that word too slight) and, as we noticed in the discussion of affective criticism, while their view offers an apparently plausible explanation of why some of us respond intensely to certain works, it offers no explanation at all of why many of us do not. Intertextual critics, by contrast, though not necessarily denying that certain symbols may have special potency, feel no necessity to locate the power of myths or symbols in the unconscious or in the extraliterary. Like the conventions of language, literary conventions are arbitrary, and they must, therefore, be learned. From this perspective, the reader who fails to respond to *King Lear*, say, or to *Moby Dick*, is not psychologically defective. He or she simply doesn't know how to read well enough.

It is the fundamental task of literary criticism to teach such readers, first by explaining what they need to know and then by showing how they may most efficiently acquire that knowledge. What they need to know, of course, are the conventions of literature, and here the only singing school is studying the monuments themselves. That is, in the intertextual view, the study of literature cannot be based on psychology, anthropology, sociology, or biography, nor can it be grounded in religious, economic, or political history. None of these contexts can directly tell us much about how literary conventions carry meaning. For similar reasons, the traditional genetic categories of author, period, and nation often prove less than ideal organizing forms for the study of literature. From the intertextual perspective, the best context for the understanding of any poem is all the other poems that employ similar conventions. These may or may not include poems by the same author or from the same historical period, but they are almost never limited to these, and they are seldom limited to the writings of a single nation or a single language.

This range suggests that in practice the intertextual study of literature may best be organized along generic lines, lines that keep our attention on conventional elements and that cut across national, temporal, and linguistic boundaries. The problem, again, is how to arrange this vast body of simultaneously existing works so that it may be most efficiently studied. Or, in terms of our definition of criticism, the problem is how to assure that the relevant information can be brought to bear on whatever work we have placed at the center of our attention. Generic concepts are helpful here, but generic distinctions are not. The critical task is not to define tragedy, or pastoral, or epic, but to assemble for our understanding the most useful comparisons. With large works, like *The Faerie Queen* or *Paradise Lost*, this purpose very quickly takes us beyond "generic" concerns to a contemplation of the vast networks of conventional images, symbols, and patterns of action that give such poems their multileveled meanings and their astonishing richness. In this view, the reader of *Ulysses* may need to know very little about Dublin at the turn of the century in the springtime, but a great deal about Western literature since Homer's time.

To be sure, nothing short of a total knowledge of all literature will guarantee that one will come to a given poem with all the relevant conventions in mind. Nevertheless, it is not difficult to imagine a course of study by which readers could acquire much of what the intertextual critics claim they must know to understand most works in the Western tradition. Such a study would concentrate early and long on the classical languages and literatures. It would emphasize the *Iliad* and the *Odyssey;* the plays of Aeschylus, Sophocles, Euripides, and Aristophanes; the dialogues of Plato. It would include some Greek lyrics, Plautus and Terence, Virgil and Ovid and Horace. It would very likely include Dante's *Commedia*, and it would certainly include intensive study of the Bible. Above all, it would conceive of Western literature as a unit, and it would largely ignore national boundaries. Obviously, this course of study resembles, in content if not in methodology, the curriculum of "liberal" education as that phrase was generally understood in the centuries before our own. And this resemblance is not surprising, for the reader who follows this curriculum would be learning the conventions of literature in much the same way that the poets he or she wants to read had learned them. As the intertextual critic sees it, these works, quite aside from their intrinsic merit, form the "grammar" and the basic

"vocabulary" of European literary language, and consequently a knowledge of them is as indispensable to readers of Barth and Borges, Pynchon and Joyce, Eliot and Stevens, as it is to readers of Spenser or Milton or Pope. For all art, says the intertextualist, is conventional.

This is the fundamental tenet. And the intertextualist can demonstrate it with even the briefest example. Consider, as a case in point, another Blake lyric, "The Sick Rose":

O Rose, thou art sick.
The invisible worm
That flies in the night
In the howling storm

Has found out thy bed
Of crimson joy,
And his dark secret love
Does thy life destroy.

To the intertextual critic, it seems pointless to look to Blake's life for the meaning of these words, and equally pointless to examine the responses of readers, until we know which readers have the best responses. Furthermore, although the poem, short as it is, exhibits a complex structure and a high degree of formal coherence, these in themselves do not account for the referential sense of the words. Now, ordinarily referential meaning implies correspondence to the world of nonverbal experience. And as a botanical description, Blake's poem is, like most poems, negligible if not downright ridiculous. But the intertextual critic argues that the real frame of reference for poetic language is not the world of nonverbal experience but the world of poetry, the world that literature creates and is.

If, ignoring considerations of rhythm and rhyme, we substitute "tulip" for "rose" in Blake's poem, and "insect" for "invisible worm," and "dawn" for "night," and so forth, we can construct a poem that would not only be equally coherent, but that would present at least as accurate a picture of the nonverbal world. As a poem, though, it would be a very poor thing, for it would lack the extensive range of conventional associations that Blake's words have. The "rose," of course, has been long established in the Western tradition as a symbol of beauty. This is not a matter of perception or "esthetics" in the basic sense. Under the aspect of eternity, we may suppose, all plants are equally beautiful, and many people may prefer tulips to roses in their gardens or vases. But not in their poems. The convention is too strong. One thinks of the *Romance of the Rose*, of Dante's Rose of Heaven, of Eliot's rose garden, of Waller's lovely rose and Housman's withered rose and Thomas's crooked rose, and on and on through a hundred other poems great and small. The only limit is our reading and our memory. And "worm," whatever its relation to real roses, has a similarly extensive literary pedigree. It calls to mind those snakes and serpents that slither through countless other poems and that have, whatever their possible psychological sources, a necessarily sinister resonance because of the pervasive influence of the Bible, a resonance reinforced here by the conventional associations of "invisible," "night," "howling storm," "dark," and "secret." Most of us do not need a Freudian analyst to tell us that "bed of joy" has sexual associations, nor that "crimson" in this context is "multivalent."

Indeed, the whole poem is wonderfully multivalent, or "plurisignificant." We can construct upon it a coherent "religious" reading, an equally coherent "sexual" reading, and any number of other readings within or around these. Short as it is, the poem can support pages of relevant commentary and not be exhausted because it is a coherent arrangement of elements that were already highly charged with poetic— that is, with "conventional"—significance. Blake didn't invent these associations any more than he invented the dictionary definitions of his words. His business as a poet was to be unusually sensitive to the conventional associations of words and to have the genius to combine deftly these already charged particles to create that supercharged verbal structure that is his poem. But that poem, the intertextualist reminds us, is fully available only to readers who have mastered the relevant conventions of literature. "The Sick Rose" has eight lines; *Paradise Lost* has 10,565. We begin to see what Eliot meant by "great labour." Happily, most of this labor consists of reading poems.

The preceding, then, is a sketch of the intertextual critic's argument, and even a skeptical reader might grant that it has much to recommend it. But he or she might also feel that the perspective raises some difficult questions. Consider, for example, the question of the poem's relationship to the world. We have noticed that the mimetic critic, by definition, and the formal critic, often more hesitantly, locate the value of poetry in its correspondence to reality, however subtly such correspondence is defined and qualified. And this "reality" is usually the empiricist's reality, the world of experience. This mimetic grounding causes difficulties, but since correspondence to reality is the definition of "truth" in most commonsense views, poetry's claim to mimetic accuracy, to "truth-revealing" powers, seems to many critics to offer the only stable ground for poetic value. Yet the intertextual critic, by arguing that poems imitate other poems and not the world of experience, appears to surrender that claim at the outset. Literature is, as I. A. Richards had said it was, a system of purely hypothetical or "pseudo" statements.

But in defense of this position, the intertextualist can urge two arguments that were not so readily available in Richards' affective context. The first argument, interestingly, simply accepts the empirical view of "truth." The poem does provide cognitive knowledge, but knowledge of imagined worlds. By showing us not what life is but in what ways it could be better of worse, poetry becomes, in Matthew Arnold's phrase, a "criticism of life." For the only standard by which we can measure actuality must be an imagined standard. The characters and actions we find in literature are, in this view, less imitations of things than things to be imitated, or shunned, images of desire or aversion. This, I assume, is what Northrop Frye means when he says that one of the functions of art is to provide the "goals of work" for civilization. Looked at this way, what we call civilization is our collective attempt to create, from the world of nature we find, something approximating the world we imagine. And in this sense, life does indeed imitate art. As that arch-antimimeticist, Oscar Wilde, reminds us, nature has good intentions, but she can't carry them out.

This argument meets the empiricists on their own ground because it assumes that the correspondence definition of truth holds and that the world experienced outside of art is the "real" world. Only now, paradoxically, the value of literature seems to inhere not in its correspondence to that world but in its difference from it. This reversal, of course, offers as many evaluative difficulties as does the correspondence standard. But such a view is at least better able to account for the many forms of literature, and it would serve to counter the modern, mimetic prejudice against forms such as epic, romance, and pastoral that flaunt their "unrealistic" conventions.

And yet, the more we contemplate the conventional aspects of poems, the more it appears that all verbal constructs are to a high degree conventional. Carried to its logical conclusion, such a view undercuts empiricism itself. It does so not by denying the existence of "reality" but by denying that it can be known apart from the structure of the mind that knows it. Perception, as Kant perceived, is itself creation, and to the extent that art organizes our perceptions, we can understand the more profound implications of Wilde's remark that "life imitates art far more than art imitates life." This remark begins to sound like Kant's structuralist answer to the empiricism that Hume had pushed to its logical and paradoxical limits, and while the intertextual perspective in criticism does not require any particular philosophical orientation, it is not surprising that many intertextual critics should feel comfortable with what we might call, broadly speaking, a "structuralist" outlook. At any rate, it is typical of neo-Kantian philosophers, such as Ernst Cassirer, and of structuralist thinkers, such as Ferdinand de Saussure and Claude Lévi-Strauss and their many followers in literary criticism, to emphasize the conventional, symbolic, and self-referential elements in all systems of thought. In such philosophies the empiricist's truth of correspondence tends to disappear. There is instead only truth of coherence.

In other words, the truth of any statement must be judged not by its correspondence to empirical reality, for this correspondence cannot be directly known, but by its coherence, its ability to fit into the system of other statements that we have already accepted as "true." And there is not only one system; there are several. Mathematics, for instance, appears to some thinkers to be a clear example of such a system of complex and totally coherent relationships that, as system, is congruent with, or corresponds to, nothing at all outside of mathematics. By analogy, what we call "history" or "sociology" or "physics" are also self-contained systems. For in this view even the physicists, the hardest of the "hard" scientists, cannot tell us if a statement corresponds to reality. They can only tell us, in the first place, if the terms of that statement have any meaning within the universe of discourse we call physics and, in the second, if the statement is consistent with other statements that constitute that universe of discourse.

And so with all systems of thought. Clearly it is beyond the scope of this introductory book to explore fully such large philosophic questions as whether truth is a matter of coherence or of correspondence. But we can at least note briefly a few of the consequences for literary criticism that are implied in a "structuralist" view of the mind's relationship to the world. Such a view suggests, in the first place, that no system of thought has a firm empirical base and that all are imaginative constructs. It follows that the critic who adopts this view is in a very different position than Richards was, for Richards denied truth of correspondence to poetry but granted it to science; the "coherence" theory denies truth of correspondence to everybody. Further, whereas mimetic critics operating with the empirical or correspondence model have difficulty separating poems from other kinds of discourse because they assume that all verbal constructs are "imitations" of reality, critics operating on the coherence model have the same difficulty for the opposite reason. If all verbal structures are imaginative structures, then what we call poems can again differ from other types of discourse only in degree, not in kind.

But, though defining poetry from this perspective may be difficult, it is also unnecessary. We need instead to define criticism, that system of discourse that is centrally concerned with the conventional elements of symbolic or metaphorical structures. In other words, clarifying the subject of study becomes more important than clarifying the object. If our analogy to physics holds, physicists do not need to sharpen their definition of "nature." Indeed, they cannot. It is enough for them to know whether a statement makes sense within the system of discourse they call physics. In the field of literary criticism, such a conception eliminates two problems that sometimes trouble critics. On the one hand, if all verbal structures are metaphorical or symbolic, literary critics need not worry about getting "out of their field" if they comment on, say, the writings of Xenophon or Thucydides, Gibbon or Hume, Mill or Marx, nor need they worry too much whether biography or autobiography is within their ken. Their business is metaphor wherever they find it, and they find it everywhere. On the other hand, the literary critic, understood in this sense, has no reason to object to the historian, the psychologist, the economist, or anyone else making statements about poems. For the statements they make would not be literary criticism simply because they were about poems; their statements would continue to be history, psychology, economics or whatever the discipline being applied was named.

To put the matter differently, it is not a question of what we study but of *how* we study. In this view, literary criticism has often appeared confused because critics have tried to define their subject of study by their object of study. They have tried to set poems apart from other verbal structures, and then they have tried to borrow their methodology—their way of seeing the object—from some other discipline. By this route we get such terms as "sociological criticism," "psychological criticism," and "historical criticism." From the perspective we are exploring here, this attempt is nonsense. One cannot borrow an approach or a methodology from another discipline because the approach or methodology *is* the discipline. Disciplines are ways of seeing, not things to be seen; subjects, not objects. And what literary critics must master is not a definition of their object, but the discipline of criticism, which involves a systematic knowledge of the conventions from which metaphoric or symbolic forms are created and through which they can be understood.

These, I believe, are a few of the consequences that follow from accepting what I have called a "structuralist" view of criticism, but one doesn't need to get to this view by way of that

label, nor is the critic who wishes to adopt an intertextual perspective compelled also to adopt this view of the mind and all that it seems to entail. As we have seen, even an empiricist can operate comfortably in the intertextual context.

But whatever their philosophic orientation may be, critics who employ the intertextual approach to literature will face some conceptual difficulties. One of these is the problem of circularity. We saw one version of this circularity in formalist theory, which holds that any part of the work could be understood and evaluated only in terms of the whole work, although (necessarily) that whole could be known only through its parts. In intertextual criticism, a similar difficulty returns on a larger scale. A particular poem can be understood only by someone who understands its conventions, but these conventions must be learned by studying similar poems, and a reading of each of these requires in turn a knowledge of conventions. But this problem, like the formalist's circularity, is less serious in practice than in theory, and again the parallel to language is instructive. We can understand, and even produce, new utterances in English because, through a complex, little understood, and never quite completed process, we have learned the conventions of our language, and this learning was gained by attending to other utterances in English. Thus the continuous interplay between convention and particular construct presents little practical difficulty at this level, however mysterious it may be to logic.

But this interplay points to a more serious problem, and that is the tendency of intertextual criticism to lose its focus on the individual work in question. Granted, this loss of focus is a problem mainly when criticism is defined, as in this book, as having as its primary goal the interpretation of particular poems. But if we hold to this conception—and most critics do—then the inclination of intertextual criticism to dissolve the particular work into an aggregate of conventions opens the approach to the charge of reductivism. If all poems are conventional, what makes some poems more effective than others? Does *Paradise Lost* have more, or better, conventions than Blackmore's *Prince Arthur*? Does *Lycidas* employ a greater number of conventional elements than lesser pastorals? Or does the better poem simply employ its conventions more effectively? Surely the latter is the case, the formalists would answer. And, while they must grant the reader's need to know the conventions used in any poem, formalists might persist in regarding such knowledge as no different in kind from a knowledge of dictionary definitions. A dictionary and *Hamlet*, they might argue, consist of conventional meanings just as a marble quarry and the Parthenon consist of stone: the particular arrangement makes all the difference.

Of course this analogy, as the intertextualists will remind us, is greatly complicated by the fact that in literature, as in architecture, the arrangement itself is largely a matter of convention. Nevertheless, formalists, the *intra*textualists, will continue to insist on the importance of "form" in their sense of the term, the special meaning that results from these particular words in this particular order, and so they will try to pull the reader's attention along the horizontal axis to the center of our diagram while the intertextual critics pull attention toward the larger context of literary and linguistic conventions. So long as the understanding of the particular poem remains the primary, if not the ultimate, goal of criticism, this tension is difficult to relax. But it is also relatively easy to live with, and the formal and intertextual perspectives are probably more compatible than other combinations that might be formed among our five contexts. Still, in spite of this compatibility, or perhaps because of it, the formalist's complaint that the intertextual critic has difficulty keeping a clear and useful focus on the individual poem is one of the most troublesome objections to the intertextual approach.

It is not, of course, the only objection. The mimetic critic, for example, will point out that if it is hard to see why we should value a poem simply because of its fidelity to empirical reality, it is also hard to see why we should value some departures from that standard more than others. The affective critic will want to know why some conventions, or some uses of conventions, will produce greater or lesser emotional impact, and the genetic critic, even if granting the importance of the conventional and communal elements in literature, will continue to maintain

that some conception of "authorial" meaning is necessary to provide a standard for valid interpretation. Only this, he or she insists, will allow us to separate what the poem does mean from what it could mean.

The intertextual perspective, in short, has not resolved all the issues. It has, however, gained many adherents. In the English-speaking world, Northrop Frye's influence alone has been considerable; it has helped to create, as it has profited from, a climate of opinion that finds many literary theorists interested in philosophers like Ernst Cassirer or art critics like E. H. Gombrich, who emphasize the role of convention in all art and thought. And on the continent, and increasingly in Britain and the United States, the concepts of structuralism and semiotics, long applied in the fields of linguistics and anthropology, are being employed to elucidate the conventional elements in literary structures. As even these few names suggest, though, we should remember that the intertextual context does not represent a single school of thought. Like the other contexts, it includes various "schools" and "movements" as well as unaffiliated individual critics, some of whom may feel a little uncomfortable in the company I have assigned them, and many of whom may want to argue with parts of the position I have sketched.

Our concern, however, is with basic orientations to the literary work, and on this principle I have classed together those critics who, despite their many differences, share a central interest in the conventional aspects of literature. This interest defines the perspective and sets it apart from the others we have considered. And, while the objections to this perspective are not negligible, the critics who adopt it enjoy some real advantages. They, like the formal and the mimetic critics, find it possible to discuss the meaning of poems without appealing to the psyches of particular authors or particular readers, and so they avoid most of the difficulties that trouble the genetic and affective approaches. By orienting the poem toward the world of poetic convention rather than toward the world of empirical reality, they eliminate the problems that haunt mimetic attempts to explain how verbal constructs can "imitate" this reality, or why we should want them to. And by arguing that poems imitate other poems and take their meaning from these literary relationships, they can account for literary form in the sense that the "formal" critics cannot. Finally, and this is by no means the least of their strengths, the intertextual critic's theory will explain, as no other theory will, why a study of poetry should help one understand poems.

Suggestions for Further Reading

In the English-speaking world, the chief figure in this context is Northrop Frye, and *Anatomy of Criticism* (1957) remains the fullest expression of his views. Among his many later books, *The Educated Imagination* (1964) may be recommended as a brief introduction to his main ideas. Ernst Cassirer in *An Essay on Man* (1944) presents a neo-Kantian perspective with implications for literary criticism. E. H. Gombrich's *Art and Illusion* (1961) is a study of perception and convention in the visual arts with similar implications. In *Metahistory* (1973), Hayden White analyzes the fictional structuring of "historical" writing, as do Paul Fussell in *The Great War and Modern Memory* (1975) and Frank Kermode in *The Genesis of Secrecy* (1979). Studies more self-consciously "structural" or "semiotic" include Roland Barthes, *Elements of Semiology* (1967), Tzvetan Todorov, *The Poetics of Prose* (1971), Edward Said, *Beginnings* (1975), Umberto Eco, *A Theory of Semiotics* (1975), Seymour Chatman, *Story and Discourse* (1978), and Michael Riffaterre, *Semiotics of Poetry* (1978). Three interpretive works in recommended order of reading: Terence Hawkes, *Structuralism and Semiotics* (1977), Jonathan Culler, *Structuralist Poetics* (1975), and Robert Scholes, *Semiotics and Interpretation* (1982).

Theory

The Critical Path

Northrop Frye

Since the middle of this century, Northrop Frye has been one of the most influential critics in the English-speaking world, and his writings provided a rationale for intertextual criticism well before structuralist and semiotic critics came to be widely known in this world. In the retrospective opening chapter to The Critical Path, *Frye describes the critical scene when he began to write, and he explains why the genetic, formal, and affective contexts seemed to him not quite the right bases for the study of literature, each being too limited and extraliterary: "I felt that no critic had given his full attention to what seemed to me the first operation of criticism: trying to see what meaning could be discovered in works of literature from their context in literature." Frye's exploration of this context led directly to his concentration on "conventions, genres, and recurring image groups," which he called "archetypal" criticism. It also led to the charge that such intertextual criticism lacks social relevance. Frye goes on to suggest that since literature provides the "models" or "goals of work" for civilization, literary study has a great deal of social relevance, and this relevance is most clearly understood by the kind of criticism that can see literature as a whole in its social context.*

THE PHRASE "THE CRITICAL PATH" IS, I UNDERSTAND, a term in business administration, and was one that I began hearing extensively used during the preparations for the Montreal Expo of 1967. It associated itself in my mind with the closing sentences of Kant's *Critique of Pure Reason*, where he says that dogmatism and skepticism have both had it as tenable philosophical positions, and that "the critical path is alone open." It also associated itself with a turning point in my own development. About twenty-five years ago, when still in middle life, I lost my way in the dark wood of Blake's prophecies, and looked around for some path that would get me out of there. There were many paths, some well trodden and equipped with signposts, but all pointing in what for me were the wrong directions. They directed me to the social conditions of Blake's time, to the history of the occult tradition, to psychological factors in Blake's mind, and other subjects quite valid in themselves. But my task was the specific one of trying to crack Blake's symbolic code, and I had a feeling that the way to that led directly through literature itself. The critical path I wanted was a theory of criticism which would, first, account for the major phenomena of literary experience, and, second, would lead to some view of the place of literature in civilization as a whole.

Following the bent that Blake had given me, I became particularly interested in two questions. One was: What is the total subject of study of which criticism forms part? I rejected the answer: "Criticism is a subdivision of literature," because it was such obvious nonsense. Criticism is the theory of literature, not a minor and non-essential element in its practice. This latter notion of it is not surprising in outsiders, or in poets, but how a critic himself can be so confused about his function as to take the same view I could not (and cannot yet) understand.

Of course criticism has a peculiar disability in the number of people who have drifted into it without any vocation for it, and who may therefore have, however unconsciously, some interest in keeping it theoretically incoherent.

Literary criticism in its turn seemed to be a part of two larger but undeveloped subjects. One was the unified criticism of all the arts; the other was some area of verbal expression which had not yet been defined, and which in the present book is called mythology. The latter seemed more immediately promising: the former I felt was the ultimate destiny of the subject called aesthetics, in which (at least at that time) relatively few technically competent literary critics appeared to be much interested. I noticed also the strong centrifugal drift from criticism toward social, philosophical and religious interests, which had set in at least as early as Coleridge. Some of this seemed to me badly motivated. A critic devoting himself to literature, but without any sense of his distinctive function, is often tempted to feel that he can never be anything more than a second-class writer or thinker, because his work is derived from the work of what by his postulates are greater men. I felt, then, that a conception of criticism was needed which would set the critic's activity in its proper light, and that once we had that, a critic's other interests would represent a natural expansion of criticism rather than an escape from it.

The other question was: How do we arrive at poetic meaning? It is a generally accepted principle that meaning is derived from context. But there are two contexts for verbal meaning: the imaginative context of literature, and the context of ordinary intentional discourse. I felt that no critic had given his full attention to what seemed to me to be the first operation of criticism: trying to see what meaning could be discovered in works of literature from their context in literature. All meaning in literature seemed to be referred first of all to the context of intentional meaning, always a secondary and sometimes the wrong context. That is, the primary meaning of a literary work was assumed to be the kind of meaning that a prose paraphrase could represent. This primary meaning was called the "literal" meaning, a phrase with a luxuriant growth

of semantic tangles around it which I have discussed elsewhere and return to more briefly here.

When I first began to write on critical theory, I was startled to realize how general was the agreement that criticism had no presuppositions of its own, but had to be "grounded" on some other subject. The disagreements were not over that, but over the question of what the proper subjects were that criticism ought to depend on. The older European philological basis, a very sound one, at least in the form in which it was expounded by August Boeckh and others in the nineteenth century, had largely disappeared in English-speaking countries. In some places, notably Oxford, where I studied in the thirites, it had declined into a much narrower conception of philology. This was partly because the shifting of the centre of literary study from the Classical to the modern languages had developed a prejudice, derived from one of the more bizarre perversions of the work ethic, that English literature at least was a merely entertaining subject, and should not be admitted to universities unless the main emphasis fell on something more beneficial to the moral fibre, like learning the classes of Old English strong verbs. In most North American universities the critical establishment rested on a mixture of history and philosophy, evidently on the assumption that every work of literature is what Sir Walter Raleigh said *Paradise Lost* was, a monument to dead ideas. I myself was soon identified as one of the critics who took their assumptions from anthropology and psychology, then still widely regarded as the wrong subjects. I have always insisted that criticism cannot take presuppositions from elsewhere, which always means wrenching them out of their real context, and must work out its own. But mental habits are hard to break, especially bad habits, and, because I found the term "archetype" an essential one, I am still often called a Jungian critic, and classified with Miss Maud Bodkin, whose book I have read with interest, but whom, on the evidence of that book, I resemble about as closely as I resemble the late Sarah Bernhardt.

The reason for this rather silly situation was obvious enough. As long as the meaning of a poem, let us say for short, is sought primarily within the context of intentional discourse, it becomes a document, to be related to some verbal area of study outside literature. Hence criticism, like Los Angeles, becomes an aggregate of suburbs, with no central area in literature itself. One of these suburbs is the biographical one, where the literary work is taken to be a document illustrating something in the writer's life. The most fashionable time for this approach was the nineteenth century, and its strongest proponent Carlyle, for whom great poetry could only be the personal rhetoric of a great man. The theory demands that Shakespeare, for instance, should be an obviously and overwhelmingly great man, which is why so much nineteenth-century critical energy was expended in trying to invent a sufficiently interesting biography for Shakespeare out of fancied allusions in the poetry. This misguided industry has now largely been restricted to the sonnets, where, as Mutt says in *Finnegans Wake*, "he who runes may rede it on all fours." Carlyle's essay on Shakespeare, in *Heroes and Hero-Worship*, comes as close to pure verbiage, to rhetoric without content, as prose sentences can in the nature of things get. Something seems to be wrong with the theory, at least in this form. One is better off with Goethe, but even there the sense of personal greatness may be connected less with the quality of the poetry than with the number of things Goethe had been able to do besides writing poetry.

I am not talking here about real biography, but about the assumption that the poet's life is the essential key to the deeper understanding of the poetry. It often happens that interesting literature is produced by an uninteresting man, in the sense of one who disappoints us if we are looking for some kind of culture-hero. In fact it happens so often that there is clearly no correlation between the ability to write poetry and any other ability, or, at least, it is clearly absurd to assume that every real poet must be a certain kind of person. Hence the formula "this poem is particularly notable for the way in which it throws light on," etc., soon ceases to carry much conviction for all but a selected group of poets. Something else, more deeply founded in a wider literary experience, is needed for critical understanding.

In these days, a biographical approach is likely to move from the manifest to the latent personal content of the poem, and from a biographical approach properly speaking to a psychological one. At the present time and place this means very largely a Freudian, or what I think of as a Luther-on-the-privy, approach. A considerable amount of determinism enters at this stage. All documentary conceptions of literature are allegorical conceptions of it, and this fact becomes even more obvious when poems are taken to be allegories of Freudian repressions, unresolved conflicts, or tensions between ego and id, or, for another school, of the Jungian process of individuation. But what is true of allegorical poetry is equally true of allegorical criticism: that allegory is a technique calling for tact. Tact is violated when the whiteness of Moby Dick is explained as a Lockian *tabula rasa*, or when Alice in Wonderland is discussed in terms of her hypothetical toilet training, or when Matthew Arnold's line in *Dover Beach*, "Where ignorant armies clash by night," is taken as a covert reference to the copulation of his parents. One is reminded of the exempla from natural history made by medieval preachers. According to Richard Rolle in the fourteenth century, the bee carries earth in its feet to ballast itself when it flies, and thereby reminds us of the Incarnation, when God took up an earthly form. The example is ingenious and entertaining, and only unsatisfying if one happens to be interested in bees.

If we tire of the shadow-play of explaining real poems by assumed mental states, we may be driven to realize that the ultimate source of a poem is not so much the individual poet as the social situation from which he springs, and of which he is the spokesman and the medium. This takes us into the area of historical criticism. Here again no one can or should deny the relevance of literature to history, but only rarely in historical criticism is there any real sense of the fact that literature is itself an active part of the historical process. Poets are assumed to have a sensitive litmus-paper response to social trends, hence literature as a whole is taken to be something that the historical process acts on, and we have still not escaped from a documentary and allegorical procedure.

Once more, some historical critics, like the biographical ones, will want to go from manifest to latent social content, from the historical context of the poem to its context in some unified overview of history. Here again determinism, the impulse to find the ultimate meaning of literature in something that is not literature, is unmistakable. At the time of which I am speaking, a generation ago, a conservative Catholic determinism was fashionable, strongly influenced by Eliot, which adopted Thomism, or at least made references to it, as the summit of Western cultural values, and looked down benignantly on everything that followed it as a kind of toboggan slide, rushing through nominalism, Protestantism, liberalism, subjective idealism, and so on to the solipsism in which the critic's non-Thomist contemporaries were assumed to be enclosed. Marxism is another enlarged historical perspective, widely adopted, and perhaps inherently the most serious one of them all. Literature is a part of a social process; hence that process as a whole forms the genuine context of literature. Theoretically, Marxism takes a social view of literature which is comprehensive enough to see it within this genuine context. In practice, however, Marxism operates as merely one more determinism, which avoids every aspect of literature except one allegorical interpretation of its content.

All these documentary and external approaches, even when correctly handled, are subject to at least three limitations which every experienced scholar has to reckon with. In the first place, they do not account for the literary form of what they are discussing. Identifying Edward King and documenting Milton's attitude to the Church of England will throw no light on *Lycidas* as a pastoral elegy with specific Classical and Italian lines of ancestry. Secondly, they do not account for the poetic and metaphorical language of the literary work, but assume its primary meaning to be a non-poetic meaning. Thirdly, they do not account for the fact that the genuine quality of a poet is often in a negative relation to the chosen context. To understand Blake's *Milton* and *Jerusalem* it is useful to know something of his quarrel with Hayley and his sedition trial. But one also needs to be aware of the vast disproportion between these minor

events in a quiet life and their apocalyptic transformation in the poems. One should also know enough of criticism, as well as of Blake, not to ascribe the disproportion to paranoia on Blake's part. Similarly, a scholar may write a whole shelf of books about the life of Milton studied in connexion with the history of his time, and still fail to notice that Milton's greatness as a poet has a good deal to do with his profound and perverse misunderstanding of the history of his time.

By the time I begun writing criticism, the so-called "new criticism" had established itself as a technique of explication. This was a rhetorical form of criticism, and from the beginning rhetoric has meant two things: the figuration of language and the persuasive powers of an orator. New criticism dealt with rhetoric in the former sense, and established a counterweight to the biographical approach which treated poetry as a personal rhetoric. The great merit of explicatory criticism was that it accepted poetic language and form as the basis for poetic meaning. On the basis it built up a resistance to all "background" criticism that explained the literary in terms of the non-literary. At the same time, it deprived itself of the great strength of documentary criticism: the sense of context. It simply explicated one work after another, paying little attention to genre or to any larger structural principles connecting the different works explicated.

The limitations of this approach soon became obvious, and most of the new critics sooner or later fell back on one of the established documentary contexts, generally the historical one, although they were regarded at first as anti-historical. One or two have even been Marxists, but in general the movement, at least in America, was anti-Marxist. Marxists had previously condemned the somewhat similar tendency in Russian criticism called "formalism," because they realized that if they began by conceding literary form as the basis for literary significance, the assumptions on which Marxist bureaucracies rationalized their censorship of the arts would be greatly weakened. They would logically have to end, in fact, in giving poets and novelists the same kind of freedom that they had reluctantly been compelled to grant to the physical scientists.

More recently, Marshall McLuhan has placed a formalist theory, expressed in the phrase "the medium is the message," within the context of a neo-Marxist determinism in which communication media play the same role that instruments of production do in more orthodox Marxism. Professor McLuhan drafted his new mosaic code under a strong influence from the conservative wing of the new critical movement, and many traces of an earlier Thomist determinism can be found in *The Gutenberg Galaxy*. An example is the curiously exaggerated distinction he draws between the manuscript culture of the Middle Ages and the book culture of the printed page that followed it.

It seemed to me obvious that, after accepting the poetic form of a poem as its primary basis of meaning, the next step was to look for its context within literature itself. And of course the most obvious literary context for a poem is the entire output of its author. Just as explication, by stressing the more objective aspect of rhetoric, had formed a corrective to the excesses of biographical criticism, so a study of a poet's whole work might form the basis of a kind of "psychological" criticism that would operate within literature, and so provide some balance for the kind that ends in the bosom of Freud. Poetry is, after all, a technique of communication: it engages the conscious part of the mind as well as the murkier areas, and what a poet succeeds in communicating to others is at least as important as what he fails to resolve for himself.

We soon become aware that every poet has his own distinctive structure of imagery, which usually emerges even in his earliest work, and which does not and cannot essentially change. This larger context of the poem within its author's entire "mental landscape" is assumed in all the best explication—Spitzer's, for example. I became aware of its importance myself, when working on Blake, as soon as I realized that Blake's special symbolic names and the like did form a genuine structure of poetic imagery and not, despite his use of the word, a "system" to which he was bound like an administrator to a computer. The structure of imagery, however, as I continued to study it, began to show an increasing number of similarities to the structures of other poets. Blake had always been regarded as a poet with a "private symbolism" locked up in his own mind, but this conception of him was so fantastically untrue that overcoming it carried me much further than merely correcting a mistaken notion of Blake.

I was led to three conclusions in particular. First, there is no private symbolism: the phrase makes no sense. There may be private allusions or associations that need footnotes, but they cannot form a poetic structure, even if the poet himself is a psychotic. The structure of the poem remains an effort at communication, however utterly it may fail to communicate. Second, as just said, every poet has his own structure of imagery, every detail of which has its analogue in that of all other poets. Third, when we follow out this pattern of analogous structures, we find that it leads, not to similarity, but to identity. Similarity implies uniformity and monotony, and any conclusion that all poets are much alike, in whatever respect, is too false to our literary experience to be tenable. It is identity that makes individuality possible: poems are made out of the *same* images, just as poems in English are all made out of the same language. This contrast of similarity and identity is one of the most difficult problems in critical theory, and we shall have to return to it several times in this book.

I was still not satisfied: I wanted a historical approach to literature, but an approach that would be or include a genuine history of literature, and not simply the assimilating of literature to some other kind of history. It was at this point that the immense importance of certain structural elements in the literary tradition, such as conventions, genres, and the recurring use of certain images or image-clusters, which I came to call archetypes, forced itself on me. T. S. Eliot had already spoken of tradition as a creative and informing power operating on the poet specifically as a craftsman, and not vaguely as a merely cultivated person. But neither he nor anyone else seemed to get to the point of identifying the factors of that tradition, of what it is that makes possible the creation of new works of literature out of earlier ones. The new critics had resisted the background approach to criticism, but they had not destroyed the oratorical conception of poetry as a personal rhetoric.

And yet convention, within literature, seemed to be a force even stronger than history. The difference between the conventions of medieval poets writing in the London of Richard II and those of Cavalier poets writing in the London of Charles II is far less than the difference in social conditions between the two ages. I began to suspect that a poet's relation to poetry was much more like a scholar's relation to his scholarship than was generally thought. Whatever one is producing, the psychological processes involved seem much the same. The scholar cannot be a scholar until he immerses himself in his subject, until he attaches his own thinking to the body of what is thought in his day about that subject. A scholar, *qua* scholar, cannot think for himself or think at random: he can only expand an organic body of thought, add something logically related to what he or someone else has already thought. But this is precisely the way that poets have always talked about their relation to poetry. From Homer onward, poets have continually insisted that they were simply places where something new in literature was able to take its own shape.

From here it is clear that one has to take a step. Criticism must develop a sense of history within literature to complement the historical criticism that relates literature to its non-literary historical background. Similarly, it must develop its own form of historical overview, on the basis of what is inside literature rather than outside it. Instead of fitting literature into a prefabricated scheme of history, the critic should see literature as a coherent structure, historically conditioned but shaping its own history, responding to but not determined in its form by an external historical process. This total body of literature can be studied through its larger structural principles, which I have just described as conventions, genres and recurring image-groups or archetypes. These structural principles are largely ignored by most social critics. Their treatment of literature, in consequence, is usually superficial, a matter of picking things out of literary works that seem interesting for non-literary reasons.

When criticism develops a proper sense of the history of literature, the history beyond literature does not cease to exist or to be relevant to the critic. Similarly, seeing literature as a unity in itself does not withdraw it from a social context: on the contrary, it becomes far easier to see what its place in civilization is. Criticism will always have two aspects, one turned toward the structure of literature and one turned toward the other cultural phenomena that form the social environment of literature. Together, they balance each other: when one is worked on to the exclusion of the other, the critical perspective goes out of focus. If criticism is in proper balance, the tendency of critics to move from critical to larger social issues becomes more intelligible. Such a movement need not, and should not, be due to a dissatisfaction with the narrowness of criticism as a discipline, but should be simply the result of a sense of social context, a sense present in all critics from whom one is in the least likely to learn anything.

There was another difficulty with new criticism which was only a technical one, but still pointed to the necessity for a sense of context. Whenever we read anything there are two mental operations we perform, which succeed one another in time. First we follow the narrative movement in the act of reading, turning over the pages and pursuing the trail from top left to bottom right. Afterwards, we can look at the work as a simultaneous unity and study its structure. This latter act is the critical response properly speaking: the ordinary reader seldom needs to bother with it. The chief material of rhetorical analysis consists of a study of the poetic "texture," and such a study plunges one into a complicated labyrinth of ambiguities, multiple meanings, recurring images, and echoes of both sound and sense. A full explication of a long and complex work which was based on the reading process could well become much longer, and more difficult to read, than the work itself. Such linear explications have some advantages as a teaching technique, but for publishing purposes it is more practicable to start with the second stage. This involves attaching the rhetorical analysis to a deductive framework derived from a study of the structure, and the context of that structure is what shows us where we should begin to look for our central images and ambiguities.

The difficulty in transferring explication from

the reading process to the study of structure has left some curious traces in new critical theory. One of them is in Ransom, with his arbitrary assumption that texture is somehow more important for the critic than structure; another is again in McLuhan, who has expanded the two unresolved factors of explication into a portentous historical contrast between the "linear" demands of old printed media and the "simultaneous" impact of the new electronic ones. The real distinction however is not between different kinds of media, but between the two operations of the mind which are employed in every contact with every medium. There is a "simultaneous" response to print; there is a "linear" response to a painting, for there is a preliminary dance of the eye before we take in the whole picture; music, at the opposite end of experience, has its score, the spatial presentation symbolizing a simultaneous understanding of it. In reading a newspaper there are two preliminary linear operations, the glance over the headlines and the following down of a story.

This point is crucial for critical theory, because the whole prose-paraphrase conception of "literal" meaning is based on an understanding which is really pre-critical. It is while we are striving to take in what is being presented to us that we are reducing the poetic to the intentional meaning, attending to what the work explicitly says rather than to what it is. The pre-critical experience of literature is wordless, and all criticism which attempts to ground itself on such experience tends to assume that the primary critical act is a wordless reaction, to be described in some metaphor of immediate and non-verbal contact, such as "taste." Verbal criticism, in this view, is a secondary operation of trying to find words to describe the taste. Students who have been encouraged to think along these lines often ask me why I pay so little attention to the "uniqueness" of a work of literature. It may be absurd that "unique" should become a value-term, the world's worst poem being obviously as unique as any other, but the word brings out the underlying confusion of thought very clearly. Criticism is a structure of knowledge, and the unique as such is unknowable; uniqueness is a quality of experience, not of knowledge, and of precisely the aspect of experience which cannot form part of a structure of knowledge.

A better word, such as "individuality," would raise deeper problems. The basis of critical knowledge is the direct experience of literature, certainly, but experience as such is never adequate. We are always reading *Paradise Lost* with a hangover or seeing *King Lear* with an incompetent Cordelia or disliking a novel because some scene in it connects with something suppressed in our memories, and our most deeply satisfying responses are often made in childhood, to be seen later as immature over-reacting. The right occasion, the right mood, the right state of development to meet the occasion, can hardly coincide more than once or twice in a lifetime. Nevertheless, the conception of a definitive experience in time seems to be the *hypothesis* on which criticism is based. Criticism, surely, is designed to reconstruct the kind of experience that we could and should have had, and thereby to bring us into line with that experience, even if the "shadow" of Eliot's *The Hollow Men* has forever darkened it. As a structure of knowledge, then, criticism, like other structures of knowledge, is in one sense a monument to a failure of experience, a tower of Babel or one of the "ruins of time" which, in Blake's phrase, "build mansions in eternity." Hence the popularity of the evaluative or taste-criticism which seems to point backwards to a greater intensity of response than the criticism itself can convey. It corresponds to a popular view of poetry itself, that whatever the poet writes down is merely salvaged from an original "inspiration" of a much more numinous kind. There is a real truth here, though it needs to be differently stated.

There are two categories of response to literature, which could be well described by Schiller's terms naive and sentimental, if used in his sense but transferred from qualities inherent in literature to qualities in the experience of it. The "naive" experience is the one we are now discussing, the linear, participating, pre-critical response which is thrown forward to the conclusion of the work as the reader turns pages or the theatre audience expectantly listens. The conclusion is not simply the last page or spoken line, but the "recognition" which, in a work of fiction particularly, brings the end into line with the beginning and pulls the straight line of response around into a parabola. A pure, self-contained pleasure of participating response is the end at which all writers aim who think of themselves as primarily entertainers, and some of them ignore, resist, or resent the critical operation that follows it.

Such pleasure is however a state of innocence rarely attained in adult life. Many of us have "favorite" authors who set up for us a kind of enclosed garden in which we can wander in a state of completely satisfied receptivity. But for each reader there are very few of these, and they are usually discovered and read fairly early. The sense of guilt about reading "escape" literature is a moral anxiety mainly derived from a feeling that it is a substitute for an unattained experience, and that if escape literature really did what it professes to do it would not be escape literature. As a rule our pleasure in direct response is of a more muted and disseminated kind. It arises from a *habit* of reading or theatregoing, and much of this pleasure comes from a greatly enlarged kind of expectation, extending over many works and many years. Instead of trying to operate the gambling machine of an ideal experience, which may never pay off, we are building something up, accumulating a total fund of experience, each individual response being an investment in it.

It is a central function of criticism to explain what is going on in the habit of reading, using "reading" as a general term for all literary experience. If reading formed simply an unconnected series of experiences, one novel or poem or play after another, it would have the sense of distraction or idle time-filling about it which so many of those who are afraid of leisure believe it to have. The real reader knows better: he knows that he is entering into a coherent structure of experience, and the criticism which studies literature through its organizing patterns of convention, genre and archetype enables him to see what that structure is. Such criticism can hardly injure the "uniqueness" of each experience: on the contrary, it rejects the evaluating hierarchy that limits us to the evaluator's reading list, and encourages each reader to accept no substitutes in his search for infinite variety.

It is simply not true that the "great" writers supply all the varieties of experience offered by the merely "good" ones: if Massinger is not a substitute for Shakespeare, neither is Shakespeare a substitute for Massinger.

Still less does the study of the recurring structural patterns of literature lead the reader to the conviction that literature is everywhere much alike. For such study, as just said, does not keep bringing the student back to similar points, but to the same point, to the sense of an identity in literary experience which is the objective counterpart to his own identity. That variety and novelty can be found only at the place of identity is the theme of much of the most influential writing in our century, of the Eliot Quartets with their garlic and sapphires clotting a bedded axletree, of the Pound Cantos which insist on "making it new" but remain at the center of the "unwobbling pivot," of that tremendous hymn to the eternal newness of the same which is *Finnegans Wake*. Twentieth-century criticism which does not understand a central theme of the literature of its own time can hardly be expected to make much sense of the literature of the past.

This brings us to the "sentimental" type of response, which starts where criticism starts, with the unity of the work being read. In modern literature there has been a strong emphasis on demanding a response from the reader which minimizes everything "naive," everything connected with suspense or expectation. This emphasis begins in English literature with the Blake Prophecies, *Milton* and *Jerusalem* particularly, which avoid the sense of linear narration and keep repeating the central theme in an expanding series of contexts. Fiction tends increasingly to abolish the teleological plot which keeps the reader wondering "how it turns out"; poetry drops its connective tissue of narrative in favor of discontinuous episodes; in Mallarmé and elsewhere it even avoids the centrifugal movement of naming or pointing to objects thought of as external to the poem. The emphasis, though it starts with unity, is not on unity for its own sake, but on intensity, a word which brings us back to the conception of an ideal experience. Hopkins with his "inscape" and "instress," Proust with his instants of remembrance and recognition, Eliot with his timeless moments at the world's axis, and a host of more recent writers with their mystiques of orgasm, drugs, and quasi-Buddhist moments of enlightenment, are all talking about a form of ideal experience, which in one way or another seems to be the real goal of life. The ideal experience itself, for the shrewder of these writers at least, never occurs, but with intense practice and concentration a deeply satisfying approximation may occur very rarely. The curious link with religion—for even writers who are not religious still often employ religious terminology or symbolism in this connexion, as Joyce and Proust do—indicates that this direct analogy of ideal experience is typically the way of the mystic or saint rather than the artist—"an occupation for the saint," as Eliot calls it, though he immediately adds that it cannot be in any sense an occupation.

Traditional Christian thought had an explanation for the dilemma of experience which at least made sense within its own postulates. According to it, Adam was capable of a preternatural power of experience before his fall, and we have lost this capacity. Our structures of reason and imagination are therefore analogical constructs designed to recapture, within the mental processes that belong to our present state, something of a lost directness of apprehension. Thus Milton can define education as "an attempt to repair the ruin of our first parents by regaining to know God aright." Similar language continues in our day. Proust concludes his colossal analysis of experience by saying that the only paradises are lost paradises; Yeats, in a much more light-hearted way, tells us in "Solomon and the Witch," anticipating the more recent orgasm cults, that a single act of perfect intercourse would restore the unfallen world. In this view, literature, philosophy and religion at least are all articulate analogies of an experience that goes not only beyond articulateness, but beyond human capacity as well.

The Christian fallen world is only one form of a conception which has run through human imagination and thought from earliest times to the present, according to which the existing world is, so to speak, the lower level of being or reality. Above it is a world which may not exist (we do not actually know that it exists even

if we seem to have an experience of it), but is not nothing or non-existence; is not a merely ideal world, because it can act as an informing principle of existence, and yet cannot convincingly be assigned to any intermediate category of existence, such as the potential. This world, related by analogy to the intelligible world of the philosopher and scientist, the imaginable world of the poet, and the revealed world of religion, is increasingly referred to in our day by the term "model." In religion, as noted, this model world is usually projected as an actually existing world created by God, though at present out of human reach. In philosophy it appears in such concepts as Aristotle's final cause, and in the more uninhibited structures of the poets it is the idealized world of romance, pastoral, or apocalyptic vision. As such it suggests a world with which we should wish to identify ourselves, or something in ourselves, and so it becomes the world indicated by the analogy of ideal experience just mentioned.

A direct experience or apprehension of such a world would be a microcosmic experience, an intelligence or imagination finding itself at the centre of an intelligible or imaginable totality, and so experiencing, for however brief an instant, without any residue of alienation. It would thus also be an experience of finally attained or recovered identity. Most of us, at least, never reach it directly in experience if it is attainable in experience at all, but only through one of the articulated analogies, of which literature is a central one. Whatever it is, it represents the end of our critical path, though we have not as yet traversed the path.

As we proceed to do this, we must keep to a middle way between two uncritical extremes. One is the centrifugal fallacy of determinism, the feeling that literature lacks a social reference unless its structure is ignored and its content associated with something non-literary. No theory is any good unless it explains facts, but theory and facts have to be in the same plane. Psychological and political theories can explain only psychological and political facts; no literary facts can be explained by anything except a literary theory. I remember a student, interested in the Victorian period, who dismissed several standard critical works in that area as "totally lacking in any sense of social awareness." I eventually learned that social awareness, for him, meant the amount of space given in the book, whatever the announced subject, to the Chartist movement. Chartism and similar social movements have their relevance to literature, certainly; but literature is all about something else, even when social protest is its explicit theme.

The other extreme is the centripetal fallacy, where we fail to separate criticism from the pre-critical direct experience of literature. This leads to an evaluating criticism which imposes the critic's own values, derived from the prejudices and anxieties of his own time, on the whole literature of the past. Criticism, like religion, is one of the sub-academic areas in which a large number of people are still free to indulge their anxieties instead of studying their subject. Any mention of this fact is apt to provoke the response: "Of course you don't understand how important our anxieties are." I understand it sufficiently to have devoted a good deal of this essay to the subject of social anxiety and its relation to genuine criticism. We notice that the two fallacies mentioned above turn out to be essentially the same fallacy, as opposed extremes so often do.

Theory

Structuralism and Literature

Jonathan Culler

Like Northrop Frye, Jonathan Culler believes we must see the individual poem within the context of literature if we are to understand it fully, and especially if we are to know how we understand it. Structuralism, as Culler views it, offers in the first place "not a new way of interpreting literary works, but an attempt to understand how it is that works do have meaning for us." So structuralist critics speak of genres and conventions and of the "system" or "institution" of literature. And they frequently take our understanding of language as the base and analogy for our understanding of literature. They may also show, as Culler does, considerable sympathy for some forms of reader-response criticism, for they will be much concerned with what the reader needs to know to attain "literary competence." At the same time, since structuralists define the competent reader as one who has mastered the relevant conventions, the number of readings they accept as competent must be considerably restricted. But this definition of competence is also the structuralists' great strength, for their theory offers a rationale for literary study as a discipline through which one can progressively come to know the conventions of literature. Structuralism, then, presents the intertextual context as the fundamental context, the one that ultimately grounds our understanding. Yet although Culler initially stresses the distinction between this generalized understanding and the interpretation of particular poems, he suggests at the end of his essay how the structuralist view may also facilitate specific interpretations.

MY MAIN PURPOSE HERE IS TO SHOW THAT DESPITE its more extreme manifestations structuralism is not an abstruse or recondite theory but that, on the contrary, a structuralist approach to literature is directly relevant to the practical study and teaching of literature. Further, I am going to assume from the first that the teaching of literature involves a concern with the fact that the objects of study are literary works rather than simply documents about inter-personal relations, and that students are supposed to learn about literature and how to read it, rather than about life and how to live.

There are, of course, good reasons for using literary works as ways of finding out about the possibilities of human experience: the images they offer are both more complex and less embarrassing to discuss than, say, another individual's account of relationships with parents or friends. And I think there would be much to be said from a structuralist or semiological point of view about the way in which attention of this kind tries to organize our world; but that is not what I am concerned with here. I shall assume that studying literature and teaching literature involve the development and mastery of special operations and procedures which are required for the reading of literature, as opposed to the reading of other kinds of texts.

First I shall try to explain what structuralism is and why it is especially relevant to the study of literature. Then I shall outline a structuralist approach to literature, both in general and with respect to several examples. But I should like to emphasize from the outset that I am not proposing a structuralist "method" of interpretation: structuralism is not a new way of interpreting literary works, but an attempt to understand how it is that works do have meaning for us.

First, then, what is structuralism? Roland Barthes once defined it, in its "most specialized and consequently most relevant version," as a method for the study of cultural artefacts derived from the methods of contemporary linguistics.[1] Now there are two possible ways of using linguistic methods in the study of literature. The first would be to describe in linguistic terms the language of literary texts. Many critics speak eloquently of the benefits of this approach, but it is not, I think, what Barthes meant by his definition nor is it the kind of structuralism with which I am concerned here. The second approach would be to take linguistics as a model which indicates how one might go about constructing a poetics which stands to literature as linguistics stands to language. In other words, one takes linguistics as an analogy which indicates how other cultural artefacts should be studied. For this kind of structuralism only a few fundamental principles of linguistics are directly relevant, of which the most important is Ferdinand Saussure's distinction between *langue* and *parole*.

La langue, the linguistic system, is what one knows when one knows English. *La parole*, specific utterances or speech acts, are instances of language, *la langue*. Saussure argued that *la langue*, the linguistic system, was the proper object of linguistics, and he went on to say that "dans la langue il n'y a que des différences, sans termes positifs." In the linguistic system there are only differences, with no positive terms. Study of *la langue* is an attempt to determine the nature of a system of relations, oppositions, and differences which makes possible *la parole*. In learning a language we master a linguistic system which makes actual communication possible, and the linguist's task is to describe and to make explicit what it is we have mastered.[2]

Taking this as a point of departure we can say that structuralism and its close relation semiology are based on two fundamental insights: first, that social and cultural phenomena do not have essences but are defined by a network of relations, both internal and external; and, secondly, that in so far as social and cultural phenomena, including literature, have meaning they are signs.

If one wished to distinguish between structuralism and semiology (and the reasons for the distinction are historical rather than logical), one could do so in these terms: structuralism studies the structures or systems of relations by which cultural objects are defined and distinguished from one another; semiology studies cultural objects as signs that carry meanings. But I think that it is extremely important *not* to make the distinction, not to try to separate the two enterprises, since one entails the other where a profitable study of literature is concerned. If the two are separated one risks either discovering patterns of relations and oppositions which are irrelevant in that they have no sign function (this is the danger of the kind of linguistic analysis best represented by Roman Jakobson[3]), or else investigating signs on a one-to-one basis without due regard to the systems of convention which produce them (this is the danger of a limited semiological approach).

The task of structural analysis, we may then say, is to formulate the underlying systems of convention which enable cultural objects to have meaning for us. In this sense structuralism is not hermeneutic: it is not a method for producing new and startling interpretations of literary works (although in another sense which I shall mention below it *is* hermeneutic). It asks, rather, how the meanings of literary works are possible.

I should perhaps digress for a moment at this point to correct a frequent misapprehension about the relative status of literary theory and critical interpretation. It is common to speak of interpretations of particular works as though they were the central activity of literary criticism and to think of literary theory as something peripheral and altogether secondary, but of course the truth is quite the reverse. Interpretations of authors and works are wholly parasitic on the activity of reading literature: the critic who writes about an author is simply producing a more thorough and perhaps more perceptive version of what readers of literature do for themselves. But to enquire about the *nature* of literature, a theoretical task, is to ask what is involved in reading something *as* literature, and this is to tackle questions which are fundamental to anyone engaged in critical interpretation in that implicit answers are necessarily presupposed both by the activity of reading literature, and by the development of a discipline concerned with the study of literature as an institution.

The best way to ease oneself into this structuralist perspective is to take linguistics as a model and to think of the relationship between an utterance and the speaker/hearer. A sentence which I utter comes to you as a series of physical events, a sequence of sounds which we might represent by a phonetic transcription. You hear this sequence of sounds and give it a meaning. The question linguistics asks is how is this possible, and the answer, of course, is that you bring to the act of communication an immense amount of implicit, subconscious knowledge. You have assimilated the phonological system of English which enables you to relate these physical sounds to the abstract and relational phonemes of English; you have assimilated a grammatical system, so complex that we are only beginning to understand it, which enables you to assign a structural description to the sentence, to ascertain the relations among its parts, and to recognize it as grammatically well-formed, even though you have never heard it before; and finally, your knowledge of the semantic component of the language enables you to assign an interpretation to this string of sounds. Now we may say, if we wish, that the phonological and syntactic structure and the meaning are *properties* of the utterance, so long as we remember that they are properties of the utterance only with respect to the complex grammar which speakers of English have assimilated. Without the complex knowledge brought to the communicative act, they have none of these properties.

Moving from language to literature, we find an analogous situation. Imagine someone who knows English but has no knowledge of literature and indeed no acquaintance with the concept of literature. If presented with a poem he would be quite baffled. He would understand words and sentences, certainly, but he would not know what this strange thing was; he would not, quite literally, know what to do with this curious linguistic construction. What he lacks is a complex system of knowledge that experienced readers have acquired, a system of conventions and norms which we might call "literary competence." And we can say that just as the task of linguistics is to make explicit the system of a language which makes linguistic communication possible, so in the case of literature a structuralist poetics must enquire what knowledge must be postulated to account for our ability to read and understand literary works.

Lest you be sceptical about the importance of this implicit knowledge that we bring to the act of reading poetry, let me offer a simple and crude example. Take a perfectly ordinary sentence, such as "Yesterday I went into town and bought a lamp," and set it down on a page as a poem:

> Yesterday I
> Went into town and bought
> A lamp.

The words remain the same, and if meanings change it is because we approach the poem with different expectations and interpretative operations. What sort of thing happens? First of all, "Yesterday" takes on a different force: it no longer refers to a particular day but to the set of possible yesterdays and serves primarily to set up a temporal opposition within the poem (between present and recent past). This is due to our conventions about the relationship of poems to the moment of utterance. Secondly, we expect the lyric to capture a moment of some significance, to be thematically viable; and we thus apply to "lamp" and "bought" conventions of symbolic extrapolation. The traditional associations of *lamp* are obvious; *buying* we can take as one mode of acquisition as opposed to others; and we thus acquire potential thematic material. Thirdly, we expect a poem to be a unified whole and thus we must attempt to interpret the fact that this poem ends so swiftly and inconclusively. The silence at the end can be read as a kind of ironic comment, a blank, and we can set up an opposition between the action of buying a lamp, the attempt to acquire light, and the failure to tell of any positive benefits which result from yesterday's action. This general structure can, of course, support a variety of paraphrases, but any interpretation of the poem is likely to make use of these three elementary operations enshrined in the institution of poetry. The conventions of the lyric create the possibility of new and supplementary meanings.

Note also, and this is important, that though in one sense these meanings are in the poem—they are public, can be argued about, and do not depend upon individual subjective associations—in another sense, which is more important given the current critical climate, they are not *in* the poem. They depend on operations performed by readers (and assumed by poets).

Though this may seem obvious, there are good reasons for insisting on it. What we still call the New Criticism, in its desire to free the text from a controlling authorial intention, wanted to convince us that meanings could be there in the language of the text. The poem was to be thought of as complete in itself, a harmonious totality, not unlike an autonomous self-sufficient natural organism. Despite the salutary effects of this Coleridgean line of criticism, which I should not in the least want to deny, it was perhaps inevitable that it should lead to the notion that the critic or reader, like a good empiricist, approaches the poem without preconceptions and attempts to appreciate fully what is there. Such a notion leads to a theoretical impasse, to a hopeless attempt to show how the language of poetry itself differs from the language of prose or everyday speech.

Structuralism leads us to think of the poem not as a self-contained organism but as a sequence which has meaning only in relation to a literary system, or rather, to the "institution" of literature which guides the reader. The sense of a poem's completeness is a function of the totality of the interpretive process, the result of the way we have been taught to read poems. And to avoid misunderstanding I should perhaps emphasize that, though it is preferable to talk about reading rather than writing, we are dealing with conventions which are assumed by the writer. He is not just setting words down on paper but writing a poem. Even when he is in revolt against the tradition, he still knows what is involved in reading and writing poems; and when he chooses among alternative words or phrases, he does so as a master of reading.

Although this notion of a literary system or of literary competence may be anathema to many, the reasons which lead one to postulate it are quite convincing. First of all, the claims of schools and universities to offer literary training cannot be lightly dismissed: it is, alas, only too clear that knowledge of English and a certain experience of the world do not suffice to make someone a perceptive reader of literature. Something else is required, something which literary training is designed to provide. And a poetics ought to be able to go some way towards specifying what is supposed to be learned. We presume, after all, to judge a student's progress towards literary competence: our examinations are not designed merely to check whether he or she has read and remembered certain books but to test his or her progress as a reader of literature. And that presumption suggests that there is something to be learnt here.

Secondly, it seems obvious that the study of one work facilitates the study of the next. We gain not only points of comparison but a sense of how to read—general formal principles and distinctions that have proved useful, questions which one addresses to certain kinds of texts, a sense of what one is looking for. We can speak if we like of extrapolating from one work to another, so long as we do not thereby obscure the fact that it is precisely this extrapolation which requires explanation. If we are to make any sense of the process of literary education we must assume, as Northrop Frye says, the possibility of "a coherent and comprehensive theory of literature . . . some of which the student unconsciously learns as he goes along, but the main principles of which are as yet unknown to us."[4]

What are the obstacles to this kind of enterprise? First, critics are accustomed to think of their task as that of producing new and subtler interpretations of literary works, and to ask them to attend to what must be taken for granted by experienced readers of literature cannot but seem an impoverishment of the critical enterprise. Just as most people are more interested in using their language than in trying to determine the nature of their linguistic competence, so most critics are more interested in exercising their understanding of literature than in investigating what it involves. But of course in the first case we do not deceive ourselves that those engaged in using their linguistic competence are thereby participating in the study of language, whereas in the second case critics have succeeded in making us believe that their discussion of individual works constitutes the study of literature. This notion is a significant obstacle; but if we are at all concerned with the nature of literature itself, and if we recognize the desirability of understanding what it is that we expect our students to learn, we would do well to grant poetics its proper status at the centre of literary studies.

The second obstacle seems more serious: the difficulty of determining what will count as evidence for literary competence, evidence about the assumptions and operations of reading. It might seem that critics differ so widely in their interpretations as to undermine any notion of a general literary competence. But I should stress first of all that this is not, in fact, an obstacle which must be overcome initially, but a matter which will resolve itself in practice. Since what one is trying to do is to determine the conventions and operations which will account for certain effects, one begins by specifying what effects in fact one is attempting to explain, and then constructs models to account for them. As it is obvious that there is a range of acceptable readings for any poem, what one attempts to discover are the operations which account for this range of readings. In the case of the brief poem which I discussed above, I assumed that the sentence had different possible meanings when set down as a poem rather than as a prose statement, and offered some crude hypotheses to explain why this should be so. If you think that it is not so, if the meanings do not strike you as acceptable in terms of your own literary competence, you will reject the hypotheses and the explanation as false. The only danger, in other words, is that you will find what I have to say irrelevant because I am trying to account for facts which you do not accept. However, even if one were to succeed only in describing in an explicit fashion one's own literary competence, that would be a significant achievement. And because literary competence is the result of an interpersonal experience of reading and discussion, any account of it will doubtless cover much common ground.

Moreover it cannot be emphasized too strongly that some kind of literary competence is presupposed by everyone who discusses or writes about literature. Any critic who claims to offer more than a purely personal and idiosyncratic response to a text is claiming that his interpretation derives from operations of reading that are generally accepted, that it is possible to convince readers of its validity because there are shared points of departure and common notions of how to read, and that both critic and audience know what counts as evidence for a reading, what can be taken for granted, and what must be explicit argued for. What I am asking is that we try to grasp more clearly this common basis of reading and thus to make explicit the conventions which make literature possible.

A structuralist approach starts by stressing the artificiality of literature, the fact that though literature may be written in the language of information it is not used in the 'language-game' of giving information. It is obvious, for example, that by convention the relationship of speaker to utterance is different when we are dealing with a poem and with another speech act. The poet does not stand in the same relation to a lyric as to a letter he has written, even if the poem be Ben Jonson's "Inviting a Friend to Supper." This initial strangeness, this artifice, is the primary fact with which we have to deal, and we can say that the techniques of reading are ways of simultaneously cherishing and overcoming this strangeness—ways of "naturalizing" the text and making it something of a communication. To naturalize a text—I use this word in preference to what some of the French theorists call *vraisemblablisation*—is to transform it so that it can be assimilated to an order of *vraisemblance*. This is absolutely basic to the reading of literature, and a simple example would be the interpretation of metaphor. When Shelley writes "my soul in an enchanted boat" we must, in order to "understand" this, naturalize the figure; we must perform a semantic transformation on "enchanted boat" so as to bring it under a particular order of *vraisemblance*, which here we might call "possible characteristics of the soul." Of course, the fact that understanding involves more than translation of this kind must be stressed: we must preserve the distance traversed in the act of translation as a sign in its own right. Here, for example, we have a sign of a particular lyric posture, of the poetical character, of the inadequacy of ordinary discourse, and so on.

Now there are various levels at which we can naturalize, various sets of conventions which can be brought into play. And of course these change with the institution of literature itself, so that once a style or mode of discourse becomes established it is possible to naturalize a poem as a comment upon this literary mode. When we read Lewis Carroll's "A-Sitting on a Gate" as a parody of Wordsworth's "Resolution and Independence" we naturalize the former and make its strange features intelligible as commentary upon the latter.

The conventions of literature guide the process of naturalization and provide alternatives to what might be called "premature naturalization." This is a direct move from poem to utterance which ignores the former's specifically literary characteristics, as if we were to naturalize Donne's "The Good Morrow" by saying: the poet was in bed with his mistress one morning when the sun rose and, being still befuddled with drink, he uttered this statement in the hope that the sun would go away and shine elsewhere. If one had no knowledge of the institution of literature this is what one might be tempted to do, but even the least advanced student knows that this is an inappropriate step, that he must naturalize at another level which takes into account some of the conventions of literature. The protest to the sun is itself a figure; the situation of the utterance of a poem is a fiction which must be incorporated in our interpretation. We are likely to naturalize "The Good Morrow" as a love poem which uses this situation as an image of energy and annoyance, and hence as a figure for a strong, self-sufficient passion.

This ought at least to indicate what I mean by naturalization: it is the process of making something intelligible by relating it to what is already known and accepted as *vraisemblable*. We are guided in this process by various codes of expectations which we ought to try to make explicit. In discussing prose fiction Roland Barthes

identifies five different codes, but I shall mention just two by way of example.[5]

What Barthes calls the semic code is an especially good case of literary conventions which produce intelligibility. As we go through a novel we pick out items which refer to the behaviour of characters and use them, as we say, to create character. Generally this involves considerable semantic transformation. Cultural stereotypes enable us to move from descriptions of dress or behaviour to qualities of persons, and we admit in fiction moves which we would not accept in ordinary circumstances. We do not believe that there is a real correlation between perfect or blemished complexions and perfect or blemished moral character, but certain *genres* permit inferences of this kind. We do not believe that blonde women as a class have different qualities from brunettes as a class, but the conventions of literature provide us with a set of opposed qualities with which the opposition between a blonde and a dark heroine may be correlated. Indeed, in order to see literature as an agent of moral education, as Christopher Butler has urged, we have to assume that literature will provide us with models of personality and ways of relating action to motive which are not the fruit of our ordinary experience; one of the things a reader of literature learns, that is to say, is how to construct personalities out of the notations that the text offers. He acquires mastery of the semic code.

The symbolic code is one of the oddest and most difficult to discuss. It is also the code with which students have the greatest difficulty, and both students and teachers ought to attempt to gain clearer notions of what it involves than we have at present. What governs the perception and interpretation of symbols? There are obviously a few symbols, consecrated by tradition, which seem to bear an intrinsic meaning, but most potential symbols are defined by complex relations with a context. The rose, for example, can lead in a variety of directions, and within each of these semantic fields (religion, love, nature) its significance will depend on its place in an oppositional structure. Sun and moon can signify almost anything, provided the opposition between them is preserved. Although, as I say, this code is poorly understood, it seems clear that symbolic extrapolation is a teleological process with a set of goals which limit the range of plausible interpretations and specify what kind of meanings serve as adequate *terminii ad quem* [ends or boundaries]. For example, there is a rule of generalization: to be told that in a phrase like "shine on my bowed head, O moon" the moon symbolizes "the quarterly production quota set by the district manager" is bathetic. We quickly learn that there is a set of semantic oppositions, such as life and death, simplicity and complexity, harmony and strife, reality and appearance, body and soul, certainty and doubt, imagination and intellect, which are culturally marked as in some way "ultimate" and hence as goals in the process of symbolic extrapolation. But we ought to be able to say a good deal more about this process which we expect students to master.

After these sketchy indications of the problems involved, I should like to turn by way of example to the kind of fundamental expectations concerning poetry which govern the operation of codes and the process of naturalization. We might start with a short poem by William Carlos Williams:

This Is Just to Say

I have eaten
the plums
that were in
the icebox

and which
you were probably
saving
for breakfast

Forgive me
they were delicious
so sweet
so cold

The fact that this is printed on a page as a poem brings into play our expectations concerning poetry (as sentences in a novel it would, of course, be read differently), the first of which we might call the convention of distance and impersonality. Although at one level the sentences are presented as a note asking forgiveness for eating plums, since poetry is by convention detached from immediate circumstances of utterance we

deprive it of this pragmatic function, retaining simply the reference to a context as an implicit statement that this kind of experience is important, worthy of poetry. By doing this we avoid the premature naturalization which says, "the poet ate the plums and left this note on the table for his wife, writing it as verse because he was a poet."

Starting then with the assumption that this is not a pragmatic utterance but a lyric in which a fictional "I" speaks of eating plums, we are faced with the question of what to do with this object, how to structure it. We expect poems to be organic wholes and we possess a variety of models of wholeness: the simplest is the binary opposition which is given a temporal dimension (not X but Y); another is the unresolved opposition (neither X nor Y but both simultaneously); next there is the dialectical resolution of a binary opposition; and finally, remaining with simple models of wholeness, the four-term homology (X is to Y as A is to B) or the series closed and summed up by a transcendent final term. In studying this poem we need to apply a model of completeness so as to secure an opening up of the poem and to establish a thematic structure into which we can fit its elements, which thus become sets of features subject to thematic expansion. Our elementary model of the opposition can here take the thematic form of rule and transgression: the plums were to be saved for breakfast but they have been eaten. We can then group various features on one side or the other: on the side of "eating" we have "delicious," "sweet" and "cold," stressed by their final position (this is a conventional rule) and implying that eating plums was indeed worth it; on the other side we have the assumed priority of domestic rules about eating (one recognizes them and asks for forgiveness), the reference to "breakfast," the orderly life represented by the hypostatization of meal-times. The process of thematic interpretation requires us to move from facts towards values, so we can develop each thematic complex, retaining the opposition between them. Thus we have the valuing of immediate sensuous experience, as against an economy of order and saving, which is also valued, though transgressed.

Then, presumably, the question we must ask

ourselves is whether this structure is complete: whether the opposition is a simple one, a move from X to Y, or whether the attitude of the poem is in fact more complex and requires us to call upon other models. And here we can take account of what we earlier set aside—the fact that the poem masquerades as a note asking forgiveness. We can say that the poem itself acts as a mediating force, recognizing the priority of conventions (by the act of writing a note) but also seeking absolution. We can also give a function at this level to the deictics, the "I" and "you" which we had set aside, taking the relationship as a figure of intimacy, and say that the note tries to bring this realm of immediate sensuous experience into the realm of interpersonal relations, where there will be tension, certainly, but where (as the abrupt ending of the poem implies) there is hope that intimacy and understanding will resolve the tension.

Although I have been naming and paraphrasing, what I am producing is, of course, a thematic structure which could be stated in various ways. The claim is simply that in interpreting a poem like this we are implicitly relying on assumptions about poetry and structural models without which we could not proceed: that our readings of the poem (which will, of course, differ) depend upon some common interpretive operations.

Interpretation might generally stop here, but if we think about the fact that these sentences are presented as a poem we can go a step further by asking "why?" Why should this sort of banal statement be a poem? And here, by an elementary reversal which is crucial to the reading of modern poetry, we can take banality of statement as a statement about banality and say that the world of notes and breakfast is also the world of language, which must try to make a place for this kind of immediate experience which sounds banal and whose value can only be hinted at. This, we could go on to say, is why the poem must be so sparse and apparently incomplete. It must produce, as it were, a felt absence, a sense of missing intensity and profundity, so that in our desire to read the poem and to make it complete we will supply what the poem itself dare not claim: the sense of significance.

Let me turn now to a poem of a rather different kind, one which is usually read as a political statement and act of engagement, Blake's "London."

> I wander through each chartered street,
> Near where the chartered Thames does flow,
> And mark in every face I meet
> Marks of weakness, marks of woe.
>
> In every cry of every Man,
> In every Infant's cry of fear,
> In every voice, in every ban,
> The mind-forged manacles I hear.
>
> How the Chimney-sweeper's cry
> Every black'ning Church appalls;
> And the hapless Soldier's sigh
> Runs in blood down Palace walls.
>
> But most thro' midnight streets I hear
> How the youthful Harlot's curse
> Blasts the new-born Infant's tear,
> And blights with plagues the Marriage hearse.

I don't want to suggest that this isn't a political poem, but I would like to impress upon you how much work we must do in order to make it a political statement and what a variety of extremely artificial conventions we must call upon in order to read it in this way.

The poem is organized as a list of things seen and heard: I mark marks; I hear manacles; I hear how. . . . And it is obvious from the outset that the things heard or seen are bad (marks of weakness, marks of woe, manacles, blasts and blights). This gives us our initial opposition between the perceiving subject and the objects of perception and provides a thematic centre which helps us to organize details. We may start with the assumption, based on the convention of unity, that we have a series which will cohere at some level (the second stanza with its repetitions of "every" is ample warrant for that). But it is quite difficult to produce this coherence. In the third stanza we can try to collate the two propositions in order to discover their common subject: I hear how the cry of the sweep and the sigh of the soldier act upon the church or palace. This gives us a sound (which fits into the series of "marks" which the "I" perceives), an actor (who, our cultural model tells us, counts among the oppressed), and an institution which they affect. The opposition between institution and oppressed is one whose parameter we know: the possibilities are those of protest and submission, the results the indifference or guilt of the institution. And in fact the structure which Blake has established is ambiguous enough to preclude our really knowing which to choose here. One critic, citing historical evidence, argues that the sigh of the soldier is the murmur of possible rebellion and that the visionary can already see the blood on palace walls in a native version of the French Revolution. But we can also say, in an alternative naturalization, that the palace is bloody because it is responsible for the blood of soldiers whom it commands. Both readings, of course, are at some distance from the "sigh running in blood," but we are sufficiently accustomed to such interpretive operations for this not to worry us.

What, though, of the chimney-sweep? One might assume that the Church is horrified ("appalled") at the conditions of child labour, but the convention of coherence invariably leads critics to reject this reading and to emphasize that "appall" means to make pale or (since by convention puns are permitted when relevant) to cast a pall over and to weaken the Church's moral authority. The "black'ning" church either becomes black, with guilt as well as soot, or makes things black by its indifference and hypocrisy; and the cry of the sweep changes its colour either by making it pale or by casting a pall of metaphorical soot over it. Our ability to perform these acts of semantic transference, moving "black" and "soot" around from sweep to church to its moral character, works as a kind of proof of the poem, a demonstration that there is a rich logical coherence and semantic solidarity here. The point, however, is that the lines do not carry an obvious meaning; they cannot be naturalized as an intimation of oppression without the help of a considerable amount of condensation and displacement.

The last stanza too has an initial strangeness which is difficult to naturalize. The speaker hears how a harlot's curse blasts a tear. We could, of course, read this as a harlot cursing at the fact that her own baby is crying, but since this is to be the climax of the poem we are constrained to reject this interpretation as prema-

ture naturalization. Indeed, such is the force of conventional expectations that no commentary I have read cites this reading, though it is the most obvious. To produce unity we must discover mind-forged manacles, and the best candidate for manacling is the infant. If we are to allow his tear to be blasted we must perform semantic operations on it: the tear can be an expression of protest and feeling, of innocence also perhaps, which is cursed and manacled not so much by the curse of the harlot (and again we become involved in semantic transfers) as by her existence. Her curse becomes her sign or mark and thus fits into the series of sounds which the narrator hears. By another transfer we can say that the infant himself is cursed, as he becomes an inhabitant of this world of harlots and charters. Similarly, in the last line we can transfer epithets to say that it is marriage itself which is blighted, so that the wedding carriage becomes a hearse, through the existence of the harlot. We could, of course, work out a casual relationship here (marriage is weakened if husbands visit harlots), but the level of generality at which the poem operates suggests that this will make coherence difficult. "London" is not after all a description of specific social evils, and that, if we read the poem as a protest, is a fact with which we must now contend.

We must ask, in other words, what we are to say about the fact that the poem goes some way towards defeating our expectations: the cries are not cries of misery only but every cry of every man, even the shouts of street vendors. What are we to make, shall we say, of this odd semiotic procedure and of the interpretive requirements which the poem imposes upon us? There is a great distance which the reader must traverse in order to get from the language of the text to political protest. What does this signify? And the answer is, I think, that here, in the kind of reading which the poem requires, we have a representation of the problems of the visionary state. The distance between every cry and mind-forged manacles is great, so great that there is a possible ambiguity about whose mind is manacled. The speaker "marks marks"; is it because he is "marking" that he sees marks? He perceives, after all, the same thing in every street cry, in every face. In order to make sense of this we must construct an identity for the "I" of the poem; we must postulate the figure of a visionary who sees what no one else sees, who can traverse these distances and read signs whose meaning is obscure to other observers. The city is not itself aware of its problems, its grief. The gap between appearance and awareness is presented, we can say, as the greatest terror of London. The true misery of manacles forged in the mind lies in the fact that they restrict the perception of misery and that no one else, not even the reader until the poem has forced him to exercise his symbolic imagination, can see the blood run down palace walls.

This has been a laboured account of what seems required if we are to read the poem as we do. It is not a structuralist interpretation for it agrees, except for the last paragraph, with customary readings of the poem. If it seems different, that is because it tries to make explicit some of the operations which we are accustomed to taking for granted. Some of these operations are highly conventional; they involve a special logic of literary interpretation, and it is not at all strange that critics prefer to take them for granted. But I think that if we are concerned with the nature of literature itself, or with dispelling the popular notion of the interpretation of literary texts as involving a complex guessing game, it is important to think more explicitly about the operations which our interpretations presuppose.

I think also, and my final remarks on "London" were designed to provide some hint of this, that the last stage in our interpretation of a poem ought to be one which returns dialectically to its source, which takes into consideration the kind of naturalization and the interpretive conventions which the poem has compelled us to use, and which asks what these demands signify. For finally the meaning of a poem will lie in the kinds of operations which it forces us to perform, in the extent to which it resists or complies with our expectations about literary

signs. It is in this sense that the structuralist poetics can be hermeneutic. If we become accustomed to thinking of literature as a set of interpretive norms and operations, we will be better equipped to see (and this is crucial in the case of the most modern and difficult texts) how and where the work resists us, and how it leads to that questioning of the self and of received modes of ordering the world which has always been the result of the greatest literature.

My readers, says the narrator at the end of *A la recherche du temps perdu*, will become "les propres lecteurs d'eux-mêmes." In my book, he says, they will read themselves and their own limits. How better to facilitate a reading of the self than by gaining a sense of the conventions of intelligibility that define the self, than by trying to make explicit one's sense of order and disorder, of the significant and the insignificant, of the naturalized and the bizarre? In its resolute artificiality, literature challenges the limits we set to the self as an agent of order and allows us to accede, painfully or joyfully, to an expansion of self. But that requires, if it is to be fully accomplished, a measure of awareness of the modes of ordering which are the components of one's culture, and it is for that reason that I think a structuralist poetics has a crucial role to play, not only in advancing an understanding of literature as an institution but also in promoting the richest experience of reading.

Notes

1. "Science versus literature," *Times Literary Supplement*, 28 September 1967, p. 897.

2. See F. de Saussure, *Course in General Linguistics*, London, Fontana, 1974.

3. See Roman Jakobson, *Questions de poétique*, Paris, Seuil, 1973. For discussion see Culler, *Structuralist Poetics*, chapter III.

4. *Anatomy of Criticism*, New York, Atheneum, 1965, p. 11.

5. Roland Barthes, *S/Z*, Paris, Sevil, 1970.

Theory

What Precisely Are the Facts?

Frank Kermode

We generally assume a distinction between fiction and nonfiction, poetry and history. Indeed, many theories of literature are founded on this assumption. But intertextual criticism calls this distinction into question. Is it based on reference or on form? And in either case, will it hold up under scrutiny? These are some of the questions explored in Frank Kermode's The Genesis of Secrecy *(1979), from which the following selection is taken. By focusing on the New Testament gospels, Kermode puts the problems in their most complex form, for these narratives are regarded by some readers as pure history, accurate records of actual events, and by other readers as pure fictions, even as supreme fictions. Curiously enough, salient features of these narratives, like their tendency to repeat events from the Old Testament (a collection of narratives having a similarly problematic status), can be used to argue either side of the question. Do any particular features of structure or style mark "historical" writings? Apparently not, because Kermode, juxtaposing historical prose with avowed fiction that imitates it such as Thomas Pynchon's* The Crying of Lot 49, *can detect no differences. Conversely, all attempts to recount events in narrative must use devices of structure and style we associate with fictional writing. Any narrative, then, is necessarily a fictional structure, and there is no simply "transparent" language. None of this is news to the structuralist, of course. But Kermode's exploration shows that the structuralist's concept of language has some disturbing implications for our usual ways of thinking about truth, history, and fiction. His*

exploration also shows that the difference between the view of language as a marvelous system of intertextual meanings and the view of language as an inescapable prison-house may be largely a matter of attitude. Kermode sees as clearly as any structuralist that "transparency" is an illusion, but he seems rather less happy about what follows from that insight: "The pleasures of interpretation are henceforth linked to loss and disappointment." And most of us, he predicts, will find it too much effort to keep from slipping back into "the old comfortable fictions of transparency."

WE HAVE SEEN SOME OF THE WAYS IN WHICH THIS history-like writing must depart from and distort the chronicle. There is another way, which I have mentioned and must now mention again. It is not peculiar to gospel history, but that it is effective in gospel history I tried to show when talking about John's version of the Leavetaking. It is, simply enough, the literary organization involved in elaborating a fable. Consider Mark's story of Peter's denial, which Jesus prophesied after he had prophesied his betrayal. Mark inserts the story of Peter in the courtyard within the account of the first Sanhedrin trial. The effect is to make the disciple's denial and the master's sole public claim to messiahship as nearly simultaneous as narrative allows. Noticing this, conventional scholarship tends to call it "homiletic." The episode is exemplary: under persecution behave like Jesus, not like Peter. But there is more to be said of this, and of Mark's other "analepses."[1] We tend not to give them the kind of attention we would think appropriate to the interpolated sequences of an epyllion, whether Alexandrian or in the imitations of Catullus or the Elizabethan erotic poets. There we see an invitation to interpret; here the word "homiletic" dismisses the case.

Reprinted by permission of the publishers, Harvard University Press, from *The Genesis of Secrecy: An Interpretation of Narrative*, pp. 114–23, by Frank Kermode. © 1979 by Frank Kermode. Notes have been renumbered.

Or, to take a more familiar example, how much interpretation has been granted to the Comices scene in *Madame Bovary*! While M. Lieuvain and M. Derozeray orate to the crowd about freedom, order, and duty, Emma and Rodolphe make love; both lovemaking and oration are punctuated by shouts about sheep, pigs, and manure; and the episode ends when Catherine Leroux is rewarded for a lifetime of servitude by a gift of twenty-five francs, which she will give to the priest for masses. We can hardly wait to begin. This famous passage is certainly more complex than Mark's, but it does share with the gospel some structural principles, notably the insertion of two narratives into the same rendering of a temporal continuum. Flaubert might have done more with Mark's idea, cutting back and forth, interspersing the cockcrows into the dialogue of the trial; but Mark does the main work, bringing together the "I am" of Jesus, his sole, brilliantly lit assertion—so unexpected that some early texts changed it to the usual noncommittal "You have said so"—and the denial of the chief and representative disciple. After that achievement the rest is only detail; John provides some, explaining how Peter got into the High Priest's courtyard in the first place, telling us that one of Peter's interlocutors was a kinsman of the servant whose ear had recently been cut off. But Mark's interest is in the space between two concurrent events. Luke abolishes that space for the sake of a moving recognition: his Jesus turns and looks upon Peter (22:61). That closes the matter; Mark does not close matters so readily. Considered diegetically, narrowly, as part of the narrative of Jesus' trial, his denial scene is null; it is for interpretation to fill the gap, to conflate denial and affirmation; to relate it to the betrayal of Judas and the flight of the other disciples; to reflect that this is the last we ever see, in the second gospel, of Peter, Matthew's rock. In Mark he blunders into mystery; his prime recognition of the Messiah, right in the middle of the book, is at once marred by his caring for the things of man and not for the things of God; whereas in Matthew he wins praise and love, in Mark he gets only an angry rebuke: Get behind me, Satan, Opponent, you whose very recognitions are denials.

We have here, in fact, a pattern of assertion and denial, recognition and falling-off, which is a structural characteristic of the whole work. It is plain that our interpretation of the Denial will turn on our sense of the whole, just as that sense will be influenced by our sense of this part, this impression-point. Yet even to say that is to imply that Mark is not a simple chronicle, such as, in the days when its priority was first being established, people hoped it might be, but a history with a literary structure. To speak so is to speak as one does of a fiction. The testimonies imply a secret narrative, a hermeneutic plot; such elaborate internal structures as I have just spoken of equally call for explanations—of the senses of sequences and junctures which are not those of chronicle, but may be those of history, and are characteristically those of fiction. And so we return to the question of fiction and history.

As I said earlier, there are some fairly simple ideas that we find it difficult to keep hold of; they require (from me at any rate) a special effort I am unwilling to make. One such is the proposition that no narrative can be transparent on historical fact. "There is no textual property," says John Searle (and why should we be dismayed?) "that will identify a stretch of discourse as a work of fiction."[2] Of course it can be labeled as such, metatextually: most novels find ways of assuring the reader that they are fictions, or what Searle calls "non-deceptive pseudo-performances," thereby ensuring the suspension of the conventions by which we normally judge the felicitousness of other kinds of discourse. Historical discourse is also guaranteed by metatextual announcements, references to sources and authorities, assurances as to the credibility of witnesses (such as John included in the narrative I began by discussing). In general, history-writing, even more than fiction, relies on third-person narration. Novels quite often have first-person narrators, but their presence in an historical account gives it a different generic feel—it becomes a memoir. The advantage of third-person narration is that it is the mode which best produces the illusion of pure reference.[3] But it *is* an illusion, the effect of a rhetorical device. We cannot escape the conclusion that "the fact can exist only linguistically, as a term in a discourse," although "we behave as if it were a simple reproduction of something or other on another plane of existence altogether, some extra-structural 'reality.' "[4]

An understanding of this, and of the dependence we have on the myth that felicitous assertion equals accurate reference, has occasionally led writers of narrative to tease us out of our delusion by "foregrounding" the differences between real and narrative time, and by destroying our illusions of narrative causality and closure. Sterne did it at the beginning of the novel, before the conventions had time to be confused with the truth; and lately it has become a dominant mode of serious narrative. Not for nothing is the purpose of the *nouveau roman* said to be "disappointment" (*déception*), and not for nothing does it wage its campaign against vulgar mimesis. We resist, drugged by the comfort of the conventional, fearing the consequences of losing an accessible truth.[5]

Historians are aware of these problems, but tend to confine discussion of them to a separate discipline called "philosophy of history." Within that enclosure they discuss, each in his own way, the relation between history and chronicle. Few, I think, maintain, when thinking along these lines, that there can be an immediate relation between history-writing and "what actually happened" (*wie es eigentlich gewesen*, in Ranke's famous formula). Indeed they seem to be most interested in questions of explanation and narrative, that is, in matters of telling and causal connection (explanations are ways of filling gaps in the causal sequence established by the narrative, a kind of modern midrash). They think that history, like story, has to have the property of "followability," to use W. B. Gallie's word;[6] that a history—in Arthur Danto's phrase—is "a narrative structure imposed upon events."[7] Such narratives will have the logical structure of other stories, though their purpose is to provide explanations by establishing connections other than those immediately suggested by a chronicle sequence.

This philosophical effort seems to be directed at the same problems that I have been discussing in relation to the Passion narratives. We are offered a narrative structure, with all its mnemonic and suasive advantages. We get the ben-

efits of followability, and whatever is followable is on the way to being acceptable. A "convincing" narrative convinces mainly because it is well-formed and followable, though for other reasons also; for instance, it reassures us by providing what appears to be an impartially accurate rendering of reality. When John gives the distance from Bethany to Jerusalem, and names the place where Pilate sat in judgment, he may well be wrong in both cases, but the detail is immediately reassuring.

Gallie observes that following a story is "a teleologically guided form of attention."[8] And as many others have argued, to make arrangements for such guidance is to have some ulterior motive, whether it is aesthetic, epistemological, or ethical (which includes "ideological"). These are Morton White's categories of metahistorical control or motive; others have more complex schemes.[9] According to William James, "the preferences of sentient creatures are what *create* the importance of topics";[10] and Nietzsche, in "The Use and Abuse of History," declared that "for a fact to exist we must first introduce meaning." All this we know, even if we behave as if we did not. The historical narrative comes to us heavily censored (as the account of a dream is censored) but also heavily interpreted (as that same account is affected by the dogmatic presuppositions of the analyst, which are, as Habermas says, "translated into the narrative interpretation.")[11] The historian cannot write, nor can we read, without prejudice. I hope we have seen that this is true of the gospel narratives.

Such a view of history-writing, suitably refined for philosophers and semiologists, might be generally acceptable; but once more we have to remember how difficult it is to behave as if it were correct. We are so habituated to the myth of transparency that we continue, as Jean Starobinski neatly puts it, to ignore *what is written* in favor of *what it is written about*.[12] One purpose of this book is to reverse that priority, which is why I am at the moment peculiarly conscious of the difficulty of doing so. And indeed the story of modern biblical exegesis (another history, with its own provision of prejudices) seems to confirm the view that it takes a powerful mind to attend to what is written at the expense of what it is written about.

The scholarly tradition that cultivated seriously this form of attention was the Jewish; and from our point of view its most influential representative was Spinoza. When he drew up his rules of scriptural interpretation in the seventh chapter of the *Tractatus Theologico Politicus* he distinguished strictly between meaning and truth (what is written and what it is written about): in exegesis "we are at work," he said, "not on the truth of passages but on their meaning." And he expressed a particular dislike for the practice of distorting meaning "in order to make it conform with some truth already entertained." He neatly convicts his illustrious predecessor Maimonides of this offense, which he thinks intellectually disreputable and liable to favor political authoritarianism. The Bible, he held, "leaves reason absolutely free"; it is of divine origin, but it is accommodated to human understanding, which may ascertain its meanings, but must not confound them with truths. "It is one thing to understand the meaning of Scripture, and quite another to understand the actual truth."[13] Five centuries of Jewish interpretative rationalism stood behind Spinoza; but he was addressing the problems of his own day, and saw that the confusion of meaning and truth might result in the suppression of religious liberty. His pious book seemed blasphemous in 1670; so powerful is the atavistic preference for truth over meaning.

It was through the English Deists, some of whom were with better cause thought shocking, that Spinoza influenced the European tradition of biblical scholarship from the late eighteenth century on. A hundred years after Spinoza, Johann Michaelis could state that there was no reason to think the evangelists inspired in their account of history; and Lessing argued that "if no historical truth can be demonstrated, then nothing can be demonstrated by means of historical truths." Kant calmly dismissed the argument about history as irrelevant: "why should we entangle ourselves in such terribly learned investigations and disputes over an historical narrative, which we should always have left where it belonged, (among the *adiaphora* [matters of indifference]) when it is with *religion* that we have to do?" And so on, to David Friedrich Strauss.

This early firmness of tone was not maintained. It was, perhaps, not easy for German scholars to shut out the echoes of Luther's voice, which had laid it down that when a text is literal rather than manifestly allegorical, and when it is also narrative, then it must be historical.[14] The consequences of this conflict are the subject of a subtle and interesting book by Hans W. Frei. One of them was the development of modern hermeneutics. The distinction between meaning and truth in the biblical narratives—whether one accepted it or denied it—required new principles of interpretation. Among the new concepts this need engendered was "history-likeness" (*Geschichtsähnlichkeit*); it was necessary to disentangle this quality from guaranteed truth.

Frei describes the evolution of various hermeneutics intended to allow for the existence of such necessary distinctions without requiring the sacrifice of everything the practitioner held dear. An example is Herder's argument that history can mean "the kind of consciousness represented by a specific kind of account. . . . To be historical . . . an account need not be of any specific occurrence that had actually taken place." Herder also said that "whoever turns a gospel of Christ into a novel has wounded my heart."[15] What he needed was the right to affirm the factual truth of scripture without having to decide whether its meaning lay in its having happened or merely in its having been written. Noting a similar compromise in Strauss, Frei explains these confusions of factuality with fact-likeness by saying that the Germans, unlike the English, had small experience of nonhistorical realistic narrative (they got the Higher Criticism but we got the Novel).[16] So the notion that the story *was* the meaning lay beyond their grasp. This is ingenious but questionable. But of the confusion between history-likeness and history there is no doubt; we still suffer from it, though later criticism reduced the historical Jesus to a shadow, and the interpretative and metahistorical motives of the evangelists have been minutely examined. The claim that the gospels are truth-centered continues for many to entail the proposition that they are in some sense factual, even though the claim takes the form of saying that the fact they refer to is a theology. It remains exceedingly difficult to treat them as stories, as texts totally lacking transparency on event.

And of course it is true that John's account of the breaking of the legs and the spear thrust, or Mark's account of Peter's denial, could hardly have achieved such success in the world had they been recorded in the manner of Pynchon's naval battle. The evangelists too were writing for a small community regarded as eccentric and possessing a communication system at odds with that of officialdom, but their object was different. It would have seemed insane to the author of John's gospel to profess not to know which ship was sent out, or where the sighting occurred, or whether either ship fired; or to allow that there was no physical evidence to prove that the encounter took place. And it would have seemed equally insane to believe that the world was a mass of interlinked communication systems bearing no messages, or only messages of the utmost triviality. He may have thought of the world as like a book; but if so the system was saturated with messages of the very highest importance. Lest they should be disbelieved or misunderstood or corrupted, there was a need for realism, and an equal need for the structure of *testimonia*, so that this sequence of events should seem a piece of, even the crown of, an historical development perceptible to the eye of the interpreter and written into the structure of the world, now seen as a book, as a codex. So it continued to be seen, by Dante at the climax of his poem, by Mallarmé at the end of the great age of the book. Pynchon's joke belongs to another age, which we have still hardly come to terms with.

The novel simulated the authority conferred on history by this perfect match of book and world. Henry James, the great master of research into the formal possibilities of fiction, continued to regard history-likeness as one of its essential characteristics. He thought the novelist was obliged to maintain the fiction that his fiction is history, and expostulated against Trollope for his carelessness in keeping up such appearances. It may be, as Hillis Miller argues,[17] that the maintenance of such fictions, and especially of the fiction that a narrative text may be transparent on fact, requires the acceptance of a culture that imposes its own conditions, in-

cluding its unexamined teleologies and its sense of endings, and that even in the nineteenth century there were signs that these beliefs and assumptions were being "demythologized." He finds attempts at demythologizing in *Middlemarch*. There may be stirrings in George Eliot of a new attitude to meaning in history (she knew Strauss, of course, as well as Charles Lyell and Darwin) but she had by no means lost the desire to report everything aright, *wei es eigentlich gewesen*, as her notebooks tell us clearly enough. What precisely are the facts? It is a very George-Eliotish question: what are the facts about the first cholera epidemic, or the 1832 Reform Act, or the laws of inheritance, or German biblical scholarship, or whatever came up and had to be consistent with history-likeness. No doubt she would have said that in reading her novels one ought to be working on meaning rather than truth (she greatly admired Spinoza) but the novels still exploit the cultural identification of the two. Nor are we, and the modern historians, so at home in a new age that we do not, for the most part, continue to countenance the benign deceit. How far we do so because of the saturation of our culture by the gospels and traditional interpretations one need not try to say.

All modern interpretation that is not merely an attempt at "re-cognition" involves some effort to divorce meaning and truth. This accounts for both the splendors and the miseries of the art. Insofar as we can treat a text as not referring to what is outside or beyond it, we more easily understand that it has internal relationships independent of the coding procedures by which we may find it transparent upon a known world. We see why it has latent mysteries, intermittent radiances. But in acquiring this privilege, the interpreters lose the possibility of consensus, and of access to a single truth at the heart of the thing. No one, however special his point of vantage, can get past all those doorkeepers into the shrine of the single sense. I make an allegory, once more, of Kafka's parable; but some such position is the starting point of all modern hermeneutics except those which are consciously reactionary. The pleasures of interpretation are henceforth linked to loss and disappointment, so that most of us will find the task too hard, or simply repugnant; and then, abandoning meaning, we slip back into the old comfortable fictions of transparency, the single sense, the truth.

Notes

1. The term is Gerard Genette's; his fuller classification would perhaps be "heterodiegetic internal analepsis," but it is interesting that none of his options seems to be a perfect fit in this case. See his *Figures III*, Paris, 1972, and Shlomith Rimmon, "A Comprehensive Theory of Narrative," *PTL: a Journal for Descriptive Poetics and Theory of Literature*, I (1976): 33–62.

2. John Searle, "The Logical Status of Fictional Discourse," *New Literary History*, 6 (1974/5): 319–332.

3. Jean Starobinski, "Le Démoniaque de Gérasa: analyse littéraire de Marc 5:1–20," in Roland Barthes and others, *Analyse structurale et exégèse biblique*, Paris, 1971, pp. 63–94; and in *Trois fureurs* ("Le Combat avec Légion"), Paris, 1974, 73–126. English translation in *New Literary History*, 4 (1973): 331–356.

4. Roland Barthes, "Le discours de l'histoire," *Social Science Information*, 6.4 (1967): 65–75.

5. Perhaps one should note here the assumption of modern semiologists that the "meaning" of a sign-vehicle never has a corresponding object (see Umberto Eco, *Theory of Semiotics*, Bloomington, 1976, pp. 58f). The social conventions governing the use of language are such that it has practical consequences: in Eco's example, if I tell you your house is on fire you will probably hurry home; but it may or may not be burning. More pointedly, the sentence "Napoleon died at Saint Helena on May 5, 1821" does not, for the semiologist, constitute something that is historically true, but merely shows that there exist in our culture codes such that sentences of this kind connote "historical truth."

6. W. B. Gallie, *Philosophy and Historical Understanding*, New York, 1964. John Drury, privately, makes the interesting point that Luke in his preface (1:1) announces that his plan is to set out his narrative sequentially (*kathexēs*), or in other words to give the story followability.

7. Arthur Danto, *Analytic Philosophy of History*, New York, 1965, p. 132.

8. Gallie, p. 64

9. Morton White, *Foundations of Historical Knowledge*, New York, 1965, p. 222.

10. Quoted in White, p. 261.

11. J. Habermas, *Knowledge and Human Interests*, trans. Jeremy Shapiro, Boston, 1971, p. 273.

12. See note 3.

13. *Works of Spinoza*, translated by R. H. M. Elwes, London, 1883, I, 101f.

14. Hans Frei, *The Eclipse of Biblical Narrative*, New Haven, 1974, p. 41.

15. Frei, p. 187.

16. Frei, pp. 142f. Frei has an interesting quotation from a letter of Richardson's, in which the novelist explains that he wishes to maintain the fiction that Clarissa's letters were real, not because he wished them to be *"thought* genuine," but, among other reasons, in order "to avoid hurting that kind of Historical Faith which Fiction itself is genuinely read with, tho' we know it to be Fiction" (p. 144). For a useful study of the relations of fact and fiction in literary theory before, during, and after the Renaissance, see W. B. Nelson, *Fact and Fiction: The Dilemma of the Renaissance Storyteller*, Cambridge, Mass., 1973.

17. J. Hillis Miller, "Narrative and History," *ELH*, 41 (1974): 455–473.

Application

Myths and *Hamlet*

P. J. Aldus

*P. J. Aldus quotes with approval Northrop Frye's
remark that "the literary anthropologist who chases
the source of the Hamlet legend from the pre-Shakespeare play to Saxo, and from Saxo to nature
myths, is not running away from Shakespeare: he is
drawing closer to the archetypal form which Shakespeare recreated"; and Aldus's book-length study of
Hamlet illustrates how such a "literary anthropologist" might go to work. Ultimately, Aldus, like
Frye, is not so much concerned with sources as he
is with recurrent images and symbols. His task is
to read the play not as a direct "mimesis" of human action, nor as a reflection of personal or social
history, but as a "text" woven from many strands
in that vast tapestry that makes up the world of literature—in short, to read it intertextually. The following selection from his chapter entitled "Myths"
shows what such a reading might look like.*

Reprinted from P. J. Aldus, *Mousetrap: Structure and
Meaning in Hamlet*, pp. 176–85. © 1977 by the University of Toronto Press. Reprinted by permission of
the University of Toronto Press.

Hyperion's curls; the front of Jove himself;
An eye like Mars, to threaten and command;
A station like the herald Mercury
New lighted on a heaven-kissing hill:
A combination and a form indeed
Where every god did seem to set his seal
To give the world assurance of a man.

The "House of Hamlet" is as marked by doom
as is the House of Kadmos. The peculiar power
of both lies in some measure in circularity: each
is the house of doomed man in its ever-recur-
ring, ever-present past. In *Hamlet* horrifying in-
tensities come in part from inversion of perspectives in the cycle: that which is within,
although we see it outwardly; the evil burden of
the past in the present, both one; night, not day,
although a malevolent light shines on its snared
and trapped figures; doomsday, here and now,
ghosts walking in judgment of men, the
"sheeted dead" squeaking and gibbering in Elsinore.

In our initial views of myth extremes at the
ends of a line—mythic substance and equally
mysterious literal fact—were postulated, and
these, to attempt a meaningful reconciliation of
paradox, were bent to form a circle. In this, beginning can be determined only by understanding the end, for they are the same. This concept
has brought us to the concurrent lines of paradox in *Hamlet*, which appear in obscurely repetitive interweavings, part of the structural
manner of Shakespeare's art. That these complexities can be reduced to the few limited topics
of essential myth emphasizes the extraordinary
invention that Shakespeare displays. But in
Plato there are two further views of invention
that have their bearings: the use of extant myths
and legends, and the controlling (and controlled) power of poetic "madness." These add
breadth and plumb depths in the myth being
invented.

The incorporation of extant literary myths,

legends, and quasi-literary stories into sophisticated literary myth has been shown in the *Phaedrus* and the *Oedipus Rex*. *Hamlet* may have fewer such allusions than either, but what there is from Greece and Rome, the Old Testament, and the Christ story invites attention. It seems reasonable that the hypothesis so far advanced should be served by such mythic-legendary-historical matter if the invention in *Hamlet* is of a piece.

Extant myths are used in *Hamlet* in two ways: occasionally as independent details to enforce a significant meaning, or in continuous symbolic parallel to the whole action. There appear to be two large, intertwined, containing patterns, one Greek, ending in death, the other beginning with the Garden and ending with doomsday. At the centre of the first is Hyperion, of the second, Christ. Frequent interplay of the two turns on Hamlet's puns on "sun–son." The concept of sacrificial ritual death appears more obviously in Christian than Greek allusions. There seem to be intermixtures of the figures of Hyperion and Phoebus Apollo; the latter's various attributes appear in Hamlet; the former's identity with Hamlet comes by way of the essential identity of Ghost-father and Hamlet-son. Within this sophisticated totality appear various independent allusions not only from the Greeks and the Old Testament, but also from folklore. The large patterns will be explored first, both substantively and in terms of their arrangements in the play.

As usual, Shakespeare's disposition of elements in his invention seems both free and ordered, in both the parts called acts and the whole play.

Act I is preponderantly Greek in emphasis, although its allusions begin with Julius Caesar and end with a parallel between Hamlet's birth and Christ's. Scene i of the act has the same containing pattern. The whole act has, between its termini, various Greek, Christian, and Old Testament allusions, so woven together in implications as to be one mythic tapestry, yet so nicely discriminated as to emphasize the nature of action and character. Its end, Hamlet's fate to be born to set right a chaotic world, is matched by a last act that, still containing Greek and Roman matter, begins in a Christian and Old Testament context and ends in a promise of the re-

telling of a mysterious and meaningful life and death.

The second and third acts, preliminary to violence with the Queen in III.iv, are almost totally Greek, with some Old Testament allusion. Within this there are brief Christian references, although the section ends in Old Testament terms.

The fourth act, obscure in other respects, as in Ophelia's dying and Hamlet's absence–presence, is no less mixed in mythic allusion. Every kind noted is present in what appears to be, but probably is not, an extravagantly casual sequence. The last act follows in terms already noted.

What is almost surely not indifferent or accidental is the direction and force of Greek allusion. It dominates the dread forebodings of I.i, the first soliloquy, critical parts of I.iv and v, almost all of the second act, all of the darkly violent Pyrrhus scene, much of the Players' play, the centre (but not the Old Testament and Christian end) of the attack on the Queen. There is little Greek myth in act IV, but that is important. It is still present, but minimally, in act V. The pattern seems to be this: where violence is sexual towards the Queen/Woman, Greek myth is dominant; where this violence is modulated into sacrificial dying, always at the end of a sequence—act or play—the emphasis is Christian. There are variables in this pattern and inclusions of disparate yet not irrelevant allusion, but not enough to qualify the thrust of the whole. Receding depths seem evident once more.

No one knows how precise Shakespeare's knowledge was of Norse and Greek myth (except as contextual meaning is a test). But sensitive readers have testified to matter and impact like that of ancient myth in their reading of *Hamlet*, notably Gilbert Murray, who writes: "Thus . . . we finally run the Hamlet-saga to earth . . . in that world-wide ritual battle of Summer and Winter, of Life and Death. . . ." The Hamlet story, he says, comes clearly from Greek or pre-Greek legends, the primeval kings in Hesiod (408–9; 405). Northrop Frye writes: ". . . the literary anthropologist who chases the source of the Hamlet legend from the pre-Shakespeare play to Saxo, and from Saxo to naturemyths, is not running away from Shakespeare:

he is drawing closer to the archetypal form which Shakespeare recreated."[1]

It may be, as has been contended by Fergusson, that Hamlet had "nothing in common with Saxo's primitive savage," or that he is, as Murray suggests, sharer of Amleth's ancestry, his father "an ancient Teutonic god connected with Dawn and the Spring" and a mother "said to be the Green Earth . . ." (408). But what is important is not Norse background, nor even the Greek in itself, which is mostly quite clear, but the interweavings of Christian and Old Testament implications with primal Greek matter. The key to this appears to be the figure of Hyperion, alluded to by Hamlet twice in extravagant encomia for a Father as over against the satyr uncle/father. If in *Hamlet* there actually is Father–Son–Ghost in the Judeo-Christian tradition, it may well be that Shakespeare chose typically to interfuse such meaning with parallels to Hyperion in scenes in the depths of the mystery.

In the most distant beginnings, according to Greek myth, Hyperion is one of ten children of the union of Sky or Heaven and Earth, Ouranos and Gaea. He is a Titan, who in turn is the father of Helios, not the sun god as Apollo, for example, but the Sun himself. In its simplest terms this appears to be parallel with, or possibly prototype for, Son, Father, and "Ghost," i.e., a reaching back into ultimate enigma.

What may strengthen the likelihood that Shakespeare is working in these terms is not only that Hyperion is the father of Moon and Dawn, both important in *Hamlet*, as well as the Sun, a critical word for Hamlet, but also that Mnemosyne, memory, is Titaness sister of Hyperion. Just as "son," "father," "mother" are of the essence of Hamlet, so is "memory." Here the force in life that generates, that is put into the form of marriage, that endlessly disrupts marriage to allow the fecund mother to procreate again, gains its most relevant word, in contemporary terms "racial memory." Murray recounts from Hesiod and through Frazer the pattern that moves towards us to the moment we are soul-shaken by *Hamlet*: Ouranos, Gaea, Kronos; Kronos, Rhea, Zeus; Laios, Jocasta, Oedipus; Agamemnon, Clytemnestra, Orestes; Hamlet/Aegisthus/Claudius, Gertrude, Hamlet.

But Shakespeare does not press the point directly: Hyperion is mentioned only twice. Even had he chosen to make the allusion frequently, it would not have altered the much richer implications that lie simply in "sun," for, on the one hand, Hyperion in his true identity has little of suggestive character that could be used, and on the other, almost everyone thinks him to be the sun god Phoebus Apollo. All of this is enriched even further by the meaningful ambiguities in "sun/son": Apollo in his various and paradoxically divided nature is prototype for Hamlet's multiple identities and puzzling ambivalences. At the same time his character as fertility god is incorporated with the sacrificial Christ figure. And just as with Hyperion, all of this is done obscurely: Apollo is mentioned only once as Phoebus; we must infer Hamlet's Apollo character through the "sun" passages, and from Hamlet, a typical obscurity. That Hercules is at times a sun god is probably not indifferent.[2]

The complexities of the several allusive patterns throughout the play can probably best be clarified by examining them in the order that Shakespeare uses them, in conjunctive clusters or individually. Each act may appear to have its identity in these terms, but there is continuous interlinkage; any major pattern that may seem to disappear is reaffirmed, sometimes almost fugitively, by some line or word. We turn then to act I at the point where, the Ghost having appeared once, the Caesar–Brutus story and "our Saviour's birth" are together one of the early tellings of the Hamlet story. In this relatively brief passage we find a complex of allusions from Roman and Christian mythic history, Greek myth, and folklore. These are interwoven as prologue for all allusion and action that follows excepting only Old Testament references, which begin in I.ii. All of this establishes probability in its matter and order for the end of the whole action; it deserves close examination.

The allusions to Caesar and Christ together are the second telling of the Hamlet story. But the two parts of this version seem to be interrupted by a brief reappearance of the silent Ghost. Although our concern at the moment is matter relevant to extant myths, it should be noted that the scene in its three parts is exactly parallel to the underlying order of the whole play: Hamlet's death, the appearance of his silent Ghost, his rebirth. There is then no interruption; whatever matter there may be in Horatio's remarks to the Ghost should be consistent with what is in the Caesar and Christ parts.

Among the omens preceding Caesar's murder are a spotted or obscured sun and a moon almost "dying" in eclipse. These terms and others in the passage almost always receive a simple-naturalistic interpretation, or one that takes into account current Elizabethan beliefs and meteorological phenomena. But Shakespeare establishes both a Roman and a Greek context. It seems reasonable to think of a moon so dark—part of the "precurse of fear'd events," "dews of blood," the murder of a King—as to be Hecate, moon goddess in Hades. Edith Hamilton identifies her as "the Goddess of the Dark of the Moon, the black nights when the moon is hidden . . . associated with deeds of darkness." She is the antithetical form of Artemis or Diana, "Huntsman-in-chief to the gods . . . 'protectress of dewy youth' . . . In her is shown most vividly the uncertainty between good and evil which is apparent in every one of the divinities" (31–2).[5]

That the "moist star" is in fact Hecate is clear in a passage that is prologue to the killing of a King:

> LUC Thou mixture rank, of midnight weeds collected,
> With Hecate's ban thrice blasted, thrice infected,
> Thy natural magic and dire property
> On wholesome life usurps immediately.

Hecate's awesome presence seems equally evident as Hamlet is about to do another dread act:

> 'Tis now the very witching time of night,
> When churchyards yawn, and hell itself breathes out
> Contagion to this world. Now could I drink hot blood . . .

There is more primal Greek myth in the omens of both Caesar's death and the harbingers of "fear'd events . . . demonstrated/Unto our . . . countrymen." Hecate/Artemis's twin brother Apollo is here and equally threatening: "As stars with trains of fire, and dews of blood,/ Disasters in the sun . . ." "Disasters" may be the

sign of some unknown sickness in the great fertility god, or of imminent destructive attack by him. These two relevances to Hamlet are borne out by several more. Apollo is musician; hunter; the healer ("O cursed spite/That ever I was born to set it right!"); god of truth, his oracle at Delphi, like Elsinore, the centre of the world ("O my prophetic soul!"—and Polonius/Hamlet, "I will find/Where truth is hid, though it were hid indeed/Within the centre"); often the sun god ("my cousin Hamlet, and my son—"; "I am too much i' th' sun").

Hamilton writes: "Apollo at Delphi was a purely beneficent power . . . the purifier . . . able to cleanse even those stained with the blood of their kindred. Nevertheless . . . [he could be] pitiless and cruel. Two ideas were fighting in him as in all the gods: a primitive, crude idea and one that was beautiful and poetic" (31). Relevant to this deep ambivalence in man projected by him into his ideal identities, the gods, is the chorus in the Parodos of the Oedipus Rex:

> [Strophe 1]
>
> What is God singing in his profound
> Delphi of gold and shadow?
> What oracle for Thebes, the sunwhipped city?
>
> Fear unjoints me, the roots of my heart tremble.
>
> Now I remember, O Healer, your power, and wonder:
> Will you send doom like a sudden cloud, or weave it
> Like nightfall of the past?

This fearful inquiry is followed by a prayer to Athene, Artemis, Zeus, and Apollo himself to save the "sunwhipped" city, from "this attack by fire," this plague which "burns on."

In the middle of the complex of Greek myth is one startling detail, in that it is Christian. The moon is "sick almost to doomsday with eclipse." "Doomsday" reappears only once again directly, in the grave-makers' scene, prologue to ritual death in v.ii. But Christian allusions beginning here are equal and interwoven with Greek myth, most clearly in the third part of the present scene.

These begin just after the cock crows, the

"bird of dawning" that "Doth . . . /Awake the god of day"; that warns ghosts and devils of coming light, that keeps evils away all night " 'gainst that season comes/Wherein our Saviour's birth is celebrated." Just as "sun–son" is *nexus* for Apollo/Christ, so is the cock, which wakens Apollo and is harbinger of the saviour-god. There is nothing directly of it in the play, but perhaps for many readers there may be here sufficient allusion to the cock's crowing at the betrayal-death of Christ shortly after his thirtieth year. Certainly the dawn observed by Bernardo, Horatio, and Marcellus is not the full glory of a brilliant Phoebus; Apollo's face is obscured by the clouds that hang on him.

Between this end and the Caesar beginning is the brief reappearance of the Ghost, to whom three appeals by Horatio that it speak are unsuccessful. What seems contextually significant is, as Kittredge points out, that Horatio's questions have "abundant illustration" in European folklore. There is, then, a consistent pattern of folklore, history, and myth in Roman–Christian terms, and Greek myth back to the beginnings, with a well-established common identity of Apollo, sun god and destroyer, and Christ, the son/sacrificial king. The second scene will add Old Testament allusions to make full the controlling pattern of myth throughout the play.

Although there are partial act and scene divisions in the Folio *Hamlet*, the artificialities of the very many imposed divisions that give the contemporary reader and theatre-goer a feeling of interruption were apparently not observed in Shakespeare's theatre. Yet there are separate identities in action, both large and small, which must have their organic interweaving. Shakespeare is a master of interlinking elements: suggestive parallels, minimal repetitions, unobtrusive, even obscure, images, rather than formal means. The Christian–Greek allusion which completes I.i is thus the first allusion in I.ii, preliminary to the critical Old Testament reference. Already dealt with, it needs only restatement: the King's inquiry why the clouds still hang on his "son," and Hamlet's cryptic response, "not so my lord. I am too much i' th' sun."

What appears to be an Old Testament allusion moments later seems much too general to be such an allusion. To persevere so, says the King, is a fault to heaven, to nature, and to reason,

> whose common theme
> Is death of fathers, and who still hath cried,
> From the first corse till he that died today,
> "This must be so."

"The first corse" seems to be so lacking in context as to refer only to the dimmest unknown dying in antiquity. But there is a context, a brother's murder. The only corse that would occupy the King's mind would be Abel's, as the prayer scene makes clear; before that, and immediately after the King's remark, Hamlet's "unweeded garden . . . things rank and gross in nature possess it merely" takes us to Genesis, to the despoiled Garden, and then, by association, to Cain.

The rank garden almost immediately merges into a series of Greek allusions. First is "Hyperion to a satyr," paraphrased two lines later in "Heaven and earth!" As Hamlet's mind dwells more and more intensely on the Queen's wicked speed to incest, other Greek allusions add their meanings.

The Queen "followed my poor father's body/ Like Niobe, all tears." The Queen wept excessively, protested her grief too much. But who was Niobe, and why did she weep? Sister of Atreus, granddaughter of Tantalus, she was a member of the tragic family of whom Orestes was one. Tantalus, a mortal son of Zeus, arranged the death of his son Pelops to show his hatred of the gods. But Pelops was restored to life by the gods, and became the father of Niobe. She in turn offended Leto, mother of Apollo and Artemis, by invidious boasting of her queenship and her children. Consequently Artemis and Apollo killed all of her children. How much here is relevant to Hamlet himself? A son killed by a demigod father; restored by divine decree to another life to become a father; his queen's children killed by the sun god and moon goddess. The initial force which creates creates that which kills, restores the killed, kills again, although it be god of light and fertility.

Next we come to an encomium of the Hyperion–father as against the satyr–uncle/father, who is

> My father's brother, but no more like my father
> Than I to Hercules.

This analogue is significant in several ways. The father already having been identified with Hyperion as sun god, Hamlet here associates him with another sun god, and himself in parallel, with uncle/father–satyr. This antithetical shift in identity from heavenly light to earthly lust is curiously carried out further in an extension of the figure as Horatio and his two companions seek to restrain Hamlet from following the Ghost. Violently fighting off their restraint, Hamlet shouts,

> My fate cries out
> And makes each petty artire in this body
> As hardy as the Nemean lion's nerve.

"My father is Herculean; I am as fiercely strong as the Nemean lion." But Hercules was the slayer of the Nemean lion. Like Tantalus, Niobe's forebear, Hamlet's father, just as the present King/uncle, is a son-slayer, at least in intent. Perhaps it is not irrelevant to remember that Laios sought to kill his son Oedipus because of Apollo's prophecy, but was killed by that son in accordance with Apollo's edict, and that that son then slept with his mother.

Hercules appears again in Hamlet's discussion of the state of the theatre with Rosencrantz/Guildenstern:

> HAM Do the boys carry it away?
> ROS Ay, that they do, my lord—Hercules and
> his load too.

Hercules once relieved Atlas of his load. More particularly, the sign of the Globe theatre, metaphoric centre, *omphalos*, of the action of *Hamlet*, was Hercules bearing all the world on his back, not an indifferent image in the meaning of *Hamlet*.

There are further details about Hercules that are likely relevant. Rose points out that he was always a man, not a god; that the original Herakles may have been a figure famous in war and hunting; that his alternate name Alkeides has an ending that "forms a patronymic, a surname signifying 'son' (or at least descendant of So-and-So)." His mother was Alkmene, his father Zeus. His mother's husband, Amphitryon, had killed his uncle, which put blood guilt upon him. He was driven mad by Hera and murdered his

sons. In his last three labours he overcame a power of the other world, or death. He is "regularly shown as amorous" (105–18 *passim*).[6]

It is not unimportant that the Nemean lion allusion comes at the moment when Hamlet will join his cursed Ghost to hear his own voice urge him on to the act whose blastments will kill him.

Following the first soliloquy Hamlet is joined by Horatio, Bernardo, and Marcellus; they will lead him to the Ghost who already possesses him. What is said to Hamlet by Horatio, their spokesman, may be within Christian implication. (Here one must note the temptation to assume Christian allusion whenever "three" is intimated or emphasized—an interpretation to be resisted, but not ignored.) Three nights, Horatio reports, the Ghost appeared, and thrice he walked in the darkness of the night, a figure entombed, yet present in the "eruption of our state."

It may seem extravagant, but not beyond belief in the context of myth, to note that at the end of I.i, the Ghost having appeared silently just after the Saviour's birth has been emphasized, Marcellus says, for the three engrossed in the mystery of the Ghost; "I this morning know/ Where we shall find him. . . ." Why this morning? Why this certainty of one of three men who will search him out, where Hamlet/Christ will be? Shortly after they have found him he bitterly speaks of the curse of the birth that will lead him to his dyings.

After the Ghost's reference to purgatory (as much a Greek as a Christian concept) he praises Hamlet:

> I find thee apt;
> And duller shouldst thou be than the fat weed
> That rots itself in ease on Lethe wharf
> Wouldst thou not stir in this.

Again Shakespeare is mildly obscure, or assumes sophistication about myth in his audience. The "fat weed" has been identified as asphodel, a flower rich in implications.

For the Greeks asphodel had antithetical meanings. As symbol of primal birth it was the flower that formed the celestial bed for Zeus and Hera, but it was also the flower of death, this with a special implication. Those who in life had been distinguished by neither virtue nor vice were sentenced to a monotonous, joyless existence in the meadows of asphodel in Hades. In Christian terms asphodel is also symbol of death and eternity, but yet is dedicated to the Virgin Mary. Finally, in the simplest sense of the "language of flowers," it is appropriate to Laertes/Hamlet, brother/lover of Ophelia, for it represents memorial sorrow—"my regrets follow you to the grave." The most interesting detail is that the Ghost avers that Hamlet is not characterized by asphodel: he will "stir" in the matter of his mother's beastly lust.

How much of this strikingly complex applicability to *Hamlet* is in fact part of Shakespeare's art one can only believe or disbelieve. But the play is so marked by images, metaphors, and symbols of comparable richness in implication, and so totally consistent in a unity, that it is difficult to disbelieve.

Notes

1. Gilbert Murray, "Hamlet and Orestes," in *Proceedings of the British Academy* (London, 1913–1914). Northrop Frye, "The Archetypes of Literature," *Kenyon Review*, 13 (1951), 101.

2. I am indebted to P. J. M. Robertson for clarifying and enforcing this and other meanings through the etymologies of the names of characters. "Polonius" appears to be a Latinized-Greek form of "Ἀπόλλωη or Apollōn," i.e. "Apollo." Particular forms and meanings seem relevant: ἀπόλλυμι, ἀπόλλω, "to destroy utterly," "to ruin"; hence "Apollyon, the destroyer"; Ἀπυλλώνιος (Apollōnios), "of or be-

longing to Apollo"; πῶλος (pōlos), "young man"; πωλέω (pōleo-polo), "to sell or offer for sale." Closely relevant are meanings lying in ὀφειλεια (ōphelia or ōpheileia) which in its verb forms can mean "to be bound to render," "to be obliged to do." Sophocles' *Philocletes* 1421 reads σοι τουτ᾽ ὀφείλεται παθείν "it is thy destiny to suffer this." The feminine noun form ὠφέλεια (opheleia) means, among other things, "spoil, booty."

3. Issue may be taken that the devil is within Christian allusion, and possibly with considerable justification. The Christian devil is, of course, God's Old Testament adversary Satan, but in a strongly Christian context, as in *Hamlet*, one tends to think of him as Christ's adversary. As myth, Satan (dark, part animal, like a satyr or a centaur) is man's projected image of his own animalistic instincts, warring within him with a higher principle, God. Monotheism adapted itself to a virtuous trinity, threatened by an objective devil cast into outer darkness. The Greeks' projection was less objective, less limited; it did not establish a formidable otherworld of God, but, with infinitely more imagination, created a race of gods who were only human beings in disguise, if often idealized, whether in slaughter, love, or lust.

4. Again I am indebted to P. J. M. Robertson for pointing out that L. *claudico -are* (n. *claudus*) means "to be lame," "to be incomplete, defective." In an action described by Hamlet as incarceration in a desolate prison, it is not indifferent that L. *claudo -ere* means "to enclose," "surround," "imprison," "confine."

5. Edith Hamilton, *Mythology* (New York, 1942).

6. H. J. Rose, *Gods and Heroes of the Greeks* (New York, 1958).

Application

Literature as Context: Milton's *Lycidas*

Northrop Frye

Northrop Frye's essay on Lycidas, *first presented as a paper to an international comparative literature conference, is an exemplary piece of intertextual criticism that simultaneously argues and illustrates Frye's critical theory. Central to that theory is the view that "the forms of literature are autonomous" and that "every problem in literary criticism is a problem in comparative literature, or simply of literature itself." As Frye moves back and forth between Milton's poem, the conventions of the pastoral elegy, and the larger cycles of death and rebirth, he reminds us that even Milton's vast reading may not include all the parallels the reader may find helpful. "Sources" are not what we're after. Neither are we after the history of the poet or his times, for these researches carry us away from the poem and involve us in irrelevant issues, such as the poet's degree of "sincerity." (Frye pauses to add a few remarks on Wordsworth's now much-debated "Slumber.") For Frye, all poetic expression is necessarily "conventional" and the greatest poems are the most conventional; that is, they are the poems that exploit the conventions of poetry most fully. The most important context for criticism, then, is the context that literature itself provides.*

From *Fables of Identity* by Northrop Frye, pp. 119–29. Copyright © 1963 by Harcourt Brace Jovanovich, Inc. Reprinted by permission of the publisher.

I SHOULD LIKE TO BEGIN WITH A BRIEF DISCUSSION of a familiar poem, Milton's *Lycidas*, in the hope that some of the inferences drawn from the analysis will be relevant to the theme of this conference. *Lycidas*, then, is an elegy in the pastoral convention, written to commemorate a young man named Edward King who was drowned at sea. The origins of the pastoral are partly classical, the tradition that runs through Theocritus and Virgil, and partly Biblical, the imagery of the twenty-third Psalm, of Christ as the Good Shepherd, of the metaphors of "pastor" and "flock" in the Church. The chief connecting link between the traditions in Milton's day was the Fourth or Messianic Eclogue of Virgil. Hence it is common enough to have pastoral images echoing both traditions at once, and not surprising to find that *Lycidas* is a Christian poem as well as a humanistic one.

In the classical pastoral elegy the subject of the elegy is not treated as an individual but as a representative of a dying spirit of nature. The pastoral elegy seems to have some relation to the ritual of the Adonis lament, and the dead poet Bion, in Moschus's poem, is celebrated with much the same kind of imagery as Bion himself uses in his lament for Adonis. The phrase "dying god," for such a figure in later pastoral, is not an anachronism: Virgil says of Daphnis, for example, in the Fifth Eclogue: *"deus, deus ille, Menalca."* Besides, Milton and his learned contemporaries, Selden, for example, or Henry Reynolds, knew at least as much about the symbolism of the "dying god" as any modern student could get out of *The Golden Bough*, which depends mainly on the same classical sources that were available to them. The notion that twentieth-century poets differ from their predecessors in their understanding or use of myth will not bear much scrutiny. So King is given the pastoral name of Lycidas, which is equivalent to Adonis, and is associated with the cyclical rhythms of nature. Of these three are of particular importance: the daily cycle of the sun across the sky, the yearly cycle of the seasons, and the cycle of water, flowing from wells and fountains through rivers to the sea. Sunset, winter, and the sea are emblems of Lycidas' death; sunrise and spring, of his resurrection. The poem begins in the morning, "Under the opening eyelids of the morn," and ends with the sun, like Lycidas himself, dropping into the western ocean, yet due to rise again as Lycidas is to do. The imagery of the opening lines, "Shatter your leaves before the mellowing year," suggests the frosts of autumn killing the flowers, and in the great roll-call of flowers towards the end, most of them early blooming flowers like the "rathe primrose," the spring returns. Again, the opening invocation is to the "Sisters of the sacred well," and the water imagery carries through a great variety of Greek, Italian, and English rivers to the sea in which the dead body of Lycidas lies.

Lycidas, then, is the "archetype" of Edward King. By an archetype I mean a literary symbol, or cluster of symbols, which are used recurrently throughout literature, and thereby become conventional. A poetic use of a flower, by itself, is not necessarily an archetype. But in a poem about the death of a young man it is conventional to associate him with a red or purple flower, usually a spring flower like the hyacinth. The historical origin of the convention may be lost in ritual, but it is a constantly latent one, not only in literature but in life, as the symbolism of the scarlet poppies in World War I shows. Hence in *Lycidas* the "sanguine flower inscrib'd with woe" is an archetype, a symbol that recurs regularly in many poems of its kind. Similarly Lycidas himself is not only the literary form of Edward King, but a conventional or recurring form, of the same family as Shelley's Adonais, the Daphnis of Theocritus and Virgil, and Milton's own Damon. King was also a clergyman and, for Milton's purposes, a poet, so, having selected the conventional archetype of King as drowned young man, Milton has then to select the conventional archetypes of King as poet and of King as priest. These are, respectively, Orpheus and Peter.

Both Orpheus and Peter have attributes that link them in imagery with Lycidas. Orpheus was also an "enchanting son" or spirit of nature; he died young, in much the same role as Adonis, and was flung into the water. Peter would have drowned too without the help of Christ; hence Peter is not named directly, but only as "The Pilot of the Galilean Lake," just as Christ is not named directly, but only as "Him that walked the waves." When Orpheus was torn to pieces by the Maenads, his head went floating "Down the swift Hebrus to the Lesbian shore." The theme of salvation out of water is connected with the image of the dolphin, a conventional type of Christ, and dolphins are called upon to "waft the hapless youth" just before the peroration begins.

The body of the poem is arranged in the form ABACA, a main theme repeated twice with two intervening episodes, as in the musical rondo. The main theme is the drowning of Lycidas in the prime of his life; the two episodes, presided over by the figures of Orpheus and Peter, deal with the theme of premature death as it relates to poetry and to the priesthood respectively. In both the same type of image appears: the mechanical instrument of execution that brings about a sudden death, represented by the "abhorred shears" in the meditation on fame and the "grim two-handed engine" in the meditation on the corruption of the Church. The most difficult part of the construction is the managing of the transitions from these episodes back to the main theme. The poet does this by alluding to his great forerunners in the pastoral convention, Theocritus of Sicily, Virgil of Mantua, and the legendary Arcadians who preceded both:

> O fountain Arethuse, and thou honour'd flood,
> Smooth-sliding Mincius, crown'd with vocal
>   reeds . . .

and later:

> Return, Alpheus, the dread voice is past
> That shrunk thy streams: return, Sicilian Muse.

The allusion has the effect of reminding the reader that this is, after all, a pastoral. But Milton also alludes to the myth of Arethusa and Alpheus, the Arcadian water-spirits who plunged underground and reappeared in Sicily, and this myth not only outlines the history of the pastoral convention, but unites the water imagery with the theme of disappearance and revival.

In pastoral elegy the poet who laments the death is often so closely associated with the dead man as to make him a kind of double or shadow of himself. Similarly Milton represents himself as intimately involved with the death of Lycidas. The theme of premature death is skilfully associated in the opening lines with the conventional apology for a "harsh and crude" poem; the poet hopes for a similar elegy when he dies, and at the end he accepts the responsibilities of survival and turns "Tomorrow to fresh woods, and pastures new," bringing the elegy to a full rich *tierce de Picardie* or major chord. By appearing himself at the beginning and end of the poem, Milton presents the poem as, in a sense, contained within the mind of the poet.

Apart from the historical convention of the pastoral, however, there is also the conventional framework of ideas or assumptions which forms the background of the poem. I call it a framework of ideas, and it may also be that, but in poetry it is rather a framework of images. It consists of four levels of existence. First is the order revealed by Christianity, the order of grace and salvation and of eternal life. Second is the order of human nature, the order represented by the Garden of Eden in the Bible and the Golden Age in classical myth, and which man in his fallen state can, up to a point, regain through education, obedience to law, and the habit of virtue. Third is the order of physical nature, the world of animals and plants which is morally neutral but theologically "fallen." Fourth is the disorder of the unnatural, the sin and death and corruption that entered the world with the Fall.

Lycidas has his connections with all of these orders. In the first place, all the images of death and resurrection are included in and identified with the body of Christ. Christ is the sun of righteousness, the tree of life, the water of life, the dying god who rose again, the saviour from the sea. On this level Lycidas enters the Christian heaven and is greeted by the "Saints above" "In solemn troops, and sweet societies," where the language echoes the Book of Revelation. But simultaneously Lycidas achieves another apotheosis as the Genius of the shore, corresponding to the Attendant Spirit in *Comus*, whose habitation is said to be a world above our own, identified, not with the Christian heaven, but with Spenser's Gardens of Adonis. The third level of physical nature is the world of ordinary experience, where death is simply a loss, and those who mourn the death have to turn to pick up their tasks again. On this level Lycidas is merely absent, "to our moist vows denied," represented only by the empty bier with its flowers. It is on this level too that the poem is contained within the mind of the surviving poet, as on the Christian level it is contained within the body of Christ. Finally, the world of death and corruption holds the drowned corpse of Lycidas, which will soon come to the surface and "welter to the parching wind." This last is an unpleasant and distressing image, and Milton touches it very lightly, picking it up again in an appropriate context:

> But swoln with wind and the rank mist they draw,
> Rot inwardly . . .

In the writing of *Lycidas* there are four creative principles of particular importance. To say that there are four does not mean, of course, that they are separable. One is convention, the reshaping of the poetic material which is appropriate to this subject. Another is genre, the choosing of the appropriate form. A third is archetype, the use of appropriate, and therefore recurrently employed, images and symbols. The fourth, for which there is no name, is the fact that the forms of literature are autonomous: that is, they do not exist outside literature. Milton is not writing an obituary: he does not start with Edward King and his life and times, but with the conventions and archetypes that poetry requires for such a theme.

Of the critical principles illustrated by this analysis, one will be no surprise to the present audience. *Lycidas* owes quite as much to Hebrew, Greek, Latin, and Italian traditions as it does to English. Even the diction, of which I have no space to speak, shows strong Italian influence. Milton was of course a learned poet, but there is no poet whose literary influences are entirely confined to his own language. Thus every problem in literary criticism is a problem in comparative literature, or simply of literature itself.

The next principle is that the provisional hypothesis which we must adopt for the study of every poem is that that poem is a unity. If, after careful and repeated testing, we are forced to conclude that it is not a unity, then we must abandon the hypothesis and look for the reasons why it is not. A good deal of bad criticism of *Lycidas* has resulted from not making enough initial effort to understand the unity of the poem. To talk of "digressions" in *Lycidas* is a typical consequence of a mistaken critical method, of backing into the poem the wrong way round. If, instead of starting with the poem, we start with a handful of peripheral facts about the poem, Milton's casual knowledge of King, his ambitions as a poet, his bitterness against the episcopacy, then of course the poem will break down into pieces corresponding precisely to those fragments of knowledge. *Lycidas* illustrates, on a small scale, what has happened on a much bigger scale in, for example, the criticism of Homer. Critics knowing something about the fragmentary nature of heroic lays and ballads approached the *Iliad* and the *Odyssey* with this knowledge in mind, and the poems obediently split up into the pieces that they wished to isolate. Other critics came along and treated the poems as imaginative unities, and today everyone knows that the second group were more convincing.

The same thing happens when our approach to "sources" becomes fragmentary or piecemeal. *Lycidas* is a dense mass of echoes from previous literature, chiefly pastoral literature. Reading through Virgil's Eclogues with *Lycidas* in mind, we can see that Milton had not simply read or studied these poems: he possessed them; they were part of the material he was shaping. The passage about the hungry sheep reminds us of at least three other passages: one in Dante's *Paradiso*, one in the Book of Ezekiel, and one near the beginning of Hesiod's *Theogony*. There are also echoes of Mantuan and Spenser, of the Gospel of John, and it is quite possible that there are even more striking parallels with poems that Milton had not read. In such cases there is not

a source at all, no one place that the passage "comes from," or, as we say with such stupefying presumption, that the poet "had in mind." There are only archetypes, or recurring themes of literary expression, which *Lycidas* has recreated, and therefore re-echoed, yet once more.

The next principle is that the important problems of literary criticism lie within the study of literature. We notice that a law of diminishing returns sets in as soon as we move away from the poem itself. If we ask, who is Lycidas? the answer is that he is a member of the same family as Theocritus' Daphnis, Bion's Adonis, the Old Testament's Abel, and so on. The answer goes on building up a wider comprehension of literature and a deeper knowledge of its structural principles and recurring themes. But if we ask, who was Edward King? What was his relation to Milton? How good a poet was he? we find ourselves moving dimly in the intense inane. The same is true of minor points. If we ask, why is the image of the two-handed engine in *Lycidas*? we can give an answer, along the lines suggested above, that illustrates how carefully the poem has been constructed. If we ask, what is the two-handed engine? there are forty-odd answers, none of them completely satisfactory; yet the fact that they are not wholly satisfactory hardly seems to be important.

Another form of the same kind of fallacy is the confusion between personal sincerity and literary sincerity. If we start with the facts that *Lycidas* is highly conventional and that Milton knew King only slightly, we may see in *Lycidas* an "artificial" poem without "real feeling" in it. This red herring, though more common among third-rate romantics, was dragged across the study of *Lycidas* by Samuel Johnson. Johnson knew better, but he happened to feel perverse about this particular poem, and so deliberately raised false issues. It would not have occurred to him, for example, to question the conventional use of Horace in the satires of Pope, or of Juvenal in his own. Personal sincerity has no place in literature, because personal sincerity as such is inarticulate. One may burst into tears at the news of a friend's death, but one can never spontaneously burst into song, however doleful a lay. *Lycidas* is a passionately sincere poem, because Milton was deeply interested in the structure and symbolism of funeral elegies, and had been practising since adolescence on every fresh corpse in sight, from the university beadle to the fair infant dying of a cough.

If we ask what inspires a poet, there are always two answers. An occasion, an experience, an event, may inspire the impulse to write. But the impulse to write can only come from previous contact with literature, and the formal inspiration, the poetic structure that crystallizes around the new event, can only be derived from other poems. Hence while every new poem is a new and unique creation, it is also a reshaping of familiar conventions of literature, otherwise it would not be recognizable as literature at all. Literature often gives us the illusion of turning from books to life, from second-hand to direct experience, and thereby discovering new literary principles in the world outside. But this is never quite what happens. No matter how tightly Wordsworth may close the barren leaves of art and let nature be his teacher, his literary forms will be as conventional as ever, although they may echo an unaccustomed set of conventions, such as the ballad or the broadside. The pretence of personal sincerity is itself a literary convention, and Wordsworth makes many of the flat simple statements which represent, in literature, the inarticulateness of personal sincerity:

No motion has she now, no force:
She neither hears nor sees.

But as soon as a death becomes a poetic image, that image is assimilated to other poetic images of death in nature, and hence Lucy inevitably becomes a Proserpine figure, just as King becomes an Adonis:

Rolled round in earth's diurnal course
With rocks, and stones, and trees.

In Whitman we have an even more extreme example than Wordsworth of a cult of personal statement and an avoidance of learned conventions. It is therefore instructive to see what happens in *When Lilacs Last in the Dooryard Bloomed*. The dead man is not called by a pastoral name, but neither is he called by his historical name. He is in a coffin which is carried the length and breadth of the land; he is identified with a "powerful western fallen star"; he is the beloved com-

rade of the poet, who throws the purple flower of the lilac on his coffin; a singing bird laments the death, just as the woods and caves do in *Lycidas*. Convention, genre, archetype, and the autonomy of forms are all illustrated as clearly in Whitman as they are in Milton.

Lycidas is an occasional poem, called forth by a specific event. It seems, therefore, to be a poem with a strong external reference. Critics who cannot approach a poem except as a personal statement of the poet's thus feel that if it says little about King, it must say a good deal about Milton. So, they reason, *Lycidas* is really autobiographical, concerned with Milton's own preoccupations, including his fear of death. There can be no objection to this unless Milton's conventional involving of himself with the poem is misinterpreted as a personal intrusion into it.

For Milton was even by seventeenth-century standards an unusually professional and impersonal poet. Of all Milton's poems, the one obvious failure is the poem called *The Passion*, and if we look at the imagery of that poem we can see why. It is the only poem of Milton's in which he is preoccupied with himself in the process of writing it. "My muse," "my song," "my harp," "my roving verse," "my Phoebus," and so on for eight stanzas until Milton abandons the poem in disgust. It is not a coincidence that Milton's one self-conscious poem should be the one that never gets off the ground. There is nothing like this in *Lycidas*: the "I" of that poem is a professional poet in his conventional shepherd disguise, and to think of him as a personal "I" is to bring *Lycidas* down to the level of *The Passion*, to make it a poem that has to be studied primarily as a biographical document rather than for its own sake. Such an approach to *Lycidas* is apt to look most plausible to those who dislike Milton, and want to see him cut down to size.

One more critical principle, and the one that I have written this paper to enunciate, seems to me to follow inevitably from the previous ones. Every poem must be examined as a unity, but no poem is an isolatable unity. Every poem is inherently connected with other poems of its kind, whether explicitly, as *Lycidas* is with Theocritus and Virgil, or implicitly, as Whitman is with the same tradition, or by anticipation, as

Lycidas is with later pastoral elegies. And, of course, the kinds of genres of literature are not separable either, like the orders of pre-Darwinian biology. Everyone who has seriously studied literature knows that he is not simply moving from poem to poem, or from one aesthetic experience to another: he is also entering into a coherent and progressive discipline. For literature is not simply an aggregate of books and poems and plays: it is an order of words. And our total literary experience, at any given time, is not a discrete series of memories or impressions of what we have read, but an imaginatively coherent body of experience.

It is literature as an order of words, therefore, which forms the primary context of any given work of literary art. All other contexts—the place of *Lycidas* in Milton's development; its place in the history of English poetry; its place in seventeenth-century thought or history—are secondary and derivative contexts. Within the total literary order certain structural and generic principles, certain configurations of narrative and imagery, certain conventions and devices and *topoi*, occur over and over again. In every new work of literature some of these principles are reshaped.

Lycidas, we found, is informed by such a recurring structural principle. The short, simple, and accurate name for this principle is myth. The Adonis myth is what makes *Lycidas* both distinctive and traditional. Of course if we think of the Adonis myth as some kind of Platonic idea existing by itself, we shall not get far with it as a critical conception. But it is only incompetence that tries to reduce or assimilate a poem to a myth. The Adonis myth in *Lycidas* is the structure of *Lycidas*. It is in *Lycidas* in much the same way that the sonata form is in the first movement of a Mozart symphony. It is the connecting link between what makes *Lycidas* the poem it is and what unites it to other forms of poetic experience. If we attend only to the uniqueness of *Lycidas*, and analyze the ambiguities and subtleties of its diction, our method, however useful in itself, soon reaches a point of no return to the poem. If we attend only to the conventional element, our method will turn it into a scissors-and-paste collection of allusive tags. One method reduces the poem to a jangle

of echoes of itself, the other to a jangle of echoes from other poets. If we have a unifying principle that holds these two tendencies together from the start, neither will get out of hand.

Myths, it is true, turn up in other disciplines, in anthropology, in psychology, in comparative religion. But the primary business of the critic is with myth as the shaping principle of a work of literature. Thus for him myth becomes much the same thing as Aristotle's *mythos*, narrative or plot, the moving formal cause which is what Aristotle called the "soul" of the work and assimilates all details in the realizing of its unity.

In its simplest English meaning a myth is a story about a god, and Lycidas is, poetically speaking, a god or spirit of nature, who eventually becomes a saint in heaven, which is as near as one can get to godhead in ordinary Christianity. The reason for treating Lycidas mythically, in this sense, is conventional, but the convention is not arbitrary or accidental. It arises from the metaphorical nature of poetic speech. We are not told simply that Lycidas has left the woods and caves, but that the woods and caves and all their echoes mourn his loss. This is the language of that curious identification of subject and object, of personality and thing, which the poet has in common with the lunatic and the lover. It is the language of metaphor, recognized by Aristotle as the distinctive language of poetry. And, as we can see in such phrases as sun-god and tree-god, the language of metaphor is interdependent with the language of myth.

I have said that all problems of criticism are problems of comparative literature. But where there is comparison there must be some standard by which we can distinguish what is actually comparable from what is merely analogous. The scientists discovered long ago that to make valid comparisons you have to know what your real categories are. If you're studying natural history, for instance, no matter how fascinated you may be by anything that has eight legs, you can't just lump together an octopus and a spider and a string quartet. In science the difference between a scientific and a pseudo-scientific procedure can usually be spotted fairly soon. I wonder if literary criticism has any standards of this kind. It seems to me that a critic practically has to maintain that the Earl of Oxford wrote the plays of Shakespeare before he can be clearly recognized as making pseudo-critical statements. I have read some critics on Milton who appeared to be confusing Milton with their phallic fathers, if that is the right phrase. I should call them pseudo-critics; others call them neo-classicists. How is one to know? There is such a variety of even legitimate critics. There are critics who can find things in the Public Records Office, and there are critics who, like myself, could not find the Public Records Office. Not all critical statements or procedures can be equally valid.

The first step, I think, is to recognize the dependence of value-judgments on scholarship. Scholarship, or the knowledge of literature, constantly expands and increases; value-judgments are produced by a skill based on the knowledge we already have. Thus scholarship has both priority to value-judgments and the power of veto over them. The second step is to recognize the dependence of scholarship on a coordinated view of literature. A good deal of critical taxonomy lies ahead of us. We need to know much more than we do about the structural principles of literature, about myth and metaphor, conventions and genres, before we can distinguish with any authority a real from an imaginary line of influence, an illuminating from a misleading analogy, a poet's original source from his last resource. The basis of this central critical activity that gives direction to scholarship is the simple fact that every poem is a member of the class of things called poems. Some poems, including *Lycidas*, proclaim that they are conventional, in other words that their primary context is in literature. Other poems leave this inference to the critic, with an appealing if often misplaced confidence.

The Symbolism of Literary Allusion in *Heart of Darkness*

Betsy C. Yarrison

Most readers of Heart of Darkness *recognize that it is a many-layered and multimodal work. It describes a journey up the Congo at the end of the nineteenth century, yet it also suggests a journey "within," a psychological exploration, as well as a journey through that echoland traversed by heroes of epic and romance literature. How does Conrad achieve this suggestiveness? Examining the various commentaries on this little work of "inexhaustible allusiveness," Betsy Yarrison is struck not only by the range of allusion to be found in Conrad's "realistic" narrative, but also by the fact that these allusions, "despite their multiplicity, do not really duplicate or contradict one another." She reminds us, then, that as intertextual critics explore the allusive richness of the literary work, they need to remember that the formalists' criteria of unity and coherence order this richness and give it thematic direction.*

Reprinted by permission from *Conradiana* 7 (1975): 155–64. Copyright © 1975 by the Textual Studies Institute, Department of English, Texas Tech University.

THE RICH AND UNMISTAKABLE LITERARY ALLU-siveness of Joseph Conrad's *Heart of Darkness* has fascinated and frustrated a generation of critics in their search for fixed patterns of symbolic meaning in the tale. Noteworthy articles have interpreted *Heart of Darkness* as a rephrasing of Book VI of the *Aeneid* of Virgil, of Dante's *Inferno*, and of the grail quests of Arthurian legend.[1] Extensive scholarship has also been done on Conrad's use of religious allusion; critics have found clear reference in the story to pagan, Christian, and Buddhist traditions.[2] The last word on the issue would appear to belong to Albert J. Guerard, who remarked in *Conrad the Novelist* (Cambridge: Harvard University Press, 1958) that "we may apply to *Heart of Darkness* Thomas Mann's words on *Death in Venice*: a little work of 'inexhaustible allusiveness' " (p. 310).

Interestingly enough, the allusions in *Heart of Darkness*, despite their multiplicity, do not really duplicate or contradict one another; they rather unearth the elements which certain religious and literary traditions share with *Heart of Darkness* and, by implication, with each other. As James Mellard has suggested in "Myth and Archetype in *Heart of Darkness*," it appears that

> some sense of organization can be achieved from this critical chaos if one is willing to back away from the story for a moment and look at it whole, to see, in other words, its most obvious character, thematic, and structural patterns. If one does this, keeping the varied interpretations in mind all the while, he may be able to reduce the story to its lowest common denominator. In literature the common denominators, that is, the basic structural and thematic patterns, may be found in myth and archetype.[3]

Mellard's comprehensive approach is highly sound, but his search for the "lowest common denominator" fails to take into account the most conspicuous characteristic of the allusions, their very multiplicity. It seems plausible that Conrad's explicit textual reference to not one but four earlier epics may have been deliberate. It is not unlikely that Conrad sought to stress the fact that the *Aeneid*, the *Inferno* and the Arthurian legends all tell the same tale that he is about to retell—the tale of a heroic pilgrimage and its effect on the man who undertakes it.

Like Aeneas and Dante, Marlow seeks illumination in the dark wood of ignorance and wishes to learn the secrets of the earth. Driven by a desire for knowledge which appears fatally prefigured, he brushes aside warnings of danger in the sepulchral city, embarks upon the river Styx, and passes from station to station deeper into a morally-structured labyrinth which resembles the classical Hades or the densely populated Hell of Dante. He undertakes a journey to the depths of his own soul and back, in search of that unknown goal which would mean achievement of his full humanity. In the course of that search he completes his education, meeting a series of human beings who have failed themselves and life, and emerging victorious from a series of trials of his own selfhood. As Feder indicates in "Marlow's Descent into Hell" (p. 280), Conrad must have been aware that the pilgrimage is an ancient image for the descent into the self. Certainly he requests a place for his own story within the literary history of the pilgrimage epic by borrowing a metaphor for Marlow's journey from earlier traditional literature—the metaphor of a descent into hell and a return to civilization.

Marlow's descent into hell and his encounters along the way may be seen to observe a structural pattern established in traditional myth and imitated by literary epic. According to this pattern: "A hero ventures forth from the world of common day into a region of supernatural wonder: fabulous forces are there encountered and a decisive victory is won: the hero comes back from this mysterious adventure with the power to bestow boons on his fellow man."[4] Moreover, as both Feder and Evans have painstakingly documented, Conrad actually incorporates into his presentation of this basic mythic descent a number of specific encounters and incidents derived from Virgil and Dante. The details of Marlow's journey have literary antecedents in a variety of traditional treatments of the voyage to hell and back. All of these traditions have been superimposed by Conrad upon his own tale of the pilgrimage of modern man into the core of his self, and as a result Marlow's entire retelling of the story of *Heart of Darkness* appears constantly to the reader as a double exposure. Strange as the tale is, it carries an uncanny quality of familiarity.

Conrad sought intentionally to introduce this quality of familiarity into the unknown world of the Congo in which his story is set. As he himself described the craft of fiction:

> In truth every novelist must begin by creating for himself a world, great or little, in which he can honestly believe. This world cannot be made otherwise than in his own image: it is fated to remain individual and a little mysterious, and yet it must resemble something already familiar to the experience, the thoughts and the sensations of his readers.[5]

Into his realistic description of the Belgian Congo, Conrad introduces a sequence of precise, striking, and unmistakable allusions to the literary masterpieces of the Western tradition. He reminds his reader of the heritage they share, thus provoking from him the realization that *Heart of Darkness* is a twice-told tale, concocted from ancient and familiar materials.

Judicious use of materials familiar from earlier literature helps Conrad to maintain an advantage over the reader, whose involuntary memory he thus controls. When Conrad presents a recognizable character, situation, or image he forces the literate reader into an automatic mental juxtaposition of the familiar item with the new context. For example, his passing reference to the brickmaker of the Central Station as a "papier-mâché Mephistopheles"[6] cannot help but lure the reader into using literary history to interpret the character and his relationship to Marlow. He recalls at once the Faust legend, which he already knows, and he is tempted to equate the two heroes and to distill elements in Marlow's being from that of Faust.

Conrad drops names, phrases, and unexplained epithets such as "papier-mâché Mephistopheles" in rapid-fire fashion throughout *Heart of Darkness*. His abrupt insertion of details from other works into his own story catches the reader's attention and tantalizes him into wondering why the brickmaker should remind Marlow of Mephistopheles or why the manager of the Central Station should recall King Arthur to him. Inhabitants of a real Congo acquire extra-literal dimensions as they are likened to the symbolic characters of traditional epic. The women knitting black wool in the waiting room of the Company offices are transformed to Fates when Marlow describes them as "uncanny and fateful . . . guarding the door of Darkness" and silently hails them with "Morituri te salutant" (p. 11). Conrad's hero is himself the first to notice that the behavior of simple Belgian working women may appear to resonate with symbolical significance.

Conrad surrounds Marlow with characters who are made through allusion to look symbolic, and he sets them into a world which is itself thematically representational. The geography of his Congo is the familiar symbolic geography of traditional epic—mournfully still groves, "primeval mud" (p. 27), "matted vegetation standing higher than the wall of a temple" (p. 27), and "rivers, streams of death in life, whose banks were rotting into mud, whose waters, thickened into slime, invaded the contorted mangroves" (p. 14). In fact, the geography is real enough, but it is carried beyond its own realism by Conrad's use of an epic style for its description. The language of *Heart of Darkness* is as condensed and as elevated as that of classical heroic verse. The story's prose must be read analytically, word by word, because of its complex syntax, its rhetorical intricacy, and its extravagant, dense, and highly developed imagery. Conrad simulates epic style in order to increase the portentous effect of his prose, to imbue it with epic "high seriousness," and thus to preclude his tale's being circumscribed by its own realism.

The author's inclusion of direct literary allusion within a story whose very style is recognizably allusive, suggests strongly to the reader that the meaning of *Heart of Darkness* is somehow to be found in its literary antecedents. Con-

rad has Marlow say, "it seemed to me I had stepped into the gloomy circle of some Inferno" (p. 17), because he wishes the realistic hell of the Congo also to be a literary hell as significant and as meaningful as the figurative Inferno of the *Divina Commedia*. The scenery and characters of *Heart of Darkness* maintain simultaneously a lifetime and a literary reality. The knitters of black wool in the Company offices do not cease to be realistic women although they are transformed in Marlow's imagination to Fates. Nor is the great river any less the Congo merely because it is also Styx, Phlegethon, Acheron, Cocytus, and the "tumid river" of Dante.

The Congo, ravaged by colonialism, is a genuine hell-hole peopled by "moribund shapes" whose existence is living death. Yet it is also a literary hell, structured as the inverse of Dante's. The imaginary reality of the *Inferno* is derived from life; Dante's shades are, in fact, people. Conrad's vision of a modern hell, on the other hand, is captured metaphorically in the real hell of the Congo, and its people are mere shades, their actions characterized by a failure, error, and frailty as terrifying to the modern reader as was sin to the fourteenth-century Florentine. Conrad uses the realism of *Heart of Darkness* to convict the reader of complicity in colonial exploitation, but by carrying the story beyond realism and making the Congo as familiar as hell, he threatens him, along with Marlow, with damnation. By asserting that his Congo is a literary hell, he insures that an extra-realistic interpretation of his story will prevail. He uses allusion to place that story within the developing sequence of literary hells envisioned by poets since the origins of literature.

Conrad creates in his novels an ambiguous atmosphere which combines familiar and exotic lifetime reality with both familiar and fresh literary reality. This atmosphere casts into artistic form the paradoxical nature of literature itself as perpetually new phrasings of old questions in familiar patterns. Through allusion, Conrad demands a place for *Heart of Darkness* within the tradition of the literature of epic quest. He unabashedly parallels Roman and British imperial civilizations by paralleling their epics. Moreover, by reasserting the quest motif in a modern context of realism, he seems to suggest that his tale partakes of a symbolic continuity allying all epics around their shared characteristics, characteristics which have become familiar precisely because they are recurrent.

A certain validity accrues around a symbol or pattern which repeats itself in tradition after tradition over a long period of literary history. Conrad was certainly aware of the phenomenon of the archetype and was much intrigued by it; he has Marlow comment at one point upon "the convention that lurks in all truth."[7] Convention lurks throughout all of Conrad's own novels—motivating behavior, dictating plot—but the archetypal familiarity of Conrad's content, rather than making his symbols seem hackneyed, succeeds in imbuing them with an uncanny incantatory power. Conrad can conjure up in his reader's mind all of the traditional meanings associated with a symbol such as—for example—snakes, without being forced to recount those meanings specifically in his own text. He guides the reader from an initially realistic perception of *Heart of Darkness* to a symbolic perception.

Conrad intends for his reader to construct patterns of meaning for *Heart of Darkness* which draw the multiple dimensions of its presentation into a symbolic whole and render it, for each individual listener, *conclusive*. Readers of Conrad are certainly prone to project universal truths from the strangely familiar facts given them by the author. In fact, Conrad drives his reader to imaginative projection by presenting those facts in an ambiguous and mysterious style. Conrad's prose is actually as vague as it is rich. He duplicates in art the infinite complex of ways in which life presents itself for man's comprehension. Thus he builds into his novels myriad suggested interpretations.

An understanding of Conrad's views on art in general tends to lead one to the conclusion that the man was perfectly aware of the bewildering suggestiveness of his novels and that he intended to leave them unexplained. In his letters and prefaces he states repeatedly the belief that the mysteries of art should remain undefined, as he considered the mysteries of life to be. He countered Richard Curle's accusation of insufficient narrative explicitness with the reproach:

> It is a strange fate that everything that I have, of set artistic purpose, laboured to leave indefinite, suggestive, in the penumbra of initial inspiration, should have that light turned on to it and its insignificance . . . exposed for any fool to comment upon or even for average minds to be disappointed with. Didn't it ever occur to you, my dear Curle, that I knew what I was doing in leaving the facts of my life and even of my tales in the background? Explicitness, my dear fellow, is fatal to the glamour of all artistic work, robbing it of all suggestiveness, destroying all illusion.[8]

Conrad's very suggestiveness of presentation, however, lures readers into the assumption that some fixed pattern of meaning is latent in the text. Critics have succumbed to Conrad's tempting offer of a prefabricated allegorical substructure in *Heart of Darkness* and have made fevered attempts to discover the precise, given meaning of Marlow's riddling experience in the Congo. But precise, given meaning in art was no component of Conrad's aesthetics. Furthermore, Conrad actually explains the aesthetics of *Heart of Darkness* within the text, when he has the first narrator observe:

> But Marlow was not typical (if his propensity to spin yarns be excepted), and to him the meaning of an episode was not inside like a kernel, but outside, enveloping the tale which brought it out only as a glow brings out a haze, in the likeness of one of those misty haloes that sometimes are made visible by the spectral illumination of moonshine. (p. 5)

The first narrator's description of Marlow's storytelling technique is too close in style and tone to Conrad's own prefaces and letters to be disregarded. The first narrator is scarcely Conrad's mouthpiece, but neither is he an uncomprehending listener. He understands Marlow as Marlow understands Kurtz, and through him the reader, unlike the Directors, gains a certain perspective on them both. He alone among the listeners appears to apprehend the extra-literal nuances of Marlow's tale.[9] His very presence helps to establish the fact that *Heart of Darkness* is less a parable, whose import would lie in a kernel of meaning, than a recounting of a symbolical experience whose import lies in its suggestiveness. Marlow's experience is triply suggestive—to himself, to the first narrator, to the reader.

It appears from Conrad's comments to Curle that he viewed the artistic quality of any work to be indexed in its suggestive power. As he explained in a letter to Barrett H. Clark,

> a work of art is very seldom limited to one exclusive meaning and not necessarily tending to a definite conclusion. And this for the reason that the nearer it approaches art, the more it acquires a symbolic character. . . . The symbolic conception of a work of art has this advantage, that it makes a triple appeal covering the whole field of life. All the great creations of literature have been symbolic, and in that way have gained in complexity, in power, in depth, and in beauty.[10]

Such a view probably arises from Conrad's belief that art should be faithful to the fluidity of truth, and it leads him to the conclusion that symbolic art is superior to literal narration because symbolism can present simultaneously a number of different facets, finely and subtly discriminated from one another. Suggestiveness, then, is a key characteristic of Conrad's symbolism. He appears to have regarded symbolism not as a one-to-one correspondence between the plane of facts and the plane of ideas, but rather as shifting effects of light illuminating the world from various changing perspectives. As he once told Curle:

> my manner of telling, perfectly devoid of familiarity as between author and reader, aimed essentially at the intimacy of a personal communication, without any thought for other effects. As a matter of fact, the thought for effects is there all the same (often at the cost of mere directness of narrative) and can be detected in my unconventional grouping and perspective, which are purely temperamental and wherein almost all my "art" consists . . . [my art] is fluid, depending on grouping (sequence) which shifts, and on the changing lights giving varied effects of perspective.[11]

In *Heart of Darkness*, Conrad's "personal communication" with his reader hinges on the reader's recognition of conventional material—principally familiar symbols—through the shifting lights. The author filters the unknown through the known, the unseen through the seen, the unfamiliar through the familiar, in order to dissuade the reader from a literal interpretation of the story. Like a prism, the symbol in Conrad's fiction is a tool for presenting the reader with a spectrum of possible meanings for the text. The symbol breaks down the bare facts of life into their component nuances and shades. It produces color, which is complex, from simple and intense white light. It produces meaning, which in Conrad's terms is "art," from direct fact, which is life. Symbolic meaning provides the margin by which Marlow's Congo experience differs from Conrad's own, on which it was based. The symbolic meaning of Marlow's adventures lies in the art of their disclosure.

The art of meaningful disclosure, according to Conrad's aesthetics, is centered in the suggestive presentation of symbolism.[12] Conrad imbues facts, characters, setting with symbolical resonance, largely through his use of an ambiguous, portentous, and mysteriously allusive epic style and through his insistent manipulation of light and darkness imagery for stage effect. A factual event in *Heart of Darkness*, such as Marlow's final lie to Kurtz's Intended, is given so oblique and incomplete a passing illumination by Conrad that the reader is obliged to develop some significance for the event in his own mind. The scene with the Intended is of particular interest in this regard, because it may be read either seriously or ironically depending on one's assessment of the meaning of *Heart of Darkness* as a whole. It is either an excellent example of the fictive brief encounter of sentimental Victorian fiction, or it is a relentless pastiche of such an encounter scene. Conrad's contemporary readers probably took the ending seriously; they would have understood Marlow to believe that to contaminate civilization with the knowledge of human atavism would accomplish nothing, would be "too dark—too dark altogether . . ." (p. 79). Our age tends toward an ironical reading, pitying Marlow his inability to reach either the girl or the Directors, who have not "breathe[d] dead hippo" (p. 50). Such a reading implies that Conrad viewed British colonialism to be premised on a colossal self-esteem. Marlow's lie then appears motivated by an unwillingness to take responsibility for puncturing England's self-delusion. In this sense, Marlow's is a sad and compromised morality.

Either of these readings is consistent with the literal text. The scene is a familiar one; is it therefore true to life because it is conventional, or is it no truer than the fiction from which it comes? The answer depends on the reader and the critic, and Conrad bequeaths to them the responsibility for interpreting his tale. He explains in a letter to Clark:

I don't think you will quarrel with me on the ground of lack of precision; for as to precision of images and analysis my artistic conscience is at rest. I have given there all the truth that is in me; and all that the critics may say can make my honesty neither more nor less. But as to "final effect" my conscience has nothing to do with that. It is the critic's affair to bring to its contemplation his own honesty, his sensibility and intelligence. The matter for his conscience is just his judgment.[13]

The meaning of a Conrad story, then, can be seen to exist largely in the mind of the reader. Conrad's words and phrases often suggest meanings beyond the literal, but the added dimensions in Marlow's character, in the Congo, in the brickmaker, actually materialize in the consciousness of the reader. Conrad's symbolism, then, depends not on a correspondence between symbol and thing symbolized, but on the effective communication of the symbolical resonance in objects to a perceiving, comprehending reader. Still, there is a potential discrepancy between Conrad's presentation of symbolic meaning and his reader's perception of it. Moreover, because of the ambiguity of its style, Conrad's work is unusually susceptible to variant readings. The "final effect" of *Heart of Darkness* remains in many respects an enigma.

How elusive, then, did Conrad intend to leave the meaning of *Heart of Darkness*? Despite his belief that "a work of art is seldom limited to one exclusive meaning and not necessarily tending to a definite conclusion," Conrad saw a core of truth in the kaleidoscope of art. He wrote in his preface to *The Nigger of the "Narcissus"*: "And art itself may be defined as a single-minded attempt to render the highest kind of justice to the visible universe, by bringing to light the truth, manifold and one, underlying its every aspect." The truth of *Heart of Darkness* is indisputably manifold. Yet it is also one, in the

sense that its symbolism, while a function of the reader's perception, is not exclusively personal. Conrad makes his reader recognize a known truth of human experience in an unknown verbal context. He establishes sufficient contact in the text between symbol and thing symbolized to guide the reader into reaching the same contact mentally. He accomplishes this feat primarily through the use of literary allusion.

Literary allusion, as Conrad uses it, unites precision of reference with infinite suggestiveness of meaning. Since allusive words and phrases exist simultaneously within and beyond the text, Conrad can play off his reader's prior acquaintance with elements in *Heart of Darkness* against the limited scope of his knowledge within the story itself. Thus he implies by the very use of allusion that part of the ultimate meaning of *Heart of Darkness* may be found by placing the story in a context of known literature. The presence of the allusions implies that literature, as a valid expression of some truth about human experience, is richer in context than in isolation. They themselves suggest that the truth of literature lies as much in its kinship with other literature as in its kinship with life. Epic self-awareness, for example, comes to human experience from literature, not from life, and Conrad writes a modern epic at least partially to show that the epic sense of life need not be lost even though the epic has ceased to exist vitally in Western literature. He thus acknowledges the responsibility of the artist to preserve literary experience within life. As Gross has indicated in his analysis of the role of the first narrator: "That the narrator is able to arrive at his moral insight through 'literature,' as Marlow had arrived at his through experience, demonstrates Conrad's faith in the moral efficacy of experience through literature" (p. 169). Therefore, as long as the literary allusions in *Heart of Darkness* continue to remain suggestive to the reader and meaningful within his experience, they may be said to symbolize in their effect the self-perpetuating continuity of literary truth.

Notes

1. See, for instance, Lillian Feder, "Marlow's Descent into Hell," *Nineteenth-Century Fiction*, 9

(March 1955), 280–92; Jerome Thale, "Marlow's Quest," *University of Toronto Quarterly*, 24 (July 1955), 351–58; Robert O. Evans, "Conrad's Underworld," *Modern Fiction Studies*, 2 (May 1956), 56–62; Guy Owens, Jr., "A Note on *Heart of Darkness*," *Nineteenth-Century Fiction*, 12 (September 1957), 168–69.

2. See William Bysshe Stein, "The Lotus Posture and *Heart of Darkness*," *Modern Fiction Studies*, 2 (Winter 1956–57), 167–70; Robert F. Haugh, *Joseph Conrad: Discovery in Design* (Norman: University of Oklahoma Press, 1957), pp. 35–40; Edwin M. Moseley, *Pseudonyms of Christ in the Modern Novel* (Pittsburgh: University of Pittsburgh Press, 1962), pp. 16–19; Kaspar Spinner, "Embracing the Universe: Some Annotations to Joseph Conrad's 'Heart of Darkness,' " *English Studies*, 43 (October 1962), 420–23.

3. *Tennessee Studies in Literature*, 13 (1968), 1–15.

4. Joseph Campbell, *The Hero with a Thousand Faces* (New York: Bollingen Foundation, 1949), p. 30.

5. "Books," in *Notes on Life and Letters* (Garden City, N.Y.: Doubleday, Page & Co., 1926), p. 6.

6. *Heart of Darkness*, ed. Robert Kimbrough (New York: Norton, 1963), p. 26. Subsequent references are to this text.

7. The comment is not in *Heart of Darkness*, but in the contemporaneous Marlow saga, *Lord Jim*, chapter eight.

8. Letter of April 24, 1922, in Richard Curle, *Conrad to a Friend* (Garden City, N.Y.: Doubleday, Doran & Co., 1928), p. 112–13.

9. Seymour Gross has made a solid and convincing case for the intelligence, sensitivity, and vision of the first narrator in "A Further Note on the Function of the Frame in 'Heart of Darkness,' " *Modern Fiction Studies*, 3 (Summer 1957), 167–70.

10. Letter of May 4, 1918, in G. Jean-Aubry, *Joseph Conrad: Life and Letters* (Garden City, N.Y.: Doubleday, Page & Co., 1927), II, 205.

11. Letter of July 14, 1923, in *Conrad to a Friend*, p. 149.

12. For related discussions of Conrad's symbolism, see Marvin Mudrick, "The Originality of Conrad," *Hudson Review*, 11 (Winter 1958–59), 545–53 and Stewart C. Wilcox, "Conrad's 'Complicated Presentations' of Symbolic Imagery," *Philological Quarterly*, 39 (January 1960), 1–17.

13. Aubry, II, 205.

A Deconstructive Epilogue

Nature to all things fix'd the Limits fit,
And wisely curb'd proud Man's pretending
    Wit.

             Pope, *Essay on Criticism*

In this book I have defined and illustrated five contexts for criticism, five ways of looking at the literary work to decide what it means. Furthermore, I have claimed that these contexts are the fundamental grounds for interpretation because questions of meaning are always decided first within one of these contexts before the significance of that meaning can then be evaluated. No doubt the wary reader was inclined to accept this distinction, and the contexts themselves, only provisionally. This same reader may have noticed that occasionally the symmetrical diagram mapped some asymmetrical concepts. The mimetic context, for example, does not go exactly on all fours with the others, since it seems to offer a standard for evaluating rather than directly determining meanings. Not surprisingly, therefore, the discussion of mimeticism opened easily to the larger concerns of significance.

All similes limp, as the proverb has it, and if the inclusion of the mimetic context has hobbled my central metaphor, it has also allowed us to touch on some ideas that have been central to Western thinking about art from ancient Greece to the present day. For not only will the explorer in this context soon meet such large questions as what is "truth" and what is "reality," but he or she will also rather quickly encounter the related question of how truth or reality, however they may be defined, can be presented, or represented, in language. And even to state the case this way may seriously beg the question since it assumes, as we often do, that there is a truth or reality independent of language that is to be present-ed or re-present-ed by means of language.

But although the paradoxes and impasses of the mimetic context appear quickly, explorers on the vertical axis of our diagram sooner or later encounter other paradoxes and impasses. The author, that solid center of genetic meaning who is the object as well as the subject of biography, gradually diminishes to the vanishing point as one pursues the day, the hour, the instant when the "real" poem was fully present to the author's consciousness. And that same apparently solid center expands, diffuses, and quite evaporates again as one pursues in the opposite direction the forces, the ideas, the "spirit of the age" that made the author that made the work. In either case the center and origin of meaning in genetic

criticism, the meaner, disappears, and only language remains. Attempts to center meaning in the reader, we have noticed, will encounter parallel problems. Critics who report on the behavior of actual readers offer us an embarrassing variety of different meanings; those who try to ground interpretation in some version of an ideal reader tend to shift the argument to one of the other contexts. And neither those critics who claim to interpret poems, nor those who claim merely to interpret readers, are ever free from the web of words.

Apparently, then, whatever critical line we follow, thought finally reaches an impasse and begins to turn back on itself. Obviously these problems do not stop us from interpreting, since we cannot read at all without interpreting. But if we pause to face the problems, we may be moved to wonder how far our practice of interpreting, and our confidence in that practice, depends on our ability to suppress these problems,

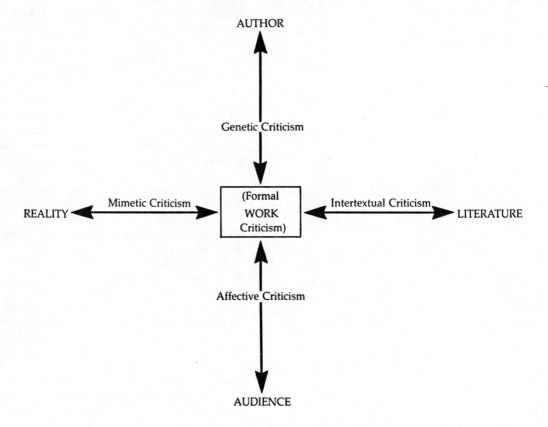

to become blind to the impasses. We have discovered often enough, as we moved from context to context, from argument to argument, that critics who were very clear-sighted in spotting the problems of other approaches appeared to be rather less perceptive about their own perceptions. Since metaphors in such discussions turn frequently to the visual, we may say we have here several variations on an old problem: it is very difficult to examine the lens you see with, to look *at* the instrument you are looking *through*.

But the visual metaphor, like all metaphors, may obscure as well as enlighten. For one constant in all these paradoxes and impasses is that they appear to arise from the nature of language itself. If language is our instrument of thought, as it is certainly our instrument of expression, then we are always in the position of trying to think about language in language. And if, as some philosophers maintain, we can escape this predicament (though the etymology of "predicament" offers little encouragement here), we must then fall into another, for we must at any rate talk about language in language, and even at this level the potential for confusion is high.

The problems of language, then, haunt all our contexts. But the formal and intertextual critics have often seemed to be most fully aware of these problems, and to have wrestled most strenuously with them. We recall that the formalist usually begins by separating the language of poetry from other kinds or uses of language. The words of a poem may be quite ordinary—as, for example, in "London" or "The Sick Rose"—but the contextual pressures within the poem itself create tensions, ambiguities, paradoxes, ironies, in short, special meanings that arise from this unique and supercharged arrangement of words. Furthermore, elements that would be irrelevant and distracting in conversation or in a laboratory report—such as rhythm, rhyme, meter, image, metaphor, and symbol—all combine in the poem to *form* meaning. As a consequence of these synergistic pressures, quite ordinary words become extraordinary language as their extensive and intensive meanings fuse in tensive balance. The result, the formalist argues, is an indissoluble unity of form and content that can express important truths,

truths that cannot be stated, or rather, imaged, in any other pattern of words.

We have already examined many aspects of this argument; here we should note three points in particular. First, by asserting the truth-telling or referential function of the poem, the formalists purchase a powerful argument for poetic value, but at a price. For now they must deal with all the difficulties of the mimetic context, most centrally the (re)presentational problems noted earlier. And the formalists' claim that the poem is a special kind of verbal structure that is in some mysterious way peculiarly suited to capture the complexities of nonverbal reality is a claim that has not been accepted by all students of language and poetry.

Second, as we saw earlier, the formalists threaten to undercut their own mimetic ground when they emphasize the poem's apparently nonreferential qualities of unity and coherence. But are unity and coherence really features or possessions of the poem, or are they simply functions of the critics' own rage for order? And can the formalists escape the relativism of affective criticism by appealing to the "text" as a stable origin and center of meaning? Or does the radically metaphorical nature of poetic language, the same metaphorical nature that the formalists have always taken as a starting point, undercut their claim? For one could argue that precisely because poetic language is radically metaphorical, it is radically indeterminate. That is, poetic language will always elude readings that seek to impose upon it a complete unity or to determine exactly its range of meanings. Other equally coherent readings will always be possible, and instead of a stable center for determinate meaning, the text becomes, from this perspective, a network for the free play of an indefinite number of meanings.

And this argument leads to the third point. For if these are the consequences of taking very seriously the metaphorical or "rhetorical" nature of poetic language, what follows if we examine closely, with a formalist's trained eye for implied image and submerged metaphor, the "nonpoetic" language used in other forms of discourse, and we discover that this language too—in fact, all language—is radically metaphorical or rhetorical? One thing that may follow is that the time-honored distinction—and it is not only the formalist's distinction—between poetry and criticism, between poetry and philosophy, between "poetic" language and any other language, will begin to dissolve. If the language explaining a poem is itself poetic, then the poet and the critic, the poem and the commentary, will begin to blur and meld in an unsettling way, all the more unsettling because here, too, the conclusion that shakes the formalist's premises appears to follow directly from those premises.

Now the intertextual critics, and particularly those most committed to a structuralist perspective, have recognized some of these difficulties. By taking the system of language as their base and model, they acknowledge more fully than do critics in any other contexts the centrality of language to all matters of interpretation. Furthermore, by stressing the self-referential nature of the system, they are able to defer (indefinitely, some would argue) the problems of mimesis or correspondence. "Meanings" are generated and deciphered within the self-contained system of signs. This statement is true on the level of an individual language such as, say, English or French, and it is also true, by extension or analogy, of any system of signs, verbal or nonverbal. For in this view we humans are essentially structuring or signifying animals, and our entire culture—the foods we eat, the clothes we wear, the sounds we utter—is a system of sign systems, a layering of codes. Hence the broad claim that all the world, at least as it can be known to *Homo significans*, is "text," and all understanding, all deciphering, is "intertextual."

This view is, of course, a radical structuralist's view of the world. Not all intertextual critics feel compelled to extend the notion of "text" this far. Yet even if we confine ourselves to more traditionally circumscribed literary problems, the intertextual emphasis on system or code seems to have wide explanatory power. Perhaps most importantly it offers to explain how readers may come to know literature in the same way that they progressively come to know their own language. At least by analogy, then, we can talk of the "language" of poetry, or of painting, of architecture, of music, and so forth. In each medium the competent "readers"—and, perforce, the competent artists—would be those who had mastered the conventions, the "language," of their art. From this perspective, the study of poetry could become the coherent, progressive discipline that Frye and others have called for, and "literary criticism" would be the name of that discipline.

Thus, intertextual critics offer their perspective as the interpretive context *par excellence*, for they undertake to show not simply what a particular poem means but how it is possible for a poem to carry meaning at all and how it is possible for the competent reader to understand that meaning. Consequently, they would argue that my diagram is misleading. In place of a number of perspectives set at equal distance from the work and from each other, with the formalist perspective apparently closer or more central than the rest, the intertextual critics would image a pyramid with the intertextual perspective at the base, since to understand anything in language at all, they would claim, is to understand "intertextually," that is, within a system of conventional signs. In other words, the textual meaning that formalists claim as their ground is in turn grounded in intertextual meaning. And so is every other kind of meaning.

But how solid is that ground? One suggestion of sponginess appears when we try to separate the "literary" elements in a work from the "non-literary" elements. "The Sick Rose" is a poem in English. It would mean little to a highly competent reader of French poetry who knew no English. But it would also mean little to a native speaker of English who knew nothing about poetry and who happened to be in search of gardening instruction. Which of these readers is closer to being a "competent" reader of the poem? Could the French critic more easily acquire enough of the "language" of English, or the English gardener enough of the "language" of poetry? And if we set about learning the language of poetry, that system of conventions somehow independent of particular linguistic systems, although always expressed within one of them, is there any principle of limitation we could apply? Or will the right side of our diagram expand indefinitely until we are driven once more to the position of the radical structuralist and must see the strands of any text interwoven with the strands of all texts? If so, then again the world becomes "text," no clear line can be drawn between one kind of text and another kind, or between one text and another text, and the meaning of any individual text becomes radically indeterminate because potentially limitless. In this view, intertextual meaning seems not merely a rather spongy ground for textual meaning but a quicksand that threatens to submerge the individual poem in a slough of signs.

This threat may not be as serious as it sounds as long as the individual reader can supply the focus. But it is not easy to see how readers are going to keep their feet on this ground either. We humans, as we have already said, are structuring animals. But it may be at least as true to say that we are structured animals, as much products as producers of systems, as much creatures as creators of our structures. Language once again supplies the paradigm. Any language is a system of systems—phonological, morphological, syntactical, lexical. Those who know the phonemes of English, for example, can immediately structure the speech sounds they hear into clusters of sounds, grouping together as one "sound" all variations that never contrast meanings in English (paying no attention, say, to the change from aspirated to unaspirated "p" in the word *pip*) but sharply distinguishing differences in sound that are significant in the system (such as the voicing of the initial consonant that changes *pip* to *bip*). We say that English listeners "structure" the sounds they hear, but only to the extent that those sounds conform to the independent and impersonal structure of English. And if the English phonemic system is the only one they know, the listeners will quite automatically "hear" any language the same way, which means that they will miss some significant sounds when listening to a different language. So it would be as accurate to say that English has structured their hearing, has formed their perceptions. In this respect, surely, we are much less creators than we are creatures of "our" language.

And language, to repeat, is the paradigm case, the simple instance of structured humanity. If our analogy holds, the idea of what qualifies one as a competent hearer of English could be expanded to explain what makes one a competent reader of *Lycidas* by showing how much of the system of English and how much of the system of "literature" such a reader would need to master—or be mastered by. Such an explanation would be immensely complex, yet at any point within these multilayered and interlocking systems the paradigm case would apply: readers could read only according to the way they had been structured. Thus the idea of the sturdy, autonomous "ego" controlling meaning as it reads begins to sink into the same slough of signs.

An equally troublesome feature of structures emerges when we try to think of their origin and development. For if the "system" must be already in place before any element in that system can have meaning, it is difficult to conceive of an origin or starting point. The problem here is not the infinite regress of the diachronic vision where each cause must have its prior cause, *ad infinitum*, but the impossibility of regressing at all. For try as we might to image in its pristine isolation the first meaningful utterance, the first systemless "sign" around which the system could form, imagination fails us. There can be no meaning, no sign, except within the system that confers meaning. So the system must be already there at the beginning; it must be always already there. And if we can't easily regress, neither can we easily progress, and for the same reasons. In short, from this perspective we can't very well account for the phenomenon of change at all, and this thoroughly synchronic vision seems to throw up new versions of the ancient paradoxes propounded by Zeno the Eleatic that appeared to show that change itself was but an illusion.

So the intertextual line, too, ends in paradox and puzzle. We start with the plausible view that meaning takes place within a conventional system, with "ordinary language" serving as the paradigm, and we construct on this ground a vision of literary criticism as a progressive and coherent discipline that might explain the system of literature as linguistics explains the system of language. Yet these premises, which promise to explain much, seem to lead logically to larger and more radical claims and to some puzzling problems. The very notion of "intertextuality," while showing how texts can have meaning, seems to undercut any way of delimiting meaning. For while it is easy to see that meaning must be limited by context, it is hard to see how context can be limited. Furthermore, the very idea of structure begins to double back on itself in odd ways if one pushes the structuralist premises far enough. At the end of the line, the coder and decoder of the message come to appear not as autonomous creators and masters of structures they employ but, at least in part, as creatures structured by the codes, employees of the system, with the notion of the autonomous ego itself being merely a device of language. The difficulty we have in thinking of the origin of the system, of imaging that first, lonely, "sign," may be a symptom of this condition. This is, perhaps, a strange conclusion to structuralist thought, but it is one that appears to follow logically from structuralist assumptions.

We may say, then, that even those contexts that have wrestled most strenuously with the problems of language have come off with, at most, nothing better than a draw. Their own premises seem to carry implications that, when fully unfolded, serve to undercut those premises. To demonstrate that this result is always the case is the main task or project of the "deconstructive" critics. The chief figure here, and the man who has provided the name and many of the key terms for the movement, is the French philosopher Jacques Derrida. Derrida's way of working—he will not call it a method—is to concentrate his considerable analytical powers on a particular text, usually a piece of discursive or "philosophical" prose, and to deconstruct or "unbuild" that text, laying bare its layers of sedimentation to show how it was constructed, to reveal its underlying metaphorical base. In this description, Derrida appears to practice some combination of formal and structural analysis, and that appearance is not entirely misleading, for Derrida could be called a superformalist or a superstructuralist, a reader who is willing to push the assumptions of the formal and structural perspectives to their logical, and paradoxical, conclusions. Above all else, he is a philosopher who takes the problems of language seriously and who argues that Western "meta-

physics" from Plato to the present has contrived to ignore or suppress those problems. As Derrida sees it, metaphysicians have typically thought of truth or ultimate reality as something above or beyond language. They have then sought, or simply assumed, an "unproblematic" language, a transparent medium that would contain or express this truth, a "philosophical discourse" that would rise above the ambiguities of ordinary language and the obscuring rhetoricity of poetry. By subjecting "philosophical" texts to careful, formal analysis, Derrida seeks to show that there is no such language. All philosophical texts, all texts of any kind, he argues, are radically metaphorical or "poetic," and thus the very nature of language undoes the metaphysicians' attempts to get through or beyond language, to convey their thoughts directly without imposing an intervening screen of rhetoric.

Some thinkers who have been acutely aware of these problems have tried to circumvent this screening effect by claiming to concentrate on those moments when the objects of thought were most fully "present" to the thinker, and the speaker of those thoughts most fully "present" to his or her hearers. Socrates' famous distrust of writing is a case in point. These attempts, according to Derrida, have led to the widespread and mistaken "privileging" of speech over writing, which has led in turn to Derrida's already notorious reversal of that priority, his counter-privileging of writing and the science of "grammatology." By such reversals and transpositions, Derrida wants to decenter our thought so we can see how it was centered in the first place. In the case of speech and writing, for example, the paradoxical position that writing is prior to speech becomes more understandable when we notice that by "writing" Derrida appears to mean something like the system of language, and in this he shows himself a thoroughgoing structuralist as well as a thoroughgoing formalist. For, as we have noted, the necessary condition for any meaningful utterance is that it be structured according to a system that is, in Derrida's phrase, "always already" in place and quite independent of the speaker—already "written," one might say.

As a formalist, then, Derrida deconstructs the

text to reveal its metaphorical basis, its inherent rhetoricity, conditions necessarily at odds with the idea of philosophical prose as a transparent, undistorting medium for present-ing nonverbal reality. As a structuralist, he deconstructs the text to show how it is structured by the system of language, a condition that once again limits the control of the speaker or author. Furthermore, as a radical structuralist, he subjects the concept of "structure" to the same deconstructive analysis. This maneuver is illustrated in his reading of the structural anthropologist Claude Lévi-Strauss in the essay "Structure, Sign and Play," which follows in this section. Here Derrida reveals at the "center" of structuralist thought an insoluble paradox: structuralists argue that they can critique empiricism because any knowledge empirically derived can be recognized as knowledge only within a system already in place; yet structuralists simultaneously argue that their own understanding of the system was empirically derived and can, therefore, be altered by new empirical discoveries. In other words, the structuralists claim to operate outside structure while claiming that such operation is impossible. And both claims are necessary to their enterprise.

This paradox haunts our attempts to think about structure at any and all levels. It is surely lurking in the tension we noted between the formalist's "empirical" view of form as the unique possession of the individual poem and the intertextualist's "structural" view of form as what the poem shares with other poems. For to make critical statements at all, each must accommodate the other's viewpoint. At a higher level of abstraction, the paradox is central to the long-playing debate between those who claim that truth is a matter of empirically discovered correspondence to "the way things are" and those who claim that truth is a matter of coherence, of conformity to a system of beliefs already in place. For empiricists must finally defend their view on the ground that it is consistent with our other beliefs, while their opponents must finally argue that the coherence theory does indeed correspond to "the way things are."

Closer to hand, the reader can discover a convenient example of the paradox in the design of this book, since it should now be apparent, if it

hasn't been all along, that our program—to examine three target texts from five different perspectives, and to measure the usefulness of these perspectives by what they revealed about the texts—could be pursued only by ignoring this empiricist-structuralist paradox. If we assume we can apply, say, a formal approach to *Hamlet*, and then a genetic approach, an intertextual approach, and so forth, and see which approach works best, or see to what extent each "works," we implicitly claim that we possess already a standard of critical adequacy independent of any approach. We will know what "works" when we see it. This is the empiricist view, and our willingness to accept this as the commonsense view shows our empirical bias. Yet if we must always read some way, within some context, then the structuralist view reasserts itself, for if we can never know the poem apart from some approach, then we can never use the "poem" to test the adequacy of an approach. We may prefer one context to another, but we could never point to the poem to ground that preference, could never claim one perspective was more "illuminating" than another, for the idea of what counted as illumination would itself be determined within the context we were defending. By such reasoning we simultaneously undercut our structures while revealing our inability to do without them.

These, then, are some of the consequences of deconstructive thought. As the sample essay illustrates, Derrida is difficult to paraphrase or summarize. Since he claims to approach each text on its own terms, even if only to show that these terms are not what the author thought they were, he claims to be something of an empiricist himself. Yet he knows full well that he cannot escape the dilemma he reveals in Lévi-Strauss's thought. Furthermore, because he is acutely aware of the metaphorical nature of language and of our tendency to overlook that nature, he has adopted a strategy of changing his key terms, his key metaphors, from book to book, or even from essay to essay, to prevent them hardening into unexamined starting points. By such shifts and dodges he hopes to keep his readers alive to the rhetorical basis of his own language and to remind us that he doesn't offer a method or a system. Rather, he offers a way of reading that focuses our attention on the problematic nature of language and that deconstructs the methods and systems of others.

Yet despite his claim to offer no method, or perhaps because of it, Derrida's way of reading has attracted a number of followers, especially in the field of literary criticism. On this side of the Atlantic, three of the most prominent figures associated with deconstruction are Paul de Man, Geoffrey Hartman, and J. Hillis Miller. Each of these men was an established critic before adopting the name and some of the aims of deconstruction, and each has a different emphasis and practices a different kind of deconstructive analysis. Hartman, for example, has been most concerned with the theoretical implications of the movement for the entire enterprise of criticism, often celebrating the ludic and "liberating" elements in deconstruction. Miller shares some of these interests but tends to downplay theory and to focus, like a good formalist, on specific texts. For him, deconstruction is yet one more critical perspective that may help him in his attempt to get at what he calls "the oddity of literary language." This focus on individual texts is even more intense in the work of Paul de Man, whose patient, probing, careful analyses are in some ways ideal formalist readings.

As even these few examples show, deconstruction is hardly a unified school of criticism, and given Derrida's starting point, that is scarcely surprising. Nonetheless, the work of Derrida and his followers has been much discussed and often imitated in the past few years, so much so that we may soon have in print a deconstructive reading of most major literary texts. And this seems, in some ways, a rather strange prospect. After all, it might be exciting and liberating to argue, as Derrida does, that "philosophical" texts are radically metaphorical or tropical, that they have not achieved a truth-bearing medium free from the distortions of rhetoric or poetry, but it can hardly be news that poems are radically metaphorical or rhetorical. The formal and intertextual critics have asserted that all along. And up to a certain point, the deconstructive critic always performs some version of formal or intertextual analysis.

But it is the mark of the deconstructive critics not to stop at any certain point. As formalists—and the rigorous analyses of Paul de Man may be taken as exemplary here—they will be concerned with the rhetorical or tropical nature of the text's language, but they will not start with the formalist assumption of unity or coherence. Instead, given their view of language, they will work from the opposite assumption and will seek to show how the rhetoricity of the text will undo or undercut any single or unified meaning. Thus the language of the poem, sharing with all language a radically rhetorical nature, shares too the condition of being radically undecidable or indeterminate. Ironically, de Man, starting from this assumption, occasionally comes to re-distinguish and re-privilege specifically "poetic" language as the only language aware of its own condition. The poem, by frankly announcing itself as a rhetorical or metaphorical structure, rather than trying to conceal this condition as "nonpoetic" language does, becomes the only truly honest language. This seems to be the deconstructivists' version of the old idea that the poet never lies because he or she never affirms. In this version, the poet's language affirms only that it lies—which at least puts it one up on everybody else's language.

As formalists, then, the deconstructive critics keep all the formalist assumptions, except the central one that coherence and unity are the defining features of poetry. Likewise, as intertextualists, they accept most of the structuralist assumptions: the poem is an utterance encoded in a system of signs, a *parole* in the *langue* of literature; the text is a dense fabric of threads stretching out to other texts. The exemplary figure here might be Roland Barthes as he carries his structuralist enterprise to its elaborate and playful conclusion in *S/Z*, a book-length reading of a Balzac short story in terms of several layered codes. Looked at one way, the book is the apogee of structuralism. Yet one gets the impression that these codes lack the firmness that the typical structuralist would want. It seems they could easily be more or fewer or other than they are, and rather than revealing a "competent" reader who has mastered a system of literary codes firmly controlling large but determinate meanings, the book displays instead a subtle and playful intelligence exulting in the creation of signs, "codes," and alternative versions of the story he is "reading." As intertextualists, then, the deconstructive critics accept the main structuralist assumptions, but refuse to accept the limits that the concepts of structure or system are generally thought to impose.

So deconstructive critics do read "literary" texts; in fact, they argue that there are really no other kinds. And deconstructive analysis is at present a rather popular activity. Nevertheless, it is important to note that deconstruction is not another "context" in any sense parallel to the five discussed earlier in this book. In the first place, each of these five has a long and rich history, and large numbers of critics have worked and continue to work in all of them. In the second place, all these contexts include one or more well-developed schools of criticism, each with a fully articulated theory and method. None of these statements would accurately describe "deconstruction." Indeed, when deconstructive critics get down to work, their reading is always some combination of formal and intertextual analysis, though with important differences. Furthermore, as Derrida's work indicates, deconstruction is less a system of criticism or a method of reading poems than a way of laying bare the paradoxes and impasses in all uses of language, and particularly in other systems and methods. As such, it may function most importantly as metacriticism, as a way of criticizing any and all systems.

For this reason, some brief discussion of deconstruction seems to me a fitting epilogue to a book that has spent so much time constructing systems of criticism, and constructing a system for containing those systems. It is salutary to be reminded that our constructs are, after all, constructs, that the metaphors we think in, and with, are metaphors. If all thinking is really analogical, and if all analogies are ultimately more or less misleading, then we should occasionally be called to face the sobering conclusion this syllogism entails. Beyond that, deconstructive critics, with their penchant for carrying to logical

and paradoxical conclusions the operating assumptions of the various schools of criticism, argue that often, perhaps always, we achieve our readings by ignoring or suppressing these paradoxes, by turning a blind eye to those impasses where thought begins to turn back on itself. We will, of course, go on thinking and speaking in metaphors, for we have no other way to think or speak. And we will go on interpreting in one context or another, for we have no other ways to interpret. But until some sage appears who can unknot these paradoxes and find a way around the impasses, the deconstructive critics may be counted on to remind us that whatever our choice of context, whatever our method of reading, it rests on a theoretical base for which we can make, at most, only modest claims. And that, too, is a salutary reminder.

Suggestions for Further Reading

For the deconstructive movement, the work of Jacques Derrida is central; *Of Grammatology* (1967) is the place to start. Roland Barthes's *S/Z* (1970) shows this protean writer in one of his poststructuralist phases. Some representative texts by American critics associated with this movement are Paul de Man, *Allegories of Reading* (1979), Barbara Johnson, *The Critical Difference* (1980), Geoffrey Hartman, *Criticism in the Wilderness* (1980), and J. Hillis Miller, *The Linguistic Moment from Wordsworth to Stevens* (1985). Although Stanley Fish has a rather different perspective, his *Is There a Text in This Class?* (1980) may be profitably read in this context. Josue V. Harari, ed., *Textual Strategies: Perspectives in Post-Structuralist Criticism* (1979) is a large collection of essays that includes a helpful introduction and a lengthy bibliography. Finally, three interpretive works in recommended order of reading: Christopher Norris, *Deconstruction: Theory and Practice* (1982), Jonathan Culler, *On Deconstruction* (1982), and Vincent Leitch, *Deconstruction: An Advanced Introduction* (1983).

Structure, Sign, and Play in the Discourse of the Human Sciences[1]

Jacques Derrida

When Jacques Derrida presented his "Structure, Sign, and Play" at a conference on the "Sciences of Man" at Johns Hopkins University in 1966, it marked the entrance of deconstruction onto the Anglo-American literary scene. While no single essay can fully represent Derrida's thought, or capture his shifting terminology, this influential paper shows some aspects of that thought in operation and introduces a number of terms—supplementarity, presence, différance—*which have become part of the lexicon of deconstructive criticism. It also displays Derrida's characteristic way of going to work. Examining the thought of Claude Lévi-Strauss, probably the world's best-known structural anthropologist, Derrida deconstructs structuralism itself. Since deconstructivists are often called "poststructuralists," it is worth noticing that this name is potentially misleading. For although Derrida's critique proceeds by uncovering an irreducible contradiction built into structuralist thought, he does not claim to pass beyond structuralism nor to replace it with another, contradiction-free system of thought. That is, the critique of structuralism presented here is exemplary. All systems of thought are subject to a similar deconstruction, since we cannot very well think of a centerless system, one that does not claim to be grounded finally on some presence, foundation, origin* (archè) *or end* (telos) *beyond freeplay. Each of the "contexts" of this book, for example, proposes a locus or ground for meaning (author, text, audience, reality, literature), and all are open to the same critique. So long as we continue to interpret interpretation, structure, sign, and freeplay*

in the hope of finding an end where interpretation itself can come to rest, Derrida concludes, we are deluded by our habits of mind and language.

PERHAPS SOMETHING HAS OCCURRED IN THE HIS-tory of the concept of structure that could be called an "event," if this loaded word did not entail a meaning which it is precisely the function of structural—or structuralist—thought to reduce or to suspect. But let me use the term "event" anyway, employing it with caution and as if in quotation marks. In this sense, this event will have the exterior form of a *rupture* and a *redoubling*.

It would be easy enough to show that the concept of structure and even the word "structure" itself are as old as the *epistèmè*—that is to say, as old as western science and western philosophy—and that their roots thrust deep into the soil of ordinary language, into whose deepest recesses the *epistèmè* plunges to gather them together once more, making them part of itself in a metaphorical displacement. Nevertheless, up until the event which I wish to mark out and define, structure—or rather the structurality of structure—although it has always been involved, has always been neutralized or reduced, and this by a process of giving it a center or referring it to a point of presence, a fixed origin. The function of this center was not only to orient, balance, and organize the structure—one cannot in fact conceive of an unorganized structure—but above all to make sure that the organizing principle of the structure would limit what we might call the *freeplay* of the structure. No doubt that by orienting and organizing the coherence of the system, the center of a structure permits the freeplay of its elements inside the total form. And even today the notion of a

Reprinted by permission from Richard Macksey and Eugenio Donato, eds., *The Languages of Criticism and the Sciences of Man*, pp. 247–265. Copyright © 1970 by The Johns Hopkins University Press.

structure lacking any center represents the unthinkable itself.

Nevertheless, the center also closes off the freeplay it opens up and makes possible. *Qua* center, it is the point at which the substitution of contents, elements, or terms is no longer possible. At the center, the permutation or the transformation of elements (which may of course be structures enclosed within a structure) is forbidden. At least this permutation has always remained *interdicted*[2] (I use this word deliberately). Thus it has always been thought that the center, which is by definition unique, constituted that very thing within a structure which governs the structure, while escaping structurality. This is why classical thought concerning structure could say that the center is, paradoxically, *within* the structure and *outside* it. The center is at the center of the totality, and yet, since the center does not belong to the totality (is not part of the totality), the totality *has its center elsewhere*. The center is not the center. The concept of centered structure—although it represents coherence itself, the condition of the *epistème* as philosophy or science—is contradictorily coherent. And, as always, coherence in contradiction expresses the force of a desire. The concept of centered structure is in fact the concept of a freeplay based on a fundamental ground, a freeplay which is constituted upon a fundamental immobility and a reassuring certitude, which is itself beyond the reach of the freeplay. With this certitude anxiety can be mastered, for anxiety is invariably the result of a certain mode of being implicated in the game, of being caught by the game, of being as it were from the very beginning at stake in the game.[3] From the basis of what we therefore call the center (and which, because it can be either inside or outside, is as readily called the origin as the end, as readily *archè* as *telos*), the repetitions, the substitutions, the transformations, and the permutations are always *taken* from a history of meaning [*sens*]—that is, a history, period—whose origin may always be revealed or whose end may always be anticipated in the form of presence. This is why one could perhaps say that the movement of any archeology, like that of any eschatology, is an accomplice of this reduction of the structurality of structure and always attempts to conceive of structure from the basis of a full presence which is out of play.

If this is so, the whole history of the concept of structure, before the rupture I spoke of, must be thought of as a series of substitutions of center for center, as a linked chain of determinations of the center. Successively, and in a regulated fashion, the center receives different forms or names. The history of metaphysics, like the history of the West, is the history of these metaphors and metonymies. Its matrix—if you will pardon me for demonstrating so little and for being so elliptical in order to bring me more quickly to my principal theme—is the determination of being as *presence* in all the senses of this word. It would be possible to show that all the names related to fundamentals, to principles, or to the center have always designated the constant of a presence—*eidos, archè, telos, energeia, ousia* (essence, existence, substance, subject) *aletheia*, transcendentality, consciousness, or conscience, God, man, and so forth.

The event I called a rupture, the disruption I alluded to at the beginning of this paper, would presumably have come about when the structurality of structure had to begin to be thought, that is to say, repeated, and this is why I said that this disruption was repetition in all of the senses of this word. From then on it became necessary to think the law which governed, as it were, the desire for the center in the constitution of structure and the process of signification prescribing its displacements and its substitutions for this law of the central presence—but a central presence which was never itself, which has always already been transported outside itself in its surrogate. The surrogate does not substitute itself for anything which has somehow pre-existed it. From then on it was probably necessary to begin to think that there was no center, that the center could not be thought in the form of a being-present, that the center had no natural locus, that it was not a fixed locus but a function, a sort of nonlocus in which an infinite number of sign-substitutions came into play. This moment was that in which language invaded the universal problematic; that in which, in the absence of a center or origin, everything became discourse—provided we can agree on this word—that is to say, when everything became a system where the central signified, the original or transcendental signified, is never absolutely present outside a system of differences. The absence of the transcendental signified extends the domain and the interplay of signification *ad infinitum*.

Where and how does this decentering, this notion of the structurality of structure, occur? It would be somewhat naïve to refer to an event, a doctrine, or an author in order to designate this occurrence. It is no doubt part of the totality of an era, our own, but still it has already begun to proclaim itself and begun to *work*. Nevertheless, if I wished to give some sort of indication by choosing one or two "names," and by recalling those authors in whose discourses this occurrence has most nearly maintained its most radical formulation, I would probably cite the Nietzschean critique of metaphyiscs, the critique of the concepts of being and truth, for which were substituted the concepts of play, interpretation, and sign (sign without truth present); the Freudian critique of self-presence, that is, the critique of consciousness, of the subject, of self-identity and of self-proximity or self-possession; and, more radically, the Heideggerean destruction of metaphysics, of onto-theology, of the determination of being as presence. But all these destructive discourses and all their analogues are trapped in a sort of circle. This circle is unique. It describes the form of the relationship between the history of metaphysics and the destruction of the history of metaphysics. *There is no sense* in doing without the concepts of metaphysics in order to attack metaphysics. We have no language—no syntax and no lexicon—which is alien to this history; we cannot utter a single destructive proposition which has not already slipped into the form, the logic, and the implicit postulations of precisely what it seeks to contest. To pick out one example from many: the metaphysics of presence is attacked with the help of the concept of the *sign*. But from the moment anyone wishes this to show, as I suggested a moment ago, that there is no transcendental or privileged signified and that the domain or the interplay of signification has, henceforth, no limit, he ought to extend his refusal to the concept and to the word sign itself—which is precisely what cannot be done. For the signification "sign" has always been comprehended and determined, in its sense, as sign-of, signifier referring to a signified, signifier different from its signified. If one erases the radical difference between signifier and signified, it is the word signifier itself which ought to be abandoned as a metapysical concept. When Lévi-Strauss says in the preface to *The Raw and the Cooked*[4] that he has "sought to transcend the opposition between the sensible and the intelligible by placing [himself] from the very beginning at the level of signs," the necessity, the force, and the legitimacy of his act cannot make us forget that the concept of the sign cannot in itself surpass or bypass this opposition between the sensible and the intelligible. The concept of the sign is determined by this opposition: through and throughout the totality of its history and by its system. But we cannot do without the concept of the sign, we cannot give up this metaphysical complicity without also giving up the critique we are directing against this complicity, without the risk of erasing difference [altogether] in the self-identity of a signified reducing into itself its signifier, or, what amounts to the same thing, simply expelling it outside itself. For there are two heterogenous ways of erasing the difference between the signifier and the signified: one, the classic way, consists in reducing or deriving the signifier, that is to say, ultimately in *submitting* the sign to thought; the other, the one we are using here against the first one, consists in putting into question the system in which the preceding reduction functioned: first and foremost, the opposition between the sensible and the intelligible. The *paradox* is that the metaphysical reduction of the sign needed the opposition it was reducing. The opposition is part of the system, along with the reduction. And what I am saying here about the sign can be extended to all the concepts and all the sentences of metaphysics, in particular to the discourse on "structure." But there are many ways of being caught in this circle. They are all more or less naïve, more or less empirical, more or less systematic, more or less close to the formulation or even to the formalization of this circle. It is these differences which explain the multiplicity of destructive discourses and the disagreement between those who make them. It was within concepts inherited from metaphysics that Nietzsche, Freud, and Heidegger worked, for example. Since these concepts are not elements or atoms and since they are taken from a syntax and a system, every particular borrowing drags along with it the whole of metaphysics. This is what allows these destroyers to destroy each other reciprocally—for example, Heidegger considering Nietzsche, with as much lucidity and rigor as bad faith and misconstruction, as the last metaphysician, the last "Platonist." One could do the same for Heidegger himself, for Freud, or for a number of others. And today no exercise is more widespread.

What is the relevance of this formal schéma when we turn to what are called the "human sciences"? One of them perhaps occupies a privileged place—ethnology. One can in fact assume that ethnology could have been born as a science only at the moment when a de-centering had come about: at the moment when European culture—and, in consequence, the history of metaphysics and of its concepts—had been *dislocated*, driven from its locus, and forced to stop considering itself as the culture of reference. This moment is not first and foremost a moment of philosophical or scientific discourse, it is also a moment which is political, economic, technical, and so forth. One can say in total assurance that there is nothing fortuitous about the fact that the critique of ethnocentrism—the very condition of ethnology—should be systematically and historically contemporaneous with the destruction of the history of metaphysics. Both belong to a single and same era.

Ethnology—like any science—comes about within the element of discourse. And it is primarily a European science employing traditional concepts, however much it may struggle against them. Consequently, whether he wants to or not—and this does not depend on a decision on his part—the ethnologist accepts into his discourse the premises of ethnocentrism at the very moment when he is employed in denouncing them. This necessity is irreducible; it is not a historical contingency. We ought to consider very carefully all its implications. But if nobody can escape this necessity, and if no one is therefore responsible for giving in to it, however little, this does not mean that all the ways of giving in to it are of an equal pertinence. The quality and the fecundity of a discourse are perhaps measured by the critical rigor with which this relationship to the history of metaphysics and to inherited concepts is thought. Here it is a question of a critical relationship to the language of the human sciences and a question of a critical responsibility of the discourse. It is a question of putting expressly and systematically the problem of the status of a discourse which borrows from a heritage the resources necessary for the deconstruction of that heritage itself. A problem of *economy* and *strategy*.

If I now go on to employ an examination of the texts of Lévi-Strauss as an example, it is not only because of the privilege accorded to ethnology among the human sciences, nor yet because the thought of Lévi-Strauss weighs heavily on the contemporary theoretical situation. It is above all because a certain choice has made itself evident in the work of Lévi-Strauss and because a certain doctrine has been elaborated there, and precisely in a *more or less explicit manner*, in relation to this critique of language and to this critical language in the human sciences.

In order to follow this movement in the text of Lévi-Strauss, let me choose as one guiding thread among others the opposition between nature and culture. In spite of all its rejuvenations and its disguises, this opposition is congenital to philosophy. It is even older than Plato. It is at least as old as the Sophists. Since the statement of the opposition—*physis/nomos*, *physis/technè*—it has been passed on to us by a whole historical chain which opposes "nature" to the law, to education, to art, to technics—and also to liberty, to the arbitrary, to history, to society, to the mind, and so on. From the beginnings of his quest and from his first book, *The Elementary Structures of Kinship*,[5] Lévi-Strauss has felt at one and the same time the necessity of utilizing this opposition and the impossiblity of making it acceptable. In the *Elementary Structures*, he begins from this axiom or definition: that belongs to nature which is *universal* and spontaneous, not depending on any particular culture or on any determinate norm. That belongs to culture, on the other hand, which depends on a system of *norms* regulating society and is therefore capable of *varying* from one social structure to another.

These two definitions are of the traditional type. But, in the very first pages of the *Elementary Structures*, Lévi-Strauss, who has begun to give these concepts an acceptable standing, encounters what he calls a *scandal*, that is to say, something which no longer tolerates the nature/culture opposition he has accepted and which seems to require *at one and the same time* the predicates of nature and those of culture. This scandal is the *incest-prohibition*. The incest-prohibition is universal; in this sense one could call it natural. But it is also a prohibition, a system of norms and interdicts; in this sense one could call it cultural.

> Let us assume therefore that everything universal in man derives from the order of nature and is characterized by spontaneity, that everything which is subject to a norm belongs to culture and presents the attributes of the relative and the particular. We then find ourselves confronted by a fact, or rather an ensemble of facts, which, in the light of the preceding definitions, is not far from appearing as a scandal: the prohibition of incest presents without the least equivocation, and indissolubly linked together, the two characteristics in which we recognized the contradictory attributes of two exclusive orders. The prohibition of incest constitutes a rule, but a rule, alone of all the social rules, which possesses at the same time a universal character (p. 9).

Obviously there is no scandal except in the *interior* of a system of concepts sanctioning the difference between nature and culture. In beginning his work with the *factum* of the incest-prohibition, Lévi-Strauss thus puts himself in a position entailing that this difference, which has always been assumed to be self-evident, becomes obliterated or disputed. For, from the moment that the incest-prohibition can no longer be conceived within the nature/culture opposition, it can no longer be said that it is a scandalous fact, a nucleus of opacity within a network of transparent significations. The incest-prohibition is no longer a scandal one meets with or comes up against in the domain of traditional concepts; it is something which escapes these concepts and certainly precedes them—probably as the condition of their possibility. It could perhaps be said that the whole of philosophical conceptualization, systematically relat-

ing itself to the nature/culture opposition, is designed to leave in the domain of the unthinkable the very thing that makes this conceptualization possible: the origin of the prohibition of incest.

I have dealt too cursorily with this example, only one among so many others, but the example nevertheless reveals that language bears within itself the necessity of its own critique. This critique may be undertaken along two tracks, in two "manners." Once the limit of nature/culture opposition makes itself felt, one might want to question systematically and rigorously the history of these concepts. This is a first action. Such a systematic and historic questioning would be neither a philological nor a philosophical action in the classic sense of these words. Concerning oneself with the founding concepts of the whole history of philosophy, deconstituting them, is not to undertake the task of the philologist or of the classic historian of philosophy. In spite of appearances, it is probably the most daring way of making the beginnings of a step outside of philosophy. The step "outside philosophy" is much more difficult to conceive than is generally imagined by those who think they made it long ago with cavalier ease, and who are in general swallowed up in metaphysics by the whole body of the discourse that they claim to have disengaged from it.

In order to avoid the possibly sterilizing effect of the first way, the other choice—which I feel corresponds more nearly to the way chosen by Lévi-Strauss—consists in conserving in the field of empirical discovery all these old concepts, while at the same time exposing here and there their limits, treating them as tools which can still be of use. No longer is any truth-value attributed to them; there is a readiness to abandon them if necessary if other instruments should appear more useful. In the meantime, their relative efficacy is exploited, and they are employed to destroy the old machinery to which they belong and of which they themselves are pieces. Thus it is that the language of the human sciences criticizes *itself*. Lévi-Strauss thinks that in this way he can separate *method* from *truth*, the instruments of the method and the objective significations aimed at by it. One could almost say that this is the primary affirmation of Lévi-Strauss; in any event, the first words of the *El-*

ementary Structures are: "One begins to understand that the distinction between state of nature and state of society (we would be more apt to say today: state of nature and state of culture), while lacking any acceptable historical signification, presents a value which fully justifies its use by modern sociology: its value as a methodological instrument."

Lévi-Strauss will always remain faithful to this double intention: to preserve as an instrument that whose truth-value he criticizes.

On the one hand, he will continue in effect to contest the value of the nature/culture opposition. More than thirteen years after the *Elementary Structures*, *The Savage Mind*[6] faithfully echoes the text I have just quoted: "The opposition between nature and culture which I have previously insisted on seems today to offer a value which is above all methodological." And this methodological value is not affected by its "ontological" non-value (as could be said, if this notion were not suspect here): "It would not be enough to have absorbed particular humanities into a general humanity; this first enterprise prepares the way for others . . . which belong to the natural and exact sciences: to reintegrate culture into nature, and finally, to reintegrate life into the totality of its physiochemical conditions" (p. 327).

On the other hand, still in *The Savage Mind*, he presents as what he calls *bricolage*[7] what might be called the discourse of this method. The *bricoleur*, says Lévi-Strauss, is someone who uses "the means at hand," that is, the instruments he finds at his disposition around him, those which are already there, which had not been especially conceived with an eye to the operation for which they are to be used and to which one tries by trial and error to adapt them, not hesitating to change them whenever it appears necessary, or to try several of them at once, even if their form and their origin are heterogenous—and so forth. There is therefore a critique of language in the form of *bricolage*, and it has even been possible to say that *bricolage* is the critical language itself. I am thinking in particular of the article by G. Genette, "Structuralisme et Critique littéraire," published in homage to Lévi-Strauss in a special issue *L'Arc* (no. 26, 1965), where it is stated that the analysis of *bricolage* could "be

applied almost word for word" to criticism, and especially to "literary criticism."[8]

If one calls *bricolage* the necessity of borrowing one's concepts from the text of a heritage which is more or less coherent or ruined, it must be said that every discourse is *bricoleur*. The engineer, whom Lévi-Strauss opposes to the *bricoleur*, should be the one to construct the totality of his language, syntax, and lexicon. In this sense the engineer is a myth. A subject who would supposedly be the absolute origin of his own discourse and would supposedly construct it "out of nothing," "out of whole cloth," would be the creator of the *verbe*, the *verbe* itself. The notion of the engineer who had supposedly broken with all forms of *bricolage* is therefore a theological idea; and since Lévi-Strauss tells us elsewhere that *bricolage* is mythopoetic, the odds are that the engineer is a myth produced by the *bricoleur*. From the moment that we cease to believe in such an engineer and in a discourse breaking with the received historical discourse, as soon as it is admitted that every finite discourse is bound by a certain *bricolage*, and that the engineer and the scientist are also species of *bricoleurs* then the very idea of *bricolage* is menaced and the difference in which it took on its meaning decomposes.

This brings out the second thread which might guide us in what is being unraveled here.

Lévi-Strauss describes *bricolage* not only as an intellectual activity but also as a mythopoetical activity. One reads in *The Savage Mind*, "Like *bricolage* on the technical level, mythical reflection can attain brilliant and unforeseen results on the intellectual level. Reciprocally, the mythopoetical character of *bricolage* has often been noted" (p. 26).

But the remarkable endeavor of Lévi-Strauss is not simply to put forward, notably in the most recent of his investigations, a structural science of knowledge of myths and of mythological activity. His endeavor also appears—I would say almost from the first—in the status which he accords to his own discourse on myths, to what he calls his "mythologicals." It is here that his discourse on the myth reflects on itself and criticizes itself. And this moment, this critical period, is evidently of concern to all the languages which share the field of the human sciences.

What does Lévi-Strauss say of his "mythologicals"? It is here that we rediscover the mythopoetical virtue (power) of *bricolage*. In effect, what appears most fascinating in this critical search for a new status of the discourse is the stated abandonment of all reference to a *center*, to a *subject*, to a privileged *reference*, to an origin, or to an absolute *archè*. The theme of this decentering could be followed throughout the "Overture" to his last book, *The Raw and the Cooked*. I shall simply remark on a few key points.

1. From the very start, Lévi-Strauss recognizes that the Bororo myth which he employs in the book as the "reference-myth" does not merit this name and this treatment. The name is specious and the use of the myth improper. This myth deserves no more than any other its referential privilege:

> In fact the Bororo myth which will from now on be designated by the name *reference-myth* is, as I shall try to show, nothing other than a more or less forced transformation of other myths originating either in the same society or in societies more or less far removed. It would therefore have been legitimate to choose as my point of departure any representative of the group whatsoever. From this point of view, the interest of the reference-myth does not depend on its typical character, but rather on its irregular position in the midst of a group (p. 10).

2. There is no unity or absolute source of the myth. The focus or the source of the myth are always shadows and virtualities which are elusive, unactualizable, and nonexistent in the first place. Everything begins with the structure, the configuration, the relationship. The discourse on this acentric structure, the myth, that is, cannot itself have an absolute subject or an absolute center. In order not to short change the form and the movement of the myth, that violence which consists in centering a language which is describing an acentric structure must be avoided. In this context, therefore it is necessary to forego scientific or philosophical discourse, to renounce the *epistèmè* which absolutely requires, which is the absolute requirement that we go back to the source, to the center, to the founding basis, to the principle, and so on. In opposition

to *epistèmic* discourse, structural discourse on myths—*mythological* discourse—must itself be mythomorphic. It must have the form of that of which it speaks. This is what Lévi-Strauss says in *The Raw and the Cooked*, from which I would now like to quote a long and remarkable passage:

> In effect the study of myths poses a methodological problem by the fact that it cannot conform to the Cartesian principle of dividing the difficulty into as many parts as are necessary to resolve it. There exists no veritable end or term to mythical analysis, no secret unity which could be grasped at the end of the work of decomposition. The themes duplicate themselves to infinity. When we think we have disentangled them from each other and can hold them separate, it is only to realize that they are joining together again, in response to the attraction of unforeseen affinities. In consequence, the unity of the myth is only tendential and projective; it never reflects a state or a moment of the myth. An imaginary phenomenon implied by the endeavor to interpret, its role is to give a synthetic form to the myth and to impede its dissolution into the confusion of contraries. It could therefore be said that the science or knowledge of myths is an *anaclastic*, taking this ancient term in the widest sense authorized by its etymology, a science which admits into its definition the study of the reflected rays along with that of the broken ones. But, unlike philosophical reflection, which claims to go all the way back to its source, the reflections in question here concern rays without any other than a virtual focus. . . . In wanting to imitate the spontaneous movement of mythical thought, my enterprise, itself too brief and too long, has had to yield to its demands and respect its rhythm. Thus is this book, on myths itself and in its own way, a myth.

This statement is repeated a little farther on (p. 20): "Since myths themselves rest on second-order codes (the first-order codes being those in which language consists), this book thus offers the rough draft of a third-order code, destined to insure the reciprocal possibility of translation of several myths. This is why it would not be wrong to consider it a myth: the myth of mythology, as it were." It is by this absence of any real and fixed center of the mythical or mythological discourse that the musical model chosen by Lévi-Strauss for the composition of his book is apparently justified. The absence of a center is here the absence of a subject and the absence of an author: "The myth and the musical work thus appear as orchestra conductors whose listeners are the silent performers. If it be asked where the real focus of the work is to be found, it must be replied that its determination is impossible. Music and mythology bring man face to face with virtual objects whose shadow alone is actual. . . . Myths have no authors" (p. 25).

Thus it is at this point that ethnographic *bricolage* deliberately assumes its mythopoetic function. But by the same token, this function makes the philosophical or epistemological requirement of a center appear as mythological, that is to say, as a historical illusion.

Nevertheless, even if one yields to the necessity of what Lévi-Strauss has done, one cannot ignore its risks. If the mythological is mythomorphic, are all discourses on myths equivalent? Shall we have to abandon any epistemological requirement which permits us to distinguish between several qualities of discourse on the myth? A classic question, but inevitable. We cannot reply—and I do not believe Lévi-Strauss replies to it—as long as the problem of the relationships between the philosopheme or the theorem, on the one hand, and the mytheme or the mythopoem(e), on the other, has not been expressly posed. This is no small problem. For lack of expressly posing this problem, we condemn ourselves to transforming the claimed transgression of philosophy into an unperceived fault in the interior of the philosophical field. Empiricism would be the genus of which these faults would always be the species. Trans-philosophical concepts would be transformed into philosophical naïvetés. One could give many examples to demonstrate this risk: the concepts of sign, history, truth, and so forth. What I want to emphasize is simply that the passage beyond philosophy does not consist in turning the page of philosophy (which usually comes down to philosophizing badly), but in continuing to read philosophers *in a certain way*. The risk I am speaking of is always assumed by Lévi-Strauss and it is the very price of his endeavor. I have said that empiricism is

the matrix of all the faults menacing a discourse which continues, as with Lévi-Strauss in particular, to elect to be scientific. If we wanted to pose the problem of empiricism and *bricolage* in depth, we would probably end up very quickly with a number of propositions absolutely contradictory in relation to the status of discourse in structural ethnography. On the one hand, structuralism justly claims to be the critique of empiricism. But at the same time there is not a single book or study by Lévi-Strauss which does not offer itself as an empirical essay which can always be completed or invalidated by new information. The structural schemata are always proposed as hypotheses resulting from a finite quantity of information and which are subjected to the proof of experience. Numerous texts could be used to demonstrate this double postulation. Let us turn once again to the "Overture" of *The Raw and the Cooked*, where it seems clear that if this postulation is double, it is because it is a question here of a language on language:

> Critics who might take me to task for not having begun by making an exhaustive inventory of South American myths before analyzing them would be making a serious mistake about the nature and the role of these documents. The totality of the myths of a people is of the order of the discourse. Provided that this people does not become physically or morally extinct, this totality is never closed. Such a criticism would therefore be equivalent to reproaching a linguist with writing the grammar of a language without having recorded the totality of the words which have been uttered since that language came into existence and without knowing the verbal exchanges which will take place as long as the language continues to exist. Experience proves that an absurdly small number of sentences . . . allows the linguist to elaborate a grammar of the language he is studying. And even a partial grammar or an outline of a grammar represents valuable acquisitions in the case of unknown languages. Syntax does not wait until it has been possible to enumerate a theoretically unlimited series of events before becoming manifest, because syntax consists in the body of rules which presides over the generation of these events. And it is precisely a syntax of South American mythology that I wanted to outline. Should new texts ap-

pear to enrich the mythical discourse, then this will provide an opportunity to check or modify the way in which certain grammatical laws have been formulated, an opportunity to discard certain of them and an opportunity to discover new ones. But in no instance can the requirement of a total mythical discourse be raised as an objection. For we have just seen that such a requirement has no meaning (pp. 15–16).

Totalization is therefore defined at one time as *useless*, at another time as *impossible*. This is no doubt the result of the fact that there are two ways of conceiving the limit of totalization. And I assert once again that these two determinations coexist implicitly in the discourses of Lévi-Strauss. Totalization can be judged impossible in the classical style: one then refers to the empirical endeavor of a subject or of a finite discourse in a vain and breathless quest of an infinite richness which it can never master. There is too much, more than one can say. But nontotalization can also be determined in another way: not from the standpoint of the concept of finitude as assigning us to an empirical view, but from the standpoint of the concept of *freeplay*. If totalization no longer has any meaning, it is not because the infinity of a field cannot be covered by a finite glance or a finite discourse, but because the nature of the field—that is, language and a finite language—excludes totalization. This field is in fact that of *freeplay*, that is to say, a field of infinite substitutions in the closure of a finite ensemble. This field permits these infinite substitutions only because it is finite, that is to say, because instead of being an inexhaustible field, as in the classical hypothesis, instead of being too large, there is something missing from it: a center which arrests and founds the freeplay of substitutions. One could say—rigorously using that word whose scandalous signification is always obliterated in French—that this movement of the freeplay, permitted by the lack, the absence of a center or origin, is the movement of *supplementarity*. One cannot determine the center, the sign which *supplements*[9] it, which takes its place in its absence—because this sign adds itself, occurs in addition, over and above, comes as a *supplement*.[10] The movement of signification adds something, which results in the fact that there is always more, but this ad-

dition is a floating one because it comes to perform a vicarious function, to supplement a lack on the part of the signified. Although Lévi-Strauss in his use of the word supplementary never emphasizes as I am doing here the two directions of meaning which are so strangely compounded within it, it is not by chance that he uses this word twice in his "Introduction to the Work of Marcel Mauss,"[11] at the point where he is speaking of the "superabundance of signifier, in relation to the signifieds to which this superabundance can refer":

> In his endeavor to understand the world, man therefore always has at his disposition a surplus of signification (which he portions out amongst things according to the laws of symbolic thought—which it is the task of ethnologists and linguists to study). This distribution of a *supplementary* allowance [*ration* supplémentaire]—if it is permissible to put it that way—is absolutely necessary in order that on the whole the available signifier and the signified it aims at may remain in the relationship of complementarity which is the very condition of the use of symbolic thought (p. xlix).

(It could no doubt be demonstrated that this *ration supplémentaire* of signification is the origin of the *ratio* itself.) The word reappears a little farther on, after Lévi-Strauss has mentioned "this floating signifier, which is the servitude of all finite thought":

> In other words—and taking as our guide Mauss's precept that all social phenomena can be assimilated to language—we see in *mana, Wakau, oranda* and other notions of the same type, the conscious expression of a semantic function, whose role it is to permit symbolic thought to operate in spite of the contradiction which is proper to it. In this way are explained the apparently insoluble antinomies attached to this notion. . . . At one and the same time force and action, quality and state, substantive and verb; abstract and concrete, omnipresent and localized—*mana* is in effect all these things. But is it not precisely because it is none of these things that *mana* is a simple form, or more exactly, a symbol in the pure state, and therefore capable of becoming charged with any sort of symbolic content whatever? In the system of symbols constituted by all cosmologies, *mana* would simply be a *valeur symbolique zéro*, that is to say, a sign marking the necessity of a symbolic content *sup-*

plementary [my italics] to that with which the signified is already loaded, but which can take on any value required, provided only that this value still remains part of the available reserve and is not, as phonologists put it, a group-term.

Lévi-Strauss adds the note:

> Linguists have already been led to formulate hypotheses of this type. For example: "A zero phoneme is opposed to all the other phonemes in French in that it entails no differential characters and no constant phonetic value. On the contrary, the proper function of the zero phoneme is to be opposed to phoneme absence." (R. Jakobson and J. Lutz, "Notes on the French Phonemic Pattern," *Word*, vol. 5, no. 2 [August, 1949], p. 155). Similarly, if we schematize the conception I am proposing here, it could almost be said that the function of notions like *mana* is to be opposed to the absence of signification, without entailing by itself any particular signification (p. 1 and note).

The *superabundance* of the signifier, its *supplementary* character, is thus the result of a finitude, that is to say, the result of a lack which must be *supplemented*.

It can now be understood why the concept of freeplay is important in Lévi-Strauss. His references to all sorts of games, notably to roulette, are very frequent, especially in his *Conversations*,[12] in *Race and History*,[13] and in *The Savage Mind*. This reference to the game or freeplay is always caught up in a tension.

It is in tension with history, first of all. This is a classical problem, objections to which are now well worn or used up. I shall simply indicate what seems to me the formality of the problem: by reducing history, Lévi-Strauss has treated as it deserves a concept which has always been in complicity with a teleological and eschatological metaphysics, in other words, paradoxically, in complicity with that philosophy of presence to which it was believed history could be opposed. The thematic of historicity, although it seems to be a somewhat late arrival in philosophy, has always been required by the determination of being as presence. With or without etymology, and in spite of the classic antagonism which opposes these significations throughout all of classical thought, it could be shown that the concept of *epistèmè* has always

called forth that of *historia*, if history is always the unity of a becoming, as tradition of truth or development of science or knowledge oriented toward the appropriation of truth in presence and self-presence, toward knowledge in consciousness-of-self.[14] History has always been conceived as the movement of a resumption of history, a diversion between two presences. But if it is legitimate to suspect this concept of history, there is a risk, if it is reduced without an express statement of the problem I am indicating here, of falling back into an anhistoricism of a classical type, that is to say, in a determinate moment of the history of metaphysics. Such is the algebraic formality of the problem as I see it. More concretely, in the work of Lévi-Strauss it must be recognized that the respect for structurality, for the internal originality of the structure, compels a neutralization of time and history. For example, the appearance of a new structure, of an original system, always comes about—and this is the very condition of its structural specificity—by a rupture with its past, its origin, and its cause. One can therefore describe what is peculiar to the structural organization only by not taking into account, in the very moment of this description, its past conditions: by failing to pose the problem of the passage from one structure to another, by putting history into parentheses. In this "structuralist" moment, the concepts of chance and discontinuity are indispensable. And Lévi-Strauss does in fact often appeal to them as he does, for instance, for that structure of structures, language, of which he says in the "Introduction to the Work of Marcel Mauss" that it "could only have been born in one fell swoop":

> Whatever may have been the moment and the circumstances of its appearance in the scale of animal life, language could only have been born in one fell swoop. Things could not have set about signifying progressively. Following a transformation the study of which is not the concern of the social sciences, but rather of biology and psychology, a crossing over came about from a stage where nothing had a meaning to another where everything possessed it (p. xlvi).

This standpoint does not prevent Lévi-Strauss from recognizing the slowness, the process of maturing, the continuous toil of factual transformations, history (for example, in *Race and History*). But, in accordance with an act which was also Rousseau's and Husserl's, he must "brush aside all the facts" at the moment when he wishes to recapture the specificity of a structure. Like Rousseau, he must always conceive of the origin of a new structure on the model of catastrophe—an overturning of nature in nature, a natural interruption of the natural sequence, a brushing aside *of* nature.

Besides the tension of freeplay with history, there is also the tension of freeplay with presence. Freeplay is the disruption of presence. The presence of an element is always a signifying and substitutive reference inscribed in a system of differences and the movement of a chain. Freeplay is always an interplay of absence and presence, but if it is to be radically conceived, freeplay must be conceived of before the alternative of presence and absence; being must be conceived of as presence or absence beginning with the possibility of freeplay and not the other way around. If Lévi-Strauss, better than any other, has brought to light the freeplay of repetition and the repetition of freeplay, one no less perceives in his work a sort of ethic of presence, an ethic of nostalgia for origins, an ethic of archaic and natural innocence, of a purity of presence and self-presence in speech[15]—an ethic, nostalgia, and even remorse which he often presents as the motivation of the ethnological project when he moves toward archaic societies—exemplary societies in his eyes. These texts are well known.

As a turning toward the presence, lost or impossible, of the absent origin, this structuralist thematic of broken immediateness is thus the sad, *negative*, nostalgic, guilty, Rousseauist facet of the thinking of freeplay of which the Nietzschean *affirmation*—the joyous affirmation of the freeplay of the world and without truth, without origin, offered to an active interpretation—would be the other side. *This affirmation then determines the non-center otherwise than as loss of the center.* And it plays the game without security. For there is a *sure* freeplay: that which is limited to the *substitution* of *given and existing*, *present*, pieces. In absolute chance, affirmation also surrenders itself to *genetic* indetermination, to the *seminal* adventure of the trace.[16]

There are thus two interpretations of interpretation, of structure, of sign, of freeplay. The one seeks to decipher, dreams of deciphering, a truth or an origin which is free from freeplay and from the order of the sign, and lives like an exile the necessity of interpretation. The other, which is no longer turned toward the origin, affirms freeplay and tries to pass beyond man and humanism, the name man being the name of that being who, throughout the history of metaphysics or of ontotheology—in other words, through the history of all of his history—has dreamed of full presence, the reassuring foundation, the origin and the end of the game. The second interpretation of interpretation, to which Nietzsche showed us the way, does not seek in ethnography, as Lévi-Strauss wished, the "inspiration of a new humanism" (again from the "Introduction to the Work of Marcel Mauss").

There are more than enough indications today to suggest we might perceive that these two interpretations of interpretation—which are absolutely irreconcilable even if we live them simultaneously and reconcile them in an obscure economy—together share the field which we call, in such a problematic fashion, the human sciences.

For my part, although these two interpretations must acknowledge and accentuate their difference and define their irreducibility, I do not believe that today there is any question of *choosing*—in the first place because here we are in a region (let's say, provisionally, a region of historicity) where the category of choice seems particularly trivial; and in the second, because we must first try to conceive of the common ground, and the *différence* of this irreducible difference.[17] Here there is a sort of question, call it historical, of which we are only glimpsing today the *conception, the formation, the gestation, the labor.* I employ these words, I admit, with a glance toward the business of childbearing—but also with a glance toward those who, in a company from which I do not exclude myself, turn their eyes away in the face of the as yet unnameable which is proclaiming itself and which can do so, as is necessary whenever a birth is in the offing, only under the species of the non-species, in the formless, mute, infant, and terrifying form of monstrosity.

Notes

1. "La Structure, le signe et le jeu dans le discours des sciences humaines." The text which follows is a translation of the revised version of M. Derrida's communication. The word "jeu" is variously translated here as "play," "interplay," "game," and "stake," besides the normative translation "free-play." All footnotes to this article are additions by the translator.

2. *Interdite:* "forbidden," "disconcerted," "confounded," "speechless."

3. ". . . qui naît toujours d'une certaine manière d'être impliqué dans le jeu, d'être pris au jeu, d'être comme être d'entrée de jeu dans le jeu."

4. *Le cru et le cuit* (Paris: Plon, 1964).

5. *Les structures élémentaires de la parenté* (Paris: Presses Universitaires de France, 1949).

6. *La pensée sauvage* (Paris: Plon, 1962).

7. A *bricoleur* is a jack-of-all trades, someone who potters about with odds-and-ends, who puts things together out of bits and pieces.

8. Reprinted in: G. Genette, *Figures* (Paris: Editions du Seuil, 1966). p. 145.

9. The point being that the word, both in English and French, means "to supply a deficiency," on the one hand, and "to supply something additional," on the other.

10. ". . . ce signe s'ajoute, vient en sus, en *supplément.*"

11. "Introduction à l'oeuvre de Marcel Mauss," in: Marcel Mauss, *Sociologie et anthropologie* (Paris: Presses Universitaires de France, 1950).

12. Presumably: G. Charbonnier, *Entretiens avec Claude Lévi-Strauss* (Paris: Plon-Julliard, 1961).

13. *Race and History* (Paris: UNESCO Publications, 1958).

14. ". . . l'unité d'un devenir, comme tradition de la vérité dans la présence et la présence à soi, vers le savoir dans la conscience de soi."

15. ". . . de la présence à soi dans la parole."

16. "Tournée vers la présence, perdue ou impossible, de l'origine absente, cette thématique structuraliste de l'immédiateté rompue est donc la face triste, *négative,* nostalgique, coupable, rousseauiste, de la pensée du jeu dont *l'affirmation* nietzschéenne, l'affirmation joyeuse du jeu du monde et de l'innocence du devenir, l'affirmation d'un monde de signes sans faute, sans vérité, sans origine, offert à une interprétation active, serait l'autre face. *Cette affirmation détermine alors le* non-centre *autrement que comme perte du centre.* Et elle joue sans sécurité. Car il y a un jeu *sûr:* celui qui se limite à la *substitution* de pièces *données et existantes, présentes.* Dans le hasard absolu, l'affirmation se livre aussi à l'indétermination *génétique,* à l'aventure *séminale* de la trace."

17. From *différer,* in the sense of "to postpone," "put off," "defer." Elsewhere Derrida uses the word as a synonym for the German *Aufschub:* "postponement," and relates it to the central Freudian concepts of *Verspätung, Nachträglichkeit,* and to the *"détours* to death" of *Beyond the Pleasure Principle* by Sigmund Freud (Standard Edition, ed. James Strachey, vol. XIX, London, 1961), Chap. V.

Semiology and Rhetoric

Paul de Man

*After reviewing some recent forms of criticism
that assume a continuity between grammar and
rhetoric, Paul de Man proceeds to challenge that assumption. Citing Kenneth Burke, Charles Sanders
Peirce, and Jacques Derrida as others who have
questioned that continuity, he begins with the playful example of a "rhetorical" question as it might be
viewed by an "archie Debunker," moves on to a deconstructive reading of four lines by Yeats, and
ends with an extended analysis of a passage from
Proust. In each case, his reading argues that rhetoric undoes grammar, and vice versa. Having
sketched an immense deconstructive project for criticism along the lines suggested by his analyses, de
Man cautions us that the superior status this
project seems to confer on the philosopher-critic is
an illusion. The poet has always been there first
and the task of the deconstructive critic is to follow
closely, like a good formalist, the text the poet has
given him. "Poetic writing is the most advanced
and refined mode of deconstruction," de Man insists and, as he demonstrates, it demands the
closest of close readers. But such readers will discover not the formalist's unity and coherence but
the text's propensity to deconstruct itself. "Literature," he concludes, "as well as criticism—the
difference between them being delusive—are condemned (or privileged) to be forever the most rigorous and, consequently, the most unreliable language
in terms of which man names and modifies himself."*

TO JUDGE FROM VARIOUS RECENT PUBLICATIONS,
the spirit of the times is not blowing in the direction of formalist and intrinsic criticism. We
may no longer be hearing too much about relevance but we keep hearing a great deal about
reference, about the non-verbal "outside" to
which language refers, by which it is conditioned and upon which it acts. The stress falls
not so much on the fictional status of literature—a property now perhaps somewhat too
easily taken for granted—but on the interplay
between these fictions and categories that are
said to partake of reality, such as the self, man,
society, "the artist, his culture and the human
community," as one critic puts it. Hence the emphasis on hybrid texts considered to be partly
literary and partly referential, on popular fictions deliberately aimed towards social and psychological gratification, on literary autobiography as a key to the understanding of the self,
and so on. We speak as if, with the problems of
literary form resolved once and forever, and
with the techniques of structural analysis refined
to near-perfection, we could now move "beyond
formalism" towards the questions that really
interest us and reap, at last, the fruits of the
ascetic concentration on techniques that prepared us for this decisive step. With the internal
law and order of literature well policed, we can
now confidently devote ourselves to the foreign
affairs, the external politics of literature. Not
only do we feel able to do so, but we owe it to
ourselves to take this step: our moral conscience
would not allow us to do otherwise. Behind the
assurance that valid interpretation is possible,
behind the recent interest in writing and reading
as potentially effective public speech acts, stands
a highly respectable moral imperative that
strives to reconcile the internal, formal, private
structures of literary language with their external, referential and public effects.

I want, for the moment, to consider briefly this tendency in itself, as an undeniable and recurrent historical fact, without regard for its truth or falseness or for its value as desirable or pernicious. It is a fact that this sort of thing happens, again and again, in literary studies. On the one hand, literature cannot merely be received as a definite unit of referential meaning that can be decoded without leaving a residue. The code is unusually conspicuous, complex and enigmatic; it attracts an inordinate amount of attention to itself and this attention has to acquire the rigor of a method. The structural moment of concentration on the code for its own sake cannot be avoided and literature necessarily breeds its own formalism. Technical innovations in the methodical study of literature only occur when this kind of attention predominates. It can legitimately be said, for example, that, from a technical point of view, very little has happened in American criticism since the innovative works of New Criticism. There certainly have been numerous excellent books of criticism since, but in none of them have the techniques of description and interpretation evolved beyond the techniques of close reading established in the thirties and the forties. Formalism, it seems, is an all-absorbing and tyrannical muse; the hope that one can be at the same time technically original and discursively eloquent is not borne out by the history of literary criticism.

On the other hand—and this is the real mystery—no literary formalism, no matter how accurate and enriching in its analytic powers, is ever allowed to come into being without seeming reductive. When form is considered to be the external trappings of literary meaning or content, it seems superficial and expendable. The development of intrinsic, formalist criticism in the twentieth century has changed this model: form is now a solipsistic category of self-reflection and the referential meaning is said to be extrinsic. The polarities of inside and outside have been reversed, but they are still the same polarities that are at play: internal meaning has become outside reference and the outer form has become the intrinsic structure. A new version of reductiveness at once follows this reversal: formalism nowadays is mostly described in

an imagery of imprisonment and claustrophobia: the "prison house of language," "the impasse of formalist criticism," etc. Like the grandmother in Proust's novel ceaselessly driving the young Marcel out into the garden, away from the unhealthy inwardness of his closeted reading, critics cry out for the fresh air of referential meaning. Thus, with the structure of the code so opaque, but the meaning so anxious to blot out the obstacle of form, no wonder that the reconciliation of form and meaning would be so attractive. The attraction of reconciliation is the elective breeding-ground of false models and metaphors; it accounts for the metaphorical model, of literature as a kind of box that separates an inside from an outside, and the reader or critic as the person who opens the lid in order to release in the open what was secreted but inaccessible inside. It matters little whether we call the inside of the box the content or the form, the outside the meaning or the appearance. The recurrent debate opposing intrinsic to extrinsic criticism stands under the aegis of an inside/outside metaphor that is never being seriously questioned.

Metaphors are much more tenacious than facts and I certainly don't expect to dislodge this age-old model in one short expository talk. I merely wish to speculate on a different set of terms, perhaps less simple in their differential relationship than the strictly polar, binary opposition between inside and outside and therefore less likely to enter into the easy play of chiasmic reversals. I derive these terms (which are as old as the hills) pragmatically from the observation of developments and debates in recent critical methodology.

One of the most controversial among these developments coincides with a new approach to poetics or, as it is called in Germany, poetology, as a branch of general semiotics. In France, a semiology of literature comes about as the outcome of the long-deferred but all the more explosive encounter of the nimble French literary mind with the category of form. Semiology, as opposed to semantics, is the science or study of signs as signifiers; it does not ask what words mean but how they mean. Unlike American New Criticism, which derived the internalization of form from the practice of highly self-conscious modern writers, French semiology turned to linguistics for its model and adopted Saussure and Jakobson rather than Valéry or Proust for its masters. By an awareness of the arbitrariness of the sign (Saussure) and of literature as an autotelic statement "focused on the way it is expressed" (Jakobson) the entire question of meaning can be bracketed, thus freeing the critical discourse from the debilitating burden of paraphrase. The demystifying power of semiology, within the context of French historical and thematic criticism, has been considerable. It demonstrated that the perception of the literary dimensions of language is largely obscured if one submits uncritically to the authority of reference. It also revealed how tenaciously this authority continues to assert itself in a variety of disguises, ranging from the crudest ideology to the most refined forms of aesthetic and ethical judgment. It especially explodes the myth of semantic correspondence between sign and referent, the wishful hope of having it both ways, of being, to paraphrase Marx in the German Ideology, a formalist critic in the morning and a communal moralist in the afternoon, of serving both the technique of form and the substance of meaning. The results, in the practice of French criticism, have been as fruitful as they are irreversible. Perhaps for the first time since the late eighteenth century, French critics can come at least somewhat closer to the kind of linguistic awareness that never ceased to be operative in its poets and novelists and that forced all of them including Sainte Beuve to write their main works "contre Sainte Beuve." The distance was never so considerable in England and the United States, which does not mean, however, that we may be able, in this country, to dispense with a preventative semiological hygiene altogether.

One of the most striking characteristics of literary semiology, as it is practiced today, in France and elsewhere, is the use of grammatical (especially syntactical) structures conjointly with rhetorical structures, without apparent awareness of a possible discrepancy between them. In their literary analyses, Barthes, Genette, Todorov, Greimas and their disciples all simplify and regress from Jakobson in letting grammar and rhetoric function in perfect continuity, and in passing from grammatical to rhetorical struc-

tures without difficulty of interruption. Indeed, as the study of grammatical structures is refined in contemporary theories of generative, transformational and distributive grammar, the study of tropes and of figures (which is how the term rhetoric is used throughout this paper, and not in the derived sense of comment or of eloquence or persuasion) becomes a mere extension of grammatical models, a particular subset of syntactical relations. In the recent *Dictionnaire encyclopédique des sciences du langage*, Ducrot and Todorov write that rhetoric has always been satisfied with a paradigmatic view over words (words substituting for each other), without questioning their syntagmatic relationship (the contiguity of words to each other). There ought to be another perspective, complementary to the first, in which metaphor, for example, would not be defined as a substitution but as a particular type of combination. Research inspired by linguisitics or, more narrowly, by syntactical studies, have begun to reveal this possibility—but it remains to be explored. Todorov, who calls one of his books a *Grammar of the Decameron*, rightly thinks of his own work and that of his associates as first explorations in the elaboration of a systematic grammar of literary modes, genres and also of literary figures. Perhaps the most perceptive work to come out of this school, Genette's studies of figural modes, can be shown to be assimilations of rhetorical transformations or combinations to syntactical, grammatical patterns. Thus a recent study, now printed in *Figures III* and entitled *Metaphor and Metonomy in Proust*, shows the combined presence, in a wide and astute selection of passages, of paradigmatic, metaphorical figures with syntagmatic, metonymic structures. The combination of both is treated descriptively and nondialectically without suffering the possiblity of logical tensions.

One can ask whether this reduction of figure to grammar is legitimate. The existence of grammatical structures, within and beyond the unit of the sentence in literary texts is undeniable, and their description and classification are indispensable. The question remains if and how figures of rhetoric can be included in such a taxonomy. This question is at the core of the debate going on, in a wide variety of apparently unrelated forms, in contemporary poetics, but I do not plan to make clear the connection between this "real" problem and the countless pseudo-problems that agitate literary studies. The historical picture of contemporary criticism is too confused to make the mapping out of such a topography a useful exercise. Not only are these questions mixed in and mixed up within particular groups or local trends, but they are often co-present, without apparent contradiction, within the work of a single author.

Neither is the theory of the question suitable for quick expository treatment. To distinguish the epistemology of grammar from the epistemology of rhetoric is a redoutable task. On an entirely naïve level, we tend to conceive of grammatical systems as tending towards universality and as simply generative, i.e. as capable of deriving an infinity of versions from a single model (that may govern transformations as well as derivations) without the intervention of another model that would upset the first. We therefore think of the relationship between grammar and logic, the passage from grammar to propositions, as being relatively un-problematic: no true propositions are conceivable in the absence of grammatical consistency or of controlled deviation from a system of consistency no matter how complex. Grammar and logic stand to each other in a dyadic relationship of unsubverted support. In a logic of acts rather than of statements, as in Austin's theory of speech acts, that has had such a strong influence on recent American work in literary semiology, it is also possible to move between speech acts and grammar without difficulty. The performance of what is called illocutionary acts such as ordering, questioning, denying, assuming etc. within the language is congruent with the grammatical structures of syntax in the corresponding imperative, interrogative, negative, optative sentences. "The rules for illocutionary acts," writes Richard Ohman in a recent paper, "determine whether performance of a given act is well-executed, in just the same way as *grammatical* rules determine whether the product of a locutionary act—a sentence—is well formed [. . .]. But whereas the rules of grammar concern the relationships among sound, syntax, and meaning, the rules of illocutionary acts con-

cern relationships among people" ("Speech, Literature, and the Space in between," *New Literary History* IV, No. 1 [Autumn 1972]; p. 50). And since rhetoric is then conceived exclusively as persuasion, as actual action upon others (and not as an intralinguistic figure or trope), the continuity between the illocutionary realm of grammar and the perlocutionary realm of rhetoric is self-evident. It becomes the basis for a new rhetoric that, exactly as is the case for Todorov and Genette, would also be a new grammar.

Without engaging the substance of the question, it can be pointed out, without having to go beyond recent and American examples, and without calling upon the strength of an age-old tradition, that the continuity here assumed between grammar and rhetoric is not borne out by theoretical and philosophical speculation. Kenneth Burke mentions *Deflection* (which he compares structurally to Freudian displacement), defined as "any slight bias or even unintended error," as the rhetorical basis of language, and deflection is then conceived as a dialectical subversion of the consistent link between sign and meaning that operates within grammatical patterns; hence Burke's well-known insistence on the distinction between grammar and rhetoric. Charles Sanders Peirce who, with Neitzsche and Saussure, laid the philosophical foundation for modern semiology, stressed the distinction between grammar and rhetoric in his celebrated and so suggestively unfathomable definition of the sign. He insists, as is well known, on the necessary presence of a third element, called the interpretant, within any relationship that the sign entertains with its object. The sign is to be interpreted if we are to understand the idea it is to convey, and this is so because the sign is not the thing but a meaning derived from the thing by a process here called representation that is not simply generative, i.e. dependent on a univocal origin. The interpretation of the sign is not, for Peirce, a meaning but another sign; it is a reading, not a decodage, and this reading has, in its turn, to be interpreted into another sign, and so on *ad infinitum*. Peirce calls this process by means of which "one sign gives birth to another" pure rhetoric, as distinguished from pure grammar, which postulates the possibility of unproblematic, dyadic meaning and pure logic, which postulates the possibility of the universal truth of meanings. Only if the sign engendered meaning in the same way that the object engenders the sign, that is, by representation, would there be no need to distinguish between grammar and rhetoric.

These remarks should indicate at least the existence and the difficulty of the question, a difficulty which puts its concise theoretical exposition beyond my powers. I must retreat therefore into a pragmatic discourse and try to illustrate the tension between grammar and rhetoric in a few specific textual examples. Let me begin by considering what is perhaps the most commonly known instance of an apparent symbiosis between a grammatical and a rhetorical structure, the so-called rhetorical question, in which the figure is conveyed directly by means of a syntactical device. I take the first example from the sub-literature of the mass media: asked by his wife whether he wants to have his bowling shoes laced over or laced under, Archie Bunker answers with a question: "What's the difference?" Being a reader of sublime simplicity, his wife replies by patiently explaining the difference between lacing over and lacing under, whatever this may be, but provokes only ire. "What's the difference" did not ask for difference but means instead "I don't give a damn what the difference is." The same grammatical pattern engenders two meanings that are mutually exclusive: the literal meaning asks for concept (difference) whose existence is denied by the figurative meaning. As long as we are talking about bowling shoes, the consequences are relatively trivial; Archie Bunker, who is a great believer in the authority of origins (as long, of course, as they are the right origins) muddles along in a world where literal and figurative meanings get in each other's way, though not without discomforts. But suppose that it is a de-bunker rather than a "Bunker," and a de-bunker of the arche (or origin), an archie Debunker such as Nietzsche or Jacques Derrida for instance, who asks the question "What is the Difference"—and we cannot even tell from his grammar whether he "really" wants to know "what" difference is or is just telling us that we shouldn't even try to find it. Confronted with the question of the difference between grammar

and rhetoric, grammar allows us to ask the question, but the sentence by means of which we ask it may deny the very possibility of asking. For what is the use of asking, I ask, when we cannot even authoritatively decide whether a question asks or doesn't ask?

The point is as follows. A perfectly clear syntactical paradigm (the question) engenders a sentence that has at least two meanings of which the one asserts and the other denies its own illocutionary mode. It is not so that there are simply two meanings, one literal and the other figural, and that we have to decide which one of these meanings is the right one in this particular situation. The confusion can only be cleared up by the intervention of an extra-textual intention, such as Archie Bunker putting his wife straight; but the very anger he displays is indicative of more than impatience; it reveals his despair when confronted with a structure of linguistic meaning that he cannot control and that holds the discouraging prospect of an infinity of similar future confusions, all of them potentially catastrophic in their consequences. Nor is this intervention really a part of the mini-text constituted by the figure which holds our attention only as long as it remains suspended and unresolved. I follow the usage of common speech in calling this semiological enigma "rhetorical." The grammatical model of the question becomes rhetorical not when we have, on the one hand, a literal meaning and on the other hand a figural meaning, but when it is impossible to decide by grammatical or other linguistic devices which of the two meanings (that can be entirely contradictory) prevails. Rhetoric radically suspends logic and opens up vertiginous possibilities of referential aberration. And although it would perhaps be somewhat more remote from common usage, I would not hesitate to equate the rhetorical, figural potentiality of language with literature itself. I could point to a great number of antecedents to this equation of literature with figure; the most recent reference would be to Monroe Beardsley's insistence in his contribution to the *Essays* to honor William Wimsatt, that literary language is characterized by being "distinctly above the norm in ratio of implicit (or, I would say ·rhetorical) to explicit meaning" (p. 37).

Let me pursue the question of rhetorical question through one more example. Yeat's poem "Among School Children," ends with the famous line: "How can we know the dancer from the dance?" Although there are some revealing inconsistencies within the commentaries, the line is usually interpreted as stating, with the increased emphasis of a rhetorical device, the potential unity between form and experience, between creator and creation. It could be said that it denies the discrepancy between the sign and the referent from which we started out. Many elements in the imagery and the dramatic development of the poem strengthen this traditional reading; without having to look any further than the immediately preceding lines, one finds powerful and consecrated images of the continuity from part to whole that makes synecdoche into the most seductive of metaphors: the organic beauty of the tree, stated in the parallel syntax of a similar rhetorical question, or the convergence, in the dance, of erotic desire with musical form:

> O chestnut tree, great rooted blossomer
> Are you the leaf, the blossom or the bole?
> O body swayed to music, O brightening glance
> How can we know the dancer from the dance?

A more extended reading, always assuming that the final line is to be read as a rhetorical question, reveals that the thematic and rhetorical grammar of the poem yields a consistent reading that extends from the first line to the last and that can account for all details in the text. It is equally possible, however, to read the last line literally rather than figuratively, as asking with some urgency the question we asked at the beginning of this talk within the context of contemporary criticism: *not* that sign and referent are so exquisitely fitted to each other that all difference between them is at times blotted out but, rather, since the two essentially different elements, sign and meaning, are so intricately intertwined in the imagined "presence" that the poem addresses, how can we possibly make the distinctions that would shelter us from the error of identifying what cannot be identified? The clumsiness of the paraphrase reveals that it is not necessarily the literal reading which is simpler than the figurative one, as was the case in

our first example; here, the figural reading, which assumes the question to be rhetorical is perhaps naïve, whereas the literal reading leads to greater complications of theme and statement. For it turns out that the entire scheme set up by the first reading can be undermined or deconstructed, in the terms of the second, in which the final line is read literally as meaning that, since the dancer and the dance are not the same, it might be useful, perhaps even desperately necessary—for the question can be given a ring of urgency, "Please tell me, how *can* I know the dancer from the dance"—to tell them apart. But this will replace the reading of each symbolic detail by a divergent interpretation. The oneness of trunk, leaf and blossom, for example, that would have appealed to Goethe, would find itself replaced by the much less reassuring Tree of Life from the Mabinogion that appears in the poem "Vacillation," in which the fiery blossom and the earthly leaf are held together, as well as apart, by the crucified and castrated God Attis, of whose body it can hardly be said that it is "not bruised to pleasure soul." This hint should suffice to suggest that two entirely coherent but entirely incompatible readings can be made to hinge on one line, whose grammatical structure is devoid of ambiguity, but whose rhetorical mode turns the mood as well as the mode of the entire poem upside down. Neither can we say, as was already the case in the first example, that the poem simply has two meanings that exist side by side. The two readings have to engage each other in direct confrontation, for the one reading is precisely the error denounced by the other and has to be undone by it. Nor can we in any way make a valid decision as to which of the readings can be given priority over the other; none can exist in the other's absence. There can be no dance without a dancer, no sign without a referent. On the other hand, the authority of the meaning engendered by the grammatical structure is fully obscured by the duplicity of a figure that cries out for the differentiation that it conceals.

Yeats' poem is not explicitly "about" rhetorical questions but about images or metaphors, and about the possibility of convergence between experiences of consciousness such as memory or emotions—what the poem calls passion, piety and affection—and entities accessible to the senses such as bodies, persons or icons. We return to the inside/outside model from which we started out and which the poem puts into question by means of a syntactical device (the question) made to operate on a grammatical as well as on a rhetorical level. The couple grammar/rhetoric, certainly not a binary opposition since they in no way exclude each other, disrupts and confuses the neat antithesis of the inside/outside pattern. We can transfer this scheme to the act of reading and interpretation. By reading we get, as we say, inside a text that was first something alien to us and which we now make our own by an act of understanding. But this understanding becomes at once the representation of an extra-textual meaning; in Austin's terms, the illocutionary speech act becomes a perlocutionary actual act—in Frege's terms, *Bedeutung* becomes *Sinn*. Our recurrent question is whether this transformation is semantically controlled along grammatical or along rhetorical lines. Does the metaphor of reading really unite outer meaning with inner understanding, action with reflection, into one single totality? The assertion is powerfully and suggestively made in a passage from Proust that describes the experience of reading as such a union. It describes the young Marcel, near the beginning of Combray, hiding in the closed space of his room in order to read. The example differs from the earlier ones in that we are not dealing with a grammatical structure that also functions rhetorically but have instead the representation, the dramatization, in terms of the experience of a subject, of a rhetorical structure—just as in many other passages, Proust dramatizes tropes by means of landscapes or descriptions of objects. The figure here dramatized is that of metaphor, an inside/outside correspondence as represented by the act of reading. The reading scene is the culmination of a series of actions taking place in enclosed spaces and leading up to the "dark coolness" of Marcel's room.

> I had stretched out on my bed, with a book, in my room which sheltered, tremblingly, its transparent and fragile coolness against the afternoon sun, behind the almost closed blinds through which a glimmer of daylight had nevertheless managed to push its yellow wings, remaining

motionless between the wood and the glass, in a corner, poised like a butterfly. It was hardly light enough to read and the sensation of the light's splendor was given me only by the noise of Camus [. . .] hammering dusty crates; resounding in the sonorous atmosphere that is peculiar to hot weather, they seemed to spark off scarlet stars; and also by the flies executing their little concert, the chamber music of summer: evocative not in the manner of a human tune that, heard perchance during the summer, afterwards reminds you of it; it is connected to summer by a more necessary link: born from beautiful days, resurrecting only when they return, containing some of their essence, it does not only awaken their image in our memory; it guarantees their return, their actual, persistent, unmediated presence.

> The dark coolness of my room related to the full sunlight of the street as the shadow relates to the ray of light, that is to say it was just as luminous and it gave my imagination the total spectacle of the summer, whereas my senses, if I had been on a walk, could only have enjoyed it by fragments; it matched my repose which (thanks to the adventures told by my book and stirring my tranquillity) supported, like the quiet of a motionless hand in the middle of a running brook the shock and the motion of a torrent of activity. (*Swann's Way*. Paris: Pléiàde, 1954; p. 83. Author's translation.)

From the beginning of the passage, inwardness is valorized positively as something desirable that has to protect itself against the intrusion of outside forces, but that nevertheless has to borrow, as it were, some of its constitutive properites from the outside. A chain of binary properties is set up and antithetically differentiated in terms of the inside/outside polarity: properties of coolness, darkness, repose, silence, imagination and totality, associated with inwardness, contrast with the heat, the light, the activity, the sounds, the senses and the fragmentation that govern the outside. By the act of reading, these static oppositions are put in motion, thus allowing for the play of substitutions by means of which the claim for totalization can be made. Thus, in a beautifully seductive effect of chiaroscuro, mediated by the metaphor of light as a poised butterfly, the inner room is convincingly said to acquire the amount of light necessary to reading. In the wake of this light, warmth can also enter the room, incarnate in the auditive synaesthesia of the various sounds. According to the narrator, these metaphorical substitutions and reversals render the presence of Summer in the room more complete than the actual experience of Summer in the outside world could have done. The text achieves this synthesis and comments on it in normative terms, comparable to the manner in which treatises of practical rhetorics recommend the use of one figure in preference to another in a given situation: here it is the substitutive totalization by metaphor which is said to be more effective than the mere contiguity of metonymic association. As opposed to the random contingency of metonymy ("par hasard"), the metaphor is linked to its proper meaning by, says Proust, the "necessary link" that leads to perfect synthesis. In the wake of this synthesis, the entire conceptual vocabulary of metaphysics enters the text: a terminology of generation, of transcendental necessity, of totality, of essence, of permanence, and of unmediated presence. The passage acts out and asserts the priority of metaphor over metonymy in terms of the categories of metaphysics and with reference to the act of reading.

The actual test of the truth of the assertion comes in the second paragraph when the absurd mathematical ratio set up at the beginning has to be verified by a further substitution. This time, what has to be exchanged are not only the properties of light and dark, warm and cool, fragment and totality (part and whole), but the properties of action and repose. The full seduction of the text can only come into being when the formal totalization of light and dark is completed by the transfer from rest to action that represents the extratextual, referential moment. The text asserts the transfer in the concluding sentence: "The dark coolness of my room [. . .] supported, like the quiet of a motionless hand in the middle of a running brook, the shock and the motion of a torrent of activity." The verb "to support" here carries the full weight of uniting rest and action ("repos et activité"), fiction and reality, as firmly as the base supports the column. The transfer, as is so often the case in Proust, is carried out by the liquid element of the running brook. The natural, representational connotation of the passage is with coolness, so

particularly attractive within the predominant summer-mood of the entire *Recherche*. But coolness, it will be remembered, is one of the characteristic properties of the "inside" world. It cannot therefore by itself transfer us into the opposite world of activity. The movement of the water evokes a freshness which in the binary logic of the passage is associated with the inward, imaginary world of reading and fiction. In order to accede to action, it would be necessary to capture one of the properties belonging to the opposite chain such as, for example, warmth. The mere "cool" action of fiction cannot suffice: it is necessary to reconcile the cool immobility of the hand with the heat of action if the claim made by the sentence is to stand up as true. The transfer is carried out, always within the same sentence, when it is said that repose supports "a torrent of activity." The expression *"torrent d'activité"* is not, or no longer, a metaphor in French: it is a cliché, a dead, or sleeping metaphor that has lost the suggestive, connotative values contained in the word "torrent." It simply means "a great deal of activity," the amount of activity that is likely to agitate one to the point of getting hot. Heat is thus surreptitiously smuggled into the passage from a cold source, closing the ring of antithetical properties and allowing for their exchange and substitution: from the moment tranquility can be active and warm without losing its cool and its distinctive quality of repose, the fragmented experience of reality can become whole without losing its quality of being real.

The transfer is made to seem convincing and seductive by the double play on the cliché "torrent of activity." The proximate, contiguous image of the brook awakens, as it were, the sleeping beauty of the dozing metaphor which, in its common use, had become the metonymic association of two words united by sheer habit and no longer by the inner necessity, the necessary link of a transcendental signification. "Torrent" functions in a double semantic register: in its reawakened literal meaning it relays the attribute of coolness that is actually part of the running water, whereas in its figural non-meaning it designates the quantity of activity connotative of the contrary property of warmth.

The rhetorical structure of this sentence is

therefore not simply metaphorical. It is at least doubly metonymic, first because the coupling of words, in a cliché, is not governed by the necessary link that reveals their potential identity but by the contingent habit of proximity; second, because the reawakening of the metaphorical term "torrent" is carried out by a statement that happens to be in the vicinity, but without there being any necessity for the proximity on the level of the referential meaning. The most striking thing is that this doubly metonymic structure is found in a text that also contains highly seductive and successful metaphors (as in the chiaroscuro effect of the beginning, or in the condensation of light in the butterfly image) and that explicitly asserts the superiority of metaphor over metonymy in terms of metaphysical categories.

That these metaphysical categories do not remain unaffected by such a reading would become clear from an inclusive reading of Proust's novel or would become even more explicit in a language-conscious philosopher, such as Nietzsche who, as a philosopher, has to be concerned with the epistemological consequences of the kind of rhetorical seductions exemplified by the Proust passage. It can be shown that the systematic critique of the main categories of metaphysics undertaken by Nietzsche in his late work, the critique of the concepts of causality, of the subject, of identity, of referential and revealed truth, etc. occurs along the same pattern of deconstruction that was operative in Proust's text; and it can also be shown that this pattern exactly corresponds to Nietzsche's description, in texts that precede *The Will to Power* by more than fifteen years, of the structure of the main rhetorical tropes. The key to this critique of metaphysics, which is itself a recurrent gesture throughout the history of thought, is the rhetorical model of the trope or, if one prefers to call it that, literature. It turns out that, in these innocent-looking didactic exercises we are in fact playing for very sizeable stakes.

It is therefore all the more necessary to know what is linguistically involved in a rhetorically conscious reading of the type here undertaken on a brief fragment from a novel and extended by Nietzsche to the entire text of post-Hellenic thought. Our first examples dealing . with the

rhetorical questions were rhetorizations of grammar, figures generated by syntactical paradigms, whereas the Proust example could be better described as a grammatization of rhetoric. By passing from a paradigmatic structure based on substitution, such as metaphor, to a syntagmatic structure based on contingent association such as metonymy, the mechanical, repetitive aspect of grammatical forms is shown to be operative in a passage that seemed at first sight to celebrate the self-willed and autonomous inventiveness of a subject. Figures are assumed to be inventions, the products of a highly particularized individual talent, whereas no one can claim credit for the programmed pattern of grammar. Yet, our reading of the Proust passage shows that precisely when the highest claims are being made for the unifying power of metaphor, these very images rely in fact on the deceptive use of semi-automatic grammatical patterns. The deconstruction of metaphor and of all rhetorical patterns such as mimesis, paranomasis or personification that use resemblance as a way to disguise differences, takes us back to the impersonal precision of grammar and of a semiology derived from grammatical patterns. Such a deconstruction puts into question a whole series of concepts that underlie the value judgments of our critical discourse: the metaphor of primacy, of genetic history and, most notably, of the autonomous power to will of the self.

There seems to be a difference, then, between what I called the rhetorization of grammar (as in the rhetorical question) and the grammatization of rhetoric, as in the de-constructive readings of the type sketched out in the passage from Proust. The former end up in indetermination, in a suspended uncertainty that was unable to choose between two modes of reading, whereas the latter seems to reach a truth, albeit by the negative road of exposing an error, a false pretense. After the de-constructive reading of the Proust passage, we can no longer believe the assertion made in this passage about the intrinsic, metaphysical superiority of metaphor over metonymy. We seem to end up in a mood of negative assurance that is highly productive of critical discourse. The further text of Proust's novel, for example, responds perfectly to an extended application of this de-constructive pattern: not only can similar gestures be repeated throughout the novel, at all the crucial articulations or all passages where large aesthetic and metaphysical claims are being made—the scenes of involuntary memory, the workshop of Elstir, the septette of Vinteuil, the convergence of author and narrator at the end of the novel—but a vast thematic and semiotic network is revealed that structures the entire narrative and that remained invisible to a reader caught in naïve metaphorical mystification. The whole of literature would respond in similar fashion, although the techniques and the patterns would have to vary considerably, of course, from author to author. But there is absolutely no reason why analyses of the kind here suggested for Proust would not be applicable, with proper modifications of technique, to Milton or to Dante or to Hölderlin. This will in fact be the task of literary criticism in the coming years.

It would seem that we are saying that criticism is the deconstruction of literature, the reduction to the rigors of grammar of rhetorical mystifications. And if we hold up Nietzsche as the philosopher of such a critical deconstruction, then the literary critic would become the philosopher's ally in his struggle with the poets. Criticism and literature would separate around the epistemological axis that distinguishes grammar from rhetoric. It is easy enough to see that this apparent glorification of the critic-philosopher in the name of truth is in fact a glorification of the poet as the primary source of this truth; if truth is the recognition of the systematic character of a certain kind of error, then it would be fully dependent on the prior existence of this error. Philosophers of science like Bachelard or Wittgenstein are notoriously dependent on the aberrations of the poets. We are back at our unanswered question: does the grammatization of rhetoric end up in negative certainty or does it, like the rhetorization of grammar, remain suspended in the ignorance of its own truth or falsehood?

Two concluding remarks should suffice to answer the question. First of all, it is not true that Proust's text can simply be reduced to the mystified assertion (the superiority of metaphor over metonymy) that our reading deconstructs. The reading is not "our" reading, since it uses only the linguistic elements provided by the text itself; the distinction between author and reader is one of the false distinctions that the deconstruction makes evident. The deconstruction is not something we have added to the text but it constituted the text in the first place. A literary text simultaneously asserts and denies the authority of its own rhetorical mode and by reading the text as we did, we were only trying to come closer to being as rigorous a reader as the author had to be in order to write the sentence in the first place. Poetic writing is the most advanced and refined mode of deconstruction; it may differ from critical or discursive writing in the economy of its articulation, but not in kind.

But if we recognize the existence of the deconstructive moment as constitutive of all literary language we have surreptitiously reintroduced the categories that this deconstruction was supposed to eliminate and that have merely been displaced. We have, for example, displaced the question of the self from the referent into the figure of the narrator, who then becomes the *signifié* of the passage. It becomes again possible to ask such naïve questions as what Proust, or Marcel's, motives may have been in thus manipulating language: was he fooling himself, or was he represented as fooling himself and fooling us into believing that fiction and action are as easy to unite, by reading, as the passage asserts? The pathos of the entire section, which would have been more noticeable if the quotation had been a little more extended, the constant vacillation of the narrator between guilt and well-being, invites such questions. They are absurd questions, of course, since the reconciliation of fact and fiction occurs itself as a mere assertion made in the text, and is thus productive of more text at the moment when it asserts its decision to escape from textual confinement. But even if we free ourselves of all false questions of intent and rightfully reduce the narrator to the status of a mere grammatical pronoun, without which the deconstructive narrative could not come into being, this subject remains endowed with a function that is not grammatical but rhetorical, in that it gives voice, so to speak, to a grammatical syntagm. The term voice, even when used in a grammatical terminology as when we speak of the passive or interrogative voice is, of course, a metaphor inferring by analogy the intent of the subject from the structure of the predicate. In the case of the deconstructive discourse that we call literary, or rhetorical, or poetic, this creates a distinctive complication illustrated by the Proust passage. The deconstructive reading revealed a first paradox: the passage valorizes metaphor as being the "right" literary figure, but then proceeds to constitute itself by means of the epistemologically incompatible figure of metonymy. The deconstructive critical discourse reveals the presence of this delusion and affirms it as the irreversible mode of its truth. It cannot pause there however. For if we then ask the obvious and simple next question, whether the rhetorical mode of the text in question is that of metaphor or metonymy, it is impossible to give an answer. Individual metaphors, such as the chiaroscuro effect or the butterfly, are shown to be subordinate figures in a general clause whose syntax is metonymic; from this point of view, it seems that the rhetoric is superseded by a grammer that de-constructs it. But this metonymic clause has as its subject a voice whose relationship to this clause is again metaphorical. The narrator who tells us about the impossibility of metaphor is himself, or itself, a metaphor, the metaphor of a grammatical syntagm whose meaning is the denial of metaphor stated, by antiphrasis, as its priority. And this subject-metaphor is, in its turn, open to the kind of deconstruction to the second degree, the rhetorical deconstruction of psycholinguistics, in which the more advanced investigations of literature are presently engaged, against considerable resistance.

We end up therefore, in the case of the rhetorical grammatization of semiology, just as in the grammatical rhetorization of illocutionary phrases, in the same state of suspended ignorance. Any question about the rhetorical mode of a literary text is always a rhetorical question which does not even know whether it is really questioning. The resulting pathos is an anxiety (or bliss, depending on one's momentary mood or individual temperament) of ignorance, not an anxiety of reference—as becomes thematically clear in Proust's novel when reading is dramatized, in the relationship between Marcel and Albertine, not as an emotive reaction to what language does, but as an emotive reaction to the impossibility of knowing what it might be up to. Literature as well as criticism—the difference between them being delusive—are condemned (or privileged) to be forever the most rigorous and, consequently, the most unreliable language in terms of which man names and modifies himself.

What Makes an Interpretation Acceptable?

Stanley Fish

Although Stanley Fish is not exactly a deconstructive critic, his latest work deserves inclusion in this deconstructive epilogue, for he too offers an overview of the larger issues. In some respects, Fish runs counter to deconstruction. Where critics like Paul de Man point to the inherent indeterminacy of language, Fish points to the inherent determinacy of interpretation. Meaning is always determinate, Fish argues, because interpreters, who make meaning, make it so. On this score his position seems to resemble Norman Holland's. But while Holland sees the reader imposing his or her individual identity on the text, producing thereby a highly individualized interpretation, Fish argues that we always read as members of an interpretive community who share an accepted interpretive strategy. Thus, Fish offers to explain both why our interpretations can agree, and why they often do not. Members of the same interpretive community may produce similar readings, and may even allow their interpretations to be "corrected" according to the rules of that community's strategy. Within such a community, interpretation can be the progressive discipline several critics have called for, and almost any literature class will furnish a microcosmic example of the process. On a larger scale, each of this book's contexts is an interpretive community, or a collection of such communities, sharing certain fundamental assumptions about where literary meaning is located and how we can get at it. But the strategies and assumptions of one context are not those of another, hence the large amount of radical disagreement in critical discussions and the apparent futility of trying to talk across the boundaries of these con-

texts or to offer a strategy they can all agree upon. Since "meaning" is itself the product of interpretation, in Fish's view, all attempts to circumvent interpretive strategies are doomed to fail. Interpretation, he reminds us, "is the only game in town." And since the acceptability of an interpretation can be decided only within an interpretive community, Fish also reminds us that the argument all along has been about what critical context one should choose.

LAST TIME I ENDED BY SUGGESTING THAT THE FACT of agreement, rather than being a proof of the stability of objects, is a testimony to the power of an interpretive community to constitute the objects upon which its members (also and simultaneously constituted) can then agree. This account of agreement has the additional advantage of providing what the objectivist argument cannot supply, a coherent account of *disagreement*. To someone who believes in determinate meaning, disagreement can only be a theological error. The truth lies plainly in view, available to anyone who has the eyes to see; but some readers choose not to see it and perversely substitute their own meanings for the meanings that texts obviously bear. Nowhere is there an explanation of this waywardness (original sin would seem to be the only relevant model), or of the origin of these idiosyncratic meanings (I have been arguing that there could be none), or of the reason why some readers seem to be exempt from the general infirmity. There is simply the conviction that the facts exist in their own self-evident shape and that disagreements are to be resolved by referring the respective parties to the facts as they really are. In the view that I have been urging, however, disagreements cannot be resolved by reference to the facts, because the facts emerge only in the context of some point of

Reprinted by permission of the publishers, Harvard University Press, from *Is There a Text in This Class?*, pp. 338–55, by Stanley Fish. © 1980 by The President and Fellows of Harvard College.

view. It follows, then, that disagreements must occur between those who hold (or are held by) different points of view, and what is at stake in a disagreement is the right to specify what the facts can hereafter be said to be. Disagreements are not settled by the facts, but are the means by which the facts are settled. Of course, no such settling is final, and in the (almost certain) event that the dispute is opened again, the category of the facts "as they really are" will be reconstituted in still another shape.

Nowhere is this process more conveniently on display than in literary criticism, where everyone's claim is that his interpretation more perfectly accords with the facts, but where everyone's purpose is to persuade the rest of us to the version of the facts he espouses by persuading us to the interpretive principles in the light of which those facts will seem indisputable. The recent critical fortunes of William Blake's "The Tyger" provide a nice example. In 1954 Kathleen Raine published an influential essay entitled "Who Made the Tyger" in which she argued that because the tiger is for Blake "the beast that sustains its own life at the expense of its fellow-creatures" it is a "symbol of . . . predacious selfhood," and that therefore the answer to the poem's final question—"Did he who made the Lamb make thee"—is, beyond all possible doubt, No."[1] In short, the tiger is unambiguously and obviously evil. Raine supports her reading by pointing to two bodies of evidence, certain cabbalistic writings which, she avers, "beyond doubt . . . inspired *The Tyger*," and evidence from the poem itself. She pays particular attention to the word "forests" as it appears in line 2, "In the forests of the night:" "Never . . . is the word 'forest' used by Blake in any context in which it does not refer to the natural, 'fallen' world" (p. 48).

The direction of argument here is from the word "forests" to the support it is said to provide for a particular interpretation. Ten years later, however, that same word is being cited in support of a quite different interpretation. While Raine assumes that the lamb is for Blake a symbol of Christ-like self-sacrifice, E. D. Hirsch believes that Blake's intention was "to satirize the singlemindedness of the Lamb": "There can be no doubt," he declares, "that *The Tyger* is a poem that celebrates the holiness of tigerness."[2] In his reading the "ferocity and destructiveness" of the tiger are transfigured and one of the things they are transfigured by is the word "forests": " 'Forests' . . . suggests tall straight forms, a world that for all its terror has the orderliness of the tiger's stripes or Blake's perfectly balanced verses" (p. 247).

What we have here then are two critics with opposing interpretations, each of whom claims the same word as internal and confirming evidence. Clearly they cannot both be right, but just as clearly there is no basis for deciding between them. One cannot appeal to the text, because the text has become an extension of the interpretive disagreement that divides them; and, in fact, the text as it is variously characterized is a *consequence* of the interpretation for which it is supposedly evidence. It is not that the meaning of the word "forests" points in the direction of one interpretation or the other; rather, in the light of an already assumed interpretation, the word will be seen to *obviously* have one meaning or another. Nor can the question be settled by turning to the context—say the cabbalistic writings cited by Raine—for that too will only be a context for an already assumed interpretation. If Raine had not already decided that the answer to the poem's final question is "beyond all possible doubt, No," the cabbalistic texts, with their distinction between supreme and inferior deities, would never have suggested themselves to her as Blake's source. The rhetoric of critical argument, as it is usually conducted in our journals, depends upon a distinction between interpretations on the one hand and the textual and contextual facts that will either support or disconfirm them on the other; but as the example of Blake's "Tyger" shows, text, context, and interpretation all emerge together, as a consequence of a gesture (the declaration of belief) that is irreducibly interpretive. It follows, then, that when one interpretation wins out over another, it is not because the first has been shown to be in accordance with the facts but because it is from the perspective of its assumptions that the facts are now being specified. It is these assumptions, and not the facts they make possible, that are at stake in any critical dispute.

Hirsch and Raine seem to be aware of this, at least subliminally; for whenever their respective assumptions surface they are asserted with a vehemence that is finally defensive: "The answer to the question . . . is beyond all possible doubt, No." "There can be no doubt that *The Tyger* is . . . a poem that celebrates the holiness of tigerness." If there were a doubt, if the interpretation with which each critic begins were not firmly in place, the account of the poem that follows from that interpretation could not get under way. One could not cite as an "obvious" fact that "forests" is a fallen word or, alternatively, that it "suggests tall and straight forms." Whenever a critic prefaces an assertion with a phrase like "without doubt" or "there can be no doubt," you can be sure that you are within hailing distance of the interpretive principles which produce the facts that he presents as obvious.

In the years since 1964 other interpretations of the poem have been put forward, and they follow a predictable course. Some echo either Raine or Hirsch by arguing that the tiger is either good or evil; others assert that the tiger is *both* good and evil, or beyond good and evil; still others protest that the questions posed in the poem are rhetorical and are therefore not meant to be answered ("it is quite evident that the critics are not trying to understand the poem at all. If they were, they would not attempt to answer its questions.")[3] It is only a matter of time before the focus turns from the questions to their asker and to the possibility that the speaker of the poem is not Blake but a limited persona ("Surely the point . . . is that Blake sees further or deeper than his *persona*").[4] It then becomes possible to assert that "we don't know who the speaker of 'The Tyger' is," and that therefore the poem "is a maze of questions in which the reader is forced to wander confusedly."[5] In this reading the poem itself becomes rather "tigerish" and one is not at all surprised when the original question—"Who made the Tyger?"—is given its quintessentially new-critical answer: the tiger is the poem itself and Blake, the consummate artist who smiles "his work to see," is its creator.[6] As one obvious and indisputable interpretation supplants another, it brings with it a new set of obvious and indisputable facts. Of course each new reading is elaborated in the

name of the poem itself, but the poem itself is always a function of the interpretive perspective from which the critic "discovers" it.

A committed pluralist might find in the previous paragraph a confirmation of his own position. After all, while "The Tyger" is obviously open to more than one interpretation, it is not open to an infinite number of interpretations. There may be disagreements as to whether the tiger is good or evil, or whether the speaker is Blake or a persona, and so on, but no one is suggesting that the poem is an allegory of the digestive processes or that it predicts the Second World War, and its limited plurality is simply a testimony to the capacity of a great work of art to generate multiple readings. The point is one that Wayne Booth makes when he asks, "Are we *right* to rule out at least some readings?"[7] and then answers his own question with a resounding yes. It would be my answer too; but the real question is what gives us the right so to be right. A pluralist is committed to saying that there is something in the text which rules out some readings and allows others (even though no *one* reading can ever capture the text's "inexhaustible richness and complexity"). His best evidence is that in practice "we all in fact" do reject unacceptable readings and that more often than not we agree on the readings that are to be rejected. Booth tells us, for example, that he has never found a reader of *Pride and Prejudice* "who sees no jokes against Mr. Collins" when he gives his reasons for wanting to marry Elizabeth Bennet and only belatedly, in fifth position, cites the "violence" of his affection.[8] From this and other examples, Booth concludes that there are justified limits to what we can legitimately do with a text, for "surely we could not go on disputing at all if a core of agreement did not exist." Again, I agree, but if, as I have argued, the text is always a function of interpretation, then the text cannot be the location of the core of agreement by means of which we reject interpretations. We seem to be at an impasse: on the one hand there would seem to be no basis for labeling an interpretation unacceptable, but on the other we do it all the time.

This, however, is an impasse only if one assumes that the activity of interpretation is itself unconstrained; but in fact the shape of that activity is determined by the literary institution which at any one time will authorize only a finite number of interpretative strategies. Thus, while there is no core of agreement *in* the text, there is a core of agreement (although one subject to change) concerning the ways of *producing* the text. Nowhere is this set of acceptable ways written down, but it is a part of everyone's knowledge of what it means to be operating within the literary institution as it is now constituted. A student of mine recently demonstrated this knowledge when, with an air of giving away a trade secret, she confided that she could go into any classroom, no matter what the subject of the course, and win approval for running one of a number of well-defined interpretive routines: she could view the assigned text as an instance of the tension between nature and culture; she could look in the text for evidence of large mythological oppositions; she could argue that the true subject of the text was its own composition, or that in the guise of fashioning a narrative the speaker was fragmenting and displacing his own anxieties and fears. She could not, however, at least at Johns Hopkins University today, argue that the text was a prophetic message inspired by the ghost of her Aunt Tilly.

My student's understanding of what she could and could not get away with, of the unwritten rules of the literary game, is shared by everyone who plays that game, by those who write and judge articles for publication in learned journals, by those who read and listen to papers at professional meetings, by those who seek and award tenure in innumerable departments of English and comparative literature, by the armies of graduate students for whom knowledge of the rules is the real mark of professional initiation. This does not mean that these rules and the practices they authorize are either monolithic or stable. Within the literary community there are subcommunities (what will excite the editors of *Diacritics* is likely to distress the editors of *Studies in Philology*), and within any community the boundaries of the acceptable are continually being redrawn. In a classroom whose authority figures include David Bleich and Norman Holland, a student might very well relate a text to her memories of a favorite aunt, while in other classrooms, dominated by the spirit of Brooks and Warren, any such activity would immediately be dismissed as nonliterary, as something that isn't done.

The point is that while there is always a category of things that are not done (it is simply the reverse or flip side of the category of things that *are* done), the membership in that category is continually changing. It changes laterally as one moves from subcommunity to subcommunity, and it changes through time when once interdicted interpretive strategies are admitted into the ranks of the acceptable. Twenty years ago one of the things that literary critics didn't do was talk about the reader, at least in a way that made his experience the focus of the critical act. The prohibition on such talk was largely the result of Wimsatt's and Beardsley's famous essay "The Affective Fallacy," which argued that the variability of readers renders any investigation of their responses ad-hoc and relativistic: "The poem itself," the authors complained, "as an object of specifically critical judgment, tends to disappear."[9] So influential was this essay that it was possible for a reviewer to dismiss a book merely by finding in it evidence that the affective fallacy had been committed. The use of a juridical terminology is not accidental; this was in a very real sense a *legal* finding of activity in violation of understood and institutionalized decorums. Today, however, the affective fallacy, no longer a fallacy but a methodology, is committed all the time, and its practitioners have behind them the full and authorizing weight of a fully articulated institutional apparatus. The "reader in literature" is regularly the subject of forums and workshops at the convention of the Modern Language Association; there is a reader newsletter which reports on the multitudinous labors of a reader industry; any list of currently active schools of literary criticism includes the school of "reader response," and two major university presses have published collections of essays designed both to display the variety of reader-centered criticism (the emergence of factions within a once interdicted activity is a sure sign of its having achieved the status of an orthodoxy) and to detail its history. None of this of course means that a reader-centered criticism is now invulnerable to challenge or attack, merely that it is now recognized as a competing literary strategy that cannot be dismissed simply by being named. It is acceptable not because everyone accepts it but because those who do not are now obliged to argue against it.

The promotion of reader-response criticism to the category of things that are done (even if it is not being done by everyone) brings with it a whole new set of facts to which its practitioners can now refer. These include patterns of expectation and disappointment, reversals of direction, traps, invitations to premature conclusions, textual gaps, delayed revelations, temptations, all of which are related to a corresponding set of authors' intentions, of strategies designed to educate the reader or humiliate him or confound him or, in the more sophisticated versions of the mode, to make him enact in his responses the very subject matter of the poem. These facts and intentions emerge when the text is interrogated by a series of related questions—What is the reader doing? What is being done to him? For what purpose?—questions that follow necessarily from the assumption that the text is not a spatial object but the occasion for a temporal experience. It is in the course of answering such questions that a reader response critic elaborates "the structure of the reading experience," a structure which is not so much discovered by the interrogation but demanded by it. (If you begin by assuming that readers do something and the something they do has meaning, you will never fail to discover a pattern of reader activities that appears obviously to be meaningful.) As that structure emerges (under the pressure of interrogation) it takes the form of a "reading," and insofar as the procedures which produced it are recognized by the literary community as something that some of its members do, that reading will have the status of a competing interpretation. Of course it is still the case, as Booth insists, that we are "right to rule out at least some readings," but there is now one less reading or kind of reading that can be ruled out, because there is now one more interpretive procedure that has been accorded a place in the literary institution.

The fact that it remains easy to think of a reading that most of us would dismiss out of hand does not mean that the text excludes it but that there is as yet no elaborated interpretive procedure for producing that text. That is why the examples of critics like Wayne Booth seem to have so much force; rather than looking back, as I have, to now familiar strategies that were once alien and strange sounding, they look forward to strategies that have not yet emerged. Norman Holland's analysis of Faulkner's "A Rose for Emily" is a case in point. Holland is arguing for a kind of psychoanalytic pluralism. The text, he declares, is "at most a matrix of psychological possibilities for its readers," but, he insists, "only some possibilities . . . truly fit the matrix": "One would not say, for example, that a reader of . . . 'A Rose for Emily' who thought the 'tableau' [of Emily and her father in the doorway] described an Eskimo was really responding to the story at all—only pursuing some mysterious inner exploration."[10]

Holland is making two arguments: first, that anyone who proposes an Eskimo reading of "A Rose for Emily" will not find a hearing in the literary community. And that, I think, is right. ("We are right to rule out at least some readings.") His second argument is that the unacceptability of the Eskimo reading is a function of the text, of what he calls its "sharable promptuary" (p. 287), the public "store of structured language" (p. 287) that sets limits to the interpretations the words can accommodate. And that, I think, is wrong. The Eskimo reading is unacceptable because there is at present no interpretive strategy for producing it, no way of "looking" or reading (and remember, all acts of looking or reading are "ways") that would result in the emergence of obviously Eskimo meanings. This does not mean, however, that no such strategy could ever come into play, and it is not difficult to imagine the circumstances under which it would establish itself. One such circumstance would be the discovery of a letter in which Faulkner confides that he has always believed himself to be an Eskimo changeling. (The example is absurd only if one forgets Yeat's *Vision* or Blake's Swedenborgianism or James Miller's recent elaboration of a homosexual reading of *The Waste Land*). Immediately the workers in the Faulkner industry would begin to reinterpret the canon in the light of this newly revealed "belief" and the work of reinterpretation would involve the elaboration of a symbolic or allusive system (not unlike mythological or typological criticism) whose application would immediately transform the text into one informed everywhere by Eskimo meanings. It might seem that I am admitting that there is a text to be transformed, but the object of transformation would be the text (or texts) given by whatever interpretive strategies the Eskimo strategy was in the process of dislodging or expanding. The result would be that whereas we now have a Freudian "A Rose for Emily," a mythological "A Rose for Emily," a Christological "A Rose for Emily," a regional "A Rose for Emily," a sociological "A Rose for Emily," a linguistic "A Rose for Emily," we would in addition have an Eskimo "A Rose for Emily," existing in some relation of compatibility or incompatibility with the others.

Again the point is that while there are always mechanisms for ruling out readings, their source is not the text but the presently recognized interpretive strategies for producing the text. It follows, then, that no reading, however outlandish it might appear, is inherently an impossible one. Consider, for another example, Booth's report that he has never found a reader who sees no jokes against Mr. Collins, and his conclusion that the text of *Pride and Prejudice* enforces or signals an ironic reading. First of all, the fact that he hasn't yet found such a reader does not mean that one does not exist, and we can even construct his profile; he would be someone for whom the reasons in Mr. Collins's list correspond to a deeply held set of values, exactly the opposite of the set of values that must be assumed if the passage is to be seen as obviously ironic. Presumably no one who has sat in Professor Booth's classes holds that set of values or is allowed to hold them (students always know what they are expected to believe) and it is unlikely that anyone who is now working in the Austen industry begins with an assumption other than the assumption that the novelist is a master ironist. It is precisely for this reason that the time is ripe for the "discovery" by an enterprising scholar of a nonironic Austen, and one can even predict the course such a discovery would take. It would begin with the uncovering of new evidence (a letter, a lost manuscript, a

contemporary response) and proceed to the conclusion that Austen's intentions have been misconstrued by generations of literary critics. She was not in fact satirizing the narrow and circumscribed life of a country gentry; rather, she was celebrating that life and its tireless elaboration of a social fabric, complete with values, rituals, and self-perpetuating goals (marriage, the preservation of great houses, and so on). This view, or something very much like it, is already implicit in much of the criticism, and it would only be a matter of extending it to local matters of interpretation, and specifically to Mr. Collins's list of reasons which might now be seen as reflecting a proper ranking of the values and obligations necessary to the maintenance of a way of life.

Of course any such reading would meet resistance; its opponents could point for example to the narrator's unequivocal condemnation of Mr. Collins; but there are always ways in the literary institution of handling this or any other objection. One need only introduce (if it has not already been introduced) the notion of the fallible narrator in any of its various forms (the dupe, the moral prig, the naif in need of education), and the "unequivocal condemnation" would take its place in a structure designed to glorify Mr. Collins and everything he stands for. Still, no matter how many objections were met and explained away, the basic resistance on the part of many scholars to this revisionist reading would remain, and for a time at least *Pride and Prejudice* would have acquired the status of the fourth book of *Gulliver's Travels*, a work whose very shape changes in the light of two radically opposed interpretive assumptions.

Again, I am aware that this argument is a tour-de-force and will continue to seem so as long as the revolution it projects has not occurred. The reading of *Pride and Prejudice*, however, is not meant to be persuasive. I only wanted to describe the conditions under which it might *become* persuasive and to point out that those conditions are not unimaginable given the procedures within the literary institution by which interpretations are proposed and established. Any interpretation could be elaborated by someone in command of those procedures (someone who knows what "will do" as a literary argument), even my own "absurd" reading of "The Tyger" as an allegory of the digestive processes. Here the task is easy because according to the critical consensus there is no belief so bizarre that Blake could not have been committed to it and it would be no trick at all to find some elaborate system of alimentary significances (Pythagorean? Swedenborgian? Cabbalistic?) which he could be presumed to have known. One might then decide that the poem was the first-person lament of someone who had violated a dietary prohibition against eating tiger meat, and finds that forbidden food burning brightly in his stomach, making its fiery way through the forests of the intestinal tract, beating and hammering like some devil-wielded anvil. In his distress he can do nothing but rail at the tiger and at the mischance that led him to mistake its meat for the meat of some purified animal: "Did he who made the Lamb make thee?" The poem ends as it began, with the speaker still paying the price of his sin and wondering at the inscrutable purposes of a deity who would lead his creatures into digestive temptation. Anyone who thinks that this time I have gone too far might do very well to consult some recent numbers of *Blake Studies*.

In fact, my examples are very serious, and they are serious in part because they are so ridiculous. The fact that they *are* ridiculous, or are at least perceived to be so, is evidence that we are never without canons of acceptability; we are always "right to rule out at least some readings." But the fact that we can imagine conditions under which they would *not* seem ridiculous, and that readings once considered ridiculous are now respectable and even orthodox, is evidence that the canons of acceptability can change. Moreover, that change is not random but orderly and, to some extent, predictable. A new interpretive strategy always makes its way in some relationship of opposition to the old, which has often marked out a negative space (of things that aren't done) from which it can emerge into respectability. Thus, when Wimsatt and Beardsley declare that "the Affective Fallacy is a confusion between the poem and its *results*, what is *is* and what it *does*," the way is open for an affective critic to argue, as I did, that a poem *is* what it does. And when the possibility of a

reader-centered criticism seems threatened by the variability of readers, that threat will be countered either by denying the variability (Stephen Booth, Michael Riffaterre) or by controlling it (Wolfgang Iser, Louise Rosenblatt) or by embracing it and making it into a principle of value (David Bleich, Walter Slatoff).

Rhetorically the new position announces itself as a break from the old, but in fact it is radically dependent on the old, because it is only in the context of some differential relationship that it can be perceived as new or, for that matter, perceived at all. No one would bother to assert that Mr. Collins is the hero of *Pride and Prejudice* (even as an example intended to be absurd) were that position not already occupied in the criticism by Elizabeth and Darcy; for then the assertion would have no force; there would be nothing in relation to which it could be surprising. Neither would there be any point in arguing that Blake's tiger is both good and evil if there were not already readings in which he was declared to be one or the other. And if anyone is ever to argue that he is both old and young, someone will first have to argue that he is *either* old or young, for only when his age has become a question will there be any value in a refusal to answer it. Nor is it the case that the moral status of the tiger (as opposed to its age, or nationality, or intelligence) is an issue raised by the poem itself; it becomes an issue because a question is put to the poem (is the tiger good or evil?) and once that question (it could have been another) is answered, the way is open to answering it differently, or declining to answer it, or to declaring that the absence of an answer is the poem's "real point."

The discovery of the "real point" is always what is claimed whenever a new interpretation is advanced, but the claim makes sense only in relation to a point (or points) that had previously been considered the real one. This means that the space in which a critic works has been marked out for him by his predecessors, even though he is obliged by the conventions of the institution to dislodge them. It is only by their prevenience or prepossession that there is something for him to say; that is, it is only because something has already been said that he can now say something different. This dependency, the reverse of the anxiety of influence, is reflected in the unwritten requirement that an interpretation present itself as remedying a deficiency in the interpretations that have come before it. (If it did not do this, what claim would it have on our attention?) Nor can this be just any old deficiency; it will not do, for example, to fault your predecessors for failing to notice that a poem is free of split infinitives or dangling participles. The lack an interpretation supplies must be related to the criteria by which the literary community recognizes and evaluates the objects of its professional attention. As things stand now, text-book grammaticality is not one of those criteria, and therefore the demonstration of its presence in a poem will not reflect credit either on the poem or on the critic who offers it.

Credit *will* accrue to the critic when he bestows the *proper* credit on the poem, when he demonstrates that it possesses one or more of the qualities that are understood to distinguish poems from other verbal productions. In the context of the "new" criticism, under many of whose assumptions we still labor, those qualities include unity, complexity, and universality, and it is the perceived failure of previous commentators to celebrate their presence in a poem that gives a critic the right (or so he will claim) to advance a new interpretation. The unfolding of that interpretation will thus proceed under two constraints: not only must what one says about a work be related to what has already been said (even if the relation is one of reversal) but as a consequence of saying it the work must be shown to possess in a greater degree than had hitherto been recognized the qualities that properly belong to literary productions, whether they be unity and complexity, or unparaphrasability, or metaphoric richness, or indeterminacy and undecidability. In short, the new interpretation must not only claim to tell the truth about the work (in a dependent opposition to the falsehood or partial truths told by its predecessors) but it must claim to make the work better. (The usual phrase is "enhance our appreciation of.") Indeed, these claims are finally inseparable since it is assumed that the truth about a work will be what penetrates to the essense of its literary value.

This assumption, along with several others, is conveniently on display in the opening paragraph of the preface to Stephen Booth's *An Essay on Shakespeare's Sonnets:*[11]

The history of criticism opens so many possibilities for an essay on Shakespeare's sonnets that I must warn a prospective reader about what this work does and doesn't do. To begin with the negative, I have not solved or tried to solve any of the puzzles of Shakespeare's sonnets. I do not attempt to identify Mr. W. H. or the dark lady. I do not speculate on the occasions that may have evoked particular sonnets. I do not attempt to date them. I offer neither a reorganization of the sequence, nor a defense of the quarto order. What I have tried to do is find out what about the sonnets has made them so highly valued by the vast majority of critics and general readers.

This brief paragraph can serve as an illustration of almost everything I have been saying. First of all, Booth self-consciously locates and defines his position in a differential opposition to the positions he would dislodge. He will not, he tells us, do what any of his predecessors have done; he will do something else, and indeed if it were not something else there would be no reason for him to be doing it. The reason he gives for doing it is that what his predecessors have done is misleading or beside the point. The point is the location of the source of the sonnets' value ("what about the sonnets has made them so highly valued") and his contention (not stated but strongly implied) is that those who have come before him have been looking in the wrong places, in the historical identity of the sequence's characters, in the possibility of recovering the biographical conditions of composition, and in the determination of an authoritative ordering and organization. He, however, will look in the right place and thereby produce an account of the sonnets that does them the justice they so richly deserve.

Thus, in only a few sentences Booth manages to claim for his interpretation everything that certifies it as acceptable within the conventions of literary criticism: he locates a deficiency in previous interpretations and proposes to remedy it; the remedy will take the form of producing a more satisfactory account of the work; and as a result the literary credentials of the work—what makes it of enduring value—will be more securely established, as they are when Booth is able to point in the closing paragraph of his book to Shakespeare's "remarkable achievement." By thus validating Shakespeare's achievement, Booth also validates his own credentials as a literary critic, as someone who knows what claims and demonstrations mark him as a competent member of the institution.

What makes Stephen Booth so interesting (although not at all atypical) is that one of his claims is to have freed himself and the sonnets from that very institution and its practices. "I do not," he declares, "intentionally give any interpretations of the sonnets I discuss. I mean to describe them, not to explain them." The irony is that even as Booth is declaring himself out of the game, he is performing one of its most familiar moves. The move has several versions, and Booth is here availing himself of two: (1) the "external-internal," performed when a critic dismisses his predecessors for being insufficiently literary ("but that has nothing to do with its qualities *as a poem*"); and (2) the "back-to-the-text," performed when the critical history of a work is deplored as so much dross, as an obscuring encrustation ("we are in danger of substituting the criticism for the poem"). The latter is the more powerful version of the move because it trades on the assumption, still basic to the profession's sense of its activities, that the function of literary criticism is to let the text speak for itself. It is thus a move drenched in humility, although it is often performed with righteousness: those other fellows may be interested in displaying their ingenuity, but *I* am simply a servant of the text and wish only to make it more available to its readers (who happen also to be my readers).

• The basic gesture, then, is to disavow interpretation in favor of simply presenting the text; but it is actually a gesture in which one set of interpretive principles is replaced by another that happens to claim for itself the virtue of not being an interpretation at all. The claim, however, is an impossible one since in order "simply to present" the text, one must at the very least describe it ("I mean to describe them") and description can occur only within a stipulative understanding of what there is to be described, an

understanding that will produce the object of its attention. Thus, when Booth rejects the assumptions of those who have tried to solve the puzzles of the sonnets in favor of "the assumption that the source of our pleasure in them must be the line by line experience of reading them," he is not avoiding interpretation but proposing a change in the terms within which it will occur. Specifically, he proposes that the focus of attention, and therefore of description, shift from the poem conceived as a spatial object which *contains* meanings to the poem conceived as a temporal experience in the course of which meanings become momentarily available, before disappearing under the pressure of other meanings, which are in their turn superseded, contradicted, qualified, or simply forgotten. It is only if a reader agrees to this change, that is, agrees to accept Booth's revisionary stipulation as to where the value and the significance of a poem are to be located, that the facts to which his subsequent analyses point will be seen to be facts at all. The description which Booth offers in place of an interpretation turns out to be as much of an interpretive construct as the interpretations he rejects.

Nor could it be otherwise. Strictly speaking, getting "back-to-the-text" is not a move one can perform, because the text one gets back to will be the text demanded by some other interpretation and that interpretation will be presiding over its production. This is not to say, however, that the "back-to-the-text" move is ineffectual. The fact that it is not something one can do in no way diminishes the effectiveness of claiming to do it. As a rhetorical ploy, the announcement that one is returning to the text will be powerful so long as the assumption that criticism is secondary to the text and must not be allowed to overwhelm it remains unchallenged. Certainly, Booth does not challenge it; indeed, he relies on it and invokes it even as he relies on and invokes many other assumptions that someone else might want to dispute: the assumption that what distinguishes literary from ordinary language is its invulnerability to paraphrase; the assumption that a poem should not mean, but be; the assumption that the more complex a work is, the more propositions it holds in tension and equilibrium, the better it is. It would not be at all unfair to label these assumptions "conservative" and to point out that in holding to them Booth undermines his radical credentials. But it would also be beside the point, which is not that Booth isn't truly radical but that he *couldn't* be. Nor could anyone else. The challenge he mounts to some of the conventions of literary study (the convention of the poem as artifact, the convention of meaningfulness) would not even be *recognized* as a challenge if others of those conventions were not firmly in place and, for the time being at least, unquestioned. A wholesale challenge would be impossible because there would be no terms in which it could be made; that is, in order to be wholesale, it would have to be made in terms wholly outside the institution; but if that were the case, it would be unintelligible because it is only within the institution that the facts of literary study—texts, authors, periods, genres—become available. In short, the price intelligibility exacts (a price Booth pays here) is implication in the very structure of assumptions and goals from which one desires to be free.

So it would seem, finally, that there are no moves that are not moves in the game, and this includes even the move by which one claims no longer to be a player. Indeed, by a logic peculiar to the institution, one of the standard ways of practicing literary criticism is to announce that you are avoiding it. This is so because at the heart of the institution is the wish to deny that its activities have any consequences. The critic is taught to think of himself as a transmitter of the best that had been thought and said by others, and his greatest fear is that he will stand charged of having substituted his own meanings

for the meanings of which he is supposedly the guardian; his greatest fear is that he be found guilty of having interpreted. That is why we have the spectacle of commentators who, like Stephen Booth, adopt a stance of aggressive humility and, in the manner of someone who rises to speak at a temperance meeting, declare that they will never interpret again but will instead do something else ("I mean to describe them"). What I have been saying is that whatever they do, it will only be interpretation in another guise because, like it or not, interpretation is the only game in town.

Notes

1. *Encounter*, June 1954, p. 50.

2. *Innocence and Experience* (New Haven: Yale University Press, 1964), pp. 245, 248.

3. Philip Hosbaum, "A Rhetorical Question Answered: Blake's *Tyger* and Its Critics," *Neophilologus*, 48, no. 2 (1964), 154.

4. Warren Stevenson, " 'The Tyger' as Artefact," *Blake Studies*, 2, no. 1 (1969–70), 9.

5. L. J. Swingle, "Answers to Blake's 'Tyger': A Matter of Reason or of Choice," *Concerning Poetry*, 2 (1970), 67.

6. Stevenson, " 'The Tyger' as Artefact," p. 15.

7. "Preserving the Exemplar," *Critical Inquiry*, 3, no. 3 (Spring 1977), 413.

8. Ibid., 412.

9. *The Verbal Icon* (Lexington: University of Kentucky Press, 1954), p. 21.

10. *5 Readers Reading* (New Haven: Yale University Press, 1975), p. 12.

11. New Haven: Yale University Press, 1969.

Index

Abrams, M. H., 119
Abstractions v. experience, 78
Adams, Richard P., 118
"Adonais" (Shelley), 257
Ad Patrem (Milton), 61
Aeneid (Virgil), 22, 23, 257, 258, 307, 308
Aesthetical normal Idea, 92
Aesthetic experience of reader, 143–144, 145
Affective criticism, 5, 73, 74; and audience-to-text continuum, 134–137; concern of, with audience, 129–130; correlation of value and form by, 77; definition of, 3–4; and elusiveness of reader, 316; as interpretive community, 350–351; and psychological theory, 130–132, 135–136; relativism of, re audience response, 132–134, 136. *See also* Audience
Affective stylistics, 136–137
Akenside, Mark, 104
Alcestis (Euripides), 132
Alice in Wonderland (Carroll), 269
Allegory, and interpretation of character, 112–113
"All in the Family" (TV program), 340
Althusser, Louis, 45–46
"Among School Children" (Yeats), 341–342
Anonymous texts, interpretation of meaning of, 35
Appearance, distinguished from reality, 195, 196
Appetencies, satisfaction of, by art, 131–132
Arcades (Milton), 21–22
Archetypal criticism, 256

Archetypes: communal nature of, 185–186; conditioning of meaning by, 310; exploration of meaning through, 186–190; and poetic recreation, 303; representation of persons as, in pastoral elegy, 300–301; response of readers to, 131; unification of themes by, . 301–302
Argument of poetry, 93, 94–95
Aristotle, 12; answer to "What is it?" 92; on essential reality, 195–197; formal analysis by, 74; on learning from art, 199; on nature of poetry, 92; on poetic imitation, 207, 208; on use of metaphor, 96
Arthurian legends, 307, 308, 309 in "A-sitting on a Gate" (Carroll), 282
Auden, W. H., 204
Audience: activation of, by textual blanks, 149, 150–153; aesthetic experience of, 143–144, 145; coherent experience of literature by, 274–275; cultural conditioning of, 145–146; Elizabethan, demonology of, 47–50, 54–55; elusiveness of, 316; exclusion of, from creation of poem, 139–142; as focus of affective criticism, 129–130; innocence of, vis-à-vis critic, 204, 205, 206; interaction of, with text, 147–153; literary competence of, 279, 280–281, 318, 319; moral response of—the effect of dramatic art, 111–113; pre-critical experience of literature by, 272–274; psychological

study of, 130–132, 135–136, 211; relative importance of, vis-à-vis text, to criticism, 134–137; and relativity of poetic value, 132–134, 136; response of, to authorial achievement, 208; response to text—conditioning of, by conventions of genre, 177–181, 182; response to text—feedback model of, 163–169; response to text—indeterminate meanings, 181–183; response to text—replication of identity in, 172–176; response to text—themes in, 160–163; response to text—variability in, 157–160; role of, in creation of poems, 140, 141, 145–146, 171–176; stripping preconceptions from, 209–210
Auerbach, Erich, 213–214
Austen, Jane, 149, 349, 352, 353
Author: archetypal inspiration of, 186–187, 190–191; body of work, considered as whole, 271; clues to mind—biographical circumstances, 10–11, 12, 13, 14; clues to mind—historical circumstances, 11, 12–13, 14; communication of meaning by, 9–10; creation of characters by, 211–212, 215–216; creativity of, 172; as creature of linguistic structure, 319, 321; as determinant of meaning, 28, 30–32, 142–145, 268–270; elusiveness of, 316; extra-aesthetic experience of, 20–22; identification of formal devices with, 208; identification with